Occasional Papers

No. 203/204   April 1996

AMERICAN LIBRARY BOOK CATALOGUES, 1801-1875:
A NATIONAL BIBLIOGRAPHY

By

Robert Singerman

Graduate School of Library and Information Science
University of Illinois at Urbana-Champaign

Manufactured in the United States of America
Printed on acid-free paper

ISSN 0276 1769
ISBN 0-87845-098-X

OCCASIONAL PAPERS deal with any aspect of librarianship and consist of papers that are too long or too detailed for publication in a periodical or that are of specialized or temporary interest. Manuscripts for inclusion in this series are invited and should be sent to: OCCASIONAL PAPERS, Graduate School of Library and Information Science, The Publications Office, University of Illinois at Urbana-Champaign, 501 E. Daniel Street, Champaign, Illinois 61820.

Papers in this series are issued irregularly, and no more often than monthly. Individual copies may be ordered; back issues are available. Please check with the publisher: *All orders must be accompanied by payment.* Standing orders may also be established. Send orders to: OCCASIONAL PAPERS, The Publications Office, Graduate School of Library and Information Science, University of Illinois at Urbana-Champaign, 501 E. Daniel Street, Champaign, Illinois 61820. Telephone 217-333-1359. Email *puboff@alexia.lis.uiuc.edu.* Make checks payable to University of Illinois. Visa, Mastercard, American Express and Discover accepted.

James S. Dowling, Managing Editor

Contents

Introduction

Kenneth E. Carpenter
Assistant Director for Research Resources
Harvard University Library

Charles Coffin Jewett, as part of preparing the first great survey of American libraries, *Notices of Public Libraries in the United States of America* (Washington, DC, 1851), issued a plea that copies of library catalogues be sent to the Smithsonian Institution: "We would also beg leave, on behalf of the Smithsonian Institution, to solicit for its Library the gift of books, pamphlets, or articles, printed or written, relative to the history, condition, or prospects of every literary, scientific, and educational establishment in the country; with catalogues (old as well as new) of all libraries. . . " (p. 6). Throughout Jewett's work, he refers to printed catalogues, for he considered record of their publication to be a crucial element of information about the libraries. Jewett also repeatedly cited information drawn from library catalogues, for they often contained historical sketches.

The next great survey of American libraries, William J. Rhees' *Manual of Public Libraries, Institutions, and Societies, in the United States, and British Provinces of North America* (Philadelphia, PA, 1859), recorded that the efforts of the Smithsonian Institution, initiated by Jewett, had been successful: "The Smithsonian Institution has endeavored for many years to procure all the catalogues of public libraries which have been printed, and it is believed has now the largest collection of this kind to be found in this country" (p. xiv). Rhees, like his predecessor, used the collection of catalogues in his work, for he often quotes from catalogues, especially from the extensive historical account that is sometimes a part of a catalogue.

The Smithsonian was right to collect library catalogues and Jewett and Rhees to use them, for they are a unique source of information about American libraries and about the reading matter available to Americans. To the historian today, library catalogues are even more useful than they were to Jewett and Rhees. They at least had the advantage of being able to send out a questionnaire–we cannot. We can only use what has come down to us, and library catalogues constitute the single largest body of primary sources for the history of American libraries before the founding of the American Library Association in 1876. Before then, we have no *Library Journal,* no proceedings of annual meetings, and few annual reports of libraries except for the largest institutions. Library catalogues are the one common source that exists for libraries of all sizes and types.

Robert Singerman's checklist reveals an extraordinary variety of types of libraries. Following is a brief sample in which the date is that of the first catalogue of a library. There are catalogues of libraries of courts (the Alabama Supreme Court, 1859); of states (California, 1855; Maine, 1839; Massachusetts, 1831; Nebraska, 1871; Nevada, 1865; Utah territorial library, 1852) to name only a few; of state agencies (Massachusetts Board of Agriculture, 1858; New York Secretary of State, 1866) of public archives (Massachusetts, 1839); schools of various sorts (Providence, RI, Reform School, 1861); bar association libraries (Ohio County, West Virginia, Law Library, 1871); legislative bodies (South Carolina General Assembly, 1826); charitable associations (National Home for Disabled Volunteer Soldiers, Milwaukee, 1875; Philadelphia Almshouse, 1824; German Society of Pennsylvania, Contributing for the Relief of Distressed Germans, 1826); railroad libraries (Boston and Albany Railroad, 1868); a regimental library (36th Illinois Infantry Regiment, sometime in the 1860s); U.S. Batallion of Engineers, Willets Point, NY, 1869?; Young Men's Association libraries (New London, CT, 1841; Milwaukee, WI, 1848; Janesville, WI, 1875); YMCA libraries (Hopkinton, MA, 1874); theological seminary libraries (Associate Presbyterian Church Seminary, Pittsburgh, PA, 1854); military institutes (Virginia Military Institute, 1855); library companies (Harrodsburg, KY, 1823; Reading, PA, 1808; Alexandria, VA, 1801; Woodbury, NJ, 1815); high school libraries (Rutland, VT, 1857); mechanics' institute libraries (Danvers, MA, 1841; Burlington, VT, 1847; Nashville, TN, 1842); mercantile libraries (Peoria, IL, 1872; St. Louis, MO, 1850; Philadelphia, PA, 1821; Galveston, TX, 1871); reading room associations (Spring Garden, Philadelphia, Free Reading Room Association, 1851); medical societies (Boston Medical Library, 1807; South Carolina, Charleston, 1806); libraries for readers of languages other than English (the Leihbibliothek of M. H. Kappelmann & Co., Charleston, SC, 1850; Deutsches Institut für Wissenschaft, Kunst und Gewerbe, St. Louis, MO, 1860; English and French Family Circulating Library, Philadelphia, PA [186-?]; Turn-Gemeinde of Cincinnati, OH, 1866); apprentices' libraries (Morristown, NJ, 1848); lyceum libraries (Franklin Lyceum of Providence, RI, 1857); historical societies (Presbyterian Historical Society, Philadelphia, PA, 1865); hospitals (Pennsylvania Hospital, Philadelphia, 1806); horticultural societies (Pennsylvania Horticultural Society, 1840); agricultural societies (Albany, 1850); scientific libraries (Franklin Institute, Philadelphia, PA, 1847); trades (Carpenters' Company, Philadelphia, PA, 1857); athenaeum libraries (Zanesville, OH, 1831); womens' libraries (libraries of colleges for women, as Wesleyan Female College of Cincnnnati, OH, 1859; Traverse City, MI, Ladies' Library Association, 1875; Ladies Society, Topsfield, MA, 1852; Ladies' Physiological Institute, Boston,

MA, 1851; Ladies' Sigourney Library, Logansport, IN, 1852); music librar-ies (Koppitz's Musical Library . . . in Possession of N. Lothian, Musical Di-rector, Boston Theatre, ca. 1875); mill and factory libraries (Boston Rub-ber Shoe Company, Malden, MA, 1873; Pacific Mills Library, Lawrence, MA, 1855); prison (Illinois State Penitentiary, 1874; Massachusetts State Prison, 1870); fraternal organizations (Odd Fellows' Library, Boston, 1875; Freema-sons, Iowa City, IA, 1873). Only one African American library catalogue survives.

To these must be added libraries that term themselves "social libraries" and later "public libraries," and, of course, church libraries and Sunday school libraries, of which thousands existed; Rhees suggests 30,000. There were also commercial circulating libraries. Colleges and universities, of course, had libraries, as did the student societies.

The variety of libraries is such that this checklist of catalogues will be useful to cultural historians with diverse interests, not only library histori-ans. As historians use it, many more catalogues will very likely be identified in collections that are not catalogued or not catalogued online.

Somewhere a copy may exist of the 52-page catalogue of Winsor's Circulat-ing Library, 1852. The 2,000 copies of this Providence circulating library cost $90 to produce, and Rhees recorded its existence; but none could be found today. Likewise, no copy is recorded today of the 1857 catalogue of the Ohio Mechanics' Institute in Cincinnati, printed in 1857 in an edition of 1,000 cop-ies. Thanks, no doubt, to the collecting of the Smithsonian Institution, one copy exists of the 1851 catalogue of the Public School Library in Poughkeepsie, New York, but none of the 1855 supplement cited by Rhees.

These works were printed and distributed locally, and rarely recorded by and distributed through booktrade channels. After all, with rare excep-tions, only those in geographical proximity to the library had access to the books listed in a catalogue or had any reason to possess a copy. Even those individuals tended not to buy copies, according to Jim Ranz (*The Printed Book Catalogue in American Libraries: 1723-1900*. Chicago, IL: American Li-brary Association, 1964, pp. 45-46). For the person who did buy a copy, the appearance of a new edition meant that the earlier was superseded and of no utility. Even those catalogues printed in large numbers and of fairly substantial size have a low survival rate, as, for example, the 1854 catalogue of the Rochester Athenaeum and Mechanics' Association. Of the 2,000 copies printed of this 106-page catalogue, only two are known to exit. It is not surprising that the 16-page, 1850 catalog of the 44-member Winnisimmet Literary Institute of Chelsea, Massachusetts, does not survive at all.

Singerman has entries for more than 3,300 catalogues, some of them being for catalogues once recorded or described in authoritative sources but are nowhere to be found today. Moreover, more than a quarter of the cata-logues are now known in only one copy. It is clear that many more must have been published, and Singerman would welcome news of their existence.

The inevitable gaps in the survival of library catalogues do not detract from the utility of this checklist. It does open a number of new possibilities. As suggested earlier, the variety of catalogues means that the student of the law in America, or science, or medicine, or prisons, or the lyceum movement, among others, will find this checklist useful. The time span, the 75 years from 1801 through 1875, and the geographical range also suggest opportunities. In what ways did libraries collect differently over time? When did popular fiction begin to be acquired? Did fiction predominate among the holdings? Do the holdings emphasize works for consultation or books for borrowing? What children's books were in libraries and did the ratio between books for children and adults change over time? What secular books were in church or Sunday school libraries? Was controversial political or religious literature acquired? Can the bases for decisions on purchases be determined? Did libraries rely on publishers' "libraries" in their buying? What was the mix between contemporary British and American authors?

When a new library was established, what was chosen for the basic collection? What, if any, are the differences in the holdings of libraries for young men and those for women, or those for mechanics and for merchant clerks? What periodicals and newspapers were acquired, and what lies behind the choices? Do libraries in various parts of the country have similar or different collections? Is there evidence of gifts of religious literature?

In his work on printed book catalogues, Ranz traced the major developments in cataloguing practices, but Robert Singerman's checklist makes it possible to determine cataloguing practices over time for different types of libraries. For instance, what subject divisions were used in 1810 and in 1840 and 1870? What is the importance of these differences?

The utility of this body of source material is greatly enhanced by the frequency with which supplements and/or new editions were issued. For example, Yale's Calliopean Society issued catalogues in 1819, 1824, 1826, 1828, 1829, 1831, 1837, 1841, and 1846. The Mercantile Library Society of Portland, Maine, issued catalogues in 1854, two years after its foundation, and then again in 1859, 1865, 1867, 1870, and 1873. The Library Company of Baltimore published a catalogue in 1802, an appendix in 1804, a new edition in 1809, supplements in 1816, 1823, 1831, 1841, and then a new catalogue in 1851. Thus, changes in emphases in collecting and recording often can be pinpointed to a limited number of years, thereby giving us an index to changing tastes. Such should particularly be the case with a circulating library, the success of which depends on the owner's capacity to judge what is most desired by the public.

The indexing greatly increases the scholarly possibilities. The subject index enables the researcher to find libraries of the same type, while the geographical index, subdivided by date, enables the researcher to identify and study a group of libraries in a particular time span. Of course, it also stimulates the researcher to raise questions. What does it mean, for example, that no catalogue was published in Florida?

Before the days of the computer, these library catalogues were primarily useful for studying the history of cataloguing and, thanks to the prefatory matter that is often present, for learning about the history of a particular library. Thanks to the computer, these catalogues give promise of being useful in studying other aspects of the history of the book, particularly the history of reading and the history of libraries. It is more than the computer, though, that gives library catalogues utility. It is also Robert Singerman's checklist, which, through recording the diverse types of libraries and catalogues and through providing locations of copies, gives the scholar the means to exploit this body of source material.

There are others, in addition to the scholars, who will actually use this bibliography and who owe a debt to its compiler. This is because it also has something to teach all concerned with preserving the sources for our nation's history. The best way of learning what it has to teach is to read through the entries for libraries in a state, particularly a state that does not have one of the old great research libraries. One will find unique copies in libraries other than those in which major preservation microfilming programs are based. (The "not in Shoemaker/not in Rinderknecht, etc." notes serve to identify material that will not be covered by preservation or bibliographical projects based on the standard checklists of imprints.) Since the sources for the history of the United States are by no means held exclusively by the large research libraries, we cannot preserve what needs to be preserved by relying solely on the entrepreneurial self-interest of major institutions. To identify, locate, and preserve our nation's historical sources, it will be necessary to do, on a broader scale, what Singerman has done here—i.e., carry out the bibliographical work that identifies unique locally published materials that never left the local area. That such is the case should not surprise, for this is a geographically widespread and decentralized nation. Few works, however, so clearly demonstrate the bibliographical consequences.

If this checklist were continued to 1910, it would even more clearly demonstrate the dispersal of material. During Singerman's period, the Smithsonian actively collected catalogues that then passed to the Library of Congress. Very likely, no such ingathering was later made in Washington. In addition, the institution with the largest number of catalogues, the American Antiquarian Society, does not emphasize the post-Singerman period. Without conscious directed effort, these and other sources that were once virtually useless will not be available for use by future generations of historians with new interests and new tools.

—Kenneth E. Carpenter

American Library Book Catalogues, 1801-1875: A National Bibliography

Author's Foreword

This checklist records 3,355 separately printed catalogues of American libraries published between 1801 and 1875. Those published before 1801 are covered by Robert B. Winans in his *A Descriptive Checklist of Book Catalogues Separately Printed in America, 1693-1800* (Worcester, MA: American Antiquarian Society, 1981). Whereas Winans records the catalogues of publishers, booksellers, book auctioneers, social and circulating libraries, and personal collections, the focus here will be strictly limited to institutional libraries (not personal ones) with coverage extending from public, college, federal, and state libraries to social, circulating, church, and Sunday school libraries among the major categories.

With so many history of the book programs now emerging in the United States, it is anticipated that the present bibliography will provide valuable sources for library, cultural, and local historians for fresh studies focusing on the sociology of American reading and literacy, the popularity and reception of authors both domestic and foreign, and, more broadly, the evolution and diffusion of the library as a social institution for intellectual advancement in the early years of the republic. Holograph catalogues, as well as library accession lists and circulation or membership records, are omitted from coverage as is any printed catalogue appearing in a newspaper.

Name entries for libraries may not conform to any accepted cataloguing code in that the form of a library's name used here is taken directly from the catalogue itself with only a minimal attempt to link different entry forms for each library by means of cross-references; no authority work has been attempted to trace the corporate genealogy of any library to the present day by recording its current name or to determine the disposition or current whereabouts of collections. When a library has more than one catalogue, arrangement is chronological.

In the note field, standard *National Union Catalog* (NUC) location symbols are given except when the number of known copies exceeds twelve, in which case an "In many libraries" notation substitutes for a lengthy string of NUC symbols. The locations include both copies examined and copies reported to be held. A conscientious effort has been made to locate copies, which means that locations, if fewer than twelve, represent all that could be found. Similarly, an effort has been made to note copies that are defective with loss of text or that are interleaved or have other manuscript additions. Occasionally, a call number is given for an item that may otherwise be difficult to find, for some catalogues in some libraries are only classified, with the pamphlet boxes or bound volumes not analyzed in the library's catalogue.

References are given to Shaw and Shoemaker's *American Bibliography: A Preliminary Checklist for 1801-19* and its continuation by Richard H. Shoemaker and others, *A Checklist of American Imprints* (up to the year 1844 as of late 1995). These can help in locating microform copies filmed under projects such as the Readex Corporations' program to film all of Shaw and Shoemaker to 1819. Some copies recorded in this checklist are not listed in those works. The collations in the checklist attempt to record any preliminary paging not consecutive with the overall pagination and the last numbered printed page; any final printed pages without numbering are counted and this is recorded within brackets.

Three indexes provide other points of access: (1) chronological by state; (2) topical, or more accurately, a modified keyword, which allows the reader to locate all catalogues for each type of library or collection— e.g., lyceum libraries or map collections—within each state; and (3) names of proprietors of circulating and rental libraries.

A few words are in order concerning the compiler's research methodology. The genesis of this checklist goes back to the research slips of the noted library historian Haynes McMullen. Those slips, recording approximately 1,500 catalogues, passed to the compiler in 1988. These were gradually searched on OCLC and RLIN, the two major bibliographical databases available to most American libraries and researchers, with the resulting data printed out and keyboarded. The search had to be item by item, because normative cataloguing practice does not require any sort of "Library catalogues" heading for the genre of library catalogues itself. Each item in the McMullen files was also searched manually in the *National Union Catalog: Pre-1956 Imprints*. Special attention was paid to verifying the McMullen slips for catalogues listed in Charles A. Cutter's inventory published in the U. S. Bureau of Education's *Public Libraries in the United States of America* (1876) or in Joseph Sabin's *Bibliotheca Americana* (1868-1936).

The hunt also branched out from McMullen's slips. It included additional searching of the utilities as well as of online files—e.g., the Library of Congress shelflist of the Z881 classification. Through extensive correspondence, other catalogues were located, and numerous visits were made to libraries and historical societies. Because McMullen, following Cutter, did not list circulating libraries or church or Sunday school libraries, to record them was particularly challenging, and it is likely that these are the types of catalogues of which additional examples are most likely to turn up, especially in churches in New England and in the archives of religious denominations.

Library catalogues are local publications, frequently issued in a small number of copies. Moreover, each catalogue had a quite limited period of utility. It is not surprising that more than 1,000 of these 3,350 catalogues exist, it seems, only in one copy or in only a trace in a published work. Very likely another 1,000 have disappeared, at the very least, from sight. Surely, the inability to visit all possible repositories of catalogues, combined with the inability of many hard-pressed librarians to respond to letters of inquiry (even when repeated and followed up with phone calls) means that more catalogues exist. In fact, one consequence of this checklist may well be to stimulate libraries both to retain these seemingly useless publications and to put in order their own historical records.

To have visited "all possible repositories" would have required travel all over the country, for bibliographical fruit tends to fall close to the tree—e.g., the library catalogue that originated in Maine will generally be found only in libraries in Maine. The American Antiquarian Society (AAS) in Worcester, Massachusetts, is the major exception to that rule, the AAS being the foremost repository of pre-1876 catalogues of every conceivable variety.

Two authoritative library histories necessary for any further study of library catalogues and the larger context of the nineteenth-century American public library and its antecedents in the social library and circulating library are by Jim Ranz (*The Printed Book Catalogue in American Libraries, 1723-1900*. Chicago, IL: American Library Association, 1964) and Jesse H. Shera (*Foundations of the Public Library: The Origins of the Public Library Movement in New England, 1629-1855*. Chicago, IL: University of Chicago Press, 1949). The once familiar circulating library and its catalogues is examined by David Kaser (*A Book for a Sixpence: The Circulating Library in America*, Pittsburgh, PA: Beta Phi Mu, 1980). These standard treatments are well known and may be profitably read for the historical background information and critical analysis they present.

The comprehensiveness of this bibliography owes a great deal to the nationwide cooperation of librarians from coast to coast. It is my special pleasure to acknowledge Haynes McMullen for the confidence placed in me when I became the custodian of his research files. Many librarians across the country responded to my requests for verification assistance, and it would be impossible to thank personally each and every one. I am especially indebted to Susan J. Wolfe (American Antiquarian Society), Mary Anne Hines (Library Company of Philadelphia), Stephen Z. Nonack

(Boston Athenaeum), Jean Rainwater (Brown University), and Mary E. Fabiszewski (Peabody and Essex Museum) for favors received. For permission to consult the shelflist at the Boston Public Library, I have to thank Gunars Rutkovskis for granting me this singular opportunity to follow up on a bibliographer's hunch that led to a large number of prized discoveries. Lewis Hurxthal (Plymouth, Massachusetts) assisted with verification work on a large number of long-forgotten bound pamphlet volumes containing library catalogues at the Boston Public Library. Martin Antonetti (Grolier Club) facilitated my on-site visit and is now thanked for his courtesies and professional interest in the collecting of library catalogues. Other librarians, some as far away from my home base in Florida as Portland, Maine, opened their doors to me by granting library privileges. Finally, Melanie Davis and Mary Gallant, Interlibrary Loan Unit at the University of Florida, were of inestimable assistance in coping with my seemingly unending torrent of borrowing and photoduplication requests.

Thank you all and to you, Kenneth Carpenter, for contributing the introduction to this project despite the varied demands on your professional time, and for your sustained encouragement to carry the task through to completion with all deliberate speed so that it could be shared with the library community.

The compiler invites the notification of additions and corrections.

—Robert Singerman

TABLE 1. NUMBER OF ENTRIES BY STATE OR MISCELLANEOUS CATEGORIES*

1,054	Massachusetts	12	Iowa
456	New York	12	North Carolina
276	Pennsylvania	12	Oregon
203	Rhode Island	10	Delaware
195	New Hampshire	10	Georgia
150	Connecticut	9	Kansas
125	District of Columbia	9	Louisiana
112	Maine	6	Railroad Libraries
88	New Jersey	6	West Virginia
82	Ohio	5	Washington
65	Maryland	4	Alabama
64	Michigan	4	Colorado
60	Vermont	3	Hawaii, Kingdom of
51	Illinois	3	Nevada
41	South Carolina	3	Tennessee
39	California	2	Nebraska
36	Virginia	2	Utah
33	Wisconsin	1	Oklahoma
27	Kentucky	2	Unidentified States
25	Indiana	1	Naval Libraries
24	Missouri	1	Regimental and Military
16	Minnesota		Libraries
15	Mississippi	1	Texas
		3,355	Total

*Does not include supplementary entries as follows: 16a (California); 493a (Maine); 830a (Massachusetts); 646a-b (Maryland); 1904a (New Hampshire); 2183a (New York); 2714a, 2718a, 2904a, 2911a (Pennsylvania); 3197a (Tennessee); 3213a, 3247a, 3248a (Vermont).

TABLE 2. VOLUMES HELD BY AMERICAN LIBRARIES BY TYPE AS OF 1875*

Social Libraries	2,052,426
College Libraries	1,949,105
Public Libraries	1,909,444
Academy and School Libraries	1,270,497
State and Territorial Libraries	834,219
Government Libraries	695,633
Theological Libraries	633,369
Mercantile Libraries	543,930
College Society Libraries	474,642
Historical Libraries	421,794
Law Libraries	339,353
Miscellaneous	305,016
Scientific Libraries	283,992
Asylum and Reformatory Libraries	223,197
Medical Libraries	159,045
Y.M.C.A. Libraries	157,557
Garrison Libraries	32,745
	12,285,964

*Statistics representing holdings of 3,682 public libraries as of 1875, adapted from United States Bureau of Education, *Public Libraries in the United States of America: Their History, Condition, and Management* ... (Washington, DC, 1876), chap. 37, "Library Reports and Statistics," pp. 797-801. Elsewhere, aggregate statistics as of 1870 for Sabbath school and church libraries (9,981,068 vols.) and circulating libraries (2,536,128 vols.) are obtained from Francis A. Walker, ed., *Compendium of the Ninth Census* (Washington, DC: USGPO, 1872), table 36, pp. 506-07.

ABBREVIATIONS

Austin
Austin, Robert B. *Early American Medical Imprints: Guide to Works Printed in the United States, 1668-1820*. Washington, DC: U.S. Dept. of Health, Education, and Welfare, Public Health Service, 1961.

Bowker
Bowker, Richard Rogers. *State Publications: Provisional List of Official Publications of the Several States of the United States from Their Organization*. New York: Publishers' Weekly, 1899-1908.

Bristol
Bristol, Roger Pattrell. *Maryland Imprints, 1801-1810*. Charlottesville: University of Virginia Press for the Bibliographical Society of the University of Virginia, 1953.

Bruntjen
Bruntjen, Scott, & Bruntjen, Carol Rinderknecht. *Checklist of American Imprints for 1831-33*. Metuchen, NJ: Scarecrow Press, 1975-79. 3 vols.

Cooper
Cooper, Gayle. *A Checklist of American Imprints for 1830*. Metuchen, NJ: Scarecrow Press, 1972.

Cutter
Cutter, Charles A. "Library Catalogues." In: United States. Bureau of Education, *Public Libraries in the United States of America: Their History Condition, and Management ...*, pp. 526-622. Washington, DC: USGPO, 1876; reprint, Totowa, NJ: Rowman & Littlefield, 1971. "List of printed catalogues of public libraries in the United States, arranged by date of publication": pp. 577-622 (spans 1723-1876).

Evans
Evans, Charles. *American Bibliography*. Chicago, IL: The Author, 1903-34; Worcester, MA: American Antiquarian Society, 1955-59. 14 vols.

Gilman
Gilman, Marcus Davis. *The Bibliography of Vermont*. Burlington, VT: Free Press Association, 1897.

Hammett
Hammett, Charles Edward. *A Contribution to the Bibliography and Literature of Newport, R.I., comprising a List of Books Published or Printed, in Newport, with Notes and Additions*. Newport, 1887.

Jewett
Jewett, Charles Coffin. *Notices of Public Libraries in the United States of America*. Washington, DC: Printed for the House of Representatives, 1851; microfiche ed., Chicago, IL: Library Resources, 1970.

"Printed by Order of Congress, as an Appendix to the Fourth Annual Report of the Board of Regents of the Smithsonian Institution."

Kaser
Kaser, David. *A Book for a Sixpence: The Circulating Library in America*. Pittsburgh, PA: Beta Phi Mu, 1980.

McKay
McKay, George Leslie. *American Book Auction Catalogues 1713-1934: A Union List*. New York: New York Public Library, 1937; reprint with additions, Detroit, MI: Gale Research Co., 1967.

Munsell
Munsell, Joel. *Bibliotheca Munselliana: A Catalogue of the Books and Pamphlets Issued from the Press of Joel Munsell from the Year 1828 to 1870*. Albany, NY, 1872; reprint, New York: Burt Franklin, 1969.

Rhees
Rhees, William Jones. *Manual of Public Libraries, Institutions, and Societies in the United States, and British Provinces of North America*. Philadelphia, PA: J. B. Lippincott, 1859; reprint, Urbana-Champaign: University of Illinois, Graduate School of Library Science, 1967.

Rinderknecht
Rinderknecht, Carol. *A Checklist of American Imprints for 1834-*. Metuchen, NJ: Scarecrow Press, 1982-.

Rink
Rink, Evald. *Technical Americana: A Checklist of Technical Publications Printed Before 1831*. Millwood, NY: Kraus International Publications, 1981.

S & S
Shaw, Ralph R., & Shoemaker, Richard H. *American Bibliography: A Checklist for 1801-19*. New York: Scarecrow Press, 1958-63. 19 vols., plus three index vols., 1965-66.

Sabin
Sabin, Joseph. *Bibliotheca Americana: A Dictionary of Books Relating to America, from Its Discovery to the Present Time*. New York, 1868-1936. 29 vols.

Sharp
Sharp, Katherine L. *Illinois Libraries*. Urbana-Champaign, 1906-08. 5 vols. Issued as *University of Illinois Bulletin*, vol. 3, no. 16; vol. 4, no. 9; vol. 5, nos. 10, 31; vol. 6, no. 9.

Shoemaker
Shoemaker, Richard H. *A Checklist of American Imprints for 1820-29*. New York: Scarecrow Press, 1964-71. 10 vols., plus two index vols., 1972-73.

Sinclair
Sinclair, Donald Arleigh. *New Jersey Libraries: A Bibliography of Their Printed Catalogs, 1758-1921*. Trenton, NJ: New Jersey Library Association, 1992.

Williamson
Williamson, Joseph. *A Bibliography of the State of Maine ...* Portland, 1896. 2 vol.

NATIONAL UNION CATALOG SYMBOLS

Symbols for selected libraries widely represented in this bibliography are given here. A complete listing of American symbols for libraries is found in vol. 754 of *The National Union Catalog, Pre-1956 Imprints* (London: Mansell, 1968-81).

C	California State Library, Sacramento
CLU	University of California, Los Angeles
CSmH	Huntington Library, San Marino
CSt	Stanford University, Stanford
CU-B	Bancroft Library, University of California, Berkeley
Ct	Connecticut State Library, Hartford
CtHi	Connecticut Historical Society, Hartford
CtY	Yale University, New Haven
DeU	University of Delaware, Newark
DeWint	Winterthur Museum, Winterthur
DLC	Library of Congress, Washington, D.C.
DNLM	National Library of Medicine, Bethesda
GU	University of Georgia, Athens
ICN	Newberry Library, Chicago
ICU	University of Chicago, Chicago
IU	University of Illinois, Urbana
InU	Indiana University, Bloomington
IaU	University of Iowa, Iowa City
KyU	University of Kentucky, Lexington
Me	Maine State Library, Augusta
MeB	Bowdoin College, Brunswick
MeHi	Maine Historical Society, Portland, Maine
MeP	Portland Public Library, Portland, Maine
MdBJ	Johns Hopkins University, Baltimore
MdBP	Peabody Institute, Baltimore
MdHi	Maryland Historical Society, Baltimore
M	State Library of Massachusetts, Boston
MA	Amherst College, Amherst
MB	Boston Public Library, Boston
MBAt	Boston Athenaeum, Boston
MH	Harvard University, Cambridge
MH-H	Houghton Library, Harvard University, Cambridge
MHi	Massachusetts Historical Society, Boston
MSaE	Essex Institute (now Peabody and Essex Museum), Salem
MWA	American Antiquarian Society, Worcester
Mi-B	Burton Collection, Detroit Public Library, Detroit
MiU	University of Michigan, Ann Arbor
MnU	University of Minnesota, Minneapolis
Nh	New Hampshire State Library, Concord
NhD	Dartmouth College, Hanover
NhHi	New Hampshire Historical Society, Concord
NjP	Princeton University, Princeton
NjR	Rutgers University, New Brunswick
N	New York State Library, Albany
NB	Brooklyn Public Library, Brooklyn

NHi	New-York Historical Society, New York
NIC	Cornell University, Ithaca
NN	New York Public Library
NNC	Columbia University, New York
NNGr	Grolier Club, New York
NcU	University of North Carolina, Chapel Hill
OClW	Case Western Reserve University, Cleveland
OKentU	Kent State University, Kent
OU	Ohio State University, Columbus
P	Pennsylvania State Library, Harrisburg
PHi	Historical Society of Pennsylvania, Philadelphia
PP	Free Library of Philadelphia, Philadelphia
PPAmP	American Philosophical Society, Philadelphia
PPL	Library Company of Philadelphia, Philadelphia
PU	University of Pennsylvania, Philadelphia
RHi	Rhode Island Historical Society, Providence
RNR	Redwood Library and Athenaeum, Newport
RPB	Brown University, Providence
ScC	Charleston Library Society, Charleston
ScU	University of South Carolina, Columbia
TxU	University of Texas, Austin
Vt	Vermont State Library, Montpelier
VtHi	Vermont Historical Society, Montpelier
Vi	Virginia State Library, Richmond
ViU	University of Virginia, Charlottesville
ViW	College of William and Mary, Williamsburg
WHi	State Historical Society of Wisconsin, Madison
WU	University of Wisconsin, Madison

ALABAMA

La Grange

La Grange College. La Fayette Society. Catalogue of the Members and Library of the La Fayette Society of La Grange College. Tuscumbia: Printed by A. C. Matthews, Franklin Democrat Office, 1844. [16] p. Not in Rinderknecht. AU.   **1**

Montgomery

Alabama Supreme Court. A Catalogue of Books belonging to the Supreme Court Library of Alabama. Montgomery: Barrett & Wimbish, 1859. 16 p. A-Ar, A-SC.   **2**

Tuscaloosa

University of Alabama. A Catalogue of the Library of the University of Alabama. By Richard Furman. Tuskaloosa: Marmaduke J. Slade, 1837. 54, [1] p. Rinderknecht 42722. A-Ar, AU, NcD.   **3**

University of Alabama. Catalogue of the Library of the University of Alabama, with an Index of Subjects. By Wilson G. Richardson, M.A., Member of the Faculty and Librarian of the University. Tuscaloosa: M. D. J. Slade, 1848. 257 p. AU, DLC, MA, MBAt, MH, MWA (defective), NhD, NNC, NcD, RPB, TxHR, ViU.   **4**

CALIFORNIA

Dutch Flat

Union Sabbath School. Catalogue of the Sabbath School Library of the Dutch Flat Union Sabbath School. San Francisco: Cubery and Co., 1869. 15 p. CU-B.   **5**

Monterey

Monterey Library Association. Constitution and Rules, together with a Catalogue of

Books, of the Monterey Library Association. Organized 1849. San Francisco: O'Meara & Painter, 1854. 17 p. CU-B, DLC.   **6**

Oakland

First Presbyterian Church. Catalogue of Books belonging to the First Independent Presbyterian Sunday School of Oakland. May 1st, 1869. San Francisco: Excelsior Press, Bacon & Co., 1869. 14 p. CU-B.   **7**

First Presbyterian Church. Catalogue of the Sunday School Library of the First Presbyterian Church, Oakland. Revised and enlarged. January, 1874. San Francisco: Winterburn & Co., 1874. 28 p. CU-B.   **8**

Oroville

Ladies' Library Society. A Catalogue of the Ladies' Library Society of Oroville. Consisting of about Five Hundred Volumes made by the Librarian. August, 1863. Oroville: [Oroville Union, Print.], 1863. 10 p. DLC.   **9**

Sacramento

California State Library. Catalogue of the California State Library. January 1, 1855. Sacramento: B. B. Redding, 1855. 172 p. C, CSmH, CSt, CU-B, DLC, ICN, MWA.   **10**

California State Library. Catalogue of the California State Library. 1857. Sacramento: J. Allen, 1857. 65 p. DLC.   **11**

California State Library. Catalogue of the California State Library. Prepared by W. C. Stratton, State Librarian. Sacramento: C. T. Botts, 1860. 409 p. C, C-L, CL-L, CLSU-L, CSmH, CU-B, DLC, M, MBAt, N, OKentU, TxU-L.   **12**

California State Library. Catalogue of the California State Library. Prepared by W. C. Stratton, State Librarian. Sacramento: O.

M. Clayes, 1866. 460, 207 p. Pt. 2, Law books. C, C-L, CLL, CSmH, CU-B, DLC, IU, M, MBAt, MWA, N. **13**

California State Library. Bibliotheca Californiae. A descriptive Catalogue of Books in the State Library of California. By Ambrose P. Dietz, A.M. Sacramento: D. W. Gelwicks, 1870-71. 2 vol. Vol. 1, Law Library; vol. 2, General Library, both compiled by Ambrose P. Dietz. Supplement to vol. 1 issued in 1876 (156 p.). C, C-L, CLL, CSmH, CU-B, DLC, M, MB, NN (film). **14**

California State Library. Law Library. Catalogue of the Law Library of the State of California. Sacramento: C. T. Botts, 1860. 210 p. CU-L. **15**

Sacramento Library. Alphabetical Catalogue of Sacramento Library. Sacramento: Record Printing House, 1872. 54 p. DLC. **16**

San Francisco

Central Methodist Episcopal Church. Catalogue and Rules of the Sunday School Library of the Central M. E. Church . . . San Francisco: Cubery and Co., 1868. 24 p. CU-B. **16a**

Central Presbyterian Church. Rules and Regulations and Catalogue of Books contained in the Central Presbyterian Church Sabbath School Library, of San Francisco. San Francisco: Winterburn & Co., [187-?]. 9 p. Running title: Catalogue of the Sunday School Library. CU-B. **17**

Emanuel Presbyterian Church. Catalogue of Books in Sunday School Library of Emanuel Presbyterian Church, San Francisco. San Francisco, 1871. 46 p. CU-B. **18**

First Congregational Church. Catalogue of the Sunday School Library of the First Congregational Church . . . together with the Constitution and By-laws and Rules for the Library, adopted by the School. San Francisco: Whitton, Towne, 1856. 54, 21 p. CtY and MH copies have suppl., Oct. 1, 1857 (21 p.). CtY, MH. **19**

First Congregational Church. Catalogue of the Sunday School Library of the First Congregational Church . . . with the Constitution, By-laws, and Rules for the Library, adopted by the School. San Francisco: Towne and Bacon, 1866. 46 p. CU-B. **20**

First Congregational Church. Catalogue of the Sunday School Library of the First Congregational Church, San Francisco. Organized, July 1849. San Francisco: A. L. Bancroft, 1872. 46 p. CU-B. **21**

First Presbyterian Church. Catalogue of the Sunday School Library of the First Presbyterian Church . . . San Francisco . . . San Francisco: Winterburn & Co., 1873. 30 p. CU-B. **22**

First Unitarian Society. Catalogue of Pilgrim Sunday School Library, First Unitarian Society, Stockton Street, San Francisco. Issued July, 1861. San Francisco: Frank Eastman, 1861. 56 p. MB. **23**

Grace Church. Catalogue of the Sunday School Library, of Grace Church Parish . . . with the Rules for the Library, adopted by the School, Feb. 1859. San Francisco: Charles F. Robbins & Freeman, 1859. 31 p. MH. **24**

Howard Presbyterian Church. Catalogue of the Sunday School Library of the Howard Presbyterian Church. San Francisco: Cubery and Co., 1868. 33 p. CU-B. **25**

Howard Presbyterian Church. Catalogue of the Sunday School Library of the Howard Presbyterian Church. San Francisco: Cubery and Co., 1874. 39 p. CU-B. **26**

Mechanics' Institute. Catalogue of the Mechanics' Institute Library of San Francisco . . . San Francisco: B. F. Sterett, 1867. xvi, 106 p. CU-B, DLC, MWA. **27**

Mercantile Library. Catalogue of the San Francisco Mercantile Library. August, 1854. San Francisco: Daily Evening News Office, 1854. vi, 197 p. Compiled by Horace Davis. CU-B (film), CtHT, DLC, MB, MBAt, MH, MWA, MnU, NjP, NHi, NN, PPL. **28**

Mercantile Library. Catalogue of Novels and Romances in the San Francisco Mercantile Library . . . San Francisco: C. A. Calhoun, 1857. 26 p. CSmH, IU. **29**

Mercantile Library. Catalogue of Novels and Romances in the Mercantile Library of San Francisco. San Francisco: Charles F. Robbins, 1860. 25 p. CSmH, CU-B. **30**

Mercantile Library. A Classified Catalogue of the Mercantile Library of San Francisco,

with an Index of Authors and Subjects . . .
Made by the Librarian. January, 1861. San
Francisco, 1861. viii, 145 p. Compiled by
Horace H. Moore, Librarian. CLU, CU-B
(film), DLC, IU, MWA, NN.   **31**

Mercantile Library. Catalogue of the Library
of the Mercantile Library Association of San
Francisco . . . San Francisco: Francis &
Valentine, 1874. vii, 958 p. The introduction is by A. E. Whitaker, Librarian.
According to Robert Ernest Cowan, *Booksellers of Early San Francisco* (Los Angeles, 1953),
pp. 93-94, Henry Kirke Goddard prepared
the catalogue. In many libraries.   **32**

Mercantile Library. Catalogue of Books
added to the Mercantile Library of San
Francisco, from February 1, 1874, to
September 1, 1875. San Francisco: Francis &
Valentine, 1875. v, 168 p. CLU, CU-B, DLC,
MA, MB, MBAt, MH, MWA, MnU, NB.   **33**

Military Library. Catalogue of the Military
Library of San Francisco, California.
February 15, 1875. San Francisco: Francis &
Valentine, 1875. 30 p. Organized by officers
of the National Guard of the State of
California. Introduction signed by David
Wilder, secretary and librarian. C, CU-B.
                                        34

St. James Church. Catalogue of the Sunday
School Library of St. James Church, San
Francisco. San Francisco: Cubery and Co.,
1869. 43, [1] p. CU-B.   **35**

San Francisco Verein. Catalogue . . . San
Francisco, 1855 or 56. Contained 1,175
titles, per Hugh S. Baker, "'Rational
Amusement in Our Midst': Public Libraries
in California, 1849-1859," *California Historical Society Quarterly* 38 (1959), p. 315, note 27
(based on *California Chronicle,* Jan. 4, 1856).
                                        36

Second Baptist Church. Catalogue of the
Sunday School Library of the Second Baptist
Church, San Francisco. Organized, October, 1860. San Francisco: Cubery and Co.,
1868. 24 p. CU-B.   **37**

Tabernacle Baptist Church. Catalogue of
the Tabernacle Baptist Sabbath School
Library . . . San Francisco: J. Winterburn,
1869. 19 p. CU-B.   **38**

Young Men's Christian Association. Catalogue of Books in the Library of the Young
Men's Christian Association, of San Francisco. January, 1856. San Francisco: Whitton,
Towne, 1856. 34 p. C, CLU, CU-B.   **39**

San Jose

San Jose Library Association. Constitution,
By-laws, Rules and Regulations of the San
Jose Library Association, with Certificate of
Incorporation, Names of Life, Annual and
Monthly Members, Names of New Books,
&c., &c. San Jose: John J. Conmy, 1872. 48 p.
CU-B, DLC.   **40**

San Quintin

State Prison. Catalogue of the State Prison
Library of the State of California, San
Quinton. Sacramento: D. W. Gelwicks,
1870. 38 p. DLC.   **41**

Stockton

Central Methodist Episcopal Church. Catalogue of the Central Methodist Episcopal
Sabbath School Library, Stockton, Cal.,
embracing the Adult and First Departments. Stockton: Independent Book and
Job Print, 1870. 22 p. CU-B.   **42**

Central Methodist Episcopal Church. Catalogue of the Central Methodist Episcopal
Sabbath School Library, Stockton, Cal.,
embracing the Second Department. Stockton: Independent Book and Job Print, 1870.
16 p. CU-B.   **43**

COLORADO

Denver

Territorial Library. Catalogue of the Territo-
rial Library of the Territory of Colorado.
Denver: Byers & Dailey, 1866. 11 p. CoD,
DLC, TxDaDF.   **44**

Territorial Library. Additional Catalogue of
the Territorial Library of Colorado . . .
Golden City: G. West, 1867. 10 p. DLC. **45**

Territorial Library. Catalogue of the Territorial
Library of the Territory of Colorado. Denver:
Woodbury & Walker, 1870. 46 p. DLC. **46**

Greeley

Greeley Public Library. Catalogue of Books contained in the Greeley Public Library, together with Rules and Regulations. Greeley: Sun Pub. Co., 1866. 70 p. IU (film).   **47**

CONNECTICUT

Ansonia

Young Men's Christian Association. Catalogue of the Y.M.C.A. Library, Ansonia, Conn. Ansonia: E. M. Jerome, 1873. 17 p. DLC. **48**

Ashford

Babcock Library. Catalogue . . . 1871. 7 p. Cf. Cutter 679.   **49**

Birmingham

Allis' Circulating Library. Catalogue of Allis' Circulating Library, Birmingham, Conn. New York: Benj. H. Tyrrel, 1868. 54 p. Conducted by George C. Allis. DLC. **50**

Bridgeport

Baldwin's Circulating Library. Catalogue of Books in J. B. Baldwin's Circulating Library, Bridgeport. [n.p., 182-?]. broadside. Not in Shoemaker. CtHi.   **51**

Bridgeport Library Association. Catalogue of the Library of the Bridgeport Library Association. January, 1860. Bridgeport: Pomeroy & Morse, 1860. 88 p. Bridgeport Public Library, DLC.   **52**

Bristol

Young Men's Christian Association. Catalogue of the Library of the Young Men's Christian Association, Bristol, Conn. Third ed. . . . Hartford: Case, Lockwood & Brainard, 1875. 66 p. DLC.   **53**

Canaan, see North Canaan.

Canterbury

Canterbury Social Library. A Catalogue of Books, belonging the "Canterbury Social Library," August 20th, 1814. [n.p.], 1814. 1

folded leaf. Not in S & S. CtHi (with ms. additions).   **54**

Canton

Congregational Church. Catalogue of the Sabbath School Library of the Congregational Church of Canton, Ct. Hartford: Case, Tiffany, 1841. 15 p. Not in Rinderknecht. CtHi.   **55**

Chester

Chester Library Association. Catalogue, Constitution and By-laws of the Chester Library Association. Chester: Francis Sheldon, 1875. 21, [2] p. Catalogue of the "Fraternal Library" on p. [22]. DLC (with suppl. leaf of additions in 1891).   **56**

Colchester

Colchester Library Association. Constitution, By-laws and Catalogue of the Colchester Library Association. Norwich: Manning, Perry, 1859. 27 p. DLC.   **57**

First Congregational Church. Catalogue, Jan. 11th, 1875, of the Sunday School Library, of the Congregational Church, Colchester. Norwich: Press of the Bulletin Co., 1875. 12 p. Ct.   **58**

Cornwall

Young Gentlemen's Society. Constitution of the Young Gentlemen's Society in Cornwall, with the Catalogue of their Library. October, 1829. Middlebury: Press of the American, 1830. 15 p. Cooper 5593. No locations provided by Cooper.   **59**

Coventry

Hale Donation Library. Catalogue of Books, belonging to the Hale Donation Library, Coventry, Conn. 1824. Hartford: P. B. Goodsell, [1824]. 12 p. Shoemaker 16378. CtHi, MWA, NHi.   **60**

Cromwell

(see also Middletown)

Friendly-Association of Upper-Middletown. Catalogue of Books belonging to the Friendly-Association of Upper-Middletown...Middletown: C. H. Pelton, 1848. 12 p. DLC.   **61**

Danbury

Danbury Library. Catalogue of the Danbury Library . . . Danbury: "News" Steam Job Printing Establishment, 1874. 56 p. MWA copy contains addenda forming pp. 57-60. DLC, MWA. **62**

Darien

Darien Library Association. The Constitution and By-laws of the Darien Library Association, with a Catalogue of Books belonging to the Association. September 1, 1842. New York: J. M. Elliott, 1842. 19 p. Not in Rinderknecht. Cf. Henry Jay Case and Simon W. Cooper, *Town of Darien, Founded 1641, Incorporated 1820* (Darien, 1935), p. 69, stating the library contained about 400 vol. **63**

Derby

Odd Fellows, Independent Order of. Ousatonic Lodge, No. 6. Catalogue of Books in the Library of Ousatonic Lodge, No. 6, I.O.F.F., Derby, Conn. . . . New Haven: Henry Bradley, 1874. 16 p. DLC. **64**

Durham

Academy Library. Catalogue of the Academy Library, Durham, Conn. Hartford: Wiley, Waterman & Eaton, 1873. 36 p. DLC ("Additions for 1874" on pp. [25]-36). **65**

Farmington

Farmington Library Company. Catalogue of the Farmington Library Company. 1850. Farmington, Conn. Hartford: Steam Press of J. Gaylord Wells, 1850. 26 p. CtHi, The Farmington Library, Farmington, Conn. **66**

Farmington Library Company. Catalogue of the Farmington Library. Hartford: Eliahu Geer, 1861. 36 p. CtHi. **67**

Guilford

Christ's Church. Catalogue of Christ's Church Sunday-School Library. Guilford, [18--]. [15] p. NNC (lost). **68**

Hartford

First Congregational Church. Catalogue of the Sabbath School Teachers' Library, of the First Congregational Church in Hartford. Hartford: J. H. Bardwell, 1851. 32 p. Ct, CtHi. **69**

Hartford Circulating Library. Catalogue of the Hartford Circulating Library. Hartford: P. Canfield, 1829. 33 p. Conducted by Henry Benton. Not in Shoemaker. CtHT, MWA. **70**

Hartford Library Company. Catalogue of Books belonging to the Hartford Library Company, and Extracts from the By-laws of said Company. Hartford: Hale & Hosmer, 1812. [22] p. Not in S & S. CtY (defective; interleaved), ICN (interleaved). **71**

Hartford Library Company. Catalogue of Books belonging to the Hartford Library, April 1st, 1818, and Extracts from the By-laws of said Company. Hartford: Hamlen & Newton, 1818. [40] p. S & S 44276. ICN (interleaved). **72**

Hartford Library Company. Catalogue No. 2, of Books added to the Hartford Library, from April 1, 1818, to April 1, 1822. Hartford: Peter B. Gleason, 1822. [8] p. Not in Shoemaker. ICN. **73**

Hartford Library Company. Catalogue of Books belonging to the Hartford Library, January 1, 1828, and Extracts from the By-laws of said Company. Hartford: Goodwin, 1828. [43] p. Shoemaker 33490. Ct, CtHi, CtHT-W, CtSoP, CtY, ICN (defective), MB, NHi. **74**

Mechanics Library. Catalogue of Books belonging to the Mechanics Library of Hartford. [Hartford 182-?]. 12 p. Not in Shoemaker. CtHi. **75**

North Congregational Church. Catalogue of the North Congregational Sabbath School Library, Hartford, Conn. 1866. Hartford: Wiley, Waterman & Eaton, 1866. 21 p. Copies: Ct. **76**

North Sabbath School. Catalogue of the North Sabbath School Library, Hartford. [Hartford]: P. B. Gleason, 1837. 23, [1] p. Not in Rinderknecht. PP. **77**

South Sabbath School. Catalogue of Books in the South S. S. Society, Hartford. April, 1830. [Hartford, 1830]. 8 p. Not in Cooper. MWA. **78**

South Sabbath School. Catalogue of Books belonging to the Library of the South Sabbath School. Scholars' Department. Hartford: Case, Tiffany, 1856. 34 p. CtHi.   **79**

Trinity College, see also Washington College.

Trinity College. Athenaeum Society. Catalogue of the Library and Members of the Athenaeum, Trinity College, Hartford. Hartford: Elihu Geer, 1853. 78 p. Copies: CtHi, DLC (defective), MB.   **80**

Washington College, see also Trinity College.

Washington College. Catalogue of Books, in the Library of Washington College. Hartford, 1832. 24 p. Bruntjen 15040. Ct, CtHi, CtHT-W, DLC, M, MA, MH, MWA, NjR, N, NN, NNGr (uncat.), RPB.   **81**

Washington College. Athenaeum Society. Catalogue of the Members of the Washington College Athenaeum Society, and of the Books in the Library . . . July, 1834. Hartford: P. Canfield, 1834. 20 p. Rinderknecht 27144. CtHT, MWA.   **82**

Washington College. Athenaeum Society. Catalogue of the Members of the Athenaeum Society, and Books in the Library . . . May, 1838. Hartford: Case, Tiffany, 1838. 32 p. Rinderknecht 53371. Ct, CtHC, CtHi, MH.   **83**

Washington College. Athenaeum Society. Catalogue of the Members of the Washington College Athenaeum Society, and of the Books in the Library. Hartford: Case, Tiffany, 1840. 37 p. Rinderknecht 40-6612. MiD-B.   **84**

Washington College. Athenaeum Society. Catalogue of the Library and Members of the Athenaeum Society, of Washington College. Hartford: Case, Tiffany & Burnham, 1844. 58 p. Rinderknecht 44-6221 (duplicated by 44-6442). Ct, CtHi, CtNhHi, InID, MA, MH, RPB.   **85**

Windsor Avenue Church. Catalogue of the Windsor Ave. Baptist Sunday School. June, 1875. [Hartford?, 1875]. broadside (stiff card). Ct.   **86**

Young Men's Institute. Catalogue of Books in the Library of the Young Men's Institute, Hartford, 1839. Hartford: Case, Tiffany & Burnham, 1839. 64 p. Rinderknecht 56176. CtHi, CtHWatk, CtSoP, CtY, ICN.   **87**

Young Men's Institute. Catalogue of the Library and Reading-Room of the Young Men's Institute, Hartford. Hartford: Case, Tiffany and Burnham, 1844. 359 p. Rinderknecht 44-2953 (duplicated by 44-2952). CtHC, CtHi, CtY, DLC, MB, MBAt, MH, MWA, NB, NN, PPL.   **88**

Young Men's Institute. Catalogue of Books added to the Library of the Hartford Young Men's Institute, since the Publication of the Catalogue in 1844. Hartford: Case, Tiffany and Burnham, 1847. 32 p. CtHi, DLC, MWA, N, NB.   **89**

Young Men's Institute. Catalogue of Books added . . . since the Publication of the Catalogue in 1847. Hartford: Case, Tiffany and Burnham, 1852. 35 p. DLC, NB.   **90**

Young Men's Institute. Catalogue of the Library of the Hartford Young Men's Institute. Hartford: [Case, Lockwood & Brainard], 1873. x, 471 p. In many libraries.   **91**

Hazardville

Hazardville Institute. Catalogue of Books belonging to the Hazardville Institute Library, Hazardville, Conn. Hazardville: J. Bridge & Sons, 1872. 25 p. CtHi.   **92**

Lebanon

Ladies' Library. A Catalogue of Books in the Ladies' Library, in Lebanon, (South Society,) Conn., November 1st, 1844. Norwich: J. G. Cooley, 1844. 6 p. Not in Rinderknecht. CtHi (with ms. additions), MWA.   **93**

Ledyard

Bill Library. Catalogue of the Bill Library, Ledyard, Conn. Norwich: Norwich Printing Co., 1867. 87 p. Includes "Sabbath School Catalogue." Ct, DLC, and ICN copies have suppl. to 1872 on pp. [89]-124. CU-SB, Ct, CtHi, DeU, DLC, ICN, MWA, NHi.   **94**

Litchfield

First Congregational Church. Catalogue of Books belonging to the First Congregational Sabbath School Library, of Litchfield, Conn. 1856. [n.p., 1856]. 24 p. Ct (defective).   **95**

St. Michael's Church. Sunday School Library of St. Michael's Church, Litchfield, Conn. [n.p., ca. 1866]. 4 p. Ct, MB.　　**96**

Manchester

Manchester Library Association. Catalogue of the Manchester Library Association, South Manchester, Conn. Hartford: Case, Lockwood & Brainard, 1873. 77 p. DLC (printed slips with additions inserted).　**97**

Meriden

Methodist Episcopal Church. Revised Catalog of the Sabbath School Library of the Methodist Episcopal Church, Meriden, Conn. Meriden: M. L. Delavan, 1871. 26 p. CtHi.　　**98**

Young Men's Christian Association. Catalogue of the Meriden Y.M.C.A. Library. January, 1873. West Meriden: Press of Citizen Association, 1873. 47 p. DLC, MWA.　**99**

Middletown

(see also Cromwell)

American Literary, Scientific, and Military Academy. Catalogue of Books in the Cadets' Library, at the American Literary, Scientific, and Military Academy . . . Middletown: E. & H. Clark, 1827. 28 p. Not in Shoemaker. NN.　　**100**

Methodist Episcopal Church. Catalogue of the Sunday School Library of the Methodist Episcopal Church, Middletown, Conn. Hartford: Case, Lockwood & Brainard, 1869. 22 p. Ct.　　**101**

Middletown Library. Catalogue of Books belonging to the Middletown Library. January 1, 1818. Middletown: T. Dunning, 1818. 16 p. S & S 44840. CSmH.　**102**

Wesleyan Theological Institute. A Catalogue of Books and Manuscripts presented to the Wesleyan Theological Institute in the Year MDCCCLIX by James Heald. [n.p., 1859?]. 290 p. Collection formed by Rev. Thomas Jackson's private library. NjMD.　**103**

Wesleyan University. Catalogue of the Library of the Wesleyan University. Middletown: William D. Starr, 1837. 50 p. Rinderknecht 48443. CtHT, DLC, IEG, MH, MWA, NN, NNC.　　**104**

Wesleyan University. Peithologian Society. Catalogue of the Members and Library of the Peithologian Society . . . September, 1838. Middletown: C. H. Pelton, 1838. 35 p. Not in Rinderknecht; Sabin 102711. CtY, MH (both locations per Sabin).　**105**

Wesleyan University. Peithologian Society. Catalogue of the Members and Library of the Peithologian Society, ofthe Wesleyan University . . . September, 1846. Middletown: W. D. Starr, 1846. 49 p., [1] p. of rules. DLC, NjR.　　**106**

Wesleyan University. Philorhetorian Society. Catalogue of the Members and Library of the Philorhetorian Society, of Wesleyan University, from its Foundation, Nov. 1, 1831, to July 12, 1837. Middletown: C. H. Pelton, 1837. 20 p. Not in Rinderknecht. MH.　　**107**

Wesleyan University. Philorhetorian Society. Catalogue of the Philorhetorian Society of the Wesleyan University. Founded, November 1, 1831. Middletown: W. Trench, 1840. 60 p. "Catalogue of the Philorhetorian Library" on pp. [11]-60. Not in Rinderknecht. DLC, NN.　　**108**

Wesleyan University. Philorhetorian Society. Catalogue of the Members, and of the Library, of the Philorhetorian Society, of Wesleyan University . . . Founded November 1, 1831. Middletown: W. D. Starr, 1846. 46 p. DLC, NN.　　**109**

New Britain

Connecticut State Normal School. Catalogue, with Rules and Regulations, of the Conn. State Normal School Library. New Britain: L. M. Guernsey, 1856. 14 p. Ct, CtNbT, DLC.　　**110**

New Britain Institute. Catalogue of the Library of the New Britain Institute. Hartford: Case, Lockwood & Brainard, 1872. 78 p. DLC, MWA.　　**111**

New Haven

Bartholomew's Select Library. Catalogue of Books at Present in Circulation at Bartholomew's Select Library. New Haven: Benham & Williams, 1872. 33 p. Operated by Lucius B. Bartholomew. DLC.　**112**

College Street Church. Catalogue of the Sabbath School Library of the College Street Church, New Haven, Conn. [New Haven]: Hoggson & Robinson, 1874. 15 p. MWA. **113**

Collegiate and Commercial Institute. Catalogue of the Library of the Collegiate and Commercial Institute, New Haven, Conn. New Haven: J. H. Benham, 1857. 23 p. MB. **114**

First Church. Catalogue of the Library of the First Church and Society in New Haven, May, 1860. [New Haven: E. Hayes, 1860]. 34 p. CtY and MB hold First Supplement . . . to March, 1861 (8 p.); MB holds Second Supplement . . . to May, 1867 (13 p.). CtY, MB. **115**

Howe and Deforest's Circulating Library. Catalogue of Books, in Howe and Deforest's Circulating Library, Chapel Street, New-Haven. [New-Haven]: Sidney's Press, 1814. 39 p. NNGr holds undated suppl., ca. 1814 (16 p.). Not in S & S. CtNhHi, NNGr. **116**

Mechanic Library Society. The Constitution and Bye-laws, of the Mechanic Library Society, of New-Haven, with a Catalogue of Books. New-Haven: Thomas Green and Son, 1801. 27 p. S & S 1008, Rink 503. CtY. **117**

Mechanic Library Society. The Constitution and Bye-laws of the Mechanic Library Society, in New-Haven. With a Catalogue of Books. [New Haven: O. Steele, 180-?]. 24 p. Not in S & S. CtY, MWA. **118**

Mechanic Library Society. The Constitution and Bye-laws of the Mechanic Library Society, in New-Haven. With a Catalogue of Books. [New Haven, 1812]. 22 p. Not in S & S; Rink 506. CtY. **119**

New-Haven Library Company. The Constitution and Bye-laws of the New-Haven Library Company, together with the Act of Incorporation, and a Catalogue of Books. [New-Haven, 1815?]. 39 p. **120**

Formed by the merger of the Mechanics' Library Society and the Social Library Company in May, 1815. S & S 35969. CtHi, CtY (entered under: New Haven. Social Library Company), MWA (entered under: The Social Library Company in New Haven).

North Church Society. Catalogue of the North Church Sunday School Library. 1860. New Haven: J. H. Benham, [1860]. 15 p. Ct. **121**

Social Library Company. The Constitution and Bye-laws of the Social Library Company, together with a Catalogue of Books. New-Haven: Oliver Steele, 1808. 12 p. S & S 15730. CtY, NN. **122**

Social Library Company. The Constitution and Bye-laws of the Social Library Company, together with the Act of Incorporation, and a Catalogue of Books. New-Haven: Joseph Barber, 1812. 19, [1] p. S & S 51224. CtY. **123**

Social Library Company. A Catalogue of Books in the New-Haven Social Library, together with the Constitution and By-laws of the Company. [New Haven]: Nathan Whiting, 1822. 25 p. Shoemaker 9647. CtNhHi, CtY, NN. **124**

Social Library Company. A Catalogue of Books in the New-Haven Social Library, together with the Constitution and By-laws of the Company. New-Haven: Baldwin & Ellis, 1833. 28 p. Bruntjen 20325. CtY, MWA. **125**

Yale University. Catalogue of Books in the Library of Yale-College, New-Haven. January, 1808. New-Haven: Oliver Steele, 1808. 79, [1] p. Compiled by James Luce Kingsley, per Sabin 105897. S & S 16771. In many libraries. **126**

Yale University. Catalogue of Books in the Library of Yale College. New Haven: Journal Office, 1823. 100, [2] p. Shoemaker 14990. In many libraries. **127**

Yale University. Brothers in Unity Society. Catalogue of Books in the Brothers' and Linonian Libraries. New Haven: Oliver Steele, 1808. 24 p. S & S 16772. CtY, MWA. **128**

Yale University. Brothers in Unity Society. Catalogue of Books belonging to the Brothers and Linonian Libraries, Yale College. New Haven: Sidney's Press, 1811. 24 p. Not in S & S. CtY, PBL, RPB. **129**

Yale University. Brothers in Unity Society. Catalogue of the Books belonging to the Brothers', Linonian, & Moral Libraries, Yale College. January, 1818. New Haven: David Kimball, 1818. 31 p. Copy held by NN has inserted "A List of Books to aid Young Preachers in the Selection of a Library" ([4] p.). Not in S & S. CtY, NN. **130**

Yale University. Brothers in Unity Society. A Catalogue of Books, belonging to the Brothers', Linonian, and Moral Libraries, Yale College. November, 1825. New Haven: Journal Office, 1825. 52 p. Shoemaker 23394. CtY, RPJCB. **131**

Yale University. Brothers in Unity Society. Catalogue of Books belonging to the Society of Brothers in Unity, Yale College. April, 1829. New Haven: Lucius K. Dow, Journal Office, [1829]. 30 p. Shoemaker 41609. CtHC, CtHT, CtY, MWA. **132**

Yale University. Brothers in Unity Society. Catalogue of Books belonging to the Society of Brothers in Unity, Yale College. September, 1832. New Haven: Whitmore and Minor, [1832]. 39 p. Bruntjen 17176. Ct, CtY, MB, NN, PPAmP. **133**

Yale University. Brothers in Unity Society. Catalogue of Books belonging to the Society of Brothers in Unity, Yale College. January, 1835. New Haven: Whitmore and Buckingham, [1835?]. 52 p. Rinderknecht 35549. Ct, CtHT, CtY, DeU, MeAug, MH, NN. **134**

Yale University. Brothers in Unity Society. Catalogue of the Library belonging to the Society of Brothers in Unity, Yale College. June, 1838. New Haven: Hitchcock & Stafford, 1838. 106 p. Rinderknecht 53767. CtY, LU, MB, MWA, MnU, N, NN, OClW. **135**

Yale University. Brothers in Unity Society. Catalogue of the Library of the Society of Brothers in Unity, Yale College. April, 1846. New Haven: B. L. Hamlen, 1846. 224 p. CtHi, CtY, DLC, NjP, N, NN, ViU. **136**

Yale University. Brothers in Unity Society. Catalogue of the Library of the Society of Brothers in Unity, Yale College. July, 1851. New Haven: Thomas J. Stafford, 1851. 294 p. Appendix contains "Index to Articles in Volumes of Essays, Speeches, and Miscellaneous Works belonging to the Library of the Brothers in Unity" (pp. [255]-94). CtHT, DLC, IU (film), MA, MB, MWA, NN, PP, RPB. **137**

Yale University. Calliopean Society. Catalogue of Books belonging to the Calliopean Society, Yale College. 1819. [New Haven, 1819?]. 8 p. Not in S & S; Sabin 105871. CtY (per Sabin) **138**

Yale University. Calliopean Society. Catalogue of the Books belonging to the Calliopean Society College. January, 1824. [New Haven, 1824]. 14 p. Shoemaker 19346. CtY, NN. **139**

Yale University. Calliopean Society. Catalogue of Books belonging to the Calliopean Society, Yale College. October, 1826. New Haven: Journal Office, 1826. 19 p. Not in Shoemaker. CtY, MWA. **140**

Yale University. Calliopean Society. Catalogue of Books belonging to the Calliopean Society, Yale College. March, 1828. New Haven: Treadway & Adams, 1828. 26 p. Shoemaker 37269. CtHT, CtY, DLC, MWA, N. **141**

Yale University. Calliopean Society. Supplement to the Catalogue of Books, belonging to the Library of the Calliopean Society, Yale College. March, 1829. [New Haven, 1829]. 8 p. Shoemaker 41610. CtY, DLC, MWA, N. **142**

Yale University. Calliopean Society. Catalogue of Books belonging to the Library of the Calliopean Society, Yale College. June, 1831. New Haven: Hezekiah Howe, 1831. 38 p. Bruntjen 10751. Ct, CtY, NBu, NN. **143**

Yale University. Calliopean Society. Catalogue of the Library of the Calliopean Society, Yale College. February 16, 1837. New Haven: Hitchcock & Stafford, 1837. 56 p. Rinderknecht 48628. CtY, MB, MWA, N, NN, PPL, PU, TNV. **144**

Yale University. Calliopean Society. Catalogue of the Library of the Calliopean Society, Yale College. October, 1841. New Haven: Hitchcock & Stafford, 1841. 84 p. Not in Rinderknecht. Ct, CtHi, CtHT, CtY, MWA, OClW, PPPrHi, RPB. **145**

Yale University. Calliopean Society. Catalogue of the Library of the Calliopean Society, Yale College. February, 1846. New Haven: B. L. Hamlen, 1846. 94 p. AU, Bridgeport (Conn.) Public Library, CtY, DLC, MA, MH, MWA, NN, PPL, ViU. **146**

Yale University. Linonian Society. Catalogue of Books in the Linonian, Brothers', and Moral Libraries, Yale College. New Haven: Oliver Steele, 1814. 27, [1] p. S & S 33744. CtU, CtY, NN. **147**

Yale University. Linonian Society. Catalogue of Books belonging to the Linonian, Brothers' and Moral Libraries, Yale College. September, 1822. New Haven: Journal Office, 1822. 39, [1] p. Shoemaker 11496. CtY, M, MH, MWA, NN, PBL, PPL, TxU. **148**

Yale University. Linonian Society. Catalogue of Books belonging to the Linonian Society, Yale College. August, 1829. New Haven: S. Babcock, [1829]. 35 p. Shoemaker 41612. CSmH, Ct, CtHT, CtY, DHEW, MWA. **149**

Yale University. Linonian Society. Catalogue of Books belonging to the Linonian Society, Yale College. October, 1831. New Haven: Baldwin & Treadway, 1831. 40 p. Bruntjen 10752. CSmH, Ct, CtY, MH, NN. **150**

Yale University. Linonian Society. Catalogue of Books belonging to the Linonian Society, Yale College. July, 1834. New-Haven: Baldwin & Peck, 1834. 50 p. Rinderknecht 29849. CSmH, CtY, MWA, NN. **151**

Yale University. Linonian Society. Supplement to the Catalogue of Books belonging to the Linonian Society, Yale College. June, 1836. New Haven: B. L. Hamlen, 1836. 15 p. Not in Rinderknecht. CtY, MB. **152**

Yale University. Linonian Society. Catalogue of the Library of the Linonian Society, Yale College. July, 1837. New Haven: B. L. Hamlen, 1837. 82 p. Rinderknecht 48630. CtHi, CtY, ICN, MB, MH, MWA, MiD-B, MnU, PPAmP. **153**

Yale University. Linonian Society. Supplement to the General Catalogue of the Library of the Linonian Society. 1840. [New Haven: B. L. Hamlen, 1840]. 16 p. Not in Rinderknecht. CtY, MnU. **154**

Yale University. Linonian Society. Catalogue of the Library of the Linonian Society, Yale College. October, 1841. New Haven: Hitchcock & Stafford, 1841. 162 p. Rinderknecht 41-5656. CtY, MHi, MWA, OCIW. **155**

Yale University. Linonian Society. Catalogue of the Library of the Linonian Society, Yale College. November, 1846. New Haven: J. H. Benham, 1846. 274 p. Ct, CtY, DLC, MBAt, MH-AH, MWA, N, NN, PHi, ViU. **156**

Yale University. Linonian Society. Catalogue of the Library of the Linonian Society, Yale College. June, 1860. New Haven: J. H. Benham, 1860. 298 p. Ct, CtY, DLC, LU, MB, MBAt, MWA, MiU, MnU, NN, RPB. **157**

Yale University. Linonian Society. Catalogue of the Linonian and Brothers' Library, Yale College. New Haven: Tuttle, Morehouse & Taylor, 1873. 334 p. CtHi, CtHT, ICN, LU, MdBJ, MBAt, MWA, MiU, MnU, NN, Vt. **158**

Yale University. Phoenix Society. Catalogue of Books in the Phoenix Library. [New Haven: O. Steele, 1806]. broadside. S & S 11904. MnU. **159**

Yale University. Sheffield Scientific School. Catalogue of the Hillhouse Mathematical Library, the Gift of Joseph E. Sheffield, and of other Mathematical Books belonging to the Sheffield Scientific School. [New Haven, 1870]. 44 p. At head of title: Appendix to the Fifth Annual Report. MB, RPB. **160**

Young Mechanics' Institute. The Constitution and By-laws, of the Young Mechanics' Institute, to which is added a Catalogue of Books belonging to the Library. New-Haven: Baldwin and Ellis, 1833. 11 p. Bruntjen 20319. CtY. **161**

Young Mechanics' Institute. The Constitution and By-laws, of the Young Mechanics' Institute, to which is added a Catalogue of Books belonging to the Library. New Haven: W. Storer, jun., 1836. 12 p. Not in Rinderknecht. CtY. **162**

Young Mechanics' Institute. The Constitution and By-laws, of the New Haven Young Mechanics' Institute, together with the Catalogue of the Library. May 1839. New Haven: Babcock & Galpin, 1839. 18 p. Not in Rinderknecht. CtY. **163**

Young Men's Institute. Catalogue of Books in the Library of the Young Men's Institute, New Haven. 1840. New Haven: James M. Patten, 1840. 36 p. Not in Rinderknecht. CtY, MWA. **164**

Young Men's Institute. Catalogue of the Library of the New Haven Young Men's Institute, with the Charter, Bye-laws, &c. New Haven: B. L. Hamlen, 1841. 65 p. Not in Rinderknecht. CtHi, CtHT, DLC, MWA, OClW. **165**

Young Men's Institute. Catalogue of the Library of the New Haven Young Men's Institute, with the Charter, Bye-laws, &c. New Haven: T. J. Stafford, 1851. 122 p. CtY, DLC. **166**

New London

Young Men's Library Association. A Catalogue of the Books, belonging to the Young Men's Library Association. 1841. New London: Star Office, 1841. 52 p. Rinderknecht 41-3759. Ct. **167**

Young Men's Library Association. A Catalogue of Books, belonging to the Young Men's Library Association, New London, Conn. 1851. New London: Star Office, 1851. 39 p. DLC. **168**

North Canaan

Douglas Library. Catalogue of Books belonging to the Douglas Library. Falls Village: C. T. Maltbie, 1860. 34 p. DLC, ICN. **169**

North Haven

Church of Christ. Catalogue of the North Haven Sunday School Library. New Haven: Tuttle, Morehouse & Taylor, 1869. 19 p. Ct. **170**

Church of Christ. Catalogue of the North Haven Sunday School Library. New Haven: Tuttle, Morehouse & Taylor, 1874. 24 p. Ct. **171**

North Haven Library. Books in the North Haven Library. [n.p., 181-?]. Not in S & S. Cf. Sheldon B. Thorpe, *North Haven Annals: A History of the Town from its Settlement* . . . (New Haven, 1892), pp. 182-83. **172**

Norwich

Norwich Circulating Library. Catalogue of the Norwich Circulating Library. Norwich, 1871. 54 p. DLC (lost). **173**

Norwich Library Association. An Alphabetical Catalogue, of Books, in the Collection of the Norwich Library Association, in the City of Norwich. Library in the Basement of Central Baptist Church. Norwich: J. G. Cooley, 1843. 22 p. Not in Rinderknecht. CtHT, New London County Historical Society, New London, Conn. **174**

Otis Library. Catalogue of Books in the Otis Library, Norwich, Conn. Norwich: J. Dunham's Press, 1850. 55 p. DLC, MWA, New London County Historical Society, New London, Conn. **175**

Otis Library. An Appendix to the Catalogue of the Otis Library. January, 1853. Norwich, 1853. 28 p. Published with the reissue of the 1850 edition. DLC, MWA. **176**

Otis Library. Catalogue of Books in the Otis Library, of the City of Norwich. Norwich: Bulletin Office, 1867. 173 p. CU-A, DLC, MB, NNC, RPB. **177**

Trinity Church. Catalogue of Books in the Library of Trinity Church Sunday School of Norwich, Conn. Norwich: Press of the Bulletin Co., 1874. 13 p. Ct. **178**

Prospect

Congregational Church. Catalogue of the Prospect Sunday School Library, Prospect, Conn. 1872. [n.p., 1872]. 12 p. Ct. **179**

Salisbury

Youth's Library. Catalogue of Books in the Youth's Library, at Salisbury, Connecticut. Feb. 20, 1806. Boston: David Carlisle, 1806. 12 p. Generally known as the Bingham Library for Youth and regarded as America's first public library. Cf. Jesse H. Shera, *Foundations of the Public Library* . . . (Chicago, 1949), pp. 158-60. S & S 11321. CtHi, MWA. **180**

Simsbury

Simsbury Free Library. Catalogue of Simsbury Free Library. January 1, 1875. Hartford: Case, Lockwood & Brainard, 1875. 25 p. DLC. **181**

Stonington

Stonington Book Club. Catalogue of Books belonging to the Stonington Book Club. [n.p., 1875?]. [10] p. DLC (with 10 p. of ms. accessions). **182**

Suffield

First Congregational Church. Catalogue of Books in the Sabbath School Library of the First Congregational Church, Suffield, Conn. 1864. Hartford: Case, Lockwood, 1864. 31 p. Ct.　　　**183**

First Congregational Church. Catalogue of Books in the First Congregational Church Sunday School Library, Suffield, Conn. Springfield, Mass.: Clark W. Bryan, 1874. 15 p. Ct, MWA.　　　**184**

Thompson

First Congregational Church. Catalogue of books belonging to the First Congregational Sabbath School Library, in Thompson, March 9, 1839 . . . Providence: H. H. Brown, [1839]. 12 p. Rinderknecht 58875. Ct.　　　**185**

Uncasville

Methodist Episcopal Church. Catalogue of Sunday School Library of the Methodist Episcopal Church, Uncasville, Conn. 1875. [n.p., 1875]. 26 p. Ct.　　　**186**

Unionville

First Congregational Church. Catalogue of the Books belonging to the Libraries of the Congregational Church & Sabbath School in Unionville, Conn. Hartford: Case, Lockwood & Brainard, 1873. 32 p. Ct. **187**

Waterbury

First Congregational Church. Catalogue of the First Congregational Sunday-School Library, Waterbury, Conn. Waterbury: E. B. Cooke, 1860. 24 p. CtHi.　　　**188**

Silas Bronson Library. Catalogue of the Silas Bronson Library of the City of Waterbury, Conn. Waterbury: American Printing Co., 1870. viii, 340 p. CU-A, DLC, ICN, IU, M, MB, MBAt, MH, MWA, MnU, Nh, NB, NRU.　　　**189**

Silas Bronson Library. Catalogue of the Silas Bronson Library of the City of Waterbury, Conn. Supplement, Books added, June 1st, 1872, to June 1st, 1873. Waterbury, 1873. [377]-390 p. DLC, ICN, MB.　　　**190**

Young Men's Institute. Supplementary Catalogue. Catalogue of Books added to the Library of the Waterbury Young Men's Institute. December, 1859. Waterbury: E. B. Cooke, 1860. 24 p. List of members for 1859-60 on pp. 19-24. CtHi.　　　**191**

West Haven

West Haven Institute. Catalogue of the West Haven Institute Library. Organized, 1867. New Haven: Tuttle, Morehouse and Taylor, 1867. 39 p. CtY (photocopy), UPB.　　　**192**

Windsor

First Congregational Church. Catalogue of the Windsor Cong. Sabbath School. Hartford: Wiley, Waterman & Eaton, 1873. 14 p. Ct.　　　**193**

Sixth School District. Catalogue of Books belonging to the Library of the Sixth School District, Windsor, Conn. Hartford: Case, Tiffany & Burnham, 1841. 12 p. Rinderknecht 41-5582. Ct, CtHi.　　　**194**

Winsted

Beardsley Library. Catalogue of the Beardsley Library, at West Winsted, Conn. Waterbury: American Printing Co., 1875. 125 p. Ct, DLC, MWA (with ms. additions), N, NRU, OCl.　　　**195**

Wolcottville

Wolcottville Library. Catalogue of the Wolcottville Library, Wolcottville, Conn. . . . Winsted: Winsted Printing Co., 1873. 32 p. DLC.　　　**196**

Woodstock

Woodstock Social Library. The Compact of the Woodstock Social Library. Woodstock: Haskell and Palmer, 1845. 21 p. "Catalogue of Books . . ." on pp. [9]-21. NHi.　　　**197**

DELAWARE

New Castle

New-Castle Library Company. A Catalogue of the Books belonging to the New-Castle Library Company, to which are prefixed the

Act of Incorporation, and the By-laws of the Company . . . Wilmington: R. Porter, 1819. 67 p. S & S 48831. DeHi, DeWi (with ms. additions).   **198**

New-Castle Library Company. A Catalogue of Books belonging to the New Castle Library Company, to which are prefixed the Act of Incorporation, and the By-laws of the Company. New Castle: Printed by John C. Clark, Philadelphia, 1840. 114 p. Not in Rinderknecht. ABAU, DeHi (2 interleaved copies, one of which has ms. additions), DeU, DLC, MWA, New Castle Public Library, NNGr.   **199**

Newark

Delaware College. Catalogue of the Books belonging to the Library of Delaware College. Wilmington: Porter & Naff, 1843. 52 p. Includes "Catalogue of Books of the Library of Newark Academy" (pp. [35]-52). Rinderknecht 43-1491. DeU, DLC, MH.   **200**

Newark Academy, see entry 200.

Wilmington

Historical Society of Delaware. Catalogue of the Historical Society of Delaware. With its History, Constitution, and By-laws, and List of Members. Wilmington: Lippincott's Press, 1871. 23 p. DeHi, DLC, IHi, MdBJ, MWA, MiD, MoSHi, NBuHi, NN, OClWHi, PPL.   **201**

Wilmington Institute Library. Catalogue of the Wilmington Institute Library. 1875. Wilmington: James & Webb, [1875]. 106 p. DeWI, DLC, MB, NNC.   **202**

Wilmington Library. Constitution, Bye-laws, and Catalogue, of the Wilmington Library. Wilmington: Robert Porter, 1815. 36 p. DLC copy has p. 14 repeated in numbering while p. 22 is skipped in numbering. S & S 36590. DeHi, DeWI, DLC.   **203**

Wilmington Library. Catalogue of Books belonging to the Wilmington Library. Wilmington: Robert Porter, 1823. 22 p. Shoemaker 14941. DeWI.   **204**

Wilmington Library. Catalogue of Books belonging to the Wilmington Library.

Wilmington: R. & J. B. Porter, 1838. 40 p. Not in Rinderknecht. DeHi, DeWI.   **205**

Wilmington Library. Catalogue of Books belonging to the Wilmington Library. Wilmington: John B. Porter, 1851. 60 p. DeHi, DeWI.   **206**

Wilmington Library. Index to the Books of the Wilmington Library and Young Men's Association. Wilmington: C. P. Johnson, 1858. 135 p. Issued with "A Historical Sketch of the Wilmington Library and Young Men's Association . . ." (32 p.). DeHi, DLC.   **207**

Young Men's Association, see entry 207.

DISTRICT OF COLUMBIA

Georgetown

Columbian Library, see entries 211-12.

Georgetown Circulating and Reference Library. Catalogue of the Georgetown Circulating and Reference Library for 1834. Kept by C. Cruikshank, Bookseller. Georgetown: H. G. Rind, 1834. 120 p. Bruntjen 24592. DGU, DLC, ScU.   **208**

Peabody Library Association. Catalogue and Rules of the Peabody Library Association, of Georgetown, D.C. Washington: W. H. Moore, [187-?]. 24 p. DLC.   **209**

Thomas, James. Catalogue of the Circulating Library, kept by James Thomas. Georgetown, 1828. 34 p. Not in Shoemaker. DLC.   **210**

Union Circulating Library. A Catalogue of the Union Circulating Library, for 1813. Kept by Joseph Milligan, Bookseller. . . Georgetown: W. Cooper, 1813. 11, 28 p. Includes "Catalogue of the Columbian Library." S & S 28618. DLC.   **211**

Union Circulating Library. A Catalogue of the Union Circulating Library, for 1815. Kept by Joseph Milligan, Bookseller . . . Georgetown: W. A. Rind, 1815-[16]. 27, 3, [25]-44 p. DLC copy includes suppl. for 1816 (3 p.) and "Catalogue of the Columbian Library" (pp. [25]-44). S & S 34777. DLC.   **212**

Washington, D.C.

Non-Governmental Libraries

Central Congregational Church. Catalogue of the Sunday School Library of the Central Congregational Church, of Washington, D.C. Jan. 1, 1870. Washington: C. W. Brown, 1870. 14 p. DLC.   **213**

Columbian College. Preliminary Catalogue of Library of Columbian College. August 13, 1871. Washington: Judd & Detweiler 1871 p. DLC, MWA.   **214**

Davis and Force's Washington Circulating Library. Catalogue of Davis & Force's Washington Circulating Library . . . Washington: Davis and Force, 1820. 46, [1] p. Shoemaker 966. DLC.   **215**

Davis and Force's Washington Circulating Library. Catalogue of Davis & Force's Washington Circulating Library . . . 2d ed. Washington: Davis and Force, 1820. 63 p. Shoemaker 967. DLC.   **216**

Davis and Force's Washington Circulating Library. Catalogue of Davis & Force's Washington Circulating Library . . . 3d ed. Washington: Davis and Force, 1821. 75 p. Shoemaker 5157. DLC (interleaved with ms. additions).   **217**

Davis and Force's Washington Circulating Library, see also entry 229.

First Baptist Church. Catalogue of the Books in the Library of the Sunday School of the First Baptist Church, Washington, D.C., July, 1857. Washington: T. McGill, 1857. 7 p. DLC. **218**

First Congregational Church. Catalogue of Library, First Congregational Sabbath-School, Washington, D.C., May 1, 1867. [Washington, 1867]. 15 p. DLC.   **219**

First Presbyterian Church. Catalogue of the Sunday School Library of the First Presbyterian Church, of Washington, D.C. [Washington], 1868. 24 p. DLC.   **220**

Fourth Presbyterian Church. Catalogue of Books in the Sabbath School Library, of the Fourth Presbyterian Church, Washington. [Washington, 182-?]. 8 p. Shoemaker 4183. DLC.   **221**

Friends, Society of. Washington Preparative Meeting. Inventory of Books belonging to

the Washington Preparative Meeting of Friends . . . Washington: Duncanson, [183-?]. broadside. Cf. Library of Congress. Rare Book Division, *Catalog of Broadsides in the Rare Book Division* (Boston, 1972), vol. 3, p. 535. Cooper 1522. DLC.   **222**

Jefferson Library. Catalogue of the Books of the Jefferson Library of Washington City. Washington: R. L. Spalding, M. T. Hunter, 1833. 27 p. DLC copy includes Constitution of the Jefferson Library . . . (8 p.). Bruntjen 19544. DLC.   **223**

New York Avenue Presbyterian Church. Catalogue of the Sabbath-School Library of the New York Avenue Presbyterian Church. Washington: T. M'Gill, 1860. 28 p. DLC.
224

New York Avenue Presbyterian Church. Catalogue of the Sabbath-School Library, May 1870. Washington: M'Gill & Witherow, 1870. 12 p. DLC.   **225**

Odd Fellows Association. Catalogue . . . 1868. 26 p. Cf. Cutter 567.   **226**

People's Circulating Library. Catalogue of the People's Circulating Library. Washington: Gideon & Pearson, [186-?]. 23 p. DLC, MWA.   **227**

People's Circulating Library. Catalogue of the People's Circulating Library . . . Washington: Gideon & Pearson, 1864. 24 p. DLC (copy 2 has library's address corrected in ms.).   **228**

Washington Circulating Library. Conditions of the Washington Circulating Library . . . Washington: Davis & Force, [182-]. 59, [1] p. Catalogue of books on pp. 3-59. Not in Shoemaker. DLC.   **229**

Washington Circulating Library, see also entries 215-17.

Washington Library. Catalogue of Books belonging to the Washington Library. June, 1815. [City of Washington, 1815]. 15 p. S & S 36488. DLC (has ms. list of shareholders and is interleaved with ms. additions). **230**

Washington Library. Catalogue of Books belonging to the Washington Library. April 5, 1819. [Washington]: National Intelligencer Office, 1819. 23 p. Not in S & S. DLC (interleaved with ms. additions).   **231**

Washington Library. Catalogue of Books belonging to the Washington Library. July 20, 1822. Washington City: Anderson and Meehan, 1822. 43 p. Shoemaker 11349. DLC, ICU.   **232**

Washington Library. Catalogue of Books in the Washington Library. January 31, 1826. City of Washington: S. A. Elliot, 1826. 87, [1] p. Not in Shoemaker. DLC (interleaved with ms. additions), MWA.   **233**

Washington Library. Catalogue of Books in the Washington Library. December, 1834. Washington: Gales and Seaton, 1835. 75 p. Rinderknecht 35274. DLC, MBAt.   **234**

Washington Library. Catalogue of the Washington Library, including the Library of Young Men's Christian Association, temporarily deposited therewith . . . Washington: Cunningham & McIntosh, 1871. xv, 51 p. DLC, NcD.   **235**

Washington Library. Supplemental Catalogue of the Washington Library in the Y.M.C.A. Building . . . Washington City: McGill & Witherow, 1873. 23 p. NcD.   **236**

Young Men's Christian Association. Catalogue of Library of the Washington City Young Men's Christian Association. Prepared by Jas. W. Walter [corrected in ms. to Walton], Esq., Librarian. Washington: H. Polkinson, 1859. 16 p. DLC.   **237**

Young Men's Christian Association, see also entries 235-36.

Washington, D.C.

Governmental Libraries

Army. Ordnance Office. Catalogue of the Ordnance Office Library. 1875. Washington: Gov't Print. Off., 1875. 78 p. DLC, PCarlMH.   **238**

Army. Signal Corps. Catalogue of the Library, Office Chief Signal-Officer, United States Army, Washington. June 30, 1872. Washington: Gov't Print. Off., 1872. 74 p. DLC.   **239**

Army Surgeon General, see entries 321-27.

Congress. Joint Committee on the Library, see entries 330-31.

Hydrographic Office. Catalogue of Books in the Library of the United States Hydrographic Office. January, 1875. Washington: Gov't Print. Off., 1875. 182 p. Printed on alternate pages. DLC, DSI.   **240**

Interior, Dept. of the. Catalogue of the Library of the Department of the Interior. Washington: Gov't Print. Off., 1861. 22 p. DLC, N.   **241**

Interior, Dept. of the. Catalogue of the Library of the Department of the Interior. Washington: Gov't Print. Off., 1871. 29 p. DLC.   **242**

Interior, Dept. of the. Alphabetical Catalogue of the Library of the Department of the Interior. Washington: Gov't Print. Off., 1873. 137 p. DLC, MBAt, NBuU, NNC.   **243**

Interior, Dept. of the. Alphabetical Catalogue of the Library of the Department of the Interior, containing the Additions made during 1873 and 1874. Washington: Gov't Print. Off., 1875. 177 p. DLC, MB, MBAt, NN, NNC, PSt.   **244**

Joint Committee on the Library, see entries 330-31.

Justice, Dept. of. Catalogue of Law Books of the Department of Justice. Washington: Gov't Print. Off., 1873. 251 p. Compiled by Henry A. Klopfer. DLC, NIC.   **245**

Library of Congress. Catalogue of Books, Maps, and Charts, belonging to the Library of the Two Houses of Congress. April, 1802. Washington City: William Duane, [1802]. 10, [2] p. S & S 3259. DGU, DLC, MH-H, MWA, NHi, PPL, ScU.   **246**

Library of Congress. Supplemental Catalogue of Books, Maps, and Charts belonging to the Library of the Two Houses of Congress, October, 1803. Washington City: James D. Westcott, [1803]. [3] p. S & S 5481. DLC, MH-H, NHi.   **247**

Library of Congress. Catalogue of Books, Maps, and Charts, belonging to the Library of the Two Houses of Congress. 1804. [Washington City, 1804]. 13 p. S & S 7489. DLC, MBAt, MWA (defective), ScU.   **248**

Library of Congress. Catalogue of the Books, Maps, and Charts, belonging to the Library established in the Capitol at the City of

Washington, for the Two Houses of Congress, to which are prefixed the Statutes and Bye-laws relative to that Institution. City of Washington: A. & G. Way, 1808. 40 p. S & S 16373. DGW, DLC, MBAt, MSaE, PPAmP, ScU. **249**

Library of Congress. Catalogue of the Books, Maps, and Charts, belonging to the Library established in the Capitol at the City of Washington, for the Two Houses of Congress, to which are prefixed the Statutes and Bye-laws Relative to that Institution. Washington City: Roger C. Weightman, 1812. 101 p. A facsimile ed., with an introduction by Robert A. Rutland and indexes by Lynda Corey Classen, was published by the Library of Congress in 1982. S & S 27120. DLC, IaU-L (copy), MWA, PPAmP, PPL, ScU. **250**

Library of Congress. Catalogue of the Library of the United States, to which is annexed, a Copious Index, alphabetically arranged. Washington: Jonathan Elliot, 1815. [8], 170 xxxii p. Half title: Catalogue of the Library of the Congress of the United States of America. The Thomas Jefferson collection, purchased in 1815. Catalogue prepared by George Watterston, per James Gilreath, "Sowerby Revirescent and Revised," *Papers of the Bibliographical Society of America* 78 (1984): 222. RNR copy contains a broadside, Additional Rules and Regulations for the Government of the Library of the United States (Washington: Jonathan Elliot, 1816). S & S 36250. In many libraries. **251**

Library of Congress. A Supplement to the Catalogue of the Library of Congress. Washington City: Daniel Rapine, 1820. 28 p. Shoemaker 4061. DLC, MH, MWA, PPAmP. **252**

Library of Congress. A Supplement to the Catalogue of the Library of Congress. Washington: Davis & Force, 1825. 40 p. Shoemaker 23131. DLC. **253**

Library of Congress. A Supplement to the Catalogue of the Library of Congress. Washington: P. Force, 1827. 109 p. Shoemaker 31516. DGW, DLC, ICN, IU, KHayF, M, MBAt, MH, MWiW, NWM, ViU, WaU. **254**

Library of Congress. An Additional Supplement to the Catalogue of the Library of Congress. Washington: Rothwell & Ustick, 1828. 16 p. Shoemaker 35637. DLC, M, PP. **255**

Library of Congress. Catalogue of the Library of Congress. December, 1830. Washington: Duff Green, 1830. 258 p. Cooper 4618. DGW, DLC, INS, IaAS, MBAt, MH, OC, PPL, ScU, TNJ, ViU, WaU. **256**

Library of Congress. Catalogue of the Library of Congress, in December, 1831, and an Index to the Names of Authors and Annotators, and to the Publications of Learned Societies, to Encyclopaedias, Newspapers, Reviews, Magazines, &c. Washington: Duff Green, 1831. 362 p. A reissue of the 1830 catalogue with suppl., Dec. 1831, the latter also published separately (see entry 258). Bruntjen 10447. DLC, MBAt, MH-L, MHi, MWiW, NNGr, PBU, ScU, WaU. **257**

Library of Congress. Supplement to the Catalogue of the Library of Congress. December, 1831. [Washington: Duff Green, 1831]. [261]-320 p. Bruntjen 10447. DLC, MH-L, MHi, ScU, WaU. **258**

Library of Congress. Additions . . . since the Publication of the Supplement to the Catalogue, in December, 1831. [Washington, 1832?]. 4 p. Not in Bruntjen. DLC. **259**

Library of Congress. Supplement to the Catalogue of the Library of Congress. December, 1833. [Washington, F. W. DeKrafft, 1833]. 92 p. Bruntjen 22435. DLC. **260**

Library of Congress. Catalogue of Additions to the Library of Congress since December, 1833. [Washington, 1834]. 13 p. Rinderknecht 27926. DLC. **261**

Library of Congress. Catalogue of Additions to the Library of Congress since December, 1834. [Washington, 1835]. 22 p. Not in Rinderknecht. DLC. **262**

Library of Congress. Catalogue of Additions to the Library of Congress since December, 1835. [Washington, 1837]. 24 p. Not in Rinderknecht. DLC. **263**

Library of Congress. Catalogue of Books in the Law Department of the Library of

Congress. January 1, 1839. [Washington, 1839]. 96 p. Advance issue of Chap. 18-23 of the general catalogue of 1840 (entry 265). Not in Rinderknecht. DLC, MBAt, ScU. **264**

Library of Congress. Catalogue of the Library of Congress, in the Capitol of the United States of America. December, 1839. City of Washington: Langtree and O'Sullivan, 1840. vii, 747 p. Not in Rinderknecht. In many libraries. **265**

Library of Congress. Supplement to the Catalogue of the Library of Congress. December, 1840. [Washington, 1840]. 28 p. Not in Rinderknecht. DLC, MBAt. **266**

Library of Congress. Supplement to the Catalogue of the Library of Congress. December, 1842. [Washington, 1842]. 29 p. Not in Rinderknecht. DLC, MBAt. **267**

Library of Congress. Supplement to the Catalogue of the Library of Congress. December, 1843. [Washington, 1843]. 33 p. Not in Rinderknecht. DLC, MBAt. **268**

Library of Congress. Supplement to the Catalogue of the Library of Congress. December 1, 1844. [Washington, 1844]. 20 p. DLC, MBAt. **269**

Library of Congress. Supplement to the Catalogue of the Library of Congress. December 1, 1845. [Washington, 1845]. 19 p. DLC, MBAt. **270**

Library of Congress. Supplement to the Catalogue of the Library of Congress. December 1, 1846. [Washington, 1846]. 12 p. DLC, MBAt. **271**

Library of Congress. Supplement to the Catalogue of the Library of Congress. December 6, 1847. [Washington, 1847]. 23 p. DLC, MBAt, N. **272**

Library of Congress. Supplement to the Catalogue of the Library of Congress. December, 1848. [Washington, 1848]. 46 p. DLC, MBAt. **273**

Library of Congress. Supplement to the Catalogue of the Library of Congress. December, 1840 to 1848. [Washington, 1848]. 8 vol. in 1. A reissue of the previously published suppl. with a collective cover-title (no suppl. issued in 1841). DLC. **274**

Library of Congress. Catalogue of the Library of Congress. June 30, 1849. [Washington, 1849]. 1022 p. Title taken from binder's title. DLC, ScU. **275**

Library of Congress. Catalogue of Books in the Law Department of the Library of Congress. December, 1849. Washington, 1849. iv, 139 p. Reissue of Chap. 18-23 of the general catalogue of 1849 (entry 275). DLC. **276**

Library of Congress. Supplement to the Catalogue of the Library of Congress. December, 1850. [Washington, 1850]. 36 p. DLC, MBAt. **277**

Library of Congress. Supplement to the Catalogue of the Library of Congress. December, 1851. [Washington, 1851]. 33 p. DLC, MBAt. **278**

Library of Congress. Additions made to the Library of Congress, since the First Day of December, 1851. November 1, 1852. Washington, L. Towers, 1852. 129 p. DLC, MB. **279**

Library of Congress. Additions made to the Library of Congress, since the First Day of November, 1852. November 1, 1853. Washington, L. Towers, 1853. 211 p. DLC, MB, MH. **280**

Library of Congress. Additions made to the Library of Congress, since the First Day of November, 1853. November 1, 1854. Washington, J. T. & L. Towers, 1854. 295 p. DLC, MB. **281**

Library of Congress. Catalogue of the Library of Congress. Chapter I. Ancient History. Complete to January, 1854. Washington, Stereotyped and Printed at the Smithsonian Institution, 1854. 19 p. Specimen text printed in double columns. DLC, WHi. **282**

Library of Congress. Catalogue of the Library of Congress. Chapter I. Ancient History. Complete to January, 1854. Washington, Stereotyped and Printed at the Smithsonian Institution, 1854. 77 p. For specimen text, see entry 282. DLC, MBAt. **283**

Library of Congress. Additions made to the Library of Congress, since the First Day of November, 1854. November 1, 1855. Washington, J. T. & L. Towers, 1855. 249 p. DLC, MB. **284**

Library of Congress. Additions made to the Library of Congress, since the First Day of November, 1855. November 1, 1856. Washington, J. T. & L. Towers, 1856. 126 p. DLC, MB, PPL (lacks pp. 123-26).   **285**

Library of Congress. Additions made to the Library of Congress, since the First Day of November, 1856. November 1, 1857. Washington, L. Towers, 1857. 93 p. DLC, MB.**286**

Library of Congress. Additions made to the Library of Congress, since the First Day of November, 1857. November 1, 1858. Washington, L. Towers, 1858. 71 p. DLC, MB.   **287**

Library of Congress. Additions made to the Library of Congress, since the First Day of July, 1859. November 16, 1859. Washington, L. Towers, 1859. 40 p. DLC.   **288**

Library of Congress. Additions made to the Library of Congress, since the Sixteenth Day of November, 1859. November 1, 1860. Washington, L. Towers, 1860. 37 p. DLC, MB.   **289**

Library of Congress. Catalogue of the Law Department of the Library of Congress. By Charles H. W. Meehan. Washington: [L. Towers], 1860. viii, 225 p. Advanced issue, Chap. 18-23, of the general catalogue of 1861 (entry 291). Added title page: Catalogue of the Library of Congress. Chapters XVIII-XXIII. Jurisprudence. DLC (film), FTaSU-L, MB, NNC-L, NNGr, Txu-L, WM.   **290**

Library of Congress. Catalogue of the Library of Congress. Washington: L. Towers, 1861. viii, 1398 p. In many libraries.   **291**

Library of Congress. Additions made to the Library of Congress, since the First Day of November, 1860. With Omissions from the Last General Catalogue. December 1, 1861. Washington: Gov't Print. Off., 1862. 80 p. Cover title: Supplementary Catalogue of the Library of Congress. December 1, 1861. Washington, 1861. CSt, DLC, MB, MH, MnU, N, NNC, PSt.   **292**

Library of Congress. Catalogue of Additions made to the Library of Congress, from December 1, 1861, to December 1, 1862. Washington: Gov't Print. Off., 1862. 151, 33 p. Law books (33 p. at end). DLC, MB, MNS, N, NRU, OCl, OU, OkU, OrU, TU, TxU.   **293**

Library of Congress. Catalogue of Additions made to the Library of Congress, from December 1, 1862, to December 1, 1863. Washington: Gov't Print. Off., 1863. 114 p. DLC, MB, MBAt, N, NNC, NRU, PSt, RPB.   **294**

Library of Congress. Alphabetical Catalogue of the Library of Congress. Authors. Washington: Gov't Print. Off., 1864. 1236 p. In many libraries.   **295**

Library of Congress. Catalogue of Additions made to the Library of Congress, from December 1, 1863, to December 1, 1864. Washington: Gov't Print. Off., 1864. 113 p. DLC, KyU, MB, MBAt, MnU, NNC, NRU, OCl, OkU, OrU, PSt, TxU.   **296**

Library of Congress. Catalogue of Additions made to the Library of Congress, from December 1, 1864, to December 1, 1865. Washington: Gov't Print. Off., 1865. 210, 29 p. Law books (29 p. at end). DLC, MB, MnU, N, NB, NNC, PSt.   **297**

Library of Congress. Catalogue of Additions made to the Library of Congress, from December 1, 1865, to December 1, 1866. Washington: Gov't Print. Off., 1866. 178, 27 p. Law books (27 p. at end). DLC, MB, MBAt, N, NB, NNC, NRU, OCl, PSt, TxU.   **298**

Library of Congress. Catalogue of Books added to the Library of Congress, from December 1, 1866, to December 1, 1867. Washington: Gov't Print. Off., 1868. 526 p. In many libraries.   **299**

Library of Congress. Catalogue of the Library of Congress. Index of Subjects. Washington: Gov't Print. Off., 1869. 2 vol. In many libraries.   **300**

Library of Congress. Catalogue of Books added to the Library of Congress, from December 1, 1867, to December 1, 1868. Washington: Gov't Print. Off., 1869. 323 p. In many libraries.   **301**

Library of Congress. Catalogue of Law Books in the Library of Congress. Arranged by Subject-matters. Washington: Gov't Print. Off., 1869. 305 p. Advance issue of law sections of the general subject catalogue issued in 1869 (entry 300). In many libraries.   **302**

Library of Congress. Catalogue of Works relating to Political Economy, and the Science of Government, in the Library of Congress. Arranged by Subject-matters. Washington: Gov't Print. Off., 1869. 65 p. DGW, DLC, MB, MH, MWiW, NhD, N, OCHP, OkHi, PP, PSt. **303**

Library of Congress. Catalogue of Books added to the Library of Congress, from December 1, 1868, to December 1, 1869. Washington: Gov't Print. Off., 1870. 415 p. DLC, MiU, N, NNC, NNUT, OkHi. **304**

Library of Congress. Catalogue of Books added to the Library of Congress, from December 1, 1869, to December 1, 1870. Washington: Gov't Print. Off., 1871. 381 p. In many libraries. **305**

Library of Congress. Catalogue of Books added to the Library of Congress during the Year 1871. Washington: Gov't Print. Off., 1872. 597 p. In many libraries. **306**

Library of Congress. Catalogue of Books added to the Library of Congress during the Year 1872. Washington: Gov't Print. Off., 1874. 492 p. In many libraries. **307**

Naval Observatory. Catalogue of the Library, U.S. Naval Observatory. [Washington, 1868]. 24 p. DLC, DN-Ob. **308**

Navy Dept. Letter from the Secretary of the Navy, transmitting a List of Newspapers and Periodical Works, with a Catalogue of the Books purchased for the use of the Navy Department, for the last Six Years; and a similar List and Catalogue for the Office of the Commissioners of the Navy . . . February 4, 1823 . . . Washington: Gales & Seaton, 1823. 14 p. Shoemaker 14569. DLC, MWA, NjP. **309**

Navy Dept. The following books will be furnished for the use of vessels of war when on a cruise, and for the use of Navy yards until otherwise ordered. Navy Department, June 10th 1839. [Washington?, 1839]. broadside. Not in Rinderknecht. MH-H (with ms. additions dated 1839 and 1841). **310**

Ordnance Office, see entry 238.

Patent Office. Catalogue of the Library of the Patent Office in 1847. Washington: J. & G. S. Gideon, 1847. 34 p. DLC, DP, MWA. **311**

Patent Office. Catalogue of Additions to the Library of the United States Patent Office. Washington: Gov't Print. Off., 1847-89. DP. **312**

Signal Corps, see entry 239.

Smithsonian Institution. Catalogue of the Berlandier Manuscripts deposited in the Smithsonian Institution, Washington, D.C. New York: Folger & Turner, 1852. 8 p. DLC, DSI, MWA, PU. **313**

Smithsonian Institution. Check-list of Periodical Publications received in the Reading-room of the Smithsonian Institution, for the Year 1853. [Washington, 1853]. 28 p. DSI, RPB. **314**

Smithsonian Institution. Catalogue of Publications of Societies and of the Periodical Works in the Library of the Smithsonian Institution. July 1, 1858. Foreign Works. Washington: Smithsonian Institution, 1859. 259 p. In many libraries. **315**

Smithsonian Institution. Catalogue of Publications of Societies and of Periodical Works belonging to the Smithsonian Institution. January 1, 1866. Deposited in the Library of Congress. Washington: Smithsonian Institution, 1866. v, 591 p. Issued as Smithsonian Miscellaneous Collections, 179. In many libraries. **316**

State, Dept. of. A Catalogue of the Library of the Department of State of the United States. 1825. [Washington, 1825]. 67 p. Shoemaker 22853. DLC, LNH, MH, NNC-L. **317**

State, Dept. of. Catalogue of the Library of the Department of State of the United States. May, 1830. [Washington, 1830]. iv, 150 p. Cooper 4619. CSmH, DLC, MH, NN, PPAmP. **318**

State, Dept. of. Catalogue of Manuscript Books, being Records of the Proceedings of Congress, the Domestic and Foreign Correspondence thereof, Military Letters, Reports of the Boards of War, Finance, Admiralty, &c., with Miscellaneous Letters and Papers relating to the War of the Revolution, and of the Confederacy, from 1774 to 1789. Deposited in the Archives of the Department of State, by an Act of Congress, approved September 15, 1789.

Washington: Blair and Rives, 1835. 24 p. Caption title: Catalogue of Manuscript Books, deposited in the Archives of the Department of State, 1774 to 1789. Not in Rinderknecht. DLC (Rare Book col. copy interleaved with ms. notes).   **319**

State, Dept. of. Catalogue of Manuscript Books, being Records of the Proceedings of Congress, the Domestic and Foreign Correspondence thereof, Military Letters, Reports of the Boards of War, Finance, Admiralty, &c., with Miscellaneous Letters and Papers relating to the War of the Revolution, and of the Confederacy, from 1774 to 1789. Deposited in the Archives of the Department of State, by an Act of Congress, approved September 15, 1789. Washington: A. O. P. Nicholson, 1855. 72 p. DLC.   **320**

Surgeon General's Office. A Catalogue of Books in the Library of the Surgeon General's Office. Washington City, 1840. [21] leaves. Not in Rinderknecht. DNLM (photocopy).   **321**

Surgeon General's Office. Catalogue of the Surgeon General's Office Library. May 10, 1864. [Washington, 1864]. 27 leaves. DLC (film), IU (film).   **322**

Surgeon General's Office. Catalogue of the Surgeon General's Office Library. October 23, 1865. [Washington, 1865]. 32 leaves. DLC (film), IU (film), KU, NcD-MC, PPC.
323

Surgeon General's Office. Catalogue of Books in the Library of the Surgeon General's Office, Washington, D.C. Alphabetically arranged, with an Appendix. [Washington], 1868. 147 p. DLC, DNLM, IU, NIC, NcD-MC.   **324**

Surgeon General's Office. Catalogue of the Library of the Surgeon General's Office, United States Army . . . Washington: Gov't Print. Off., 1872. 454 p. DLC, DNLM, KyLou-HS, MBAt, NcD-MC, PBL, PPC, TxDaS.   **325**

Surgeon General's Office. Supplement to Catalogue. No. I. List of American Medical Journals. Washington: Gov't Print. Off., 1872. 26 p. DLC, DNLM.   **326**

Surgeon General's Office. Catalogue of the Library of the Surgeon General's Office, United States Army . . . Washington: Gov't Print. Off., 1873-74. 3 vol. Vol. I-II and suppl. DHEW, DLC, DNLM, GU, ICU, MB, MBAt, MiU, ScU, WU-M.
327

Treasury Dept. Letter from the Secretary of the Treasury, transmitting (pursuant to a Resolution of the House of Representatives of the 20th ult.) Statements shewing the Newspapers, Journals, Charts, Instruments, Maps, &c, which are taken in the Treasury Department, at the Public Expense; also, a Catalogue of the Books, which have been procured, for the use of said Department, during the last Six Years. February 25, 1823 . . . Washington: Gales & Seaton, 1823. 29 p. Shoemaker 14591. DLC, NjP.   **328**

Treasury Dept. Catalogue of the Library of the Treasury Department. July 1, 1873. Washington: Gov't Print. Off., 1873. 131 p. DLC, IU, N.   **329**

United States. Congress. Joint Committee on the Library. Annual Report of the Library Committee of the Two Houses of Congress. April 11th, 1808. Printed by Order of the Senate. Washington: R. C. Weightman, 1808. 18 p., 3 folded tables. "The following donations . . . have been received since . . . (11th February, 1807)": pp. 4-6. S & S 16366. DLC, NN (defective).   **330**

United States. Congress. Joint Committee on the Library. Annual Report of the Library Committee of the Two Houses of Congress for the Year 1808. January 27th, 1809. Printed by Order of the Senate. Washington: R. C. Weightman, 1809, 18 p., 3 folded tables. "List of Donations": pp. [3]-6. S & S 18813. DLC, MWA.   **331**

War Dept. Letter from the Secretary of War, transmitting pursuant to a Resolution of the House of Representatives, Reports of the Newspapers, Journals, and other Periodical Publications, Charts, and Instruments, Maps, and Prints, taken at the Public Expense in the War Department; also, a Catalogue of the Books, which have been purchased on Public Account, with the last Six Years. Feb. 11, 1823 . . . Washington: Gales & Seaton, 1823. 35 p. Shoemaker 14620. DLC, NjP, MiU-C.   **332**

GEORGIA

Athens

University of Georgia. A Catalogue of Books in the Library of Franklin College, University of Georgia. [n.p., 184-?]. [14]-43 p. NN.   **333**

University of Georgia. Catalogue of Books, in the Library of the University of Georgia, by Prof. James Jackson, Librarian. Athens: Southern Banner Print., 1847. 69 p. DLC, GU, LU, MH, MWA. **334**

University of Georgia. Catalogue of Books in the Library of the University of Georgia, by Prof. James Jackson, Librarian . . . Athens: Franklin Job Office, 1850. 146 p. DLC and GU hold an undated appendix, ca. 1853 (32 p.). DLC, GHi, GU (with ms. additions), MA, ScU. **335**

University of Georgia. Catalogue of Books in the Library of the University of Georgia . . . Richard M. Johnston, John D. Easter, William Bradford, Committee. William Rutherford, Jr., Librarian. Athens, 1858. 192 p. DLC, GU (with ms. additions). **336**

University of Georgia. Demosthenian Society. Catalogue of the Books, belonging to the Library of the Demosthenian Society, Franklin College. Athens: "Gazette" Job Office, 1849. 32 p. GHi. **337**

University of Georgia. Demosthenian Society. Catalogue of the Books, belonging to the Library of the Demosthenian Society, Franklin College. Athens: Southern Banner Office, 1855. 31 p. DLC. **338**

Atlanta

Georgia State Library. Catalogue of the Georgia State Library. 1869. By John L. Conley, State Librarian. Atlanta: Samuel Bard, 1869. iv, 286 p. See also entry 341. Ct, DLC, GEU, GU, IU, M, OKentU, T, Vi, WHi, WU. **339**

Augusta

Young Men's Library Association. Catalogue of the Library of the Young Men's Library Association, Augusta, Ga. Founded, 1848. [Augusta, 1868]. 45, [1] p. DLC. **340**

Milledgeville

Georgia State Library. Catalogue of the State Library of Georgia. 1859. By C. J. Wellborn, State Librarian. Milledgeville: Federal Union Print., 1859. 142 p. See also entry 339. GEU, M, MBAt. **341**

Savannah

Savannah Library Society. A Catalogue of the Books belonging to the Savannah Library

Society. Instituted in the Year 1809, and re-organized in the Year 1838, with its Charter and By-laws, to which is added a Brief Account of the Origin and Progress of the Society from its Commencement to 1839. Savannah: Thomas Purse, 1839. 69 p. Rinderknecht 58365. GHi, NcD. **342**

HAWAII, KINGDOM OF

See Entries 3353-55

ILLINOIS

Alton

Alton Public Library Association. Constitution, By-laws and Catalogue of the Alton Public Library Association. Alton: Telegraph Steam Job Printing House, 1874. 35 p. DLC. **343**

Belleville

German Library Society of St. Clair County. Numeral-Katalog der Deutschen Bibliothek von St. Clair County, Ill. [Belleville?, 1854?]. 24 p. DLC. **344**

Belleville Sängerbund and Library Society. Numeral-Katalog der Bibliothek Belleviller Sängerbundes und der Bibliotheks-Gesellschaft, Belleville, 1863. Belleville: Gedruckt in der Offizin der "Belleviller Zeitung" von F. Rupp, [1863?]. 24 p. DLC holds suppl., 1867 (4 p.) and 1871 (4 p.) DLC. **345**

Bloomington

Bloomington Library Association. List of Books. January, 1868 . . . 1868. 52 p. Cf. Sharp, p. 751. Sharp also reports suppl., Feb. 1870 (27 p.). **346**

Ladies' Library. Catalogue of the Ladies' Library of Bloomington . . . Bloomington: Daily Pantagraph Printing House, 1864. 29 p. IHi. **347**

Bushnell

Bushnell Library Association. Constitution and Regulations with Catalogue of Books belonging to the Bushnell Library Association of Bushnell, Illinois. Quincy: Cadogan & Gardner, 1875. 33 p. DLC. **348**

Chicago

Chicago Public Library. Temporary Finding Lists for Alcoves A. to L. July, 1874. [Chicago, 1874]. Cf. Jim Ranz, *The Printed Book Catalogue in American Libraries, 1723-1900* (Chicago, 1964), p. 127. An edition dated May, 1874, is reported by Sharp, p. 753.   **349**

Chicago Public Library. Temporary Finding Lists. February, 1875. 2d ed. Chicago: Hazlitt & Reed, 1875. Cf. Jim Ranz, *The Printed Book Catalogue in American Libraries, 1723-1900* (Chicago, 1964), p. 128.   **350**

Cobb's Library. Sixth Annual Catalogue of the Books in Cobb's Library, 36 Monroe Street, Palmer House. December, 1874. Chicago: L. M. Cobb, [1874]. 56 p. Operated by Lucius M. Cobb. DLC.   **351**

Excelsior Society. Catalogue . . . Chicago, 1851. Cf. Rhees, p. 35.   **352**

First Universalist Sabbath School. Catalogue of Books belonging to the Library of the First Universalist Sabbath School, Chicago, March 4th, A.D. 1867. Chicago: Jameson & Morse, 1867. 79, [5] p. MnU.   **353**

Mechanics' Institute. Catalogue . . . Chicago, 1843. Not in Rinderknecht. Cf. Cutter 235, Jewett, p. 177, Rhees, p. 35.   **354**

Mechanics' Institute. Catalogue . . . Chicago, 1847. 30 p. Cf. Cutter 282, Jewett, p. 177, Rhees, p. 35.   **355**

Mechanics' Institute. Catalogue of the Library of the Mechanics' Institute of the City of Chicago, with the Charter, Constitution and By-laws. Organized February 23, 1842, and incorporated February, 1843. Chicago: Hyatt Brothers, 1859. 80 p. IC.   **356**

Skinner Library Association. Catalogue of the Library of the Skinner Library Association of the City of Chicago. 1862. Chicago: Isaac A. Pool, 1862. 43 p. ICHi, MWA.   **357**

West Side Library. Catalogue of Books and Magazines in the West Side Library . . . Chicago: Emerson & Kennedy, [1875]. 95 p. Operated by George W. Emerson and John W. Kennedy. DLC.   **358**

Young Men's Association. Catalogue of the Library of the Young Men's Association of the City of Chicago . . . Chicago: Whitmarsh & Fulton, 1852. 44 p. MH, MHi.   **359**

Young Men's Association. Catalogue of the Library of the Young Men's Association of the City of Chicago . . . Chicago: Hays & Thompson, 1856. 120 p. DLC, MH, MWA, MnU.   **360**

Young Men's Association. Catalogue of the Library of the Young Men's Association of the City of Chicago, together with the Charter, Rules, Regulations, etc., of the Association. Chicago: Press & Tribune Print, 1859. 119 p. ICHi, MWA.   **361**

Young Men's Association. Catalogue of the Books belonging to Young Men's Association, of the City of Chicago. Volume I. Containing the Titles added from the Foundation of the Library to April 1st, 1865 ... Compiled by John M. Horton, Librarian. Chicago: Rounds & James, 1865. xxvii, 249, [1] p. DLC, ICHi, ICJ, ICN, IU, MB, MHi, NNGr, PPL.   **362**

Young Men's Christian Association Free Library. Catalogue of the Books belonging to the Y.M.C.A. Free Library of Chicago. Vol. I. Containing a List of the Books in the Library up to January 1st, 1871 ... Chicago: Shark & Thain 1871 viii, 120, ix-16 p. No more published. DLC, ICHi, ICN (interleaved with ms. additions), NN.   **363**

Danville

Culbertson Library. Catalogue ... 1867. 11 p. Cf. Cutter 545, Sharp, p. 757.   **364**

Decatur

Ladies' Library Association. Catalogue . . . Decatur, 1868. Cf. Sharp, p. 757.   **365**

Ladies' Library Association. Catalogue of Books belonging to the Ladies' Library Association of Decatur, Ill. Decatur: Hamsher & Mosser, 1871. 42 p. DLC holds suppl. (9 p.). DLC.   **366**

Edwardsville

Edwardsville Library. A Complete Catalogue of all the Books now in, or belonging to, the Edwardsville Library ... Drawn for the use of the Share-holders, at the Library Room,

Edwardsville. Nov. 30, 1819. John H. Randle, Librarian. Edwardsville: H. Warren, [1819]. broadside. Not in S & S; Sabin 47784. IEd.   **367**

Elgin

Elgin Public Library. Catalogue of the Elgin Public Library, Elgin, Illinois. Established in 1874, by the Town of Elgin. Elgin: Advocate Power Print., 1874. 32 p. DLC, MWA. **368**

Universalist Church. Catalogue of New Books in the Sunday School Library belonging to the Universalist Church in Elgin. Elgin: Elgin Gazette Printing Co., 1871. 8 p. MWA. **369**

Evanston

Free Public Library. Catalogue of the Free Public Library of Evanston, Illinois. Chicago: Bright Side Co., 1873. 36 p. DLC. **370**

Northwestern University. Catalogue of the Books in the Library of the Northwestern University. Volume I . . . Chicago: Spalding & LaMontes, 1868. 47 p. IEN. **371**

Joliet

Illinois State Penitentiary. Catalogue . . . 1872. Cf. Bowker, p. 242.   **372**

Illinois State Penitentiary. A Catalogue of the Illinois State Penitentiary Library. Founded A.D., 1872, by the Board of Commissioners and supported by the Visitors' Fund. Comprising the Books purchased in the Winter of 1873, as the Second Accession to the Library since its Establishment in the Beginning of the Year 1872. Joliet: Sun Steam Printing Co., 1874. 128, 11 p. Catalogue of the "Deutsche Bibliothek" (11 p. at end). DLC, IC.   **373**

Kewanee

Kewanee Public Library. Catalogue of the Kewanee Public Library. 1875. Organized April 7th, 1875. Kewanee: Independent Book and Job Office, 1875. 24 p. DLC. **374**

Lebanon

McKendree College. Philosophian Society. Catalogue . . . Lebanon, 1850. Cf. Rhees, p. 38. **375**

McKendree College. Platonian Literary Society. Catalogue of the Members, Constitution, and By-laws, and Library of the Platonian Literary Society of McKendree College, Lebanon, Illinois. Lebanon: Journal Office, 1867. 38 p. IU.   **376**

Mendota

Mendota Library Association. Catalogue of the Mendota Library Association. Mendota: Mendota Bulletin Print, 1874. 18 p. DLC. **377**

Monmouth

Warren County Library. Catalogue of Books of the Warren County Library and Reading Room Association, Monarch, Illinois. November 1, 1874. Reading Room opened 1868; Library 1871. Monmouth: Jno. S. Clark & Son, [1874]. 51, 4 p. DLC, NN. **378**

Onarga

Onarga Library. Catalogue of the Onarga Library . . . Onarga: E. Rumley, 1865. [34] p. DLC.   **379**

Peoria

Peoria City Library. Catalogue of the Peoria City Library, with its Constitution and By-laws. Peoria: Benj. Foster, 1860. 96 p. DLC. **380**

Peoria deutscher Leseverein. Catalog der Bibliothek des deutschen Lesevereins in Peoria. Peoria: C. Rummel, 1865. 29 p. IHi holds "Anhang zum Catalog des Peoria Lesevereins" (8 p.). IHi.   **381**

Peoria Mercantile Library. Catalogue of the Peoria Mercantile Library . . . Peoria, 1872. xv, 109 p. CU-A, DLC, IU, MB.   **382**

Polo

Polo Library Association. Catalogue of the Books belonging to the Polo Library Association. Also, Catalogue of Book belonging to the Polo Public School Library, Polo, Illinois. May 1st, 1873. Polo: Ogle Co. Press Print, 1873. 29, 10 p. N (Misc. pamphlet box, 018.1).   **383**

Quincy

Quincy Library. Catalogue of Books, Pamphlets, Apparatus, &c. of the Quincy Library, located in the City of Quincy; to which is prefixed, the Constitution and By-laws of the Association organized March 1841. Quincy, 1848. 23 p. DLC (with ms. additions of books purchased since Jan. 1848), IQ.   **384**

Quincy Library. Catalogue of the Quincy Library . . . to which is prefixed the Charter, Constitution and By-laws of the Association . . . Quincy: Herald Book and Job Office, 1868-[72]. 3 pts. DLC (with printed additions to June 1, 1870 and from June 1, 1870 to Feb. 1, 1872).   **385**

Rock Island

Rock Island City Library and Reading Room Association. Constitution and Catalogue of the Books and Periodicals of the R. Island City Library & Reading Room. Organized September 22, 1855. Rock Island: Pershing & Connelly, 1856. 16 p. ICHi.   **386**

Rockford

Rockford Public Library. Catalogue of the Rockford Public Library, together with the First Annual Report of the Board of Directors, By-laws, Rules, etc. Rockford, 1873. 86 p. Sharp, p. 763, records suppl. no. 1, March 1874. DLC, MB.   **387**

Rockford Public Library. Catalogue of the Public Library of Rockford, Illinois. Supplement No. 2, April 1875. Rockford: Register Co., 1875. 60 p. DLC.   **388**

Rockford Seminary. Catalogue of Rockford Seminary Libraries. Prepared by Caroline A. Potter. September, 1875. Rockford: Register Co., [1875]. 30 p. DLC, IU.   **389**

Springfield

Illinois State Library. Catalogue . . . 1848. 47 p. Cf. Cutter 297.   **390**

Illinois State Library. Catalogue of the Illinois State Library. Springfield: Illinois Journal Printing Office, 1869. 43 p. DLC (film), I, M.   **391**

Illinois State Library. Catalogue of the Illinois State Library. Springfield: State Journal Printing Office, 1871. 52 p. DLC (film), I, IHi, M.   **392**

Springfield Library Association. Articles of Association, By-laws, and Catalogue of Books of the Springfield Library Association. February 15, 1871. Springfield: Illinois State Journal Print., 1871. 111 p. DLC, WU (School of Library and Information Studies).   **393**

INDIANA

Bloomington

Indiana State University. Catalogue of the Library of Indiana State University . . . Bloomington: M. L. Deal, [1842]. 50 p. Rinderknecht 42-2526. DLC, InU   **394**

Crawfordsville

Wabash College. Calliopean Society. Catalogue of the Calliopean Society of Wabash College, Crawfordsville, Ind., 1848-1855. Indianapolis: Cameron & McNealy, 1856. 31 p. "Catalogue of Books" on pp. 13-31. ICU, InCW (Archives, Tuttle Miscellany).
                                         395

Wabash College. Lyceum Society. Catalogue of the Lyceum Society of Wabash College, Crawfordsville, Ind., 1847-53. Indianapolis: Indiana State Journal Office Press Print., 1854. 16 p. "Catalogue of Books" on pp. 11-16.   InCW (Archives, Tuttle Miscellany).   **396**

Fort Wayne

Catholic Circulating Library Association. Catalogue of Books belonging to the Fort Wayne Catholic Circulating Library Association. Established July 1st, 1871. Incorporated August 4th, 1874 . . . [Fort Wayne: Sentinel Steam Printing House, 1874]. 37, 8 p. Cutter 887 reports "Deutsche Bücher" (8 p.) and "Livres français" (8 p.). DLC (includes "Deutsche Bücher" at end).
                                         397

Indianapolis

Indiana State Library. Catalogue of Books in the Indiana State Library. November 1, 1841. Indianapolis: Dowling and Cole, 1841.

36 p. Rinderknecht 41-2730. MWA, OCHP, OKentU. **398**

Indiana State Library. Report of Mr. Sweetser, in relation to the State Library, presented to the General Assembly. The following is a List of the Books belonging to the State Library . . . [Indianapolis, 1841?]. [527]-67 p. At head of title: Doc. No. 52. H. of R. List of missing books on pp. 564-67. In (text in *Documentary Journal of Indiana, Reports, 1840*). **399**

Indiana State Library. Catalogue of the Indiana State Library, for the Year 1859. Compiled and arranged by J. R. Bryant, State Librarian. Indianapolis: John C. Walker, 1859. v, 95, [1] p. Ct, DLC (film), OKentU, Vi. **400**

Indiana State Library. Catalogue of the Indiana State Library, for the Year 1865. Indianapolis, 1865. 86 p. M. **401**

Indiana State Library. Catalogue and Rules and Regulations of the Indiana State Library. Arranged by M. G. McLain, State Librarian. Indianapolis: Alexander H. Conner, 1869. 91 p. MB. **402**

Indiana State Library. Catalogue, and Rules and Regulations of the Indiana State Library. Arranged by James De Sanno, State Librarian. Indianapolis: R. J. Bright, 1872. 100 p. Ct, DLC (film), InStme, LU, M, MB, Vi. **403**

Indiana Supreme Court. A Catalogue of the Indiana Supreme Court Library. December, 1870. Indianapolis: Braden & Burford, 1870. 71 p. In, In-SC (photocopy?). **404**

Indiana Supreme Court. A Catalogue of Law Books contained in the Supreme Court Library, of the State of Indiana. April, 1872. Indianapolis: R. J. Bright, 1872. 100 p. DLC, In-SC, M, MB, MWA, Vi. **405**

Indianapolis Library Association. Catalogue of Books belonging to the Indianapolis Library Association . . . Indianapolis: H. C. Chandler, 1869. 41 p. In. **406**

Indianapolis Library Association. Catalogue of Books belonging to the Indianapolis Library Association . . . Indianapolis: Indianapolis Journal Company, 1871. 56 p. In, InI, ViU. **407**

Indianapolis Public Library. Catalogue of the Public Library of Indianapolis. 1873.

Indianapolis: Press of Printing and Publishing House, 1873. xii, 365 p. In many libraries. **408**

La Porte

McClure Library. Catalogue . . . 1860. Cf. Ella Lonn, "The History of an Unusual Library," *Indiana Magazine of History* 19 (1923): 213-14, note 16. **409**

Logansport

Ladies' Sigourney Library. Catalogue of the Ladies' Sigourney Library, Logansport, Indiana. Organized February 15, 1848. Logansport: Pharos Press, 1852. 8 p. InHi. **410**

Madison

Madison Library Association. Catalogue of the Books belonging to the Madison Library Association . . . Madison: Printed at the Courier Job Office, 1856. 106 p. DLC, In, InFrlC, InHi, IaHi. **411**

New Harmony

Harmony Township, see entry 412.

Workingmen's Institute Library. The Catalogue, Constitution, By-laws and History of the Workingmen's Institute Library, New Harmony, Ind. Also the Catalogue of Harmony Township and School Libraries and a Sketch of the History of New Harmony. Evansville: Healy, Isaacs, 1870. 79 p. DLC, In, InFrlC, InNhW, InU. **412**

Richmond

Earlham College. Catalogue of the Libraries of Earlham College. Richmond: Telegram Steam Book and Job Press, 1870. 88 p. Includes the Yearly Meeting Reference Library, Ionian Library, and the Phoenix Library. In. **413**

Friends' Boarding School. Alphabetic Catalogue of the Books contained in the Library of Friends' Boarding School, Richmond, Ind. 1857. Richmond: Holloway & Davis, Printers, 1857. 36 p. InHi. **414**

Morrisson Library. Catalogue of the Morrisson Library, Richmond, Ind. July, 1864. Cincinnati: R. Clarke, 1864. vi, 132 p. DLC. **415**

Morrisson Library. Supplement No. 1, to the
Catalogue of the Morrisson Library. July,
1864 to May 1871. Richmond: Democratic
Herald Print, 1871. 71 p. DLC.   **416**

Vincennes

Vincennes Library. Catalogue . . . 1813. Not
in S & S. Cf. Cutter 64, Rhees, p. 52.   **417**

Vincennes Library. A Catalogue of the
Vincennes Library, with the Charter and
Constitution prefixed. Vincennes: R. Y.
Caddington, 1838. 19 p. Not in Rinderknecht.
In U (Lilly Library).   **418**

IOWA

Burlington

Congregational Church. Manual of the
Congregational Church in Burlington,
Iowa. A.D. 1857. [Burlington]: C. Dunham,
1857. 46 p. "Catalogue of the Church
Library" on pp. 17-22. CSmH.   **419**

Public Library. Catalogue of the Public
Library of Burlington, Iowa. With a List of
Stockholders, and the Rules. April, A.D.
1870. Burlington: Osborn, Snow, 1870.
38, [2] p. DLC, MWA.   **420**

Cedar Falls

Cedar Falls Library Association. Catalogue of
the Cedar Falls Library Association. [Cedar
Falls, 187-]. 15 p. DLC holds two suppl.,
1875-? (5 p., 6-8 p.). DLC.   **421**

Clinton

Young Men's Association. Library Catalogue . . .
February, 1869. Lyons: Beera & Eaton, 1869.
19 p. DLC (lost).   **422**

Davenport

Griswold College. Catalogue of Books in the
John Farr Library, Griswold College,
Davenport, Iowa. A Case of Books for the
Theological Department, presented by

Thomas H. Powers, of Philadelphia, Pa.
Philadelphia: Collins, 1861. 15 p. DLC,
MWA.   **423**

Young Men's Literary Association. Catalogue
of the Library of the Young Men's Literary
Association, with the President's Annual
Report. Davenport: Luse, Lane, 1859.
11, [1] p. IaDaM.   **424**

Des Moines

State Library of Iowa. Catalogue of the Iowa
Territory. Library. 1839. Burlington: James
E. Edwards, 1839. 18 p.   Rinderknecht
56505. IaCrM, MH.   **425**

State Library of Iowa. Catalogue . . . 1845. 18
p. Cf. Bowker, p. 308, Cutter 257, Jewett, p.
186, Rhees, p. 53.   **426**

State Library of Iowa. Catalogue of the Iowa
State Library. 1872. Compiled by Mrs. Ada
North, Librarian. Des Moines: G. W.
Edwards, 1872. 142 p. Ct, DLC, GU-L, IU,
IaHi, IaU, M, OKentU.   **427**

Dubuque

Young Men's Library Association. Catalogue
of the Library of the Young Men's Library
Association of Dubuque, Iowa. 1874.
Dubuque: Daily Times Power Printing
House, 1874. iv, 144 p. DLC.   **428**

Iowa City

Freemasons. Iowa. Grand Lodge. Catalogue
of the Library of the Grand Lodge of Iowa.
June 1, 1873. By Theodore S. Parvin, Grand
Secretary. Iowa City: Davenport Day, Egbert
& Fidlar, 1873. 144 p. Parvin's "Catalogue of
Books and Periodicals . . . June, 1858"
appears in *Proceedings of the Grand Lodge of
Iowa* . . . (Muscatine, 1858), pp. [593]-614.
MBAt, MWA, WM, Museum of Our National
Heritage, Lexington, Mass.   **429**

Keokuk

Keokuk Library Association. Catalogue of Books
belonging to the Keokuk Library Association,
with a Historical Sketch. Keokuk: Gate City
Book and Job Office, 1866. 166 p. CLobS,
DLC, IaHi, IaU, MH, PPL.   **430**

KANSAS

Fort Dodge

Fort Dodge Post Library. Catalogue . . . Fort Dodge?, 1873. 13 p. Cf. Cutter 813.   **431**

Lansing

Kansas. Prison Library. Catalogue . . . 1874. 32 p. Cf. Cutter 889.   **432**

Leavenworth

Clough & Wheat. Catalogue of the Law Library of Clough & Wheat. April 28, 1870 . . . Leavenworth: Geo. L. Hathaway, 1870. 24 p. MoKu.   **433**

Leavenworth Law Library Association. Act of Incorporation and Articles of Association of the Leavenworth Law Library Association, together with a Catalogue of Books belonging to said Association. February 1, 1870. Leavenworth: Geo. L. Hathaway, 1870. 16 p. KHi.   **434**

Leavenworth Law Library Association. Catalogue of the Law Library of the Leavenworth Law Library Association. February 1, 1871, Leavenworth City, Kansas. [Leavenworth?]: Times Printing Co., 1871. 14 p. MoKu.   **435**

Leavenworth Mercantile Library. Catalogue of the Leavenworth Mercantile Library, together with a History of the Association, Constitution, By-laws, etc., etc. Leavenworth: Times and Conservative Book and Job House, 1869. 61 p. KLe.   **436**

Topeka

Kansas State Library. Catalogue of the Kansas State Library. 1871. By D. Dickinson, State Librarian. Topeka: S. S. Prouty, 1871. 50, [1] p. CtY-BR (interleaved), DLC, IaHi, K, KHi, WHi.   **437**

Kansas State Library. Catalogue of the Law and Miscellaneous Books in the Kansas State Library. D. Dickinson, State Librarian. Topeka: Geo. W. Martin, 1873. vii, 67 p. DLC, K, KHi, KKC, M, NbHi, OKentU.   **438**

Topeka Library Association. Catalogue of Books of the Topeka Library Association. Nos. 1 to 863. October, 1873. Topeka: Kansas Magazine Job Rooms, 1873. 65 p. KHi.   **439**

KENTUCKY

Frankfort

Kentucky State Library. Catalogue of Books belonging to the State Library of Kentucky. January 3, 1854. [Frankfort, 1854]. 13 p. At head of title: Legislative Document, No. 13. In many libraries as part of the *Kentucky Legislative Document* set.   **440**

Kentucky State Library. Report of the State Librarian of Kentucky. January 10, 1856. [Frankfort, 1856]. 13 p. At head of title: Legislative Document, No. 15. This "Report to the General Assembly" transmits a catalogue. In many libraries as part of the *Kentucky Legislative Document* set.   **441**

Kentucky State Library. Catalogue of Law Books, belonging to the State Library of Kentucky. July, 1857. Frankfort: A. G. Hodges, 1857. 16 p. MWA.   **442**

Kentucky State Library. Catalogue of Law Books in the State Library of Kentucky. August 1, 1862. Frankfort: W. E. Hughes, 1862. 24 p. MH.   **443**

Kentucky State Library. Catalogue of Books in the Kentucky State Library. August, 1872. Frankfort: Kentucky Yeoman Office, 1872. 40 p. DLC.   **444**

Kentucky State Library. Catalogue of Books in the Kentucky State Library. December, 1875. Frankfort: Kentucky Yeoman Office, 1875. 97 p. KyU.   **445**

Georgetown

Georgetown College. Catalogue of Books, Maps, Statuary, &c. belonging to Georgetown College, Kentucky. Cincinnati: E. Shepard, 1848. 72, [4] p. DLC, Georgetown College, MoU.   **446**

Harrodsburg

Harrodsburg Library Company. A Catalog of the Books belonging to the Harrodsburg

Library Company, to which is prefixed the By-laws and Regulations. Incorporated December 1823. Harrodsburg: H. Miller, 1824. 17 p. Not in Shoemaker. KyLoF. **447**

Lexington

Lexington Library. Catalogue of the Books belonging to the Lexington Library, to which is prefixed, an Abstract from the By-laws. Lexington: Daniel Bradford, 1804. 16 p. S & S 6648. KyLo, MWA. **448**

Lexington Library. Catalogue of the Books in the Lexington Library. Lexington: F. Bradford, 1815. 72 p. "Abstract of the By-laws" on pp. 71-72. S & S 35101. ICU, InU (photocopy), KyLx. **449**

Lexington Library. Addition to the Catalogue of the Lexington Library. Lexington: F. Bradford, jr., 1817. 26 p. Copy held by KyLx has 44 p. of ms. additions. S & S 41257 (duplicated by 41258). ICU, KyLx. **450**

Lexington Library Company. A Catalogue of the Books, belonging to the Lexington Library Company, to which is prefixed, a Concise Narrative of the Origin and Progress of the Institution, with its Charter, Laws & Regulations. Lexington: Thomas Smith, 1821. xiv, 172 p., [2] p. of errata and index. Shoemaker 5819. CLSU, DLC, ICU, KyLx, KyLxT, KyRE, KyU, MoU, NN (with a 15 p. "Additional Catalogue"), OC (defective), OFH, OOxM, ViU. **451**

Lexington Library Company. Additions to the Catalogue of Books belonging to the Lexington Library Company, from the Time of its Publication in 1821, to the Present, and the Additional Laws for its Governance. Lexington: A. W. Elder, 1852. 112, [1] p. DLC, ICU, KyLx (with ms. notes), KyU, OC. **452**

Louisville

Kentucky Mechanics' Institute. Catalogue of the Library of the Kentucky Mechanics' Institute. Louisville: J. F. Brennan, 1854. 56 p. DLC. **453**

Kentucky Mechanics' Institute. Catalogue of Library. Kentucky Mechanics' Institute, Louisville. Louisville: J. F. Brennan, 1855. 57, 15 p. KyLo. **454**

Louisville Circulating Library. Catalogue of Books in the Louisville Circulating Library, established August, 1838. Louisville, 1838. 22 p. Not in Rinderknecht. KyU (entered under: Lyons, D. J.). **455**

Louisville Circulating Library. Catalogue of Books in the Louisville Circulating Library... Louisville: W. N. Haldeman, 1842. 13 p. Rinderknecht 42-3045. DLC, InU, NcU. **456**

Louisville Law Library. Catalogue . . . Louisville, 1852. Cf. Rhees, p. 60. **457**

Louisville Library Association. List of Books belonging to the Louisville Library Association... E. G. Booth, Librarian. Louisville: J. P. Morton, 1871. 40 p. DLC. **458**

Louisville Library Association. List of Books belonging to the Louisville Library Association... E. G. Booth, Librarian. Louisville: J. P. Morton, 1872. 64 p. DLC, KyU. **459**

Louisville Mercantile Library. Catalogue of the Louisville Mercantile Library, and a List of the Newspapers and Periodicals in the News-room, with an Appendix, containing the Library Regulations and a List of the Officers and Life Members. Louisville: Prentice and Weissinger, 1843. 101, [2] p. DLC copy has ms. corrections to the library regulations. Not in Rinderknecht. DLC, KyLo, KyLoF, MB, MBAt. **460**

Louisville Mercantile Library Association. Catalogue . . . Louisville, 1828. 12 p. Not in Shoemaker. Cf. Cutter 114 (same as Cutter 299 for a 1848 ed?). **461**

Louisville Odd Fellows' Library Association. Catalogue . . . 1873. 45 p. Cf. Cutter 815 (a ghost edition confused by Cutter with entry 466 infra?). **462**

University of Louisville. Medical Department. Catalogue of the Library of the Medical Department of the University of Louisville. Louisville: Prentice and Weissinger, 1847. 91 p. KyLoU-HS. **463**

Young Men's Christian Association. Catalogue of the Library of the Young Men's Christian Association of Louisville, Kentucky. Louisville: Davidson Brothers, 1871. 21 p. DLC. **464**

Maysville

Maysville Circulating Library. Catalogue of Books in the Maysville Circulating Library, containing above 3000 Vol. in the various Branches of Literature, kept by Edward Cox, for Sale or Hire at his Book and Music Store, Front Street. Maysville: L. Collins, 1832. 24 p. Not in Bruntjen. OCHP. **465**

Newport

Odd Fellows' Library Association. Catalogue of the Odd Fellows' Library Association, Newport, Ky. Cincinnati: Applegate, Pownsford, 1873. 45 p. DLC. **466**

LOUISIANA

Baton Rouge

Louisiana State Library, see entries 469-70.

New Orleans

Ellis' Circulating Library. Catalogue of Books in Ellis' Circulating Library. New Orleans: George Ellis & Brother, 1871. 42, [1] p. LNT. **467**

Ellis' Circulating Library. Sixth Annual Catalogue Ellis' Circulating Library. Established October, 1868. New Orleans: George Ellis & Brother, 1874. 66 p. DLC. **468**

Louisiana State Library. Catalogue of the Louisiana State Library. 1869. Albert Bovee, State Librarian. New Orleans: Printed at the Republican Office, 1869. 146 p. DLC, IU, L-L, LN, LNT, M, MiU, Vi. **469**

Louisiana State Library. Catalogue of the Louisiana State Library. 1871. Harriet S. Ball, State Librarian. New Orleans: Republican Printing Co., 1871. 158 p. DLC, L-L, LU, M. **470**

Lyceum and Library Society. Catalogue of the Library of the Lyceum and Library Society, First District, City of New Orleans. New Orleans: R. C. Kerr, 1858. 124 p. AU, CU-A, DLC, LN, LNT, LU, MBAt, MiU, N. **471**

Lyceum and Library Society. Catalogue of the Juvenile Library of the Lyceum and Library Society, First District, City of New Orleans. New Orleans: R. C. Kerr, 1858. 22 p. LN. **472**

New Orleans Circulating Library. Catalogue of Books, in the New Orleans Circulating Library, No. 34, St. Charles Street, opposite the Exchange Hotel. New Orleans, 1840. 59 p. Operated by J. A. Noble. Not in Rinderknecht. LNT. **473**

New Orleans Commercial Library. Catalogue of the Books and Periodicals of the N. O. Commercial Library and Reading Room. New Orleans: Charles Small, 1838. 93 p. Rinderknecht 51895. CtHT, LN. **474**

Public School and Lyceum Library. Catalogue of the Public School Library of Municipality No. Two. New Orleans, 1848. viii, 155 p. CtHT, DLC, LN, LNT, MWA, N, PPL. **475**

MAINE

Auburn

Young Men's Christian Association. Catalogue of Books in the Y.M.C.A. Library, Auburn, Maine. Lewiston: Printed at the Journal Office, 1874. 44 p. DLC, MeB. **476**

Augusta

Kennebec Law Library. Catalogue of Books belonging to the Trustees of Kennebec Law Library, together with a Copy of their By-laws. Augusta: Elias G. Hedge, 1859. 22 p. MWA. **477**

Maine State Library. Catalogue of Maine State Library. Arranged and prepared by Philip C. Johnson, Secretary of State. December, 1839. Augusta: Smith & Robinson, 1839. 59 p. Not in Rinderknecht. CtY, Me, MWA. **478**

Maine State Library. A Catalogue of Books, contained in the Maine State Library. Arranged and prepared by Philip C. Johnson, Secretary of State. Augusta: Wm. R. Smith, 1843. 88 p. Rinderknecht 43-3226. CtY, Me, M, MWA. **479**

Maine State Library. Catalogue of Books, belonging to the Maine State Library. Arranged and prepared by Ezra B. French, Secretary of State. January 1, 1846. Augusta: Wm. T. Johnson, 1846. 119 p. Me. **480**

Maine State Library. Catalogue of the Maine State Library, 1850. Arranged and prepared by Abner Oakes, Assistant Librarian, under the Direction of Ezra B. French, Secretary of State. Augusta: W. T. Johnson, 1850. 248 p. DLC (interleaved), IU, Me, M, MA, MH, NN, OKentU, P, Vt, Vi.   **481**

Maine State Library. Appendix to the Catalogue of the Maine State Library, 1854. Augusta: W. T. Johnson, 1854. 47 p. DLC (interleaved), Me, MH, MWA, T.   **482**

Maine State Library. Catalogue of the Maine State Library, 1856. Arranged and published agreeably to Resolve approved April 4, 1856, under Direction of Caleb B. Ayer, Secretary of State. Augusta: Fuller & Fuller, 1856. 439 p. DLC, Me, MeHi, NN.   **483**

Maine State Library. Catalogue of the Maine State Library. 1862. [Augusta: Stevens & Sayward, 1862]. 304 p. CtY, DLC, Me, MeHi, MB, MMeT, MWA, Nh,   **484**

Maine State Library. Supplement. Catalogue of the Maine State Library. 1867. Augusta: Owen & Nash, 1868. 75 p.   DLC (interleaved), Me, MB, MWA, NNC. **485**

Bangor

Bangor Circulating Library. Catalogue of the Bangor Circulating Library. Bangor, 1836. Not in Rinderknecht. Cf. Williamson, vol. 1, p. 72 (library was operated by E. J. Duren).   **486**

Bangor Library Association. Catalogue of Books . . . [Bangor]: Benjamin A. Burr, 1873. 146 p. MeBa.   **487**

Bangor Mechanics' Association. Catalogue of Books in the Library of the Bangor Mechanics' Association. January, 1853. [Bangor]: Bartlett & Burr, 1853. 46 p. MeBa. **488**

Bangor Mechanics' Association. Catalogue of Books in the Library of the Bangor Mechanics' Association. January, 1860. Bangor: Samuel S. Smith, 1860. 43 p. NN.
489

Bangor Mechanics' Association. Catalogue of Books in the Library of the Bangor Mechanics' Association. 1870. Bangor: Samuel S. Smith, 1870. 51 p. DLC, MeHi.
490

Bangor Mercantile Association. Catalogue of Books in the Library of the Bangor Mercantile Association. April, 1848. Bangor: Samuel S. Smith, 1848. 33 p. MeBa.   **491**

Bangor Mercantile Association. Catalogue of Books in the Library of the Bangor Mercantile Association. 1855. Bangor: Samuel S. Smith, 1855. 55 p. DLC, MeB, MeBa, MeHi.   **492**

Bangor Mercantile Association. Catalogue of Books . . . Bangor: B. A. Burr, 1873. 244 p. Reissued, with supplementary material, by the Bangor Mechanic Association in 1876. DLC, MeBa, MB, NN.   **493**

Belfast

Belfast Circulating Library. Catalogue of the Belfast Circulating Library, kept by Noyes P. Hawes. [Belfast]: J. Dorr, 1831. 22 p. Not in Bruntjen. TxHR.   **493a**

Biddeford

Public Library. Catalogue of the Public Library, of the City of Biddeford. Biddeford: O. A. Dearing, 1863. 54 p. DLC, MB, MWA.
494

Brunswick

Bowdoin College. Catalogue of the Library of Bowdoin College, in Brunswick, Maine. Brunswick: Joseph Griffin, 1821. iv, 120 p. Shoemaker 4813. CtY, MeB, MeHi, MB, MH, MHi, MWA, MnU, NN, NNC, PPAmP, PPiPT, ViW.   **495**

Bowdoin College. A Catalogue of the Library of Bowdoin College, to which is added, an Index of Subjects. Brunswick, 1863. vi, 832 p. Compiled by William P. Tucker. In many libraries.   **496**

Bowdoin College. Athenaean Society. Catalogue of the Library of the Athenaean Society of Bowdoin College. September, 1822. [Brunswick?, 1822]. 12 p. Shoemaker 8160. CtY, MeB.   **497**

Bowdoin College. Athenaean Society. Catalogue of the Library of the Athenaean Society of Bowdoin College . . . Brunswick: Joseph Griffin, 1824. 24 p.   Not in Shoemaker. MH (lost).   **498**

Bowdoin College. Athenaean Society. Catalogue of the Library of the Athenaean Society of Bowdoin College. August, 1830. Brunswick: Joseph Griffin, 1830. 48 p. Cooper 629. MH, MWA (defective), MeB. **499**

Bowdoin College. Athenaean Society. Catalogue of the Library of the Athenaean Society of Bowdoin College. August, 1834. Brunswick: Joseph Griffin, 1834. 55 p. Rinderknecht 23525. CtY, MeB, MHi. **500**

Bowdoin College. Athenaean Society. Catalogue of the Athenaean Society. To which is added a List of the Books belonging to the Library. Brunswick: Joseph Griffin, 1838. 24, 24 p. Rinderknecht 49389. DLC, Me, MeB, MeHi, MHi, MnU. **501**

Bowdoin College. Athenaean Society. Catalogue of the Athenaean Library, Bowdoin College. 1861. Brunswick: J. Griffin, 1861. 86 p. DLC, MeB, MHi, MWA. **502**

Bowdoin College. Medical School. Catalogue of the Library of the Medical School of Maine, at Bowdoin College. February, 1823. Brunswick: Joseph Griffin, 1823. 24, 16 p. ("Appendix," Dec. 1823, 16 p. at end). Shoemaker 11964-11965. CtY-M, MeB, MH (lacks Appendix), MHi (lacks Appendix), MWA, PPPAmP. **503**

Bowdoin College. Medical School. Catalogue of the Library of the Medical School of Maine, at Bowdoin College. February, 1825. Brunswick: Joseph Griffin, 1825. 62 p. Shoemaker 19838. MeB (with continuously paged suppl., 82 p., 1827), MH. **504**

Bowdoin College. Medical School. Catalogue of the Library of the Medical School of Maine, at Bowdoin College. February, 1830. Brunswick: Joseph Griffin, 1830. 84, [2] p. Cooper 626. MeB, MeHi, MWA, WU. **505**

Bowdoin College. Medical School. Catalogue of the Library of the Medical School of Maine, at Bowdoin College. February, 1834. Brunswick: J. Griffin, 1834. 73 p. Rinderknecht 23527. CtY-M, MeB, MBM, MH, Nh, NN. **506**

Bowdoin College. Peucinian Society. Catalogue of the Library of the Peucinian Society, Bowdoin College. Hallowell: Goodale, Glazier, 1823. 26 p. Henry

Wadsworth Longfellow was involved as a compiler, per Jacob Blanck, *Bibliography of American Literature*, #12035. Shoemaker 11967. FU, MeB, PPL. **507**

Bowdoin College. Peucinian Society. Catalogue of the Library of the Peucinian Society, Bowdoin College. January, 1829. Brunswick: George Griffin, 1829. 42 p. Shoemaker 37918. DLC, MeB, MiD-B. **508**

Bowdoin College. Peucinian Society. Catalogue of the Library of the Peucinian Society, of Bowdoin College. December, 1834. Brunswick: Joseph Griffin, 1834. 67 p. Rinderknecht 23528. MeB, MeHi, MHi, RPB. **509**

Bowdoin College. Peucinian Society. Catalogue of the Library of the Peucinian Society of Bowdoin College, Brunswick, Maine. Brunswick: Joseph Griffin, 1843. 40 p. Rinderknecht 43-710. MB, MeHi, MnHi. **510**

Bowdoin College. Peucinian Society. Catalogue of the Peucinian Library, Bowdoin College. 1859. Lewiston: Printed at the Journal Office, 1859. 86 p. MHi has undated "Addenda" (Brunswick: J. Griffin) forming pp. [87]-97. DLC, MeB, MeHi, MH, MHi, MWA, NNGr. **511**

Bucksport

Bucksport Social Library. Catalogue . . . 1847. Cf. Rhees, p. 71. **512**

Dresden

Dresden Social Library. Catalogue of Books in the Dresden Social Library. [n.p., ca. 1840]. Not in Rinderknecht. Cf. Charles Edwin Allen, *History of Dresden, Maine* . . . (Augusta, 1931), pp. 818-20, giving the contents of the catalogue. **513**

Eastport

Eastport Athenaeum. Catalogue . . . 1836. 46 p. Not in Rinderknecht. Cf. Cutter 169. **514**

Gardiner

Mechanics' Association. Catalogue . . . 1847. 20 p. Cf. Rhees, p. 71. **515**

Mechanics' Association. Catalogue of the Library of the Mechanics' Association, Gardiner, Maine, with its By-laws, Library Rules, &c. Gardiner: A. M. C. Heath, 1856. 57 p. DLC.   **516**

Mechanics' Association. Catalogue of the Library of the Mechanics' Association, Gardiner, Maine, with its By-laws, Library Rules, &c. Gardiner: H. K. Morrell, 1868. 52 p. MB.   **517**

Public Library. Catalogue of the Public Library of Gardiner, comprising the Rules and Regulations, Alphabetical Catalogue of Books, and Alphabetical Catalogue of Authors, with their Works . . . Gardiner: H. K. Morrell & Son, 1873. 164 p. Cutter 817 reports suppl. (9 p.). DLC, MB.   **518**

Hallowell

Hallowell Circulating Library. Catalogue of the Hallowell Circulating Library . . . Kept by Goodale, Glazier & Co., at the Hallowell Bookstore. Hallowell: Goodale, Glazier, 1820. 48 p. Shoemaker 1494. No locations given by Shoemaker.   **519**

Hallowell Social Library. Catalogue of Books in the Hallowell Social Library. April, 1843. Hallowell: Glazier, Masters & Smith, [1843]. 24 p. DLC holds "Additional Catalogue for 1847" (6 p.). Not in Rinderknecht. DLC, MeB, MB, MWA.   **520**

Kennebunk

Wells Social Library. Catalogue of Books, in the Wells Social Library (Established at Kennebunk.). [Kennebunk: J. K. Remich, 181-?]. broadside. Not in S & S. MWA.**521**

Lewiston

Harper Library Association. Catalogue of the Harper Library Association. Lewiston, 1855. Cf. Williamson, vol. 1, p. 702.   **522**

Manufacturers' and Mechanics' Library Association. Catalogue of the Manufacturers' and Mechanics' Library Association of Lewiston, with the Charter, Constitution and By-laws . . . Incorporated, 1861. Lewiston, 1861. 68 p. MeB, MB.   **523**

Manufacturers' and Mechanics' Library Association. Catalogue of the Manufacturers' and

Mechanics' Library Association of Lewiston. With the Charter, Constitution and By-laws. Lewiston: Journal Steam Printing Office, 1869. 69 p. DLC and NN hold suppl. #1-3 to July, 1875. DLC, MeU, MB, NN.   **524**

Park Street Methodist Episcopal Church. Catalogue of Books in the Park Street Methodist Episcopal Sabbath-School Library, of Lewiston, with a Brief History of the Origin and Progress of the School. Lewiston: Journal Steam Printing Office, 1871. 32 p. Cf. Williamson, #5438.   **525**

Limington

Limington Social Library. Catalogue of Books in Limington Social Library. January 1, 1837. [Limington? 1837]. 8 p. Not in Rinderknecht. MeB, MeHi, MWA.   **526**

Machias

Machias Social Library. Catalogue . . . 1841. Not in Rinderknecht. Cf. Rhees, p. 73.**527**

Portland

Apprentices' Library. Catalogue of Books composing the Apprentices' Library, founded by the Voluntary Contributions of the Citizens of Portland, July, 1820 . . . Portland: Printed at the Argus Office, 1843. 38 p. DLC copy has "Additions to August 1, 1845" (pp. 39-50, but lacks pp. 41-47). Not in Rinderknecht. DLC.   **528**

Casco Street Church. Catalogue of Casco St. S. S. Library. 1871. Portland: Stephen Berry, 1871. 11 p. MeP.   **529**

Chestnut Street Methodist Episcopal Church. Catalogue of Books in the Sunday School Library of the Methodist Episcopal Church, Chestnut Street, Portland, Me. [Portland]: Staples & Lunt, 1854. 17 p. MeHi.   **530**

Colman and Chisholm's Circulating Library. Catalogue of Colman and Chisholm's Circulating Library, kept at their Bookstore . . . [Portland, 1837?]. 25 p. Not in Rinderknecht. MeHi.   **531**

Colman's Public Library. Catalogue of the Public Library. 1831. [Portland, 1831]. 14 p. This "public library and literary reading room" was managed by S. Colman. Not in Bruntjen. MeHi. **532**

Colman's Public Library. Catalogue of Coleman's Public Library. [Portland, 1834]. 48 p. Not in Rinderknecht. MeHi (additional "List of Books" on paper wrappers). **533**

Congress Street Methodist Episcopal Church. Catalogue of Books in the Congress Street Methodist Episcopal Church Sunday-School. Portland: Ford & Perry, 1874. 16 p. Cf. Williamson, #8145. **534**

Cumberland Law Library. Catalogue of the Cumberland Law Library. Portland: Shirley and Hyde, 1830. 22 p. Cooper 1048. MeHi. **535**

Cumberland Law Library. A Catalogue of Books in the Library of the Bar, of Cumberland County, Maine, with the Library Regulations, Bar Rules, &c. . . . Portland: Foster, Gerrish, 1853. 76 p. MeP, MWA. **536**

First Baptist Church. Catalogue of Sunday-School Books. Portland: David Tucker, 1868. 16 p. Cf. Williamson, #8143. **537**

First Baptist Church. Catalogue of First Baptist S. S. Library, Portland. Re-organized September, 1875. Portland: Harmon, Paine, 1875. 32 p. MeHi. **538**

Free Street Baptist Church. Catalogue of the Sunday School Library . . . Portland, 1870. MeHi (lost). **539**

Free Street Baptist Church. Catalogue of Free Street Baptist S. S. Library. Reorganized Sept. 1874. Portland: Stephen Berry, 1874. 31 p. MeHi (lost), MeP. **540**

High Street Church. Catalogue of High Street Sabbath School Library. September, 1874. Portland: B. Thurston, 1874. 16 p. MeP. **541**

India Street Universalist Church. Catalogue of Books in the Library of the India Street Universalist Church Sunday-School. Portland: Geo. B. Bagley, 1874. 24 p. Cf. Williamson, #8146. **542**

Maine Charitable Mechanic Association. Catalogue . . . 1855. 57 p. Cf. Rhees, p. 73. **543**

Maine Charitable Mechanic Association. Catalogue of the Books of the Library of the Maine

Char'ble Mechanic Association . . . Revised March, 1859. Portland, 1859. 78 p. DLC.**544**

Maine Charitable Mechanic Association. Catalogue of the Books of the Library of the Maine Char'ble Mechanic Association. Founded July, 1820 . . . Revised June, 1867. Portland: N. A. Foster, 1867. 94 p. DLC. **545**

Maine Charitable Mechanic Association. Catalogue of the Books of the Library of the Maine Charitable Mechanic Association. Founded July, 1820. Revised June, 1875. Portland: B. Thurston, 1875. 128, 28 p. A "Congressional Library" section forms second group (28 p.). MeHi, MeP. **546**

Mechanics' Library, see Maine Charitable Mechanic Association.

Mercantile Library Association. Catalogue of the Portland Mercantile Library. Portland: Foster & Gerrish, 1854. 52 p. DLC. **547**

Mercantile Library Association. Catalogue of Books in the Library of the Mercantile Library Association. Incorporated March, 1852. Portland: Horace C. Little, 1859. 63 p. MeP. **548**

Mercantile Library Association. Catalogue of Books in the Library of the Mercantile Library Association, incorporated March, 1852 . . . Portland: David Tucker, 1865. 106 p. MeP. **549**

Mercantile Library Association. Catalogue of Books in the Library of the Mercantile Library Association. Incorporated March, 1852 . . . Portland: David Tucker, 1867. 77 p. MeP. **550**

Mercantile Library Association. Catalogue of Books in the Library of the Mercantile Library Association. Incorporated March, 1852. Portland: David Tucker, 1870. 118 p. MeHi, MeP (interleaved). **551**

Mercantile Library Association. Catalogue of Books in the Library of the Mercantile Library Association. Incorporated March, 1852. Portland: David Tucker, 1873. 163, [1] p. Cutter 818 reports suppl. (14 p.); MeP has an interleaved suppl. with 48 p. DLC, MeP.**552**

Park Street Church. Catalogue of the Park Street Sabbath School Library. 1867.

Portland: Stephen Berry, 1867. 31 p. (p. 31 blank). MeHi.   **553**

Portland Athenaeum. Catalogue . . . [Portland, 182-?]. 31 p. Not in Shoemaker. MeHi (interleaved copy; lacks title page).
554

Portland Athenaeum. Catalogue of the Books in the Portland Athenaeum, with the By-laws and Regulations of the Institution. Portland: Shirley & Hyde, 1828. 52 p. MeHi and MWA hold suppl. of books purchased in 1828 and 1829 (8 p.). Shoemaker 34848. MeB, MeHi (with added leaf numbered 47 laid in opposite p. 47), MeP (interleaved), MWA, NN (with added leaf numbered 47 laid in opposite p. 47).   **555**

Portland Athenaeum. Catalogue of the Books in the Portland Athenaeum, with the Library Regulations. Portland: Thomas Todd, 1832. 42 p. Bruntjen 14335. MeB, MeHi, NN.   **556**

Portland Athenaeum. Catalogue of the Library of the Portland Athenaeum, with the By-laws and Regulations of the Institution. Portland: A. Shirley, 1839. 88 p. Rinderknecht 58023. LNT, Me, MeHi, MeP, MeWC, MH, MWA.   **557**

Portland Athenaeum. Supplement to the Catalogue of the Library of the Portland Athenaeum, containing the Books added from 1839 to 1845. Portland: A. Shirley & Son, 1846. 38 p. MeP.   **558**

Portland Athenaeum. Catalogue of the Library of the Portland Athenaeum, with the Bye-laws of the Institution, adopted Feb. 19, 1849. Portland: Wm. E. Edwards, 1849. 150, [1] p. DLC, ICN, Me, MeHi, MeP, MBAt, MH, MWA, M.   **559**

Portland High School. Catalogue of the Girls' Library of the Portland High School. Portland: Stephen Berry, 1866. 36 p. Cf. Williamson, #8132.   **560**

Portland Institute and Public Library. Finding List for Books in the Portland Institute and Public Library, April 1, 1869, with a Supplementary List to June 1, 1869, the Charter, Laws, Regulations, Names of Officers and Life Members, and List of Donations to the Library. Portland: [B. Thurston], 1869. 119 p. DLC, MeB, MeHi, MeP, MeU, MB, MWA, NNC.   **561**

Portland Library. By-laws of the Proprietors of Portland Library, with the Names of the Proprietors, and Catalogue of the Books. Portland: Thomas B. Wait, 1806. 14 p. S & S 11196. CSt, MeHi, MeP.   **562**

Portland Library. By-laws of the Proprietors of the Portland Library, with the Names of the Proprietors, and a Catalogue of the Books. Portland: Arthur Shirley, 1811. 14 p. Not in S & S. MeP (with 3 p. of ms. additions).
563

Portland Library. By-laws of the Proprietors of Portland Library, with the Names of the Proprietors, and Catalogue of the Books. Portland: A. & J. Shirley, 1815. 28 p. S & S 35683. CSt, MeHi, MeP, MWA.   **564**

Portland Library. By-laws of the Proprietors of Portland Library, with the Names of the Proprietors, and a Catalogue of the Books. Portland: Arthur Shirley, 1821. 32 p. Shoemaker 6514. MeHi.   **565**

Portland Library. By-laws of the Proprietors of Portland Library, with the Names of the Proprietors, and a Catalogue of the Books. Portland: Hill, Edwards, 1826. 33, [3] p. Shoemaker 25812. MeHi, MeP, MWA, PPL.
566

St. Luke's Cathedral. Catalogue of St. Luke's Cathedral Sunday School Library. Portland: Stephen Berry, 1873. 11 p. MeP.   **567**

State Street Church. State Street Sabbath School Library. April, 1869. Portland: B. Thurston, 1869. 16 p. MWA.   **568**

State Street Church. Catalogue of State Street Sabbath School Library. October, 1872. Portland: B. Thurston, 1872. 24 p. MeHi (lost).   **569**

Washington Circulating Library. Catalogue of Books belonging to the Washington Circulating Library, kept at the Bookstore of Pearson & Little. Portland: Day & Fraser, 1829. 23 p. Shoemaker 41438. MiD-B (erroneously catalogued as located in Washington, Maine).   **570**

Waverly Circulating Library. Catalogue of the Waverly Circulating Library, No. 8, Mussey's Row, Middle-Street. Portland: James Adams, jun., 1828. 12 p. Shoemaker 37106. MWA (entered under: Robinson & Wyatt), MiD-B (erroneously catalogued as located in Waverly, Maine). **571**

Readfield

Maine Wesleyan Seminary. Calliopean Society. Catalogue of the Library of the Calliopean Society of the Maine Wesleyan Seminary, Readfield. August, 1835. Hallowell: Glazier, Masters & Smith, 1835. 12 p. Not in Rinderknecht. MeB. **572**

Rockland

Rockland Athenaeum. Catalogue . . . 1850. Cf. Rhees, p. 76. **573**

Saco

Saco Athenaeum. Catalogue of Books, By-laws, and Rules and Regulations of the Saco Athenaeum Library. Biddeford: John Hanscom, 1868. 38 p. DeU. **574**

Saco Circulating Library. A Catalogue of the Books contained in the Saco Circulating Library, kept by A. E. Small . . . Saco: W. J. Condon, 1834. 12 p. Rinderknecht 26613. MeHi, MWA. **575**

York Library. Catalogue of Books in the York Library, Saco. July, 1839. Saco: S. &. C. Webster, 1839. 16 p. Not in Rinderknecht. Cf. Williamson, #8813. **576**

Skowhegan

Skowhegan Library. Catalogue of the Skowhegan Library. Skowhegan: Smith & Emery, 1869. 52 p. DLC, MeHi, MB, MWA, NB. **577**

Thomaston

Ladies' Home Library. Catalogue . . . 1853. Cf. Rhees, pp. 76-77. **578**

Togus

National Home for Disabled Volunteer Soldiers. Catalogue of the Library of the National Home for Disabled Volunteer Soldiers (Eastern Branch), Togus, (near) Augusta, Maine. May 1st, 1872. Sprague: Owen & Nash, 1872. 100 p. DLC, M. **579**

Waterville

Universalist Church. Catalogue of the Universalist S. S. Library, West Waterville, Me. 1874.[Waterville?, 1874]. 12 p. MeHi. **580**

Waterville College. Catalogue of the Library of Waterville College, in Waterville, Maine. Waterville: Edgar H. Gray, 1835. 30 p. Not in Rinderknecht. MeB, MeBa. **581**

Waterville College. Catalogue of the Library of Waterville College, in Waterville, Maine. Waterville: John S. Carter, 1845. 47 p. DLC, MeBa, MeHi, MB, MH, MWA. **582**

Waterville College. Literary Fraternity Society. Catalogue of the Members and Library of the Literary Fraternity Society of Waterville College. Instituted 1824, incorporated 1828. Portland: B. Thurston, 1852. 53 p. LU, MeWC, NRAB. **583**

Westbrook

Westbrook Social Library. Finding List of the Westbrook Social Library. Portland: Harry H. Baker, 1835. 20, [2] p. Rinderknecht 35347. MeWebr. **584**

Winthrop

Friends, Society of. Catalogue of Books belonging to the Friends' Sabbath School Library, Winthrop, Maine. Portland: Steven Berry, 1874. 12 p. MeHi. **585**

Wiscacasset

Lincoln Law Library Association. Catalogue of Books of the Lincoln Law Library Association. 1842. [Wiscacasset?, 1842]. 4 p. Not in Rinderknecht. MeHi. **586**

Yarmouth

First Congregational Church. Catalogue of the First Parish Sunday School Library, Yarmouth, Maine. Portland: Stephen Berry, 1873. 12 p. MeHi. **587**

MARYLAND

Annapolis

Maryland State Library. A Catalogue of Books in the Maryland State Library. Annapolis: J. Green, [1827]. 8 p. Shoemaker 29637. MdBP. **588**

Maryland State Library. Catalogue of Law Books belonging to the State Library. Annapolis: J. Green, 1832. 18 p. Bruntjen 13584. MdLL, PHi. **589**

Maryland State Library. Catalogue of the Library of the State of Maryland. D. Ridgely, Librarian. December, 1832. Annapolis: Jeremiah Hughes, 1833. v, 111 p. Bruntjen 19979. CtHWatk, CtY-L, MdHi, MWA, NN, NcD. **590**

Maryland State Library. Catalogue of the Library of the State of Maryland. D. Ridgely, Librarian. December, 1837. Annapolis: Jeremiah Hughes, 1837. 132 p. DLC copy is interleaved with ms. additions to 1841. Rinderknecht 45460. DLC, IU (film), MdBE, MdBP, MdLL, MH. **591**

Maryland State Library. Catalogue of the Maryland State Library. 1851. Arranged and prepared by Richard Swann, State Librarian. Annapolis: Riley and Davis, 1851. 226 p. DLC, MdBE, MdLL, PP, T. **592**

Maryland State Library. Catalogue of the Maryland State Library. 1862. Arranged and prepared by Edwin M. Shipley. Annapolis: Robert F. Bonsall, 1862. 220 p. MdBE, MdLL, MdU, MWA. **593**

Maryland State Library. Supplemental Catalogue . . . Annapolis: R. P. Bayly, 1863. 34 p. Prepared by Hanson P. Jordan. MdU. **594**

Maryland State Library. Supplemental Catalogue . . . December, 1864. [Annapolis?, 1865?]. 28 p. Bowker, p. 666, records supplements published in *Report of the Joint Committee on the State Library,* 1865, 1867. MdBE. **595**

Maryland State Library. Catalogue of the Maryland State Library. 1874. Compiled by William T. Iglehart . . . Annapolis: Office of the Anne Arundel Advertiser, 1874. 4, 394 p. Ct, DLC, MdBE, MdBJ, MdLL, M, OKentU, Vt, Vi. **596**

St. John's College. Catalogue of Books, belonging to the Library of St. John's College, Annapolis, Md. [Annapolis]: Riley & Davis, 1847. 36, [2] p. DLC, MH, NN. **597**

United States Naval Academy. Catalogue of the Library of the U.S. Naval Academy, Annapolis, Maryland. June 30, 1860. Annapolis: Robert F. Bonsall, 1860. vi, 251 p. CtHT, DLC, DSI, MdAN, MH, MWA, NHi, RPB. **598**

Baltimore

Apprentice's Library. Catalogue of the Apprentice's Library in Baltimore, to be loaned gratis, to Apprentices and other Young Persons, with the Names of the Donors. Baltimore: Thomas Murphy, 1822. 12 p. Shoemaker 7885, Rink 514. MdHi. **599**

Baltimore Athenaeum. Catalogue of Books belonging to the Library of the Baltimore Athenaeum. Baltimore: John D. Toy, 1827. 172+ p. Shoemaker 27955 gives the printer as Edes and Leakin. MdBP (defective). **600**

Baltimore Circulating Library. [Catalogue of Additional Books]. Baltimore, 1802. Advertised in the *Baltimore Republican,* July 14, 1802. Cf. Bristol #82, S & S 1805. **601**

Baltimore Circulating Library. A Catalogue of the Baltimore Circulating Library, kept by William Munday . . . to which is prefixed, Rules and Regulations for said Library . . . Baltimore: John W. Butler, 1807. 112 p. S & S 12033. DLC (film), MdHi (entered under: Munday, William). **602**

Baltimore Circulating Library. First Supplement to the Catalogue of the Baltimore Circulating Library, kept by William Munday. [Baltimore, 1809]. 24 p. S & S 16898. MdHi (entered under: Munday, William). **603**

Baltimore Circulating Library. A Catalogue of the Baltimore Circulating Library, kept by William Munday . . . to which is prefixed, Rules and Regulations, for said Library. Baltimore: William Warner, 1812. 43 p. S & S 24696. MdHi (entered under: Munday, William). **604**

Baltimore Circulating Library. First Supplement to the Catalogue of the Baltimore Circulating Library, kept by William Munday. Baltimore: William Warner, 1813. 8 p. S & S 27782. MdHi (entered under: Munday, William). **605**

Baltimore Circulating Library. Second Supplement to the Catalogue of the Baltimore Circulating Library, kept by William Munday. Baltimore: William Warner, 1814. 21 p. Not in S & S. MdHi (entered under: Munday, William). **606**

Baltimore Library Company, see Library Company of Baltimore.

Concordia Gesellschaft. Catalog der Bibliothek der Concordia. Baltimore: C. W. Schneidereith, 1869. 48 p. DLC. **607**

Fell's Point Circulating Library. Catalogue . . . Baltimore: Samuel Barnes, 1809. Referred to in the *Baltimore Evening Post*, April 13, 1809. Cf. Bristol #728, S & S 17500. Operated by Samuel Barnes, per Kaser, p. 138. **608**

Fell's Point Circulating Library. Catalogue . . . Baltimore, 1810. Advertised in the *Baltimore Whig*, Dec. 17, 1810. Cf. Bristol #845, S & S 20101. Operated by Samuel Barnes, per Kaser, p. 138. **609**

Gunpowder Library Association of Friends. Constitution of Gunpowder Library Association of Friends, together with the Rules and Regulations, and a Catalogue of Books. [n.p.]: E. F. Church, 1853. 14 p. If not actually in Baltimore, probably somewhere in Baltimore County? PSC-Hi. **610**

Hunter & Robinson's Circulating Library. Catalogue . . . Baltimore, 1809. Advertised in the *Baltimore Evening Post*, Oct. 27, 1809. Cf. Bristol #746, S & S 17786. Operated by James A. Hunter and Joseph Robinson, per Kaser, p. 144. **611**

Hunter & Robinson's Circulating Library. First Supplementary Catalogue . . . Baltimore, 1809. Advertised in the *Baltimore Evening Post*, Dec. 5, 1809. Cf. Bristol #747, S & S 17787. Operated by James A. Hunter and Joseph Robinson, per Kaser, p. 144. **612**

Hunter & Robinson's Circulating Library. General Catalogue . . . Baltimore, 1810.

Advertised in the Baltimore *Federal Republican*, June 26, 1810. Cf. Bristol #862, S & S 20408. Operated by James A. Hunter and Joseph Robinson, per Kaser, p. 144. **613**

Library Company of Baltimore. A Catalogue of the Books, &c. belonging to the Library Company of Baltimore, to which are prefixed, the Act for the Incorporation of the Company, their Constitution, their By-laws, and an Alphabetical List of the Members. Baltimore: Prentiss & Cole, 1802. xxiii, 98 p. S & S 2531. DGU, MdBD, MdHi, MB, MWA. **614**

Library Company of Baltimore. Appendix to the Catalogue. [Baltimore, 1804]. 18 p. S & S 5766. MdHi. **615**

Library Company of Baltimore. A Catalogue of the Books, &c. belonging to the Library Company of Baltimore, to which are prefixed, the Act for the Incorporation of the Company, their Constitution, their By-laws, and an Alphabetical List of the Members. Baltimore: Edes & Leakin, 1809. 196 p. S & S 16901 (duplicated by 3717 for a ghost 1803 ed., and 17913). CLU, CtHT, DLC, MdBE, MdHi, MdBP, MBAt, MHi, MWA, MiU-C, NN, NNC, PHi, PPL, PU. **616**

Library Company of Baltimore. A Supplement to the Catalogue of Books, &c. belonging to the Library Company of Baltimore. 1816. Baltimore: J. Robinson, 1816. iv, 36 p. S & S 38072. CLU, MdBP, MdHi, MHi, MWA, MiU-C, NNC, PHi, PPL. **617**

Library Company of Baltimore. A Supplement to the Catalogue of Books, &c. belonging to the Library Company of Baltimore. No. 2, 1823. Baltimore: John D. Toy, 1823. 40 p. Shoemaker 13105. CLU, MdBP, MdHi, MWA, MiU-C, NNC, PP, PPL. **618**

Library Company of Baltimore. Third Supplement to the Catalogue of Books, &c. belonging to the Library Company of Baltimore. 1831. Baltimore: John D. Toy, 1831. 21 p. Bruntjen 7971 (duplicated by 5892). CLU, MdBP, MdHi, MiU-C, NNC, PP, PPL. **619**

Library Company of Baltimore. Fourth Supplement to the Catalogue of Books, &c. belonging to the Library Company of

Baltimore. 1841. Baltimore: John D. Toy, 1841. 28 p. Rinderknecht 41-345. MdHi. **620**

Library Company of the Baltimore Bar. Catalogue of Books, in the Law Library of the Baltimore Bar. June, 1851. Baltimore: John D. Toy, 1851. 53 p. NN. **621**

Library Company of the Baltimore Bar. A General Catalogue of Books of the Law Library of the Library Company of the Baltimore Bar, formed April 13, 1840-- Incorporated January 8, 1841. Compiled by J. Campbell Dorry, Librarian. June, 1860. Baltimore: John D. Toy, 1860. 143 p. DLC (film), MdBE, MdBP, MdHi, MB. **622**

Maryland Circulating Library. A Catalogue of the Books, &c. belonging to the Maryland Circulating Library . . . Baltimore: Frederick G. Schaeffer, [1822?]. [8], 119, 20 p. Operated by Nathaniel P. Bixby, per Kaser, p. 148. Shoemaker 2131 (under 1820). MdHi, MWA. **623**

Maryland Circulating Library. No. 2. Supplement to the Catalogue of Books, &c. belonging to the Maryland Circulating Library . . . Baltimore, 1822. 34, [2] p. Operated by N. P. Bixby. Shoemaker 9392. MdHi. **624**

Maryland Historical Society. Catalogue of the Manuscripts, Maps, Medals, Coins, Statuary, Portraits and Pictures; and An Account of the Library of the Maryland Historical Society, made in 1854, by Lewis Mayer, Assistant Librarian. Baltimore: John D. Toy, 1854. 49, [2] p. In many libraries. **625**

Maryland Institute for the Promotion of the Mechanic Arts. Catalogue of Books in the Library of the Maryland Institute, for the Promotion of the Mechanic Arts. In Two Parts. Part First.--Alphabetical. Baltimore: "The Printing Office," 1857. 132 p. DLC (interleaved), MB, PPAmP. **626**

Maryland Institute for the Promotion of the Mechanic Arts. Catalogue of Books in the Library of the Maryland Institute, for the Promotion of the Mechanic Arts . . . Baltimore: James Young, 1865. 176 p. DLC, MdBP. **627**

Maryland Sunday School Union. Catalogue of Books belonging to the Juvenile Circulating

Library of the Maryland Sunday School Union. Baltimore: Lucas and Deaver, 1835. 24 p. Not in Rinderknecht. MdHi. **628**

Medical and Chirurgical Faculty of the State of Maryland. Catalogue of Books belonging to the Library of the Medical and Chirurgical Faculty of Maryland. Baltimore: John D. Toy, 1835. 28 p. Rinderknecht 32962. DNLM (interleaved with 51 p. of ms. additions), DSG. **629**

Medical and Chirurgical Faculty of the State of Maryland. Catalogue of Books belonging to the Library of the Medical and Chirurgical Faculty, of Maryland. Baltimore: J. W. Woods, 1852. 66 p. DLC, DNLM, MdBP. **630**

Mercantile Library Association. Catalogue of the Mercantile Library Association of Baltimore. Baltimore, 1842. Not in Rinderknecht. Cf. Jewett, p. 134. **631**

Mercantile Library Association. First Supplement to the Catalogue of the Mercantile Library Association of Baltimore up to February 8th, 1844. [Baltimore]: Robert Neilson, [1844]. 27 p. Not in Rinderknecht. MdBE. **632**

Mercantile Library Association. Catalogue of the Mercantile Library Association of Baltimore. 1848. Baltimore, 1848. 118 p. Cf. Cutter 301, Jewett, p. 134. **633**

Mercantile Library Association. Catalogue of the Mercantile Library of Baltimore. 1851. Baltimore: John W. Woods, 1851. 338 p. Rhees, p. 85, reports suppl., 1854. DLC, MdBE, MdHi, MA, NN. **634**

Mercantile Library Association. Catalogue of the Mercantile Library of Baltimore. Baltimore: Sherwood & Co., 1858. 477 p. A reissue of the Catalogue of 1851, with "Supplementary Catalogue. January 1, 1858" on pp. [339]-477 p. MdBE, NN, PP (suppl. only). **635**

Mercantile Library Association. Catalogue of the English Prose Fiction, including Translations and Juvenile Fiction, in the Mercantile Library Association, of Baltimore, to October, 1874. Baltimore: John W. Woods, 1874. 116 p. C, CU, DLC, ICN, MdBE, MdU, MB, MBAt, MH, MWA, Mi, NN, NcU, PPL. **636**

Odd Fellows, Independent Order of. Catalogue of the Library of the I.O.O.F. of Baltimore. 1852. Baltimore: H. E. Huber, [1852]. 59 p. MdBP.   **637**

Odd Fellows, Independent Order of. Catalogue of Books in the Library of the Independent Order of Odd-fellows, of the City of Baltimore . . . Baltimore: John Y. Slater, 1872. 193 p. DLC.   **638**

Peabody Institute. Alphabetical Catalogue of Books proposed to be purchased for the Library of the Peabody Institute, Baltimore. Baltimore: John D. Toy, 1861. 415 p. Running title: Alphabetical Index. DLC, MdBE, MdBP, MBAt, MH, MnU, NNC, NNGr, NcD, PPL.   **639**

Peabody Institute. No. 2. Catalogue of Books to be purchased by the Peabody Institute of the City of Baltimore. No. 2. Baltimore: John D. Toy, 1863. 218 p. CtHT-W, DLC, MdBE, MdBP, MBAt, MH, NN.   **640**

Roach's Circulating Library. Catalogue of Roach's Circulating Library, No. 38 Market-street, Baltimore . . . Baltimore, [ca. 1822-23]. 104 p. Operated by J. Roach. For dating, see Rollo G. Silver, "The Baltimore Book Trade, 1800-1825," *Bulletin of the New York Public Library* 57 (1953): 349. S & S 13463 (under 1807). MdHi (lost).   **641**

Robinson's Circulating Library. Catalogue of Robinson's Circulating Library . . . Baltimore, 1816. 154 p. Operated by Joseph Robinson. S & S 38824. MdBE, MdHi, MWA.   **642**

Robinson's Circulating Library. First Supplement for 1816 to the Catalogue of Robinson's Circulating Library, No. 96, Market-Street. [Baltimore, 1816]. 15 p. Operated by Joseph Robinson. S & S 38825. MdBE, MdHi, MWA.   **643**

Robinson's Circulating Library. Second Supplement, for 1817-1818, to the Catalogue of Robinson's Circulating Library . . . Baltimore: J. Robinson, 1818. 12 p. Operated by Joseph Robinson. S & S 44566 MdBE, MdHi, NN.   **644**

Robinson's Circulating Library. Third Supplement, for 1816, to the Catalogue of Robinson's Circulating Library . . . Baltimore: J. Robinson, 1819. 12 p.

Operated by Joseph Robinson. S & S 49310. MdBE, MdHi.   **645**

Robinson's Circulating Library. General Catalogue to Robinson's Circulating Library . . . Baltimore: J. Robinson, 1823. 211 p. Operated by Joseph Robinson. Shoemaker 13972. MdHi (defective; pp. 161-72 lacking).   **646**

Robinson's Circulating Library. Catalogue . . . Baltimore, 1828. Cf. Robinson's advertisement for the American edition of *Falkland* in *American & Commercial Daily Advertiser* (Baltimore), July 3, 1830, p. 3. Not in Shoemaker.   **646a**

Robinson's Circulating Library. Catalogue . . . Baltimore, 1830. Cf. Robinson's advertisement for a new catalogue ("part 1st . . . will be ready this day") in *American & Commercial Daily Advertiser* (Baltimore), Dec. 7, 1830, p. 4. Not in Cooper.   **646b**

Robinson's Circulating Library. Catalogue of Robinson's Circulating Library, Baltimore. Part I. History, Voyages, Travels, &c. Part II. Miscellaneous. Part III. Novels, Tales and Romances. [Baltimore], 1839. 80 p. Operated by Joseph Robinson. "Parts IV, V, & VI, containing Poetry, The Drama, and Magazines and Reviews, and the works in French and Italian, will be published shortly." Rinderknecht 58268. MdBP.   **647**

Young Men's Christian Association. Catalogue of the Library of the Young Men's Christian Association of Baltimore. Baltimore: J. B. Rose, 1865. 30 p. MdBP.   **648**

Hagerstown

Dietrick's Circulating Library. Catalogue of Jacob D. Dietrick's Circulating Library, consisting of History, Voyages, Novels, etc. now kept in Hagers-Tow . . . Hagers-Town: John Gruber, 1801. 110 p. Includes a section of German books, per Karl John Richard Arndt and Reimer C. Eck, *The First Century of German Language Printing in the United States of America* (Göttingen, 1989), #1259. S & S 415 (calling for 98 p.). MdHag (defective).   **649**

New Windsor

New Windsor Library Company. Catalogue of Books belonging to the New Windsor Library

Company. Baltimore: Richard J. Matchett, 1841. 12 p. Not in Rinderknecht. MWA.**650**

Sandy Spring

Sandy Spring Library Company. Catalogue . . . 1843. 12 p. Not in Rinderknecht. Cf. Jewett, p. 137. **651**

Sandy Spring Library Company. Catalogue . . . 1854. Cf. Rhees, pp. 89-90. **652**

MASSACHUSETTS

Amesbury

Public Library of Amesbury and Salisbury. Catalogue of the Public Library of Amesbury and Salisbury. Salem: G. W. Pease, 1866. 49 p. DLC holds suppl., 1873? (22 p.). DLC. **653**

Union Evangelical Sabbath School of Amesbury & Salisbury, Mass. Catalogue. Salisbury: H. E. Morrill, 1874. 15 p. MH. **654**

Union Straw Works. Catalogue of the Union Library, Union Straw Works. Foxboro: William H. Thomas, 1866. 17 p. MHi. **655**

Amherst

Amherst College. Catalogue of Books belonging to the Library of Amherst College. September, 1827. Amherst: J. S. and C. Adams, 1827. 38 p. Shoemaker 27861. DLC, IU, MA, MH, MWA, N. **656**

Amherst College. Catalogue of Amherst College Library. Amherst: William Faxon, 1855. iv, 177, [1] p. In many libraries. **657**

Amherst College. Catalogue of Amherst College Library, 1821-1871. Amherst: H. P. Montague, 1871. 177, 207 p. A reissue of the Catalogue of 1855, with a Catalogue of Books . . . added from July, 1855 to July, 1871. DLC, MA, MAJ, MH, N (only the 207 p. cat.), ViW. **658**

Amherst College. Athenian Society. Catalogue of the Library, and Names of Members, of the Athenian Society from its Formation in 1821, to 1836. Boston: John Ford, 1836. 43 p. Rinderknecht 35767. MA, MBC, MH, MWA, MiD-B, WHi. **659**

Amherst College. Athenian Society. Catalogue of the Library of the Athenian Society, Amherst College, with an Index. Amherst: William Faxon, 1855. 66 p. MA, MWA. **660**

Massachusetts Agricultural College. Library Catalogue of the Massachusetts Agricultural College. Amherst: H. M. M'Cloud, 1875. 30 p. On cover: Catalogue of the Libraries of the Massachusetts Agricultural College and its Literary Societies. M, MAA, MAJ. **661**

Public Library. Catalogue of the Public Library, Amherst, Mass. Amherst: H. M. M'Cloud, 1873. 26 p. Cutter 819 reports suppl. (10 p.). DLC, MAJ, MH. **662**

Andover

(see also North Andover)

Andover Social Library. The Laws and Regulations of the Social Library in Andover. Haverhill: Printed at the Gazette and Patriot Office, 1823. 10 p. "Catalogue of the Books in Andover Social Library" on pp. 7-10. Not in Shoemaker. MSaE. **663**

Andover Social Library. Catalogue . . . 1837. Not in Rinderknecht. Cf. Sarah Loring Bailey, *Historical Sketches of Andover . . .* (Boston, 1880), p. 531. **664**

Andover Theological Seminary. Catalogue of the Library belonging to the Theological Institution in Andover. Andover: Flagg and Gould, 1819. 161 p. S & S 46999. In many libraries. **665**

Andover Theological Seminary. Outline of the Course of Study in the Department of Christian Theology, with References to the Books in the Library, pertaining to that Department. Andover: Flagg & Gould, 1822. 53 p. Shoemaker 7817. In many libraries. **666**

Andover Theological Seminary. Outline of the Course of Study pursued by the Students of the Theological Seminary, Andover, in the Department of Christian Theology, with References to the Books in the Library pertaining to that Department. Andover: Flagg & Gould, 1825. 38 p. Shoemaker 19437. GDC, IWW, InIT, MH-AH, MHi (2 copies, each with ms. notes), MnNS, NjPT, NNG, OKentU, ViRUT. **667**

Andover Theological Seminary. Outline of the Course of Study pursued by the Students

of the Theological Seminary, Andover, in the Department of Christian Theology, with References to the Books in the Library pertaining to that Department. [Andover, 1830]. [211]-54 p. Not in Shoemaker. MHi.
668

Andover Theological Seminary. Catalogue of the Library of the Theol. Seminary in Andover, Mass. By Oliver A. Taylor. Andover: Gould & Newman, 1838. 531 p. Rinderknecht 48850. In many libraries.
669

Andover Theological Seminary. Outline of the Course of Study pursued by the Students of the Theological Seminary, Andover, in the Department of Christian Theology, with References to the Principal Books in the Library pertaining to that Department. [Andover, 1840]. 48 p. Rinderknecht 40-213. IEG, MB, MH, NNUT.
670

Andover Theological Seminary. Catalogue of the Library of the Theological Seminary, in Andover, Mass. First Supplement. Andover: J. D. Flagg and W. H. Wardwell, 1849. 66 p. DHEW, MH, MH-AH, MHi, MWA, RPB.
671

Andover Theological Seminary. Porter Rhetorical Society. Catalogue of Books in the Library of the Rhetorical Society at the Theological Seminary, Andover. July, 1827. Andover: Flagg & Gould, [1827]. 8 p. Not in Shoemaker. NN.
672

Andover Theological Seminary. Porter Rhetorical Society. Catalogues of the Libraries, belonging to the Porter Rhetorical Society, and the Society of Inquiry, in the Theological Seminary, Andover. Andover: Flagg & Gould, 1830. 36 p. Cooper 153. CtY, MH, MSaE.
673

Andover Theological Seminary. Porter Rhetorical Society. Catalogue of Books belonging to the Library of the Porter Rhetorical Society, Theological Seminary, Andover, Mass. April, 1839. Andover: Gould, Newman, and Saxton, 1839. 53 p. Rinderknecht 54003. CSmH, MAnHi, MBC, MNaP, RPB.
674

Christ Church. Catalogue of the Parish Library, of Christ Church, Andover. [Andover?, 1845?]. 12 p. MSaE, MWA.
675

Memorial Hall Library. Catalogue of the Memorial Hall Library, Andover, Mass. Lawrence: Geo. S. Merrill & Crocker, 1874. xix, 180 p. DLC, LU, MAnHi, MB, MBAt, MH, MSaE, MWA, Memorial Hall Library.
676

Phillips Academy. Catalogue of the Associate Library of Phillips Academy, Andover, Mass. Instituted 1825. Andover: John D. Flagg, 1854. 23 p. CtY, MB, MWA.
677

Phillips Academy. Catalogue of the Associate Library, of Phillips Academy, Andover, Mass. Instituted 1825. Andover: Sargent & Merrill, 1858. 24 p. MSaE.
678

Phillips Academy. Catalogue of the Associate Library of Phillips Academy, Andover, Mass. . . . Andover: W. F. Draper, 1860. 24 p. CtY.
679

Phillips Academy. Catalogue of the Associate Library of Phillips Academy, Andover, Mass. . . . Lawrence: G. S. Merrill, 1870. 20 p. CtY.
680

Arlington

(see also West Cambridge)

Arlington Public Library. Catalogue of the Arlington Public Library, with the By-laws. Woburn: J. L. Parker, 1873. 142 p. Cutter 820 reports suppl., 1873 (10 p.). DLC.
681

Arlington Town Library. Catalogue of Books of the Town Library, Arlington, Mass. Boston: Wright & Potter, 1867. 58 p. MH, MWA. **682**

Ashfield

Ashfield Library Association. Catalogue . . . 1867. Cf. *Ninth Report of the Free Public Library Commission of Massachusetts* (1899), p. 22.
683

Assonet

(later Freetown)

Assonet Union Library. Catalogue of Books, of the Assonet Union Library. [n.p., 185-?]. 8 p. NN.
684

Auburn

Auburn Sabbath School. Catalogue of the Books in the Library of the Auburn Sabbath School. July 1865. Worcester: Tyler & Seagrave, 1865. 16 p. MWA.
685

Auburn Sabbath School. Catalogue of the Books in the Library of the Auburn Sabbath School. May, 1867. Worcester: Tyler & Seagrave, 1867. 13 p. MWA.   **686**

Ayer

Town Library. Catalogue of the Town Library of Ayer. 1873. Ayer: John H. Turner, 1873. 16 p. MH, MWA.   **687**

Barre

Barre Public Library. Catalogue of the Public Library, Barre, Mass. 1872. Barre: J. Henry Goddard, [1872]. 76 p. DLC, MWA, N (misc. pamphlet box, 018.1).   **688**

Barre Town Library. Catalogue of Books, and Regulations of the Barre Town Library. [Barre?, 185-?]. 8 p. MWA.   **689**

Barre Town Library. Catalogue of Books in the Town Library of Barre, Mass. 1861. Barre: J. Henry Goddard, 1861. 12 p. MWA.   **690**

Barre Town Library. Catalogue of the Town Library of Barre, Mass. 1865. Barre: J. Henry Goddard, [1865]. 19 p. MWA.   **691**

Belmont

Belmont Public Library. Catalogue of the Belmont Public Library. 1872. Boston: Rand, Avery, 1872. 52 p. DLC holds suppl., 1874? (8 p.). M reported owning catalogues for 1871 and 1872, but both are now withdrawn. Cf. *Catalogue of the State Library of Massachusetts* (Boston, 1880), p. 66. DLC.   **692**

Bernardston

Cushman Library. Catalogue of Cushman Library, Bernardston, Mass., as compiled by William Dwight, Librarian. Athol Depot: R. Putnam, 1866. 42 p. CU-SB, DLC, NNC.   **693**

Cushman Library. Catalogue of the Cushman Library, Bernardston, Mass., as compiled by the Librarian. 1875. Amherst: H. H. McCloud, 1875. 46 p. DLC.   **694**

Beverly

Beverly Public Library. Catalogue of the Public Library of the Town of Beverly. Salem: T. J. Hutchinson, 1856. 108 p. MBAt, MH, MSaE, MWA.   **695**

Beverly Public Library. Catalogue of the Public Library, of the Town of Beverly. Boston: C. C. P. Moody, 1862. 108 p. DLC, M, MB, MBev, MH, MSaE.   **696**

Beverly Public Library. Second Supplement... 1870 [i.e. 1872?]. 12 p. Cf. Cutter 635.   **697**

Beverly Public Library. First Supplement... 1872? [i.e. 1870?]. 8 p. Cf. Cutter 750.   **698**

Beverly Public Library. Catalogue of the Public Library of the Town of Beverly. Boston: G. L. Keyes, 1875. 145 p. DLC, MB, MBev, MSaE.   **699**

Beverly Second Social Library. Regulations of Beverly Second Social Library. Salem: Joshua Cushing, 1806. 21 p. "Catalogue of Beverly Second Social Library" on pp. [9]-14. S & S 9961. MBev (lost), MH.   **700**

Social Library in Beverly. Laws and Regulations for the Social Library in Beverly. Salem: Joshua Cushing, 1805. 6, [10] p. Contains a catalogue of books ([10] p.) at end. S & S 9388. CSt, MSaE, MWA (with ms. notes).   **701**

Blackstone

Blackstone Library Association. Catalogue of the Blackstone Library Association. Organized Oct. 4, 1856 [i.e. 1855]. Library Room in Blackstone Block. Woonsocket: S. S. Foss, 1856. 51 p. MH, MWA, RPB.   **702**

Bolton

Bolton Town Library. The Bolton Town Library. [Bolton, 1860?]. 22 p. Historical note and catalogue. DLC.   **703**

Bolton Town Library. Catalogue of Books in the Town Library of Bolton. November, 1863. Clinton: E. Ballard, 1863. 36 p. (blank pages included in pagination). DLC.   **704**

Bolton Town Library. Catalogue of Books in the Town Library of Bolton. April, 1867. Clinton: Courant Book and Job Office, 1867. 34 p. DLC.   **705**

Bolton Town Library. Catalogue of the Town Library in Bolton. Clinton: Courant Power

Printing Establishment, 1871. 27 p. DLC holds annual suppl., 1872-74. DLC. **706**

Boston

(see also listings under Boston Highlands, Brighton, Charlestown, Dorchester, East Boston, Jamaica Plain, Mattapan, Roxbury, West Roxbury)

American Academy of Arts and Sciences. Catalogue of Books, in the Library of the American Academy of Arts and Sciences, Boston, 1802. [Boston], 1802. 68 p. S & S 1751. CtHT, DeU, DLC, FU, ICU, MB, MBAt, MH-H, MWA, NN, NNC, NcD, PPAmP. **707**

American Academy of Arts and Sciences. Books missing from the Printed Catalogue of the Library of the American Academy of Arts and Sciences, May, 1817. [Boston, 1817]. 1 folded leaf printed on 1 side. Not in S & S. MH-H, MWA. **708**

American and Foreign Circulating Library. Catalogue of the American and Foreign Circulating Library kept by E. P. Peabody . . . [Boston, 185-?]. 36 p. Not in Rinderknecht. MH-H (entered under: Peabody, Elizabeth Palmer). **709**

American and Foreign Circulating Library, see also entries 823-24.

Anthology Reading Room and Library, see entry 715.

Architectural Library of Boston. The Constitution of the Proprietors of the Architectural Library of Boston, instituted 15th November, 1809. Boston: T. Kennard, 1809. 10, 5, [1] p. Library catalogue on pp. [1]-5 (2d group). Not in S & S; Rink 2518-19. CaQMCCA, MWA. **710**

Arlington-Street Church. Catalogue of the Libraries, for Adults and for Children, of the Arlington-Street Church. Boston: John Wilson and Son, 1863. 55 p. MB, MBAt. **711**

Arlington-Street Church. Catalogue of the Libraries, for Adults and for Children, of the Arlington-Street Church. Boston: John Wilson and Son, 1863 [i.e., 1871]. 75 p. A reissue of the 1863 catalogue (pp. 1-46), with new suppl. for 1871 (pp. [47]-75). MB, MWA. **712**

Baldwin Place Church. Catalogue of the Library of the Baldwin Place Church, Boston. Opened May 2, 1828. Boston: J. B. Hall, 1844. 12 p. Not in Rinderknecht. MWA. **713**

Berry Street Vestry. Books added to the Berry Street Vestry Library, since the Catalogue was printed in 1840. Boston: I. R. Butts, 1842. 8 p. Not in Rinderknecht. DLC, MHi. **714**

Boston Athenaeum. Anthology Reading Room and Library. [Boston, 1807]. 8 p. Contains a list of periodicals ordered by the Anthology Society of Boston, soon thereafter chartered as the Boston Athenaeum. Not in S & S. MH-H, MWA. **715**

Boston Athenaeum. Catalogue of the Books in the Boston Athenaeum. [Boston, 1810]. 266 p. S & S 19597. MBAt, MH-H. **716**

Boston Athenaeum. Catalogue of Books in the Boston Atheneum [sic] to which are added the By-laws of the Institution, and a List of its Proprietors and Subscribers. Boston: William L. Lewis, 1827. 356 p. Shoemaker 28236. In many libraries. **717**

Boston Athenaeum. Catalogue of Books added to the Boston Athenaeum since the Publication of the Catalogue in January, 1827. [Boston]: W. L. Lewis, [1829?]. 64 p. Includes "Books ordered Oct. 1, 1829, but not yet received." Shoemaker 37898. MB, MBAt, MH, MHi, MWA (interleaved), NN, NcD, PPAmP. **718**

Boston Athenaeum. Catalogue of Books added to the Boston Athenaeum, in 1830-1833. Boston: Eastburn's Press, 1834. 80 p. Rinderknecht 23497. DLC, MB, MBAt, MH, MHi, MWA, MnHi. **719**

Boston Athenaeum. Catalogue of Books added to the Boston Athenaeum, since the Publication of the Catalogue in January, 1827. Boston: Eastburn's Press, 1840. 178, [1] p. Rinderknecht 40-932. DeU, DLC, IGK, MB, MBAt, MH-AH, MHi, MWA. **720**

Boston Athenaeum. Catalogue of a Large Collection of Books, being the Duplicates of the Boston Athenaeum, to be sold by Auction, on Wednesday and Thursday, Jan. 29 and 30, 1862, in the Library Sales-Room of Leonard & Co. . . . Boston: John Wilson and Son, 1862. 28 p. McKay 939. DLC, MB, NYPL. **721**

Boston Athenaeum. List of Books added to the Library of the Boston Athenaeum, from December 1, 1862, to 1871. [Boston, 1863-71]. 6 vol. DLC (1862/63, 1865/66-1866/67, 1869), MB (1862-71; lacking only 1870, #6 and 1871, #2), MBAt (6 pts, 1862/63-1867/68), MH (1862/63), MWA (6 pts, 1862/63-1867/68), N (6 pts, 1862/63-1867/68), NN (6 pts, 1862/63-1867/68), PPL (1862/63-1863/64, 1867/68), PU (1862/63, 1864/65). **722**

Boston Athenaeum. Catalogue of the Library of the Boston Athenaeum. 1807-1871. Boston, 1874-82. 5 vol. Compiled by Charles Ammi Cutter. In many libraries. **723**

Boston Athenaeum. [Order-slips, containing Brief Titles of the more Important New Books Received]. No. 1-97; Sept. 5, 1874-Feb. 3, 1877. Boston, 1874-77. broadsides. MH. **724**

Boston Circulating Library. Catalogue of Books in the Boston Circulating Library, No. 3. School-Street. [Boston]: E. Lincoln, Printer, 1805. 76 p. On p. 76: Printed by J. T. Buckingham, Winter-Street. Operated by William P. Blake, per Kaser, p. 131. See also entry 2337. Not in S & S. MBAt. **725**

Boston City Hospital. Catalogue of the Boston City Hospital Library. Boston: J. E. Farwell, 1864. 71 p. MB. **726**

Boston City Hospital. Catalogue of the Boston City Hospital Library. Boston: Rockwell & Churchill, 1873. 24 p. DLC, DNLM, MB (interleaved), MH (interleaved), MWA. **727**

Boston Hospital for the Insane. Catalogue of the Library of the Boston Hospital for the Insane. Boston: A. Mudge & Son, 1869. 22 p. MB. **728**

Boston Hospital for the Insane, see also entry 745.

Boston Library. Catalogue of Books in the Boston Library, May 1, 1802. [Boston, 1802]. 24 p. S & S 1932. MH-H. **729**

Boston Library. Catalogue of Books in the Boston Library. Jan. 1, 1805. [Boston, 1805]. 27, [1] p. S & S 50504. CtY, PU. **730**

Boston Library. Catalogue of Books in the Boston Library. Nov. 1, 1807. Boston:

Snelling and Simons, 1807. 41 p., [3] p. of advertisements. S & S 12181. CtY, DLC, MB, MH-H, MWA, WHi, WU (School of Library and Information Studies). **731**

Boston Library. Catalogue, No. 1, of Books in the Boston Library. October 1, 1815. Incorporated in 1794, and kept in the Room over the Arch, in Franklin Place. Boston: John Eliot, 1815. 64 p. S & S 34171. InU, MB, MBAt, MH-H, MHi, MWA (interleaved with ms. additions), MnU, PPL. **732**

Boston Library. Catalogue, No. 2, of Books in the Boston Library, Franklin Place. [Boston, 1817]. 16 p. Contains "Livres françois" (pp. [1]-9) and "English Books, added since October, 1815" (pp. 10-16). S & S 40291. MBAt, MH-H, MHi, MWA, PPL. **733**

Boston Library. Catalogue, No. 2, of Books in the Boston Library, Franklin Place . . . English Books. [Boston, 1819?]. 15 p. Not in S & S. MHi, PPL. **734**

Boston Library. Livres françois. [Boston, 1819]. 15, [1] p. Not in S & S. MBAt, MHi, PPL. **735**

Boston Library. Catalogue of Books in the Boston Library. June, 1824 . . . Boston: Munroe and Francis, 1824. 96, [1] p. Shoemaker 15519. DLC, MB, MBAt, MBL, MCM, MH, MH-AH, MHi (bound with Boston Library Catalogue, No. 2, 1817), MWA. **736**

Boston Library. Catalogue of Books, added to the Boston Library, since printing the General Catalogue. [Boston, 1829?]. [91]-98 p. Not in Shoemaker. MB (with ms. additions), MHi (with ms. additions), PPL (defective). **737**

Boston Library. Catalogue of Books in the Boston Library, June, 1830 . . . in Franklin Place. Boston: John H. Eastburn, 1830. 107 p. Cooper 605. CU-S, DLC (interleaved with ms. additions), ICN, MB, MBAt, MH, MHi (2 copies, one with ms. additions and one with ms. alterations in the by-laws section), MWA, N, NNC, OClWHi, RPAt, WHi, WU (School of Library and Information Studies). **738**

Boston Library. Catalogue of Books added to the Boston Library from the Time of Printing the General Catalogue to January,

1835. [Boston, 1835?]. [109]-48 p. Not in Rinderknecht. ICN (to p. 124 only?), MB, MH (with ms. additions), MHi, WU (School of Library and Information Studies).   **739**

Boston Library. Catalogue of Books added to the Boston Library from the Time of Printing the Supplementary Catalogue in January, 1835 to April, 1838. [Boston, 1838?]. [149]-71 p. Not in Rinderknecht. MB, MH, MHi, WU (School of Library and Information Studies).   **740**

Boston Library Society. Catalogue of the Books of the Boston Library Society, in Franklin Place. January, 1844. Boston: T. R. Marvin, 1844. x, 335 p., [2] p. of errata. Rinderknecht 44-896. DeU, DLC, ICN, ICU, MB, MBAt, MH, MHi, N, NNC, NcD, PP.   **741**

Boston Library Society. Books in the Boston Library relating to America, its History, Biography, Productions, Climate, Soil, etc. [Boston, 1849?]. 24 p. Running title: Supplemental Catalogue of the Boston Library. MH, MHi.   **742**

Boston Library Society. Supplemental Catalogue of the Boston Library. 1849. [Boston, 1849]. 72 p. DLC, ICN, MB (with ms. additions), MBAt, MH, MHi, MWA, N. **743**

Boston Library Society. Supplemental Catalogue to the Boston Library. 1855. [Boston, 1855]. 66 p. DLC, MBAt, N.   **744**

Boston Lunatic Hospital. Catalogue of the Library of the Boston Lunatic Hospital . . . Boston: Rockwell and Churchill, 1875. 42 p. MB (interleaved).   **745**

Boston Lunatic Hospital, see also entry 728.

Boston Medical Library. An Abstract of the Rules of the Boston Medical Library. [Boston, ca. 1807]. 1 folded leaf printed on 2 sides. Includes "List of Books now in the Library." Not in S & S; Austin 252. MBM, MHi (photostat copy in J. C. Warren Papers, vol. 6).   **746**

Boston Medical Library. Catalogue of Books in the Boston Medical Library, and the Rules and Regulations concerning the same. Also, a Statement of the Trustees to the Proprietors. Boston: Thomas Fleet, 1808. 16 p. S & S 14554, Austin 254. CtY, CtY-M, DLC, MBM, MH-H, MH-M.   **747**

Boston Medical Library. Catalogue of Books in the Boston Medical Library, and the Rules and Regulations concerning the same. [Boston, 1810?]. 20 p. Probably identical to S & S 12182 (under 1807), Austin 255. DNLM (film), MH-M (with ms. notes), MSaE.   **748**

Boston Medical Library. Catalogue of Books in the Boston Medical Library, and the Rules and Regulations concerning the same. Boston: Munroe and Francis, 1816. 46 p. S & S 37049, Austin 256. DNLM (interleaved), MBM, MHi (interleaved; pp. 17-18 misbound), NNNAM.   **749**

Boston Medical Library. Catalogue of Books in the Boston Medical Library, and the Rules and Regulations concerning the same. Boston: J. H. A. Frost, 1823. iv, 36 p. Shoemaker 11945. DNLM, MB, MHi (defective), NN.   **750**

Boston Neck Mission. Catalogue of the Boston Neck Mission Sunday School Library, Concord Street, Boston. Boston: Alfred Mudge & Son, 1864. 23 p. MB. **751**

Boston Public Library. Report of the Committee on the Library, in Relation to the Donations received from the City of Paris. With a Catalogue of the Reciprocal Gifts exchanged between the Two Cities, with the Names of the Donors. Together with the Proceedings of the City Government upon the Subject of International Exchanges. Boston: J. H. Eastburn, 1849. 72 p. Issued as *City Document,* No. 46. MB, MBSi, MH, PPA, RPB.   **752**

Boston Public Library. [Catalogue of the Books presented to the City of Boston by Edward Everett. With accompanying Correspondence]. [Boston, 1851]. 28 p. Issued as City Document, No. 51. DLC, MB, MHi, NN.   **753**

Boston Public Library. Catalogue of the Public Library of the City of Boston. Boston: John Wilson & Son, 1854. iv, 180 p. In many libraries.   **754**

Boston Public Library. Catalogue of American Books desirable for the Boston Public Library. [Boston 1857] 25 p. MB.   **755**

Boston Public Library. Index to the Catalogue of a Portion of the Public Library of the City of

Boston, arranged in the Lower Hall. Boston: Geo. C. Rand and Avery, 1858. iv, 204 p. DLC, MBAt hold suppl. 1-8; M holds suppl. 1-4; Dec. 20, 1858-Nov. 1, 1861; MB holds suppl. 1-7; Dec. 20, 1858-Sept. 1, 1864; MWA holds suppl. 1-6; Dec. 20, 1858-Sept. 1, 1863; WU (School of Library and Information Studies) holds suppl. 1-2. In many libraries.   **756**

Boston Public Library. Index to the Catalogue of Books in the Upper Hall of the Public Library of the City of Boston. Boston: Geo. C. Rand and Avery, 1861. vii, 902 p. Compiled by Charles C. Jewett, assisted by Frederic Vinton and William E. Jillson. In many libraries.   **757**

Boston Public Library. List of Duplicates. [Boston, 1864]. 27 p. DLC, M, MB, MH.
758

Boston Public Library. Index to the Catalogue of Books in the Bates Hall of the Public Library of the City of Boston. Second Stereotype Edition. Boston: J. E. Farwell, 1865. vii, 902 p. In many libraries.   **759**

Boston Public Library. Index to the Catalogue of Books in the Bates Hall of the Public Library of the City of Boston. First Supplement. Boston: J. E. Farwell, 1866. iv, 718, 21 p. Compiled by Charles C. Jewett, assisted by Frederic Vinton and William E. Jillson. At end: "Index to the City Documents, from 1834 to 1865." In many libraries.   **760**

Boston Public Library. Lower Hall. Finding List for Alcoves II, IX, XII, and XIX. History, Politics, etc. [Boston, 1866]. 27 p. DLC, M, MB.   **761**

Boston Public Library. Lower Hall. Finding List for Alcoves IV and VII. [First Edition. Fiction and Juvenile Works]. [Boston, 1866]. 34 p. MB.   **762**

Boston Public Library. Lower Hall. Finding List for Alcoves IV and VII. [Second Edition, Dec. 1866. Fiction and Juvenile Works]. [Boston, 1866]. 41 p. DLC, M, MB, MH, N.
763

Boston Public Library. Bulletins, showing Titles of Books added to the Library, with Bibliographical Notes, etc. Vol. 1, no. 1-vol. 2, no. 35; Oct. 1867-Oct. 1875. Title varies.

Ceased publication with vol. 14; Jan. 1896. In many libraries.   **764**

Boston Public Library. Lower Hall. Finding List for Part of Alcoves X and XX: French, German and Italian Books. [Boston, 1867]. 45 p. DLC, ICN, M, MB, MH, NIC, NN.
765

Boston Public Library. Lower Hall. Finding Lists for Alcoves I and XI and Part of X and XX, containing Works in the Sciences, Arts, and Professions (Theology, Medicine, Law). [Boston, 1867]. 59 p. DLC, M, MB, MH.**766**

Boston Public Library. Catalogue of the American Portion of the Library of the Rev. Thomas Prince. With a Memoir, and List of his Publications, by Wm. H. Whitmore. Boston: J. K. Wiggin & Wm. Parson Lunt, 1868. xxv, 166 p. See also entries 768, 772, 895. In many libraries.   **767**

Boston Public Library. The Prince Library. The American Part of the Collection which formerly belonged to the Reverend Thomas Prince, by him bequeathed to the Old South Church, and now deposited in the Public Library of the City of Boston. [Boston, 1868]. 70 p. A "Preliminary Issue" (see also entries 767, 772, 895). DLC, MdBP, MB, MWA, MiU-C, NB, NN, NcD, RPJCB.   **768**

Boston Public Library. Lower Hall. Finding Lists for Alcoves V, VI, XV, and XVI. Biography and Travels. [Boston, 1868]. 52 p. DLC, M, MB, MH.   **769**

Boston Public Library. Lower Hall. Finding List for Alcoves IV, VII, XIV, and XVII. Fiction and Juvenile Works. Third Edition. August, 1868. [Boston, 1868]. 57 p. M, MB, MBAt, MH.   **770**

Boston Public Library. Lower Hall. Class List for English Prose Fiction, including Juvenile Fiction. Fourth Edition. October, 1869. [Boston, 1869]. 66 p. DLC, MBAt, MH, PPL, RPB.   **771**

Boston Public Library. The Prince Library. A Catalogue of the Collection of Books and Manuscripts which formerly belonged to the Reverend Thomas Prince, and was by him bequeathed to the Old South Church, and is now deposited in the Public Library of the City of Boston. Boston: Alfred Mudge &

Son, 1870. xvii, 160 p. See also entries 767-68, 895. CSmH, CtY, DLC, ICN, MB, MH-AH, MWA, MiEM, MiU, MoS, NhD, NB, NNUT, PPL, RPB.   **772**

Boston Public Library. Lower Hall. Class List for Poetry, the Drama, Rhetoric, Elocution, Collections, Periodicals, and Miscellaneous Works. First Edition. July, 1870. [Boston 1870]. 128 p. DLC, ICN, M, MB, MBAt, MH, MiU, MnU, NIC, NN, NNC, PP, PPL.   **773**

Boston Public Library. Periodicals currently received; and Works of Reference in the Reading Room and at the Desk in Bates Hall. First Edition. September, 1870. [Boston, 1870]. 31 p. MB, MWA.   **774**

Boston Public Library. Lower Hall. Historical Fiction. Novels, Plays, Poems. First Edition. April, 1871. [Boston, 1871]. 9 p. DLC, M, MBAt, MWA, N (film).   **775**

Boston Public Library. Lower Hall. Class List for English Prose Fiction, including Translations and Juvenile Fiction. Fifth Edition. August, 1871. [Boston, 1871]. 76 p. DLC, MB, MBAt, MH, MWA, MnU, NjP, NIC, PPL.   **776**

Boston Public Library. Lower Hall. Class List for Works in the Arts and Sciences, including Theology, Medicine, Law, Philosophy . . . Second Edition September, 1871. [Boston 1871]. 71 p. CSmH, DLC, ICN, M, MB, MH, MiU, MnU, NIC, NN, NNC, PHi, PPL.   **777**

Boston Public Library. East Boston Branch. List of Books, arranged by Authors, Titles and Subjects. February, 1871. [Boston, 1871]. 90 p. DLC, MB, MBAt, NN.   **778**

Boston Public Library. Roxbury Branch (1873), see entry 1439.

Boston Public Library. South Boston Branch. List of Books, arranged by Authors, Titles, and Subjects. First Edition. May, 1872. [Boston, 1872]. 71 p. MB, MBAt, MH, MnU, NIC.   **779**

Boston Public Library. A Catalogue of Books belonging to the Lower Hall of the Central Department, in the Classes of History, Biography, and Travel . . . Second, or Consolidated Edition. July, 1873. Boston: Rockwell and Churchill, 1873. 304 p. N.B. MB holds Justin Winsoɪ's copy with diverse

inserted materials, printed and ms. In addition, MB has Second Edition (Boston, 1872), consisting of 128 pages of text representing all signatures printed at time of a fire on Nov. 9, 1872. In many libraries.   **780**

Boston Public Library. Periodicals currently received, and Works of Reference in Reading Room, and at Desk in Bates Hall. Second Edition. April, 1873. [Boston, 1873]. 23 p. DLC, MB, MH.   **781**

Boston Public Library. A Chronological Index to Historical Fiction, including Prose Fiction, Plays and Poems. Second and Enlarged Edition. Boston, 1875. 32 p. Preface signed by the compiler, Justin Winsor. CSmH, DLC, MB, MH, MHi, MWA, MnU, PPL, RPB.   **782**

Boston Public Library. Dorchester Branch (1875), see entry 1105.

Boston Society of Natural History. Catalogue of the Library of the Boston Society of Natural History. Boston: Freeman and Bolles, 1837. 16 p. Not in Rinderknecht. ICN, MA, MH (Museum of Comparative Zoology), MWA, NhD, NmLcU, PBL, PPL, TxDaM.   **783**

Boston Society of Natural History. Catalogue of the Library of the Boston Society of Natural History. Boston: Freeman and Bolles, 1837-[41?]. 27, [1] p. "Additions to the Library . . . since 1837" on pp. [17]-27. Rinderknecht 43361. CtY, DLC, MB, MBAt, MBM, MHi, MWA, NhD, PBL, PPL (pp. 1-16 only), WHi.   **784**

Boston Society of the New Jerusalem. A Catalogue of the Books in the Library of the Sunday School of the Boston Society of the New Jerusalem. January, 1868. Boston: David Clapp & Son, 1868. 40 p. MB holds suppl., Jan. 1870 (7 p.). MB, NN.   **785**

Boston Union Circulating Library, see Union Circulating Library.

Boston Universalist Young Men's Institute. Constitution of the Boston Universalist Young Men's Institute, with a List of Members, and a Catalogue of the Library. Boston: George P. Oakes, 1837. 12 p. Rinderknecht 43363. MMeT.   **786**

Boston Young Men's Christian Association. Catalogue of the Library of the Boston Young

Men's Christian Association. Rooms, Tremont Temple. Boston: Geo. C. Rand & Avery, 1857. 64 p. DeU, MB, MHi, NB, NN, WHi.   **787**

Boston Young Men's Christian Union. Catalogue of the Library of the Boston Young Men's Christian Union. Incorporated 1852. Boston, 1855. 48 p. DLC, ICN, MB (with ms. additions) MWA, NN, WHi.   **788**

Boston Young Men's Society. Catalogue of Books belonging to the Subscription Circulation Library of the Boston Young Men's Society. Boston, 1833. 16 p. Bruntjen 17911. MBAt, WHi.   **789**

Bowditch Library. Report of the Proprietors of the Bowditch Library. Boston: I. R. Butts, 1841. 16 p. "Donations to the Library . . . which have been received since Commencement of the Library" on pp. 5-15. Rinderknecht 41-785. MB, MHi, MWA, PPAmP.   **790**

Bowdoin Square Church. Catalogue of Books in the Bowdoin Square Baptist Sabbath School Library. 1015 Volumes. January, 1845. Boston: John Putnam, [1845]. 35 p. MB.   **791**

Bowdoin Street Church. Bowdoin Street Sabbath School Library, 1833. [Boston, 1833]. 17 p. Not in Bruntjen. MWA. **792**

Boylston Circulating Library. Catalogue of the Boylston Circulating-library . . . Sept. 1828. [Boston, 1828]. [72] p. Not in Shoemaker. MH-H, NNGr.   **793**

Boylston Circulating Library. Catalogues of the Boylston Circulating-Library. Boston: David Francis, [1830]. [130] p. Caption title: Alphabetical and Numerical Catalogues of the Boylston Circulating Library. Not in Cooper. MH-H.   **794**

Boylston Circulating Library. Supplementary Catalogue of the Boylston Circulating-Library. Jan. 1833. Boston: David Francis, [1833]. [12] p.   Not in Rinderknecht. NNGr (bound with the 1828 Catalogue).   **795**

Boylston Circulating Library. Catalogue of the Boylston Circulating Library. David Francis, 364 Washington Street, Boston . . . Boston, 1837. 94 p. Rinderknecht 43385

(calls for 83 p.).   MB (also a copy with ms. additions), MH-H (defective, but has 14 p. of ms. additions).   **796**

Boylston Circulating Library. Catalogue of a Part of the Boylston Circulating Library, being Duplicate Copies. Also, a Large Assortment of upwards of 500 Juvenile Books, and Forty-seven Volumes of Old Pamphlets . . . to be sold at Public Auction, by Howe, Leonard & Co. . . . on Thursday, May 21, 1846 . . . [Boston]: Munroe & Francis, [1846]. 30 p. McKay 418. MWA.   **797**

Brattle Square Church. Catalogue of the Library belonging to the Church in Brattle Square. Boston: J. E. Hinckley, 1834. 12 p. Not in Rinderknecht.   Congregational Library, Boston, MB, MHi, MWA.   **798**

Brattle Square Church. A Catalogue of Books, in the Brattle Square Sabbath School Library, Boston. January 1, 1847. Boston: Benjamin H. Greene, 1847. 16 p. MHi (interleaved). **799**

Brattle Square Church. A Catalogue of Books, in the Brattle Square Sabbath School Library, Boston. November 11, 1848. Boston: Benjamin H. Greene, 1848. 15 p. MHi.   **800**

Brattle Square Church. Catalogue of the Sunday School Library of the Brattle Square Church, Boston. Boston: Benjamin H. Greene, 1850. 16 p. MB.   **801**

Brattle Square Church. Catalogue of the Sunday School Library . . . Boston, 1854. MBAt (lost).   **802**

Brattle Square Church. Catalogue of the Sunday-School Library of the Brattle-Square Church. 1861. Boston: John Wilson and Son, 1861. 28 p. MHi (interleaved with ms. additions).   **803**

Brattle Square Church. Catalogue of the Sunday-School Library of the Brattle-Square Church. 1865. Boston: John Wilson and Son, 1865. 32 p. MHi.   **804**

Brattle Square Church. Catalogue of the Sunday School Library of the Brattle-Square Church . . . Boston: Alfred Mudge & Son, 1873. 24 p. MHi (interleaved with ms. additions).   **805**

Campbell's Circulating Library. Catalogue of Campbell's Circulating Library .. Boston.

April, 1870. Boston, [1870]. 47 p. Operated by James Campbell. MB. **806**

Campbell's Circulating Library. Supplement to Catalogue of Campbell's Circulating Library . . . July, 1870. No. 1. [Boston, 1870]. 45-48 p. Operated by James Campbell. MWA. **807**

Children's Mission to the Children of the Destitute. Catalogue of the Library of the Children's Mission Sunday School. 1869. Boston: S. O. Thayer, 1869. 15 p. MHi (interleaved). **808**

Church of the Disciples. Catalogue of Books belonging to the Sunday-School Library of the Church of Disciples. Superintendent: Rev. James Freeman Clarke. Boston: Prentiss & Deland, 1867. 34 p. MWA. **809**

Church of the Redeemer. Sabbath-School Library Catalogue . . . Boston: Wright & Potter, 1866. 12 p. MB. **810**

Church of the Redeemer. Sunday-School Library Catalogue . . . Boston: John Wilson and Son, 1870. 15 p. MB, MnU. **811**

Church of the Unity. Catalogue of Books in the Sunday-School Library connected with the Church of the Unity. Boston: Nathan Sawyer, 1864. 34 p. MBAt (with ms. additions). **812**

Church Street Methodist Episcopal Church. Catalogue of the Church Street M. E. Sunday School Library. South Boston: Mattapan Register Press, 1859. 24 p. MB. **813**

Columbian Circulating Library, see entry 840.

Columbian Social Library. Catalogue of Books in the Columbian Social Library, Instituted, January, 1813. Boston: Rowe and Hooper, 1815. 8 p. S & S 34408. MB. **814**

Essex Street Church. Catalogue of the Essex Street Sabbath School Library. Boston: Geo. C. Rand & Avery, 1859. 24 p. DLC. **815**

Essex Street Church. Catalogue of the Essex Street Sabbath School Library. April, 1863. Boston: Geo. C. Rand & Avery, 1863. 31 p. MBAt. **816**

Essex Street Church. Supplement to Catalogue of the Essex Street Sabbath School Library. October, 1866. [Boston, 1866]. 4 p. MBAt. **817**

Federal Street Baptist Church. Catalogue of Books in the Library of the Federal Street Baptist Sabbath School, Boston. Boston: William D. Ticknor, 1840. 22 p. Not in Rinderknecht. DLC. **818**

Federal Street Congregational Society. Catalogue of the Parish Library of the Federal Street Congregational Society. January 1, 1848. Boston: Andrews & Prentiss, 1848. 28, [1] p. DLC and MHi copies include suppl. leaf of books added since Jan. 1, 1848. DLC, MB, MHi. **819**

Federal Street Congregational Society. Catalogue of the Parish Library of the Federal Street Congregational Society in Boston. Boston: John Wilson and Son, 1858. 47 p. DLC, MB, MHi. **820**

First Church. Catalogue of the Library of the First-Church Sunday School, Boston. Boston: John Wilson and Son, 1863. 16 p. MBAt (with ms. notes). **821**

First Presbyterian Church. Catalogue of Books in the Sunday-School Library of the First Presbyterian Church . . . Boston: Alfred Mudge & Son, 1864. 30 p. MB. **822**

Foreign Circulating Library. Catalogue of the Foreign Circulating Library, No. 13, West Street. Boston: A. P. Clark, 1849. 30 p. Operated by Elizabeth Palmer Peabody. See also entries 709, 824. MH-H (entered under: Peabody, Elizabeth Palmer). **823**

Foreign Library. Catalogue of the Foreign Library, No. 13, West Street. Boston: S. N. Dickinson, 1840. 12 p. Operated by Elizabeth Palmer Peabody. See also entries 709, 823. Rinderknecht 40-907. Text of catalogue reprinted in Madeleine B. Stern, "Elizabeth Peabody's Foreign Library (1840)," in the author's *Books and Book People in 19th-Century America* (New York, 1978), pp. 121-35. MB, MH-H (entered under: Peabody, Elizabeth Palmer), MWA. **824**

Fourth Social Library, see Theological Library.

Fourth Universalist Church. Catalogue of Books in the Sabbath School Library of the Fourth Universalist Society. January, 1861. Boston: Eugene Bettes, 1860. 24 p. MB. **825**

Franklin Circulating Library. Catalogue of the Franklin Circulating Library . . . to which Additions are continually making . . . Boston: Sylvester T. Goss, 1820. 62 p. Operated by Sylvester T. Goss. Shoemaker 1282. MH-H, MWA.   **826**

Franklin Typographical Society. Catalogue of the Franklin Typographical Society's Library. Founded A.D. 1830. Boston, 1848. 18 p. DLC.   **827**

Franklin Typographical Society. Constitution and Catalog of Library of the Franklin Typographical Society. Instituted 1824, Incorporated 1825. Boston: Snow & Wilder, 1850. 32 p. DLC, MB, WHi.   **828**

Franklin Typographical Society. Catalogue. November, 1873. Boston: Rhodes, 1873. 47 p. IaU holds undated suppl. #1-2. IaU, MB, MBAt.   **829**

General Theological Library. Annual Report. Boston, 1863-. Contains a librarian's report listing periodicals (1863-64) or additions to the library (1865-75, etc.) CtY, DLC, MH-AH, MWA.   **830**

Halliday's Circulating Library. Catalogue of Halliday's Circulating Library, on Washington Street, opposite "ye Old South Meeting House" . . . Boston: W. H. Halliday & Co., {186-?}. 32 p. Operated by William H. Halliday. NNGr.   **830a**

Halliday's Circulating Library. Halliday's Circulating Library. Boston: W. F. Brown, 1872. 29, 4, [6] p. Operated by William H. Halliday. MWA.   **831**

Handel and Haydn Society. Act of Incorporation and By-laws of the Handel and Haydn Society, with the Trust Deed creating a Permanent Fund, a Complete List of the Officers and Members of the Society, from its Formation, and an Abstract from the Catalogue of the Society's Library. Instituted April, 1815. Incorporated February, 1816. Boston: E. L. Balch, 1867. 82 p. MB, MH, NN.   **832**

Harvard Musical Association. Catalogue of the Library of the Harvard Musical Association, with a List of Members, and an Appendix . . . Boston: Charles C. P. Moody, 1851. 28 p. MB, MBHM.   **833**

Harvard Musical Association. Catalogue of the Library of the Harvard Musical Association. 1857 . . . Boston: Edward L. Balch, 1857. 11 p. Copy held by MB includes "Additions to the Library" for 1857 and 1859 (each a single leaf). MB.   **834**

Hollis Street Church. Catalogue of the Hollis Street Sunday School Library. Boston: Printed for Weeks, Jordan & Co., 1837. 18 p. Not in Rinderknecht.   NN (with ms. "Extracts from the Library Regulations").   **835**

Hollis Street Church. Catalogue of the Hollis Street Sunday School Library. Boston: S. O. Thayer, 1867. 28 p. MBAt.   **836**

Hollis Street Church. Catalogue of the Hollis Street Sunday School Library. Boston: Alfred Mudge & Son, 1875. 37 p. MB.   **837**

Howard Sunday School. Catalogue of the Howard Sunday School Libraries. Boston: John Wilson and Son, 1866. 43 p. MBAt.   **838**

Koppitz's (Chas.) Musical Library. Catalogue to the late Chas. Koppitz's Musical Library, now in Possession of N. Lothian, Musical Director, Boston Theatre. [Boston, ca. 1875]. 16 p. MWA.   **839**

Ladies' Circulating Library. Catalogue of the Ladies' Circulating Library, Boston . . . Boston: Putnam & Hunt, 1829. 66 p. On title page of MH-H copy, the word "Ladies" is lined out and "Columbian" is written above it. Shoemaker 39242. MH-H.   **840**

Ladies' Physiological Institute. Synopsis of the Proceedings of the Second Annual Meeting of the Ladies' Physiological Institute, of Boston and Vicinity. With the Secretary's Report, and the Constitution and By-laws of the Society, with Catalogue of Library. Boston: Alfred Mudge, 1851. 27 p. DLC.   **841**

Ladies' Physiological Institute. Catalogue of Books belonging to the Ladies' Physiological Institute, of Boston and Vicinity. Boston: Alfred Mudge and Son, 1855. 8 p. MWA.   **842**

Loring's Select Circulating Library. Books most called for at Loring's Library . . . [Boston, 186-?]. 4 p. Operated by Aaron K. Loring. MB (defective).   **843**

Loring's Select Circulating Library. Catalogue of Loring's Select Library. Established June, 1859. Boston: Franklin Printing House, 1860. 20 p. Operated by Aaron K. Loring. ViU. **844**

Loring's Select Circulating Library. Catalogue of Loring's Select Circulating Library. Established June, 1859. [Boston: J. E. Farwell], 1863. 40 p. At head of title: English Division. Operated by Aaron K. Loring. DLC, MB, MWA. **845**

Mason Street Sabbath School. Descriptive Catalogue of Books in the Mason Street Sabbath School Library . . . Boston: Perkins & Marvin, 1837. 63 p. Rinderknecht 43330. WHi. **846**

Massachusetts. Board of Agriculture. Catalogue of the Agricultural Library in the Office of the Secretary of Massachusetts Board of Agriculture. Boston: William White, 1858. 29 p. M, MWA. **847**

Massachusetts. General Court, see also Massachusetts. State Library.

Massachusetts. General Court. Catalogue of the Library of the General Court. Boston: Dutton & Wentworth, 1831. 43 p. Bruntjen 8189. DeU, ICN, IaHi, LNT, M, MB, MBAt, MH-L, MHi, MWA, Nh, NN. **848**

Massachusetts. General Court. Catalogue of the Library of the General Court. Boston: Dutton & Wentworth, 1839. [102] p. Rinderknecht 57167 (duplicated by 57177). CtHT, ICU, IU, M (blank pages inserted at end of each letter), MB, MBAt (with ms. additions), MHi, MWA. **849**

Massachusetts. General Court. Catalogue of the Library of the General Court. Boston: Dutton & Wentworth, 1846. 141 p. DeU, M (interleaved with ms. additions), MB, MBAt, MH-L, MHi, MWA, Nh, NNC-L, PPL. **850**

Massachusetts. General Court. Senate. Catalogue of Books belonging to the Senate Chamber. Prepared by Order of the Senate. March 1, 1843. By Lewis Josselyn, Clerk. Boston: Dutton and Wentworth, 1843. 9 p. Not in Rinderknecht. MWA. **851**

Massachusetts. Public Archives. Statement of the Books, Manuscripts and Documents belonging to the Public Archives. [Boston, 1839]. 12 p. At head of title: House. No. 21. Rinderknecht 57176. MBC, MHi, MWA. **852**

Massachusetts. State Library, see also Massachusetts. General Court.

Massachusetts. State Library. Analytical Catalogue of Books, Maps, Charts, Medals, etc. presented by Alexandre Vattemare to the State Library, in conformity with his System of International Exchanges. [Boston, 1849]. 13-52 p. (also appears with pagination of 40 p.). Appendix to *Report on International Literary Exchanges.* Issued as Massachusetts General Court House Doc. 151. M. **853**

Massachusetts. State Library. Catalogue of the State Library of Massachusetts. Boston: William White, 1858. xxiv, 338 p. Additions appear in the *Report of the Librarian of the State Library* beginning in 1859. In many libraries. **854**

Massachusetts Charitable Mechanic Association. Catalogue of the Library of the Massachusetts Charitable Mechanic Association. 1853. Boston: Damrell & Moore, 1853. 12 p. MH, MHi. **855**

Massachusetts Historical Society. Catalogue of the Books, Pamphlets, Newspapers, Maps, Charts, Manuscripts, &c., in the Library of the Massachusetts Historical Society. Boston: John Eliot, jun., 1811. vi, 96 p. Compiled by Timothy Alden. Copy 2 held by MHi has ms. additions. S & S 23344. In many libraries. **856**

Massachusetts Historical Society. Catalogue of the Private Library of Thomas Dowse, of Cambridge, Mass., presented to the Massachusetts Historical Society. July 30, 1856. Boston: John Wilson & Son, 1856. 214 p. "Twenty-five Copies Printed for Private Distribution." See also entry 859. MHi, MeB, NHi, NN. **857**

Massachusetts Historical Society. Catalogue of the Library of the Massachusetts Historical Society. Boston, 1859-60. 2 vol. The Ellis Hall copy held by MHi has ms. annotations of the old Massachusetts Historical Society classification system. In many libraries. **858**

Massachusetts Historical Society. Catalogue of the Private Library of Thomas Dowse, of Cambridge, Mass., presented to the Massachusetts Historical Society, July 30, 1856. Boston: J. Wilson & Son, 1870. 214 p. See also entry 857. In many libraries. **859**

Massachusetts Horticultural Society. Constitution and By-laws of the Massachusetts Horticultural Society, with the Act of Incorporation, &c., &c. Boston: Dutton and Wentworth, 1842. 88, x p. Catalogue of books and list of members forms second group (x p.). Rinderknecht 42-3306. MB-FA, MH, MHi, MWA, NN, NNNBG, PPL. **860**

Massachusetts Horticultural Society. Transactions of the Massachusetts Horticultural Society for the Years 1843-4-5-6 . . . Boston: Dutton and Wentworth, 1847. xxv, 192, 26 p. "Catalogue of Books in the Library of the Massachusetts Horticultural Society, February 7, 1847" on pp. [185]-92. MHi, MWA. **861**

Massachusetts Horticultural Society. Transactions of the Massachusetts Horticultural Society. Vol. 1. Boston: William D. Ticknor, 1847. x, 102, vi, 215 p. "Catalogue of Books in the Massachusetts Horticultural Society's Library" on pp. [211]-15. In many libraries. **862**

Massachusetts Horticultural Society. Catalogue of Books in the Library of the Massachusetts Horticultural Society. January, 1854. Boston: Cross & Freeman, 1854. 33 p. New acquisitions are listed in the Society's *Transactions* beginning in 1858. DLC, MB, MWA. **863**

Massachusetts Horticultural Society. A Catalogue of the Library of the Massachusetts Horticultural Society. Boston: Henry W. Dutton & Son, 1867. 65, [1] p. New acquisitions are listed in the Society's *Transactions* beginning in 1858. DLC, M, MB, MBAt, MWA, NIC, NNBG. **864**

Massachusetts Horticultural Society. A Catalogue of the Library of the Massachusetts Horticultural Society. Boston: A. A. Kingman, 1873. 155 p. New acquisitions are listed in the Society's *Transactions* beginning in 1858. DLC copy contains "List of Duplicates

and Books Wanted" (4 p.). CU, DLC, MeU, M, MB, MHi, MU, MWA, MiEM, NNBG, PSt. **865**

Massachusetts Mechanic Association, see Mechanic Apprentices' Library Association.

Massachusetts Medical College. A List of Books belonging to the Library of the Mass. Medical College. For the use of Students until a Catalogue properly arranged is published. Boston: David Clapp, 1847. 23 p. MB (entered under: Harvard College. Medical School), MH (Archives), MH-M. **866**

Massachusetts Medical College. A Catalogue of Books belonging to the Library. Boston: David Clapp, 1854. 48 p. MB (entered under: Harvard College. Medical School), MoSW-M. **867**

Massachusetts Medical Society. Catalogue of Books in the Library of the Massachusetts Medical Society. July, 1810. [Boston, 1810]. 4, [2] p. S & S 20691 (duplicated by S & S 37808, a ghost 1816 ed.). CtY-M, DLC, DNLM, MBCo, MWA, PPC. **868**

Massachusetts Medical Society. A Catalogue of Books, belonging to the Massachusetts Medical Society. 17th June, 1822. [Boston, 1822]. 12 p. Shoemaker 9427. CtY-M, DLC, DNLM, MB, MBCo, MBM, MH-M, MHi, NNNAM, PPL. **869**

Mayhew and Baker's Central Circulating Library. Catalogue of Mayhew and Baker's Central Circulating Library . . . Boston: Mayhew and Baker, 1860. 30 p. Operated by Matthew A. Mayhew and George M. Baker. MB. **870**

Mayhew and Baker's Juvenile Circulating Library. Catalogue of Mayhew and Baker's Juvenile Circulating Library . . . Boston: Mayhew and Baker, 1860. 16 p. Operated by Matthew A. Mayhew and George M. Baker. MHi. **871**

Mechanic Apprentices' Library Association. Catalogue of the Apprentices' Library in Boston, to be loaned gratis, under the Superintendence of the Massachusetts Mechanic Association . . . Boston: Munroe and Francis, 1820. 24 p. Shoemaker 2197, Rink 512. MBAt (defective), MBBS. **872**

Mechanic Apprentices' Library Association. Catalogue of Books, in the Mechanic Apprentices' Library, with the Constitution, By-laws, &c., of the Association. Boston: Shepley & Wright, 1836. 46 p. Rinderknecht 36290. MB, MnHi, NNGr (uncat.). **873**

Mechanic Apprentices' Library Association. Catalogue of the Books in the Mechanic Apprentices' Library, with the Constitution, By-laws, &c. of the Association. Boston: Samuel N. Dickinson, 1838. 45 p. Rinderknecht 49352. MB, MBAt, MHi, WHi. **874**

Mechanic Apprentices' Library Association. Catalogue of Books of the Mechanic Apprentices' Library Association, with the Constitution, By-laws, etc. Boston: S. N. Dickinson, 1841. 48 p. Rinderknecht 41-753. IC, MB. **875**

Mechanic Apprentices' Library Association. Catalogue of Books in the Mechanic Apprentices' Library Association, with the Constitution, By-laws, &c. Boston: David H. Ela, 1845. 64 p. MB, NNGr (uncat.). **876**

Mechanic Apprentices' Library Association. Catalogue of Books of the Mechanic Apprentices' Library Association, with the Constitution, By-laws, &c. Boston: White & Potter, 1847. 68 p. DLC, MHi, MWA. **877**

Mechanic Apprentices' Library Association. Catalogue of Books of the Mechanic Apprentices' Library Association, with the Constitution, By-laws, &c. Boston: Damrell & Moore, 1851. 75 p. DLC, MB. **878**

Mechanic Apprentices' Library Association. Catalogue of Books of the Mechanic Apprentices' Library Association, with the Constitution, By-laws, &c. Boston: Robinson and Richardson, 1856. 88 p. MB. **879**

Mechanic Apprentices' Library Association. Catalogue of Books of the Mechanic Apprentices' Library Association, with a List of Honorary Members. Boston: Wright & Potter, 1867. 79 p. MHi. **880**

Mechanic Apprentices' Library Association. Catalogue of Books of the Mechanic Appren-tices' Library Association, Rules and Regulations of the Library, with a List of Honorary Members. Boston: Brown Type-setting Machine Co., 1873. 116 p. DLC. **881**

Mercantile Library Association. Catalogue of Books, in the Mercantile Library, Boston. June, 1821. Boston: W. W. Clapp, [1821]. 26 p. Not in Shoemaker. MWA. **882**

Mercantile Library Association. Constitution and By-laws of the Mercantile Library Association, together with a Catalogue of Books. Boston: D. K. Hitchcock, 1837. 75 p. Not in Rinderknecht. DeU. **883**

Mercantile Library Association. Constitution and By-laws of the Mercantile Library Association, together with a Catalogue of Books, and Names of Members. Instituted 1820. Boston: Dow & Jackson, 1839. x, 77 p. Rinderknecht 54581. CU-S, CtY, DLC, MB, MHi, NN. **884**

Mercantile Library Association. A Catalogue of Books of the Boston Mercantile Library Association, together with a History of the Institution, Constitution, By-laws, etc. Boston: Freeman and Bolles, 1844. 100 p. Rinderknecht 44-877 (duplicated by 44-4189). MB, MBAt, MH, MHi, MWA, NN, PU, WHi. **885**

Mercantile Library Association. A Supplementary Catalogue of Books, of the Mercantile Library Association of Boston, together with the Act of Incorporation, By-laws and Regulations adopted May, 1845, and the Annual Report for 1845-6. May, 1846. Boston, 1846. xx, 24 p. MB, MWA. **886**

Mercantile Library Association. A Catalogue of Books of the Mercantile Library Association, of Boston, together with the Act of Incorporation, and the By-laws an Regulation adopted January, 1848. Boston, 1848. 135 p. List of newspapers and magazines appears in the *Annual Report* for 1849-50. MB, MBAt, MHi, MWA, MnU, NNC. **887**

Mercantile Library Association. A Catalogue of Books of the Mercantile Library Association, of Boston, together with the Act of Incorporation, and the By-laws and Regulations adopted December 1, 1850. Boston: Damrell & Moore 1850. 135, 35 p. An undated "Supplementary Catalogue" constitutes the second group (35 p.). "List of Books added . . ." appears in the *Annual Report of the Mercantile Library Association.* DLC, MChB, MH, MHi, NN (film), OKentU. **888**

Mercantile Library Association. Supplementary Catalogue of Books of the Mercantile Library Association, of Boston, together with the Act of Incorporation, and the By-laws and Regulations adopted December 1, 1850. Boston: Damrell & Moore 1851. 20 p. MHi. **889**

Mercantile Library Association. Catalogue of the Mercantile Library of Boston. Boston: John Wilson & Son, 1854. xxiii, 298 p. William F. Poole, Librarian. Copy held by ICN has 50 leaves of ms. additions. "List of Books added . . ." or "List of Newspapers and Maga-zines" appear in the *Annual Report of the Mercantile Library Association*. In many libraries. **890**

Mercantile Library Association. Supplement to the Catalogue of the Mercantile Library Association of Boston. Boston: J. Wilson and Son, 1858. 52 p. List of newspapers and magazines appears in the *Annual Report* for 1865-68. CSmH, DLC, MA, MB, MH, NNUT, OKentU. **891**

Mercantile Library Association. Index to the Catalogue of Books of the Mercantile Library Association of Boston. Compiled by Charles William Baker. Boston: A. Mudge & Son, 1869. xxii, 221, [2], [11]-19 p. List of newspapers and magazines appears in the *Annual Report* for 1873. CSmH, DLC, MB (2 copies; copy "A" is interleaved), MBAt, MHi, MWA, PPL. **892**

New Circulating Library. A Catalogue of the New Circulating Library, kept at No. 82, Newbury-Street, to which is prefixed, the Conditions of said Library. Boston: Munroe & Francis, 1804. 24 p. S & S 6866. MWA. **893**

Odd Fellows' Library. Catalogue of Books contained in the Odd Fellows' Library, with a Short History of the Library, Regulations, etc., etc. Boston, 1875. x, [2], 71, [1] p. Compiled by Fred. W. Calkins, Assistant Librarian. DLC (includes suppl., Jan. 1877 and April 1881, consecutively paged to p. 86). **894**

Old South Church. Catalogue of the Library of Rev. Thomas Prince, Former Pastor of Old South Church. Presented by him to the Old South Church and Society. Compiled by G. H. Whitman. Boston: Crocker and Brewster, 1846. 112 p. Collection was deposited in the Boston Public Library in 1866 (see entries 767-68, 772). CSmH, DLC, MH, MHi, NhD, N, NN, RHi, TU, ViU, ViW. **895**

Old South Church. Catalogue of Books in the Old South Sabbath School Library. [Boston, 1861?]. 16 p. MB. **896**

Park Street Church. [Catalogue of the Library of the Sabbath School Library]. [Boston, 1864?]. 16 p. MB (defective). **897**

Pelham's Circulating Library. Catalogue of Pelham's Circulating Library, No. 59, Cornhill, consisting of a chosen Assortment of Books in the various Branches of Literature. Charlestown: Samuel Etheridge, 1801. 51 p., [5] p. of advertisements. Conducted by William Blagrove. S & S 1110. MBC, MH-H, MWA, PU. **898**

Pelham's Circulating Library. Catalogue of Pelham's Circulating Library, No. 5, School Street . . . Boston: Munroe & Francis, 1804. 62 p. Conducted by William Blagrove. Not in S & S. MWA **899**

Phillips, Sampson, & Co. Phillips, Sampson, & Co.'s Catalogue of their Select Circulating Library. Established June, 1859. Boston: Phillips, Sampson, [1859?]. 18 p. MB. **900**

Pitts-Street Chapel. Catalogue of the Parish Library of Pitts-Street Chapel, Boston. Boston: John Wilson, 1850. 23 p. MWA. **901**

Rowe Street Baptist Church. Catalogue of the Rowe Street Sabbath School Library. Boston: Gould and Lincoln, 1857. 32 p. MHi. **902**

St. Matthew's Church. Catalogue of the Sunday School Library, together with the Constitutions of the Charitable Societies in St. Matthew's Church, Boston. Boston: Putnam & Hunt, 1830. 36 p. Not in Cooper. MWA. **903**

St. Paul's Church. Catalogue and By-laws of the Sears Library of St. Paul's Church, Boston. Also, the Catalogue of the Sunday School Library of St. Paul's Church. Boston: John Cotton, 1827. 52 p. Not in Shoemaker. MWA. **904**

St. Paul's Church. Catalogue of St. Paul's Church Sunday School Library. September, 1860. Boston: Mudge and Son, 1860. 8 p. MB. **905**

St. Stephen's Church. Catalogue of St. Stephen's Sunday School Library. Boston: Mudge, 1859. 14 p. MB (defective). **906**

St. Stephen's Church. Catalogue of St. Stephen's Sunday School Library. Boston: A. Mudge & Son, 1861. 15 p. MB (interleaved). **907**

St. Stephen's Church. Catalogue of the Sunday School Library of St. Stephen's Church, Purchase St., Boston. Boston: A. Mudge & Son, 1863. 11 p. MB. **908**

Second Church. Catalogue of Books belonging to the Library of the Second Church, Bedford Street. Boston: I. R. Butts, 1854. 56 p. MB, MWA. **909**

Second Church. Catalogue of the Sunday-School Library connected with the Second Church. Boston: John Wilson & Son, 1858. 24 p. MB **910**

Second Church. Catalogue of Books in the Sunday-School Library connected with the Second Church, Boston. Boston: J. Wilson and Son, 1862. 22 p. MiU. **911**

Second Church. Catalogue of Books in the Sunday-School Library connected with the Second Church, Boston . . . Boston: W. F. Brown, 1868. 25 p. MB. **912**

Second Social Library. A Catalogue of Books, in the Second Social Library in the Town of Boston. Instituted January, 1805, Incorporated 1806. Boston: Emerald Printing Office, 1808. 12 p. S & S 16161. MB, MWA. **913**

Second Social Library. Supplementary Catalogue of Books, added to the Second Social Library, from January, 1809, to May, 1811. [Boston, 1811]. 12 p. Not in S & S. MB. **914**

Shakespeare Circulating Library. Catalogue of Books in the New Circulating Library, No. 11, Marboro'-Street. Boston: T. G. Bangs, 1815. 57 p. Caption title: Catalogue of the Shakespeare Circulating Library, No. 12, Cornhill. Conducted by Charles Callender. S & S 35911. MB, MSaE. **915**

Shakespeare Circulating Library. Catalog of the Shakspeare [!] Circulating Library . . . to which Additions are continually making.

Boston: Printed for Charles Callender, Librarian and Proprietor, 1819. 48 p. S & S 47495. MHi. **916**

Shakespeare Circulating Library. Catalogue of the Shakespeare Circulating Library . . . to which Additions are continually making. Boston: Printed for Charles Callender, Librarian and Proprietor, 1820. 48 p. Shoemaker 3183. MB, MHi, MWA. **917**

Shakespeare Circulating Library. A Circulating Library to be retailed at Auction. On Monday, the 26th Day of the Present Month (October) . . . at No. 25, School-Street will commence the Sale of the Shakspeare [!] Circulating Library . . . consisting of upwards of Four Thousand Volumes . . . [Boston, 1829?]. 56 p. Caption title (p. 5): Catalogue of the Shakspeare [!] Circulating Library, No. 25, School-Street, Boston. Stock offered by Charles Callender. Not in Shoemaker or McKay. NN. **918**

Social Law Library. Rules and Catalogue of the Social Law Library. Boston: John Eliot, 1814. 24 p. S & S 32809. M (interleaved), MB (defective), MH-H, MWA, NhD, PPL. **919**

Social Law Library. Rules and Catalogue of the Social Law Library. Boston: Phelps and Farnham, 1824. 32 p. Shoemaker 18027. MB, MBAt, MH-H (interleaved), MWA, N, NNC-L, NNE, PPL, WaU-L. **920**

Social Law Library. A Catalogue of the Social Law Library, in Boston. Second Edition. Boston, 1849. xii, 197 p. Includes Act of Incorporation and By-laws. M, MB, MBAt, MBS (interleaved and extensively annotated by Joel Bishop?), MH, MWA, N. **921**

Social Law Library. Catalogue of Social Law Library in Boston. Third Edition. Boston, 1865. xv, 281 p. Includes Act of Incorporation and By-laws. In many libraries. **922**

Social Library, No. 1. Catalogue of Books in Social Library, No. 1. March, 1823. Boston, [1823]. 36 p. Shoemaker 11948. MB. **923**

Social Library, No. 1. A Catalogue of Books in the Social Library, No. 1. February, 1831. Boston, 1831. 35 p. Not in Bruntjen. DLC, MH-H. **924**

Society of Natural History, see entries 783-84.

Society of the New Jerusalem, see entry 785.

South Boston Circulating Library. Catalogue of the South Boston Circulating Library . . . Boston: A. J. Wright's Steam-Press Printing Establishment, 1849. 36 p. MH-H (entered under: Caleb Gill & Co.).   **925**

South Congregational Church. Catalogue of the South Congregational Sunday-School Library, Union-Park Street. Boston: Walker, Wise, 1862. 32 p. MB, MWA.   **926**

South-End Mission. Catalogue of the South-End Mission Sunday School Library. 1864. Boston: Mudge & Son, 1864. 12 p. MB.
927

State Library of Massachusetts, see Massachusetts. State Library.

Suffolk Circulating Library. Catalogue of the Suffolk Circulating Library, Corner of Court and Brattle Streets, Boston . . . [Boston]: N. S. & J. Simpkins, 1821-22. 3 pts. in 1 vol. Operated by Nathaniel S. Simpkins and John Simpkins. Not in Shoemaker. MH-H (includes 1st suppl., 1821, and 2d suppl., 1822).   **928**

Theological Library. Catalogue of Books, in the Theological Library, in the Town of Boston, March 1, 1808. Boston: Snelling and Simons, 1808. 33 p. S & S 14561. CSmH, DeU, MB, MH-H, MWA, NN, NNGr, PPL.   **929**

Third Church, see Old South Church.

Third Social Library. By-laws. [Boston, 1834]. 7 p. Catalogue of books on pp. 3-7. Rinderknecht 23495. MBA, MWA, WHi.   **930**

Twelfth Congregational Church. Catalogue of the Juvenile Library of the Twelfth Congregational Sunday School, Boston. Boston: C. C. P. Moody, 1861. 24 p. MH-H.
931

Union Circulating Library. Catalogue of the Union Circulating Library . . . Boston: Munroe & Francis, 1806. 82 p. Conducted by William Blagrove. S & S 11491. MWA.
932

Union Circulating Library. Catalogue of the Union Circulating Library, No. 3, School-Street. Boston: Samuel Avery, 1810. 80 p. Conducted by William Blagrove. S & S 21547. MWA.   **933**

Union Circulating Library. Catalogue of the Boston Union Circulating Library, No. 3, School-Street. Boston: S. H. Parker, 1812. 76 p. Conducted by Samuel H. Parker. Not in S & S. MB, MBAt.   **934**

Union Circulating Library. Catalogue of the Boston Union Circulating Library and Reading Room . . . Boston: Samuel H. Parker, 1815. 110 p. Caption title (p. [5]): Catalogue of the Boston Circulating Library. Running title variously reads Boston Circulating Library or Boston Union Circulating Library. Conducted by Samuel H. Parker. S & S 34176. MWA.   **935**

Union Circulating Library. Catalogue of the Boston Union Circulating Library . . . Boston: Samuel H. Parker, 1820. 128 p. Shoemaker 2650 (under S. H. Parker). MB, MWA.   **936**

Universalist Young Men's Institute, see Boston Universalist Young Men's Institute.

Urbino's Foreign Circulating Library. Catalogue of S. Urbino's Foreign Circulating Library. Boston: Office of the Neu England Zeitung, [185-?]. 31 p. Operated by Sampson Urbino. MWA (with ms. notes).
937

Washington Circulating Library. Catalogue of the Washington Circulating Library . . . [Boston]: T. G. Bangs, 1817. 60, 12 p. Following p. 60: "Catalogue of Books, for Private Sale, at Reduced Prices" (12 p.). S & S 42831. MWA.   **938**

Washington Circulating Library. Catalogue of the Washington Circulating Library . . . Boston: I. R. Butts, 1833. 66 p. Not in Bruntjen. MH-H.   **939**

West Church. West Parish Association. Constitution of the West Parish Association, together with Reports of Committees on the Sunday Schools, and Library. Boston: Wm. Bellamy, 1825. 24 p. "Catalogue of Books, which it is proposed to obtain for the formation of the library of the West Parish Association" on pp. [19]-24. Shoemaker 19828. ICMe, MB, MH, MH-AH, MHi, MWA, MiD-B, NNUT.   **940**

West Church. West Parish Association. Catalogue of the Library of the West Parish

Association in Boston. Cambridge: Hilliard & Metcalf, 1826. 11 p. Shoemaker 23901. MHi. **941**

West Church. West Parish Association. Catalogue of the Library of the West Parish Association in Boston. Boston, 1830. 14 p. Cooper 619. MHi. **942**

West Church. West Parish Association. Catalogue of the Library of the West Parish in Boston. Boston: John Wilson, 1850. 24 p. MWA. **943**

West Church. West Parish Association. Catalogue of Books in the Parish Library connected with the West Church. Boston: John Wilson and Son, 1859. 22 p. MB (2 copies with ms. additions), MWA. **944**

Young Men's Christian Union, see entry 788.

Young Men's Society, see entry 789.

Boston Highlands

(see also Roxbury)

Eliot Church. Catalogue of the Eliot Sabbath School Library, Boston Highlands. October 1, 1868. Boston: T. R. Marvin & Son, 1868. 14 p. MB (entered under: Roxbury. Eliot Church). **945**

Walnut Avenue Sabbath School. Catalogue of Books of the Walnut Avenue Sabbath School Library, Boston Highlands. Boston: A. K. Brown, 1874. 24 p. MWA. **946**

Boylston

Boylston Sabbath School. Catalogue of the Boylston Sabbath School Library. 1856. [Boston?, 1856]. 16 p. MWA. **947**

Braintree

Union Social Library. Catalogue of Books, belonging to the Union Social Library of Braintree and Weymouth. Sept. 1829. [Boston, 1829]. broadside. Not in Shoemaker. MWA. **948**

Bridgewater

(see also North Bridgewater)

Bridgewater Natural History Society. Catalogue of the Library of the Bridgewater Natural History Society. Boston: J. E. Farwell, 1856. 16 p. DLC, DSI. **949**

First Congregational Church. Catalogue of the Library of the Sunday School of the First Congregational Society in Bridgewater. 1864. Boston: Geo. C. Rand & Avery, 1864. 20 p. MB. **950**

Brighton

Brighton Library Association. Catalogue ... 1857. Cf. Cutter 404. **951**

Brighton Library Association. Catalogue of Books belonging to the Brighton Library Association. Boston: C. H. Crosby, 1859. 40 p. DLC, N. **952**

Brighton Social Library. Catalogue ... 1824? Cf. Cutter 96. **953**

Brighton Social Library. Catalogue of Books, belonging to the Brighton Social Library. January 1, 1836. With the Constitution. Boston: Dutton & Wentworth, 1836. 24 p. Rinderknecht 36368. MB, N. **954**

Evangelical Church. Catalogue of the Evangelical Sabbath School Library, Brighton. Boston: Davis & Farmer, 1859. 23 p. MB. **955**

First Parish. Catalogue of Books in the Library of the Sunday School. Boston: Tuttle & Dennett, 1842. [12] p. Rinderknecht 42-742. MB.**956**

Holton Library. Catalogue of the Holton Library of Brighton. Boston: Charles H. Crosby, 1866. 105, [3] p. Copy held by DeU contains "Corrections and Additions." Lists of added books appear in the Holton Library's 4th-6th *Annual Report* for 1868-70. DeU (interleaved), MB, MBAt, MH, N (interleaved). **957**

Holton Library. Second Catalogue of the Holton Library of Brighton, Mass. Comprising Rules and Regulations; Names of Officers; Dictionary of Pseudonyms; Donations, with Names of Donors; and Bulletin No. 1. Boston: Alfred Mudge & Son, 1872. xviii, 336 p. Preface signed F.A.W. [Frederick Augustus Whitney]. DLC, ICN, IU, M, MB, MBAt, MH, MWA, N, NN, NNC. **958**

Holton Library. Bulletin. No. 1-3; March 1872-Jan. 1874. ICN, M (#2; March, 1873), MB (#1-3), MWA (#2-3; March 1873-Jan. 1874), N (#1-3). **959**

Brockton

Brockton Public Library. Catalogue of the
Public Library, of the Town of Brockton.
Established 1867. Brockton: Gazette Steam
Job Printing Establishment, 1874. 155 p.
DLC.   **960**

Brookfield

(see also North Brookfield)

Evangelical Congregational Church. Cata-
logue of the Sabbath School Library of the
Evangelical Congregational Church of
Brookfield, Mass. 1871. Worcester: Charles
Hamilton, [1871?]. 7 p. MWA.   **961**

Merrick Public Library. Catalogue of the
Merrick Public Library, of Brookfield. 1867.
Worcester: Charles Hamilton, 1867. 42 p.
MB and MWA hold "Additional Catalogue,"
March, 1869 (pp. [43]-52) and "Second
Additional Catalogue," April, 1870 (pp.
[53]-66); MH and N hold "Second
Additional Catalogue" only. MWA.   **962**

Merrick Public Library. Catalogue of the Merrick
Public Library of the Town of Brookfield.
November 1, 1872. Cambridge: Welch, Bigelow,
1872. vi, 115 p. DLC, M, MB, MWA, N.   **963**

Brookline

Brookline Public Library. Catalogue of the
Public Library of Brookline. December 2,
1857. Boston: Alfred Mudge & Son, 1857.
24 p. MBr.   **964**

Brookline Public Library. A Classed Catalogue of the Brookline Public Library, with
an Alphabetical Index. Boston: J. E. Farrell,
1859. xii, 95 p. MB, MBr.   **965**

Brookline Public Library. Catalogue of the
Public Library of Brookline. Boston: John
Wilson and Son, 1865. x, 165 p. DeU, MB,
MBAt, MBr, MH, PPL.   **966**

Brookline Public Library. Finding List for
Alcoves I, II, IX and X. Fiction, Juvenile
Department, etc. [n.p., 1871?]. 89 p. MBr.
                                       967

Brookline Public Library. Catalogue of the
Public Library of Brookline. Cambridge:
John Wilson and Son, 1873. xii, 623 p.
Suppl. appears in the Library's 17th *Annual
Report*, 1874. DLC (film), ICN, ICU, IU, MA,

MB, MBr, MH, MWA, MnU, NhD, NjP, N,
NN, PPL.   **968**

Brookline Social Library. Catalogue ... 1827.
Not in Shoemaker. Contained nearly 300
vol., per Louis A. Cook, ed., *History of Norfolk
County, Massachusetts, 1622-1918* (New York,
1918), vol. 1, p. 406.   **969**

First Parish Church. Catalogue of the Library of
the First Parish Sunday-School in Brookline.
September, 1857. Cambridge: Metcalf, 1857.
24 p. MBAt (with ms. additions).   **970**

Burlington

Burlington Town Library. Catalogue of Books
belonging to the Town Library of Burlington.
1858. Boston, 1858. 18 p. M (lost).   **971**

Burlington Town Library. Catalogue of Books
belonging to the Burlington Town Library.
1868. Boston: L. Rhodes, 1868. 22 p. DLC.
                                       972

Cambridge

(see also Cambridgeport, West Cambridge)

Boylston Medical Library, see Harvard
University. Boylston Medical Library.

Cambridge Athenaeum. [Catalogue of Li-
brary]. Appendix. [n.p., 1857?]. [33]-43 p.
MB (holds Appendix only).   **973**

Cambridge Circulating Library. Catalogue of
the Cambridge Circulating Library. September, 1858. [Cambridge]: John Bartlett,
1858. 24 p. Sabin 10147 reports a catalogue
dated Dec. 1858 (7 p.). MHi.   **974**

Cambridge Circulating Library. Catalogue of
the Cambridge Circulating Library. September, 1859. [Cambridge]: Sever and Francis,
1859. 31 p. MWA.   **975**

Cambridge Circulating Library. Catalogue of
the Cambridge Circulating Library, University
Bookstore, Harvard Square. [Cambridge]:
Sever and Francis, 1861. 32 p. MB.   **976**

Cambridge High School. A Classed Catalogue
of the Library of the Cambridge High
School, with an Alphabetical Index. To
which is appended a List of the Philosophical and other Apparatus belonging to the
School. Cambridge: John Bartlett, 1853.
239 p. Compiled by Ezra Abbot, jr. In many
libraries.   **977**

Dana Library. Catalogue of the Dana Library, Cambridge. Cambridge: Riverside Press, 1865. 83 p. DLC, MB, MH.   978

Dana Library. Catalogue of the Dana Library, Cambridge. Cambridge: Riverside Press, 1870. 125 p. Reissue of the catalogue of 1865 with suppl. on pp. 84-125. DLC, MB.   979

Dana Library. Catalogue of the Dana Library, Cambridge. Cambridge: John Metcalf and Son, 1875. 252 p. MB, MBAt, MH, MWA.   980

First Parish. Catalogue of the First Parish Sunday School Library, Cambridge. October, 1845. Cambridge: Metcalf, 1845. 36 p. MB.   981

First Parish. A Catalogue of the Library of the First Parish in Cambridge. Cambridge: Metcalf, 1854. vi, 32 p. MB, MHi.   982

First Parish. Catalogue of the Library of the First Parish Sunday School in Cambridge. May, 1858. Cambridge: Metcalf 1858. 24 p. MBAt (with ms. additions).   983

Harvard Law School. Catalogue of the Library of the Law School of Harvard University. Cambridge: Hilliard & Metcalf, 1826. 25, [1] p. Shoemaker 24802. CLU, DLC, MB, MH (Archives), MH-L, MHi, NhD, PPL, ViU-L, WU-L.   984

Harvard Law School. A Catalogue of the Law Library of Harvard University in Cambridge, Massachusetts. Cambridge: Charles Folsom, 1834. viii, 80 p. Rinderknecht 24845. IU, MA, MB, MH (Archives), MWA, MeB, NhD, PPAmP, ViW.   985

Harvard Law School. Supplement to the Catalogue of the Law Library of Harvard University in Cambridge, Massachusetts. Cambridge: Charles Folsom, 1835. 16 p. Rinderknecht 32073.   LNH, MB, MH (Archives), MHi, MWA, OCHP.   986

Harvard Law School. A Catalogue of the Law Library of Harvard University in Cambridge, Massachusetts. Second Edition. Cambridge: Folsom, Wells and Thurston, 1841. xii, 228 p. Preface by William R. Woodward, Librarian. Constitutes the third ed., with the catalogues of 1826 and 1834 considered the first and second ed., respectively. Rinderknecht 41-2418. DLC, IU, MeB, M, MB, MH (Archives), MHi, N, PPL.   987

Harvard Law School. A Catalogue of the Law Library of Harvard University in Cambridge, Massachusetts. Fourth Edition. Cambridge: Metcalf, 1846. 354 p. In many libraries.   988

Harvard Medical School (collection was housed at the Massachusetts Medical College in Boston; see entries 866-67).

Harvard Musical Association, see entries 833-34.

Harvard University. Catalogue of Books, which may be taken from the Library of Harvard University by Members of the Freshman Class. Cambridge, 1814. 12 p. S & S 31658. DHEW, MH (Archives).   989

Harvard University. Catalogue of Books to be sold by Public Auction at Francis Amory's Auction Room, Boston, immediately after the Sales advertised to commence December 20, 1815. [Boston, 1815]. 16 p. A sale of duplicates from Harvard's library. S & S 33857, McKay 178. DLC, MH (Archives), NN.   990

Harvard University. Catalogue of Duplicates in the Library of Harvard University, for Sale. [Cambridge?, 1823?]. 31, [1] p. Shoemaker 16464 (under 1824), probably duplicated by Bruntjen 19230 (under 1833) for undated MBAt copy. CLU, DLC, MB, MBAt, MH (Archives), MHi, MWA (dated 1824?), NN, NNGr, NhD.   991

Harvard University. A Catalogue of the Library of Harvard University in Cambridge, Massachusetts. Cambridge: E. W. Metcalf, 1830-31. 3 vol. in 4. Vol. 3, pt. 2 has title: A Catalogue of the Maps and Charts in the Library of Harvard University in Cambridge, Massachusetts (Bruntjen 7465). Benjamin Peirce, librarian. Cooper 1772. In many libraries.   992

Harvard University. A Catalogue of the Library of Harvard University in Cambridge, Massachusetts. First Supplement. Cambridge: Charles Folson, 1834. 260 p. Rinderknecht 24846. In many libraries.   993

Harvard University. Catalogue of the Bound Historical Manuscripts collected by Jared Sparks, and now deposited in the Library of Harvard University (1871), see entry 2298.

Harvard University. Bulletin of the more Important Accessions. No. 1; 1875. MH.   994

Harvard University. Boylston Medical Library. Catalogue of Books in the Boylston Medical Library, at Harvard University, Cambridge. Instituted in 1802. [Cambridge?, 180-?]. 20 p. Not in S & S; Austin 886. DLC, DNLM, MBM, MH (Archives). **995**

Harvard University. Boylston Medical Library. Catalogue of Books in the Boylston Medical Library, at Harvard University, Cambridge. Boston: Ezra Lincoln, 1824. 36 p. Shoemaker 16463. DNLM, MBCo, MH (Archives; 3 copies, one of which is interleaved and annotated), MWA. **996**

Harvard University. Deipnophagoi Club. Catalogue of Books in the Library of the Deipnophagoi Club, Harvard College. Cambridge: Hilliard and Metcalf, 1816. 12 p. S & S 37809. MWA. **997**

Harvard University. Hasty Pudding Club. A Catalogue of the Members and Library of the Hasty-Pudding Club in Harvard University. Instituted 1795 . . . Cambridge: Metcalf, Torry, & Ballou, 1838. 35 p. Rinderknecht 50754. DLC, MB, MH (Archives), MLexHi, MWA. **998**

Harvard University. Hasty Pudding Club. A Catalogue of the Members and Library of the Hasty-Pudding Club in Harvard University. Cambridge: Metcalf, Torry, and Ballou, 1841. 48 p. Not in Rinderknecht. MB, MH (Archives), MnU, NN. **999**

Harvard University. Institute of 1770. Catalogue of the Honorary and Immediate Members of the Institute of 1770, of Harvard University. Cambridge: E. W. Metcalf, 1832. 44 p. "Library of the Institute of 1770" on pp. [25]-44. Bruntjen 12836. CtY, DLC, MHi, MWA, N (holds library section only), OClWHi. **1000**

Harvard University. Knights of the Square Table. Library of the Order of Knights of the Square Table, Harvard University, Cambridge, Mass. Instituted 1809. Cambridge: E. W. Metcalf, 1829. 16 p. Cover title: Knights' Library. Not in Shoemaker. MH (Archives). **1001**

Harvard University. Law Library, see Harvard Law School.

Harvard University. Medical School (collection was housed at the Massachusetts Medical College in Boston; see entries 866-67).

Harvard University. Porcellian Club. Catalogue of Books in the Library of the Porcellian Club, Harvard College. Cambridge: Hilliard and Metcalf, 1816. 12 p. S & S 37810. MH (Archives), MWA. **1002**

Harvard University. Porcellian Club. Catalogue of Books in the Library of the Porcellian Club of Harvard University, Cambridge, Mass. Cambridge: Hilliard, Metcalf, 1827. 19 p. Shoemaker 29167. CLU, MH (Archives), MHi. **1003**

Harvard University. Porcellian Club. Catalogue of the Honorary and Immediate Members of the Procellian Club, of Harvard University. Instituted, 1791. Cambridge: E. W. Metcalf, 1831. 63, [1] p. Library catalogue on pp. 37-63. CLU, MB, MH (Archives), PPL. **1004**

Harvard University. Porcellian Club. Catalogue of the Honorary and Immediate Members, and of the Library of the Porcellian Club of Harvard University. Instituted 1791. Cambridge: Metcalf, Torry and Ballou, 1834. 75, [1] p. Rinderknecht 24844. DLC, MB, MH (Archives), MH-L, MHi, PPL. **1005**

Harvard University. Porcellian Club. Catalogue of the Honorary and Immediate Members, and of the Library of the Porcellian Club of Harvard University. Instituted 1791. Cambridge: J. H. Eastburn, 1839. 95 p. Rinderknecht 56191. DLC, MB, MH (Archives), OClWHi. **1006**

Harvard University. Porcellian Club. Catalogue of the Honorary and Immediate Members, and of the Library of the Porcellian Club of Harvard University. Instituted, 1791. Cambridge: Metcalf, 1846. 107 p. MB, MH (Archives). **1007**

Harvard University. Porcellian Club. Catalogue of the Honorary and Immediate Members, and of the Library of the Porcellian Club of Harvard University. Instituted 1791. Cambridge: Metcalf, 1850. 113 p. MB. **1008**

Harvard University. Porcellian Club. Catalogue of the Honorary and Immediate Members, and of the Library of the Porcellian Club of Harvard University.

Instituted 1791. Cambridge: Metcalf, 1854. 119, [1] p. CSmH, DLC, MB. **1009**

Harvard University. Porcellian Club. Catalogue of the Honorary and Immediate Members, and of the Library of the Porcellian Club of Harvard University. Instituted 1791. Cambridge: Allen and Farnham, 1857. 67, 103 p. DLC, MB, MH (Archives). **1010**

Harvard University. Porcellian Club. Catalogue of the Porcellian Club of Harvard University. Instituted in 1791. Cambridge, 1865. 67, 94, 95-95u, [96]-103 p. The catalogue of 1857 with suppl. dated June, 1865, on pp. 95-95u. DLC, IU (film), MB, MH (Archives; MH also has film). **1011**

Harvard University. Porcellian Club. Catalogue of the Porcellian Club of Harvard University. Instituted 1791. Cambridge, 1867. 74, 199 p. Library catalogue on pp. 1-199 (2d group). DLC, MB, NN. **1012**

Cambridgeport

(see also Cambridge, West Cambridge)

Cambridgeport Parish. Cambridgeport Parish Library. [n.p.], 1849. 8 p. A report and catalogue of books. NN. **1013**

Cambridgeport Parish. Cambridgeport Parish Library. Cambridge: John Ford, 1854. 22 p. MHi. **1014**

Canton

Canton Public Library. Catalogue. [Canton: Wm. Bense, 187-?, but no later than July 7, 1875, per Bureau of Education date stamp on DLC copy]. 15 p. DLC. **1015**

Canton Social Library. Catalogue . . . 1835. Not in Rinderknecht. Contained around 500 vol., per Daniel T. V. Huntoon, *History of the Town of Canton, Norfolk County, Massachusetts* (Cambridge, Mass., 1893), p. 572. **1016**

Charlestown

Baker's Circulating Library. Catalogue of T. M. Baker's Circulating Library . . . Charlestown: G. Davidson, 1826. 24 p. See also entry 1019. Not in Shoemaker. MWA. **1017**

Charlestown Circulating Library. Catalogue of the Charlestown Circulating Library . . .

Charlestown, 1815. 13 p. S & S 34327. MH. **1018**

Charlestown Circulating Library. Catalogue of the Charlestown Circulating Library . . . Boston: True & Weston for T. M. Baker, 1819. 56 p. Caption title: Catalogue of T. M. Baker's Circulating Library . . . See also entry 1017. S & S 47572. MH. **1019**

Charlestown Public Library. Catalogue of the Public Library of the City of Charlestown. Charlestown: Caleb Rand, 1862. xv, 199, [1] p. DLC, ICU, MdBP, MB, MBAt, MH, MWA. **1020**

Charlestown Public Library. Supplement to Catalogue. Books added to the Library from October 1, 1862 to August 1, 1863. [Charlestown, 1863]. 12 p. DLC, MH. **1021**

Charlestown Public Library. Second Supplement to Catalogue. Books added to the Library from August 1, 1863, to August 1, 1865. [n.p., 1866?]. 27 p. Copy held by MWA appended to *Report of the Trustees of the Public Library of the City of Charlestown, November 1, 1865* (Boston: W. & E. Howe, 1866). DLC, MH, MWA. **1022**

Charlestown Public Library. Catalogue of the Public Library of the City of Charlestown. Supplementary Catalogue. Boston, 1872. viii, 166 p. Covers 1862-72. MB, MWA. **1023**

Charlestown Union Library. Catalogue of Books in the Charlestown Union Library. [Boston, 1822]. 19, [1] p. Not in Shoemaker. MWA. **1024**

Charlestown Union Library. Catalogue of Books in the Charlestown Union Library. [Charlestown, 1835?]. 31 p. Shoemaker 723. DLC (film), MB (defective), MH-H, MWA. **1025**

First Baptist Church. Catalogue of the Sabbath School Library of the First Baptist Church, Charlestown. Boston: John Putnam, 1849. 16 p. MWA. **1026**

First Parish. Library of Sabbath School, First Parish in Charlestown. 1860. Catalogue. [n.p., 1860?]. 11 p. DLC, MWA. **1027**

First Universalist Church. Catalogue of Books in the Library of the Universalist Sabbath

School in Charlestown. January, 1861. Charlestown: Caleb Rand, 1861. 31 p. DLC.
1028

Harris's Circulating Library. Catalogue of Books in J. Harris's Circulating Library . . . Charlestown: Caleb Rand, 1841. 18 p. Not in Rinderknecht. MH-H.
1029

Harvard Church. Catalogue of Harvard Church Sunday-School Library. Charlestown: A. B. Morss, 1853. 20 p. MWA.
1030

Harvard Church. Catalogue of Harvard Church Sunday School Library, Charlestown. Charlestown: Caleb Rand, 1856. 24 p. MWA.
1031

Harvard Church. Catalogue of the Harvard Church Sunday School Library, Charlestown, Mass. Charlestown: Printed at the Chronicle Office, 1870. 34 p. MWA.
1032

Massachusetts. State Prison. Catalogue of Books in the Library of the Massachusetts State Prison. Boston: J. M. Hewes, 1870. 55, 8, 10 p. MWA.
1033

Mishawum Literary Association. By-laws of the Mishawum Literary Association, together with the Catalogue of Books. Charlestown: C. Rand, 1853. 24 p. MB, MWA.
1034

Mishawum Literary Association. By-laws and Catalogue of Books, of the Mishawum Literary Association, Charlestown, Mass. Founded September, 1851. Boston: W. & E. Howe, 1857. 40 p. MH and MWA copies include suppl., Nov. 1, 1859, forming pp. [41]-46. DLC, MH, MWA.
1035

St. John's Church. Catalogue of Books in the St. John's Church Sunday School Library, Charlestown. Boston: Willard L. Goodnow, 1859. 20 p. MWA.
1036

Warren School. Catalogue of Books belonging to the Warren School, Charlestown, Mass. Charlestown: Press of the Bunker-Hill Aurora, 1840. 12 p. Not in Rinderknecht. MWA (with ms. additions).
1037

Chelmsford

Chelmsford Social Library. Institution and Regulations . . . 1801. Not in S & S. Contains a list of books, per Wilson Waters, *History of Chelmsford, Massachusetts* (Lowell, 1917), p. 584.
1038

Chelsea

Chelsea Library Association. Catalogue . . . 1856. Cf. Rhees, p. 140.
1039

Chelsea Public Library. Catalogue of the Public Library of the City of Chelsea. Chelsea: Telegraph and Pioneer Press, 1869. 78 p. MB holds suppl., 1870 (53 p.). DLC, MB, OU.
1040

Chelsea Public Library. Catalogue . . . 1871. Cf. *Catalogue of the San Francisco Free Public Library*, no. 4, May, 1884, p. 51.
1041

Chelsea Unitarian Church. Catalogue of the Library of Chelsea Unitarian Sunday School. 1869. Boston: J. E. Farwell, [1869?]. 16 p. MWA.
1042

Chestnut Street Congregational Church. Catalogue of Books in the Library of the Chestnut Street Congregational Sabbath School, Chelsea. Boston: Fred Rogers, 1859. 32 p. MB.
1043

Winnisimmet Congregational Church. Catalogue of Books in the Winnisimmet Congregational Sabbath School Library. October 20, 1844. Boston: S. N. Dickinson, 1844. 12 p. MWA.
1044

Winnisimmet Literary Institute. Alterations and Amendments of the Constitution of the Winnisimmet Literary Institute. Adopted May 27th, 1850. [Chelsea?, 1850]. 16 p. Catalogue of books on pp. 5-16. MB (presumably defective without title page).
1045

Cherry Valley

Cherry Valley Sunday School. Catalogue of the Cherry Valley Sunday School Library. Worcester: Charles Hamilton, 1873. 16 p. MWA.
1046

Cheshire

Cheshire Library Association. Catalogue of Books belonging to the Cheshire Library Association, of Cheshire, Mass. Boston: Wright & Potter, 1868. 24 p. DLC copy contains entries #801-1278 in ms. DLC (film), GU, IQC, TxDW.
1047

Chesterfield

Chesterfield Town Library. Catalogue . . . 1873. Cf. *Ninth Report of the Free Public Library*

Commission of Massachusetts (1899), pp. 81-82.
1048

Chicopee

Cabot Institute. Constitution and By-laws of the Cabot Institute, with a Catalogue of the Books contained in the Library. Springfield: Horace S. Taylor, 1846. 35 p. MChi (uncat.). **1049**

Chicopee Falls School Library. Catalogue of the Chicopee Falls School Library . . . and the Regulations for its Government. Springfield: John M. Wood, 1848. Cf. Sabin 12685. **1050**

Chicopee Town Library. Catalogue . . . 1846. Cf. Cutter 270, *Ninth Report of the Free Public Library Commission of Massachusetts* (1899), p. 82. **1051**

Chicopee Town Library. A Catalogue of the Books contained in the Chicopee Town Library, together with the General Regulations of the same. Chicopee, 1853. 36 p. MChi (uncat.), Pocumtuck Valley Memorial Association Library, Deerfield, Mass. **1052**

Chicopee Town Library. A Catalogue of the Books contained in the Chicopee Town Library, together with the General Regulations of the same. Chicopee, 1859. 60 p. MB, MChi (uncat.). **1053**

Chicopee Town Library. Supplement . . . 1862. Cf. Cutter 476, *Ninth Report of the Free Public Library Commission of Massachusetts* (1899), p. 82. **1054**

Chicope Library Supplement Book adde sinc July, 1859. March, 1866. Chicopee: G. V. Wheelock, 1866. 23 p. MB, MChi (uncat.; defective). **1055**

Chicopee Town Library. Catalogue of the Chicopee Town Library, its History and Regulations . . . [Springfield: Weaver, Shipman, 1875]. vi, 160 p. CtHT, DLC, ICN, MB, MWA. **1056**

School District No. Six. Permanent Regulations and By-laws, School District No. Six, Chicopee Falls, and a Catalogue of the School Library, with the Regulations for its Government. Chicopee, Mass. 1849. Springfield: G. W. Wilson, 1849. 23 p. MB. **1057**

Clinton

Bigelow Free Public Library. Catalogue of the Bigelow Free Public Library of the Town of Clinton. 1874. Clinton: W. J. Coulter, 1874. vii, 241 p. DLC, MB, NN. **1058**

Bigelow Library Association. Catalogue . . . 1853. 42 p. Cf. Rhees, p. 141. **1059**

Bigelow Library Association. Catalogue . . . Supplement . . . 1854. Cf. Rhees, p. 141 (also reporting suppl., 1855). **1060**

Bigelow Library Association. Catalogue of the Bigelow Library Association, Clinton, Mass. Incorporated June 19, 1852. Clinton: Printed at the Office of the Saturday Courant, 1861. xii, 148 p. ICU, MB, MH. **1061**

Bigelow Mechanics' Institute. Catalogue . . . 1850. Cf. Andrew E. Ford, *History of the Origin of the Town of Clinton, Massachusetts, 1653-1865* (Clinton, 1896), p. 411, stating the library contained 308 vol. **1062**

Bigelow Mechanics' Institute. Catalogue . . . 1852. 148 p. Cf. Cutter 345, Andrew E. Ford, *History of the Origin of the Town of Clinton, Massachusetts, 1653-1865* (Clinton, 1896), p. 411, stating the library contained 667 vol. **1063**

Concord

Charitable Library Society. Catalogue . . . 1805. Not in S & S. Cf. George B. Bartlett, *The Concord Guide Book*, Second Edition, Revised (Boston, 1880), pp. 92-93, stating the library contained 250 vol. May or may not be identical with the catalogue for 1808 cited in the *Ninth Report of the Free Public Library Commission of Massachusetts* (1899), p. 87. **1064**

Concord Free Public Library, for earlier entries, see Concord Town Library.

Concord Free Public Library. Additions to the Concord Free Public Library during the Six Months ending October 1, 1873. Boston: Tolman & White, 1873. 60 p. Concord Free Public Library, MB. **1065**

Concord Free Public Library. Catalogue of the Free Public Library of Concord, Mass. Jan. 1, 1875. Concord: Tolman & White, 1875. 470 p. DLC, ICN, MB, MBAt, MWA, N. **1066**

Concord Social Library. Catalogue of Concord Social Library. Concord, 1836. 23 p. Not in Rinderknecht. Concord Free Public Library, NN. **1067**

Concord Town Library. Catalogue of the Books belonging to the Concord Town Library. 1852. Concord: Middlesex Freeman Office, 1852. 20 p. Concord Free Public Library. **1068**

Concord Town Library. Catalogue of Books belonging to the Concord Town Library. 1855. Concord: Benjamin Tolman, 1855. 41 p. Concord Free Public Library, MB, MH. **1069**

Concord Town Library. Catalogue of Books belonging to the Concord Town Library. January, 1865. Concord: Benjamin Tolman, 1865. 137 p. Concord Free Public Library holds annual List of Books Added . . . for 1865-1868/69; MWA has 1865-67; MB has 1866. Concord Free Public Library, MH, MWA. **1070**

Concord Town Library, for later entries, see Concord Free Public Library.

Lenox Agricultural Library. Catalogue of Books in the Lenox Agricultural Library. Furnished by John Raynolds. Principal Office and Depository . . . Concord, Mass. . . . [n.p., 185-?]. broadside. For related broadsides, see entries 1156, 1173. MHi. **1071**

Middlesex Law Library Association. A Catalogue of Books belonging to the Middlesex Law Library Association. Concord: Herman Atwill, 1828. 10 p. Shoemaker 34135. MHi. **1072**

Stacy's Circulating Library. Catalogue of Books in Stacy's Circulating Library, likewise, Catalogue of Books, Stationery and Fancy Goods, for Sale by Albert Stacy, Concord, Mass. [Concord?, 185-?]. 24 p. Concord Free Public Library. **1073**

Stacy's Circulating Library. Catalogue of Books in Stacy's Circulating Library, also Catalogue of Books, Stationery and Fancy Goods, for Sale by Albert Stacy, Concord, Mass. [Concord]: Benjamin Tolman, 1860. 22, 12 p. Concord Free Public Library, MWA. **1074**

Cummington

Cummington Library. Catalogue of the Cummington Library. New York: Evening Post Steam Presses, 1873. 122 p. CU-A, DeU, DLC, MWelC. **1075**

Cummington Library. Supplementary Catalogue of the Cummington Library. Additions made 1873 and 1874. New York: Evening Post Steam Presses, 1875. 21 p. DLC. **1076**

Dalton

Dalton Library. Catalogue of the Dalton Library. March, 1873. Pittsfield: W. H. Phillips, 1874. 21 p. DLC. **1077**

Danvers

(for South Danvers, see Peabody)

Danvers Mechanic Institute. Catalogue of Books belonging to the Library of the Danvers Mechanic Institute. 1841. Salem: Register Press, 1841. viii, 29 p. Includes Act of incorporation, constitution, and list of members. Rinderknecht 41-1439. MPeHi. **1078**

Danvers Mechanic Institute. Catalogue of Books belonging to the Library of the Danvers Mechanic Institute. 1841. Salem: Register Press, 1841 [i.e. 1842]. viii, 33 p. "Additions to the Library of the Danvers Mechanic institute, 1842": pp. [30]-33. Includes Act of incorporation, constitution, and list of members. Not in Rinderknecht. MH-H, MSaE. **1079**

Danvers Mechanic Institute. Additions to the Library of the Danvers Mechanic Institute. 1843-44. [South Danvers: George R. Carlton, 1843-44]. 48 p. Rinderknecht 43-1426. MPeHi. **1080**

Danvers Mechanic Institute. Constitution, By-laws, Officers and Members of Danvers Mechanic Institute, with a Catalogue of Books, belonging to the Library. February 1st, 1846. Danvers: G. R. Carlton-Courier Press, 1846. 63 p. MSaE. **1081**

Danvers Mechanic Institute. Supplement containing the Additions to the Library of the Danvers Mechanic Institute to January, 1849. Boston, 1850. 16 p. MSaE. **1082**

First Congregational Church. Catalogue of the Sabbath School Library, First Congregational Church, Danvers, Mass. Boston: Alfred Mudge & Son, 1863. 19 p. MB.**1083**

First Universalist Church. Catalogue of the Library, of the First Universalist Sunday School, Danvers, Mass. Dec. 1, 1855. Salem: Printed at the Gazette Office, 1855. 22 p. MSaE. **1084**

Franklin Circulating Library. Catalogue of the Franklin Circulating Library . . . Salem: W. & S. B. Ives, 1834. 24 p. Conducted by Amos Trask, jun. Rinderknecht 24491. MB, MHi, MSaE, MWA, NNGr. **1085**

Peabody Institute, Danvers Branch, see under Peabody.

Second Congregational Church. Catalogue of the Library, belonging to the Sabbath School of the Second Congregational Church, Danvers. 1846. Danvers: G. R. Carlton, 1846. 34 p. MSaE. **1086**

Second Congregational Church. A Supplementary Catalogue of the Sabbath School Library, of the Second Congregational Society, Danvers. Boston: William C. Lears, 1853. 27 p. MSaE. **1087**

Dartmouth

Smith's Neck Union S. S. Library. Catalogue of Books in the Smith's Neck Union S. S. Library, Dartmouth. January 1st, 1873. [n.p., 1873]. 12 p. MNBedf. **1088**

Dedham

Bussey Social and Circulating Library. Catalogue of the Bussey Social and Circulating Library, Mill Village, Dedham. Dedham: H. Mann, 1837. 40 p. Not in Rinderknecht. MWA. **1089**

Dedham Evangelical Sabbath School Library. Catalogue of the Dedham Evangelical Sabbath School Library. [Dedham?, ca. 1834]. 11 p. Not in Rinderknecht. MWA. **1090**

Dedham Public Library. Catalogue of the Dedham Public Library. [Dedham: H. H. McQuillen, 1875]. 75 p. DLC, MWA. **1091**

First Parish. Catalogue of Books in the Library of the First Parish in Dedham. [Dedham, ca. 1828]. 7, [1] p. Not in Shoemaker. MWA. **1092**

First Parish. Catalogue of Books belonging to the Library of the First Parish. Dedham, 1860. 12 p. MWA. **1093**

First Parish. Catalogue of the Juvenile Library, First Parish, Dedham. [n.p., 1864]. 18 p. MB. **1094**

First Social Library. Extracts of the Bye-laws of the First Social Library in Dedham. [n.p., 183-?]. 4 p. "Catalogue of Books" on pp. 1-4. Not in Cooper, Bruntjen, or Rinderknecht. MWA. **1095**

Norfolk Circulating Library. Catalogue of the Norfolk Circulating Library . . . Dedham: H. & W. H. Mann, 1823. 28 p. Caption title: Catalogue of H. Mann & Sons' [sic] Circulating Library. Operated by Herman Mann and Samuel Chandler Mann. Not in Shoemaker. MWA. **1096**

Norfolk Circulating Library. Catalogue of the Norfolk Circulating Library, with Additions. Newly arranged by S. C. & E. Mann. October, 1833. [Dedham]: Dedham Patriot Press, 1833. 56 p., 3 p. of "Additions." On cover: Catalogue of a Valuable Circulating Library to be sold at Auction, on Wednesday and Thursday next, May 3 and 4 . . . comprising about 3000 Volumes . . . at J. L. Cunningham's Auction Room . . . Not in Bruntjen. DLC (with ms. corrections), MB. **1097**

Norfolk Law Library. A Catalogue of the Norfolk Law Library, Court House, Dedham, Nassachusetts. [Dedham], 1863. 44 p. MWA. **1098**

St. Paul's Church. Catalogue of Books in the Sunday School Library of St. Paul's Church, Dedham. Boston: J. E. Farwell, [186-?]. 16 p. MH (with ms. additions). **1099**

South Parish. Catalogue of the Social Circulating Library, in Dedham, South Parish, with the Proprietors' Names, and the Constitution of the Library. Boston: T. R. Marvin, 1844. 16 p. Rinderknecht 44-1889. No holdings given by Rinderknecht. **1100**

Deerfield

Second Social Library. Catalogue of Books in the Second Social Library, Deerfield, with the Bye Laws of the Company, and the Rules and Regulations under which Books are loaned from the Library. Walpole, N.H.: From the Press of Thomas & Thomas, by D. Newhall, 1803. 12 p. Not in S & S. Pocumtuck Valley Memorial Association Library, Deerfield, Mass. **1101**

Social Library. A Catalogue of Books in the Social Libary, Deerfield. Deerfield: Charles J. Newcomd [!], 1818. 12 p. S & S 43824. MA, Pocumtuck Valley Memorial Association Library, Deerfield, Mass. **1102**

Social Library. Catalogue . . . 1835. Not in Rinderknecht. Cf. George Sheldon, *A History of Deerfield, Massachusetts* (Deerfield, 1896), vol. 2, pp. [823]-24, stating the library contained 947 vol. **1103**

Dighton

Dighton Social Library. Catalogue and Regulations of the Dighton Social Library. Taunton: Daily Gazette Press, 1869. 28 p. MB, NN. **1104**

Dorchester

Boston Public Library. Dorchester Branch. List of Books, arranged by Authors, Titles, and Subjects. First Edition. March, 1875. [Boston, 1875]. 102 p. DLC, ICN, MB, MBAt, NN. **1105**

Boston Public Library. Dorchester Branch. First Supplemental List. August, 1875. [Boston, 1875]. 51 p. ICN. **1106**

Dorchester and Milton Circulating Library. Catalogue of the Dorchester and Milton Circulating Library. Dedham: Cox & Hutchins, 1854. 41 p. DLC, MB, MMilt. **1107**

Dorchester Athenaeum. Catalogue of Books of the Dorchester Athenaeum. 1857. Boston: McIntire & Moulton, 1857. 24 p. MWA. **1108**

Dorchester Athenaeum. Catalogue of Books of the Dorchester Athenaeum. Supplement No. 1. 1865. [n.p., 1865?]. 16 p. MWA. **1109**

Dorchester Athenaeum. Catalogue of Books of the Dorchester Athenaeum. 1870. Boston: Rand, Avery, & Frye, 1870. 85 p. DLC, MB (with ms. additions), MWA. **1110**

Dorchester Library. Rules and Orders of the Dorchester Library, with a Catalogue of the Books. September, MDCCCI. Boston: I. Thomas and E. T. Andrews, 1801. 12 p. S & S 50209. MWA. **1111**

Dorchester Library. Rules and Orders of the Dorchester Library, with a Catalogue of the Books. July, MDCCCVII. Boston: Belcher and Armstrong, 1807. 13 p. S & S 12459. CtY, MH (defective), MWA, NN. **1112**

First Church and Society. A Catalogue of the Social Religious Library of the First Church and Society in Dorchester. Boston: Minot Pratt, 1835. 16 p. Not in Rinderknecht. MWA. **1113**

First Church and Society. Catalogue of the Library of the First Parish Sunday School in Dorchester. April, 1863. Boston: John Wilson and Son, 1863. 29 p. MBAt. **1114**

Gardner Library Association. Catalogue of Books of the Gardner Library Association, with the By-laws, List of Members, &c. Boston: McIntire & Moulton, 1857. 30 p. MB. **1115**

Mattapan Library. Catalog of the Mattapan Library, Dorchester, Mass. Boston: David Clapp, 1853. 20 p. DeWint, MB, MWA. **1116**

Mattapan Library. Mattapan Library, Harrison Square, Dorchester. Boston: Prentiss, Sawyer, 1859. 32 p. MWA. **1117**

Mattapan Literary Association. A Catalogue of Books of the Mattapan Literary Association; with the Provisions of the Constitution and By-laws relating to the Library. Boston, 1853. 50 p. NNGr. **1118**

Mattapan Literary Association. Constitution and By-laws of the Mattapan Literary Association; with a List of the Officers and Members, and a Catalogue of the Library. Association founded April 18, 1848. Library Established 1852. Boston: David Clapp, 1857. 60 p. The library catalogue is on pp. [27]-60. Cutter 405 for a catalogue of 34 p. in 1857 is probably an analytical for this edition or a newly paginated reprint edition? MH, MHi, MWA. **1119**

St. Mary's Church. Catalogue of the Sunday School Books, belonging to St. Mary's

Church, Dorchester. Boston: Charles Stimpson, 1854. 16 p. MWA. **1120**

St. Mary's Church. Catalogue of the Sunday School Library of St. Mary's Church, Dorchester. September, 1858. Boston: David Clapp, 1858. 15 p. MHi. **1121**

St Mary's Church. Catalogue of the Sunday School Library, of St. Mary's Church, Dorchester. 1866. Boston: Alfred Mudge & Son, 1866. 23 p. MBAt. **1122**

Dover

Dover Library. Catalogue of Books in the Dover Library, with the Constitution for the Management and Regulation of said Library. Dedham: Ebenezer Fish, 1832. 16 p. Not in Bruntjen. MWA. **1123**

East Boston

(see also Boston)

East Boston Library Association. Catalogue of the East Boston Library Association, with the Constitution and Act of Incorporation. East Boston: Ledger Press, Tyler & Blanchard, 1856. 20 p. MBAt. **1124**

Sumner Library Association. Catalogue of the Books of the Sumner Library Association, East Boston. Boston: Spooner and Cobb's Press, 1863. 52 p. MB (2 copies; one is defective and one has ms. additions), MWA. **1125**

East Bridgewater

East Bridgewater Library Association. Catalogue of Books belonging to the East Bridgewater Library Association. East Bridgewater: J. Burrell, 1871. 21 p. DLC. **1126**

East Walpole

East Walpole Library. Catalogue of the East Walpole Library. 1872. Boston: Wright & Potter, 1872. 15 p. DLC. **1127**

East Walpole Library. Supplementary Catalogue . . . 1875. 7 p. Cf. Cutter 967. **1128**

Easthampton

Public Library Association. Catalogue of the Public Library Association of Easthampton,

Mass. East Hampton: F. A. Bartlett, 1871. 114 p. DLC holds undated suppl. (29 p.), ca. 1874, per Bureau of Education date stamp, Dec. 2, 1874. DLC, MB. **1129**

Fairhaven

First Congregational Church. Catalogue of Books in the Library of the Sabbath School of the First Congregational Church, Fairhaven. 1869. [n.p., 1869]. 16 p. MNBedf. **1130**

Fall River

Fall River Athenaeum. Catalogue of the Fall River Athenaeum Library, with an Appendix containing the Rules and Regulations of the Library, By-laws . . . etc. A List of Officers of Proprietors. Fall River: Hammond and Earl, 1838. 56 p. Rinderknecht 50270. MA, MBAt, RPAt. **1131**

Fall River Athenaeum. Catalogue of the Fall River Athenaeum Library, containing the Rules, Regulations, and By-laws of the Institution, and a List of its Officers. Boston: Damrell & Moore, 1855. 36 p. DLC. **1132**

Fall River Public Library. Catalogue of the Public Library, of the City of Fall River. Established 1861. Fall River: Almy & Milne's Steam Press, 1861. 100 p. ICU holds Appendix, Oct. 1861; MB and MF hold Appendix for Oct. 1861 (12 p.), Nov. 1863 (39 p.), Jan. 1868 (53 p.), MF holds Appendix for April 1870 (50 p.). ICU, MB, MF. **1133**

Fall River Public Library. Catalogue of the Public Library of the City of Fall River. Established 1861. Boston: Rand, Avery, 1874. xii, 383 p. Compiled by C. M. Smith and Geo. W. Rankin. DLC, MB, MBAt, MF, NhD, N, NNGr, RU, Salem Athenaeum. **1134**

Fall River Public Library. Catalogue of the Public Library of the City of Fall River. Established 1861. Appendix No. 1. Boston: Rand, Avery, 1875. 96 p. DLC, MB, MBAt, MWA, N. **1135**

Fall River Social Library. Catalogue of Books. [n.p., 1826?]. 9-18 p. Not in Shoemaker. MWA. **1136**

Falmouth

First Congregational Church. Catalogue of
Titles and of Authors of the Church Library
of the First Congregational Church of
Falmouth. Boston: Bazin and Chandler,
1859. 47 p. DLC.   **1137**

First Congregational Church. Catalogue of
the Library of the Sabbath School of the
First Congregational Church in Falmouth.
New Bedford: E. Anthony & Sons, 1871.
12 p. MNBedf.   **1138**

Fitchburg

Athenaeum Library. Catalogue of Books in
the Athenaeum Library, in Fitchburg, Mass.
Fitchburg: E. &. J. F. D. Garfield, 1854. 20 p.
MFi, MWA.   **1139**

Calvinistic Congregational Society. Catalogue
of Books of the Sabbath School Library,
connected with Calvinistic Congregational
Society, Fitchburg, Mass. Fitchburg: J.
Garfield, 1840. 12 p. Not in Rinderknecht.
MWA.   **1140**

Calvinistic Congregational Society. Catalogue
of Books, in the Sabbath School Library,
connected with Calvinistic Cong. Society, in
Fitchburg, Mass. Fitchburg: J. Garfield,
1843. 8 p. Not in Rinderknecht. MWA.
                                         1141

Calvinistic Congregational Society. Catalogue
of the Calvinistic Congregational Sabbath
School Library in Fitchburg. July, 1857.
Fitchburg: E. & J. F. D. Garfield, 1857. 28 p.
MWA.   **1142**

Fitchburg Public Library. Catalogue of the
Fitchburg Public Library, Fitchburg, Mass.
Fitchburg: E. & J. F. D. Garfield, 1859. 50 p.
MB, MBAt, MH, MWA.   **1143**

Fitchburg Public Library. Catalogue of the
Public Library, Fitchburg, Mass. Established
1859. Fitchburg: Caleb C. Curtis, 1862. 35 p.
MB holds annual suppl., 1864, 1866-67,
1869; Cutter 696 reports suppl., 1871. MB.
                                         1144

Fitchburg Public Library. Catalogue of the
Public Library. Fitchburg: Reveille Steam
Printing Works, 1873. 100 p. DLC holds
suppl., 1874; NNGr holds suppl., 1874-80.
DLC, MWA, NNGr.   **1145**

South Gardner Social Library. Catalogue of
Books in the South Gardner Library,
February 15, 1867. Instituted November 8,
1841. Fitchburg: Printed at the Sentinel
Office, [1867?]. 28 p. ICN.   **1146**

Worcester North District Medical Society. By-
laws, List of Members, and Catalogue of
Books, of the Wor. No. Dist. Medical
Society. Established 1858. Fitchburg: Rev-
eille Printing Works, 1874. 23 p.   DLC,
DNLM.   **1147**

Foxborough

Baptist Sabbath School. Catalogue of Books in
the Baptist Sabbath School Library, Foxboro'.
Boston: J. M. Hewes, 1868. 11 p. MWA.
                                         1148

Baptist Sabbath School. Catalogue of the Baptist
Sabbath School Library, Foxboro'. Boston:
William H. Thomas, 1872. 23 p. MWA.   **1149**

Boyden Library. A List of Books. December,
1870. [n.p., 1870?]. 21 p. MWA.   **1150**

Boyden Public Library. Catalogue of the
Boyden Public Library, Foxboro', Mass.
Foxboro': Thomas's Printing Office, 1872.
71 p. MWA.   **1151**

Foxborough Social Library. Catalogue of the
Foxborough Social Library. Edson Carpenter, Librarian. [n.p., ca. 1854]. 9 p. MWA.
                                         1152

Franklin First Social Library, see entry 1153.

Franklin Library. [A Catalogue of those Books
in Franklin Library which belong to the
Town . . . n.p., 1812]. 7 p. Catalogue of the
First Social Library on pp. [5]-7. S & S
25451. MWA (defective).   **1153**

Franklin Library. Catalogue of Books in the
Franklin Library. Founded A.D. 1786, by
Benjamin Franklin, L.L.D. Re-organized
Dec. 1871. Franklin: Rogers & Baker, 1871.
10 p. CtY, Franklin Public Library.   **1154**

Franklin Library Association. Catalogue of Books
of the Franklin Library Association. February,
1875. Boston: Rockwell and Churchill, 1875.
80 p. MWA holds suppl., Dec. 1875 (9 p.). DLC,
Franklin Public Library, MWA.   **1155**

Freetown (see Assonet).

Georgetown

Georgetown Agricultural Library. Catalogue of Books in the Georgetown Agricultural Library. Supplied by John Raynolds . . . Concord, Mass. . . . [n.p., 1859?]. broadside. For related broadsides, see entries 1071, 1173. MSaE. **1156**

Georgetown Agricultural and Social Library. Catalogue of Books in the Georgetown Agricultural and Social Library Association. [n.p., 1860?]. 12 p. MSaE. **1157**

Georgetown Agricultural and Social Library. Catalogue of Agricultural and Social Library of the Town of Georgetown. Organized 1860. Salem: Geo. W. Pease, 1863. 43 p. MSaE holds Appendix #2 (pp. 53-59). MSaE. **1158**

Georgetown Peabody Library. Catalogue of the Georgetown Peabody Library. Salem: George W. Pease, 1869. 159 p. DLC and MSaE hold four suppl., [1870?-73?]. DLC, Georgetown Peabody Library, MB, MSaE, MWA. **1159**

Globe Village

Hamilton Free Library. Catalogue of the Hamilton Free Library . . . Southbridge: Morse & Whitaker, 1873. 76 p. DLC, MH. **1160**

Gloucester

Procter Public Library. Catalogue of the Procter Public Library. Established January 1, 1851, by Francis Procter. Gloucester: Procter Brothers, 1875. 173, [1] p. DLC. **1161**

Sawyer Free Library. Catalogue of the Sawyer Free Library, Gloucester, Mass. Gloucester: John S. E. Rogers, 1872. 160 p. Rules and regulations on pp. [161-62]. DLC, M, MB, MH, MWA, N **1162**

Grafton

Free Public Library. Catalogue of Books, and the By-laws of the Free Public Library and Reading Room of the Town of Grafton. Boston: L. B. Eilder, 1868. 63 p. M, MB. **1163**

Free Public Library. Addenda to Public Library . . . [Grafton?, 1871]. 31 p. DLC, M. **1164**

Free Public Library. Second Addenda . . . 1874. [Grafton?, 1874]. 24 p. DLC, M. **1165**

Unitarian Congregational Society. Catalogue of the Sunday School Library of the Unitarian Congregational Society, Grafton, Mass. 1873. Worcester: Charles E. Nye, [1873?]. 18 p. MWA. **1166**

Great Barrington

Great Barrington Library Association. Catalogue . . . 1862. 19 p. Cf. Cutter 478. **1167**

Greenfield

Greenfield Library Association. Catalogue of the Library of the Greenfield Library Association . . . 1869. Greenfield: Franklin Job Printing Office, 1869. ix, 81 p. DLC. **1168**

Greenfield Library Association. Supplement to Catalogue. Greenfield Library Association . . . 1874. Greenfield: Franklin Job Printing Office, 1874. 23 p. DLC. **1169**

Greenfield Social Library. Greenfield Social Library Catalogue. Jan. 1, 1835. Greenfield: Ths. Prince, [1835]. 8 p. Not in Rinderknecht. Pocumtuck Valley Memorial Association Library, Deerfield, Mass. **1170**

Groton

First Parish Church. A Catalogue of the First Parish Library, Groton. Instituted 1841. Boston: Albert Morgan, 1842. 8 p. Not in Rinderknecht. Groton Public Library. **1171**

First Parish Church. A Catalogue of the First Parish Library, Groton. Instituted 1841. Lowell: Stearns & Taylor, 1844. 12 p. Rinderknecht 44-2834. DLC, Groton Public Library, MeHi, MB, MH, MHi, MWA, N (misc. pamphlet box, 018.1), NHi, NNGr, PPL. **1172**

Groton Agricultural Library. Catalogue of Books in the Groton Agricultural Library. Supplied by John Raynolds . . . Concord, Mass. . . . [n.p., 1858?]. broadside. For

related broadsides, see entries 1071, 1156.
MHi (photostat copy).   **1173**

Groton Public Library. Catalogue of the
Groton Public Library, with the By-laws and
Regulations. Groton: Geo. H. Brown, 1855.
26 p. CtY, DLC, Groton Public Library, ICN,
IU,M, MB, MBAt, MHi, MWA, Nh, N, NRU,
ViU, WU (School of Library and Informa-
tion Studies).   **1174**

Groton Public Library. Catalogue of the
Groton Public Library, at Groton, Mass.
Groton Junction: Henry L. Brown, 1862.
53 p. ICN, MB, MWA and N hold suppl.,
1870 ([4] p.). DLC, Groton Public Library,
MA, MB, MBAt, MWA, N, PPL, ViU. **1175**

Groton Public Library. Catalogue . . . 1868.
Cf. Sabin, vol. 7, p. 470. MB (per Sabin).
1176

Groton Public Library. Catalogue of the
Groton Public Library, at Groton, Mass.
Ayer: J. H. Turner, 1875. 81 p. DLC, Groton
Public Library, ICN, M, MA, MB, MWA, Nh,
WU (School of Library and Information
Studies).   **1177**

Lawrence Academy. Catalogue of the Library
of Lawrence Academy, Groton, Mass. 1850.
Lowell: S. J. Varney, 1850. 206, [1] p.
Preface signed by James Mason. In many
libraries.   **1178**

Union Church and Society. Catalogue of the
Congregational Library, of the Union
Church and Society, Groton. [Groton?,
185-?]. 16 p. MB, MHi, MWA.   **1179**

Unitarian Society. Catalogue of Unitarian
Sabbath School Library. March, 1869. Groton
Junction: John H. Turner, 1869. 12 p. Groton
Public Library, MB (16 p. ed.), MH.   **1180**

Groton Centre

North Middlesex Circulating Library. Catalogue of North Middlesex Circulating
Library, Groton Centre, Mass. Charles
Woolley, Jr., Proprietor. Groton Junction:
John H. Turner, 1866. 16 p. Copy at MH-H
includes "New Books added to Woolley's
Circulating Library, January 1st, 1867"
(4 p.). Groton Public Library, MH-H
(entered under: Woolley, Charles).   **1181**

Woolley's Circulating Library, see entry 1181.

Groton Junction, see Ayer.

Harvard

Harvard Public Library. Catalogue of the
Public Library of the Town of Harvard.
January 1st, 1868. Groton Junction: John H.
Turner, 1868. 20 p. MB, MWA, NNGr
(uncat.), WU (School of Library and
Information Studies).   **1182**

Haverhill

Haverhill Athenaeum. Catalogue of the
Library of the Haverhill Athenaeum, at
Haverhill, Mass. Incorporated February,
1852. Haverhill: E. H. Safford, 1853.
23, 11 p. DLC, MWA (23 p. section only).
1183

Haverhill Athenaeum. Catalogue. [n.p.,
1856?]. 36 p. MHa copy includes undated
suppl. (11 p.). MHa (defective without title
page).   **1184**

Haverhill Circulating Library. Catalogue . . .
1855. 36 p. Operated by O. W. Flanders. Cf.
Rhees, p. 145.   **1185**

Haverhill Library. Catalogue of Haverhill
Library. [n.p., 180-?]. 16 p. Not in S & S.
MHa.   **1186**

Haverhill Library Association. Catalogue of the
Haverhill Library Association, Haverhill,
Mass., to which is added an Historical Sketch
of the Library, the Constitution, Names of
Shareholders, List of Officers, etc. Compiled
by Geo. W. Chase, Librarian. Haverhill: E. G.
Frothingham, 1860. 112 p. MSaE holds
undated suppl. (18 p.). MSaE.   **1187**

Haverhill Social Library. Catalogue of Books
in Haverhill Social Library. January, 1821.
[n.p., 1821]. 15 p. Shoemaker 5560. MHa,
MSaE.   **1188**

Hinsdale

Public Library Association of Hinsdale.
Catalogue of the Public Library Association
of Hinsdale. Springfield: Samuel Bowles,
1868. 57 p. MB.   **1189**

Holbrook

Holbrook Public Library. Catalogue of the
Holbrook Public Library, Holbrook, Mass.
Boston: A. Williams, 1874. ii, 133 p. DLC.
1190

Holliston

Holliston Circulating Library. Catalogue of Books in the Holliston Circulating Library . . . Plimpton & Clark, Proprietors. Holliston, 1863. 17 p. MWA.   **1191**

Parker & Plimpton's Circulating Library. Regulations and Catalogue of Parker & Plimpton's Circulating Library, Holliston, Mass. 1854. [n.p., 1854]. 11 p. MH-H.
1192

Plimpton's Select Circulating Library. Catalogue of Books in Plimpton's Select Circulating Library . . . Holliston, 1861. 12 p. MWA.   **1193**

Holyoke

Holyoke Public Library. Catalogue of Books of the Holyoke Public Library, Holyoke, Mass. Holyoke: Transcript Printing House, 1875. 2 pt. in 1 vol. DLC, MBAt.   **1194**

Hopkinton

Congregational Sabbath School. Catalogue of Congregational Sabbath School Library, Hopkinton. May 1, 1872. Boston: Alfred Mudge & Son, 1872. 10 p. MWA.   **1195**

Young Men's Christian Association. Catalogue of the Library of the Young Men's Christian Association, Hopkinton, Mass. . . . Hopkinton: D. B. Ryder, 1874. 25 p. DLC.
1196

Hubbardston

Hubbardston Public Library. Catalogue of the Hubbardston Public Library . . . Gardner: A. G. Bushnell, [1873]. 70 p. DLC.   **1197**

Hudson

Hudson Public Library. Catalogue of the Hudson Public Library, Hudson, Massachusetts. Established 1868. Boston: Geo. C. Rand & Avery, 1868. 29 p. DLC holds suppl. #2-4, ca. 1871-74. DLC (with blank pages for additions), MB.   **1198**

Hyde Park

Hyde Park Public Library. Catalogue of the Hyde Park Public Library. 1874. Hyde Park:
Norfolk County Gazette Office, 1874. 108, [1] p. DLC, MB, N (with blank leaves for additions).   **1199**

Ipswich

First Congregational Church. Catalogue of Books belonging to the Sabbath School Library connected with the First Congregational Church, Ipswich. Salem: Register Press, 1860. 14 p. MSaE.   **1200**

Ipswich Public Library. Laws for the Regulation of the Ipswich Public Library. Instituted 1791. With a List of the Subscribers and a Catalogue of the Books. Ipswich: F. Pawsey, 1836. 51 p. Rinderknecht 38213. CtY.   **1201**

Ipswich Public Library. List of Books in Ipswich Public Library. 1869. Boston: L. Rhodes, 1869. 39 p. DLC.   **1202**

Ipswich Public Library. Catalogue of the Free Public Library, Ipswich, Mass. Boston: Alfred Mudge & Son, 1875. 168 p. "Catalogue of Books presented by Daniel Treadwell of Cambridge, Mass." on pp. [151]-68. DLC, N.   **1203**

Jamaica Plain

Eliot Library Association. Catalogue of Books belonging to the Eliot Library Association, Jamaica Plain, Mass., with the Act of Incorporation and the By-laws. Boston: John Wilson & Son, 1858. viii, 39 p. MHi, RPB.   **1204**

Unitarian Church. Catalogue of the Jamaica Plain Unitarian Sabbath School Library. June, 1857. Boston: Hollis & Gunn's Press, 1857. 24 p. NcD.   **1205**

Unitarian Church. Catalogue. [Boston: John Wilson and Son, 186-?]. 34 p. MBAt (defective without title page).   **1206**

Lakeville

Lakeville Library Association. Lakeville Library Association, Lakeville, Mass. [n.p., 187-?]. 11, [1] p. MNBedf.   **1207**

Lancaster

Lancaster Library Club. Catalogue of Lancaster Library Club. [Lancaster?, 1854]. 12 p. DLC (with ms. additions), MWA.   **1208**

Lancaster Town Library. Catalogue of the Lancaster Town Library. Clinton: E. Ballard, 1865. vii, 33, [1] p. DLC, MB, MBSi, MWA, NNGr.   **1209**

Lancaster Town Library. Catalogue of the Lancaster Town Library. 1868. Clinton: Wm. J. Coulter, [1868] vii, 108 p. DLC and MWA copies include undated suppl. (31 p.). "List of Books added . . ." appears in the *Report of the Committee of the Lancaster Town Library* for 1872-75, etc. DLC, M, MB, MWA.   **1210**

Lawrence

Franklin Library Association. Catalogue . . . 1848. 14 p. Cf. Jewett, p. 37.   **1211**

Franklin Library Association. The Act of Incorporation, of the Franklin Library Association, at Lawrence, Mass., with the Revised Constitution and By-laws, of said Institution. Incorporated, April, 1847. Lawrence: J. F. C. Hayes, 1855. 46, [4] p. "Catalogue of Books contained in the Franklin Library . . ." on pp. [17]-46. MSaE, MWA, NN.   **1212**

Free Public Library. Catalogue of the Free Public Library of the City of Lawrence. 1873. Lawrence: Geo. S. Merrill & Crocker, 1873. vii, 341 p. MB holds suppl. Bulletin, #1-[35]; June 15, 1873-Oct. 1, 1882; MBSi holds #1-4; MSaE holds #1-4, 7, 13-17, 19-25, 27-34, issued by the Lawrence Public Library. DLC, ICU, M, MB, MBAt, MBSi, MH, MSaE, MWA, Nh, N, NB, Salem Athenaeum.**1213**

Pacific Mills Library. Catalogue of the Pacific Mills Library, Lawrence, Mass. Opened August 21, 1854. Boston: Damrell and Moore, 1855. 101 p. DLC and MWA copies contain 1st and 2d suppl. included in pagination (184 p.). CtHT, DLC, MWA.   **1214**

Pacific Mills Library. Bulletin . . . [Boston?]. DLC (Sept. 1868-June 1874, incomplete).   **1215**

Lee

Lee Public Library. Catalogue of the Lee Public Library, Lee, Mass., 1874. Lee: Gleaner Printing Establishment, 1874. 44, [2] p. DLC.   **1216**

Leicester

Leicester Academy. Social Fraternity. An Alphabetical Catalogue of Books in the Library belonging to the Social Fraternity of Leicester Academy. July 29, 1816. Leicester: Hori Brown, 1816. broadside. Not in S & S. MStuO, MWA.   **1217**

Leicester Public Library. Catalogue of the Leicester Public Library, with the Regulations for its use. Worcester: Henry J. Howland, [1861 or 62]. 40 p. MWA. **1218**

Leicester Public Library. Catalogue of the Leicester Public Library, with the Regulations for its use. Second Edition. Worcester: Chas. Hamilton, 1869. 48 p. MB, MWA.   **1219**

Leicester Public Library. Catalogue of the Leicester Public Library, with the Regulations for its use. Third Publication. Worcester: Charles Hamilton, 1873. 74, [1] p. DLC, MB, MWA, N.   **1220**

Lenox

Lenox Library. Rules, By-laws, and Catalogue. January 1st, 1855. Lee: French & Royce, 1855. 20 p. ICJ, IU.   **1221**

Leominster

Free Public Library. Catalogue . . . 1854. 88 p. Cf. Cutter 368.   **1222**

Free Public Library. Catalogue of the Leominster Public Library. Fitchburg: C. C. Curtis, 1864. 55 p. MBSi.   **1223**

Free Public Library. Catalogue of the Free Public Library, Leominster. Worcester: Charles Hamilton, [ca. 1871]. vii, 180 p. DLC and MWA hold 1st suppl., ca. 1872 (32 p.), and 2d suppl., ca. 1874 (34 p.). DLC, M, MB (cataloguing gives date as [1864]), MWA.   **1224**

Lexington

Cary Library. Catalogue of the Cary Library in Lexington, Mass. Established, 1868. Boston: T. R. Marvin & Son, 1869. 28 p. MLex has suppl. "Catalogue of Books added April 17, 1869" (4 p.). MHi, MLex.   **1225**

Cary Library. Catalogue of the Cary Library in Lexington, Mass. Boston: T. R. Marvin & Son, 1871. 47 p. DLC holds suppl. catalogue of books added from July 1, 1871 to Jan. 1, 1873, and a catalogue of books added during 1873. DLC, MWA, WU (School of Library and Information Studies). **1226**

Cary Library. Catalogue of the Cary Library, in Lexington, Mass. Established 1868. 1875. Boston: Frank Wood, 1875. 64 p. MB, MLex. **1227**

Lexington Social Library. Catalogue of Books in the Lexington Social Library. January, 1831. Boston: Munroe & Francis, 1831. 4 p. Bruntjen 7965. MH, MLex. **1228**

Lowell

City Library. Catalogue of the City Library, Lowell, Mass. Established May 20, 1844. Lowell: Stone & Huse, 1861. 411, [1] p. DLC, M, MA, MB, MBAt, MH, MWA, NN, Salem Athenaeum. **1229**

City Library. Catalogue of the City Library, Lowell, Mass. Supplement to the Catalogue. Lowell: Knapp & Morey, 1861?- DLC (1861?, 1872, 1877), MB (1869, 1872, 1877), MH (1869). **1230**

City Library. Catalogue of the City Library, Lowell, Mass. Lowell: Stone & Huse, 1873. xii, 373 p. DLC, MWA. **1231**

City School Library. Catalogue of the City School Library, Lowell, Mass. Established May 20, 1844. Lowell: Stearns & Taylor, 1845. 66 p. Jewett, p. 37, notes four annual suppl. MH (with undated suppl., 8 p.). **1232**

City School Library. Fourth Supplement to the Catalogue of the City School Library. November, 1848. Lowell: James Akinson, [1848]. 28 p. NNGr. **1233**

City School Library. Catalogue of the City School Library, Lowell, Mass. Established May 20, 1844. Lowell: S. J. Varney, 1853. 154 p. Cutter 352 records "Addenda to 1854, 8 pp. of slips." DLC, KU, MBAt, MWA. **1234**

City School Library. Catalogue of the City School Library, Lowell, Mass. Established May 20, 1844. First Supplement. Lowell: S. J. Varney, 1855. 16 p. DLC, MWA. **1235**

City School Library. Catalogue of the City School Library, Lowell, Mass. Established May 20, 1844. Lowell: S. N. Merrill, 1858. v, 214 p. DLC, M, MA, MB, MBAt, MH, NN. **1236**

First Unitarian Society. Catalogue of Books of the Parish Library. Lowell: S. J. Varney, 1854. 40 p. DLC, N. **1237**

Lowell Circulating Library. Catalogue of Books, contained in the Lowell Circulating Library, connected with the Lowell Bookstore, Tyler's Building . . . Conducted by Stevens & Co. . . . Lowell: Stevens & Co., [1834?]. 76 p. Not in Rinderknecht. MB. **1238**

Lowell Circulating Library. Catalogue of Books contained in Lowell Circulating Library, connected with the Central Bookstore . . . conducted by Powers, Bagley & Co. Lowell: Stearns & Taylor, 1848. 83 p. NNGr. **1239**

Lowell Circulating Library. Catalogue. [Lowell?, ca. 1856]. 32 p. MWA. **1240**

Middlesex Mechanic Association. A Catalogue of the Library of the Middlesex Mechanic Association, at Lowell, Mass., with the Act of Incorporation, and the Constitution and By-laws of said Institution. Lowell: Leonard Huntress, 1840. 168 p. Rinderknecht 40-4633. DeU, MB, MBAt, MH, MWA, MnU, MStuO, NN, NNGr, PPL. **1241**

Middlesex Mechanic Association. Supplement to the Catalogue of the Library of the Middlesex Mechanic Association. July, 1846. Lowell: Joel Taylor, 1846. 22 p. MWA. **1242**

Middlesex Mechanic Association. Catalogue . . . 1851. 32 p. Cf. Cutter 341. **1243**

Middlesex Mechanic Association. A Catalogue of the Library of the Middlesex Mechanic Association, at Lowell, Mass., with the Act of Incorporation, and the Constitution and By-laws of said Institution. Lowell: S. J. Varney, 1853. 165, [1] p. DLC, MAnHi, MLowU, MWA, RPB. **1244**

Middlesex Mechanic Association. Supplementary Catalogue of the Library of the

Middlesex Mechanic Association. Lowell: Daily Courier Steam Press, 1856. 28 p. DLC, MLowU.   **1245**

Middlesex Mechanics' Association. Catalogue of the Middlesex Mechanics' Association, with the Charter, By-laws, Rules of the Library and Reading-room, Historical Sketch of the Association, &c. Lowell: Vox Populi Book Press, 1860. 299, [1] p. DLC, MB, MBAt, MH, MHi, MLowU, MWA, NN, NNC, OCl, PP.   **1246**

St. Anne's Church. The Rector's Library of St. Anne's Church, Lowell, Mass. Boston: James B. Dow, 1845. 7 p. DLC, NHi. **1247**

St. Anne's Church. Catalogue . . . Sunday School Library. DLC (lost).   **1248**

Worthen Street Methodist Episcopal Church. Catalogue of the Sunday School Library of the Worthen Street, M.E. Church, Lowell, Mass. Lowell: B. H. Penhallow, 1847. 20 p. MnU.   **1249**

Lunenburg

Lunenburg Philomathean Society. Constitution and By-laws of the Lunenburg Philomathean Society, together with a Catalogue of Books in the Library, and Rules for its Regulation. Fitchburg: E. & J. F. D. Garfield, 1855. 12 p. MWA.   **1250**

Lunenburg Town Library. Catalogue of Books in the Lunenburg Town Library. Established, 1852. June, 1868. Fitchburg: Fitchburg Sentinel Office, [1868]. 30 p. MB, MWA (with ms. additions).   **1251**

Lunenburg Town Library. Catalogue of Books, in the Lunenburg Town Library. Established 1852. July, 1875. Fitchburg: Piper & Boutelle, 1875. 41 p. DLC, MWA.   **1252**

Lynn

Free Public Library. Catalogue of the Free Public Library, Lynn, Mass. Boston: A. Mudge & Son, 1863. vii, 181 p. DLC, ICU, MB, MBAt, MLy, MSaE, N, ViU.   **1253**

Free Public Library. A Supplement to the Catalogue of the Free Public Library, Lynn, Mass. Lynn: Thos. P. Nichols, 1868. 111 p.

DLC and MB hold suppl. Bulletin, #1-4; 1869-[73]; MLy holds #1-9; 1869-May 1882, etc., to 1921. DLC, MB, MLy, MSaE, N.
1254

Lynn Library Association. Catalogue of the Library of the Lynn Library Association. Incorporated, March 24, 1855. Lynn: W. W. Kellogg, 1856. xi, 84 p. DLC, MSaE (copy 2 has ms. notes).   **1255**

Malden

Boston Rubber Shoe Company. Library of the Boston Rubber Shoe Company, Malden, Mass. Boston: Alfred Mudge & Son, 1873. 37 p. MB, MWA.   **1256**

Universalist Church. Catalogue of Books in the Library of the Universalist Sabbath School, Malden, Mass. 1866. Boston: C. C. P. Moody, 1866. 24 p. MWA.   **1257**

Manchester

Manchester Public Library. Catalogue of the Manchester Public Library, Manchester, Mass. Gloucester: Advertiser Office, 1871. 46 p. DLC holds 1st-2d suppl. DLC, MB.
1258

Mansfield

Baptist Church. Catalogue of Library belonging to Baptist Sabbath School, Mansfield, Mass. 1867. Providence: A. Crawford Greene, 1867. 12 p. MWA.   **1259**

Marblehead

First Baptist Church. Catalogue of the Sunday School Library, of the First Baptist Church, Marblehead, Mass. Salem: T. J. Hutchinson, 1869. 16 p. MSaE.   **1260**

Marblehead School Library. Catalogue of Marblehead School Library. Boston: William B. Fowle & Nahum Capen, 1845. 24 p. MSaE, MWA.   **1261**

St. Michael's Church. Catalogue of the Sunday School Library of St. Michael's Church, Marblehead. Salem: Ives and Pease, 1860. 12 p. MWA.   **1262**

Marion

Marion Congregational Church. Marion Congregational Sabbath-School Library. New Bedford: E. Anthony & Sons, 1870. 12 p. MNBedf.					**1263**

Marion Congregational Church. Library of the Marion Congregational Bible School. [New Bedford?, 187-?]. 11, [1] p. MNBedf.					**1264**

Marlborough

Marlborough Public Library. Catalogue of the Marlborough Public Library. Established 1870 . . . Worcester: Charles Hamilton, 1871. 78 p. MWA holds suppl., July 1871-Sept. 1872 (31 p.). MB, MWA.					**1265**

Unitarian Society. Catalogue of the Parish Library of the Second Parish in Marlborough. Boston: J. Wilson, 1849. 16 p. DLC.					**1266**

Unitarian Society. Supplement to the Catalogue of the Parish Library of the Second Parish in Marlborough. Boston: J. Wilson & Son, 1852. 8 p. DLC.					**1267**

Unitarian Society. Catalogue of Books of the Parish Library of the Unitarian Society . . . Cambridge: J. Wilson and Son, 1873. 45 p. DLC, MB.					**1268**

Mattapoisett

Congregational Church. Catalogue of Books belonging to the Congregational Sabbath-School, Mattapoisett. Aug. 1, 1860. New Bedford: Standard Steam Printing-House, 1860. 15, [1] p. MNBedf.					**1269**

Universalist Church. Catalogue of Books in the Mattapoisett Universalist Sabbath-School Library, together with the Rules for the Legislation of the same. New Bedford: Standard Steam Printing-House, 1860. 12 p. MNBedf.					**1270**

Medfield

Library Society. A Catalogue of Books, together with the Constitution of the Incorporated Library Society in Medfield, and the Names of the Proprietors. Dedham: Herman Mann, 1810. 18 p. S & S 20708. MBedHi.					**1271**

Medfield Social Library. Medfield Library. [Dedham: Dedham Gazette Office, 1816]. 24 p. Contains a history of the library, its constitution, a list of the proprietors, and a catalogue. S & S 38211. MdHi, WHi, WU (School of Library and Information Studies).					**1272**

Second Social Library. A Catalogue of the Second Social Library of Medfield. Boston: W. W. Clapp, 1828. 32 p. Not in Shoemaker. MWA.					**1273**

Medford

Medford Public Library. Catalogue of the Public Library of the Town of Medford. 1862. Boston: W. F. Brown, [1862]. viii, 55 p. MB.					**1274**

Medford Public Library. Catalogue of the Public Library of the Town of Medford. 1867. Boston: W. F. Brown, [1867?]. 89 p. MB.					**1275**

Medford Public Library. Catalogue of the Public Library, of the Town of Medford. September 1, 1871. Cambridge: Welch, Bigelow, 1871. 210 p. On cover: 1872. MB holds suppl., Aug. 1873. DLC, MB, MBAt, MH, N.					**1276**

Medford Social Library. Catalogue . . . 1827. Not in Shoemaker. Cf. M.E.F. Sargent "The Evolution of the Medford Public Library," *Medford Historical Register* 2 (1899): 81.					**1277**

Medford Social Library. Catalogue . . . 1837. Not in Rinderknecht. Cf. M.E.F. Sargent "The Evolution of the Medford Public Library," *Medford Historical Register* 2 (1899): 81-82, indicating library held 695 vol.					**1278**

Medford Tufts Library. Catalogue of Books, belonging to the Medford Tufts Library. 1856. Boston: J. M. Usher, 1856. 36 p. MB.					**1279**

Medway

Dean Library Association. Catalogue of Books, and By-laws of the Dean Library Association of Medway. Founded by Dr. Oliver Dean, of Franklin. Incorporated Mar. 1860. Boston: Watson's Press, 1871. 35 p. DLC holds suppl., 1873 (4 p.) and 1874 (5 p.). DLC.					**1280**

West Parish Library. Constitution of the Library, with a Catalogue of the Books. Dedham, 1817. 8 p. S & S 41398. MBC.
1281

Melrose

Melrose Public Library. Catalogue of the Melrose Public Library, Melrose, Mass. 1871. Boston: Alfred Mudge & Son, 1871. 49 p. IU, MB, MWA.
1282

Melrose Public Library. Catalogue of the Melrose Public Library, Melrose, Mass. Established 1871. Boston: T. W. Ripley, 1875. 82 p. DLC, MB, MWA, N.
1283

Methuen

Public Library. Catalogue of the Public Library of Methuen, Mass. Lawrence: G. S. Merrill & Crocker, 1874. 22 p. DLC holds Bulletin #1, Books added May, 1874-May, 1875 (11 p.). DLC.
1284

Middleboro, see Middleborough.

Middleborough

First Parish. Catalogue of Books in the First Parish Sunday School Library, Middleborough. Middleborough: James M. Coombs, 1869. 11, [1] p. MNBedf.
1285

Middleborough Social Library. Catalogue of the Middleborough Social Library. Founded 1832. Taunton: Edmund Anthony, 1848. 15 p. CSmH.
1286

Robinson Brothers' Circulating Library. Revised Catalogue of Robinson Bros' Circulating Library, 11 Water Street, Middleboro', Mass. Middleborough: J. M. Coombs, 1872. 13 p. MNBedf.
1287

Milford

Milford Library Association. Catalogue of Books, and Constitution, of the Milford Library Association. Boston: John Wilson and Son, 1859. 44 p. MWA.
1288

Milford Town Library. Catalogue of Books and By-laws of Milford Town Library. Founded August, 1858. Milford: Milford Journal Job Press, 1859. 36 p. CU-SB, Nh (holds first 12 p. only).
1289

Milford Town Library. Catalogue of Books and the By-laws of Milford Town Library. Founded August, 1858. Milford: G. W. Stacy, 1873. 88 p. Cutter 974 reports suppl. to March, 1875 (18 p.). DLC, MB, MWA.
1290

Millbury

First Congregational Church. Catalogue of Sabbath School Library of First Congregational Church, Millbury. July, 1875. Worcester: Chas. Hamilton, 1875. 37 p. MWA.
1291

Millbury Academy. Social Friends. Catalogue of Books belonging to the Social Friends' Library, Millbury Academy. [n.p., 185-?]. 4 p. MWA.
1292

Millbury Town Library. Catalogue of the Millbury Town Library. 1872. Worcester: E. R. Fiske, 1872. 43 p. Cutter 838 reports suppl., 1873. (12 p.). DLC.
1293

Milton

Dorchester and Milton Circulating Library, see entry 1107.

First Congregational Parish. Catalogue of the Library of the First Congregational Parish in Milton. Boston: John Wilson and Son, 1858. 26 p. MWA.
1294

Milton Agricultural Library. Catalogue . . . [Milton?, 186-?]. Contains around 178 titles, per Nathaniel Thayer Kidder, *The First Sixty Years of the Milton Public Library, 1870-1931* (Milton, 1932), p. 8. Milton Public Library (Teele Collection).
1295

Milton Public Library. Catalogue of the Milton Public Library of Milton, Mass. Boston: Rockwell & Churchill, 1869. vii, 460 p. DLC, MBAt, UPB.
1296

Milton Public Library. Catalogue of Milton Public Library. 1871. Boston: Alfred Mudge & Son, 1871. 216 p. MB holds suppl. Bulletin, 1871/72-1875. MB, MBAt, MH, MWA, Milton Public Library, NN, UPB.
1297

Monson

Monson Academy. Linophilian Society. Catalogue of the Linophilian Library of Monson

Academy, Monson, Mass. 1859. Springfield: S. Bowles, 1859. 28 p. MnU.   **1298**

Nahant

Nahant Public Library. Catalogue of the Public Library of Nahant. 1872. Boston: Rockwell & Churchill, 1872. 23 p. MWA, NN, WU (School of Library and Information Studies).   **1299**

Nahant Public Library. Catalogue No. 2, of the Public Library of Nahant. 1872. Boston: Alfred Mudge & Son, 1872. 31 p. MWA.   **1300**

Nahant Public Library. Catalogue of the Public Library of Nahant. 1875. Boston: W. F. Brown, 1875. 103 p. DLC.   **1301**

Nantucket

Nantucket Atheneum. Catalogue of Books in the Nantucket Atheneum, to which are added the Charter and By-laws of the Institution. Nantucket: T. J. Worth, 1835. 36 p. Not in Rinderknecht. MB.   **1302**

Nantucket Atheneum. Catalogue of the Library of the Nantucket Atheneum, with the By-laws of the Institution. Nantucket, 1841. v, 72 p. Printed in Boston by Freeman and Bolles. Rinderknecht 41-3678. MNan, MWA, PPL, RNR (with ms. additions).   **1303**

Natick

Citizen's Library. Catalogue . . . 1852. Contained 432 vol., per Samuel Adams Drake, *History of Middlesex* County, Massachusetts (Boston, 1880), vol. 2, p. 197; *Ninth Report of the Free Public Library Commission of Massachusetts* (1899), p. 246.   **1304**

Morse Institute. Class List of Prose, Fiction, and Juvenile Works. Boston: A. Mudge & Son, 1875. 108 p. Includes class list of history, biography, travels, and miscellaneous works (pp. 58-108). DLC, NN (pp. 58-108 only).   **1305**

Natick Social Library. Catalogue . . . [181-]. Not in S & S. Contained 94 vol., per Samuel Adams Drake, *History of Middlesex County, Massachusetts* (Boston, 1880), vol. 2, p. 196.   **1306**

Natick Town Library. Regulations and Catalogue of the Books in the Natick Town Library, established in 1857. Boston: J. B. Chisholm, 1857. 24 p. MWA.   **1307**

Natick Town Library. Catalogue of the Natick Town Library . . . Boston: S. Chism, 1866. 50 p. DLC holds suppl., 1869?-72. DLC, MB (also undetermined suppl.; all lost?).   **1308**

Needham

First Parish Church. Catalogue of Books belonging to the Library of the Sabbath School, connected with the First Parish Church, Needham. Boston: Alfred Mudge & Son, 1857. 12 p. MB.   **1309**

New Bedford

Allen Street Methodist Episcopal Church. Catalogue of the Allen Street Methodist Episcopal Sabbath School Library. New Bedford: E. Anthony, 1858. 22 p. MNBedf.   **1310**

Allen Street Methodist Episcopal Church. Catalogue of Books in the Allen Street M. E. Sabbath School Library, New Bedford, Mass. [New Bedford, 187-?]. 25, [1] p. MNBedf.   **1311**

Bonney Street Christian Sabbath School. Catalogue of Books in the Library of the Bonney Street Christian Sabbath-School. New Bedford: E. Anthony & Sons, 1866. 16 p. MNBedf.   **1312**

Bonney Street Christian Sabbath School. Catalogue of Books in the Library of the Bonney Street Christian Sabbath-School. New Bedford: E. Anthony & Sons, 1875. 12 p. MNBedf.   **1313**

First Christian Sabbath School. Catalogue of Books in the Library of the First Christian Sabbath School, New-Bedford. New-Bedford: Evening Standard Steam Press, 1862. 23, [1] p. MNBedf.   **1314**

First Christian Sabbath School. Catalogue of Books in the Library of the First Christian Sabbath School, New-Bedford. New-Bedford: Evening Standard Steam Press, 1864. 30 p. MNBedf.   **1315**

First Christian Sabbath School. Catalogue of Books in the Library of the First Christian

Sabbath School, New-Bedford. New Bedford: E. Anthony & Sons, 1867. 30 p. MNBedf. **1316**

First Congregational Church. Catalogue of the Sunday School Library of the First Congregational Church, New Bedford, Mass. New Bedford: Benjamin Lindsey, 1851. 16 p. MNBedf. **1317**

First Universalist Society. Catalogue of Books in the Library of the Sabbath School, of the First Universalist Society, of New-Bedford. New-Bedford: Daily Evening Standard Press, 1856. 20 p. MNBedf. **1318**

First Universalist Society. Catalogue of Books in the Library of the Sabbath School, of the First Universalist Society, of New-Bedford. New-Bedford: Evening Standard Steam Press, 1860. 18 p. MNBedf. **1319**

Fourth Street Methodist Episcopal Church. Catalogue of the Fourth Street Methodist Episcopal Sabbath School Library. August, 1843. New Bedford: William Canfield, 1843. 11, [1] p. Rinderknecht 43-3652. MNBedf. **1320**

Friends' Academy. Catalogue of the Friends' Academy, New Bedford. April, 1859. New Bedford: Benjamin Lindsey, 1859. 16 p. MWA. **1321**

Friends' First-Day School. Catalogue of the Library of Friends' First-Day School, New Bedford. Revised 1868. New Bedford: Taber Bros., 1868. 16 p. MNBedf. **1322**

Middle Street Church. Catalogue of Books in the Library of the Middle Street Sabbath School, New Bedford. New-Bedford: Evening Standard Steam Press, 1864. 8 p. MNBedf. **1323**

Middle Street Church. Catalogue of Books in the Library of the Middle Street Sabbath School, New Bedford. New Bedford: E. Anthony & Sons, 1865. 12 p. MNBedf. **1324**

Middle Street Church. Catalogue of Books in the Library of the Middle Street Christian Sunday School. New Bedford: E. Anthony & Sons, 1871. 15, [1] p. MNBedf. **1325**

Middle Street Church. Catalogue of Books in the Library of the Middle Street Christian Sunday School. New Bedford: E. Anthony & Sons, 1874. 16 p. MNBedf. **1326**

New Bedford Free Public Library. Catalogue of the Free Public Library, New Bedford, Mass. New Bedford: B. Lindsey, 1858. vii, 354, [2] p. Supplementary lists appear in the *Annual Report of the Trustees of the Free Public Library in New Bedford;* e.g., "New Bedford Documents" in *Report* for 1864-65; "Lists of Periodicals currently received . . ." in *Report* for 1870, 1873-74. In many libraries. **1327**

New Bedford Free Public Library. Supplement to the Catalogue of the Free Public Library, New Bedford, Mass. New Bedford: E. Anthony, 1869. 313, [3] p. In many libraries. **1328**

New Bedford Free Public Library. Catalogue of Fiction and Juveniles, added to the Library 1869-74. [New Bedford, 1874?]. 40 p. MNBedf. **1329**

New Bedford Free Public Library. Bulletin . . . List of Books added . . . No. 1- ; Jan. 1874-. New Bedford. DLC (#1-7; Jan. 1874-Sept. 1875), MB (#1-16; Jan. 1874-April 1883, etc.). **1330**

New Bedford Library. Catalogue of Books, belonging to New-Bedford Library. 1812. [New Bedford, 1812]. [12] p. Not in S & S. PPL (with ms. notes). **1331**

New Bedford Library. Catalogue of Books, belonging to New-Bedford Library. 1821. [New Bedford: Benj. Lindsey, 1821]. 13, 3 p. Shoemaker 6192. MNBedf. **1332**

New Bedford Social Library. Catalogue of Books, belonging to New-Bedford Social Library. 1827. New Bedford: Benjamin Lindsey, 1827. 24 p. Shoemaker 29919. MNBedf. **1333**

New Bedford Social Library. A Catalogue of Books, belonging to New-Bedford Social Library. 1832. [New Bedford?, 1832]. 23, [1] p. Not in Bruntjen. MNBedf. **1334**

New Bedford Social Library. Supplement to the Catalogue of Books in the New Bedford Social Library. 1836. [New Bedford?, 1836?]. 16, [2] p. Rinderknecht 39164. MNBedf. **1335**

New Bedford Social Library. Catalogue of Books belonging to the New-Bedford Social Library... New Bedford: Benjamin Lindsey, 1839. 48 p. Rinderknecht 57440. MNBedf, MWA, MiD-B. **1336**

New Bedford Social Library. Catalogue of Books belonging to the New Bedford Social Library... New Bedford: Benjamin Lindsey, 1843. 74, [2] p. Rinderknecht 43-3655 (duplicated by 43-3653). MNBedf, MWA, MiD-B, RPA. **1337**

New Bedford Social Library. Catalogue of Books belonging to the New Bedford Social Library, arranged in the Order of the Letters of the Alphabet. New Bedford: Benjamin Lindsey, 1847. iv, 198 p. DLC, MNBedf, MnU. **1338**

North Congregational Church. Catalogue of Books belonging to the Sabbath School Library of the North Congregational Church. New-Bedford: Benjamin Lindsey, 1840. 11, [1] p. Rinderknecht 40-4882. MNBedf. **1339**

North Congregational Church. Catalogue of Books in the Library of the North Congregational Sabbath School, New Bedford. New Bedford: E. Anthony, 1858. 26 p. (library regulations on back cover). MNBedf. **1340**

North Congregational Church. Catalogue of Books in the Library of the North Congregational Sabbath School, New Bedford. New Bedford: E. Anthony & Sons, 1864. 12 p. (library regulations on back cover). MNBedf. **1341**

North Congregational Church. Catalogue of Books in the Library of the North Congregational Sabbath School, New Bedford. New Bedford: E. Anthony & Sons, 1866. 12 p. (library regulations on back cover). MNBedf. **1342**

North Congregational Church. Catalogue of Books in the Library of the North Congregational Sabbath School, New Bedford. New Bedford: E. Anthony & Sons, 1869. 16 p. MNBedf. **1343**

Pleasant Street Methodist Episcopal Church. Catalogue of Books in the Library of the Pleasant-Street Methodist Episcopal Sabbath-School, New Bedford. New Bedford: Standard Steam Printing House, 1859. 18 p. MNBedf. **1344**

Pleasant Street Methodist Episcopal Church. Catalogue of Books in the Library of the Pleasant Street Methodist Episcopal Sabbath-School, New Bedford. New Bedford: Standard Steam Printing House, 1861. 30 p. MNBedf. **1345**

Pleasant Street Methodist Episcopal Church. Catalogue of Books in the Library of the Pleasant Street Methodist Episcopal Sabbath-School. New Bedford: E. Anthony & Sons, 1866. 30 p. MNBedf (incomplete copy?). **1346**

Pleasant Street Methodist Episcopal Church. Catalogue of Books in the Library of the Pleasant Street Methodist Episcopal Sabbath School. New Bedford: E. Anthony & Sons, 1869. 36 p. MNBedf (incomplete copy?). **1347**

Rockdale Church. Catalogue of Books in the Library of the Rockdale Sabbath School. New Bedford: E. Anthony & Sons, 1871. 8 p. MNBedf. **1348**

South Christian Church. Catalogue of the Sabbath School Library, of the South Christian Church. April, 1859. New-Bedford: Standard Steam Printing House, 1859. 18 p. MNBedf. **1349**

Trinitarian Church. Catalogue of Books in the Library of the Trinitarian Sabbath-School. 1859. New Bedford: Standard Steam Printing House, 1859. 18 p. MNBedf. **1350**

Trinitarian Church. Catalogue. Trinitarian Sabbath School Library. [New Bedford?, 187-?]. 8 p. MNBedf. **1351**

Universalist Church. Catalogue of Books in the Universalist Sunday School Library, New Bedford. [New Bedford, 187-?]. 15, [1] p. MNBedf. **1352**

William Street Baptist Church. Catalogue of Books in the Library of the William Street Baptist Sabbath School, New-Bedford. New Bedford: Evening Standard Steam Press, 1863. 8 p. MNBedf. **1353**

William Street Baptist Church. Catalogue of Books in the Library of the William Street Baptist Sabbath School, New Bedford. New Bedford: E. Anthony & Sons, 1868. 16 p. MNBedf. **1354**

William Street Baptist Church. Catalogue of Books in the Library of the William Street Baptist Sabbath School, New Bedford. New Bedford: E. Anthony & Sons, 1870. 19, [1] p. MNBedf.   **1355**

Newbury

First Parish. The Constitution of the Social Library in the First Parish in Newbury; with a Catalogue of the Books, annexed. Newburyport: Abel Whitton, 1848. 12 p. MWA.   **1356**

Newburyport

Gilman's Circulating Library. Catalogue of Books in the Circulating Library kept by W. & J. Gilman, Booksellers . . . [Newburyport]: W. & J. Gilman, [182-]. 46 p. For second part, see entry 1358. Not in Shoemaker. MSaE, MWA.   **1357**

Gilman's Circulating Library. Catalogue of Books in the Circulating Library, kept by W. & J. Gilman, Booksellers . . . [Newburyport]: W. & J. Gilman, [1828]. 12 p. Forms the second part (#1185-1475) of entry 1357. On p. 12, the library is referred to as the Merrimack Circulating Library. Not in Shoemaker. MSaE.   **1358**

Merrimack Circulating Library, see entry 1358.

Newburyport Athenaeum. A Catalogue of Books in the Newburyport Athenaeum. [Newburyport, 1810?]. 12 p. Not in S & S. MSaE.   **1359**

Newburyport Athenaeum. Catalogue of Books belonging to the Newburyport Atheneaum. January, 1841. Newburyport: J. Gilman, 1841. 24 p. Rinderknecht 41-3866. MNe, MSaE (with ms. additions).   **1360**

Newburyport Circulating Library. Catalogue of Books in the Newburyport Circulating Library, kept at Charles Whipple's Bookstore . . . [Newburyport]: C. Norris, 1816. 107 p. See also entry 1368. Not in S & S. MSaE, MWA (entered under: Whipple, Charles), NN (entered under: Whipple, Charles).   **1361**

Newburyport Sabbath School Library. Catalogue of the Newburyport Sabbath School Library, kept at S. N. Tenney's Bookstore,

No. 2 State Street. Newburyport: E. W. Allen, 1826. 16 p. Shoemaker 25586. MNe, MSaE.   **1362**

Public Library. Catalogue of the Public Library, of the City of Newburyport, founded by Hon. Josiah Little. Newburyport: Wm. H. Huse, 1857. 207 p. Supplements appear in the *Annual Report of the Directors of the Public Library of the City of Newburyport*. DLC, IU, M, MA, MB, MBAt, MSaE, MWA, N, NB, PP, Salem Athenaeum, UPB, ViW.   **1363**

Religious Library. The Constitution and Catalogue of Books of the Religious Library in Newburyport. Organized July 9, 1804. Newburyport: William B. Allen, 1816. 21 p. S & S 38772. MiD-B.   **1364**

Social Library. The Bye-laws and Catalogue of Books, of the Social Library in the Town of Newburyport. Newburyport: Allen & Stickney, 1802. 20 p. S & S 3092. MWA.   **1365**

Social Library. By-laws, and Catalogue of Books, of the Social Library, in the Town of Newburyport. Newburyport: W. and J. Gilman, 1810. 32 p. S & S 20912. MSaE, MWA.   **1366**

Social Library. Catalogue of Books, belonging to the Proprietors of the Newburyport Social Library, saved from the late Fire, and to be sold at Public Auction on Wednesday, August 21, 1811 . . . [Salem: W. & J. Gilman, 1811]. broadside. S & S 23560. MSaE.   **1367**

Whipple's (Charles) Circulating Library. Catalogue No. 2 of Charles Whipple's Circulating Library, and of Books for sale . . . [Newburyport, 1818?]. 67 p. See also entry 1361. Not in S & S. MSaE.   **1368**

Newton

(see also West Newton)

Eliot Church. Catalogue of the Eliot Sabbath School Library, Newton . . . Boston, 1854. 20 p. Cf. Sabin 55086. MH (per Sabin).   **1369**

Free Public Library. Catalogue of the Free Public Library, Newton, Mass. Waterbury: American Printing Co., 1871. xiii, 248 p. Cutter 704 reports suppl. Bulletin, 1872-74.

ICU, MB, MNtcA, N, Newton Free Library, RPB. **1370**

Grace Church. Catalogue of the Sunday School Library, of Grace Church, Newton. 1857. Boston: Alfred Mudge & Son, [1857?]. 20 p. Cf. Sabin 55086. MH (per Sabin). **1371**

Grace Church. Catalogue of the Parish Library, of Grace Church, Newton. 1858. Boston: Thomas Groom, [1858]. 19 p. Private collection (photocopy of copy held by Grace Church). **1372**

Grace Church. Second Catalogue of Books in the Grace Church Sunday School Library, Newton, Mass. June, 1864. Boston: Thomas Groom, 1864. 20 p. MB, Private collection (photocopy of copy held by Grace Church). **1373**

Second Unitarian Society. Catalogue of the Sunday School Library, belonging to the Second Unitarian Society in Newton. Boston: J. Howe, 1854. 16 p. Cf. Sabin 55086. MH (per Sabin). **1374**

Newton Center

Baptist Church. Catalogue of Books of the Library of the Baptist Sabbath School, Newton Centre. December, 1848. Boston: John Putnam, 1848. 16 p. NHi. **1375**

Baptist Church. Catalogue of Books for the use of the Baptist Sunday School Library, Newton Centre, Mass. 1871. Boston: Cutter, Tower, 1871. 16 p. MWA. **1376**

Newton Centre Library Association. Catalogue of Books, and the By-laws of the Newton Centre Library Association. Founded, 1859. Boston: Franklin Printing House, 1860. 28 p. MNt. **1377**

Newton Theological Institution. Catalogue of Books belonging to the Library of the Newton Theological Association. August 1, 1833. Boston: Lincoln, Edmands, 1833. 29 p. Not in Bruntjen. MWA. **1378**

Newton Lower Falls

Free Library. Catalogue of the Free Library at Newton Lower Falls, Massachusetts. Estab-

lished January, 1867. F. D. Lord, M.D., Librarian. Boston: J. M. Hewes, 1872. 40 p. DLC holds suppl. for March 1874 (7 p.) and 2d suppl., Feb. 1875 ([3] p.). DLC. **1379**

Newtonville

Central Congregational Church. Revised Catalogue of . . . the Sunday School Library of the Central Congregational Church, Newtonville, Mass. Boston: Chas. T. Valentine, 1870. 12 p. Cf. Sabin 55102. **1380**

North Adams

North Adams Library Association. Catalogue . . . ca. 1870. Cf. W. F. Spear, *History of North Adams, Mass., 1749-1885* (North Adams, 1885), p. 115. **1381**

North Andover

(see also Andover)

North Andover Library. Catalogue of the North Andover Library . . . Lawrence: G. S. Merrill & Crocker, 1875. iv, 29, [1] p. DLC. **1382**

North Bridgewater

(see also Bridgewater, Brockton)

Public Library. Catalogue of the Public Library, of the Town of North Bridgewater . . . [North Bridgewater]: North Bridgewater Gazette, 1867. 80 p. DLC, MB. **1383**

Public Library. Catalogue of the Public Library, of the Town of North Bridgewater. Appendix. [North Bridgewater, 186-]. 22 p. DLC, MB. **1384**

Public Library. Catalogue of the Public Library, of the Town of North Bridgewater. Supplement. May 1st, 1870-April 1, 1872. [North Bridgewater, 1870-72]. 2 vol. DLC. **1385**

North Brookfield

(see also Brookfield)

Ladies' Library Association. Catalogue, Constitution, and By-laws, of the Ladies' Library Association, North Brookfield, Mass. West Brookfield: Thomas Morey, 1872. 14 p. MWA. **1386**

Ladies' Library Association. Catalogue, Constitution, and By-laws, of the Ladies' Library Association, North Brookfield, Mass. North Brookfield: Journal Printing Office, 1875. 15 p. MWA. **1387**

Northampton

Boys' High School. Catalogue of the Library connected with the Boys' High School, Northampton. 1839. [Northampton?, 1839]. 20 p. Not in Rinderknecht. DLC (marked copy), MWA. **1388**

Northampton Agricultural Library, see entries 1390-91.

Northampton Book Club. Catalogue of . . . the Library of the Northampton Book Club. [n.p., 184-?]. [12] p. Cf. Sabin 55762; *Ninth Report of the Free Public Library Commission of Massachusetts* (1899), p. 262. MB (per Sabin). **1389**

Northampton Public Library. Catalogue of the Northampton Public Library, including the Agricultural Library. Northampton: Trumbull & Gere, 1862. iv, 75 p. MA (entered under: Forbes Library). **1390**

Northampton Public Library. Catalogue of the Northampton Public Library, including the Agricultural Library, with Supplements. Northampton: Trumbull and Gore, 1868. 75 p. MB holds 1st suppl. (8 p.) and 2d suppl. (13 p.). MB. **1391**

Northampton Public Library. Catalogue of the Northampton Public Library . . . 1874. Northampton: Gazette Printing Co., 1874. 2 pt. in 1 vol. DLC, ICN, MB, MnU, NjP. **1392**

Northampton Young Men's Institute. Catalogue of Books in the Library of the Northampton Young Men's Institute. October, 1846. [Cambridge]: Metcalf, [1846]. 28 p. CtY (interleaved). **1393**

Northampton Young Men's Institute. Catalogue of the Library of the Young Men's Institute . . . Northampton: Hopkins, Bridgman, 1857. 133 p. Cf. Sabin 55763; *Ninth Report of the Free Public Library Commission of Massachusetts* (1899), p. 263. **1394**

Northborough

Northborough Free Library. Catalogue of the Free Library, of Northboro', Mass. Clinton:

W. J. Coulter, 1873. 128 p. DLC holds suppl., 1875 (26 p.). DLC, MWA, N. **1395**

Northfield

Northfield Social Library. Catalogue . . . 1825. Not in Shoemaker. Contained 500 titles, per Herbert Collins Parsons, *A Puritan Outpost: A History of the Town and People of Northfield, Massachusetts* (New York, 1937), p. 263. **1396**

Northfield Social Library. Catalogue of the Northfield Social Library . . . Albany: J. Munsell, 1866. 53 p. DLC. **1397**

Orange

Free Public Library. Catalogue of the Free Public Library, of Orange, Mass. 1869. Athol Depot: E. F. Jones, 1869. 43 p. DLC. **1398**

Free Public Library. Supplementary Catalogue . . . 1869. Orange: Journal of Industry Office, 1874. 23 p. DLC. **1399**

Oxford

Free Public Library. Catalogue of the Free Public Library of Oxford, Mass. January, 1871. Worcester: Goddard & Nye, [1871]. 30 p. MWA. **1400**

Free Public Library. Revised Catalogue of the Books in the Free Public Library, Oxford, Mass. 1874. Worcester: Tyler & Seagrave, 1874. 44 p. DLC, MWA. **1401**

Social Library. A Catalogue of Books belonging to the Social Library in Oxford, March 1st, 1818, with their Prices annexed. [Worcester?, 1818]. 1 sheet. Not in S & S. DeU, MWA. **1402**

Peabody

(formerly South Danvers)

Peabody Institute. Catalogue of the Library of the Peabody Institute, South Danvers, Mass. Boston: John Wilson and Son, 1855. xix, 102 p. Contains "Historical Sketch" on pp. [vii]-xiii. DLC, ICN, MeB, MB, MBAt, MH, MPeal (Danvers Archival Center), MSaE, N, NNUT, ScU, TxU. **1403**

Peabody Institute. Catalogue of the Branch Library of the Peabody Institute, Danvers, Mass. Boston: John Wilson and Son, 1857. xv, 75 p. Contains "Historical Sketch of the

Branch Library at Danvers" on pp. [vii]-xi.
DLC, MA, MPeal (Danvers Archival Center), MSaE, MWA, N.   **1404**

Peabody Institute. Supplement to Catalogue of the Library of the Peabody Institute, South Danvers, Mass. July, 1857. [South Danvers, 1857]. 26 p. Suppl. for Aug. 1857-Feb. 1859 appears in the *Seventh Annual Report of the Trustees of the Peabody Institute of South Danvers* for 1859 (8 p. at end). MeB, MB, MBAt, MSaE, MWA.   **1405**

Peabody Institute. Catalogue of New Books added to the Library of the Peabody Institute, Danvers, Mass. Feb. 1859-Aug. 1871. [Danvers?]. Vol. for 1859-64 called: Branch Library of the Peabody Institute. Books added since the Catalogue was Published. DLC (complete?), MPeal (Danvers Archival Center, 4 vol., 1859-64), MSaE (4 vol., 1859-64), MWA (4 vol., 1859-64), N (4 vol., 1859-64).   **1406**

Peabody Institute. Supplement to Catalogue of the Library of the Peabody Institute, South Danvers, Mass. January, 1865. South Danvers: Charles D. Howard, 1865. 116 p. DLC, ICN, MSaE, N, NNUT.   **1407**

Peabody Institute. Catalogue of New Books added to the Peabody Institute, Danvers, Mass. October, 1869. [n.p., 1869]. 26 p. Contains all books added since Feb. 1864. MPeal (Danvers Archival Center), MWA, N.   **1408**

Peabody Institute. Catalogue of the Library of the Peabody Institute, Peabody, Mass. Peabody: Chas. D. Howard, 1872. viii, 483 p. CSmH, DLC, MB, MBAt, MBSi, MH, MSaE, NcU, ScU.   **1409**

South Church. A Catalogue of the Sabbath School Library, of the South Church, South Danvers. Salem: Wm. Ives and G. W. Pease, 1857. 32 p. MSaE.   **1410**

South Danvers Lyceum. Catalogue of Books in the South Danvers Lyceum Library. 1836. Salem: W. &. S. B. Ives, [1836]. 12 p. Not in Rinderknecht. MWA.   **1411**

Universalist Society. Catalogue of Books belonging to the Library of the Universalist Society, South Danvers. 1857. Salem: Gazette and Essex County Mercury Press, 1857. 16 p. MSaE.   **1412**

Phillipston

Phillips Free Public Library. Catalogue of the Phillips Free Public Library, of Phillipston, Mass. Athol Depot: R. Putnam, 1862. 22 p. MWA.   **1413**

Phillips Free Public Library. Catalogue of the Phillips Free Public Library, Phillipston, 1871. Athol Depot: E. F. Jones, [1871]. 44 p. DLC holds Catalogue of New Books . . . 1872 (entries 2319-2627). Cutter 706 reports suppl. for 1872-74. DLC.   **1414**

Pittsfield

Berkshire Medical Institution. Catalogue of Books, belonging to Henry H. Childs, John P. Batchelder, and the Berkshire Medical Institution. Pittsfield: Phinehas Allen, 1825. 35 p. Not in Shoemaker. MWA.   **1415**

Pittsfield Athenaeum. Catalogue of the Library of the Pittsfield Athenaeum, Pittsfield, Mass. Founded 1850. Pittsfield: Chickering & Axtell, 1872. 140, [1] p. of rules. DLC, MPB.   **1416**

Pittsfield Athenaeum. First Supplement to the Catalogue of the Library of the Pittsfield Athenaeum, Pittsfield, Mass. Pittsfield: W. H. Phillip, 1873. 22 p. DLC.   **1417**

Pittsfield Library. Catalogue of Books belonging to the Pittsfield Library. Established October, 1862. Pittsfield: Daniel T. Neal, 1865. [42] p. (includes suppl.). MB. **1418**

Pittsfield Library Association. Catalogue, Constitution, By-laws, &c. of the Pittsfield Library Association. Pittsfield: Reed, Hull & Peirson, 1855. 14 p. MWA.   **1419**

Plymouth

Plymouth Library. Catalogue of the Plymouth Library, Plymouth, Mass. 1858. Plymouth, 1858. 16 p. MB (lost).   **1420**

Plymouth Library. Catalogue of the Plymouth Library, Plymouth, Mass. 1867. Plymouth: Memorial and Rock Press, 1867. 67 p. MWA.   **1421**

Princeton

Princeton Ladies' Reading Society. Catalogue of the Library of the Princeton Ladies'

Reading Society. January, 1858. Worcester: Henry J. Howland, [1858]. 11 p. MWA.
1422

Princeton Ladies' Reading Society. Catalogue of Books in the Library of the Princeton Ladies' Reading Society. January, 1862. Worcester: Chas. Hamilton, [1862]. 16 p. MWA.
1423

Provincetown

Provincetown Public Library. Catalogue of the Public Library, Provincetown, Mass. 1874. Provincetown: Advocate Steam Job Printing Establishment, 1874. 53 p. DLC, N (errata leaf inserted).
1424

Quincy

Evangelical Congregational Church. Catalogue of Books belonging to the Library of the Sabbath School connected with the Evangelical Congregational Church, Quincy, Mass. Boston: Alfred Mudge, 1862. 12 p. MB.
1425

First Church. Catalogue of Books in Sunday School Library, First Church, Quincy. Boston: Alfred Mudge & Son, 1875. 20 p. MH-AH.
1426

Hancock Street Church. S. S. Library. Hancock Street Church, Quincy. June, 1865. [Boston: Mudge & Son, 1865]. 10 p. MB.
1427

Quincy Public Library. Deeds and other Documents relating to the several Pieces of Land, and to the Library presented to the Town of Quincy, by President Adams, together with a Catalogue of the Books. Cambridge: Hilliard and Metcalf, 1823. 67 p. Transferred to the Boston Public Library in 1894. Shoemaker 11529. CSmH, DLC, ICN, IU, MB, MHi, MWA, NN, NNC, PU, WHi.
1428

Quincy Public Library. List of Books in the Quincy Public Library, on the 1st of January, 1872. Boston: Rockwell & Churchill, 1872. 26, [2] p. DLC, MB, MQ, NN.
1429

Quincy Public Library. Catalogue of the Public Library of Quincy, Mass. Boston: Rockwell & Churchill, 1875. 288 p. DLC, ICN, IU, MdBP, M, MBAt, MH, MQ, MiEM, MnU, NB, NN, NNC.
1430

Unitarian Church. Catalogue of Books belonging to the Quincy Unitarian Sunday School Library. June, 1849. Boston: John Wilson, 1849. 16 p. NB.
1431

Randolph

Randolph Ladies' Library Association. Catalogue . . . 1868. 19 p. Cf. Cutter 582.
1432

Reading

Reading Public Library. Catalogue of Books belonging to the Public Library, Reading, Mass. July 16, 1870. Boston: Hollis & Gunn, 1870. 72 p. DLC, MB.
1433

Reading Public Library. Supplementary Catalogue, No. 1. Books added to the Library since July, 1870. Boston: Hollis & Gunn, 1874. 34 p. MWA.
1434

Rehoboth

Rehoboth Village Sabbath School. Catalogue of Books belonging to the Rehoboth Village Sabbath School Library. July, 1866. Providence: Knowles, Anthony, 1866. 16 p. MWA.
1435

Rochester

Trinitarian Church. Catalogue of Books in the Trinitarian Sabbath School Library, Rochester. [n.p., 187-?]. 8, [4] p. MNBedf.
1436

Rockland

Rockland Library Association. Catalogue of the Rockland Library Association. Rockland: Standard Steam Press, 1874. 60 p. DLC holds 1st suppl., 1874 (4 p.). DLC.
1437

Rockport

Rockport Public Library. Catalogue . . . 1872. 27 p. Cf. Cutter 761.
1438

Roxbury

(see also Boston Highlands)

Boston Public Library. Roxbury Branch. List of Books arranged by Authors, Titles, and Subjects. Roxbury Branch, including Fellowes Athenaeum. First Edition. October, 1873. Boston, 1873. 140 p. ICN, MB.
1439

Fellowes Athenaeum, see entry 1439.

Roxbury Athenaeum. Catalogue of Books in the Roxbury Athenaeum, to which are added the By-laws of the Institution, an Account of its Incorporation, and a List of its Proprietors. Roxbury: W. B. Ewer, 1849. 115, xv p. CtY, MB, MWA, PP.   **1440**

Roxbury Circulating Library. Catalogue of the Roxbury Circulating Library . . . Roxbury: Reynolds & Gill, 1837. 30 p. Conducted by Reynolds & Gill at their bookstore. Not in Rinderknecht. MB.   **1441**

Roxbury Library. A Catalogue of the Books comprising the Roxbury Library. Boston: Bellamy and Green, 1819. 10 p. S & S 49330. PHi.   **1442**

Roxbury Library. Catalogue of Books in the Roxbury Library. September, 1829. Regulations . . . Boston: Munroe and Francis, 1829. 16 p. Not in Shoemaker. MWA.   **1443**

Social Library. Catalogue of Books in the Social Library of Roxbury. January 1, 1832. Boston: Munroe and Francis, 1832. Not in Bruntjen. Cf. Jesse H. Shera, *Foundations of the Public Library* (Chicago, 1949), p. 292.   **1444**

Social Library. Catalogue of Books in the Social Library of Roxbury. October 1, 1836. To which is prefixed the By-laws, adopted July 23, 1831. Boston: Munroe and Francis, 1836. 35 p. Not in Rinderknecht. MWA.   **1445**

Warren Street Methodist Episcopal Church. Catalogue of the Warren-Street M. E. Sabbath-School Library, Roxbury. Boston: Geo. C. Rand & Avery, 1867. 31 p. MB.   **1446**

Rutland

Rutland Public Library. Catalogue of the Public Library, Rutland, Mass. 1873. Barre: Cook & Crandall, [1873]. 17 p. DLC. **1447**

Salem

Barton Square Church. Catalogue of the Teachers' and Scholars' Libraries, belonging to the Barton Square Sunday School, Salem, Mass. Salem: Printed at the Gazette

Office, 1856. 32 p. MSaE (with ms. additions).   **1448**

Barton Square Church. Catalogue of the Scholars' Library belonging to the Barton Square Sunday School, Salem, Mass. Salem: Printed at the Salem Gazette Office, 1867. 19 p. MSaE.   **1449**

Crombie Street Church. Catalogue of the Crombie Street Sabbath School Library, Salem, Mass. Salem: Ives and Frank, 1858. 16 p. MSaE.   **1450**

Cushing & Appleton, see Essex Circulating Library.

Dabney, John. Catalogue of Books, for Sale or Circulation, in Town or Country, by John Dabney at his Book and Stationary Store, and Circulating Library in Salem. [Salem?], 1801. 50 p. (pp. 49-50 are advertisements). S & S 376. MH-H, MHi, MSaE, MWA, MnU (defective).   **1451**

Dabney, John. Catalogue of the Salem Bookstore and Circulating Library, by John Dabney. Salem, 1813. 36 p. S & S 28264. MWA.   **1452**

Dabney, John. Valuable Catalogue of Books, being the Extensive Library belonging to John Dabney, Esq., consisting of between 6 and 7000 Volumes . . . to be Sold at Auction, at the Store, Corner of Liberty-Street . . . Salem, by Jonathan P. Saunders, Auctioneer, on Tuesday, 8th September, and each successive Day till all are sold . . . [Salem, 1818]. 57 p. S & S 46626. MWA.   **1453**

East Church. Catalogue of the Sabbath School Library of the East Church, Salem. Salem: T. J. Hutchinson, 1875. 13 p. MSaE.   **1454**

East-India Marine Society. The East-India Marine Society of Salem. [Salem: W. Palfray, jr., 1821]. 100 p. Contains "Catalogue of the Journals of the Voyages." Shoemaker 6699. DLC, DSI, MB, MBAt, MH-BA, MHi, MSaE, NhD, NjP, NNC, PPAmP, PPL.   **1455**

East-India Marine Society. The East-India Marine Society of Salem. [Salem: Salem Press, Palfray, Ives, Foote & Brown, 1831]. 178 p. Contains "Catalogue of the Journals of the Voyages." Bruntjen 9084. DLC, ICN, MB, MH, MHi, MSaP, MWA.   **1456**

East-India Marine Society. Supplement to the Catalogue of the Articles in the Museum, Journals, &c. of the East-India Marine Society of Salem. Salem: William Ives, 1837. 24 p. Rinderknecht 46647. CSmH, MB, MHi, MSa. **1457**

Essex Agricultural Society. Transactions of the Essex Agricultural Society, for 1849. Boston: George R. Carlton, 1849. 193 p. "A Catalogue of Books belonging to the Essex Agricultural Society" on pp. [182]-91. MSaE. **1458**

Essex Agricultural Society. Transactions of the Essex Agricultural Society, for 1858. Newburyport: Herald Job Press, 1858. 224 p. "Catalogue of the Library of the Essex Agricultural Society" on pp. [207]-22. MSaE. **1459**

Essex Circulating Library. Catalogue of Books, for Sale or Circulation, by Cushing & Appleton . . . Salem: Thomas C. Cushing, 1818. 100, 7 p. S & S 43958. MSaE, MWA. **1460**

Essex Circulating Library. A Supplementary Catalogue of the Essex Circulating Library, kept by Cushing & Appleton . . . for 1820. Salem: John D. Cushing, 1820. 12 p. Shoemaker 1123. MSaE, MWA (entered under: Cushing & Appleton). **1461**

Essex Circulating Library. A Catalogue of the Essex Circulating Library, kept by John M. Ives at His Book, Stationary, and Music Store, Essex Street, Salem. Salem: John D. Cushing and Brothers, 1822. 83, [1] p. Cover title: Catalogue of John M. Ives' Circulating Library, Essex Street, Salem. Shoemaker 8637. MSaE, MWA, MiD-B. **1462**

Essex Circulating Library. A Catalogue of the Essex Circulating Library . . . consisting of Five Thousand Volumes . . . Salem: Andrews & Foote, at the Gazette Office, 1826. 83, [1] p. Conducted by John M. Ives. Shoemaker 24444. DeU, MH-H, MSaE, MWA (entered under: Ives, John M.), PPL (entered under: Ives, John M.). **1463**

Essex County Law Library. A Catalogue of the Essex County Law Library. Salem: Salem Press, 1872. vii, 40 p. MSaE. **1464**

Essex South District Medical Society. Catalogue of Books belonging to the Essex Southern District Medical Society. Salem: Warwick Palfray, jun., 1824. 15 p. Shoemaker 16072. DLC, MBCo, MHi, MSaE (copy 2 has ms. additions), MWA. **1465**

Essex South District Medical Society. Catalogue of Books belonging to the Essex South District Medical Society. May, 1836. Salem, 1836. 12 p. Rinderknecht 37328. MBCo, MBM, MSaE (copy 2 has ms. additions). **1466**

First Baptist Church. Catalogue of the Sunday School Library of the First Baptist Society in Salem. [Salem, 1843]. 12 p. MWA. **1467**

First Baptist Church. Catalogue of the First Baptist Sabbath School Library, Salem. Salem: C. W. Swasey, 1861. 21 p. MSaE. **1468**

First Church. A Catalogue of the Library of the First Church in Salem. Salem: Foote & Brown, 1829. 30 p. MSaE holds suppl. (8 p.). Shoemaker 40348. CtY, MBAt, MH, MSaE, MWA, NNGr (uncat.). **1469**

First Church. Supplement, to November, 1838. [Salem, 1838]. 4 p. Not in Rinderknecht. MSaE. **1470**

First Church. Catalogue of the Sunday School Library of the First Church, Salem, Mass. Salem: Printed at the Observer Office, 1863. 17 p. MSaE. **1471**

First Church. Catalogue of the Sunday School Library of the First Church, Salem, Mass. Salem: Salem Press, 1871. 36 p. MSaE. **1472**

Fourth Social Library. Rules and Regulations of the Fourth Social Library in Salem. Instituted July 21, 1806. Salem: Pool & Palfray, 1807. 16 p. "Catalogue" on pp. 12-16. Not in S & S. MSaE. **1473**

Ives, John M., see Essex Circulating Library.

Library of Arts and Sciences. Rules and Regulations of the Library of Arts and Sciences. Salem: Thomas C. Cushing, 1802. 8, [8] p. "Catalogue of the Library of Arts & Sciences": [8] p. at end. S & S 2532, Rink 504. MSaE. **1474**

North Society. Catalogue of North Society Sunday School Library. Salem: Ives & Pease, 1842. 22 p. MSaE. **1475**

North Society. A Catalogue of Books in the North Society Sunday School Library. April, 1856. Salem: Salem Gazette Office, [1856]. 15 p. MSaE. **1476**

North Society. A Catalogue of Books in the North Society Sunday School Library. January, 1863. Salem: Salem Gazette and Mercury, 1863. 24 p. MSaE. **1477**

North Society. A Catalogue of Books in the North Society, Sunday School Library. 1864. Salem: Salem Gazette Office, 1864. 23 p. MSaE. **1478**

St. Peter's Church. A Catalogue of the Sunday School Library of St. Peter's Church, Salem. Salem: T. J. Hutchinson, 1862. 9 p. MSaE. **1479**

St. Peter's Church. Catalogue of St. Peter's Church Sunday School Library, Salem, Mass. September, 1874. Salem: Salem Observer Office, 1874. 28 p. MSaE. **1480**

Salem Athenaeum. Catalogue . . . 1809. 42 p. Cf. Jewett, p. 40, Rhees, p. 158. **1481**

Salem Athenaeum. Catalogue of the Books belonging to the Salem Athenaeum, with the By-laws and Regulations. Salem: Thomas C. Cushing, 1811. 72 p. S & S 23864. CSmH, CtY, DeU, DLC, InU, MBAt, MH, MHi, MSaE (interleaved with ms. additions), MWA (with ms. notes), MnU, Nh, NN, PPL. **1482**

Salem Athenaeum. Catalogue of the Books belonging to the Salem Athenaeum, with the By-laws and Regulations. Salem: W. Palfrey, jun., 1818. 79 p. S & S 45616. CtY, DLC, InU, MBAt, MH, MSaE, MWA, NNGr (with ms. notes), NNU, PPiPT, PU, Salem Athenaeum, UPB. **1483**

Salem Athenaeum. Catalogue of the Books belonging to the Salem Athenaeum, with the By-laws and Regulations. Salem: Warwick Palfrey, jun., 1826. 95 p. MWA holds suppl. of additions to 1833 (12 p.) Shoemaker 26006. MH, MSaE (interleaved with ms. additions), MWA, MiD-B, N, PPAmP, Salem Athenaeum. **1484**

Salem Athenaeum. Catalogue of the Books belonging to the Salem Athenaeum, with the By-laws and Regulations. Salem: Foote & Chisholm, 1834. 95 p. Not in Rinderknecht. MSaE (interleaved), MWA. **1485**

Salem Athenaeum. Catalogue of the Library of the Athenaeum, in Salem, Massachusetts. With the By-laws and Regulations. Salem: Printed at the Office of the Gazette, 1842. xvi, 171 p. Rinderknecht 42-4383. CLSU, Ct, DLC, LU, MeP, M, MB, MH, MHi, MSaE, MWA, NN, NNC, PU, RPB, Salem Athenaeum. **1486**

Salem Athenaeum. Supplement to the Catalogue of the Library of the Athenaeum, in Salem, Massachusetts. 1849. [Salem, 1849]. 13 p. MHi, MSaE, PU. **1487**

Salem Athenaeum. A Catalogue of the Library of the Salem Athenaeum, in Salem, Massachusetts. To which is prefixed a brief Historical Account of the Institution with its Charter and By-laws. Boston: John Wilson and Son, 1858. xxi, 179 p. In many libraries. **1488**

Salem Evangelical Library. Rules & By-laws of the Salem Evangelical Library. Instituted Feb. 7, 1818. [Salem]: W. Palfray, jr., [1818]. 24 p. Catalogue of books on pp. 6-24. S & S 45620. MSaE. **1489**

Salem Evangelical Library. Extracts from the Rules & Catalogue of Books. [Salem?, 1830?] 32 p. Not in Cooper. MSaE. **1490**

Salem Library. A Catalogue of Books belonging to Salem Library. [Salem?, 1810?]. 4 p. S & S 21269. No locations given by S & S. **1491**

Salem Mechanic Library. Rules and By-laws of the Salem Mechanic Library. Instituted August 1820. Salem: Warwick Palfray, jun., 1821. 16 p. Catalogue of books on pp. 5-16. Shoemaker 6704, Rink 513. MSaE. **1492**

Salem Mechanic Library. Rules & By-laws of the Salem Mechanic Library. Instituted Aug. 1820. Salem: W. Palfray, jr., 1823. 24 p. Catalogue of books on pp. 5-24. Shoemaker 14036, Rink 523. MSaE, MWA. **1493**

Salem Mechanic Library. Catalogue of the Salem Mechanic Library, with the Rules and By-laws. Instituted August 1820. Salem: W. Palfray, jr., 1830. 31 p. Cooper 3390, Rink 573. MB, MHi, MSaE. **1494**

Salem Mechanic Library. Catalogue of the Salem Mechanic Library, together with the

Rules and By-laws. Instituted August, 1820. [Salem]: Foote and Brown, 1832. 32 p. Not in Bruntjen. MSaE, MWA. **1495**

Salem Mechanic Library. A Catalogue of the Salem Mechanic Library, together with the Rules and By-laws. Instituted August 1820. Salem: Palfray and Chapman, 1837. 35 p. Not in Bruntjen. MH, MSaE. **1496**

Salem Mechanic Library. Catalogue of the Salem Mechanic Library togethe Rule By-laws Instituted, August, 1820. Salem: Gazette Press, 1840. 48 p. Not in Bruntjen. MSaE, MWA. **1497**

Salem Mechanic Library. Catalogue of the Salem Mechanic Library, together with the Rules & By-laws. Instituted August, 1820. Salem: Register Press, 1851. 96 p. DLC, MH, MSaE, MWA. **1498**

Salem Mechanic Library. Supplement . . . 1854. Cf. Rhees, p. 161. **1499**

Salem Mechanic Library. Catalogue of the Salem Mechanic Library, together with the Rules and By-laws. Salem: Printed at the Observer Office, 1865. 84 p. MSaE. **1500**

Salem Mechanic Library. Catalogue of the Salem Mechanic Library, together with the Rules & By-laws. Instituted August, 1820. Salem: T. J. Hutchinson, 1871. 92 p. DLC, MHi, MsaE. **1501**

Salem Mechanic Library. Supplement . . . 1875. 15 p. Cf. Cutter 980. **1502**

Salem Social Library of Religion and Literature. Rules and Regulations of the Salem Social Library of Religion and Literature. Salem: Haven Pool, 1807. 15 p. Catalogue of books on pp. [9]-15. S & S 13540. MSaE, MWA. **1503**

Salem Teachers' Library. Salem Teachers' Library Catalogue. [Salem, 1875?]. 3 p. MSaE. **1504**

Second Baptist Church. A Catalogue of the Second Baptist Sunday School Library, in Salem. [Salem]: Salem Gazette Press, 1833. 16 p. Not in Bruntjen. MSaE. **1505**

Social Library. By-laws and Regulations of the Proprietors of the Social Library in Salem, with a Catalogue of the Books belonging to the Library. Salem: Thomas C. Cushing,

1809. 42 p. S & S 18650. The 1801 ed. called for by S & S 1286 is really the [1797?] ed. (Evans 32800). MH-H, MSaE, MWA. **1506**

South Church. Library Catalogue of the South Church Sabbath School, Salem. Salem: Printed at the Salem Press, 1871. 23 p. MSaE. **1507**

Tabernacle Church. Catalogue of the Library of the Tabernacle Sabbath School, Salem, Mass. Salem: Hutchinson's Printing Establishment, [1858?]. 11 p. MSaE. **1508**

Tabernacle Church. Catalogue of the Library of the Tabernacle Sabbath School, Salem, Mass. Salem: T. J. Hutchinson, 1861. 12 p. MSaE. **1509**

Tabernacle Church. Library of the Tabernacle Sabbath School, Salem, Mass. . . . Salem: T. J. Hutchinson, 1870. 16 p. MSaE. **1510**

Tabernacle Ministerial and Social Library. Rules and Regulations of the Tabernacle Ministerial and Social Library, with a Catalogue of the Books. Salem: Printed at the Register Office, 1826. 16 p. Not in Shoemaker. MSaE. **1511**

Salisbury

Public Library of Amesbury and Salisbury, see entry 653.

Union Evangelical Sabbath School of Amesbury & Salisbury, see entry 654.

Sherborn

Sherborn Town Library. Catalogue of Books and the Regulations of Sherborn Town Library. Instituted March, 1860. Boston: John Wilson, 1860. 48 p. NB. **1512**

Shrewsbury

Methodist Episcopal Sabbath School. Catalogue of the M. E. Sabbath School Library, Shrewsbury. 1871. Worcester: Chas. Hamilton, 1871. 15 p. MWA. **1513**

Somerville

First Congregational Society. Catalogue of the Sunday-School Library of the First Congregational Society, Somerville. Boston: Geo. C. Rand & Avery, 1867. 16 p. MB. **1514**

Somerville Public Library. [Catalogue]. Boston: J. A. Cummings, 1873. 84 p. Cutter 981 reports suppl., 1875? MB (defective).**1515**

Winter Hill School. Catalogue of the Winter Hill Juvenile Library. [Shrewsbury?]: Edmund Tufts, 1841. 8 p. Not in Rinderknecht. MWA. **1516**

South Danvers, see Peabody.

South Scituate

James Library. Catalogue of the James Library, South Scituate, Mass. Boston: W. F. Brown, 1874. 24 p. DLC holds undated suppl. #1 ([4] p.). DLC. **1517**

South Woburn, see Winchester.

Southborough

Fay Library. By-laws and Catalogue of the Fay Library, South Borough. Boston: Charles H. Crosby, 1859. 46 p. MB. **1518**

Fay Library. By-laws and Catalogue of the Fay Library, Southborough. Boston: Wright & Potter, 1869. 64 p. DLC holds suppl., March, 1872 (12 p.) and May, 1875 (2 p.). Cutter 605 reports suppl. for 1872, 1873, 1875. CtY, DLC, MB. **1519**

Southbridge

Southbridge Public Library. Catalogue of the Southbridge Public Library, Southbridge, Mass. Opened Feb. 4, 1871. Southbridge: Morse & Whitaker, 1871. 122 p. Cutter 708 reports suppl., 1872 (28 p.). DLC, MWA. **1520**

Southbridge Public Library. Supplement to Catalogue of the Southbridge Public Library. October 1, 1873. Miss A. Jeannette Comins, Librarian. [Southbridge?, 1873]. 58 p. DLC, MWA. **1521**

Spencer

Spencer Free Public Library. Catalogue of the Spencer Free Public Library. Worcester: E. R. Fiske, 1871. 40 p. DLC holds suppl., 1875? (11 p.). DLC (interleaved). **1522**

Spencer Library. Catalogue of the Spencer Library. Worcester: Chas. Hamilton, 1865. 24 p. MWA. **1523**

Springfield

(see also West Springfield).

City Library Association. Catalogue of the Library of the City Library Association, Springfield, Mass. Springfield: Samuel Bowles, 1871. xii, 668 p. CtW, DLC (film), DNLM, M, MA, MB, MSCV, MShM, MWelC, MWA, N, OKentU, PU. **1524**

Hampden Mechanic Association. Catalogue of Books in the Apprentices' Library belonging to the Hampden Mechanic Association, Springfield, Mass. [n.p., 1834?]. 12 p. Not in Cooper, Bruntjen, or Rinder-knecht. MSCV. **1525**

High School Library. A Catalogue of the High School Library, with the Regulations for its Government. Springfield, Mass. 1850. Springfield: G. W. Wilson, 1850. 19 p. MB. **1526**

Springfield Institute, see Young Men's Institute Library.

Young Men's Institute Library. Catalogue of the Institute Library, with the Constitution & By-laws. Springfield: Howard S. Taylor, 1847. 78, [1] p. DLC, MA, MB, MH, MSCV. **1527**

Young Men's Library Association. Catalogue . . . Springfield: C. W. Bryan, 1873. 41 p. DLC. **1528**

Sterling

Sterling Public Library. Catalogue of the Sterling Public Library. 1874. Clinton: W. J. Coulter, 1874. 90 p. DLC. **1529**

Stockbridge

Berkshire Republican Library. Catalogue . . . [n.p., 181-?]. "Undoubtedly two editions of a catalogue were issued or at least planned . . ." Cf. Harry M. Lydenberg, "The Berkshire Republican Library at Stockbridge, 1794-1818," *Proceedings of the American Antiquarian Society* 50 (1940): 124. **1530**

Stoneham

Methodist Episcopal Church. Catalogue of the Methodist Episcopal Sabbath School Library, Stoneham, Mass. 1869. Boston: J. W. Pitman & Son, 1869. 16 p. MBSi. **1531**

Public Library. Catalogue of the Public Library of the Town of Stoneham. Re-catalogued April, 1866. Boston: J. E. Farwell, 1866. 76 p. DLC holds Appendix A . . . July, 1870 (30 p.) and Appendix B . . . September, 1872 (24 p.). DLC, MB, NN.
1532

Stoneham Social Library. Catalogue of Books in the Stoneham Social Library. Organized, March 1st, 1792. Names of Proprietors and By-laws. Stoneham, 1853. 17 p. DLC. **1533**

Stoughton

Stoughton Library. Catalogue of Books, belonging to the Stoughton Library. [Stoughton?, 183-?]. broadside. Not in Cooper, Bruntjen, or Rinderknecht. Stoughton Public Library. **1534**

Stoughton Public Library. Catalogue of the Public Library, Stoughton, Mass. Stoughton: Office of the "Stoughton Sentinel," 1875. 23, [1] p. DLC, MB. **1535**

Stoughton Public Library. Catalogue of the Public Library, Stoughton, Mass. Stoughton: Office of the "Stoughten Sentinel," 1875. 38, ix p. NN. **1536**

Sturbridge

Sturbridge Public Library. Catalogue of the Sturbridge Public Library, Sturbridge, Mass. November, 1873. Southbridge: Printed at the Journal Office, 1873. 19 p. Cutter 843 reports suppl., Books added during 1873-74 (39 p.). DLC. **1537**

Sudbury

Goodnow Library. Catalogue of the Goodnow Library, Sudbury, Mass., funded by the Munificence of John Goodnow, late of Boston, to his Native Town, and opened to the Citizens of the Town on Saturday, April 4, 1863. Concord: Benjamin Tolman, 1867. 97 p. MB holds suppl., 1869 (15 p.). Cutter 552 reports suppl., 1871 (11 p.). DLC, MB.
1538

Goodnow Library. Catalogue of the Goodnow Library, Sudbury, Mass. Sudbury, 1874. 108 p. DLC holds suppl. #1, Dec. 1874 (5 p.). DLC, MB. **1539**

Sunderland

Sunderland Library. Catalogue of Books, in the Sunderland Library. Amherst: Storrs & M'Cloud, 1870. 43 p. Cutter 647 reports suppl., 1871 (4 p.). DLC. **1540**

Sutton

Sutton Free Library. Catalogue of the Sutton Free Library. Established March 15, 1875. D. T. Thurston, Librarian. Worcester: Charles Hamilton, 1875. 18 p. MWA. **1541**

Taunton

Social Library. By-laws of the Proprietors of the Social Library in the Town of Taunton. Taunton: Edmund Anthony, 1836. 36 [i.e. 34] p. "Catalogue" on pp. [9-30]. Rinderknecht 40414. CSmH. **1542**

Social Library. Catalogue of the Taunton Social Library, in the Town of Taunton, with an Appendix, containing the By-laws of the Library. And a List of the Officers for the Year 1841. Taunton: Israel Amsbury, jr., 1841. 47 p. Not in Rinderknecht. MB, MWA (with blank leaves for additions), NN (interleaved with ms. additions). **1543**

Taunton Public Library. Catalogue of the Public Library of the City of Taunton. Established, 1866. Taunton: [C. A. Hack & Son], 1866. 234 p. A periodicals list appears in the *Annual Report of the Trustees of the Public Library of Taunton* for 1867-73, etc. MWA holds suppl., 1869/70 (20 p.) DLC, MB, NN, Old Colony Historical Society (Taunton). **1544**

Taunton Public Library. Supplementary Catalogue of New Books added from the Opening to Jan. 1, 1873. Taunton: Republican Steam Printing Rooms, 1873. 165 p. DLC, NN. **1545**

Taunton Public Library. Supplementary Catalogue of New Books added during 1873. Taunton: Republican Steam Printing Rooms, 1874. 39 p. DLC. **1546**

Trinitarian Congregational Church. Catalogue of Books in the Sabbath School Library of the Trinitarian Congregational Church, Taunton, Mass. Taunton: American Republican Office, 1859. Cf. F. A.

Briggs, "Sunday School Libraries in the 19th Century," *Library Quarterly* 31 (1961): 173, note 37. **1547**

Templeton

Boynton Free Public Library. Catalogue of the Boynton Free Public Library, Templeton, Mass. Gardner: A. G. Bushnell, 1873. 48 p. MWA holds undated suppl., #1-4. DLC, MB, MWA. **1548**

Ladies' Social Circle. Catalogue of Books in the Library of the Ladies' Social Circle of the First Parish, Templeton, Mass. Fitchburg: E. & J. F. D. Garfield, 1857. 12 p. DLC copy (20 p.) includes entries for 1857-1866 imprints. DLC, MWA. **1549**

Tisbury

Holmes Hole Baptist Church. Catalogue of Books in the Library of the Holmes Hole Baptist Sabbath-School, Tisbury, Mass. New Bedford: Standard Steam Printing House, 1859. 17, [1] p. MNBedf also holds a later (?) catalogue, lacking the title page and all pages after p. 8. MNBedf. **1550**

Topsfield

Ladies' Society. Catalogue of the Books belonging to the Ladies' Society, Topsfield. Salem: Gazette Press, 1852. 8 p. MSaE, MWA (with blank leaves for additions). **1551**

Topsfield Town Library. Catalogue of the Topsfield Town Library. 1875. Salem: Press of the Essex County Mercury, 1875. 46 p. MWA, Topsfield Historical Society, Topsfield, Mass. **1552**

Upton

Methodist Sunday School. Catalogue of Books in the Library of the Methodist Sunday School, Upton, Mass. [n.p., 187-?]. 12 p. MNBedf. **1553**

Upton Town Library. Catalogue of Books and By-laws of the Upton Town Library. Upton, Mass. Founded March, 1871. Milford: Cook & Sons, 1874. 20 p. DLC. **1554**

Uxbridge

Free Public Library. Catalogue . . . Uxbridge, 1874. M formerly held the 1874 catalogue as well as Appendix #1-2 (1875). Cf. *Catalogue of the State Library of Massachusetts* (Boston, 1880), p. 878. **1555**

Wakefield

Beebe Town Library. Catalogue . . . 1872. 35 p. Cf. Cutter 748. **1556**

Walpole

Walpole Social Library. Catalogue . . . 1826. Not in Shoemaker. Cf. Willard De Lue, *The Story of Walpole, 1724-1924* (Norwood, Mass., 1925), pp. 302-3. **1557**

Walpole Town Library. Catalogue of the Walpole Town Library. October, 1869. Boston: Wright & Potter, [1869]. 31 p. MB, MWA. **1558**

Waltham

Manufacturers' Library. Catalogue of Books, in the Manufacturers' Library, Waltham. Boston: True & Green, 1822. 18+ p. Not in Shoemaker; Rink 516. DeGe (defective). **1559**

Public Library. Catalogue of the Public Library of Waltham. Waltham: Hastings' Sentinel Office, 1865. 108 p. MB holds first suppl. (5 p.). MB. **1560**

Public Library. Catalogue of the Public Library of Waltham. Waltham: Hastings' Sentinel Office, 1870. 150 p. MB holds suppl. #1-3; 1870-71. DLC, MB. **1561**

Public Library. Catalogue of the Public Library of Waltham. January, 1875. Waltham, 1875. iii, 259, [1] p. DLC, MB. **1562**

Rumford Institute. Catalogue of the Books belonging to the Rumford Institute, Waltham. Cambridge: E. W. Metcalf, 1831. 28 p. Brunjen 9048. MB. **1563**

Rumford Institute. Catalogue of the Books belonging to the Rumford Institute, Waltham, Mass. Waltham: Josiah Hastings, 1848. 32 p. MWA. **1564**

Rumford Institute. Catalogue of Books belonging to the Rumford Institute, Waltham, Mass. Waltham: Josiah Hastings, 1860. 72 p. MWA. **1565**

Watertown

First Congregational Society. Catalogue of the Library of the Sunday School connected with the First Congregational Society, Watertown. Boston: Crosby, Nichols, 1853. 32 p. NB.   **1566**

Free Public Library. Catalogue of the Free Public Library of the Town of Watertown. January, 1870. Boston: S. Chism, Franklin Printing House, 1870. 188 p. DLC holds suppl. #2-5; 1871/72-Springfield 5; MWat hold suppl., 1871-77; MWA holds suppl., 1870/71-1871/72 Suppl. #1-9 (1870/71-79) also appear in the Library's *Annual Report*. DLC, M, MB, MWat, MWA, N, RPB, Watertown Free Public Library.   **1567**

Harrington, J. B. Catalogue of J. B. Harrington's Circulating Library, Watertown, Ms. August, 1837. Watertown, 1837. 22 p. Not in Rinderknecht. MH, MWat.   **1568**

Wayland

Public Library. Catalogue of the Public Library of the Town of Wayland. Boston: Franklin Press, Rand, Avery, 1875. 128 p. DLC.   **1569**

Wayland Town Library. Catalogue of Books belonging to the Wayland Town Library. 1853. Boston: John Wilson & Son, 1853. 79, [1] p. DLC, MWA, ViW, WU (School of Library and Information Studies).   **1570**

Wayland Town Library. Catalogue of Books belonging to the Wayland Town Library. 1865. Waltham: Hastings' Sentinel Press, 1865. 58 p. DLC holds suppl., 1867-72. DLC, MB (also undetermined suppl.; all lost?).   **1571**

Webster

Baptist Sabbath School. Catalogue of Books in the Baptist S. School Library, Webster, Ms. July, 1844. Worcester: H. J. Howland, [1844]. 21 p. Not in Rinderknecht. MWA.   **1572**

Congregational S. S. Library. Catalogue of the Congregational S. S. Library, Webster, Mass. [Webster?]: Times Office, 1865. 15 p. MWA.   **1573**

Wendell

Social Library. Catalogue of Books, belonging to the Social Library, in Wendell. June, 1829. [Cambridge?]: John Metcalf, 1829. 8 p. Not in Shoemaker. MWA.   **1574**

Wenham

Wenham Library Association. Catalogue of the Library of the Wenham Library Association, with the Names of the Officers for the Year 1868, and a List of the Members. Salem: T. J. Hutchinson, 1868. 12 p. MWA.   **1575**

West Brookfield

Public Library. Catalogue of the Public Library of the Town of West Brookfield. April 1, 1874. West Brookfield: Thomas Morey, 1874. 30 p. DLC holds "Supplementary Catalogue (A)," ca. 1875 (16 p. but pp. 15-16 blank), per Bureau of Education date stamp, March 2, 1875. DLC.   **1576**

West Cambridge

(see also later name Arlington)

Orthodox Congregational Church. Catalogue of the West Cambridge Orthodox Congregational Sabbath School Library. July, 1864. Boston: Geo. C. Rand & Avery, 1864. 16 p. NB.   **1577**

Orthodox Congregational Church. [Catalogue of the West Cambridge Orthodox Congregational Sabbath School Library]. [Boston, 1866]. 12 p. MB (defective without title page; entered under: Arlington, Mass. Orthodox Congregational Church).   **1578**

West Cambridge Juvenile Library. Catalogue of Books in the West Cambridge Juvenile Library, West Cambridge, Mass. Boston: W. & E. Howe, 1861. 44 p. MB.   **1579**

West Cambridge Social Library. Catalogue of Books in the West-Cambridge Social Library. To which are prefixed, the By-laws of the Institution. Boston: Munroe and Francis, 1835. 22 p. Not in Rinderknecht. MWA.   **1580**

West Cambridge Social Library. Catalogue of the Books in West-Cambridge Social Library. Arlington, 1843. Not in Rinderknecht.

Robbins Library, Arlington, Mass. (not veri-
fied because the Historical Collection was in
storage).   **1581**

West Newton

(see also Newton)

Newton Athenaeum. Catalogue of Books in the
Newton Athenaeum, with a Sketch of the
Origin and Object of the Institution. Boston:
Bazin & Chandler, 1856. 41 p. MB.   **1582**

Newton Athenaeum. Catalogue of the New-ton
Athenaeum Library, West Newton. Boston:
Stacy & Richardson, 1860. 56 p. WU (School
of Library and Information Studies).   **1583**

Newton Athenaeum. Catalogue of the Newton
Athenaeum Library. West Newton. Boston: A.
A. Kingman, 1871. xv, 110 p. Cutter 703
reports suppl., 1874 (23 p.). DLC, MB. **1584**

West Roxbury

(see also Roxbury)

First Parish Sunday School. Catalogue of
Books in the Library of the First Parish
Sunday School, West Roxbury. Dedham: H.
H. McQuillen, 1873. 22 p. DLC holds suppl.,
1874 ([2] p.). DLC.   **1585**

West Roxbury Free Library. Catalogue of the West
Roxbury Free Library, with the Regulations for its
use. Boston: Wright & Potter, 1863. 39 p. DLC
holds undated suppl., Books added . . . since
September, 1863 (11 p.). DLC.   **1586**

West Roxbury Free Library. Catalogue . . .
Additions, 1869-74 . . . 1874. 32 p. Cf. Cutter
919.   **1587**

West Springfield

(see also Springfield)

West Springfield Library Association. Catalogue of the Books of the West Springfield
Library Association. 1873. Springfield: C. W.
Bryan, 1873. 36 p. DLC (interleaved with
ms. additions).   **1588**

Westboro

Westboro' Mechanic Association. Catalogue
of the Westboro' Mechanic Association's
Library. August, 1848. [n.p., 1848?]. 16 p.
MWA (defective).   **1589**

Westboro' Town Library. Catalogue of
Westboro' Town Library. April, 1874.
Boston: Rand, Avery, 1874. 61 p. DLC.
                                        1590

Westborough, see Westboro.

Westfield

Normal Lyceum and Library Association.
Constitution, By-laws, and Catalogue of the
Library of the Normal Lyceum and Library
Association, Westfield, Mass. July, 1858.
Springfield: Samuel Bowles, 1858. 12 p.
MH, Westfield Athenaeum.   **1591**

Westfield Athenaeum. Catalogue of the
Westfield Athenaeum, of Westfield, Mass.
[Westfield]: Clark & Story, 1873. 135 p.
DLC, Westfield Athenaeum.   **1592**

Westford

Public Library of Westford. Catalogue of the
Public Library, Westford. Lawrence: Printed
at Sentinel Office, 1871. 69 p. A suppl.
(12 p.), published Lowell, 1874, is held by
the J. V. Fletcher Library, Westford, Mass.
DLC.   **1593**

Westford Social Library. Catalogue of Books
in Westford Social Library. 1816. [n.p.,
1816]. 4 p. Not in S & S. J. V. Fletcher
Library, Westford, Mass.   **1594**

Westford Social Library. Catalogue of Books
in Westford Social Library. Lowell: S. J.
Varney, 1852. 12 p. J. V. Fletcher Library,
Westford, Mass.   **1595**

Westminster

Westminster Literary Society. Catalogue of
Books belonging to the Westminster Liter-
ary Society Library. Fitchburg: E. & J. F. D.
Garfield, 1855. 8 p. MWA.   **1596**

Weston

Weston Town Library. Catalogue of the
Weston Town Library . . . 1859. 60 p. MB
(lost).   **1597**

Weston Town Library. Catalogue of the
Weston Town Library. 1871. Boston: Rand,
Avery, & Frye, [1871]. 72 p. DLC, M, MH,
MWA.   **1598**

Westport

Pacific Union Sabbath School. Catalogue of Books in the Library of the Pacific Union Sabbath School, Westport. New Bedford: E. Anthony & Sons, 1875. 16 p. MNBedf.
1599

Weymouth

First Social Library. Catalogue of Books, belonging to the First Social Library in Weymouth. [Boston: W. W. Clapp, 1829?]. 8 p. Not in Shoemaker. MWA.   **1600**

Union Social Library of Braintree and Weymouth, see entry 948.

Universalist Sunday School. A Catalogue of the Universalist Sunday School Library in Weymouth, Ms. Boston: J. N. Bang, 1846. 8 p. MWA.   **1601**

Whitinsville

Whitinsville Social Library. Catalogue of Books in the Whitinsville Social Library. Woonsocket: S. S. Foss, 1855. 27 p. MB holds suppl. for 1856 and 1857 (2 p. each). MB.   **1602**

Wilbraham

Wesleyan Academy. Catalogue of Books in the Library of Wesleyan Academy. Springfield: Union Printing Co., 1868. 48 p. MB copy includes suppl. (4 p.). MB.   **1603**

Williamstown

Jackson Theological Library, see entry 1612.

Mills Theological Society. Catalogue of the Mills Theological Society, with a Short Sketch of its History, by Prof. Albert Hopkins. Williamstown, 1853. 58 p. Library catalogue on pp. 27-58. MWiW.   **1604**

Williams College. Catalogue of Books in the Library of Williams College, Williamstown. Stockbridge: Heman Willard, 1802. 16 p. S & S 3565. CtHT, MBC, MWiW.   **1605**

Williams College. Catalogue of Books in the Library of Williams College, Williamstown. Stockbridge: Heman Willard, [1812]. 36 p. Catalogue of the Adelphic Union Library on pp. 25-36. S & S 27563. MWA, MWiW.
1606

Williams College. Catalogue of Books in the Library of Williams College, Williamstown. Albany: Websters & Skinners, 1821. 36 p. Catalogue of the Adelphic Union Library on pp. [25]-36. Shoemaker 7675. DGW, MWA, MWiW, N, NN, NNebgWM.   **1607**

Williams College. Catalogue of Books in the Library of Williams College, Williamstown. Williamstown: Ridley Bannister, 1828. 40 p. Catalogue of the Adelphic Union Library on pp. [29]-40. Shoemaker 37199. MWA, MWiW, MnU.   **1608**

Williams College. Catalogue of Books in the Library of Williams College, Williamstown. Troy: Norman Tuttle, 1836. Rinderknecht 42494. MH.   **1609**

Williams College. Catalogue of Books in the Library of Williams College, Williamstown. Boston: T. R. Marvin, 1845. 51 p. CU-SB, DLC, MH, MWiW, MWA, MiU.   **1610**

Williams College. Catalogue of Books in the Library of Williams College, Williamstown. Boston: T. R. Marvin 1852. 62 p. DLC, MBAt, MH, MHi, MWiW, MWA, MnU.
1611

Williams College. Catalogue of Books in the Library of Williams College, Williamstown. 1861. Boston: T. R. Marvin & Son, 1861. 87, [1] p. Catalogue of the Jackson Theological Library on pp. 86-87. DHEW, ICN, IU, M, MA, MB, MH, MHi, MWiW, MWA, N. **1612**

Williams College. Supplementary Catalogue of Williams College. January 1, 1867. Boston: T. R. Marvin & Son, 1867. 20 p. IU, MB, MH, MHi, MWiW.   **1613**

Williams College. Catalogue of the Library of Williams College, Williamstown, Mass. 1875. North Adams: James T. Robinson & Son, 1875. 233 p. DLC, IU, M, MA, MB, MBAt, MH, MHi, MWiW, MWA, NhD, N, OO.
1614

Williams College. Adelphic Union, see also entries 1606-8.

Williams College. Adelphic Union. Catalogue of the Adelphic Union Library. [n.p., 1831]. 22 p. Not in Bruntjen. MWA.   **1615**

Williams College. Lyceum of Natural History. Catalogue of the Lyceum of Natural History of Williams College. Instituted A.D. 1835. Williamstown, 1852. 60 p. Library catalogue on pp. 45-48. CtY, MB, MH, MWiW, NIC, PU. **1616**

Williams College. Philologian Society. Catalogue of the Philo-Logian Library, Williams College. 1843. Troy: N. Tuttle, [1843]. 24 p. Rinderknecht 43-5303. MH, MWiW, N (misc. pamphlet box, 017.1), NH, NN, NNC. **1617**

Williams College. Philologian Society. Triennial Catalogue of the Philo-Logian Society, Williams College. June, 1847. Springfield: Horace S. Taylor, 1847. 51 p. Library catalogue on pp. 35-51. MB, MH, MWiW. **1618**

Williams College. Philologian Society. Triennial Catalogue of the Philologian Society of Williams College. Founded A.D. 1795. Williamstown, 1850. 110 p. Library catalogue on pp. 43-110. MWiW. **1619**

Williams College. Philologian Society. Catalogue of the Philologian Library of Williams College. Williamstown, 1853. 74 p. MWiW, MnU. **1620**

Williams College. Philologian Society. Catalogue of the Philologian Library of Williams College. 1856. Williamstown, 1856. 81 p. MWiW, MWA. **1621**

Williams College. Philologian Society. Library Catalogue and the Constitution and By-laws of the Philologian Society, Williams College. 1862. Williamstown, 1862. 89 p. KyU (lacks pp. 83-89), MH. **1622**

Williams College. Philotechnian Society. Triennial Catalogue of the Philo-Technian Society of Williams College. Formed 1795. Troy: J. C. Kneeland, 1844. 32 p. Library catalogue on pp. 25-32. Not in Rinderknecht. MWiW. **1623**

Williams College. Philotechnian Society. Triennial Catalogue of the Philo-Technian Society, Williams College. June, 1847. Springfield: Horace S. Taylor, 1847. 49 p. Library catalogue on pp. 35-49. MB, MWiW. **1624**

Williams College. Philotechnian Society. Triennial Catalogue of the Philotechnian Society of Williams College. Instituted A.D.

1795. Williamstown, 1850. 112 p. Library catalogue on pp. 47-111. MWiW. **1625**

Williams College. Philotechnian Society. Triennial Catalogue of the Philotechnian Society of Williams College. Instituted A.D. 1795. Williamstown, 1853. 120 p. Library catalogue on pp. 49-120. DLC (pp. 49-120 only), MWiW. **1626**

Williams College. Philotechnian Society. Catalogue of the Philotechnian Library of Williams College. 1856. Williamstown, 1856. 79 p. MWA. **1627**

Williams College. Philotechnian Society. Library Catalogue and the Constitution and By-laws of the Philotechnian Society of Williams College. Williamstown, 1861. 82 p. MH, MWiW, MWA. **1628**

Williams College. Philotechnian Society. Library Catalogue and the Constitution and By-laws of the Philotechnian Society of Williams College. 1867. Williamstown, 1867. 77 p. MWiW, MWA. **1629**

Winchendon

Winchendon Public Library. Catalogue of the Winchendon Public Library. 1867. Winchendon, 1867. 21 p. MB. **1630**

Winchendon Public Library. List of New Books Added. Winchendon, 1869-. DLC (1869, 1871-73), MB (1869). **1631**

Winchester

(formerly South Woburn)

South Woburn Library Association. Catalogue of Books belonging to the South Woburn Library Association. Established 1848. Boston: Abner Forbes, [ca. 1848-50]. 15 p. Later incorporated as the Winchester Library Association. DeU, MWA. **1632**

Winchester Library Association. Constitution and Catalogue of Books of the Winchester Library Association. Established 1848. Boston: Damrell & Moore, 1851. 24 p. MWA. **1633**

Winchester Library Association. The Constitution and Catalogue of Books belonging to the Winchester Library Association. April, 1856. [n.p., 1856]. 32 p. MWA. **1634**

Winchester Town Library. By-laws and Catalogue of the Public Library of the Town of Winchester. Boston: William A. Hall, 1859. 24 p. MWA.   **1635**

Winchester Town Library. Catalogue of Books purchased for the Winchester Town Library. May, 1860. [n.p., 1860]. 2 p. MWA holds similar catalogue, May, 1861. MWA.   **1636**

Winchester Town Library. Catalogue . . . 1864. Cf. Cutter 501.   **1637**

Winchester Town Library. By-laws and Catalogue of the Town Library, Winchester, Mass. Woburn: Middlesex Journal Office, H. C. Gray, Printer, 1869. 39 p. Cutter 613 reports two suppl. MB.   **1638**

Winchester Town Library. By-laws and Catalogue of the Town Library, Winchester, Mass. Woburn: John L. Parker, 1874. 108 p. DLC, MB, MWA, N.   **1639**

Woburn

Charitable Religious Library. Constitution of the Charitable Religious Library in Woburn, and Catalogue of Books which it contains. Woburn, 1807. 8 p. Not in S & S. Was connected with the First Congregational Church, per Samuel Sewall, *The History of Woburn, Middlesex County, Mass.* (Boston, 1868), p. 516; D. Hamilton Hurd, *History of Middlesex County, Massachusetts* (Philadelphia, 1890), vol. 1, p. 409.   **1640**

Charitable Religious Library. Catalogue . . . June, 1856. 12 p. Cf. Rhees 172 (under "Religious Charitable Library"); D. Hamilton Hurd, *History of Middlesex County, Massachusetts* (Philadelphia, 1890), vol. 1, p. 409.   **1641**

Charitable Religious Library. Catalogue . . . 1868. Cf. D. Hamilton Hurd, *History of Middlesex County, Massachusetts* (Philadelphia, 1890), vol. 1, p. 409.   **1642**

First Unitarian Parish. [Catalogue of the Sunday School Library]. [Boston, 1868?]. 17 p. MB (defective).   **1643**

New Bridge Library Association. Catalogue of Books belonging to New Bridge Library Association. Woburn: Fowle & Brother, 1852. 12 p. Woburn Public Library.   **1644**

New Bridge Library Association. Catalogue of Books belonging to New Bridge Library

Association. [Woburn?, 185-?]. 15 p. Woburn Public Library.   **1645**

North Woburn Library Association. Catalogue of Books belonging to the North Woburn Library Association. Boston: Geo. L. Keyes, 1874. 24 p.   Woburn Public Library.   **1646**

Pippy's Circulating Library. Catalogue of Pippy's Circulating Library, at the Woburn Book Store. Woburn: John J. Pippy, 1857. 13 p., [3] p. of advertisements.   MWA, Woburn Public Library.   **1647**

Woburn Circulating Library. Catalogue of the Books in the Woburn Circulating Library . . . at the Apothecary Store of J. M. Grosvenor & Co. Boston: Alfred Mudge & Son, 1867. 15 p. Woburn Public Library.   **1648**

Woburn Public Library. Catalogue of the Public Library of the Town of Woburn. Woburn: John J. Pippy, 1856. 61 p. NN, Woburn Public Library.   **1649**

Woburn Public Library. Catalogue of the Woburn Library. Appendix (I.). Woburn: E. T. Moody, 1862. 36 p.   Woburn Public Library.   **1650**

Woburn Public Library. Catalogue of the Woburn Public Library. Opened July, 1856. Woburn: E. Marchant, 1865. 66 p. DLC copy contains appendices for 1866-70 (15 p.) and 1871 (7 p.); MB holds appendices for 1866-72; Woburn Public Library holds suppl. (1873) containing all the accessions from 1866 to 1873 (46 p.). New books are listed in the 18th *Report of the Library Committee of the Town of Woburn,* 1875. DLC, M, MB, MWA, NN, Woburn Public Library.   **1651**

Woburn Young Men's Library. Catalogue of Books in the Woburn Young Men's Library. Jan. 1st, 1852. [Woburn, 1852]. 4 p. Woburn Public Library.   **1652**

Woburn Young Men's Society. Constitution, By-laws and Regulations of the Woburn Young Men's Society, together with a Catalogue of the Books contained in their Library. January 1, 1835. Boston: Webster and Southard, [1835]. 16 p. Not in Rinderknecht. Woburn Public Library.   **1653**

Worcester

All Saints Church. Catalogue of the Sunday School Library of All Saints Church, Worcester. Worcester: Goddard & Nye, 1868. 19 p. MWA. **1654**

American Antiquarian Society. A Catalogue of Books in the Library of the American Antiquarian Society, in Worcester Massachusetts. Worcester: Henry Howland, [1836]-37. various pagings. Compiled by Christopher C. Baldwin and completed by Maturin L. Fisher. MWA copy, in 3 vol., has ms. notes. Rinderknecht 35721. In many libraries. **1655**

Baptist Sabbath School. Catalogue of Books in the Baptist Sabbath School Library, Worcester, January, 1836 . . . Worcester: Henry J. Howland, 1835. 12 p. Not in Rinderknecht. MWA. **1656**

Calvinist Sabbath School. Catalogue of the Calvinist Sabbath School Library, Worcester. Worcester: Edward R. Fiske, 1854. 29 p. MWA, N. **1657**

Chamberlin's Circulating Library. Revised Catalogue of Miss Chamberlin's Circulating Library . . . Worcester: Tyler & Seagrave, 1870. 37 p. Operated by Lottie Chamberlin. MWA. **1658**

Chamberlin's Circulating Library. Catalogue of Circulating Library, at Chamberlain's [!] News Room . . . Worcester: Goddard & Nye, 1872. 20 p. Operated by Lottie Chamberlin. MWA. **1659**

Dorman's Circulating Library. Revised Catalogue of Mrs. Dorman's Circulating Library . . . Worcester: Tyler & Seagrave, [ca. 1870]. 22 p. Operated by Mrs. James A. Dorman. MWA. **1660**

First Parish. Catalogue of the Sabbath School Library, First Parish, Worcester. [Worcester, 185-?]. 21 p. MWA. **1661**

First Parish. Catalogue of the Sabbath School Library, First Parish, Worcester. Worcester: Chas. Hamilton, 1852. 27 p. MWA. **1662**

Free Public Library. Supplementary Index of Additions and Corrections to the Free Public Library, Worcester. July, 1860. [Worcester, 1860]. 36 p. MWA. **1663**

Free Public Library. Catalogue of the Circulating Department, Worcester, 1861. Worcester: Chas. Hamilton, 1861. 186 p. DLC and MWA hold "Addenda, 1864" (187-220 p.); MWA and N hold "Addenda, 1867" (84 p.); MB and MWA hold "List of Books added . . . for the Year ending May 1, 1868" (46 p.). New books also listed in *Annual Report of the Free Public Library, Worcester.* DLC, M, MB, MBAt, MH, MW, MWA, N. **1664**

Free Public Library. Catalogue of the Circulating Department, Worcester, 1870. Worcester: Chas. Hamilton, 1870. 349 p. MWA holds semi-annual "List of Books added to the Free Public Library" for Jan. 1-June 1, 1874 (24 p.), June 1, 1874-Jan. 1, 1875 (36 p.), Jan. 1-July 1, 1875 (36 p.), July 1, 1875-Jan. 1, 1876 (34 p.). New books also listed in *Annual Report of the Free Public Library, Worcester.* CtY, DLC, M, MB, MBAt, MH, N. **1665**

Free Public Library. Supplement to the Catalogue of the Circulating Department. Worcester, 1874. Worcester: Chas. Hamilton, 1874. 251 p. New books also listed in *Annual Report of the Free Public Library,* Worcester. DLC, MB, MBAt, MWA, N, OHi. **1666**

Grace Methodist Episcopal Church. Catalogue of Books in the Sabbath School Library of Grace M. E. Church, Worcester, Mass. [Worcester]: Charles E. Nye, 1874. 29 p. MWA. **1667**

Harris's (Clarendon) Circulating Library. A Catalogue of Clarendon Harris's Circulating Library at the Worcester Book-Store . . . Worcester: M. W. Grout, 1835, 36 p. Not in Rinderknecht. MWA. **1668**

Jail and House of Correction. Catalogue of Books in the Library of the Jail and House of Correction, in Worcester. Worcester: Chas. Hamilton, 1860. 16 p. MWA. **1669**

Main Street Baptist Church. Catalogue of Books in the Library of the Main Street Baptist Sabbath School, Worcester, Mass. September 1, 1869. Worcester: Tyler & Seagrave, [1869]. 30 p. MWA. **1670**

Park Street Methodist Episcopal Church. Catalogue of the Books in the Park Street M. E. Sabbath School Library. 1855. Worcester: C. B. Webb, [1855]. 11 p. MWA. **1671**

Park Street Methodist Episcopal Church. Catalogue of Books in the Sabbath School Library of the Park Street M. E. Church, Worcester. Worcester: S. Chism, 1857. 16 p. MWA.   **1672**

Plymouth Church. Catalogue of the Plymouth Church Sabbath School Library, Worcester, Mass. Worcester: Goddard & Nye, 1871. 31 p. MWA.   **1673**

Salem Street Church. Catalogue of the Salem Street Sabbath School Library, Worcester. July, 1852. Worcester: Henry J. Howland, [1852]. 25 p. MWA.   **1674**

Second Congregational Church. Catalogue of Books in the Library of the Second Parish. January, 1837. Worcester: Printed at the Spy Office, [1837]. 16 p. Not in Rinderknecht. MWA.   **1675**

Second Congregational Church. Catalogue of Books in the Library of the Second Parish. November, 1838. Worcester: Henry J. Howland, 1838. 16 p. Not in Rinderknecht. MWA.   **1676**

Second Congregational Church. Catalogue of Books in the Sunday School Library of the Second Parish, Worcester. 1853. Worcester: Henry J. Howland, [1853]. 16 p. MWA.   **1677**

Second Congregational Church. Catalogue of Books in the Sunday School Library of the Second Parish, Worcester. 1857. Worcester: Henry J. Howland, [1857]. 16 p. MWA.   **1678**

Second Congregational Church. Catalogue of the Sunday School Library of the Second Parish, Worcester. Worcester: Chas. Hamilton, 1875. 22 p. MWA.   **1679**

Tucker's Circulating Library. Catalogue of E. N. Tucker's Circulating Library, in the Worcester Book Store. Worcester: C. Buckingham Webb, [ca. 1850]. 40 p. Operated by Erastus N. Tucker. MWA.
                                               1680

Universalist Sabbath School. Catalogue of Books in the Library of the Universalist Sabbath School. February 10, 1864. [Worcester, 1864]. 20 p. MWA.   **1681**

Universalist Sabbath School. Catalogue of the Books in the Library of the Universalist

Sabbath School, Worcester, Mass. Worcester: Tyler & Seagrave, 1871. 40 p. MWA.
                                               1682

Valley Falls Church. Catalogue of Valley Falls Sabbath School Library, Worcester, Mass. [Worcester]: Charles E. Nye, 1872. 8 p. MWA.   **1683**

Ward's (A. H.) Select Circulating Library. Revised Catalogue of A. H. Ward's Select Circulating Library, at the Bookstore, No. 2 American House Block, Main Street. Worcester: A. H. Ward, 1860. 16 p. MWA.
                                               1684

Worcester County Horticultural Society. Transactions of the Worcester County Horticultural Society, for the Year 1855, containing the Annual Reports, Triennial Festival, the Officers of the Society for 1855, a List of the New Members, and Catalogue of the Library. Worcester: Fiske & Reynolds, 1855. 50 p. A library catalogue also appears in the *Transactions* for 1857/64; lists of additions appear in some of the subsequent volumes. MWA, PPL.   **1685**

Worcester County Law Library. Catalogue of the Worcester County Law Library. 1864. Worcester: Chas. Hamilton, [1864]. 60 p. CtY-L, DLC, ICJ, ICU, MU, MWA.   **1686**

Worcester County Mechanics Association. Constitution of the Worcester County Mechanics Association, with a List of Members and Catalogue of the Library. January, 1849. Worcester: Henry J. Howland, [1849]. 56 p. CtHT, MWA.   **1687**

Worcester County Mechanics Association. Historical Sketch of the Worcester County Mechanics Association, with the Charter and By-laws, a List of Members, and Catalogue of the Library. July, 1854. Worcester: Henry J. Howland, [1854]. 78 p. ICN, MB, MWA.   **1688**

Worcester County Mechanics Association. Catalogue of the Library of the Worcester County Mechanics Association. April, 1857. Worcester: Henry J. Howland, [1857]. 83 p. MWA holds suppl., April, 1858. DLC, MWA, NNC.   **1689**

Worcester County Mechanics Association. Catalogue of the Library. 1865. Worcester:

Chas. Hamilton, [1865]. 69 p. MWA holds "Additions to June 1, 1869" (8 p.). MWA. **1690**

Worcester County Mechanics Association. Catalogue of the Library. 1871. Worcester: Snow Brothers, 1871. 99 p. MWA holds "Additions, July 1, 1873," forming pp. [101]-16, and "Additions, July 1, 1874," forming pp. [117]-34. Cutter 713 reports Additions for 1872 (12 p.). DLC, MWA. **1691**

Worcester County Mechanics Association. Catalogue of the Library. 1875. Worcester: Charles Hamilton, 1875. 235 p. DLC, MB, MWA. **1692**

Worcester District Medical Society. By-laws and Catalogue of Library of the Worcester District Medical Society. Worcester: Henry J. Howland, 1838. 30 p. Not in Rinderknecht. MWA. **1693**

Worcester District Medical Society. By-laws of the Worcester District Medical Society, with a List of Members and Catalogue of Library . . . Worcester: Edward R. Fiske, [1853?]. 40 p. MWA. **1694**

Worcester District Medical Society. Catalogue of the Library of the Worcester District Medical Society. With a List of the Present Members. Worcester: Chas. Hamilton, 1860. ix, 128 p. MWA holds suppl. #[1]-2. DeU, DNLM, M, MB, MWA, NNC-M, NNGr, RPB. **1695**

Worcester District Medical Society. Catalogue of the Library of the Worcester District Medical Society. Worcester: Edward R. Fiske, 1865. 144 p. MWA holds annual suppl., 1867/68-1877/78. DLC, DNLM, MWA, NNC-M, OMC, PPC. **1696**

Worcester Law Library Association. Rules and Regulations of the Worcester Law Library Association. [Worcester?, 1832]. 15 p. "Catalogue of the Law Library" on pp. [5]-15. Not in Bruntjen. MWA. **1697**

Worcester Lyceum. Catalogue of Books in the Library of the Worcester Lyceum. [Worcester, 1835]. 12 p. Rinderknecht 35522 (under Worcester Natural History Society). MW, MWA. **1698**

Worcester Lyceum. Additions to Catalogue. November, 1837. [Worcester, 1837]. 13-14 p. Not in Rinderknecht. MWA. **1699**

Worcester Lyceum. Catalogue. Additions of 1838 and 1839. [Worcester, 1839]. 15-16 p. Not in Rinderknecht. MWA. **1700**

Worcester Lyceum. Catalogue of the Books in the Library of the Worcester Lyceum. Worcester, 1843. 19 p. Rinderknecht 43-5399 (under Worcester Natural History Society). MB, MWA, MWHi. **1701**

Worcester Lyceum. Catalogue of the Books in the Library of the Worcester Lyceum. Worcester: Henry J. Howland, 1844. 24 p. Rinderknecht 44-6747 (under Worcester Natural History Society). MWA, MWHi, NNC. **1702**

Worcester Lyceum. Catalogue of the Library of the Worcester Lyceum and Library Association . . . Worcester: Henry J. Howland, 1859. 96 p. MWA, N. **1703**

Worcester Social Library. Catalogue of Books belonging to the Worcester Social Library. [Worcester?, 1812?]. 12 p. S & S 27625. See Sabin 105437 concerning a 12 p. suppl. once bound with MWA's copy but no longer present. InU, MWA. **1704**

Young Men's Library Association. Catalogue of the Library of the Young Men's Library Association, of Worcester, with the Act of Incorporation, By-laws, List of Officers, &c. Worcester: Henry J. Howland, 1853. 34 p. DLC, MB, MWA, N. **1705**

Yarmouthport

Universalist Church. Catalogue of Books in the Universalist Sunday-school Library, Yarmouthport, Mass. Boston: John Wilson and Son, 1862. 16 p. NB. **1706**

MICHIGAN

Adrian

Adrian Public Schools. Catalogue of the Public Library of the Adrian Public Schools. April 1874. Adrian: Times and Expositor Pioneer Print, 1874. 60, 10, 6 p. DLC, MB, MiU. **1707**

Ladies' Library Association. Catalogue of Books, Articles of Association, By-laws and Officers of the Ladies' Library Association of Adrian, Mich. Organized Sept. 8, 1868.

Adrian: Adrian Times Steam Print., 1869.
30 p. Mi.   **1708**

Ladies' Library Association. Appendix to the
Catalogue of the Ladies' Library, of Adrian,
Mich., from No. 935 to No. 1448, inclusive.
Adrian: Adrian Times Steam Print., 1871.
16 p. Mi.   **1709**

Ann Arbor

Ladies' Library Association. Catalogue of the
Ladies' Library Association of Ann Arbor,
Mich. Edition of 1873. Incorporated April,
1866. Ann Arbor: Michigan Argus Office,
1873. 32 p. MiU holds "Supplement of April
1875" (3 p.). MiD-B, MiU.   **1710**

University of Michigan. Catalogue of the
Library of the University of Michigan. 1846.
Ann Arbor, 1846. 48 p. "Printed by the order
of the Board of Regents under the direction
of S. S. Schoff, assistant librarian." Mi, MiD-
B, MiU, MiU-Hi, OMC.   **1711**

Bay City

Library Association. Catalogue of the Library
Association of Bay City, Mich., with the
Articles of Association, By-laws, etc. Bay
City: Culbert, Warren and Kroencke, 1871.
56 p. Copy held by MWA has wrappers with
different imprint and is dated 1873. MWA,
MiD-B, MiSW.   **1712**

Coldwater

Ladies' Library Association. Catalogue of the
Ladies' Library Association. of Coldwater,
Michigan. Incorporated, 1869. Coldwater:
Sentinel Book and Job Print, 1870. 22 p. Mi
holds separately paged Addenda (3, 5, 3 p.).
Mi.   **1713**

Ladies' Library Association. Catalogue of the
Ladies' Library Association, of Coldwater,
Michigan, for 1875. Incorporated, 1869.
Coldwater: Republican Steam Printing
House, 1875. 45 p. DLC holds "Books added
to Library since 1874, also those omitted in
Catalogue" (8 p.). DLC.   **1714**

Detroit

Detroit Mechanics' Society, see Mechanics'
Society.

Detroit Public Library. Catalogue of the
Public Library of the City of Detroit, with the

Rules concerning its use. Detroit: Free Press
Steam Book and Job Printing Establishment, 1865. 100 p. DLC, MiD-B, NcD.**1715**

Detroit Public Library. Catalogue of the
Public Library of the City of Detroit . . . Also
the Rules concerning its use. Detroit:
Advertiser and Tribune Steam Printing Co.,
1868. vii, 149 p. DLC, ICN, IU, MB, MiD-B,
MiDW, MiU, NN.   **1716**

Detroit Public Library. Supplement A to
Catalogue of the Public Library of the City
of Detroit . . . June, 1871. [Detroit, 1871].
73 p. DLC, ICN, MB.   **1717**

Detroit Young Men's Society. Catalogue of
Books in the Library of the Detroit Young
Men's Society. 1839. Detroit: J. S. & S. A.
Bagg, 1839. 23 p. Not in Rinderknecht.
MiD-B.   **1718**

Detroit Young Men's Society. Act of
Incorporation, By-laws and Standing Rules,
of the Detroit Young Men's Society, with the
Names of Regular and Honorary Members,
and of the Presidents and Vice Presidents of
the Society, and a Catalogue of Books in the
Library. Detroit: Morgan Bates, 1842. 43 p.
Not in Rinderknecht. CSmH, DLC, MiD-B,
MiU-C.   **1719**

Detroit Young Men's Society. Act of
Incorporation, By-laws and Standing Rules,
of the Detroit Young Men's Society, and a
Catalogue of Books in the Library. Detroit:
Duncklee, Wales, 1851. 45 p. MiD-B. **1720**

Detroit Young Men's Society. Catalogue of
Books in the Library of the Detroit Young
Men's Society, also, the Act of Incorpora-
tion and By-laws, and Standing and Library
Rules of the Society. Detroit: Palmer, Luce
& Fleming, 1857. 67 p. DLC, MiD.   **1721**

Detroit Young Men's Society. Catalogue of
Books in the Library of the Detroit Young
Men's Society, also, the Act of Incorpora-
tion, and By-laws, and Standing and Library
Rules of the Society. Reported by Commit-
tee on Library, March, 1859. Detroit: Barns,
French & Way, 1859. 63, 12 p. IU, Mi, MiD.
                                             1722

Detroit Young Men's Society. Catalogue of
the Library of the Detroit Young Men's
Society, with a Historical Sketch. Detroit: O.
S. Gulley's Steam Power Presses, 1865.
169 p. DLC, MiD-B.   **1723**

First Presbyterian Church. Catalogue of the Sunday School Library of the First Presbyterian Church, 1874-75. Detroit: W. E. Tunis, 1874. 24 p. MiD-B. **1724**

Mechanics' Society. Catalogue of Books in the Library of the Mechanics' Society of the City of Detroit. 1846. Detroit: M. Geiger, 1846. [26] p. MiD-B. **1725**

Mechanics' Society. The Charter with its Amendments and the Constitution and By-laws of the Mechanics' Society of the City of Detroit, together with the By-laws of the Society's Library, and a Catalogue of the Books in the Library. Detroit: W. Harsha, 1851. 35 p. DLC, M, Mi, MiD-B. **1726**

Mechanics' Society. Catalogue of Books in the Library of the Detroit Mechanics' Society, with the Rules for the Regulation of the Library. Detroit: Free Press Book and Job Printing House, 1860. 86 p. DLC (with ms. additions to 1872?), Mi, MiD-B. **1727**

Mechanics' Society. Appendix . . . 1870. 43 p. Cf. Cutter 651. **1728**

Dowaciac

(later Dowagiac)

Dowaciac Ladies' Library Association. Catalogue of Books of Books of the Dowaciac Ladies' Library Association, Dowaciac, Michigan. Kalamazoo: Ihling Brothers, 1872. 16 p. Mi. **1729**

Flint

Ladies' Library Association. Catalogue of the Ladies' Library Association. Instituted, March 1851. Incorporated, March 1853. Flint: Jenny & Lyon, 1862. 17 p. Mi. **1730**

Ladies' Library Association. Constitution and Catalogue of the Ladies' Library Association of Flint, Michigan. Flint: Rankin & Warren, 1869. 47 p. DLC, MB, Mi, MiFli, MiFliC, WU (School of Library and Information Studies). **1731**

Grand Rapids

Central School Library. Catalogue of the Central School Library . . . Grand Rapids: Printed at the Daily Eagle Office, 1862. 15, [1] p. DLC. **1732**

Public School Library. Catalogue of the Public School Library, of the City of Grand Rapids. Grand Rapids: Democrat Steam Book and Job Printing House, 1872. 30, [1] p. DLC. **1733**

Public School Library. Catalogue of the Public School Library of Grand Rapids, Michigan. Grand Rapids: Eagle Steam Printing House, 1875. 34 p. DLC. **1734**

Jackson

Young Men's Association. Catalogue of the Young Men's Association Library of Jackson, Michigan. Jackson: Daily Citizen, 1871. 74 p. DLC. **1735**

Kalamazoo

Kalamazoo College. Philolexian Society. Catalogue of the Officers, Students and Books of the Philolexian Society, in Kalamazoo College. Kalamazoo: Stone Brothers, 1868. Cf. Catharine Penniman Storie, "What Contribution Did the American College Society Library Make to the History of the American College Library? A Supplementary Chapter in the History of the American College Library," Master's Thesis (M.S.L.S.), Columbia University, 1938, pp. 38, 95. MiKC (per Storie, p. 38). **1736**

Kalamazoo College. Sherwood Rhetorical Society. Catalogue of the Officers, Members and Books of the Sherwood Rhetorical Society of Kalamazoo College, together with the Constitution and By-laws. Kalamazoo: Clark & Cadman's Power-Press Print., 1868. 16 p. Cf. Catharine Penniman Storie, "What Contribution Did the American College Society Library Make to the History of the American College Library? A Supplementary Chapter in the History of the American College Library," Master's Thesis (M.S.L.S.), Columbia University, 1938, pp. 38, 95. MiKC (per Storie, p. 38). **1737**

Kalamazoo College. Sherwood Rhetorical Society. Catalogue . . . Constitution, By-laws and Rules of Order. Kalamazoo: Stone & Smith, 1871. 19 p. Library catalogue on pp. 12-19. Cf. Catharine Penniman Storie, "What Contribution Did the American College Society Library Make to the History

of the American College Library? A Supplementary Chapter in the History of the American College Library," Master's Thesis (M.S.L.S.), Columbia University, 1938, pp. 38, 95. MiKC (per Storie, p. 38).
1738

Kalamazoo College. Sherwood Rhetorical Society. Catalogue . . . Constitution, By-laws and Rules of Order. Kalamazoo: Herald & Torchlight Pub. Office, 1873. 19 p. Library catalogue on pp. 12-19. Cf. Catharine Penniman Storie, "What Contribution Did the American College Society Library Make to the History of the American College Library? A Supplementary Chapter in the History of the American College Library," Master's Thesis (M.S.L.S.), Columbia University, 1938, pp. 38, 95. MiKC (per Storie, p. 38).
1739

Ladies' Library Association. Catalogue . . . 1853. Cf. Rhees, p. 186.   **1740**

Ladies' Library Association. Catalogue . . . 1856. 14 p. Cf. Rhees, p. 186.   **1741**

Ladies' Library Association. Catalogue of Books belonging to the Ladies' Library Association of Kalamazoo, Michigan. Organized January 1852. Kalamazoo: James H. Stone, 1873. 50 p. DLC, Mi.   **1742**

School District No. 1. Catalogue . . . 1873. 63 p. Cf. Cutter 849.   **1743**

Young Men's Library Association. Catalogue of Books belonging to the Young Men's Library Association .. Kalamazoo, 1867. 27 p. DLC.   **1744**

Lansing

Library and Literary Association. Catalogue of Books belonging to the Library and Literary Association, Lansing, Mich. Lansing: W. S. George, 1872. 22 p. Mi.   **1745**

Library and Literary Association. Catalogue of Books belonging to the Library and Literary Association, Lansing, Mich. Lansing: W. S. George, 1874. 27 p. Mi.   **1746**

Michigan (Territory). Legislative Council. "Catalogue of Books belonging to the Legislative Council of the Territory of Michigan. May 9th, 1828." In: *Journal of the Legislative Council of the Territory of Michigan,*

being the First Session of the Third Council, begun and held at the City of Detroit, May 5, 1828 ([Detroit]: John P. Sheldon, 1828), pp. 67-70. Prefaced by a report, library rules, and concludes with a separate catalogue of missing books. Not in Shoemaker. In many libraries.   **1747**

Michigan State Library. Catalogue of Books in the State Library. [Lansing?, 1846]. 19 p. MiD, MiU, OMC.   **1748**

Michigan State Library. Catalogue of Michigan State Library. Henry Tisdale, State Librarian. Lansing: R. W. Ingals, 1850. 30 p. DLC, Mi, Mi-L, MiD-B.   **1749**

Michigan State Library. [Catalogue of Michigan State Library]. [Lansing, 1854 or 55?]. 42 p. MiU (defective; title page lacking).   **1750**

Michigan State Library. Catalogue of the Michigan State Library, for the Year 1857. Lansing: Hosmer & Fitch, 1857. 47 p. DLC, Mi.   **1751**

Michigan State Library. Catalogue . . . 1858. Lansing, 1858. Cf. Bowker, p. 258.   **1752**

Michigan State Library. Catalogue of the Michigan State Library, for the Year 1859. Lansing: Hosmer & Kerr, 1859. 63 p. Ct, M, MiEM (defective), MiU.   **1753**

Michigan State Library. Catalogue of the Michigan State Library, for the Year 1861. J. E. Tenney, State Librarian. Lansing: Hosmer & Kerr, 1861. 88 p. DLC, Mi, MiU.   **1754**

Michigan State Library. Catalogue of the Michigan State Library, for the Year 1863. Prepared by J. E. Tenney, State Librarian. November 30, 1862. Lansing: John A. Kerr, 1862. 107 p. MWA, Mi, MiD-B, MiU.   **1755**

Michigan State Library. Catalogue of the Michigan State Library, for the Year 1865. Prepared by J. E. Tenney, State Librarian. November 30, 1864. Lansing: John A. Kerr, 1864. 112 p. IU, Mi, MiD.   **1756**

Michigan State Library. Catalogue of the Michigan State Library, for the Year 1867. Prepared by J. E. Tenney, State Librarian. November 30, 1866. Lansing: John A. Kerr, 1866. 131 p. Mi.   **1757**

Michigan State Library. Catalogue of the Michigan State Library, for the Year 1869. Prepared by J. E. Tenney, State Librarian. November 30, 1868. Lansing: John A. Kerr, 1868. 142 p. MB, Mi, MiD-B, MiU. **1758**

Michigan State Library. Catalogue of the Michigan State Library, for the Years 1870-71. Prepared by H. A. Tenney, State Librarian. November 30, 1870. Lansing: W. S. George, 1870. 222 p. DLC, M, Mi, MiD-B, MiS, MiU, MiU-H. **1759**

Michigan State Library. Catalogue of the Michigan State Library, for the Years 1873-4. Prepared by H. A. Tenney, State Librarian. January 1, 1873. Lansing: W. S. George, 1873. viii, 293 p. Ct, DLC, ICN, IU, M, MB, MWA, Mi, MiD, MiEM, MiU, NB, NN, OKentU, TxU. **1760**

Michigan State Library. Catalogue of the Michigan State Library, for the Years 1875-76. Prepared by Harriet A. Tenney, State Librarian. January 1, 1875. Lansing: W. S. George, 1875. vi, 228 p. DAU, DLC, IU, M, MB, MWA, Mi, MiD, MiEM, MiU, NB, OKentU. **1761**

Marshall

Ladies' Library Association. Catalogue . . . 1873. 37 p. Cf. Cutter 850. **1762**

Monroe

Monroe City Library. Catalogue of the Monroe City Library. [Monroe?, ca. 1864]. 16 p. DLC (defective). **1763**

Owosso

Ladies' Library and Literary Association. Articles of Association, By-laws, and Catalogue of Books of Ladies' Library and Literary Association of Owosso City. Organized May 5, 1867. Chartered November 16, 1870. Owosso: J. H. Champion, 1870. 25 p. Mi copy includes "Additional Books" (3 p.). Mi. **1764**

Port Huron

Ladies' Library Association. Catalogue of the Library of the Ladies' Library Association of Port Huron . . . also, the Rules concerning its use, and a Historical Sketch. Detroit: Daily News Post Printing Establiment, 1869.

32 p. DLC holds Appendix to Catalogue, 1871 (14 p.). DLC. **1765**

Saginaw

Saginaw Public Schools. Catalogue of the Library of the Saginaw Public Schools . . . Saginaw: Daily Republican Office, 1873. 25 p. MiU. **1766**

Traverse City

Ladies' Library Association. Catalogue and Constitution & By-laws of the Ladies' Library Association of Traverse City. Traverse City: Traverse Bay Eagle Steam Print, 1875. 19 p. DLC. **1767**

Ypsilanti

Ladies' Library Association. Catalogue . . . 1869. Cf. A. F. Bixby and A. Howell, *Historical Sketches of the Ladies' Library Associations of the State of Michigan* (Adrian, 1876), p. 139. **1768**

Ladies' Library Association. Catalogue . . . 1871. Cf. A. F. Bixby and A. Howell, *Historical Sketches of the Ladies' Library Associations of the State of Michigan* (Adrian, 1876), p. 139. **1769**

Ladies' Library Association. Catalogue . . . 1874. Cf. A. F. Bixby and A. Howell, *Historical Sketches of the Ladies' Library Associations of the State of Michigan* (Adrian, 1876), p. 139. **1770**

MINNESOTA

Duluth

Duluth Library Association. Catalogue of the Duluth Library Association for the Year 1870. Duluth: Minnesotian Printing Co., 1870. 32 p. DLC, MnHi. **1771**

Rochester

Rochester Library. Catalogue . . . 1867. 19 p. Cf. Cutter 560. **1772**

St. Cloud

Union Library. Catalogue of the Union Library of Saint Cloud, Minnesota. Alphabetically arranged. Nov. 1, A.D. 1874. D. H.

Selby, Librarian. St. Cloud: Times Book and Job Print., 1874. 36 p. DLC. **1773**

St. Paul

Central Presbyterian Church. Catalogue of the Sunday-School Library of the Central Presbyterian Church, Saint Paul. St. Paul: Pioneer Printing Co., 1858. 20 p. MnHi. **1774**

First Presbyterian Church. Catalogue of Books belonging to the First Presbyterian Church Sabbath School. [St. Paul, 186-?]. 20 p. MnHi. **1775**

Hunt's Circulating Library. Catalogue of Hunt's Circulating Library . . . Saint Paul, Minnesota. St. Paul: John Jay Lemon, 1873. 43 p. Operated by Howard A. Hunt. MnHi. **1776**

Mercantile Library Association. Catalogue of the Mercantile Library Association, Saint Paul, Minn. [St. Paul, 1863]. 13 p. MnHi. **1777**

Saint Paul Library Association. Catalogue of the St. Paul Library Association, 1864. St. Paul: David Ramaley, 1864. 82 p. (pp. 81-82 contain 1st suppl.). MB holds 2d suppl. (8 p.) and 3d suppl. (10 p.). MB, MBAt, MnHi, NN. **1778**

Saint Paul Library Association. Catalogue of the St. Paul Library Association. 1868. St. Paul: Ramaley & Hall, 1868. 99 p. MnHi. **1779**

Saint Paul Library Association. Catalogue of the St. Paul Library Association, 1873. St. Paul: Ramaley, Chaney, 1873. 134 p. DLC. **1780**

Territorial Library of Minnesota. Catalogue of the Territorial Library of Minnesota. St. Paul: James M. Goodhue, 1850. 30, [1] p. DLC, MWA, MnHi, MnU, OKentU. **1781**

University of Minnesota. An Alphabetical Catalogue of Authors. Complete to March 31, 1872. St. Paul: Ramaley, Chaney, 1872. [51]-225 p. Reprinted from the *Annual Report of the Board of Regents* for 1871. Also issued in a 177 page ed. (Copies at DLC, NN). DLC, IaAS, MH, MnHi, MnU, N, RPB. **1782**

Young Men's Christian Association. Catalogue of the Library, of the Young Men's Christian Association, Saint Paul, 1861. [St. Paul, 1861]. 11 p. MnHi, MnS. **1783**

St. Peter

St. Peter Library Association. Catalogue of the Saint Peter Library Association. 1870. St. Peter: J. K. Moore, 1870. 37, [2] p. DLC, MnHi. **1784**

Stillwater

Stillwater Library Association. Catalogue of Books belonging to the Stillwater Library Association. August, 1874. Stillwater: Gazette Print, 1874. 16 p. DLC (with ms. additions). **1785**

Winona

Winona Library. Catalogue of the Winona Library. Alphabetical and Classified. Winona: Winona Herald Book and Job Office, 1872. 35 p. DLC. **1786**

MISSISSIPPI

Jackson

Mississippi State Library. A Catalogue of the Library of the State of Mississippi . . . To which are prefixed, the Rules and Regulations provided for its Government. Jackson: B. D. Howard, 1839. 27 p. Rinderknecht 57304. DLC. **1787**

Mississippi State Library. A Catalogue of the Library of the State of Mississippi . . . To which are prefixed, the Rules and Regulations provided for its Government. Jackson: G. R. Fall, 1841. 34 p. Rinderknecht 41-3568. DLC, MWA. **1788**

Mississippi State Library. A Catalogue of the Library of the State of Mississippi . . . To which are prefixed, the Rules and Regulations provided for its Government. Jackson: Price & Fall, 1845. 43 p. DLC. **1789**

Mississippi State Library. A Catalogue of the Library of the State of Mississippi . . . To which are prefixed, the Rules and Regulations provided for its Government.

Jackson: C. M. Price & G. R. Fall, 1847. 61 p.
DLC.   **1790**

Mississippi State Library. A Catalogue of the
Library of the State of Mississippi . . . To
which are prefixed the Rules and Regulations, provided for its Government. Jackson:
Fall & Marshall, 1849. 51 p. DLC.   **1791**

Mississippi State Library. A Catalogue of the
Library of the State of Mississippi . . . To
which are prefixed the Rules and Regula-
tions provided for its Government. Jackson:
Fall & Marshall, 1851. 55 p. On cover: 1852.
DLC.   **1792**

Mississippi State Library. A Catalogue of the
Library of the State of Mississippi . . . To
which are prefixed the Rules and Regulations provided for its Government. Jackson:
Palmer & Pickett, 1854. 58 p. DLC.   **1793**

Mississippi State Library. Catalogue of the
Library of the State of Mississippi . . . To
which are prefixed the Rules and Regulations provided for its Government. Jackson:
E. Barksdale, 1857. 61 p. DLC.   **1794**

Mississippi State Library. A Catalogue of the
Library of the State of Mississippi . . . To
which are prefixed the Rules and Regulations provided for its Government. Benjamin F. [corrected in ms. to W. on DLC
copy] Sanders, Librarian. Jackson: E.
Barksdale, 1858. 87 p. DLC.   **1795**

Mississippi State Library. Catalogue of the
Mississippi State Library, with the Laws,
Rules and Regulations . . . O. H. Crandall,
Librarian. Jackson, 1869. 132 p. Cf. Bowker,
p. 878.   **1796**

Mississippi State Library. Catalogue of the
Mississippi Library. Together with the Laws,
Rules and Regulations providing for its
Government. I. N. Osborn, Librarian.
Jackson: Kimball, Kaymond, 1872. 116, [2] p.
DLC, IU, N, OKentU, Vt, Vi.   **1797**

Mississippi State Library. Catalogue . . .
September 1873. Cf. Bowker, p. 878. **1798**

Oxford

University of Mississippi. Catalogue of the
Library of the University of Mississippi.

[Oxford?], 1858. 50 p. Cf. Boyd Childress,
"The 1868 Catalog of the University of
Mississippi," *Libraries & Culture* 26 (1991):
534. For only surviving copy, see entry 1800.
                                            1799

University of Mississippi. Catalogue of the
Library of the University of Mississippi.
Revised and corrected by Giles M. Hillyer,
A.M. Oxford, 1868. 90 p. A ledger book
consisting of pasted pages of the printed
1858 catalogue and ms. entries represent-
ing additions. Cf. Boyd Childress, "The 1868
Catalog of the University of Mississippi,"
Libraries & Culture 26 (1991): 532-39. MsU
(Dept. of Archives and Special Collections).
                                            1800

Washington

Jefferson College. The Charter and Statutes
of Jefferson College, Washington, Mississippi, as revised and amended, together
with a Historical Sketch of the Institution
from its Establishment to the Present Time.
To which is prefixed a List of Trustees,
Officers and Faculty, the Acts of Congress
and of the Legislature relating to the
Institution, and a Catalogue of its Library,
Apparatus, &c. Natchez: Book and Job
Office, 1840. 90, [2] p. Rinderknecht 40-
3598. DLC, KyLoF, LU, MH, MBC, MWA,
NcD, PHi, RPB, TxU.   **1801**

MISSOURI

Brunswick

Library Association of Brunswick. Catalogue
of Books belonging to the Library Association of Brunswick, Mo. Brunswick: Naylor &
Balthis, 1875. [14] p. MoSHi.   **1802**

Columbia

University of Missouri. Catalogue of the
Books belonging to the Library of the
University of Missouri, to which are
appended Catalogues of the Books belong-
ing to the Libraries of the Literary Societies.
Columbia: Union Democrat Book and Job
Office, 1857. 31 p. The literary societies are
the Athenaean Society and the Union
Literary Society. MoHi, MoU.   **1803**

Hannibal

Mercantile Library. Catalogue of Books in the Hannibal Mercantile Library, Hannibal, Missouri. 1874. Hannibal: Winchell & Ebert Printing and Lithographing Co., 1874. 51 p. DLC (with ms. entries #2163-2223). **1804**

Jefferson City

Missouri State Library. Catalogue of State Library of Missouri. N. C. Burch, Librarian . . . Jefferson City: Horace Wilcox, 1871. 57 p. Running title: Catalogue of the State Law Library. DLC, Or. **1805**

St. Joseph

Fülling, Carl. Catalog der Leihbibliothek von Carl Fülling in St. Joseph, Mo. . . . [St. Joseph, 1875?]. 118 p. Mostly German books (to p. 110), followed by a selection of French and English books. DLC. **1806**

Saint Joseph Public School Library. A Catalogue of the Saint Joseph Public School Library, prepared by John S. Crosby . . . St. Joseph: Woolworth, 1872. 54 p. DLC. **1807**

St. Louis

City Circulating Library. Catalogue of the City Circulating Library, No. 32 Chestnut Street, (opposite the Post Office), containing upwards of Ten Thousand Volumes . . . R. Jones Woodward, Proprietor . . . St. Louis: Printed at the New Era Office, 1842. 90 p. Not in Rinderknecht. MWA, MoS. **1808**

Concordia Theological Seminary. Katalog der Theologischen Bibliothek des Evangelisch-lutherischen Concordia Collegiums zu St. Louis, Mo. St. Louis: Druckerei der Synode von Missouri, Ohio u. a. Staaten, 1874. 81 p. CtY-D, InFwCT, InValU, MH-AH, MnSCC, MoS. **1809**

Deutsches Institut für Wissenschaft, Kunst und Gewerbe. Catalog der Bibliothek des Deutschen Instituts für Wissenschaft, Kunst und Gewerbe (Chartered November 21, 1857, and March 5, 1859,) [gegründet im Dezember, 1856,] nebst Charter und Statuten, Mitglieder-Verzeichniss, u.s.w. Saint Louis: Klünder & Scholz, 1860. [74] p. MoS. **1810**

St. Joseph's Church. Verzeichniss der Bücher der Rozenkranz-Bibliothek an der St. Joseph's-Kirche zu St. Louis, Mo. St. Louis: F. Saler, 1866. 21, 10 p. MoSHi, MoSW. **1811**

St. Joseph's Church. Verzeichniss der Bibliothek der Marianischen Jünglings-Sodalität an der St. Joseph's-Kirche zu St. Louis, Mo. St. Louis: F. Saler, 1871. 34 p. MoSW. **1812**

St. Louis Academy of Science, see entry 1824.

St. Louis Law Library Association. Charter, Constitution, By-laws, and Catalogue of Books of the St. Louis Law Library Association of St. Louis. Founded A.D. 1838. St. Louis: Chambers & Knapp, 1845. 24 p. MoSHi, MoSU. **1813**

St. Louis Law Library Association. Catalogue . . . 1853. 71 p. Cf. Rhees, p. 201. **1814**

St. Louis Law Library Association. A Descriptive Catalogue of the Books in the Library of the Law Library Association of Saint Louis, on July 1, 1870. Together with an Index to the same, and the Constitution and By-laws of the Association. Saint Louis: Levison & Blythe, 1870. 227, [1] p. DLC, IU. **1815**

St. Louis Law School, see entry 1824.

St. Louis Library. Constitution, By-laws, and Catalogue of the St. Louis Library, St. Louis. St. Louis: St. Louis Enquirer Office, [1824 or 25?]. 30 p. For dating, see John Francis McDermott, "Public Libraries in St. Louis, 1811-39," *Library Quarterly* 14 (1944): 15. Not in Shoemaker. MoS. **1816**

St. Louis Library Association. Constitution, Bye-laws and Catalogue of the St. Louis Library Association. St. Louis: Charless & Paschall, 1834. 47 p. Not in Rinderknecht. DLC, MoS. **1817**

St. Louis Library Association. Charter, Constitution, By-laws and Catalogue of the St. Louis Library Association. St. Louis: William Weber, 1839. x, 43 p. Not in Shoemaker. MoS (with ms. notes), MoSW. **1818**

St. Louis Mercantile Library Association. Catalogue of Books belonging to the Saint

Louis Mercantile Library Association. January, 1850. St. Louis: Chambers & Knapp, 1850. 315 p. Compiled by William P. Curtis. Lists of new additions published in *Annual Report of the Board of Directors of the Mercantile Library Association of Saint Louis, Missouri,* 1850-67. In many libraries.   **1819**

St. Louis Mercantile Library Association. Supplement to the Catalogue of the St. Louis Mercantile Library comprising the Additions made during the Year 1850. St. Louis: Printed at the Republican Office, 1851. 107 p. Lists of new additions published in *Annual Report of the Board of Directors of the Mercantile Library Association of Saint Louis, Missouri,* 1850-67. DLC, IU, MWA, MoS, MoSM, PPL.   **1820**

St. Louis Mercantile Library Association. Catalogue, Systematic and Analytical, of the Books of the Saint Louis Mercantile Library Association. Prepared . . . by Edward Wm. Johnston. December, 1858. St. Louis: R. P. Studley, 1858. xvi, 559, ccxlv p. Lists of new additions published in *Annual Report of the Board of Directors of the Mercantile Library Association of Saint Louis, Missouri,* 1850-67. In many libraries.   **1821**

St. Louis Mercantile Library Association. Classified Catalogue of Saint Louis Mercantile Library . . . St. Louis: Democrat Lithographing and Printing Co., 1874. xii, 762 p. In many libraries.   **1822**

St. Louis Public School Library. Systematic Index to the Books of the St. Louis Public School Library, together with the Charter, Regulations and By-laws of the Society, and the Rules and Regulations of the Library and Reading Room. St. Louis: Missouri Democrat Book and Job Printing House, 1866. 54 p. CLSU, DLC, M, MB, MBAt, MH, MnHi, NNC.   **1823**

St. Louis Public School Library. Catalogue, Classified and Alphabetical, of the Books of the St. Louis Public School Library. Including, also, the Collections of the St. Louis Academy of Science, and St. Louis Law School. Prepared . . . by Jno. Jay Bailey, Librarian. St. Louis: Missouri Democrat Book and Job Printing House, 1870. xvi, 384 p. In many libraries.   **1824**

St. Louis Public School Library. Catalogue . . . First Supplement. November, 1872. [St. Louis]: St. Louis Democrat Litho. & Print. Co., [1872 or 73]. 102 p. DLC, M, MH, PPAmP, PPL.   **1825**

NEBRASKA

Lincoln

Nebraska State Library. Catalogue of the Nebraska State Library . . . By Guy A. Brown . . . Des Moines: Mills, 1871. 51 p. DLC, IU.   **1826**

Omaha

Omaha Library Association. Catalogue of the Books of the Omaha Library Association. 1872. Omaha: Omaha Daily Herald and Job Printing House, 1872. 45 p. NN.   **1827**

NEVADA

Carson City

Nevada State Library. Catalogue of the Nevada State Library, for the Year 1865 .. Carson City: John Church, 1865. 32 p. "List of Books received by Exchange and Donation" appears in *Third Annual Report of the Board of Directors of the State Library, for the State of Nevada* (Carson City, 1867), pp. 9-11. A "Catalogue of Books in the Nevada State Library received since January 1st, 1871" appears in *Report of the Board of Directors of the Nevada State Library, for the Years 1871 and 1872* (Carson City, 1873), pp. 9-27. IU, M.   **1828**

Nevada State Library. Catalogue of the Nevada State Library. 1872, J. D. Minor, Secretary of State, and Ex-officio State Librarian. Carson City: Charles L. Perkins, 1872. 116 p. DLC, IU, M, Nv, WHi.   **1829**

Nevada State Library. Catalogue of the Nevada State Library. 1874, J. D. Minor, Secretary of State, and Ex-officio State Librarian. Carson City: C. A. V. Putnam, 1874. 132 p. DLC, IU, M, NjP.   **1830**

NEW HAMPSHIRE

Amherst

Franklin Society. A Catalogue of Books belonging to the Franklin Society, Amherst,

N.H. [Amherst]: Joseph Cushing, 1808. 6 p. Not in S & S. MWA.   **1831**

Andover

Andover Social Library. Rules and Regulations of the Andover Social Library, adopted March 21, 1814. Concord: Isaac Hill, 1817. 12 p. Catalogue of books on pp. 7-9; names of proprietors on pp. 10-12. Not in S & S. NhHi.   **1832**

Atkinson

Congregational Church. Catalogue of Books in the Congregational Sabbath School Library, Atkinson, New Hampshire. [n.p., 186-?]. broadside. NhD.   **1833**

Boscawen

Boscawen Social Library. A Catalogue of Books in the Boscawen Social Library, alphabetically arranged under the following Heads: Theological, Historical, and Miscellaneous. Concord: George Hough, 1811. 8 p. S & S 22430. NhHi.   **1834**

Brentwood

Social Library. Rules and Regulations of the Social Library of Brentwood, adopted Sep. 5, 1805. Exeter: Ranlet & Norris, 1806. 15 p. Half-title: Brentwood Social Library. Incorporated June 9, 1802. "Catalogue of Books belonging to the Social Library, Brentwood" on pp. 9-14. S & S 11393. MWA.   **1835**

Brookfield, see entry 2020.

Canterbury

Canterbury Library. Catalogue of the Canterbury Library. [n.p., 186-?]. 8 p. NhHi.**1836**

Charlestown

Charlestown Social Library. Charter, Byelaws, and Catalogue of Books, of the Charlestown Social Library. January 1, 1818. [Bellows Falls: Bill Blake, 1818?]. 19, [1] p. S & S 43587. WU (School of Library and Information Studies).   **1837**

Charlestown Social Library. Charter, Byelaws, and Catalogue of Books of the

Charlestown Social Library. January 1, 1826. [n.p., 1826]. 18, [2] p. Shoemaker 24068. MWA, WU (School of Library and Information Studies).   **1838**

First Public Library. Regulations and Catalogue of the First Public Library, in Chalestown [!], N.H. Charlestown: Webber & Bowman, 1830. 16 p. Cooper 834. MB.
                                         1839

Claremont

Fiske Free Library. Catalogue of the Fiske Free Library. Claremont: National Eagle Office, 1873. 32 p. DLC holds suppl., 1874 (4 p.). DLC, Nh, NN.   **1840**

Concord

Asylum Library, see New Hampshire Asylum for the Insane.

Concord Library. Catalogue of Books, belonging to Concord Library. December 1807. Concord: J. C. Tuttle, 1808. 16 p. S & S 14756. Concord Public Library, NhHi.
                                         1841

Concord Public Library. Catalogue of the Public Library, Concord, N.H. Concord: Independent Democrat Office, Fogg & Hadley, 1857. 48 p. Concord Public Library, MWA.   **1842**

Concord Public Library. Catalogue of the Public Library, Concord, N.H. Concord: Independent Democrat Office, Fogg & Hadley, 1858. 57 p. Suppl., June, 1859 (15 p.) at Concord Public Library, MStuO, Nh, and NhHi; suppl. #2, Feb. 1860 (8 p.) at Concord Public Library and MStuO; suppl. #3, Jan. 1862 (15 p.) at Concord Public Library and NhHi. Concord Public Library, MStuO, Nh.   **1843**

Concord Public Library. Catalogue of the Concord Public Library, Concord, N.H. Concord: Fogg, Hadley, 1863. 94 p. Concord Public Library holds suppl. [#1], 3-4, Jan. 1866, April 1870-Jan. 1872; DLC holds suppl. #4, Jan. 1872; MB and NhHi hold suppl. [#1]-2, Jan. 1866-Nov. 1868; Nh holds suppl. [#1], Jan. 1866. Concord Public Library, MB, Nh, NhHi.   **1844**

Concord Public Library. Catalogue of the Concord Public Library, Concord, N.H. Concord: Republican Press Association, 1874. 168 p. Nh. **1845**

First Baptist Church. Catalogue of the First Baptist Sunday School Library, Concord, N.H. Revised November, 1858. Concord: Jones & Cogswell, 1858. 23 p. NhHi. **1846**

First Congregational Church. Catalogue of Books in the First Congregational Sabbath School Library, Concord, N.H. [Concord, 1868?]. 8 p. MnU, NhHi. **1847**

First Universalist Society. Catalogue of Books belonging to the Scholars' Library, of the First Universalist Sabbath School, School Street, Concord, N.H., 1864. Nashua: N. P. Greene, 1864. 20 p. NhHi. **1848**

First Universalist Society. Catalogue of Books in the Library of the Universalist Society of Concord, N.H. Concord: Daily Monitor Office, 1867. 24 p. NhHi. **1849**

Merrill's Circulating Library. Merrill's Circulating Library, containing Popular Works on Biography, Agriculture and Domestic Economy, Voyages and Travels, Ancient and Modern History, Novels and Romances, Miscellaneous and Periodicals . . . Concord: Rufus Merrill, 1852. 20 p. NhD. **1850**

Methodist General Biblical Institute. Catalogue of the Methodist General Biblical Institute, Concord, N.H. 1853. Concord: Ervin B. Tripp, [1853]. 31 p. MH-AH.**1851**

New Hampshire Asylum for the Insane. Catalogue of the Asylum Library, Concord, N.H. Concord: Cogswell & Sturtevant, 1864. 15 p. NhHi. **1852**

New Hampshire Asylum for the Insane. Catalogue of the Asylum Library, Concord, N.H. Concord: Morrill & Silsby, 1874. 48 p. DLC. **1853**

New Hampshire Medical Society. Laws of the New-Hampshire Medical Society's Library. [Concord?, 1807]. 16 p. "A Catalogue of Books in the Library of the New-Hampshire Medical Society" on pp. 6-16. S & S 13201, Austin 1371. DLC, MWA. **1854**

New Hampshire Medical Society. Laws of the New-Hampshire Medical Society's Library.

[Concord?, 1815?]. 23 p. "A Catalogue of the New-Hampshire Medical Society and Eastern District Society's Library" on pp. [4]-23. Not in S & S; Austin 1372. DLC. **1855**

New Hampshire State Library. Catalogue of the Books, Pamphlets and Maps in the State Library of New-Hampshire . . . 1846. Concord: Asa McFarland, 1847. 57 p. DLC, ICN, IaHi, MB, MWA, Nh, NhHi, NhD, T. **1856**

New Hampshire State Library. Catalogue of the Books, Pamphlets and Maps in the State Library of New Hampshire. Concord: Jones & Cogswell, 1857. 47, [1] p. DLC, IaHi, M, MB, MWA, Nh, NhHi, PPL. **1857**

New Hampshire State Prison. Catalogue of Books in the N.H. State Prison Library. Concord: George E. Jenks, 1867. 32 p. NhHi. **1858**

Second Congregational Society. Catalogue of Books in the Library of the Sabbath School, Second Congregational Society, Concord. April, 1830. [Concord, 1830]. 20 p. MWA and NhHi copies have blank pages 9-16. Not in Cooper. MWA, NhHi. **1859**

Unitarian Church. Catalogue of Books in the Unitarian Sabbath School Library, Concord, N.H. Nov. 1st, 1867. Concord: A. G. Jones, [1867]. 19 p. NhHi. **1860**

Unitarian Church. Catalogue of Books in the Unitarian Sunday School Library, Concord, N.H. Revised May 1871. [Concord, 1871]. 63 p. NhHi. **1861**

Dover

Dover Agricultural Library. Catalogue of the Books in Dover Agricultural Library. Organized January 29, 1862. [Dover?, 1862]. 8 p. Nh. **1862**

Dover Library. A Catalogue of the Books in Dover Library. Incorporated Nov. 14, 1850. Dover: Dover Gazette Power Press, 1853. 42 p. NhD, NhDo. **1863**

Dover Library. Catalogue of Dover Library, organized November, 1850. Dover: Morning Star Steam Job Print Establishment, 1874. 95 p. DLC, NhDo. **1864**

First Congregational Church. Catalogue of Books belonging to the First Congregational Sabbath School Library, Dover, N.H. Dover: H. H. Goodwin, 1865. 28 p. MH, NhHi.   **1865**

Franklin Library. Constitution and By-laws with a Catalogue. [Dover?], 1833. Rinderknecht 18604. NhDo (lost and withdrawn?).   **1866**

New Hampshire Medical Society. Strafford District. A Catalogue of the Books in the Library of the Strafford District N.H. Medical Society, in their Rooms at Dover, N.H. Dover: Geo. Wadleigh, 1859. 8 p. NhD, NhDo.   **1867**

Unitarian Church. Catalogue of the Unitarian Sunday School Library, Dover, N.H. Dover: G. H. S. E. Twobley, 1862. 20 p. NhHi.   **1868**

Exeter

Exeter Circulating Library. Catalogue of the Exeter Circulating Library, kept by Francis Grant . . . Exeter: John J. Williams, 1822. 31, [1] p. Not in Shoemaker. NhD.   **1869**

Exeter Town Library. Catalogue and Regulations of the Town Library, Exeter, N.H. [Exeter]: Smith, Hall and Clarke, 1855. 20 p. DLC, NhHi (16 p.).   **1870**

Exeter Town Library. Catalogue of the Books in the Town Library, Exeter, N.H. Exeter: Hall and Clark, 1856. 64 p. NN copy has 11 suppl. pages, 1857; Nh and NhHi copies contain suppl., pp. 65-80 (1861). Nh, NhHi, NN.   **1871**

Exeter Town Library. Catalogue of the Books in the Town Library, Exeter, N.H. Exeter: News-letter Printing Establ., 1871. iv, 61 p. DLC and NhHi hold suppl., ca. 1873 (10 p.). DLC, NhM.   **1872**

Phillips Exeter Academy. Golden Branch Society. Constitution, By-laws, and Catalogue of the Library of the Golden Branch of Phillips Exeter Academy. Exeter, 1857. 34 p. MWA.   **1873**

Phillips Exeter Academy. Golden Branch Society. Constitution, By-laws, and Catalogue of the Library of the Golden Branch of Phillips Exeter Academy. Exeter, 1869. 67 p. MWA.   **1874**

Farmington

Farmington Library. Catalogue of Books in Farmington Library. July, 1853. Dover: George Wadleigh, 1853. 16 p. DLC.   **1875**

Young Men's Christian Association. Catalogue of the Young Men's Christian Association Library, Farmington, N.H. Organized, Jan. 28, 1869. Rochester: C. W. Folsom, 1870. 32 p. Nh.   **1876**

Fisherville

(later Penacook)

Library Association. Catalogue of Books of the Library Association, Fisherville, N.H. Concord: McFarland & Jenks, 1866. 31 p. Nh.   **1877**

Library Association. Catalogue of Books of the Library Association, Fisherville, N.H. Concord: McFarland & Jenks, 1869. 40 p. DLC, Nh, NhHi.   **1878**

Fitzwilliam

Fitzwilliam Town Library. Catalogue of the Fitzwilliam Town Library, with the Rules, Fitzwilliam, N.H. March 1, 1875. Keene: Wm. B. Allen, 1875. [31]-44 p. DLC and Nh copies have suppl., March 1, 1876 ([2] p.). DLC, Nh, NhHi.   **1879**

Franklin

Franklin Library Association. Catalogue of Books belonging to the Frankin Library Association, Franklin, N.H. January, 1869. Concord: McFarland & Jenks, 1869. 45 p. Cutter 618 reports Additions to April, 1871 (4 p.). DLC, MWA, Nh.   **1880**

Gilmantown

Gilmantown Social Library. The Act of Concorporation and By-laws of Gilmantown Social Library, together with the Names of the Proprietors and a Catalogue of the Books. Gilmantown: Leavitt & Clough, 1804. 14 p. S & S 6390. MA.   **1881**

Gilmantown Theological Seminary. Catalogue of Books in the Library of the Theological Seminary, at Gilmantown. Gilmantown: Alfred Prescott, 1839. 36 p. Rinderknecht 55879. Nh, NhD, NhHi.   **1882**

Goffstown

Baptist Church. Catalogue of the Baptist Sabbath School Library, Goffstown Centre, N.H. [n.p., 186-?]. 16 p. NhHi. **1883**

Great Falls

(later Somersworth)

First Congregational Church. Catalogue of Books, belonging to the Library of the First Congregational S. School. Great Falls: Great Falls Advertiser Press, 1857. 14 p. Private Collection. **1884**

Manufacturers' and Village Library. Catalogue of Books belonging to the Manufacturers and Village Library at Great Falls, from No. 1 to 1628. Jan'y 1, 1847. Great Falls: Transcript Press, Henderson & Wingate Printers, [1847]. [14 p.]. DLC holds four suppl., April 1852-Feb. 1855. DLC. **1885**

Manufacturers' and Village Library. Catalogue . . . 1856. 104 p. Cf. Rhees, p. 210. **1886**

Hanover

Dartmouth College. A Catalogue of Books in Dartmouth College Library. [Hanover: C. & W. S. Spear, 1809?]. 24 p. Not in S & S. CLU, MHi (with ms. notes), MWA, NhD, NIC, PPL, PU. **1887**

Dartmouth College. A Catalogue of the Books in the Library of Dartmouth College . . . November, 1825. Concord: George Hough, 1825. 44 p. Shoemaker 20259. CSmH, CtY, DeWint, ICN, MH, MHi, MWA, MnU, NhD, NhHi, N, NN, NNC, NNGr (uncat.), PPL. **1888**

Dartmouth College. A Catalogue of the Library of Dartmouth College. Hanover: Dartmouth Press, 1868. 264 p. DeWint, DLC, MH, NhD, NjP, OClWHi. **1889**

Dartmouth College. Appendix to the Catalogue of the College Library. [Hanover, ca. 1873]. 30 p. NhD (bound with the Library's 1868 catalogue). **1890**

Dartmouth College. Chandler Scientific Department. Philotechnic Society. Catalogue of Books in the Library of the Philotechnic Society of the Chandler Scientific Department of Dartmouth College. Hanover: Dartmouth Press, 1862. 14 p. NhD. **1891**

Dartmouth College. Chandler Scientific Department. Philotechnic Society. Catalogue of Books in the Library of the Philotechnic Society, Chandler Scientific Department, Dartmouth College, Hanover, N.H. Hudson, Mass.: Wood & Rawson, 1872. 61 p. NhD. **1892**

Dartmouth College. Society of Social Friends. Catalogue of the Books belonging to the Social Friends Library. Hanover: C. & W. S. Spear, [1810?]. 16 p. Not in S & S. NhD. **1893**

Dartmouth College. Society of Social Friends. Catalogue of Books belonging to the Library of Social Friends. September, 1813. Hanover: Charles Spear, 1813. 24 p. S & S 28277. MWA, NhHi. **1894**

Dartmouth College. Society of Social Friends. Catalogue of Books belonging to the Social Friends' Library. August 1817. Hanover: Charles Spear, 1817. 23 p. Not in S & S. NhD. **1895**

Dartmouth College. Society of Social Friends. Catalogue of Books in the Library. Hanover, 1820. Shoemaker 957. MH. **1896**

Dartmouth College. Society of Social Friends. Catalogue of Books in the Social Friends' Library at Dartmouth College. March, 1824. Concord: Isaac Hill, 1824. 43 p. Not in Shoemaker. MH, MWA, NhD, NhHi. **1897**

Dartmouth College. Society of Social Friends. Catalogue of the Books in the Social Friends' Library, at Dartmouth College. June, 1824. Concord: Isaac Hill, 1824. 47 p. Not in Shoemaker. MWA. **1898**

Dartmouth College. Society of Social Friends. Catalogue of the Books belonging to the Social Friends' Library at Dartmouth College. October, 1831. Hanover: Thomas Mann, 1831. 64 p. Bruntjen 6779. CSmH, CtY, MH, MWA, NhD, NhHi, N, NN, NNGr. **1899**

Dartmouth College. Society of Social Friends. Catalogue of Books in the Social Friends' Library, Dartmouth College. March, 1841. Hanover: E. A. Allen, 1841. 136 p. Not in Rinderknecht. DHEW, DLC, ICN, MH, MWA, NhD, NhHi. **1900**

Dartmouth College. Society of Social Friends. Catalogue of Books in the Social Friends' Library, Dartmouth College. July, 1852. Hanover: Dartmouth Press, 1852. 88 p. NhD holds suppl., Books presented to the Social Friends' Library of Dartmouth College by . . . the Senior Class of 1853 ([91]-94 p.). NhD, OClW.   1901

Dartmouth College. Society of Social Friends. Catalogue of Books in the Social Friends Library, Dartmouth College. January, 1857. Hanover: McFarland & Jenks, 1856. 146 p. Date on cover: 1857. NhD holds nine suppl. to 1869 with title: Catalogue of Books presented . . . by the Class of . . . MH, MWA, NhD, NhHi.   1902

Dartmouth College. United Fraternity. Catalogue of the Books in the Library of the United Fraternity, at Dartmouth College. April, 1812. Hanover: Charles Spear, 1812. 24 p. Not in S & S. NhD.   1903

Dartmouth College. United Fraternity. Catalogue of Books in the Library of the United Fraternity, at Dartmouth College. August, 1815. [Hanover]: Charles Spear, 1815. 24 p. Not S & S; Sabin 97876. PPL.   1904

Dartmouth College. United Fraternity. Catalogue of Books in the Library of the United Fraternity, at Dartmouth College. August, 1819. Concord: George Hough, 1819. 30 p. Not S & S. MWA.   1904a

Dartmouth College. United Fraternity. Catalogue of Books in the Library of the United Fraternity, at Dartmouth College. August, 1820. Hanover: [Bannister & Thurston], 1820. 44 p. Shoemaker 958. MH, MWA, NhD (lacks index, pp. 43-44).   1905

Dartmouth College. United Fraternity. Catalogue of Books in the United Fraternity's Library, at Dartmouth College. June, 1824. Concord: Isaac Hill, 1824. 47 p. Shoemaker 15931. MH, MHi, MWA, NhD, NhHi, NN, PPL.   1906

Dartmouth College. United Fraternity. Catalogue of Books in the Library of the United Fraternity, Dartmouth College. April, 1835. [Windsor, Vt.: Chronicle Press, 1835]. 80 p. Rinderknecht 31255. DHEW, KHi, LNH, MdBJ, MB, MH, MWA, NhD, NhHi, N, NN, NNC, OCHP, VtU.   1907

Dartmouth College. United Fraternity. A Catalogue of the United Fraternity's Library, of Dartmouth College. July, 1852. Hanover: Dartmouth Press, 1852. 192 p. Supplements have title: Catalogue of Books presented to the Library of the United Fraternity, of Dartmouth College by Brothers . . . of the Senior Class of . . . Copies: DLC (1852-54), MH (1853-55), NhD (1852-55), NhHi (1853, 1855), OClW (1852-54). DLC, IU, MH, MWA, Nh, NhD.   1908

Dartmouth College. United Fraternity. A Catalogue of the United Fraternity's Library, of Dartmouth College. Sept., 1859. Hanover: Dartmouth Press, 1859. 198 p. NhD has suppl. Catalogue of Books presented . . . by Brothers of the Senior Class of . . . (1861-69, 1871). Nh, NhD, NjP.   1909

Second Social Library. Catalogue of Books in the Second Social Library in Hanover. January, 1835. Hanover: L. Wyman, jr., 1835. 28 p. Not in Rinderknecht. NhD (interleaved).   1910

Haverhill

Congregational Church. Catalogue of Books in the Sabbath School Library of the Congregational Church, Haverhill, N.H. Haverhill: S. Reding, 1870. 9 p. MWA.   1911

Hollis

Hollis Social Library. Catalogue of the Social Library in Hollis. Incorporated 1799. Nashua: Gazette Power-Presses, 1853. 16 p. DeU, MWA, Nh, NhHi.   1912

Hollis Social Library. Catalogue of the Hollis Social Library. Nashua: R. W. Berry, 1872. 69 p. DLC, Nh, NhHi.   1913

Hollis Social Library. Appendix, comprising Books added to the Hollis Library from July 1872 to July 1874. [Nashua: Hildredth, 1874]. 11 p. DLC.   1914

Hopkinton

Hopkinton Public Library. Catalogue of the Hopkinton Public Library, Hopkinton, N.H.

Organized March 17, 1871. Concord: The People Steam Press, 1872. 25 p. DLC, Nh, NhHi. **1915**

Keene

Cheshire Athenaeum. Rules and Regulations of the Cheshire Athenaeum, with a Catalogue of the Library. 1830. Keene: Nahum Stone, 1830. 15 p. Not in Cooper. Nh, NhHi. **1916**

Keene Circulating Library. Catalogue of Books in the Keene Circulating Library, kept by George Tilden. August, 1831. Keene: J. &. J. W. Prentiss, 1831. 23 p. Not in Bruntjen. NhHi. **1917**

Keene Circulating Library. Catalogue of Books in the Keene Circulating Library, kept by George Tilden. September, 1834. Keene: J. &. J. W. Prentiss, 1834. 26 p. Not in Rinderknecht. MWA, NhHi. **1918**

Keene Public Library. Catalogue of the Keene Public Library, with the Regulations. Keene: Horatio Kimball, 1859. 41 p. Nh, NNGr (with ms. additions). **1919**

Keene Public Library. Catalogue of the Keene Public Library, with the Regulations. Keene: Sentinel Printing Co., 1875. 57 p. Nh. **1920**

Lancaster

Lancaster Public Library. Catalogue of the Lancaster Public Library. May, 1871. Lancaster: Emerson, Hartshorn, [1871]. 28 p. DLC. **1921**

Littleton

Littleton Village Library. Catalogue of the Littletown Village Library. Concord: McFarland & Jenks, 1867. 16 p. DLC holds suppl., 1871 (8 p.). DLC. **1922**

Lyme

Social Library. Catalogue of Books in the Social Library in Lyme, also the By-laws, and the Names of the Proprietors. Hanover: Dartmouth Press, 1855. 48 p. NhD copy contains 12 p. of ms. additions. MWA, Nh, NhD. **1923**

Manchester

First Baptist Church. Catalogue of the First Baptist Sabbath School Library, Manchester, N.H. Manchester: William H. Fisk, 1870. 16 p. Nh. **1924**

First Baptist Church. Catalogue of the First Baptist Sunday School Library, Manchester, N.H. Manchester: Campbell & Hanscom, 1874. 15 p. Nh. **1925**

First Congregational Church. Catalogue of Books in the Sabbath School Library of the First Congregational Church, Manchester, N.H. Revised January, 1866. Manchester: Henry A. Gage, 1866. 12 p. Nh. **1926**

First Congregational Church. Catalogue of Books in the Sabbath School Library of the First Congregational Church, Manchester, N.H. Revised June, 1867. Manchester: William H. Fisk, 1867. 15 p. Nh. **1927**

First Congregational Church. Catalogue of Books in the Sabbath School Library of the First Congregational Church, Manchester, N.H. Revised April, 1869. Manchester: Henry A. Gage, 1869. 16 p. Nh. **1928**

First Congregational Church. Catalogue of Books in the Sabbath School Library of the First Congregational Church, Manchester, N.H. Revised June, 1870. Manchester: Henry A. Gage, 1870. 16 p. Nh. **1929**

First Congregational Church. Catalogue of Books in the Sabbath-School Library of the First Congregational Church, Manchester, N.H. Revised, November, 1873. Manchester: John B. Clarke, 1873. 16 p. Nh. **1930**

Franklin Street Church. Catalogue of the Franklin Street Sabbath School Library. Manchester: Daily Mirror Mammoth Job Printing Establishment, 1857. 32 p. Nh. **1931**

Franklin Street Church. Catalogue of the Franklin Street Sabbath School Library. Manchester: Gage & Farnsworth, 1861. 28 p. Nh. **1932**

Franklin Street Church. Catalogue of the Franklin-Street Sabbath School Library. Manchester: Flanders, Challis, 1875. 20 p. Nh. **1933**

Lowell Street Universalist Church. Catalogue of the Universalist Sabbath School Library, Manchester, N.H. Revised 1854. Manchester: Abbott, Jenks, 1854. 17 p. Nh.   **1934**

Lowell Street Universalist Church. Catalogue of Books in the Sabbath School Library of the Lowell Street Universalist Church, Manchester, N.H. Revised, July 1860. Manchester: John B. Clarke, 1860. 20 p. Nh.   **1935**

Lowell Street Universalist Church. Catalogue of the Lowell-Street Universalist Sunday School Library, Manchester, N.H. Manchester: C. F. Livingston, 1867. 14 p. Nh. **1936**

Lowell Street Universalist Church. Catalogue of the Lowell-Street Universalist Sunday School Library, Manchester, N.H. Manchester: C. F. Livingston, 1872. 15 p. Nh. **1937**

Manchester Art Association. Manchester Art Association, containing Articles of Incorporation, By-laws, List of Members, Catalogue of Books, &c. Manchester: John B. Clarke, 1875. 24 p. Nh.   **1938**

Manchester Athenaeum. A Catalogue of Books belonging to the Manchester Athenaeum. 1845. Manchester: Printed at the American Office, 1845. 23 p. Nh, NhM, NN.   **1939**

Manchester Athenaeum. Catalogue of the Library of the Manchester Athenaeum, and Index of Titles and Authors, to which is added the Constitution and By-laws, and a List of the Officers and Proprietors. Manchester: Union Steam Printing Works, Campbell & Gilmore, 1853. xv, 112 p. DLC, MB, MWA, Nh, NhM, N.   **1940**

Manchester City Library. Supplementary Catalogue of the Manchester City Library. April, 1855. Manchester: Adams, Hildreth, 1855. 39 p. DLC, Nh, NhM.   **1941**

Manchester City Library. Catalogue of the Manchester City Library, Manchester, N.H. Manchester: Abbott & Warren, 1856. iv, 82 p. Nh, NhM, NN.   **1942**

Manchester City Library. Supplementary Catalogue of the Manchester City Library, Manchester, N.H. [Manchester, 1858]. 20 p. Nh, N.   **1943**

Manchester City Library. Second Supplementary Catalogue of the Manchester City Library. Manchester: Goodale & Farnsworth, 1859. 36 p. MB, MWA, Nh, N.   **1944**

Manchester City Library. Third Supplementary Catalogue of the Manchester City Library. Manchester: C. F. Livingston, 1861. 18 p. Nh, N.   **1945**

Manchester City Library. Index Catalogue of the Manchester City Library, with the Rules and Regulations, the Contract of the City of Manchester with the Manchester Athenaeum, and a Supplement, containing the Books added to the Library, to February 9, 1863. Compiled by S. N. Bell. Manchester: C. F. Livingston, 1863. vii, 158 p. MWA holds suppl. #4-10 (1865-71); NhHi holds suppl. [#1], Feb. 9 to Dec. 31, 1863 and #6-9 (1867-70); NhM holds #4 (Jan. 1-Dec. 1, 1865); N holds suppl. #4-10. DLC, MB, MH, MWA, Nh, NhD, NhM.   **1946**

Merrimack Street Baptist Church. Catalogue of Books in the Merrimack-St. Baptist Sabbath School Library, Manchester, N.H. Manchester: C. F. Livingston, 1868. 15 p. Nh.   **1947**

Merrimack Street Baptist Church. Catalogue of Books in Merrimack-St. Baptist Sabbath School Library, Manchester, N.H. Manchester: C. F. Livingston, 1874. 10 p. Nh. **1948**

Merrimack Street Baptist Church. Catalogue of the Merrimack-St. Free Baptist Sabbath School Library, Manchester, N.H. Manchester: T. H. Tuson, 1875. 16 p. Nh.   **1949**

St. Paul's Methodist Episcopal Church. Catalogue of Books in the Sabbath School Library of the St. Paul's M. E. Church, Manchester, N.H. Revised September, 1866. Manchester: William H. Fisk, 1866. 12 p. Nh.   **1950**

St. Paul's Methodist Episcopal Church. Catalogue of Books in the Sabbath School Library of the St. Paul's M. E. Church, Manchester, N.H. Revised January, 1870. Manchester: Henry A. Gage, 1870. 16 p. Nh.   **1951**

St. Paul's Methodist Episcopal Church. Catalogue of Books in the S. S. Library of the

St. Paul's M. E. Church, Manchester, N.H. Revised September, 1872. Manchester: Livingston's Power Book and Job Office, 1872. 16 p. Nh. **1952**

Unitarian Church. Catalogue of Unitarian Sunday School Library at Manchester, N.H. [Manchester]: C. F. Livingston, 1859. 31 p. Nh. **1953**

Unitarian Church. Catalogue of the Unitarian Sunday School Library, Manchester, N.H., including the Parish, Adult, and Juvenile Collections. Manchester: Wm. E. Moore, 1870. 29 p. Nh. **1954**

Marlborough

Frost Free Library. Catalogue of the Frost Free Library, Marlborough, N.H. 1867. Boston: Alfred Mudge & Son, 1867. 56 p. MH, Nh, NhD, NHi. **1955**

Meredith Bridge

Meredith Bridge Social Library. The Act of Incorporation, and the By-laws, of Meredith Bridge Social Library. Instituted December 1803, and Incorporated June 1807, with the Names of the Proprietors, and a Catalogue of the Books. Concord: George Hough, 1808. 24 p. S & S 15584. Nh, NhHi. **1956**

Meriden

Kimball Union Academy. Catalogue . . . [ca. 1835]. Not in Rinderknecht. Cf. Jewett, p. 14. **1957**

Kimball Union Academy. Philadelphian Society. Catalogue of Books in the Library of the Philadelphian Society, Kimball Union Academy. Hanover: Dartmouth Press, 1854. 16 p. DLC, NhD. **1958**

Kimball Union Academy. Philadelphian Society. Catalogue of Books in the Library of the Philadelphian Society, Kimball Union Academy. Fall Term, 1856. Concord: McFarland & Jenks, 1856. 32 p. Nh. **1959**

Kimball Union Academy. Philadelphian Society. Catalogue of Books in the Library of the Philadelphian Society, Kimball Union Academy. Fall Term, 1862. Concord: McFarland & Jenks, 1862. 21, [1] p. Nh, NhD. **1960**

Milford

Milford Free Library. Catalogue of the Milford Free Library. April, 1868. Milford: Blanchard's Job Office, 1868. 12 p. Nh. **1961**

Milford Free Library. Catalogue of the Milford Free Library, Milford, N.H. Milford: J. M. Blanchard, 1870. 47 p. MWA holds suppl., July, 1871 (13 p.). Cutter 655 reports suppl., 1871 (24 p.). MWA, Nh. **1962**

Nashua

Chapel of the Good Shepherd. S. S. Library of the Chapel of the Good Shepherd. Nashua: E. Clement, 1875. 19 p. Nh. **1963**

First Baptist Society. Catalogue of the Sunday School Library of the First Baptist Society, Nashua, N.H. Nashua: Whittemores' Press, 1868. 30 p. Nh. **1964**

First Baptist Society. Catalogue of the First Baptist Sabbath School Library, Nashua, N.H. Nashua: Moore & Langley, 1873. 17 p. Nh. **1965**

First Universalist Society. Catalogue of the Universalist S. S. Library, Nashua. January, 1858. Nashua: Whittemores' Press, 1858. 18 p. MWA. **1966**

First Universalist Society. Catalogue of Books belonging to the Sunday School Library of the First Universalist Society, Nashua, N.H. Nashua: Moore & Langley, 1870. 36 p. NhHi. **1967**

Public Library. Catalogue of the Public Library of the City of Nashua. Manchester: John B. Clarke, 1868. 138 p. DLC, Nh. **1968**

Public Library. Supplement to the Catalogue of the Nashua City Library, containing the Books added . . . since the First Catalogue was printed . . . Nashua, 1874. [141]-320 p. DLC, Nh. **1969**

Union Athenaeum Library. Catalogue of the Union Athenaeum Library, of Nashua and Nashville. Nashville: Albin Beard, 1852. 15 p. MWA. **1970**

Union Athenaeum Library. Catalogue of the Union Athenaeum Library, Nashua, N.H.

August, 1855. Nashua: Albin Beard, 1855. 21 p. MWA holds "Addition" (4 p.). MWA, NhHi. **1971**

Union Athenaeum Library. Catalogue of the Union Athenaeum Library, Nashua, N.H. Nashua: Albin Beard, 1860. 32 p. ICN. **1972**

Nashville, see entry 1970.

New Hampton

Academical and Theological Institution. Literary Adelphi. A Catalogue of the Books in the Library of the Literary Adelphi, New Hampton, N.H. Concord: McFarland & Jenks, 1871. 24 p. DLC. **1973**

Academical and Theological Institution. Social Fraternity. A Catalogue of the Books in the Library of the Social Fraternity, New Hampton, N.H. New Hampton: C. D. Thyng, 1873. 23 p. DLC. **1974**

New London

New London Literary and Scientific Institute. Euphemian Association. Catalogue of Books in the Library of the Euphemian Association of the New-London Literary and Scientific Institution, New-London, N.H. Concord: Hale & Ela, 1857. [16] p. Nh. **1975**

North Enfield

North Enfield Union Library Association. Constitution, By-laws and Catalogue of Books of the North Enfield Union Library Association. Concord: McFarland & Jenks, 1856. 12 p. Nh. **1976**

Nottingham

Nottingham Social Library. Rules and Regulations of the Nottingham Social Library, adopted Feb. 15, 1802. [Nottingham?, 1802?]. 16 p. Catalogue of books on pp. 7-11. S & S 2815. MWA. **1977**

Orford

People's Circulating Library. Catalogue of Books in the People's Circulating Library of Orford, N.H., and Vicinity (established in 1860). April, 1861. Hanover: Dartmouth Press, 1861. 54 p. MB, Nh, NhHi. **1978**

Penacook, see Fisherville.

Peterborough

Peterborough Town Library. Catalogue of Books in the Town Library, at Peterborough. 1837. Keene: John Prentiss, 1837. 16 p. Not in Rinderknecht. Peterborough Town Library (copy 1 has ms. additions). **1979**

Peterborough Town Library. Catalogue of Books in the Town Library in Peterborough, N.H. June, 1860. Peterborough: K. C. Scott, 1860. 34 p. Peterborough Town Library. **1980**

Peterborough Town Library. Catalogue of Books, in the Peterboro' Town Library. May, 1857. Peterborough: K. C. Scott, 1857. 26 p. Nh (errata page inserted). **1981**

Peterborough Town Library. List of Books in the Town Library in Peterborough, N.H. June, 1860. Peterborough: K. C. Scott, 1860. 34 p. Nh. **1982**

Peterborough Town Library. Catalogue of the Town Library, Peterboro', N.H. 1867. Peterborough: Transcript Office, Farnum & Scott, Proprietors, 1867. 53 p. MWA, Nh, Peterborough Town Library. **1983**

Unitarian Congregational Church. Catalogue of the Unitarian Congregational Sunday-School Library, Peterboro', N.H. Peterboro': "Transcript" Print, 1863. 16 p. MWA. **1984**

Unitarian Congregational Church. Catalogue of the Unitarian Congregational Sunday School Library, Peterborough, N.H. Peterboro': Transcript Office, 1870. 24 p. MWA, Peterborough Town Library. **1985**

Unitarian Church. Catalogue of the Unitarian Sunday School Library, Peterboro', N.H. Peterboro': Farnum and Scott, 1875. 16 p. MWA. **1986**

Pittsfield

Pittsfield Library. Catalogue of Books belonging to the Pittsfield Library. Established October, 1862. Pittsfield: Daniel T. Neal, 1865. 38 p. MWA holds suppl. (8 p.). MWA, NhHi. **1987**

Portsmouth

Exchange Circulating Library. Catalogue of the Exchange Circulating Library at the

Book Store of John S. Harvey . . .
Portsmouth: Millers and Gray, 1852. 48 p.
MWA (defective; has only printed wrappers), Nh.   **1988**

Mercantile Library Association. Constitution,
By-laws, and Library Catalogue of the
Mercantile Library Association of Portsmouth, N.H. Portsmouth: C. W. Brewster,
1856. 32 p. NhPoA (Portsmouth Historical
Society Collection).   **1989**

Mercantile Library Association. Catalogue of
Books belonging to the Mercantile Library
Association of Portsmouth, N.H. Portsmouth: Daily Evening Times Steam Print.
Establishment, 1870. 32 p. DLC holds
Appendix, Sept. 1, 1872 (8 p.). DLC. **1990**

Miller, Tobias Ham. Catalogue of the
Circulating Library, kept at T. H. Miller's
Book-Store . . . Portsmouth, [ca. 1820]. 12 p.
Not in Shoemaker. NhPoA.   **1991**

Miller, Tobias Ham. Catalogue of the
Circulating Library, kept at the Book-Store
and Printing-Office of T. H. Miller . . .
Portsmouth, [ca. 1823]. 12 p. Not in
Shoemaker. NhPoA.   **1992**

North Parish Library. Catalogue . . . Jan. 1,
1826. Portsmouth, 1826. 4 p. Shoemaker
25814. MBC.   **1993**

North Parish Library. Catalogue . . . Jan. 1,
1827. Portsmouth, 1827. 12 p. Shoemaker
30314. MBC.   **1994**

North Parish Library. North Parish Library,
1828. While the Library consisted of only a
few Volumes . . . It is therefore Necessary at
this Time to Print a Catalogue of those
Books only which have been added to the
Library in the course of the past Year.
[Portsmouth, 1828]. [2] leaves (cover letter
and suppl. designated p. 13). Shoemaker
34856. MBC.   **1995**

North Parish Library. The Parishioners are
presented with a Catalogue of the Books
which have been added to the Library
during the past Year. [Portsmouth, 1829].
[2] leaves (cover letter and suppl.
designated p. 14). Shoemaker 40132.
MBC.   **1996**

North Parish Library. At the Commencement
of this Year, the Directors Report . . . 50
Volumes have been added since the
Printing of the Last Annual Catalogue, a
List of which is annexed. [Portsmouth,
1830]. 1 leaf designated p. 15). Cooper
3144. MBC.   **1997**

Peirce, Charles. Catalogue of Books for Sale
and Circulation by Charles Peirce, at his
Brick Book-Store, in Daniel Street . . .
Portsmouth, 1806. 103 p. At head of title:
Circulating Library and for Sale. S & S
11113 is based on the incomplete copy
(74 p.) at NN. MWA, MiU-C, NN (defective).   **1998**

Peirce, Charles. C. Peirce's Catalogue of
Classical & School Books, also Seamen's and
Singing Books, Military Discipline, Blank
Books . . . Portsmouth, 1812. 20, [4] p.
"Conditions of C. Peirce's Circulating
Library" on last printed page. S & S 26401.
MWA.   **1999**

Portsmouth Apprentices' Library. Catalogue
of Books, belonging to the Portsmouth
Apprentices' Library. Portsmouth: Gazette
Office, 1824. 19 p. Not in Shoemaker.
MWA.   **2000**

Portsmouth Athenaeum. Catalogue of Books
in the Portsmouth Athenaeum. [Portsmouth]: Charles Turell, 1823. 32 p. Not in
Shoemaker. NN.   **2001**

Portsmouth Athenaeum. Catalogue of Books
in the Portsmouth Athenaeum. [Portsmouth]: Charles Turell, 1827. 24 p.
Shoemaker 30313. NhHi, NhPoA.   **2002**

Portsmouth Athenaeum. Catalogue of Books
in the Portsmouth Athenaeum, to which are
added the By-laws of the Institution, and a
List of its Proprietors. Portsmouth: Miller
and Brewster, 1833. 108 p. Bruntjen 20787.
DLC, MWA (with ms. notes), Nh, NhD,
NhPoA, Salem Athenaeum.   **2003**

Portsmouth Athenaeum. Catalogue of Books
added to the Library of the Portsmouth
Athenaeum, from May, 1833, to January,
1839. Portsmouth: C. W. Brewster, 1839.
31 p. Not in Rinderknecht. DLC, NhPoA.
                                       2004

Portsmouth Athenaeum. Books Missing. List
of Books Missing from the Library, January
5th, 1848 . . . Albert R. Hatch, Secretary.
[Portsmouth?, 1848]. broadside. NhHi.
                                       2005

Portsmouth Athenaeum. Catalogue of Books in the Portsmouth Athenaeum, to which are added the By-laws of the Institution, and a List of its Proprietors. Portsmouth: Charles W. Brewster, 1849. 192 p. NhPo holds "Additions" for 1849 (8 p.) and 1850 (4 p.). DeWint, DLC, MH, MnU, NhPoA.   **2006**

Portsmouth Athenaeum. Catalogue of Books in the Portsmouth Athenaeum, to which are added the By-laws of the Institution, and a List of its Proprietors. Portsmouth: Charles W. Brewster & Son, 1862. 252 p. DLC, MsHall, Nh, NhPoA, PP.   **2007**

Portsmouth Circulating Library. Catalogue of the Portsmouth Circulating Library, at the Book and Stationery Store of J. F. Shores & Son . . . [Portsmouth]: C. W. Brewster, 1843. 48 p. Not in Rinderknecht. Nh.   **2008**

Portsmouth Circulating Library. Catalogue of the Portsmouth Circulating Library at the Book and Stationery Store of James F. Shores, jr. . . . [Portsmouth]: Charles W. Brewster, 1851. 54 p. MWA holds Appendix, June, 1854 (7 p.). MWA, Nh.   **2009**

Portsmouth Circulating Library. Catalogue of the Portsmouth Circulating Library. Founded 1792. James F. Shores, jr., Proprietor . . . Nov. 1862. [Portsmouth]: C. W. Brewster & Son, [1862]. 64 p. Nh.   **2010**

Portsmouth Circulating Library. Catalogue of the Portsmouth Circulating Library, Established 1792. James F. Shores, jr., Proprietor . . . December, 1866. Portsmouth: C. W. Brewster & Son, 1866. 64 p. Running title: J. F. Shores, Jr.'s Circulating Library. NN holds Appendix, November, 1868 (8 p.). NhDo, NN.   **2011**

Shores' Circulating Library. Catalogue of James F. Shores' Circulating Library. Containing History, Biography, Voyaegs [sic], Travels . . . Portsmouth: R. Foster, 1821. 24 p. Not in Shoemaker. MWA.   **2012**

South Parish. Catalogue of Books belonging to the South Parish Library, established 1820. [Portsmouth]: C. W. Brewster, 1840. 20 p. Rinderknecht 40-5510. DLC.   **2013**

South Parish. Catalogue of Books belonging to the South Parish Library. Established 1820. Portsmouth: C. W. Brewster & Son, 1865. 12 p. MBAt (includes ms. "Catalogue of the South Parish Sunday School Library," 12 p.).   **2014**

Tappan, Charles. Tappan's Catalogue. A Catalogue of Books for Sale and Circulating, by Charles Tappan, at his Book-store and Circulating Library . . . Portsmouth: Stephen Sewall, 1809. 34, [2] p. Not in S & S. MWA.   **2015**

Young Men's Christian Association. Catalogue . . . 1856. 24 p. Cf. Rhees, p. 217.   **2016**

Rochester

First Congregational Church. Catalogue of Books in the First Congregational Sunday School Library, Rochester, N.H. . . . Rochester: Chas. W. Folsom, 1875. [8] p. MnU, NhD.   **2017**

Salisbury

First Social Library. Catalogue of Books in the First Social Library, in Salisbury, 1833. [n.p., 1833]. 8 p. Not in Bruntjen. MWA.   **2018**

Salmon Falls

Salmon Falls Library Association. Catalogue. Pawtucket: A. W. Pearce, 1852. 16 p. DLC.   **2019**

Somersworth, see Great Falls.

Wakefield

Wakefield and Brookfield Union Library. Catalogue of the Books composing the Wakefield & Brookfield Union Library. [Wakefield?, ca. 1854-55]. 4 p. DLC (ms. additions on 5 suppl. pages; dating is from holograph title page).   **2020**

Wilton

Wilton Public Library. Catalogue of Wilton Public Library. 1874. Peterboro': Transcript Office, Farnum & Scott, 1874. 98 p. DLC.   **2021**

Winchester

Washington Library. Catalogue of Books in the Washington Library at Winchester,

N.H. Keene: J. Printiss, 1837. 8 p. Not in Rinderknecht. MStuO (photocopy). **2022**

Washington Library Association. By-laws and Catalogue of Washington Library Association, N.H. Brattleboro, Vt.: G. E. Selleck, 1870. 27 p. DLC (with ms. additions).**2023**

Windham

Nesmith Library. Catalogue of the Nesmith Library, of Windham, N.H. Lawrence: Geo. S. Merrill, 1872. 73 p. DLC holds 1st suppl., Nov. 1872 (13 p.); Nh holds 2d suppl., Aug. 1875 (11 p.). DLC, Nh. **2024**

Windham Library. Windham Library: Subscribers' Names; Act of Incorporation; By-laws and Catalogue of Books. Haverhill, 1811. Not in S & S. Contained 60 vol., per Leonard A. Morrison, *The History of Windham in New Hampshire (Rockingham County), 1719-1883* (Boston, 1883), pp. 281-83. **2025**

NEW JERSEY

Bergen

Bergen Library. Catalogue . . . Jersey City, 1866? Sinclair 104. See also Sinclair 105 for an unlocated 2d ed., 1868. **2026**

Bergen Library. Catalogue of Bergen Library. 3d ed., Enlarged. Jersey City: Pangborn, Dunning & Dean, 1872. 75 p. DLC holds suppl., 1874 (pp. [77]-87). Sinclair 106-107. DLC, NjJ, NN. **2027**

Bricksburg

(later Lakewood)

Bricksburg Library. Catalogue of the Bricksburg Library. January, 1871. Bricksburg: Printed at the Times Office, [1871]. 16 p. Sinclair 2. NjLak, NjR (copy). **2028**

Bridgeton

Public Library. Catalogue of the Public Library, of Bridgeton, in New-Jersey. Established on the Eighth of April, 1811. Philadelphia: Thomas Town, 1813. 11 p. Not in S & S; Sinclair 3. NjP, NjR (copy). **2029**

Young Men's Christian Association. Catalogue . . . 1872. 23 p. Not in Sinclair. Cf. Cutter 772. **2030**

Burlington

Apprentice's Library Company. A Catalogue of the Books belonging to the Burlington Apprentice's Library Company. Instituted 1822. Burlington: D. Allinson, 1824. [26] p. Shoemaker 15601, Sinclair 4, Rink 524. DLC (with ms. additions). **2031**

Burlington Social Library. By-laws and Catalogue of the Burlington Social Library. Burlington, [ca. 1850]. 8 p. Sinclair 12, based on Sabin 9337. **2032**

Library Company of Burlington. A Catalogue of Books belonging to the Library Company of Burlington, taken November 15th, 1806, to which is prefixed a List of the Present Members, and a Copy of the Existing Regulations, and, in an Appendix, is added a Summary of the Laws of the Company. Burlington: S. C. Ustick, 1807. 50, [2] p. S & S 12248, Sinclair 8. NjBu, NjR, PHi. **2033**

Library Company of Burlington. Additional Catalogue of Books, of the Burlington Library. 1816. [Burlington, 1816]. 51-54 p. Not in S & S; Sinclair 9. NjBu, PHi. **2034**

Library Company of Burlington. Additional Catalogue of Books belonging to the Burlington Library. 1824. [Burlington, 1824]. 51-62 p. Not in Shoemaker; Sinclair 10. NjBu, NjR. **2035**

Dover

First Presbyterian Church. Catalogue of the Library of the Dover Presbyterian S. School., N.J. New York: William S. Dorr, 1862. 20 p. Sinclair 283. NjR. **2036**

Dunellen

First Presbyterian Church. Catalogue of Sunday School Library of the First Presbyterian Church, Dunellen, N.J. Plainfield: Central New Jersey Times Print., 1872. 15 p. Not in Sinclair. MWA. **2037**

East Orange

First Presbyterian Church. Catalogue of Books in the Library of the Sunday School of the First Presbyterian Church, at East Orange, N.J. February 28th, 1869. Newark: Jennings Brothers, 1869. 17 p. Sinclair 284. NjR.   **2038**

Elizabeth

Elizabeth-town Religious Library Company. Constitution of the Elizabeth-town Religious Library, together with a Catalogue of the Books and the Names of the Stockholders. [n.p.], 1821. 16 p. Not in Shoemaker or Sinclair. NHi.   **2039**

Flemington

Flemington Library Company. Regulations ordained & established by the Trustees for the Government of "The Flemington Library Company;" together with a Catalogue of Books belonging to said Library. Trenton: Sherman & Mershon, 1802. 11 p. Catalogue of books on pp. 9-11. Not in S & S; Sinclair 23. NjFlHi, NjR (copy).   **2040**

Freehold

Freehold Circulating Library [Catalogue]. Freehold: James S. Yard, 1875. 25 p. Sinclair 25. NjFrHi (defective).   **2041**

Freehold Institute. A Catalogue of the Library of Freehold Institute, with a Catalogue of Teachers, and a Circular annexed. New-York: James D. Torrey, 1853. 32 p. Sinclair 274. DLC (lost?), NjR.   **2042**

Second Reformed Church. Catalogue of the Sabbath School Library, of the Reformed Church, Freehold, N.J. [Freehold, 1871]. 8 p. Sinclair 285. NjFrHi.   **2043**

Haddonfield

Haddonfield Library Company. The Constitution and By-laws of the Haddonfield Library Company, with a Catalogue of the Books belonging to the same. Philadelphia: James Humphreys, 1805. 32 p. S & S 8576, Sinclair 28. DLC, NjHHi, PHi.   **2044**

Haddonfield Library Company. Constitution of the Haddonfield Library Company, together with a Catalogue of the Books, and the Library Regulations. Philadelphia: Duross Brothers, 1862. 14 p. Sinclair 28a. NjHHi.   **2045**

Haddonfield Library Company. Articles of Association and Constitution of the Haddonfield Library Company, with Library Regulations and List of Books. Philadelphia: William Mann, 1875. 60 p. The catalogue on pp. [13]-60 is dated 1876. Sinclair 28b. NjH, NjHHi.   **2046**

Hightstown

Presbyterian Church. Catalogue of the Presbyterian S. School Library, Hightstown, N.J. [Hightstown, ca. 1868]. broadside. Sinclair 286. NjHi, NjR (copy).   **2047**

Hoboken

Franklin Lyceum. Catalogue of the Library of the Franklin Lyceum . . . Hoboken, N.J. New York: Livesey Bros., 1873. 31 p. Sinclair 24. DLC.   **2048**

Hopewell

Hopewell Library Company. A Catalogue of Books belonging to the Hopewell Library Company. [Trenton?], 1804. Not in S & S; Sinclair 29.   **2049**

Jersey City

Public School Free Library. Catalogue . . . Jersey City, 1874. Sinclair 276. NjJ (lost?).   **2050**

Keyport

Calvary Methodist Episcopal Church. Catalogue of the Library of the Calvary M. E. Sunday School, Keyport, N.J. New York: C. H. Conrow, 1863. 11 p. NjR holds updated suppl. (11 p.). Sinclair 287. NjR.   **2051**

Kingston

Kingston Library Company. [Constitution, Rules, Catalogue of Books, and Names of Present Proprietors of the Kingston Library]. [New Brunswick?: Lewis Deare?, 1812]. 16 p. Sinclair 34. NjPHi (defective), NjR (copy).   **2052**

Lakewood, see Bricksburg.

Livingston

Baptist Church. Catalogue of the Livingston Baptist Sunday-School Library. [Livingston, ca. 1875]. [3] p. Sinclair 290. NjR. **2053**

Montclair

Montclair Library. Catalogue of the Montclair Library, Montclair, N.J. 1871. [n.p., 1871?]. 15 p. Not in Sinclair. MWA.   **2054**

Montclair Library. Catalogue of the Montclair Library, Montclair, N.J. Organized, 1869. Incorporated, 1871. Montclair: E. Madison, 1873. 39 p. Not in Sinclair. MWA.   **2055**

Moorestown

Moorestown Library Company. Constitution and Bye-laws of the Moorestown Library Company, New-Jersey. Instituted Anno Domini Eighteen Hundred and Eight. Philadelphia: W. Hall, jun., & G. W. Pierie, 1809. 13, [2] p. Catalogue of books on pp. [14-15]. S & S 18114, Sinclair 41. MWA, NjMor.   **2056**

Morristown

Apprentices Library Association. Catalogue of the Apprentices Library Association of Morristown, N.J. Instituted June 16th, 1848. Morristown, S. P. Hull, 1850. 14 p. Sinclair 1. DLC (may be an incomplete copy?).   **2057**

Emmell's Circulating Library. Catalogue of Books in the Circulating Library of Morris-Town, belonging to S. B. Emmell. [Morristown]: S. P. Hull, 1836. 22 p. Not in Rinderknecht; Sinclair 18. NjHi.   **2058**

Emmell's Circulating Library. Catalogue of books in the Circulating Library of Morristown, belonging to S. B. Emmell. Morristown, 1845. 15 p. Sinclair 19. NjMo (lost?).   **2059**

New Brunswick

First Presbyterian Church. Catalogue of the First Presbyterian Church Sunday School Library. 1875. New Brunswick: A. L. Blue, 1875. 43 p. Sinclair 293. Private Collection (Joseph J. Felcone, per Sinclair).   **2060**

New Brunswick Library Company. A Catalogue of the Books, belonging to the New-Brunswick Library Company, to which are prefixed such Extracts from the Constitution . . . [New Brunswick: William Myer, 1821]. 16 p. NHi copy has ms. additions and supplementary pages of books added. Not

in Shoemaker; Sinclair 45-46 (see for dating). NHi (catalogued as 1826), NjNb, NjR (copy).   **2061**

New Brunswick Library Company. Catalogue of the Books belonging to the New Brunswick Library Co. New Brunswick: Times Press: 1847. 28 p. NjNb and NjR (copy) each hold an undated suppl. (4 p.). Sinclair 47. MWA, NjNb, NjR, NjT.   **2062**

Rutgers College. Catalogue of Books in the Library of Rutgers College, New Brunswick, N.J. July 7, 1832. New Brunswick: Terhune & Letson, 1832. 35 p. Not in Bruntjen; Sinclair 368. NjR.   **2063**

Rutgers College. Philoclean Society, Catalogue of the Library of Philoclean Society, Rutgers College, New Brunswick, N.J. New Brunswick: Terhune & Van Anglen's Press, 1875. 35 p. Sinclair 83. NjR.   **2064**

Young Men's Christian Association. Catalogue of Books in Library of the Young Men's Christian Association, of New Brunswick, N.J. 1870. New Brunswick: Terhune & Van Anglen, [1870]. 34 p. Sinclair 99. NjR.   **2065**

Young Men's Christian Association. Supplementary Catalogue, No. 1, of Books of the Y.M.C.A. Library . . . New Brunswick, N.J. New Brunswick: Times Steam Printing House, 1871. 16 p. Cover title: Supplementary Catalogue, No. 1, of Books in Library, Young Men's Christian Association, New Brunswick, N.J. 1872. Sinclair 100. NjR.
2066

Newark

First Presbyterian Church. Catalogue of the Sunday School Library of the First Presbyterian Church, Newark, N.J. Senior Department. Newark: A. L. Dennis & Brother, 1858. 24 p. Sinclair 296. NjHi.   **2067**

First Presbyterian Church. Catalogue of the Sunday School Library of the First Presbyterian Church, Newark, N.J. Senior Department. Newark: Daily Advertiser Office, 1864. 31 p. Sinclair 297. NjHi.
2068

Newark Library Association. Catalogue of the Newark Library Association. Newark: Daily Advertiser Office, 1847. iv, 102 p. Sinclair 48. DLC.   **2069**

Newark Library Association. Books of the
Newark Library Association. Newark: Daily
Advertiser Office, 1849. 27 p. Sinclair 49.
NjHi (also a copy with ms. additions).**2070**

Newark Library Association. Catalogue of the
Newark Library Association. Chartered
February 19, 1847. Newark: Daily Advertiser
Office, 1850. iv, 102 p. Sinclair 50. DLC,
NjN, N(interleaved).   **2071**

Newark Library Association. Additions to
Catalogue of the Newark Library Association. [Newark, 1852?]. 28 leaves (blank
versos). Sinclair 51 DLC.   **2072**

Newark Library Association. Catalogue of the
Library of the Newark Library Association.
Newark: Douglass & Starbuck, 1857. 148 p.
DeU and NjP copies (139 p., [1] p.) lack
addenda while the book was in press.
Sinclair 52. DeU, DLC, MB, MBAt, MWA,
MiD, NjHi, NjN, NjP, NjR, NjUN, N, NNC,
PPL.   **2073**

Newark Library Association. Appendix to the
Catalogue of the Library of the Newark
Library Association (Books added since
1857). Newark: Francis Starbuck, 1861.
68 p. Sinclair 53. DeU, DLC, NjHi, NjN,
NjP, NjR, N.   **2074**

Newark Library Association. Second Appendix to the Catalogue of the Library of the
Newark Library Association (Books added
since 1861). Newark: A. Stephen Holbrook,
1868. 76 p. Sinclair 54. DLC, NjHi, NjN,
NjR, N.   **2075**

Newark Library Society. Catalogue of Books,
belonging to the Newark Library Society. September 26, 1821. [Newark, 1821]. broadside.
Not in Shoemaker; Sinclair 55. NjHi.   **2076**

Newark Library Society. Catalogue of Books,
belonging to the Newark Library Society,
regularly classed and alphabetically arranged. Newark: W. Tuttle, 1830. 17 p. Not
in Cooper; Sinclair 56. MWA, NjHi, NjR,
NjRuF.   **2077**

Young Men's Christian Association. Catalogue . . . 1875. Not in Sinclair. Cf. Cutter
989.   **2078**

Newton

Newton Library Association. First Catalogue
of the Dennis Library, belonging to the

Newton Library Association, Newton, N.J.
Newark: M. R. Dennis, 1873. 95 p. Sinclair
16. DLC, MB, NjNet.   **2079**

Orange

Orange Baptist Sunday School. Alphabetical
Catalogue of the Orange Baptist Sunday
School Library . . . New York: Baker &
Godwin, 1861. 26 p. Not in Sinclair. MWA.
                                        2080

Orange Library Association. Catalogue of the
Library of the Orange Library Association,
Orange, New Jersey. May, 1859. New York:
C. O. Jones, 1860. 47 p. Not in Sinclair.
MWA.   **2081**

Princeton

College of New Jersey. American Whig
Society. Catalogue. [Princeton?, 184-]. 45 p.
Caption title. Sinclair 63. NjP, NjR, PPL
(cataloguing dated [1843?]).   **2082**

College of New Jersey. American Whig
Society. The Catalogue of the American
Whig Society Library, College of New Jersey.
New York: Charles Scribner, 1853. 95 p.
(some pages blank for additions). Sinclair
64. CSmH, DLC, MH, PPL, ViU.   **2083**

College of New Jersey. American Whig
Society. Catalogue of the Library of the
American Whig Society, College of New
Jersey. New York: Frank McElroy, 1862. 59 p.
Sinclair 65. NjP, ViU.   **2084**

College of New Jersey. American Whig
Society. Catalogue of the Library of the
American Whig Society of the College of
New Jersey. Philadelphia: Spangler & Davis,
1865. 106 p. NjP copy includes suppl.
(1867). Sinclair 66-67. MdBJ, NjP.   **2085**

College of New Jersey. American Whig
Society. Library Catalogue of the American
Whig Society of Princeton College.
Princeton: Charles S. Robinson, 1870. 128
p. NjHi and NjP hold copies with 119 p.;
other copies listed below contain a suppl. on
pp. [121]-28. Sinclair 68-69. CtY, DHEW,
IU, MWA, NjHi, NjP.   **2086**

College of New Jersey. Cliosophic Society.
Catalogue of the Cliosophic Society,
instituted in theCollege of New Jersey,

1765. Princeton: John Bogart, 1840. 39 p.
Rinderknecht 40-5562; Not in Sinclair. MB,
NjR, NN, OClW, PPL, PU, WM.   **2087**

College of New Jersey. Cliosophic Society.
Catalogue of the Library of the Cliosophic
Society, Princeton, N.J. 1855. Philadelphia:
J. B. Chandler, 1855. 54 p. NjP and ViU hold
an undated appendix (4 p.). Sinclair 70-71.
DLC, NjP, ViU.   **2088**

College of New Jersey. Cliosophic Society.
Catalogue of the Library of the Cliosophic
Society, Princeton, N.J. 1859. Newark:
Holbrook, 1859. 63 p. Sinclair 72. NjP, NjR,
NjVHi.   **2089**

College of New Jersey. Cliosophic Society.
Catalogue of the Library of the Cliosophic
Society, College of New Jersey. Princeton,
1864. 55 p. Sinclair 73. MnU, ViU. **2090**

College of New Jersey. Cliosophic Society.
Catalogue of the Library of the Cliosophic
Society, College of New Jersey. Princeton,
N.J. Princeton, 1870. 118 p. Sinclair 74.
NjP, NjR.   **2091**

College of New Jersey. Cliosophic Society.
Catalogue of the Library of the Cliosophic
Society, College of New Jersey, Princeton,
N.J. Princeton, 1873. iv, 52, 4 p. Sinclair 75.
NjP.   **2092**

College of New Jersey. Philological Society.
Catalogue of Books belonging to the Library
of the Philological Society of Nassau-Hall,
together with those deposited for use of its
Members. Princeton: Connolly & Madden,
1828. 60 p. Shoemaker 34888, Sinclair 81.
ICN, NjP, NN, PPAmP, WMSF.   **2093**

Princeton Library Company. Catalogue of
Books belonging to the Princeton Library
Company. January 1, 1825. Princeton: D. A.
Borrenstein, [1825]. 12 p. Shoemaker
21974, Sinclair 62. NjP, Phi.   **2094**

Princeton University, see College of New
Jersey.

Salem

Public Library. Catalogue of the Public
Library of Salem, in New-Jersey . . .
Philadelphia: Hall and Pierie, 1811. [16] p.
Not in S & S; Sinclair 37. NjR, NjSalHi
(copy).   **2095**

Public Library. Catalogue of the Public
Library of Salem, in New-Jersey . . .
Philadelphia: Hall and Atkinson, 1818. 21 p.
Not in S & S; Sinclair 38. NjR, NjSalHi
(copy).   **2096**

Shiloh

Union Library Company. A Catalogue of
Books belonging to the "Union Library
Company," Shiloh, Cum. Co., N. Jersey.
[n.p., 185-?]. [8] p. Sinclair 92. Nj, NjR
(copy of original held by Nj and dated by
NjR's cataloguing as ca. 1837).   **2097**

South Orange

South Orange Library Association. Catalogue
. . . 1869. 36 p. Not in Sinclair; Cutter 619.
                                      2098

Trenton

Fourth Presbyterian Church. Catalogue of
Books belonging to the Library of the
Fourth Presbyterian Church Sunday School
of Trenton, N.J. Trenton: W. S. Sharp, 1875.
30 p. Sinclair 302a. NjR.   **2099**

Law Library Association of New-Jersey.
Catalogue of Books belonging to the Law
Library Association of New-Jersey. July 1st,
1846. Trenton, 1846. Sinclair 309. Nj
(lost?).   **2100**

Law Library Society of New Jersey. Catalogue
of Books belonging to the Law Library
Society of New-Jersey. January 1, 1830.
Trenton: George Sherman, 1830. 16 p. Not
in Cooper; Sinclair 310. CtY-L, NjR (copy).
                                      2101

Law Library Society of New Jersey. Catalogue
of the Books belonging to the Law Library
Society of New Jersey. January 1, 1842.
Trenton: Phillips and Boswell, 1842. 15 p.
Not in Rinderknecht; Sinclair 311. Nj, NjR
(copy).   **2102**

New Jersey State Library. Catalogue of teh
Books in the New Jersey State Library.
January 1,1838. Trenton: Phillips and
Boswell, 1838. 36 p. Rinderknecht 51889,
Sinclair 157. Nj, Phi, PPM.   **2103**

New Jersey State Library. Catalogue of the
Books belonging to the New Jersey State

Library. January 1, 1847. Trenton: Sherman and Harron, 1847. 37 p. Sinclair 158. DLC, Nj, NjHi, NjR. **2104**

New Jersey State Library. Catalogue of the Books belonging to the New Jersey State Library. By Authority of the Seventy-seventh Legislature. Trenton: True American Office, 1853. 117 p. Sinclair 159. DLC: IU, M (interleaved), MA, Nj, NjHi, NjP, NjR, NN, OKentU, PHi, Vi. **2105**

Trenton Circulating Library. Catalogue and Rules and Regulations of the Trenton Circulating Library, instituted May, 1797. Trenton: True American Office, 1866. 59 p. Sinclair 86. NjT. **2106**

Trenton Library Association. Catalogue of the Trenton Library Association, with their Rules and Regulations. Trenton: Sherman and Harron, 1853. 35 p. Sinclair 87. NjR, NjT, PP. **2107**

Trenton Library Company. Laws and Regulations of the Trenton Library Company, agreed to by the said Company on the First Monday in May, 1797. Trenton: James Oram, 1804. 27 p. "A Catalogue of Books belonging to the Library Company of Trenton . . ." on pp. 11-27. S & S 7384, Sinclair 89. NjT, NHi. **2108**

Trenton Library Company. Laws and Regulations of the Trenton Library Company, agreed to by the said Company on the First Monday in May, 1797. Trenton: J. Justice, 1819. 24 p. "A Catalogue of Books belonging to the Library Company of Trenton . . ." on pp. [9]-24. Not in S & S; Sinclair 90. NjR (copy), PPAmP. **2109**

Young Men's Christian Association. Catalogue . . . 1872. 55 p. Not in Sinclair; Cutter 773. **2110**

Woodbury

Woodbury Library Company. A Catalogue of Books, and Rules of the Woodbury Library Company, with a List of the Member's Names. Instituted 24th of April, 1794. Philadelphia: John Bioren, 1815. 27 p. Not in S & S; Sinclair 94. PHi. **2111**

Woodbury Library Company. A Catalogue of Books, and Rules of the Woodbury Library Company, with a List of the Member's Names. Instituted April 24, 1794. Woodbury: A. S. Barber, 1835. 24 p. Not in Rinderknecht; Sinclair 95. NjWdHi (also a copy with ms. additions). **2112**

Woodside

Presbyterian Church. Catalogue of the Sunday School Library of the Presbyterian Church, Woodside, N.J. Newark: Holbrook's Steam Printery, 1873. 8 p. Not in Sinclair. RPB. **2113**

NEW YORK

Albany

Albany Apprentices' Library. Catalogue of the Albany Apprentices' Library. Incorporated March 31, 1821. Albany: Websters & Skinners, E. & E. Hosford, Packard & Van Benthuysen, and G. J. Loomis, 1822. [4], 33, [3] p. Not in Shoemaker. MWA. **2114**

Albany Apprentices' Library. Catalogue of Books, belonging to the Albany Apprentices' Library . . . Albany: Webster & Skinners, 1832. 48 p. Not in Bruntjen. MWA. **2115**

Albany Apprentices' Library. Catalogue of Books belonging to the Albany Apprentices' Library. Albany: T. G. Webb, 1835. 70 p. Not in Rinderknecht. N (lost?). **2116**

Albany Apprentices' Library. Catalogue of the Apprentices' Library. Albany: Joel Munsell, 1838. Cf. Munsell, p. 8. **2117**

Albany Institute. Catalogue of the Albany Institute Library. Founded 1793. Prepared by George Wood. Albany: J. Munsell, 1855. 454 p. Issued as *Transactions of the Albany Institute*, vol. 3. CSt, DLC, ICJ, ICN, MB, MWA, MnU, NN, NNC, O, PPRF. **2118**

Albany Library. A Catalogue of the Books belonging to the Albany Library. January 20, 1802. Albany: Whiting and Leavenworth, 1802. 36 p. Not in S & S. MiD. **2119**

Albany Library. A Catalogue of Books in the Albany Library. January, 1806. Albany: Charles R. and George Webster, 1806. 40 p. Not in S & S. MiD. **2120**

Albany Library. Catalogue of Books in the Albany Library. October, 1821. Albany: E. &

E. Hosford, 1821. 75 p. Shoemaker 4443. Colpies: DLC (film), MB, N. **2121**

Albany Library. Catalogue of Books in the Albany Library. July, 1828. Albany: Websters and Skinners, 1828. 81, [3] p. Shoemaker 31917. MB, MWA, NjR, N, NN. **2122**

Arbor Hill Methodist Episcopal Church. Catalogue of the Sabbath School Library connected with the Arbor Hill M. E. Church. Albany: Joel Munsell, 1851. 8 p. Cf. Munsell, p. 44. **2123**

Arbor Hill Methodist Episcopal Church. Catalogue of the Arbor Hill M. E. Church Sabbath School Library. Albany: Joel Munsell, 1858. 16 p. NAlUHL. **2124**

Dutch Reformed Church. Catalogue of the Sabbath School Library of the Dutch Reformed Church. Albany: Joel Munsell, 1840. Cf. Munsell, p. 11. **2125**

First Baptist Church. Catalogue of the Scholars' Library of the Sabbath School Association connected with the First Baptist Church of Albany. Organized May 16, 1858. Albany: Frank H. Little, 1858. 16 p. NAlUHL. **2126**

First Baptist Church. Catalogue of the Teachers' Library of the Sabbath School Association connected with the First Baptist Church of Albany. Organized May 16, 1858. Albany: Frank H. Little, 1858. 8 p. NAlUHL. **2127**

First Baptist Church. Catalogue of the Scholars' Library of the Sabbath School connected with the First Baptist Church of Albany. Organized May 16, 1858. Albany: Joel Munsell, 1860. 20 p. Cf. Munsell, p. 104. **2128**

First Baptist Church. Catalogue of the Scholar's Library of the Sabbath School connected with the First Baptist Church of Albany. Organized May 16, 1858. Albany: Frank H. Little, 1863. 19 p. MH. **2129**

First Baptist Church. Catalogue of Books in the First Baptist Sunday School Library, Corner of Philip and Hudson Streets, Albany, N.Y. Albany: George B. Carter, 1873. 22 p. N (misc. pamphlet box, 018.1). **2130**

First Congregational Church. Catalogue of Books in the Library of the First Congregational Sabbath School. June, 1869. Albany: Joel Munsell, 1869. 30 p. Cf. Munsell, p. 157. **2131**

First Congregational Church. Catalogue of Books in the Library of the First Congregational Sabbath School. Albany: Joel Munsell, 1871. 32 p. Cf. Munsell, p. 166. **2132**

First Lutheran Church. Catalogue of the Sunday School Library of the First Lutheran Church in the City of Albany. Albany: Joel Munsell, 1870. 19 p. Cf. Munsell, p. 162. **2133**

First Presbyterian Church. Catalogue of the First Presbyterian Church Sunday School Library. Albany: Joel Munsell, 1837. 36 p. Cf. Munsell, p. 6. **2134**

First Presbyterian Church. Church Library of the First Presbyterian Church of the City of Albany. Albany: Joel Munsell, 1843. 8 p. Rinderknecht 43-82. NAlUHL. **2135**

First Presbyterian Church. Catalogue of Books in the Sabbath School Library of the FirstPresbyterian Church. January 1, 1850. Albany: Weed, Parsons, 1850. 29 p. N (misc. pamphlet box, 018.1). **2136**

First Presbyterian Church. Catalogue of Books in the Sabbath School Library of the First Presbyterian Church January 1, 1852. Albany: Joel Munsell, 1852. 16 p. Cf. Munsell, p. 50. **2137**

First Presbyterian Church. Catalogue of Books in the Library of the First Presbyterian Church Sunday School. Albany: Joel Munsell, 1857. 38 p. N, NAlUHL. **2138**

First Presbyterian Church. Catalogue of Books in the Library of the First Presbyterian Church Sunday School. Albany: Joel Munsell, 1859. 20 p. Cf. Munsell, p. 97. **2139**

Garretson Station Methodist Episcopal Church. Catalogue of the Sunday School Library of the Garretson Station M. E. Church. Albany: Joel Munsell, 1859. 16 p. Cf. Munsell, p. 98. **2140**

Grace Church. Library of Grace Church Sunday School, Albany. [Albany, 1874]. 15 p. NNC (lost). **2141**

Hudson Street Methodist Episcopal Church. Catalogue of the Sunday School Library of the Hudson Street Methodist Episcopal Church, Albany. Jan. 15, 1852. Albany: Joel Munsell, 1852. 25 p. Cf. Munsell, p. 51.
2142

Methodist Episcopal Church. Catalogue of Books in the Sunday School Library of the Methodist Episcopal Church, Ferry Street, Albany. Albany: Joel Munsell, 1859. 16 p. Cf. Munsell, p. 97.
2143

Middle Dutch Church. Catalogue of the Middle Dutch Church Library. Albany: Joel Munsell, 1844. 24 p. Cf. Munsell, p. 20.
2144

New York. Secretary of State. Catalogue of Maps and Surveys in the Offices of the Secretary of State, of the State Engineer and Surveyor, and in the New-York State Library . . . Albany: Weed, Parsons, 1851. 288 p. DLC, MBAt, MWA, MiD, MiU, N, NRU, NSySC, NWM, PP, PPL, RPB, Vi.
2145

New York. Secretary of State. Catalogue of Maps and Surveys, in the Office of the Secretary of State, State Engineer and Surveyor, and Comptroller, and the New York State Library. Printed by Order of the Assembly and under the Direction of the Secretary of State, 1851, and revised, corrected and enlarged by Order of the Assembly and under the Direction of the Secretary of State, by David E. E. Mix, C.E. Albany: C. Van Benthuysen, 1859. 375 p. In many libraries.
2146

New York. Secretary of State. List of Books and Papers in the Office of the Secretary of State . . . Albany: Weed, Parsons, 1866. 8 p. NN (film).
2147

New York State Agricultural Society. Transactions of the New York State Agricultural Society . . . Vol. 1-34; 1841-1883/86. Albany: Charles Van Benthuysen, etc., 1842-89. Vol. 7-9 (1847-49), 19 (1859), 21 (1861), 24-26 (1864-66), 28-31 (1868-71) contain "Additions to Library and Museum" (title and publisher varies); vol. 9 (1849) contains "Catalogue of the Library . . . Jan. 1, 1850" on pp. [xxiii]-xxx. In many libraries. **2148**

New York State Library. Annual Report of the Trustees of the State Library made to the Senate . . . Vol. 1-87; 1818-1905. Albany. Reports for 1818, 1822-25, 1827-43 contain catalogues of the library. In many libraries.
2149

New York State Library. "A Catalogue of Books received into the State Library." In: *Journal of the Assembly of the State of New-York at their Forty-second Session begun and held at the Capitol, in the City of Albany, the Fifth Day of January, 1819.* (Albany: J. Buel, 1819), pp. 148-53. MWA.
2150

New York State Library. Catalogue of the New-York State Library, in the City of Albany. Jan. 1st, 1820. Albany: E. & E. Hosford, 1820. 20 p. Shoemaker 2481. CtW. **2151**

New York State Library. Catalogue of Books, Maps, &c. belonging to, and remaining in the State Library. January 1, 1838. [Albany: E. Croswell, 1838]. 115 p. Issued as part of *Annual Report of the Trustees of the State Library,* contained in *Documents of the Senate of the State of New-York,* Sixty-first Session, 1838, vol. 1. Copy held by N is interleaved with ms. notes. Not in Rinderknecht. In many libraries as part of New York *Documents of the Senate* set. **2152**

New York State Library. Catalogue of the New-York State Library. January 1, 1846. Albany: C. Wendell, 1846. 2 vol. in 1. Catalogue of Law Library (252 p.) and Catalogue of Miscellaneous Library (294 p.). Catalogues of additions or donations appear in *Annual Report of the Trustees of the State Library,* 1847-1875, etc. DLC, MBAt, MH, MWA, N, NCH, NHi, NN, NNGr, RPB, Vi.
2153

New York State Library. Catalogue of Historical Papers and Parchments received from the Office of the Secretary of State, and deposited in the New York State Library. Made by the Regents of the University, Feb. 13, 1849. Albany: Weed, Parsons, 1849. 55 p. For related catalogue, see entry 2155. DLC, MB, MWA, NBC, NN.
2154

New York State Library. Report of the Regents of the University on the Historical and other Papers and Parchments received from the Office of the Secretary of State for Deposit in the State Library . . . [Albany, 1849]. 55 p. At head of title: State of New-York. No. 148. In Assembly, Feb. 24, 1849.

Half-title (p. 9): Manuscripts, received from the Office of the Secretary of State, and deposited in the State Library, in pursuance of a Joint Resolution of the Senate and Assembly, passed Dec. 15, 1847. For related catalogue, see entry 2154. MWA, PPL (contains p. 55, "Addenda," "Errata"), WHi. **2155**

New York State Library. Catalogue of the New York State Library. January 1, 1850. Albany: Charles Van Benthuysen, 1850. 1058 p. Catalogues of additions or donations appear in *Annual Report of the Trustees of the State Library*, 1847-1875, etc. In many libraries. **2156**

New York State Library. Catalogue of Maps and Surveys . . . (1851), see entry 2145.

New York State Library. Catalogue of the New-York State Library: 1855. General Library. Albany: Charles Van Benthuysen, 1856. x, 987 p. Compiled by Henry Augustus Homes. Catalogues of additions or donations appear in *Annual Report of the Trustees of the State Library*, 1847-1875, etc. In many libraries. **2157**

New York State Library. Catalogue of the New-York State Library: 1856. Maps, Manuscripts, Engravings, Coins, &c. Albany: Charles Van Benthuysen, 1857. xii, 274 p. In many libraries. **2158**

New York State Library. Catalogue of the Books on Bibliography, Typography and Engraving, in the New-York State Library. Albany: Charles Van Benthuysen, 1858. 143 p. In many libraries. **2159**

New York State Library. Catalogue of Maps and Surveys . . . (1859), see entry 2146.

New York State Library. Catalogue of the New-York State Library. 1861. General Library: First Supplement. Albany: Charles Van Benthuysen, 1861. x, 1084 p. Catalogues of additions or donations appear in *Annual Report of the Trustees of the State Library*, 1847-1875, etc. In many libraries. **2160**

New York State Library. Catalogue of the New York State Library. 1872. Subject-index of the General Library. Albany: Van Benthuysen Printing House, 1872. xvii, 651 p. Explanatory note signed: H. A. H. [Henry Augustus Homes]. In many libraries. **2161**

New York State Library. Law Library. Catalogue of the Law Books in the New-York State Library . . . December, 1849. Albany: Charles Van Benthuysen, 1849. 376 p. AAP, DLC, N. **2162**

New York State Library. Law Library. Catalogue of the New York State Library. 1855. Law Library. Albany: Charles Van Benthuysen, 1856. x, 402 p. In many libraries. **2163**

New York State Library. Law Library. Catalogue of the New-York State Library. 1865. Law Library: First Supplement. Albany: Charles Van Benthuysen, 1865. 180 p. In many libraries. **2164**

North Dutch Church. Catalogue of Books in the North Dutch Church Sabbath School Library. Albany: Joel Munsell, 1862. 32 p. WHi. **2165**

North Pearl Street Baptist Church. Catalogue of Books in the North Pearl Street Baptist Sabbath School Library. Albany: Joel Munsell, 1857. 18 p. NAlUHL. **2166**

Park Chapel. Catalogue of the Library of Park Chapel Sunday School. Albany: Joel Munsell, 1870. 16 p. Cf. Munsell, p. 162. **2167**

Pearl Street Baptist Church. Catalogue of Books in the Sabbath School Library of the Pearl Street Baptist Church. Albany: Joel Munsell: 1852. 24 p. Cf. Munsell, p. 50. **2168**

Pearl Street Baptist Church. Catalogue of Books in the Sabbath School Library of the Pearl Street Baptist Church. Albany: Joel Munsell, 1855. 20 p. NAlUHL. **2169**

Pearl Street Baptist Church. Catalogue of the Pearl Street Baptist Sabbath School Library. Albany: Joel Munsell, 1864. 16 p. Cf. Munsell, p. 128. **2170**

Rensselaer Street Mission. Catalogue of Books in the Library of the Rensselaer Street Mission Sunday School. February 2, 1850. Albany: Joel Munsell, 1850. 17 p. N. **2171**

Rensselaer Street Mission. Catalogue of Books in the Library of the Rensselaer Street Mission Sunday School. Albany: Joel Munsell, 1856. 20 p. Cf. Munsell, p. 76. **2172**

St. Peter's Church. Catalogue of Books in the Sunday School Library of St. Peter's Church. Albany: Joel Munsell, 1837. 23 p. Not in Rinderknecht. Cf. Munsell, p. 6.
2173

Second Reformed Protestant Dutch Church. Catalogue of Books in the Library of the Second R. P. Dutch Church, Albany, N.Y. Albany: Joel Munsell, 1854. 8 p. NAlUHL.
2174

Second Reformed Protestant Dutch Church. Catalogue of the Library of the Second R. P. Dutch Church Sabbath School Library, Albany, N.Y. Albany: Joel Munsell, 1860. 32 p. Cf. Munsell, p. 104.
2175

Second Reformed Protestant Dutch Church. Catalogue of the Library of the Second R. P. Dutch Church Sabbath School, Albany, N.Y. Albany: J. Munsell, 1865. 36 p. Copy held by N has "Appendix," forming pp. [37]-47. N (misc. pamphlet box, 027.8).
2176

Sixth Presbyterian Church. Library of the Sixth Presbyterian Church Sabbath School. November, 1873. Albany: Joel Munsell, 1873. 28 p. NNC.
2177

Society for the Promotion of Useful Arts. A Catalogue of Books in the Library of the Society for the Promotion of Useful Arts. March 7, 1818. [Albany, 1818]. 4 p. S & S 45752, Rink 509. MB, MHi, N.
2178

State Street Presbyterian Church. Catalogue of the Library of the State Street Presbyterian Church Sabbath School. Albany: Joel Munsell, 1864. 29 p. Cf. Munsell, p. 128.
2179

State Street Presbyterian Church. Catalogue of State Street Presbyterian Sunday School Library. Albany: Joel Munsell, 1866. 40 p. Cf. Munsell p. 142, Sabin 90650.
2180

State Street Presbyterian Church. Catalogue of the Library of the State Street Presbyterian Church Sabbath School. Albany: Joel Munsell, 1868. 43 p. Cf. Munsell, p. 153.
2181

Third Reformed Protestant Dutch Church. Catalogue of Books in the Library of the Third Dutch Church Sabbath School, in the City of Albany. Albany: Joel Munsell, 1851. 11 p. DLC.
2182

Third Reformed Protestant Dutch Church. Catalogue of Books in the Sabbath School of the Third Reformed Dutch Church . . . in the City of Albany. Albany: Joel Munsell, 1859. 36 p. Cf. Munsell, p. 97.
2183

Third Reformed Protestant Dutch Church. Catalogue of the Third R.P.D. Church S. School, Albany, N.Y. Albany, 1864. 19 p. Copies: The British Library, London.
2183a

Trinity Methodist Episcopal Church. Catalogue of the Library of the Trinity M. E. Church Sabbath School . . . Albany: Joel Munsell, 1872. 30 p. MWA, N (misc. pamphlet box, 018.1), PPL.
2184

Unitarian Church. Catalogue of the Unitarian Sunday School Library. Albany: Joel Munsell, 1866. 25 p. Cf. Munsell, p. 143.
2185

Washington Avenue Church. Catalogue of the Washington Avenue Sunday School Library. Albany: Joel Munsell, 1865. 20 p. Cf. Munsell, p. 134.
2186

Young Men's Association. Catalogue of Books in the Library of the Young Men's Association for Mutual Improvement in the City of Albany. Albany, 1837. 33 p. Rinderknecht 48654. MHi, NAl.
2187

Young Men's Assopciation. Catalogue of the Library of the Young Men's Association for Mutual Improvement in the City of Albany. Albany: Joel Munsell, 1840. 50 p. Rinderknecht 40-7190. MHi, NAlUHL.
2188

Young Men's Association. Catalogue of Books in the Library of the Young Men's Association for Mutual Improvement in the City of Albany. Albany: Joel Munsell, 1843. 54 p. Rinderknecht 43-5440. MH, N, NAl, NN.
2189

Young Men's Association. Catalogue of Books in the Library of the Young Men's Association for Mutual Improvement in the City of Albany. January, 1848. Albany: Charles Van Benthuysen, 1848. 102, [1] p. Cutter 304 reports suppl. for 1848, 1849, 1850. DLC (film), NAlUHL.
2190

Young Men's Association. Catalogue of the Library of the Young Men's Association,

Albany. 1853. Albany: Cuyler & Henly, 1853. 148 p. DLC, MA, MB, MBAt, MH, MWA, MnU, NjP, NAlUHL, NHi, NN, NNC, PPL. **2191**

Albion

Albion Library Association. Catalogue of the Library of the Albion Library Association, together with the Officers, Standing Committees, Constitution and By-laws. Albion: Orleans American Steam Press, 1874. 32 p. MWA. **2192**

Batavia

Batavia Library Association. Catalogue of the Library of the Batavia Library Association, together with the Charter, By-laws, Officers, Standing Committees, etc. Batavia: "The Spirit of the Times" Steam Press, 1873. 38 p. DLC. **2193**

Union School Library. Catalogue of the Union School Library, District No. 2, Batavia, N.Y., together with the Officers of the Board of Education, Instructors, By-laws, etc. Batavia: "The Spirit of the Times" Steam Press, 1873. 40 p. DLC. **2194**

Bath

Bath Library Association. Catalogue of the Bath Library Association. April, 1874. Bath: A. L. Underhill, 1874. 59 p. DLC. **2195**

Bethlehem

Second Reformed Church. Catalogue of Books in the Library of the Second Reformed Church Sabbath School, Bethlehem, N.Y. Albany: Weed, Parsons, 1870. 18 p. MWA. **2196**

Binghamton

Binghamton Library Association. First Catalogue of Books in the Library of the Binghamton Library Association. Incorporated May 4, 1874. Binghamton: Republican Print, 1874. 36 p. DLC. **2197**

Union School Library. Catalogue and Regulations of the Union School Library, Binghamton, N.Y. Binghamton: Republican Print, 1874. 128 p. DLC. **2198**

Blooming Grove

Blooming-Grove Library Association. Catalogue of the Blooming-Grove Library Association, established Jan. 1836. Newburgh: Chas. U. Cushman, [1836?]. 12 p. Not in Rinderknecht. MWA. **2199**

Brooklyn

(see also listings under Flatbush)

Apprentices' Library Association, see Brooklyn Apprentices' Library Association.

Brooklyn Apprentices' Library Association. Catalogue . . . Brooklyn, 1824. Not in Shoemaker. Cf. Ralph Foster Weld, *Brooklyn Village, 1816-1834* (New York, 1938), p. 198 (based on notice in the *Long Island Star,* March 4, 1824). **2200**

Brooklyn Apprentices' Library Association. Catalogue of Books, belonging to the Brooklyn Apprentices' Library Association. Instituted in November 1823. Brooklyn: A. Spooner, 1826. 35, 4 p. Shoemaker 23931, Rink 535. NBLiHi (copy not located per Rink). **2201**

Brooklyn Apprentices' Library Association. Catalogue of Books, belonging to the Brooklyn Apprentices' Library Association. Brooklyn: A. Spooner, 1828. 35 p. Shoemaker 32484, Rink 548. NBLiHi. **2202**

Brooklyn Apprentices' Library Association. Catalogue of Apprentices' Library. Brooklyn: Stationer's Hall Works, 1842. 68 p. Rinderknecht 42-758. MB, NB. **2203**

Brooklyn Athenaeum and Reading Room. A Catalogue of the Brooklyn Athenaeum and Reading Room, with the Rules of the Library Committee. November 1, 1853. New York: N. Lane, 1853. 64 p. DLC, MB, NB, NBLiHi, NN, NNC. **2204**

Brooklyn Circulating Library. Catalogue of Books in the Brooklyn Circulating Library, kept at the Office of the Long-Island Star, Fulton Street, Brooklyn. Brooklyn: E. Worthington, 1821. 34 p. Presumably operated by Erastus Worthington. Shoemaker 4841. NB, NBLiHi. **2205**

Brooklyn City Library. Act of Incorporation, By-laws and Catalogue of the Brooklyn City Library. Brooklyn: A. Spooner & Son, 1840. 80 p. Rinderknecht 40-1039. CU, DLC, MH, NB, NN, NRU, WHi. **2206**

Brooklyn Collegiate and Polytechnic Institute. Library of the Brooklyn Collegiate & Polytechnic Institute. [Brooklyn?], 1861. 58 p. Cover title: Catalogue of the Library of the Brooklyn Collegiate and Polytechnic Institute, and of the Zetalethean Society. DLC, NN. **2207**

Brooklyn Institute of Arts and Sciences. A Supplement to the Youths' Free Library Catalogue . . . Brooklyn, 1844. 23 p. Not in Rinderknecht. NB. **2208**

Brooklyn Institute of Arts and Sciences. Catalogue of the Youths' Free Library, Brooklyn Institute . . . New York: John R. M'Gown, 1849. 114 p. DLC, MWA, NN. **2209**

Brooklyn Institute of Arts and Sciences. Supplement to the Catalogue of the Youths' Free Library, Brooklyn Institute . . . New York: L. Van Anden's Print, 1851. 8 p. NN holds suppl. #2 (8 p.) and #3 (4 p.), both 1852. NN. **2210**

Brooklyn Institute of Arts and Sciences. Catalogue of the Youths' Free Library, Brooklyn Institute . . . New York: Edward T. Callender, 1857. 118 p. NB has annual suppl., 1858-63; NN has suppl. for 1858-59. DLC, NB, NBLiHi, NN. **2211**

Brooklyn Institute of Arts and Sciences. Catalogue of the Youths' Free Library, Brooklyn Institute . . . New York: J. H. Tobbit, 1867. 88 p. NN. **2212**

Brooklyn Institute of Arts and Sciences. Catalogue of the Youths' Free Library, Brooklyn Institute . . . Brooklyn: Daily Union Job Printing Establishment, 1873. 116 p. NN holds suppl., 1875 (6 p.). NN. **2213**

Brooklyn Library Association of the Eastern District. Catalogue of the Brooklyn Library Association, of the Eastern District, May, 1866 . . . Organized, January 9th, 1865, Incorporated, April 3, 1865. Brooklyn, E.D.: Broach & Herring, 1866. 272 p. MB, NN. **2214**

Brooklyn Mercantile Library. A Catalogue of the Books in the Mercantile Library of the City of Brooklyn, N.Y. August, 1858. Brooklyn, Baker & Godwin, 1858. 138 p. CSmH, DLC, MB, MBAt, MH, NjP, NB, NN (interleaved), NRU. **2215**

Brooklyn Mercantile Library. Catalogue of the Mercantile Library of the City of Brooklyn. Brooklyn, 1859. 138, 76 p. A reissue of the Catalogue of 1858, with suppl. (76 p.). CU-S, DLC, IU, MB, MH, MnU, NjP, NB (with ms. additions), NNGr. **2216**

Brooklyn Mercantile Library. Alphabetical List of the Works of Fiction in the Brooklyn Mercantile Library. 1869. [Brooklyn, 1869]. 36 p. DLC, MB, MWA, NBLiHi, NN. **2217**

Brooklyn Mercantile Library. Bulletin of New Books. No. 1-40; Nov. 1869-Dec. 1901. No. 8-9 called Book List. DLC (complete), MB (#1-39; Nov. 1869-Dec. 1899), MWA (#1-4, 1869-71), NN (complete, but #8 is bound with Class List of English Prose Fiction . . . 2d ed. Brooklyn, 1875). **2218**

Brooklyn Mercantile Library. English Prose Fiction. Nov., 1873. [Brooklyn, 1873]. 59 p. MB. **2219**

Brooklyn Mercantile Library. Works of Fiction in the Brooklyn Mercantile Library. [Brooklyn, 1874]. 64, [1] p. Suppl., Nov. 1873-Nov. 1874, on pp. 61-64. DLC, MA, MBAt, NBLiHi. **2220**

Brooklyn Mercantile Library. Class List of English Prose Fiction, including Juveniles and Translations. 2d ed., with Supplement, to Dec. 1874. Brooklyn, 1875. 64 p. NBLiHi, NN (only the Supplementary Class List, Nov. 1873-Nov. 1874, forming pp. 61-64.) **2221**

Church of the Holy Trinity. Alphabetical Catalogue of the Sunday School and Parish Library of the Church of the Holy Trinity, Brooklyn. Brooklyn: Bloomfield & Farmer, 1861. 16 p. NN. **2222**

First Presbyterian Church. Catalogue of the Sabbath-School Library of the First Presbyterian Church. Brooklyn: "The Union" Steam Presses, 1864. 26 p. NN (preservation copy). **2223**

First Reformed Dutch Church. Descriptive Catalogue of the Library of the Sunday-School attached to the First Ref. Dutch Church, Brooklyn, E.D., edited under the Pastoral Care of Rev. Elbert S. Porter, D.D. By the Superintendent. New-York: John A. Gray, 1860. 65 p. DLC. **2224**

Kings County Penitentiary. Catalogue of Library of Kings County Penitentiary, Brooklyn, N.Y. 1871. Brooklyn: H. M. Gardner, jr., [1871]. 22 p. MB. **2225**

Long Island Historical Society. Medical Department of the Library of the Long Island Historical Society. An Account of its Formation, with a Catalogue of the Books. Brooklyn, 1870. 31 p. Printed in New York by William Felt. CtY, DLC, DNLM, NB, NBLiHi, NHi, NN, OClWHi. **2226**

Mercantile Library, see Brooklyn Mercantile Library.

Plymouth Church of the Pilgrims. Catalogue of the Library of the Plymouth Sabbath School, Brooklyn, N.Y., with the Organization and Rules of the School. New York: M. B. Brown, 1867. 38, 3 p. (pagination continues on wrappers). NN. **2227**

Plymouth Church of the Pilgrims. Catalogue of Books belonging to the Sabbath School of the Church of the Pilgrims . . . New York: Pelletreau & Raynor, 1873. 10 p. NN. **2228**

Plymouth Church of the Pilgrims. Catalogue of the Library of the Plymouth Church Sabbath-School. 1875. [Brooklyn?]: Union Print., [1875]. 52 p. NN. **2229**

St. John's Church. Catalogue of the Sunday School Library of St. John's Church, Brooklyn. New York: John F. Trow, 1857. 18 p. NHi. **2230**

School District No. 5. Classified Catalogue of Books belonging to the School District Library, No. 5, Brooklyn, L.I. . . . Brooklyn: I. Van Anden's Press, 1848. 36 p. NN. **2231**

Seventeenth District Common School Library. Catalogue of the Seventeenth District Common School Library, Brooklyn . . . Brooklyn: Printed at the Times Office, 1855. 52 p., 2 leaves. DLC. **2232**

Seventeenth District Common School Library. Supplement to Catalogue of the 17th Dist. Common School Library, Brooklyn. Brooklyn: George C. Bennett, 1858. 8 p. DLC. **2233**

United States Naval Lyceum. Catalogue of the Library belonging to the U.S. Naval Lyceum, at the New York Navy Yard. 1856.

New York: E. T. Callender, [1856]. 57 p. (blank leaves for additions). DLC, DN, NB. **2234**

United States Naval Lyceum. Catalogue of the Library of the U.S. Naval Lyceum, at the Navy Yard, Brooklyn. 1872. Hempstead: Inquirer Office, 1872. 75 p. Catalogue of the Museum on pp. 65-75. DLC, CN, NBhi. **2235**

Young Men's Christian Association. Catalogue of the Library of the Young Men's Christian Association, of Brooklyn, N.Y. Brooklyn, 1862. 103 p. NN. **2236**

Young Men's Christian Association. Catalogue of Books in Library of the Brooklyn Young Men's Christian Association. 1872. Brooklyn: Daily Union Book and Job Printing Establishment, 1872. 189 p. DLC, NN. **2237**

Young Men's Christian Association. Supplementary Catalogue of Books in Library of the Brooklyn Young Men's Christian Association. 1872. Brooklyn, [1872?]. 24 p. DLC holds suppl. and mounted accessions for 1873-75. DLC, NN (with additional mounted entries). **2238**

Youth's Free Library of the Brooklyn Institute, see Brooklyn Institute of Arts and Sciences.

Buffalo

Apprentices' Society. Constitution and By-laws of the Apprentices' Society, to which is annexed a Catalogue of Books comprising the Library. Buffalo: David L. Wood, 1837. 17 p. Not in Rinderknecht. Cf. "Contributions Towards a Bibliography of the Niagara Region. Pamphlets and Books Printed in Buffalo Prior to 1850." *Publications of the Buffalo Historical Society* 6 (1903): 578. **2239**

Black's Circulating Library. Book Catalogue of R. Black's Circulating Library . . . Buffalo: Geo. J. Bryan, 1859. 35 p. Operated by Robert Black. Not In Rinderknecht. N (misc. pamphlet box, 018.1). **2240**

Buffalo Catholic Institute. Catalogue . . . 1874. 56 p. Cf. Cutter 939. **2241**

German Young Men's Association. Catalog über die Bibliothek der Deutschen Jung-Männer Gesellschaft in Buffalo. Buffalo: Reinecke & Zesch, 1869. 146 p. DLC (interleaved with ms. additions). **2242**

Russell's (Jared) Circulating Library. Catalogue of Jared Russell's Circulating Library. Buffalo: Press of Eastabrooks and Runcie, Office of the Daily Sun, 1840. 12 p. Not in Rinderknecht. NBuHi. **2243**

Young Men's Association. Catalogue of Books in the Library of the Young Men's Association of the City of Buffalo. Founded 22d February, 1836, Incorporated March 3d, 1837. Buffalo: Oliver G. Steele, 1837. 34 [i.e., 42] p. Rinderknecht 48656 (duplicated by 43470). ICLaw, NBu. **2244**

Young Men's Association. Catalogue of the Library of the Young Mens' [sic] Association of the City of Buffalo. Buffalo: Jewett, Thomas, 1848. 146 p. Annual list of new books or periodicals appears in *Annual Report of the Executive Committee of the Young Men's Association of the City of Buffalo.* DLC, NBu. **2245**

Young Men's Association. Catalogue of the Library of the Young Men's Association of Buffalo . . . Buffalo: A. M. Clapp, 1865. x, 351 p. Annual list of new books or periodicals appears in *Annual Report of the Executive Committee of the Young Men's Association of the City of Buffalo.* NBu, NBuC, NBuHi. **2246**

Young Men's Association. Bulletin of Books recently added to the Library of the Young Men's Association of Buffalo, N.Y. March 1st to June 1st, 1870, with a List of Periodicals and Newspapers on File in the Reading Rooms. Buffalo: Baker, Jones & Smith, 1870. 21 p. Cover title: Bulletin of Books added to the Library . . . DLC, MWA, N, NBu. **2247**

Young Men's Association. Catalogue of Novels, Tales, Romances and Juvenile Books, in the Library of the Young Men's Association. Buffalo, 1871. 28 p. NBu, NHi. **2248**

Young Men's Association. Catalogue of the Young Men's Association Library of the City of Buffalo. Buffalo: Matthews & Warren, 1871. 416 p. Annual list of new books or periodicals appears in *Annual Report of the*

Executive Committee of the Young Men's Association of the City of Buffalo. In many libraries. **2249**

Young Men's Association. First Supplement to the Catalogue of the Young Men's Association Library of the City of Buffalo (Accessions, November, 1870 to August, 1872). Buffalo, 1872. 154 p. NNGr copy includes Novels, Tales and Juvenile Books added . . . from November, 1870 to August, 1872 (15 p.). DLC, NBu, NHi, NNGr.**2250**

Cambridge

Washington Academy. Catalogue of the Library of Cambridge Washington Academy. 1875. Cambridge: Washington County Post Steam Printing House, 1875. 20 p. MWA. **2251**

Canandaigua

Wood Library Association. Catalogue of the Wood Library Association, Canandaigua, Ontario Co., N.Y. Canandaigua: Printed at the Repository Office, 1861. 47 p. NCanHi. **2252**

Wood Library Association. Catalogue of the Wood Library Association, Canandaigua, Ontario Co., N.Y. Canandaigua: Ontario County Times Office, 1868. 28 p. DLC. **2253**

Catskill

Reformed Dutch Church. Catalogue of Books belonging to the Library of the Reformed Church Sunday School, Catskill, N.Y. Catskill: J. B. Hall's Steam Presses, 1873. 8 p. MnU. **2254**

Cazenovia

Oneida Conference Seminary. Catalogue of the Members, Library & Reading Room of the Seminary Lyceum, from November 6, 1833, to January 1, 1839. Cazenovia, 1839. 24 p. Not in Rinderknecht. IaU. **2255**

Clinton

Hamilton College. Catalogue of Hamilton College Library. January, 1826. [Utica?, 1826]. 24 p. Shoemaker 24785. IU, MH, MWA, NCH, NN, WHi. **2256**

Hamilton College. Phoenix Society. Catalogue of Books belonging to the Phoenix Society, Hamilton College. August, 1827. [Auburn: Office of the Free Press, 1827]. 8 p. Not in Shoemaker. NCH.   **2257**

Hamilton College. Phoenix Society. Triennial Catalogue of the Members and Books belonging to the Phoenix Society, Hamilton College, Clinton. October, 1836. Utica: Bennett & Bright, 1836. 23 p. Rinderknecht 37888. CSmH, N, NBuC, NCH.   **2258**

Hamilton College. Phoenix Society. Triennial Catalogue of the Phoenix Society, Hamilton College, Clinton. October, 1839. Utica: Bennett, Backus, & Hawley, [1839]. 27 p. Library catalogue on pp. [15]-27. Rinderknecht 56136. MWA, N, NCH.**2259**

Hamilton College. Phoenix Society. Triennial Catalogue of the Phoenix Society, Hamilton College, Clinton. October, 1842. Utica: Bennett, Backus, & Hawley, [1842]. 36 p. Library catalogue on pp. [17]-29. Rinderknecht 42-2194. NCH, PPPrHi.   **2260**

Hamilton College. Phoenix Society. Triennial Catalogue of the Phoenix Society, Hamilton College, Clinton. November, 1844. Utica: R. W. Roberts, 1844. 48 p. Library catalogue on pp. [25]-40. Rinderknecht 44-2893. NCH.   **2261**

Hamilton College. Phoenix Society. Triennial Catalogue of the Phoenix Society, Hamilton College, Clinton. November, 1847. Utica: Roberts, Sherman & Colston, 1848. 61 p. Library catalogue on pp. [25]-44. NCH.   **2262**

Hamilton College. Phoenix Society. Triennial Catalogue of the Phoenix Society, Hamilton College, Clinton. January, 1851. Utica: Roberts & Sherman, 1851. 61 p. Library catalogue on pp. [27]-44. NCH.   **2263**

Hamilton College. Phoenix Society. Triennial Catalogue of the Phoenix Society, Hamilton College, Clinton. June, 1855. Utica: Curtiss & White, 1855. 46, [4] p. Library catalogue dated July, 1855, on pp. [29]-46. LNT, NCH.   **2264**

Hamilton College. Union Society. Triennial Catalogue of the Union Society of Hamilton College, Clinton, October, 1835. Utica:

Northway & Johnson, 1835. 28 p. Library catalogue on pp. [17]-28. Rinderknecht 32036. N, NCH.   **2265**

Hamilton College. Union Society. Triennial Catalogue of the Union Society of Hamilton College, Clinton. November, 1838. Utica: William Williams, 1838. 39 p. Library catalogue on pp. [21]-34. Rinderknecht 50714. MWA, NCH.   **2266**

Hamilton College. Union Society. Triennial Catalogue of the Union Society of Hamilton College, Clinton. January, 1842. Rome: R. Waldby, [1842]. 45 p. Library catalogue on pp. [23]-35. Not in Rinderknecht. N (misc. pamphlet box, 017.1; holds library catalogue section only), NCH.   **2267**

Hamilton College. Union Society. Triennial Catalogue of the Union Society of Hamilton College, Clinton. June, 1844. Utica: R. W. Roberts, 1844. 46 p. Library catalogue on pp. [23]-36. Rinderknecht 44-2894. NCH, NUt.   **2268**

Hamilton College. Union Society. Triennial Catalogue of the Union Society of Hamilton College, Clinton. 1847. Utica: H. H. Curtiss, 1847. 55 p. Library catalogue on pp. [29]-42. NCH.   **2269**

Hamilton College. Union Society. Triennial Catalogue of the Members, Library, and Cabinet, of the Union Society of Hamilton College. 1851. Utica: Roberts & Sherman, 1851. 64 p. Library catalogue on pp. [31]-47. NCH.   **2270**

Hamilton College. Union Society. Triennial Catalogue of the Members, Library, and Cabinet, of the Union Society of Hamilton College. 1858. Utica: Roberts, 1858. 62 p. Library catalogue on pp. [35]-49. NCH.   **2271**

Cohoes

City Library. Catalogue of the City Library, Cohoes, N.Y. January 1, 1874. Cohoes: Clark & Foster, 1875. 62 p. DLC (with additions, March, 1875).   **2272**

Cohoes District School Library. Catalogue of Books in the Cohoes District School Library. Albany: Joel Munsell, 1854. 31 p. Cf. Munsell, p. 62.   **2273**

Cohoes District School Library. Catalogue of the Cohoes District School Library. January 1, 1857. Cohoes: J. H. Masten, 1857. 29 p. NAlUHL.   **2274**

Cohoes District School Library. Catalogue of the Cohoes District School Library. June 1, 1864 [i.e., 1863?]. Albany: Joel Munsell, 1863. 41 p. Cf. Munsell, p. 121 (classified under 1863).   **2275**

Cohoes District School Library. Cohoes School District Library Catalogue. Albany: Joel Munsell, 1864. 40 p. Cf. Munsell, p. 129.   **2276**

Cooperstown

Franklin Library. Catalogue of Books. [n.p., 1832?]. 8 p. Not in Bruntjen. MWA. **2277**

Young Men's Association. Catalogue of the Library of the Young Men's Association and Reading Room, Cooperstown, N.Y. Cooperstown: Republican and Democrat Office, 1872. 23 p. NCooHi.   **2278**

Cortland

Presbyterian Church. Catalogue of the Presbyterian Sabbath School Library, Cortland, N.Y. Cortland: Wm. H. Livermore, 1869. 16 p. PPPrHi.   **2279**

Coxsackie

Methodist Episcopal Church. Catalogue of Books contained in the Library of the M. E. Church Sabbath School of Coxsackie. Albany: Joel Munsell, 1870. 16 p. Cf. Munsell, p. 161.   **2280**

Dunkirk

Dunkirk Library. Catalogue of the Dunkirk Library. 1873. Dunkirk: Journal Printing Co., 1873. 42 p. DLC.   **2281**

Flatbush

(see also Brooklyn)

Erasmus Hall Academy. Catalogue of the Library of Erasmus Hall Academy, Flatbush, L.I., with an Appendix containing the Rules and Regulations of the Hall and the Rules of the Library. New-York: Lewis Nichols, 1835. 29 p. Not in Rinderknecht. MWA. **2282**

Flushing

Flushing Library Association. Catalogue of Books in the Library of the Flushing Library Association. Flushing: C. R. Lincoln, 1861. 36 p. NJQ.   **2283**

Flushing Library Association. Catalogue . . . 1871. 80 p. Cf. Cutter 721, also reporting suppl. for 1872 (7 p.).   **2284**

Fordham

St. John's College. Catalogue of the Students' Library, St. John's College, Fordham. New York: Baker & Godwin, 1871. 59 p. MWA, NNF.   **2285**

Geneseo

Atheneum Library. Catalogue of the Atheneum Library, at Geneseo, New-York. Founded and endowed by the late James Wadsworth, in 1844. Geneseo: James T. Norton, 1858. 95 p. NRU.   **2286**

Geneva

Hobart Free College. A Catalogue of the Library of Hobart Free College, in Geneva, N.Y. Geneva: S. H. Parker, 1859. 63 p. DLC, MH, MWA, NN.   **2287**

Trinity Church. A Catalogue of the Parish Library of Trinity Church, Geneva, N.Y. . . . December, 1837. Geneva: J. T. Bradt, 1837. 14 p. Not in Rinderknecht. MB.   **2288**

Gloversville

Congregational Church. Catalogue of the Library of the Congregational Church Sabbath School, Gloversville, N.Y. Albany: Joel Munsell, 1871. 22 p. Cf. Munsell, p. 166.   **2289**

Greenbush

First Presbyterian Church. Catalogue of the Sabbath School Library, First Presbyterian Church, Greenbush. 1873. Albany: S. R. Gray, 1873. 30 p. NNC.   **2290**

Greenbush Methodist Episcopal Church. Catalogue of the Greenbush Methodist Episcopal Sunday School Library. Albany: Joel Munsell, 1866. Cf. Munsell, p. 142. **2291**

Greene

School Library. Catalogue of School Library of District No. 4, including the Village of Greene. February, 1872. Norwich: Chenango Union Power Press, 1872. 32 p. (pp. 27-32 blank for additions). DLC.   **2292**

Hartwick

Hartwick Seminary. Catalogue of Books in the Theological Library of Hartwick Seminary. [Hartwick?, ca. 1829-30]. 14 p. "Catalogue of Books belonging to the Philophronean Society of Hartwick Seminary" on pp. [13]-14. See also entry 2502. Not in Shoemaker or Cooper. DLC, MWA, NCooHi.   **2293**

Hudson

Franklin Library Association. By-laws and Catalogue of Books of the Franklin Library Association of the City of Hudson. Hudson: Bryan & Moons, 1849. 21 p. DLC.   **2294**

Franklin Library Association. By-laws and Catalogue of Books of the Franklin Library Association of the City of Hudson. Hudson: R. Van Antwerp, 1855. 35 p. DLC, WU (School of Library and Information Studies).   **2295**

Franklin Library Association. By-laws and Catalogue of Books of the Franklin Library Association, Hudson, N.Y. Hudson: Bryan & Webb, 1862. 48 p. MWA, WU (School of Library and Information Studies).   **2296**

Franklin Library Association. Catalogue and Index to Authors, of the Franklin Library, and By-laws of the Franklin Library Association, Hudson, N.Y., March, 1872. Hudson: Bryan & Webb, 1872. 176 p. (pp. 162-76 blank for additions). Cutter 776 reports suppl., 1873 (39 p.). DLC, IU, N.
2297

Ithaca

Cornell University. Catalogue of the Library of Jared Sparks, with a List of the Historical Manuscripts collected by Him and now deposited in the Library of Harvard University. Cambridge: Riverside Press, 1871. iv, 230, [1] p. The library was purchased at auction by Cornell University

in 1872. The manuscripts remained at Harvard and are also described in a separate reissue of the appendix, Catalogue of the Bound Historical Manuscripts collected by Jared Sparks, and now deposited in the Library of Harvard University. Cambridge, 1871 (20 p.). Compiled by Charles Ammi Cutter. Official copy held by MH-H has a ms. index. In many libraries.   **2298**

Cornell University. The Library of the Cornell University. No. 1. [Ithaca, 1873]. 12 p. DLC, MH.   **2299**

Jamaica

Sleight's Circulating Library. Catalogue of H. C. Sleight's Circulating Library, Jamaica, L.I. [Jamaica: Sleight, 1824]. 24 p. Shoemaker 17996. NBLiHi.   **2300**

Lima

Genesee College. Catalogue of the Library of Genesee College and Genesee Wesleyan Seminary, Lima, Livingston Co., N.Y. Rochester: C. D. Tracy, Rochester Evening Express, 1861. 32 p. NRU.   **2301**

Genesee Wesleyan Seminary, see entry 2301.

Lockport

Union School District Library. Catalogue of Union School District Library. Lockport: Richardson & Freeman, 1860. 23 p. DLC.
2302

Union School District Library. Catalogue of Union School District Library. Lockport: Skeels & Boyce, 1872. 30 p. DLC.   **2303**

Louisville

Butternuts Library. By-laws of the Butternuts Library at Louisville, with a Catalogue of Books. Library arranged Feb. 14, 1815. Constitution recorded March 19, 1821. By-Laws revised and adopted Feb. 18, 1837. New-Berlin: J. W. Marble, 1837. 10 p. Not in Rinderknecht. MWA.   **2304**

Middletown

Middletown Lyceum. Catalogue of the Library and Reading Room of the

Middletown Lyceum. Middletown: "Press" Printing Establishment, 1860. 60 p. DLC.
2305

Millbrook

Millbrook Reformed Church. Catalogue . . . 1874. 12 p. Cf. Cutter 942. **2306**

New York City

American Academy of the Fine Arts. The Charter and By-laws of the American Academy of the Fine Arts, instituted February 12, 1802, under the Title of the American Academy of the Arts. With an Account of the Statues, Busts, Paintings, Prints, Books, and other Property belonging to the Academy. New-York: David Longworth, 1817. 34 p. "Library" on pp. 29-30. S & S 39970. DLC, MH, MHi, MWA, NjP, PHi, PPAmP. **2307**

American Bible Society. Catalogue of Editions of the Holy Scriptures in various Languages, and other Biblical Works, in the Library of the American Bible Society. New York: Daniel Fanshaw, 1837. 31 p. Rinderknecht 42777. CtY, MB, NjP, NNUT, PPDrop. **2308**

American Bible Society. Catalogue of Books contained in the Library of the American Bible Society, embracing Editions of the Holy Scriptures in various Languages, and other Biblical and Miscellaneous Works. New York: American Bible Society's Press, 1855. 120 p. DLC, MH, MiU, NHi, NN, NNUT, PPLT. **2309**

American Bible Society. Catalogue of Books contained in the Library of the American Bible Society, embracing Editions of the Holy Scriptures in various Languages, and other Biblical and Miscellaneous Works. New York: American Bible Society's Press, 1863. 168 p. "Appendix" (36 p.) issued in 1870 held by DLC, MB, MWA, NHi. DLC, MdBP, MB, MWA, NhD, NBuU, NN, NNAN, OClW, OO, PP, PPLT, TxH, ViW. **2310**

American Bible Union. Catalogue of the Library of the American Bible Union. New York, 1857. 104 p. DLC (film), NNUT. **2311**

American Bible Union. Catalogue of the Library of the American Bible Union.

Prepared by T. J. Conant. New York: J. J. Little, [1875?]. 162 p. The collection is being offered for sale. CtY-D, KyLoS, NN, NNUT, PCC, TxHU. **2312**

American Ethnological Society. "Catalogue of Books belonging to the American Ethnological Society." In: *Transactions of the American Ethnological Society,* vol. 2 (New York: Bartlett & Welford, 1848), pp. [xiii]-xix. In many libraries. **2313**

American Geographical and Statistical Society. Catalogue of the Library of the American Geographical and Statistical Society. Compiled by E. R. Straznicky. New York: G. B. Teubner, 1857. 32 p. CtHT-W, DLC (film), DNLM, MdBJ, NN, OU, Vi, WHi (film). **2314**

American Institute. Catalogue of the Library of the American Institute, of the City of New York, with the Rules and Regulations of the same. New York: Hopkins & Jennings, 1841. 64 p. Rinderknecht 41-206. DeWint, DLC, NjR, N, NN. **2315**

American Institute. Alphabetical and Analytical Catalogue of the American Institute Library. With the Rules and Regulations, &c. New York: W. L. S. Harrison, 1852. 8, 212 p. DeWint, DLC, KyU, MB, MH, MWA, MiU, NN, NNC, NNGr, PKsL, PPL, UPB, Vt. **2316**

American Institute. Alphabetical and Analytical Catalogue of the American Institute Library. First Supplement. New York: John W. Amerman, 1857. 132 p. MWA, NN, NNGr. **2317**

Anthon Memorial Church. Catalogue of the Parish Library. New York: Russell Brothers, [187-?]. 33 p. NNC. **2318**

Apprentices' Library. Catalogue of the Apprentices' Library, instituted by the Society of Mechanics and Tradesmen of the City of New-York, on the 25th November, 1820, with the Names of Donors. To which is added an Address delivered on the Opening of the Institution by Thomas R. Mercein. New-York: William A. Mercein, 1820. 48, 22 p. NHi holds suppl. to April 1, 1821 (15 p.). Shoemaker 2520, Rink 511. MWA, NHi, NN. **2319**

Apprentices' Library. Catalogue of the Apprentices' Library, for the Years 1833-34, instituted by the Society of Mechanics and Tradesmen of the City of New-York, November 25, 1820. New York: E. B. Clayton, 1833. 168 p. Not in Rinderknecht. OKentU. **2320**

Apprentices' Library. A Catalogue of the Books in the Apprentices' Library. April, 1839. New York: William E. Dean, 1839. 126 p. Not in Rinderknecht. MWA, N, NN. **2321**

Apprentices' Library. Catalogue of the Miscellaneous Library, bequeathed by the late B. De Milt, esq. . . . New York: Benjamin W. Van Norden, 1846. 35 p. NN holds undated suppl. (31 p.). NHi. **2322**

Apprentices' Library. Catalogue of the Apprentices' Library. October, 1849. New York: John F. Trow, 1849. 96 p. DeWint. **2323**

Apprentices' Library. Catalogue of the Apprentices' and De Milt Libraries, New-York . . . July 1, 1855. New-York: John W. Amerman, 1855. xi, 248 p. DLC, MWA, N, NN, NNC, NNGr, NNUT, PPL. **2324**

Apprentices' Library. Catalogue of the Apprentices' Library in New-York. Established and supported by the General Society of Mechanics and Tradesmen. January, 1860. New-York: John W. Amerman, 1860. 308 p. MBAt, NHi, NN (with an extra 36 p. section), NNC, UPB. **2325**

Apprentices' Library. Catalogue of the Apprentice's Library in New-York. Established and supported by the General Society of Mechanics and Tradesmen. September, 1865. New York: A. W. King, 1865. 345 p. DeWint holds suppl. (72 p.). CtY, DeWint, DLC, MB, MH (film), MWA, N, NN, PPL. **2326**

Apprentices' Library. Second Supplement, classified and alphabetical, to the Catalogue of Books in the Apprentices' Library, of the City of New York. Established and supported by the General Society of Mechanics and Tradesmen, including a Classification of the Books in the last Supplement (Accessions from June 1, 1871 to Nov. 1, 1872) compiled . . . by J. Schwartz, jr.,

Librarian. New York: Russells' American Steam Printing House, 1872. 46 p. DLC, MB. **2327**

Apprentices' Library. Catalogue of the Apprentices' Library, established and supported by the General Society of Mechanics and Tradesmen of the City of New York . . . With a Supplement of Additions and Omissions, and a Special Catalogue of Prose Fiction and Juvenile Literature. Compiled by J. Schwartz, jr., Librarian. September, 1874. New York: Chatterton & Parker, 1874. [vii], 419, 16, 99 p. Copy held by N has ms. notes. In many libraries. **2328**

Astor Library. Alphabetical Index of the Astor Library. Part I. Books bought in 1849. To which is prefixed a Concise Classified Bibliography. New York: R. Craighead, 1849. xxx, 232 p. Compiled by J. G. Cogswell. Annual lists of books presented appear in the *Annual Report of the Trustees of the Astor Library* . . ., 1850-75, etc. DLC, MWA. **2329**

Astor Library. Alphabetical Index to the Astor Library or Catalogue, with Short Titles, of the Books now collected and of the Proposed Accessions, as submitted to the Trustees of the Library for their Approval, Jan. 1851. New York: R. Craighead, 1851. iv, 446 p. Compiled by J. G. Cogswell. Copies also exist with preliminary paging containing the "Bibliography" section from the Catalogue issued in 1849 (copies at NNC, NNGr). Annual lists of books presented appear in the *Annual Report of the Trustees of the Astor Library* . . ., 1850-75, etc. In many libraries. **2330**

Astor Library. Catalogue of Books in the Astor Library relating to the Languages and Literature of Asia, Africa, and the Oceanic Islands. New York: Astor Library Autographic Press, 1854. 424 p. Compiled by F. L. O. Roehrig and completed by J. G. Cogswell. In many libraries. **2331**

Astor Library. List of Periodicals & Transactions of Societies taken in at the Astor Library. 1855. [New York, 1855]. 26 p. Lithographed copy of manuscript list. NNC, PPL. **2332**

Astor Library. Catalogue or Alphabetical Index of the Astor Library . . . New York: R.

Craighead, 1857-61. 4 vol. For subject index, see entry 2334. Annual lists of books presented appear in the *Annual Report of the Trustees of the Astor Library* . . ., 1850-75, etc. CSt, CU, DLC (film), DNLM, FTaSU, MBAt, MH, MWA, MnU, NN, NNC, PPL, PSt.   **2333**

Astor Library. Supplement to the Astor Library Catalogue, with an Alphabetical Index of Subjects in all the Volumes. New York: R. Craighead, 1866. 605 p. Annual lists of books presented appear in the *Annual Report of the Trustees of the Astor Library* . . ., 1850-75, etc. CSt, DLC, FTaSU-L, MBAt, MH, MWA, NNC, PPL.   **2334**

Barlass' Circulating Library. A Catalogue of Books, in W. Barlas' [!] Circulating Library, No. 6, Liberty-Street. New-York, 1809. various pagings. Operated by William Barlass. Not in S & S. MWA.   **2335**

Bartlett's Circulating Library, see entries 2338-39.

Berrian's Increasing and Circulating Library. A Catalogue of Samuel Berrian's Increasing and Circulating Library . . . New-York: G. & R. Waite, 1803. 91 p. The suppl. on pp. [73]-91 has a separate title page. S & S 3785. NN.   **2336**

Blake (William P.) & Co.'s Circulating Library. Catalogue of Books . . . New-York: Printed for Wm. P. Blake & Co., 1818. 55, [1] p. See also entry 725. Not in S & S. NN.   **2337**

Bowery Circulating Library. Catalogue of Books belonging to the H. & S. Raynor's (formerly Bartlett's) Circulating Library . . . New-York: J. W. Harrison Book and Job Printing, 1840. 127 p. Running title: Raynor's Library. Operated by Hiram and Samuel Raynor. Not in Rinderknect. MH-H (defective).   **2338**

Bowery Circulating Library. Supplement to the Catalogue of H. & S. Raynor's (formerly Bartlett's) Circulating Library . . . New York: C. C. Childs Book and Job Printer, 1846. 24 p. Running title: Raynor's Library. Operated by Hiram and Samuel Raynor. MH-H (with ms. additions).   **2339**

Brotherhead & Co. Catalogue of Brotherhead & Co's Library, 129 East Seventeenth Street

. . . W. Brotherhead, A. Sutton . . . [New York, ca. 1870]. 100 p. Operated by William Brotherhood and Andrew J. Sutton. See also entries 2798-99. MB.   **2340**

Caritat's Circulating Library. A Catalogue of Approved Books in English, French, Spanish, Greek, Latin, &c. in all Arts & Sciences, just Imported for the New York Literary Assembly, and for Sale and Circulation . . . London: W. Lane, 1802. iv, 126 p. Operated by Hocquet Caritat. NN, PPL.   **2341**

Caritat's Circulating Library. Explanatory Catalogue of H. Caritat's Circulating Library. No. 1, City Hotel, Broad-Way, New-York. New York: G. & R. Waite, [1804?]. xii, 322 p. Operated by Hocquet Caritat. Newly edited by George Gates Raddin, *An Early New York Library of Fiction, with a Checklist of Fiction in H. Caritat's Circulating Library, No. 1, City Hotel, Broadway, New York, 1804* (New York, 1940). S & S 3932. MiU, NHi, NN (defective).   **2342**

Caritat's Literary Room. A Catalogue of the Library of H. Caritat's Literary Room, New-York. New York: Isaac Collins & Son, 1803. vi, 36 p. Operated by Hocquet Caritat. S & S 3931. NHi, NN.   **2343**

Century Association. Constitution and By-laws of The Century. Adopted January 8th, 1870. Amended June 6, 1874; February 6, 1875. New York: Martin's Printing House, 1875. 72 p. "Catalogue of the Library of The Century" on pp. [29]-61. DLC, NHi, PHi.   **2344**

Chamber of Commerce of the State of New York. Catalogue of the Chamber of Commerce of the State of New York. New York: J. W. Amerman, 1862. 25 p. DLC, NN.   **2345**

Charter's Circulating Library. A Catalogue of Books in G. Charter's Circulating Library. New-York: Van Winkle, Wiley, 1817. 84 p. Operated by George Charter. MWA copy contains suppl., 1817 ([16] pages). Not in S & S. MWA, NHi.   **2346**

Chatham Circulating Library. Catalogue of the Chatham Circulating Library, containing upwards of Six Thousand Volumes. J. & H. E. Langley, Booksellers & Stationers . . .

New-York: J. L. Buckingham, 1837. 155 p. Rinderknecht 45116. DLC. **2347**

Church of the Ascension. Catalogue of the Parish Library of the Church of the Ascension. New-York: Baker, Godwin, 1851. 24 p. Private Collection. **2348**

Church of the Ascension. Catalogue. Sunday-School Library of the Church of the Ascension, New York. [New York, 1859?]. 24 p. Private Collection. **2349**

Church of the Holy Communion. Catalogue of Books in the Library of the Sunday-School of the Church of the Holy Communion . . . New York: American Church Press Co., 1871. 68 p. On cover: New York: T. Whittaker, 1871. DLC. **2350**

Church of the Most Holy Redeemer. Bücher-Verzeichniss der Leih-Bibliothek an der Kirche zum allerheiligsten Erlöser. New-York: Gebrüder Erdmann's Buchdruckerei, 1860. 44 p. DLC. **2351**

Columbia University. Catalogue of Duplicates for Sale in Columbia College Library. March 10, 1838. [New York, 1838]. 7 p. Rinderknecht 49809. ICN, MH, NNC. **2352**

Columbia University. Catalogue of the Books and Pamphlets in the Library of Columbia College, New York. New York: John W. Amerman, 1874. 412 p. Compiled by John F. Meyer. In many libraries. **2353**

Columbia University. Columbian Peithologian Society. Catalogue of the Books of the Columbian Peithologian Society Library. New-York, 1813. 16 p. Not in S & S. NHi. **2354**

Columbia University. Philolexian Society. Constitution, Catalogue of Library, and List of Members of the Philolexian Society. New York, 1825. 35 p. Not in Shoemaker. IU (with ms. additions; film, entered under: Columbia University. Philoxenian Society), NNC (with additions; film, entered under: Columbia University. Philoxenian Society). **2355**

Columbia University. School of Mines. Catalogue of the Library of the School of Mines of Columbia College, New York. May, 1869. New York: S. Angell, 1869. 58 p. DLC, MWA, MiU, NN, NNC. **2356**

Columbia University. School of Mines. A Catalogue of the Books and Pamphlets in the Library of the School of Mines of Columbia College. July 1st, 1875. New York: John W. Amerman, 1875. 399 p. DLC (film) and NNC hold advance sheets of section devoted to periodical publications (pp. [147]-90). In many libraries. **2357**

Cooper Union. Catalogue of the Library of the Cooper Union. New York: Printed at the Cooper Union, 1861. 80, [1] p. DLC, NN. **2358**

Cooper Union. Catalogue of Papers and Magazines in the Reading Room. [New York, 186-?]. [4] p. MB. **2359**

Corporation Library. Catalogue of the Corporation Library of the City of New York. January 1, 1857. New York: C. W. Baker, 1857. 15 p. NN. **2360**

Eastburn, James. Plan of the Literary Rooms, instituted by James Eastburn & Co. . . . Second Edition, Corrected and Enlarged. New-York: Abraham Paul, 1817. 15, [1] p. of "Terms of Subscription." See pp. 7-8 for a list of serials (reviews, magazines, periodicals) proposed for the collection. S & S 40715. For earlier ed. (1813), see S & S 28393. MWA. **2361**

Enterprize Library. Catalogue of Books in the Enterprize Library, No. 403, Broadway, April, 1828. New York: Vanerpool & Cole, 1828. 4, 82 p. Conducted by James Herring, jr. Not in Shoemaker. NHi. **2362**

Fifth Avenue Baptist Church. Catalogue of Library of Sunday School attached to Fifth Avenue Baptist Church. New York: T. Holman, 1861. 16 p. Private Collection. **2363**

Fifth Avenue Presbyterian Church. Catalogue of the Fifth Ave. Presbyterian Church Sunday School. [New York?], 1875. 33 p. NN. **2364**

Fireman's Lyceum. Catalogue of Books in the Fireman's Lyceum of the City of New York . . . Charles de F. Burns, Librarian and Superintendent. New York: Baker & Godwin, 1869. 60 p. NHi, NNC, NNGr. **2365**

Free Academy, see New York Free Academy.

Friends, Society of. New York Preparative Meeting. The Rules and Catalogue of the Library of the Preparative Meeting of Friends of New York. [New York]: R. & G. S. Wood, 1830. 16 p. Cooper 1516. MH.
2366

Friends, Society of. New York Preparative Meeting. Catalogue of the Library of the Preparative Meeting of Friends of New York. New York: William Wood, 1873. 25 p. NN.
2367

General Society of Mechanics and Tradesmen. Apprentices' Library, see Apprentices' Library.

General Theological Seminary of the Protestant Episcopal Church in the United States. A Catalogue of the Library belonging to the General Theological Seminary of the Protestant Episcopal Church in the United States. New-York: Vanderpool & Cole, 1824. ii, 52 p. Shoemaker 17411. MBD, MH, N, NNG, PHi, ViW.
2368

General Theological Seminary of the Protestant Episcopal Church in the United States. The First Supplement to the Catalogue of the Library belonging to the General Theological Seminary of the Protestant Episcopal Church in the United States, New York, November, 1826. New York: T. and J. Swords, 1826. 14 p. Shoemaker 25573. N, NNG, ViW.
2369

Goodrich's Circulating Library. Goodrich and Co.'s New-York Circulating Library and Reading-Room . . . Catalogue of Books . . . New-York, 1813. 55, [1] p. Not in S & S. MWA.
2370

Goodrich's Circulating Library. Goodrich's Circulating Library, Book and Stationary Store . . . Catalogue of Books . . . New-York, 1815. 105, [3] p. NN holds suppl., March-Nov. 1815 (10 p.). Not in S & S. NN.**2371**

Goodrich's Circulating Library. Goodrich and Co.'s Circulating Library and Bookstore . . . New-York: C. S. Van Winkle, 1818. 112 [i.e. 120] p. S & S 44183. DLC, NN (film).
2372

Goodrich's Circulating Library. Goodrich's Circulating Library and Bookstore . . . New-

York: J. &. J. Harper, 1826. 119 p. Not in Shoemaker. NN.
2373

Harlem Library. A Catalogue of Books belonging to the Harlem Library Association. October 1, 1831. New York: J. Post, 1831. 16 p. Bruntjen 7444. NN (copy of original held by the Harlem Library Branch).
2374

Harlem Library. Catalogue of the Harlem Library. 1874. New York: Wynkoop & Hallenbeck, 1874. 64 p. N.B. Compiler unable to determine if The Harlem Library (New York, 1872), 23, [1] p., at DLC (lost) is a library catalogue. DLC.
2375

Irving Circulating Library. Catalogue of the Irving Circulating Library, 129 Nassau Street. Conducted by William H. Attree. New York, 1842. 108 p. At head of title: 20,000 Volumes. Caption title: Part I. Novels, Tales, and Romances. Not in Rinderknecht. DLC (lacks pp. 3-4), MnU (photocopy of DLC copy).
2376

Libreria italiana di New York. Lorenzo da Ponte a suoi rispettabili allievi, amice e concittadini . . . Prezzo della sottoscrizione cinque talleri . . . [New York, 1826]. 11 p. See also entry 2429. Not in Shoemaker. MH-H (entered under: Da Ponte, Lorenzo).
2377

Lyceum of Natural History. Charter, Constitution and Bye-laws of the Lyceum of Natural History, incorporated April 20, 1818. New York: E. Conrad, 1823. 22 p. Catalogue of books as of Nov. 1822 on pp. [13]-22. See also supplementary "Catalogue of Books in the Library of the Lyceum of Natural History" in *Annals of the Lyceum of Natural History of New-York* 1:1 (1824): 12 p. following p. 192 (suppl. for Dec. 1824); 1:2 (1825): 392-402 (suppl. for Dec. 1825), and 2 (1828): unpaged section following p. 451 (suppl. for Dec. 1827). Shoemaker 13558 (under New York Academy of Sciences). CU, MdBM, MB, MWA, NN, NNC.
2378

Lyceum of Natural History. Index to the Library of the Lyceum of Natural History of New-York. 1830. New York: J. Seymour, [1830]. 72 p. Cooper 2818 (entered under New York Lyceum of Natural History). CU, DLC, DNLM, MBAt, MHi, MWA, NHi, NN, NNC, NRU, PHi, PPL, TNJ, ViU.
2379

Madison Square Presbyterian Church. Catalogue of the Sunday-School Library of the Madison Square Presbyterian Church. New York: John F. Trow, 1855. 31 p. NHi. **2380**

Madison Square Presbyterian Church. Catalogue of the Sunday School Library of the Madison Square Presbyterian Church. New York: Walter Gibson, 1866. 31 p. NHi. **2381**

Mechanics' Institute. Catalogue of the Library of the Mechanics' Institute of the City of New-York. Regulations of the Reading Room and Library, with an Alphabetical List of Authors, and References pointing out their various Works in the Library. New-York: Windt & Conrad, 1835. 25 p. Rinderknecht 32959. DLC, PPL. **2382**

Mechanics' Institute. Catalogue of the Library of the Mechanics' Institute of the City of New-York, with the Regulations of the Reading Room and Library. New-York: W. B. & T. Smith, 1838. 32 p. Rinderknecht 51909. DLC, InHi. **2383**

Mechanics' Institute. Catalogue of the Library of the Mechanics' Institute, of the City of New-York; Regulations of the Reading Room and Library; and Circular to the Public. New-York: A. Baptist, jr., 1844. iv, 64 p. Rinderknecht 44-4535. DLC, MH. **2384**

Mercantile Library Association. Constitution, Rules, and Regulations, of the Mercantile Library Association, of the City of New-York, formed November 27, 1820, with a Complete Catalogue of the Books belonging thereto. New-York: Manly B. Fowler, 1821. 33, [1] p. Shoemaker 6278. MH (transferred to MH-H?), MWA. **2385**

Mercantile Library Association. Catalogue of the Books belonging to the Mercantile Library Association of the City of New-York, to which are prefixed, the Constitution and the Rules and Regulations of the same. New-York: Hopkins & Morris, 1825. 106 p. MH-BA, NHi, and NN hold suppl., [1826] (36 p.). Shoemaker 21688, Rink 531. DeU, ICJ, ICN, IU (film), MH-BA, MWA, NHi, NN, PPL. **2386**

Mercantile Library Association. Catalogue of the Books belonging to the Mercantile Library Association of the City of New-York, to which are prefixed, the Constitution and the Rules and Regulations of the same. New-York: J. & J. Harper, 1828. 188 p. Shoemaker 34545, Rink 549. FU, MWA, N, NHi, NN, NNS, RPA. **2387**

Mercantile Library Association. Catalogue of the Books belonging to the Mercantile Library Association of the City of New-York, to which are prefixed, the Constitution and the Rules and Regulations of the same. New-York: J. & J. Harper, 1830. 160 p. Cooper 2819, Rink 570. MWA, NBu, NN, ViU. **2388**

Mercantile Library Association. Catalogue of Books belonging to the Mercantile Library Association of the City of New-York, to which are prefixed, the Constitution and the Rules and Regulations of the same. Institution in Clinton Hall. New-York: Harper & Brothers, 1834. 199 p. PPL copy has at end: "Agreement between the Clinton Hall Association and the Mercantile Library Association, Nov. 2, 1830" ([2] p.). Rinderknecht 25668. FTaSU, MWA, NBu, NHi, PPL. **2389**

Mercantile Library Association. Systematic Catalogue of Books in the Collection of the Mercantile Library Association of the City of New-York With a General Index, and one of Dramatic Pieces, together with an Appendix, containing the Constitution, and the Rules and Regulations of the Association. New-York Harper & Brothers, 1837. xi, 312 p. DeWint, MHi, NHi, NN, PPAmP, and ScU hold suppl., 1838 (54 p.). Rinderknecht 45836, 51912. In many libraries. **2390**

Mercantile Library Association. Systematic Catalogue of Books in the Collection of the Mercantile Library Association of the City of New-York. With a General Index, and One of Dramatic Pieces; Together with an Appendix, Containing the Constitution, and the Rules and Regulations of the Association. New-York: Harper & Brothers, 1840. xi, 312, [271]-385, [1] p. Reissue of the 1837 catalogue, with "A Supplementary Catalogue . . . July, 1837, to January, 1840." New York: H. Ludwig, 1840. Rinderknecht 45838; Rinderknecht 40-4979 for Supplementary Catalogue only. DLC, MdBP, MB, MH, NBu, NHi (suppl. only), NN, NNGr, OKentU, PPL. **2391**

Mercantile Library Association. Catalogue of the Mercantile Library in New York. New York: Edward O. Jenkins, 1844. 300 p. Rinderknecht 44-4536 (duplicated by 44-4542). In many libraries.   **2392**

Mercantile Library Association. Catalogue of the Mercantile Library in New York. New York: Baker, Godwin, 1850. 376, 34 p. Includes "Catalogue of the Cabinet of the Mercantile Library Association" (34 p.) Additions and/or periodical lists appear in *Annual Report of the Board of Direction of the Mercantile Library Association of the City of New York* beginning in 1851. In many libraries.   **2393**

Mercantile Library Association. First Supplement to the Catalogue of the Mercantile Library in the City of New York. January, 1852. New York: R. Craighead, 1852. 48 p. DLC, MB, MH, MWA, N, NB, NHi, NNUT, PPL.   **2394**

Mercantile Library Association. Catalogue of Novels, Tales, &c. May 1, 1856. New York: Baker & Godwin, 1856. 41 p. ViU.   **2395**

Mercantile Library Association. Catalogue of Books in the Mercantile Library of the City of New York. With a Supplement to August 1, 1856. New York: Baker & Godwin, 1856. 376, 214 p. Additions and/or periodical lists appear in *Annual Report of the Board of Direction of the Mercantile Library Association of the City of New York* beginning in 1851. CU-A, DLC, IU, MdBP, MBAt, MH, MWA, NjP, NB, NN, NNGr, NNU.   **2396**

Mercantile Library Association. Supplement to the Catalogue of the Mercantile Library of the City of New York containing the Additions made to August, 1856. New York: Baker, Godwin & Co., 1856. 214 p. CSt, MiU, NB, NHi, OMC, RPB.   **2397**

Mercantile Library Association. Bulletin. No. 1-3; Dec. 1858-[?], 1860? MB (#2-3), MWA (#1, 3).   **2398**

Mercantile Library Association. List of Principal New Works. December 1st, 1860. [4] p. MWA.   **2399**

Mercantile Library Association. Catalogue of Novels, Tales, and Works in Foreign Languages, in the New York Mercantile Library. Sept. 1, 1861. New York: Baker & Godwin, 1861. 92 p. MH, MWA, NN. **2400**

Mercantile Library Association. Catalogue of the Mercantile Library, of the City of New York, with a Supplement to August 1, 1856. To which is added: A List of Novels, and Works in Foreign Languages, brought down to January 1, 1863. New York: Baker & Godwin, 1863. various pagings. DLC, IU, MdBP, NjP, NN.   **2401**

Mercantile Library Association. Catalogue of Books in the Mercantile Library, of the City of New York. New York: F. T. Taylor, 1866. 699 p. In many libraries.   **2402**

Mercantile Library Association. Supplement to the Catalogue of Books in the Mercantile Library of the City of New York. Accessions March, 1866 to October, 1869. New York: John Medole, 1869. 250, 15 p. NHi holds suppl. Accessions List to Dec. 15, 1869; Accessions List for Dec. 15, 1869-Dec. 14, 1870 at NNC. C, CtW, DLC, MB, MBAt, MH, MWA, MnU, N, NB, NHi, NNC, NNF, NNGr, NNUT, OKentU, UPB, Vi.   **2403**

Mercantile Library Association. Second Supplement to the Catalogue of Books in the Mercantile Library of the City of New York (Accessions, October, 1869, to April, 1872). New York: James Sutton, 1872. 296 p. C, CSmH, CSt, DLC, IU, IaHi, MB, MBAt, MH, MWA, MiU, MnU, N, NB, NNC, NNGr, NNUT, RPB, Salem Athenaeum.   **2404**

Mission School, No. 17. Catalogue of the Library of Mission School, No. 17, Third Avenue, between Thirtieth & Thirty-first Sts., connected with the Madison Square Presbyterian Church . . . Oct. 15, 1860. New York: John W. Oliver, 1860. 36 p. NHi (defective).   **2405**

Mission School, No. 17. Catalogue of the Library of Mission School, No. 17, Third Avenue, between Thirtieth & Thirty-first Sts., connected with the Madison Square Presbyterian Church, Nov. 15, 1860. New York: John F. Trow, 1861. 35 p. NHi. **2406**

Murden's (Edward) Circulating Library. Catalogue of Edward Murden's Museum Circulating Library, No. 4 Chamber, near Chatham St. . . . New-York, 1822. 34 p. Not in Shoemaker. NN.   **2407**

Murden's (Edward) Circulating Library. Catalogue of E. M. Murden's Circulating Library & Dramatic Repository . . . New-York, 1823. 90 p. Not in Shoemaker. DLC.
2408

Nash's Circulating Library. Explanatory Catalogue of M. Nash's Circulating Library, No. 79, Beekman-Street, New-York . . . serving also, for a Sale-Catalogue . . . New-York: Sage and Clough, 1803. 32, [1] p. Operated by Melatiah Nash. Copy held by NHi has holograph note: "12 pages more to be printed in a few days." S & S 4705. NHi, NN.
2409

New York Free Academy. Catalogue of the Library of the New York Free Academy. New York: W. C. Bryant, 1860. lxxxviii, 368 p. CSt, DLC, DSI, MnU, NNC, NNR, NRU.
2410

New York Herald. Catalogue of the New York Herald Library. July, 1870. New York: Metropolitan Job Printing Establishment, 1870. 115, [1] p. CSmH, DLC, NNGr (interleaved).
2411

New York Historical Society. Catalogue of the Books, Tracts, Newspapers, Maps, Charts, Views, Portraits, and Manuscripts, in the Library of the New-York Historical Society. New-York: J. Seymour, 1813. vii, 139 p. Compiled by Timothy Alden. Copy held by MH-H has cancelled gatherings with replacement leaves. S & S 29353. In many libraries.
2412

New York Historical Society. Catalogue of Books, Manuscripts, Maps, &c. added to the Library of the New-York Historical Society since January, 1839. New-York: Joseph W. Harrison, 1840. 32 p. Rinderknecht 40-5050. DLC, MB, MH, MiEM, NAlU, NHi, NIC, NN, NNGr, PPL, WHi.
2413

New York Historical Society. Catalogue of Printed Books in the Library of the New-York Historical Society. New-York, 1859. viii, 653 p. Issued as *Collections of the New-York Historical Society*, 2d ser., vol. IV. In many libraries.
2414

New York Historical Society. The De Peyster Collection. Catalogue of Books in the Library of the New-York Historical Society, presented by John Watts De Peyster. Part I. January, 1868. New-York, 1868. 24 p. DLC, ICN, NHi, NN, NNGr.
2415

New York Historical Society. A Memorial of Francis L. Hawks, D.D., LL.D., by Evert A. Duyckinck, esq., read before the New-York Historical Society, May 7th, 1867. With an Appendix of Proceedings, etc. New York, 1871. 166, [1] p. "The Hawks-Niblo Collection. Catalogue of Books in the Library of the Rev. Francis L. Hawks . . . presented in the New-York Historical Society by William Niblo": pp. [47]-166. DeU, DLC, ICN, MH, N, NHi, NIC, NN, NcU, OO, PHi, PPL.
2416

New York Hospital. A Brief Account of the New-York Hospital. New-York: Isaac Collins & Son, 1804. 62, 67 p. "Catalogue of Books belonging to the New-York Hospital Library" forms 2d group (67 p.). A "Catalogue of the Books" also forms chap. 5 (pp. 46-61) in 1st group. Some copies may exist with additional leaves for "Appendix to the Library of the New-York Hospital" inserted after p. 60 in first group, per Austin 1792. S & S 6922 (S & S 6923 is an analytical for the Catalogue section found in 2d group), Austin 1791. DLC, DNLM, MBCo, MH, MWA, NHi, NN, NNNAM, PPL, PU.
2417

New York Hospital. An Account of the New-York Hospital. New York: Collins, 1811. 65, 74 p. "Catalogue of Books belonging to the New-York Hospital Library" forms 2d group (74 p.). S & S 23958, Austin 1789 (Austin 1400 is for the 74 p. catalogue). CtY-M, DLC (film), DNLM, MB, MBCo, MH-M (holds only the 74 page catalogue), MWA, NjP, NHi, NNC-M (holds only the 74 page cat.), NcD-MC.
2418

New York Hospital. A Catalogue of the Books belonging to the Library of the New-York Hospital and the Regulations for the use of the same. New York: Collins, 1818. 125 p. S & S 45070 (duplicated by 45753), Austin 1401. CtHT-W, CtY-M, DLC, MA, MB, MBAt, MWA, NNC, NNNAM (interleaved with ms. additions), PPL.
2419

New York Hospital. A Catalogue of the Books belonging to the Library of the New-York Hospital and the Regulations for the use of the same. New York: G. F. Hopkins & Son, 1829. 132 p. Shoemaker 40479. DNLM, LU, MB, MWA, MiU, NjNCM, NN, NNNAM, PPAmP.
2420

New York Hospital. Supplementary Catalogue of the New-York Hospital Library. November, 1831. New-York: Office of the Medico-Chirurgical Review, 1831. 12 p. Not in Bruntjen. MWA. **2421**

New York Hospital. Supplementary and Analytical Catalogue of the New York Hospital Library . . . New York: Mahlon Day, 1839. 50 p. Rinderknecht 58601. NjNCM, NNNAM. **2422**

New York Hospital. A Catalogue of the Books belonging to the Library of the New York Hospital, arranged alphabetically and analytically, and the Regulations for the use of the same. New York: R. Craighead, 1845. v, 194 p. DLC, DNLM, ICAH, MnU-B, NHi, NNBG, NNC-M, PPC. **2423**

New York Hospital. Supplementary Catalogue of the Books belonging in the Library of the New York Hospital. No. [I]-VI. New York: R. Craighead, 1861-86. 6 vol. Printers vary. DLC, NHi (#1-3), NNC-M (#1-2). **2424**

New York Law Institute. Catalogue of the Library of the New York Law Institute . . . together with the Charter, By-laws, and Officers and Members of the Institute, the Rules and Regulations of the Library and a Chronological List of the Contemporary English Reporters from 1216 to the Present Time, July 1, 1842. Prepared by Lewis H. Sandford, Librarian, and Chairman of the Library Committee. New York: J. M. Elliott, 1843. 111 p. Rinderknecht 43-3794. C-L, MiU-L, N, NHi, NIC, NNC, TxU-L. **2425**

New York Law Institute. Catalogue of the Books in the Library of the New York Law Institute. New York: Martin's Steam Printing House, 1874. li, 614 p. In many libraries. **2426**

New York Society Library. A Catalogue of the Books belonging to the New-York Society Library, together with the Charter and By-laws of the same. New York: C. S. Van Winkle, 1813. 8, 49, 240 p. MWA copy has extra "Novels" section (16 p. at end). S & S 29360. DLC (defective), MBAt, MH-H, MWA, MiU-C, MnU, N, NHi, NN, NNC, NNS, PPAmP, PPL, ViW, WU (School of Library and Information Studies; defective). **2427**

New York Society Library. Supplement to the Catalogue of the Books belonging to the New-York Society Library. New York: C. S. Van Winkle, 1825. 135, [1] p. Not in Shoemaker. DLC, DNLM, MH, MWA, NNS, WU (School of Library and Information Studies). **2428**

New York Society Library. Catalogue of Italian Books, deposited in the N.Y. Society Library, for the Permanent use of L. Da Ponte's Pupils and Subscribers. New York: Gray & Bunce, 1827. 12, [3] p. Appears with a separate title page in editions of Lorenzo Da Ponte's *Storia della lingua e letteratura italiana in New-York.* New-York: Gray & Bunce, 1827 (Shoemaker 28659). See also entry 2377. Not in Shoemaker. MHi, MWA, MiU.**2429**

New York Society Library. Alphabetical and Analytical Catalogue of the New-York Society Library. With a Brief Historical Notice of the Institution, the Original Articles of Association in 1754, and the Charter and By-laws of the Society. New York: James Van Norden, 1838. xxviii, 328 p. Prepared by Philip J. Forbes. Rinderknecht 51977. CLU, CSmH, DeWint, DLC, ICN, MH, Mi, MnU, N, NHi, NNC, NNS, NRU, PPAmP, RPB, ScU, ViU, WU (School of Library and Information Studies); variant ed. (xx, 322 p.), CtNbC, DeU, LU, MWA, MiU, NcD, OKentU. **2430**

New York Society Library. Supplementary Catalogue of the New-York Society Library. New York: J. Van Norden, 1841. vii, 72 p. Rinderknecht 41-3858. MBAt, MH-H, MWA, MiU, N, NHi, NN, NNC, NNS. **2431**

New York Society Library. Alphabetical and Analytical Catalogue of the New York Society Library. With the Charter, By-laws, &c., of the Institution. New York: R. Craighead, 1850. xlviii, 621 p. "Supplement to the Alphabetical Catalogue" on pp. [xxxv]-xlviii. Annual list of added books and periodicals list appear in *Annual Report of the Trustees of the New York Society Library.* In many libraries. **2432**

New York Society Library. List of Members of the New York Society Library and of Books added from April, 1860 to April, 1861. New York: W. H. Tinson, 1861. 36 p. MWA, NN (defective), NNC. **2433**

New York Society Library. Catalogue of Books from the Circulating Library of the late James Hammond, of Newport, R.I., presented to the New-York Society Library by Robert Lenox Kennedy, 1868. New-York: John W. Amerman, 1868. 31 p. See also entries 2976-84. MWA, NN.   **2434**

New York Sunday School Union, see entry 2450.

New York Typographical Society, see Printers' Free Library.

New York Unitarian Book Society. Annual Report of the New-York Unitarian Book Society, with the Rules of the Society, and Catalogues of the Library and Tracts, for 1823. New-York: Joseph C. Spear, 1823. 43 p. Shoemaker 13579. CBPac, M, MH, MHi, MWA, NHi, PPAmP.   **2435**

New York Unitarian Book Society. Catalogue of the Library of the New-York Unitarian Book Society, with the Rules of the Society, and an Index of the Principal Authors, their Writings, &c. &c. New-York: Clayton & Van Norden, 1829. 41 p. Not in Shoemaker. INC, NNC.   **2436**

Parthenon Circulating Library. Catalogue of Books, for Sale, by S. C. Schenk, at the Parthenon Circulating Library and Reading Room... New-York: J. Seymour, 1826. 70 p. Copies of most books are also available in the library. See also entry 2458. Not in Shoemaker. NHi.   **2437**

Presbyterian Church in the U. S. A. Board of Foreign Missions. A Catalogue of the Books and Maps belonging to the Library of the Board of Foreign Missions of the Presbyterian Church. New York: Mission House, 1847. 54 p. DLC, NN.   **2438**

Presbyterian Church in the U.S.A. Board of Foreign Missions. A Catalogue of the Books and Maps belonging to the Library of the Board of Foreign Missions of the Presbyterian Church. New York: Mission House, 1861. 94 p. CtY, DLC, NN, PPPrHi. **2439**

Printers' Free Library. Catalogue of the Printer's Library, under the Direction of the New York Typographical Society. New York: G. F. Nesbitt, 1850. 99 p. DLC.   **2440**

Printers' Free Library. Catalogue of the Printer's Library, under the Direction of the New York Typographical Society. New York: Baker, Godwin, 1852. 81 p. MWA, NNC.   **2441**

Printers' Free Library. Catalogue of the Printer's Free Library, under the Direction of the New York Typographical Society. New York: Baker, Godwin, 1855. 81, [22] p. Reissue of the 1852 ed., with a new [22] page suppl. DLC, MWA, NNC.   **2442**

Public School, No. 12. Catalogue of the Library of Public School, No. 12. New-York: Mahlon Day, 1833. 15 p. Bruntjen 20346. CtHT, IHi.   **2443**

Raynor's Circulating Library, see entries 2339-40.

Remney, John. A Catalogue of Books, consisting of History, Biography, Arts & Sciences, Antiquities, Magazines & Reviews, Miscellaneous and Voyages and Travels. New-York: Printed for E. Sargeant, 1809-[16?]. 128 p. (issued in four continuously paged parts). Part [2], called "First Supplement," printed in New-York by E. Conrad; parts [3-4] are without imprint statement. Shoemaker 18493 (for pt. 1) and 29642 (for pt. 2). MH-H (holds pt. 1-2 and 2d suppl., Aug. 1, 1816, to p. [80]), NHi (complete?), NN (pt. 2).   **2444**

St. George's Church. Sunday School Library of St. George's Church. New York: John A. Gray, 1852. 15 p. NHi holds suppl., Oct. 1853. NHi.   **2445**

St. Thomas' Church. Catalogue of the Library of the Sunday School of St. Thomas' Church, New-York. New York: G. F. Nesbitt, 1854. 27 p. NN.   **2446**

Schirmer's Circulating Music Library. G. Schirmer's Catalogue of Circulating Music Library & Imported Music... New York: G. Schirmer, 1869. 4 vol. Operated by Gustav Schirmer, also a publisher of music. MdBJ (Peabody Music Library has v. 1), MiU (v. 1-4).   **2447**

Seaman's New-York Circulating Library. Catalogue of Books belonging to J. V. Seaman's New-York Circulating Library, and Reading Room, 221 Broadway... New York: R. Tyrell, 1825. 59 p. Operated by James V. Seaman. Not in Shoemaker. NHi.   **2448**

Second Unitarian Church. Catalogue of the Juvenile Library of the Second Unitarian Church, New-York . . . [New York?, ca. 1829]. 8 p. Not in Shoemaker. MB. **2449**

Society of the New York Hospital, see New York Hospital.

South Dutch Church. Catalogue of Books in the Library of the Sabbath School of the South Dutch Church, and Number One of the New-York Sunday-School Union. Revised, September, 1866. New York: McKay & Wynkoop, 1866. 48 p. NNC. **2450**

Spingler Institute. Catalogue . . . 1852. Cf. Rhees, p. 295. The Institute appears to be attached to the Abbot Collegiate Institute for Young Ladies (name varies slightly). **2451**

Stuyvesant Circulating Library. Catalogue of the Stuyvesant Circulating Library, containing upwards of 1500 Volumes. George Miller, Bookseller & Stationer . . . New-York: W. B. & T. Smith, 1839. 23 p. Not in Rinderknecht. NHi. **2452**

Sunday School Teachers' Reading Room and Exchange. Catalogue of the Library of the Sunday School Teachers' Reading Room and Exchange, No. 15, Bible House (Eighth Street, bet. Third and Fourth Avenues,) New York. New York: Eckler, [1872 or 73?]. 84 p. Copies held by NHi and NN contain a slip with additional contributions for 1871 and 1872. NHi, NN, RPB. **2453**

Sutton, Andrew, see entry 2341.

Union League Club. A Catalogue of the Library of the Union League Club of New York. New York, 1867. 20 p. NN. **2454**

Washington Circulating Library. Catalogue of Books, at the Washington Circulating Library. New-York: Printed for Olmstead, Levy and Co., 1810. 156 p. Presumably operated by Olmstead, Levy and Co., whose advertisements appear here. S & S 21954. NHi, NN. **2455**

Washington Heights Library. Catalogue . . . 1871. 22 p. Cf. Cutter 723. **2456**

Washington Square Reformed Dutch Church. Catalogue of the Library of the Washington Square Reformed Dutch Sunday School. New York: Wm. M. Taylor, 1866. 16 p. MWA. **2457**

Waverley Circulating Library. Catalogue of the Waverley Circulating Library. New York: Charles Roe, [1858?]. 82 p. Conducted by Charles Roe. Running title begins: Parthenon Circulating Library . . . See also entry 2437. CU-A. **2458**

Woman's Library. Catalogue of Books in the Woman's Library, of New York . . . New York: Baptist & Taylor, 1861. 23 p. NHi. **2459**

Young Men's Christian Association. Catalogue of the Library of the New York Young Men's Christian Association, Clinton Hall, Astor Place. New York: J. A. Gray, 1855. 65 p. DLC. **2460**

Young Men's Christian Association. Eastern Branch. Catalogue of the Library of the Eastern Branch Y.M.C.A., 473 Grand Street, N.Y. [New York, 1872]. 14 p. MWA. **2461**

Newburgh

First Presbyterian Church. Catalogue of the Library of the First Presbyterian Church, Newburgh, N.Y. 1858. Newburgh: Gray, Lawson, [1858?]. 16 p. Cf. Sabin 54901. MH (per Sabin). **2462**

Mechanics' Library Association. Catalogue of Mechanics' Library Association of Newburgh, with the Act of Incorporation . . . Newburgh: S. T. Callahan, 1843. 16 p. Not in Rinderknecht; Sabin 54901. MH (per Sabin). **2463**

Newburgh Free Library. Catalogue of Books in the Newburgh Free Library. Newburgh: E. M. Ruttenber, 1868. 125 p. DLC (also suppl. #1-3), NN (also suppl. #1-2). **2464**

Shawangunk Society Library. Catalogue of Books in the Shawangunk Society Library. [Newburgh, 1827]. broadside. Not in Shoemaker. MWA. **2465**

Theological Seminary of the Associate Reformed Church. Catalogue . . . 1848. 16 p. Cf. Jewett, p. 84. **2466**

Washington's Headquarters. Catalogue of Manuscripts and Revolutionary Relics deposited in Washington's Head Quarters, Newburgh, N.Y. Newburgh: Highland Courier Press, 1858. 49 p. CLobS, CSmH, MWA, MiU-C, WHi. **2467**

Washington's Headquarters. Catalogue of Manuscripts and Relics in Washington's Head-quarters, Newburgh, N.Y., with Historical Sketch. Prepared for the Trustees under Act of May 11, 1874, by E. M. Ruttenber. Newburgh: E. M. Ruttenber & Son, 1874. 74 p. DLC, MWA, NBuHi, NIC, NN. **2468**

Niagara Falls

St. Andrews' Church. Catalogue of the Congregational Library of St. Andrew's Church. [Niagara: Gleaner Press, 1834]. 16 p. Not in Rinderknecht. PPPrHi. **2469**

Ossining

Union Free School. Catalogue of the Library of the Union Free School, District No. 1., Ossining, N.Y. Sing Sing: Printed at the Office of "The Republican," 1866. 34 p. DLC. **2470**

Oswego

Oswego City Library. Catalogue of the Oswego City Library. Oswego, 1857. 46 p. Sabin 57837. N (per Sabin). **2471**

Oswego City Library. First Catalogue of the Oswego City Library. Founded by Gerrit Smith, 1855. New York: Baker & Godwin, 1858. 103 p. Also suppl., 1863 (18 p.), per Cutter 428. MWA. **2472**

Oswego City School. Catalogue . . . 1869. 98 p. Cf. Cutter 621. **2473**

Poughkeepsie

Christ Church. Catalogue of the Christ Church Parish Library, Poughkeepsie. Poughkeepsie: Platt & Schram, 1844. 8 p. Not in Rinderknecht. NHi. **2474**

Poughkeepsie Lyceum of Literature, Science and Mechanic Arts. Catalogue . . . 1845. Cf. Cutter 262, Jewett, p. 98. **2475**

Potter & Wilson's Circulating Library. Catalogue of Books belonging to Potter & Wilson's Circulating Library . . . Poughkeepsie: Jackson & Schram, 1837. 48 p. Not in Rinderknecht. NCooHi. **2476**

Public School Library. Catalogue of the Public School Library, in Poughkeepsie. July, 1851. Poughkeepsie: Platt & Schram, [1851]. 96 p. Rhees, p. 298, reports suppl., 1855. DLC. **2477**

Public School Library. Catalogue of the Public School Library, in Poughkeepsie. January, 1858. Poughkeepsie: Osborne & Killey, 1858. 120 p. NIC. **2478**

Public School Library. Catalogue of the Public School Library, in Poughkeepsie. Poughkeepsie: Farmer Steam Printing Office, 1870. 209 p. NCooHi copy includes suppl., 1877 (78 p.). NCooHi. **2479**

Red Hook

St. Paul's Evangelical Lutheran Church. Catalogue of Library of St. Paul's Evangelical Lutheran Sabbath School, Red Hook, N.Y. Albany: Joel Munsell, 1869. 23 p. Cf. Munsell, p. 157. **2480**

Rhinebeck

Starr Institute. Catalogue of the Starr Institute, Rhinebeck, N.Y. 1862. New York: James Miller, 1862. 46 p. "Catalogue of the Standard Library" on pp. [17]-46. NN. **2481**

Rochester

New York. Court of Appeals. Catalogue . . . Library of the Court of Appeals. Rochester, 1847, 55 p. Cf. Jewett, p. 98. **2482**

Rochester Athenaeum and Mechanics' Association. Catalogue . . . 1847. 40 p. Cf. Cutter 289, Jewett, p. 98. **2483**

Rochester Athenaeum and Mechanics' Association. Catalogue of the Rochester Athenaeum and Mechanics' Association, with the Constitution of the Association. Rochester: A. Strong, 1850. 36 p. NBu, NRHi, NRU. **2484**

Rochester Athenaeum and Mechanics' Association. Catalogue of the Library of the Rochester Athenaeum and Mechanics' Association. Rochester: Daily Democrat Office, 1854. 106 p. NN, NRHi. **2485**

Rochester Athenaeum and Mechanics' Association. Catalogue of the Rochester Athenaeum and Mechanics' Association Library. Rochester: Benton & Andrews, 1866. 124 p. DLC. **2486**

Rochester City Library. Catalogue of the Rochester City Library, April, 1839, with a Notice of the City Reading Rooms, &c., under the care of the Young Men's Association. Rochester: Shepard, Strong and Dawson, 1839. At head of title: Rochester Athenaeum-Young Men's Association. DLC, NN, and NRHi hold "Additional Catalogue . . . May 1840" (6 p.). Rinderknecht 58272, 40-5811. DLC, NN, NR, NRHi, NRU.   **2487**

Rochester Public Schools. Catalogue of Central Library of Rochester Public Schools. Rochester: Tracy & Rew, Express Printing House, 1870. 67 p. MB, NRU.   **2488**

Rondout

Rondout Circulating Library Association. Catalogue of the Rondout Circulating Library Association, Rondout, Ulster Co., N.Y. Rondout: J. P. Hageman, 1854. 24 p. N (misc. pamphlet box, 017.1).   **2489**

Society Library. Catalogue of Books belonging to the Society Library of Rye. New York: John F. Trow, 1866. 16 p. MB.   **2490**

Sag Harbor

Library Company of Sag-Harbor. Books belonging to the Library Company of Sag-Harbor. [Sag Harbor]: Alden Spooner, 1806. 8 p. S & S 11315. NEL.   **2491**

Library Company of Sag-Harbor. Catalogue of Books belonging to the Library Company of Sag-Harbor. Jamaica: H. C. Straight, 1821. 8 p. Shoemaker 7726a. NJQ.   **2492**

Salem

United Presbyterian Church. Catalogue of Books in the Sabbath School Library of the United Presbyterian Church, Salem, Washington County, N.Y. . . . [Salem]: Salem Press Print, 1874. 16 p. N (misc. pamphlet box, 027.8).   **2493**

Saratoga Springs

Bedortha's Saratoga Circulating Library. Catalogue of Dr. N. Bedortha's Saratoga Circulating Library . . . Brainard T.

Bedortha, Librarian. Saratoga Springs: Potter & Judson, 1867. 10 p. NSar.   **2494**

Saratoga Circulating Library. Catalogue of Books in the Saratoga Circulating Library, kept by G. M. Davison. 1829. [Saratoga Springs?, 1829]. 10 p. Operated by Gideon Miner Davison. Not in Shoemaker. NSar.   **2495**

Union Free School. A Catalogue of the Union Free School Library, Saratoga Springs, N.Y. Saratoga Springs: A. S. Baker, 1870. 19 p. DLC.   **2496**

Saugerties

Saugerties Circulating Library Association. Catalogue. January, 1873. New York: Dennison, Smith, [1873]. 28 p. DLC. **2497**

Schenectady

District School Library. Catalogue of Books belonging to the District School Library of Schenectady. Schenectady: Riggs & Norris, 1840. 8 p. N holds suppl., 1840, forming pp. [11]-16. Not in Rinderknecht. N. **2498**

District School Library. Catalogue of Books belonging to the District School Library of Schenectady. Schenectady: I. Riggs, 1845. 45 p. CSmH.   **2499**

Lancaster School. Catalogue of Books, belonging to the Lancaster School Library of Schenectady. [Schenectady?]: A. A. Keyser, 1850. 48 p. N.   **2500**

Miller's Public Circulating Library. Catalogue of Books belonging to Miller's Public Circulating Library . . . Schenectady: Riggs & Norris, 1840. 44 p. Conducted by Robert Miller. Rinderknecht 40-4656. N (misc. pamphlet box, 018.1), NSchHi, NschU.   **2501**

Union College. Catalogue of Books, Manuscripts, Maps and Charts, belonging to the Library of Union College. 1815. Schenectady: Riggs and Stevens, 1815. 46 p. Library holdings of the Hartwick Library on pp. [27]-46 (see also entry 2293). S & S 36142. DLC, MB, MH-H, MWA, N, NN, NSchU, PHA.   **2502**

Union College. Donation to the Library, Apparatus & Museum, of Union College.

Annual Catalogue. 1842-1843/44. Schenectady: I. Riggs, 1842-44. 3 vol. Vol. for 1842/43 and 1843/44 have title: Annual Catalogue of Donations to the Library, Apparatus and Museum, of Union College. Rinderknecht 42-4930 for 1842; 43-5027 for 1842/43, 44-6291 for 1843/44. 1842: N, NSchU; 1842/43: MB, MWA, N, NSch-Hi, WHi; 1843/44: NN, NSchU, PPPrHi, WHi. **2503**

Union College. Catalogue of the Books, Maps, &c., belonging to the Library of Union College, 1846. Schenectady: I. Riggs, 1846. 80 p. (p. 79 omitted in numbering). Copies held by MH and N have 79 p. with no misnumbering. DLC, IU (film), MA, MH, MWA, N, NN. **2504**

Union College. Adelphic Society. Catalogue of Books belonging to the Library of the Adelphic Society, in Union College. 1827. Schenectady: Isaac Riggs, 1827. 50 p. Not in Shoemaker. N. **2505**

Union College. Adelphic Society. Catalogue of the Adelphic Union Library. 1831. [Schenectady, 1831]. 22 p. Not in Bruntjen. MWA. **2506**

Union College. Adelphic Society. Catalogue of Books belonging to the Library of the Adelphic Society, in Union College. 1832. Schenectady: C. G. & A. Palmer, 1832. 36 p. Bruntjen 15080. MH, MHi, MWA. **2507**

Union College. Adelphic Society. Catalogue of Books belonging to the Library of the Adelphic Society, in Union College. 1836. Schenectady: S. S. Riggs, 1836. 34 p. Not in Rinderknecht. MiU-C, NSchU. **2508**

Union College. Adelphic Society. Catalogue of Books belonging to the Library of the Adelphic Society, in Union College. 1843. Troy: N. Tuttle, 1843. 36 p. Not in Rinderknecht. MWA, NSchU. **2509**

Union College. Adelphic Society. Catalogue of Books belonging to the Library of the Adelphic Society, in Union College. 1847. Schenectady: Riggs, 1847. 39 p. DLC, N, NSchU. **2510**

Union College. Adelphic Society. Catalogue of Books belonging to the Library of the Adelphic Society, in Union College. 1852. Schenectady: Riggs, 1852. 48 p. NSchU. **2511**

Union College. Adelphic Society. Catalogue and Regulations of the Library of the Adelphic Society, in Union College. 1856. Founded, 1796. Albany: Weed, Parsons, 1856. 82 p. NSchU. **2512**

Union College. Adelphic Society. Catalogue and Regulations of the Library of the Adelphic Society, in Union College. Founded, 1796. 1868. Syracuse: B. Hermon Smith, [1868]. 54 p. N, NSchU. **2513**

Union College. Philomathean Society. Catalogue of Books in the Philomathean Society Library, in Union College, 1812. Schenectady: I. Riggs, [1812]. 28 p. S & S 26929. DLC (film), N. **2514**

Union College. Philomathean Society. Catalogue of Books belonging to the Library of the Philomathean Society, in Union College. 1820. Schenectady: Isaac Riggs, 1820. 52 p. Not in Shoemaker. N. **2515**

Union College. Philomathean Society. Catalogue of the Books belonging to the Library of the Philomathean Society, in Union College. 1823. Schenectady: Printed at the Cabinet Printing-House, Isaac Riggs, Printer, 1823. 57, [3] p. Not in Shoemaker. MWA, NSchU. **2516**

Union College. Philomathean Society. Catalogue of the Books belonging to the Library of the Philomathean Society, in Union College. 1828. Pittsfield: Printed at the Argus Office, 1828. 44 p. Not in Shoemaker. MH, NSchU. **2517**

Union College. Philomathean Society. Catalogue of the Library of the Philomathean Society, in Union College. 1833. Schenectady: S. S. Riggs, 1833. 39 p. Bruntjen 21605. MHi, N (lacks pp. 37-39), NSchU. **2518**

Union College. Philomathean Society. Catalogue of the Library of the Philomathean Society, in Union College. 1840. Schenectady: James Riggs, 1840. 36 p. Not in Rinderknecht. NSchU. **2519**

Union College. Philomathean Society. Catalogue of the Library of the Philomathean Society, in Union College. 1841. Schenectady: James Riggs, 1841. 36 p. Not in Rinderknecht. NSchU. **2520**

Union College. Philomathean Society. Catalogue of the Library of the Philomathean Society, in Union College. Schenectady: Riggs, 1848. 40 p. NSchU.   **2521**

Union College. Philomathean Society. Catalogue of the Semicentennial Contribution to the Philomathean Society of Union College. [Schenectady?, 1849]. 12 p. NSchU.   **2522**

Union College. Philomathean Society. Catalogue of the Library of the Philomathean Society, Union College. Founded Oct. 17, 1793. Schenectady: Riggs, 1852. 60 p. NSchU.   **2523**

Union College. Philomathean Society. Catalogue of the Library of the Philomathean Society, Union College. Founded Oct. 17, 1793. Schenectady: Riggs, 1856. 70 p. NSchU.   **2524**

Union College. Philomathean Society. Catalogue of the Library of the Philomathean Society, in Union College. 1863. Founded, Oct. 17, 1793. Albany: J. Munsell, 1863. 110 p. DLC, N, NSchU.   **2525**

Young Men's Association. Catalogue of Books belonging to the Young Men's Association of Schenectada [!]. Schenectada [!]: Printed at the Office of the Democrat, 1839. 22 p. Not in Rinderknecht. N.   **2526**

Schodack Landing

Reformed Dutch Church. Catalogue of Books in the Reformed Dutch Church Sabbath School, Schodack Landing, N.Y. June, 1872. Albany: S. R. Gray, 1872. 8 p. NNC. **2527**

Setauket

Franklinean Library Company. Catalogue of Books, contained in the Franklinean Library, of Setauket. Instituted June 7, 1806. Sag-Harbor: Alden Spooner, 1807. 12 p. S & S 12596. DLC, NSmB.   **2528**

Stamford

Stamford Seminary. Catalogue of the Judson Circulating Library Company of Stamford Seminary. 1872. Albany: J. Munsell, 1872. 47 p. DLC.   **2529**

Syracuse

Central Library. Catalogue of the Syracuse Central Library, Board of Education Rooms, City Hall Building. Syracuse: Masters & Lee, 1860. 107, [1] p. MB, NBu.   **2530**

Central Library. Catalogue of Books, in the Central Library of the City of Syracuse, N.Y. Syracuse: Truair & Smith, 1869. 173 p. DLC, MB, MWA, N.   **2531**

Central Library. Catalogue of Books . . . Supplement . . . Accessions, March, 1870 to June, 1872. Syracuse: Truair, Smith, 1872. 68 p. DLC.   **2532**

Franklin Institute. Catalogue of the Franklin Institute Library, of Syracuse. Syracuse: S. Haight, 1851. 28 p. DLC.   **2533**

Franklin Institute. Catalogue of the Franklin Institute Library, of Syracuse. Syracuse: Evening Chronicle Book and Job Office, 1855. 28 p. MWA.   **2534**

Franklin Institute. Catalogue of the Franklin Institute Library, Syracuse. July 1, 1857. Syracuse: Daily Journal Print, 1857. 74 p. Includes constitution and a brief history of the Institute. N.   **2535**

Plymouth Congregational Church. Catalogue of the Sunday School Library of Plymouth Congregational Church . . . April 1st, 1875. Syracuse: Masters, Lee & Stone, 1875. 7 p. MWA.   **2536**

Tarrytown

Young Men's Lyceum. Catalogue of the Books contained in Library of Young Men's Lyceum, Tarrytown . . . New-York: Alfred Cobb, 1869. 16 p. DLC.   **2537**

Young Men's Lyceum. Supplementary Catalogue of Books contained in Library of Young Men's Lyceum, Tarrytown. New York: "Argus" Printing Office, 1870. 14 p. DLC.   **2538**

Troy

Franklin Circulating Library. Catalogue of Books, belonging to the Franklin Circulating Library, of E. & D. W. Platt, at their

Franklin Book Store . . . Together with the Terms, Rules, and Regulations of the same. Troy: Z. Clark, 1823. 34, [2] p. Operated by Ebenezer Platt and Daniel Wright Platt. Not in Shoemaker. MWA. **2539**

Hosford's Circulating Library. Catalogue of Books, belonging to Hosford's Circulating Library . . . Troy, N. Y. Together with the Rules and Regulations. Troy: J. Hosford, 1832. 50 p. Operated by Jasper Hosford. Not in Bruntjen. N. **2540**

St. Joseph's Provincial Seminary. Catalogue . . . 1870. 75 p. Cf. Cutter 663. **2541**

Troy Library. Laws' and Catalogue of Troy Library. Incorporated January 15th, 1800. Troy: Robert Moffitt, [1805?]. 20 p. Evans 38674 (in error); not in S & S; Sabin 97074. MBAt, MWA (film). **2542**

Troy Library. Catalogue of Books in the Troy Library. January, 1821. Troy: William S. Parker, 1821. 14 p. Not in Shoemaker. CSmH, MB. **2543**

Troy Library, see also entry 2544.

Troy Young Men's Association. A Catalogue of the Books, Maps, Charts and Bound Newspapers of the Troy Young Men's Association, with a Catalogue of the Troy Library kept at the Rooms of the Association . . . March, 1840. Troy: N. Tuttle, 1840. 48 p. Not in Rinderknecht. NT. **2544**

Troy Young Men's Association. Catalogue of the Library of the Troy Young Men's Association of the City of Troy. 1845. Troy: N. Tuttle, 1845. 32 p. DLC. **2545**

Troy Young Men's Association. Catalogue of the Library of the Troy Young Men's Association of the City of Troy. 1850. Troy: Johnson and Davis, 1850. 54 p. DLC, NT. **2546**

Troy Young Men's Association. Catalogue of the Library of the Troy Young Men's Association of the City of Troy. 1850. Together with a Supplementary Catalogue, and a Further List of Books added to the Library, down to Feb. 20, 1853. Troy: Johnson and Davis, 1850-[53]. 113 p. DLC, NT. **2547**

Troy Young Men's Association. Catalogue of the Library of the Troy Young Men's

Association. Troy, 1859. iv, 230 p. In many libraries. **2548**

Troy Young Men's Association. Supplementary Catalogue of Books in the Library of the Troy Young Men's Association. Troy: Wm. H. Young, 1866. 114 p. DLC, MWA, NNC, NT. **2549**

Troy Young Men's Association. Second Supplementary Catalogue of Books in the Library of the Troy Young Men's Association. Troy: Troy Daily Press, 1871. 68 p. DLC, NT. **2550**

Utica

Merrell & Hastings' Circulating Library. Catalogue of Books, belonging to Merrell & Hastings' Circulating Library, kept at their Book Store . . . Together with the Rules & Regulations. Utica: [Merrell & Hastings], 1823. 12 p. Shoemaker 13305. NUt. **2551**

School District Library. Alphabetical Catalogue of the School District Library, of the City of Utica. May 1, 1843. Utica: Bennett, Backus, & Hawley, 1843. various pagings. N and NN hold suppl. (3 p.) of books added to May 1, 1844 (Rinderknecht 44-6325); NN has suppl. of books added to Jan. 1, 1846 (7 p.). Not in Rinderknecht. NN, NUtHi. **2552**

School District Library. Catalogue of the School District Library, of the City of Utica. September 1, 1851. Utica: H. H. Curtiss, 1851. 66, [1] p. NCH, NUtHi. **2553**

School District Library. Catalogue of the School District Library, of the City of Utica. September, 1875. Utica: Curtiss & Childs, 1875. 120 p. Cutter 994 reports a catalogue of juvenile books (24 p.). DLC, NUtHi. **2554**

Utica Library. The Utica Library, Incorporated the 5th of March, 1825 . . . Act under which the Utica Library was incorporated, By-laws, and Catalogue of Books. Utica: William Williams, 1829. 43 p. Shoemaker 41354. NUt. **2555**

Utica Library. Catalogue of the Utica Library, incorporated March 5th, 1825, containing the Act of Incorporation. Utica: R. Northway, jr., 1835. 21 p. Rinderknecht 35168. NUt. **2556**

Young Men's Association. Catalogue of the Library of the Young Men's Association of the City of Utica, containing the Acts of Incorporation, Constitution and By-laws, April, 1840. Utica: E. Morrin, [1840?]. 35 p. Rinderknecht 40-7191. NUt.   **2557**

Watertown

Sterling & Mosher's Select Circulating Library. Catalogue of Sterling & Mosher's Select Circulating Library. Watertown, 1873. 40 p. Operated by John C. Sterling. NRU.   **2558**

Young Men's Association. Catalogue of the Library of the Young Men's Association of the Village of Watertown, containing the Act of Incorporation, Constitution and Laws. December, 1841. Watertown: Knowlton & Rice, 1841. 24 p. Not in Rinderknecht. MWA.   **2559**

Watervliet

Watervliet Union Sunday School. Catalogue of the Library of the Watervliet Union Sunday School. Albany: Joel Munsell, 1871. 8 p. Cf. Munsell, p. 166.   **2560**

West Point

United States Military Academy. Catalogue of Books in the Library of the Military Academy. August 1822. Newburgh: W. M. Gazlay, 1822. 31 p. Not in Shoemaker. A facsimile edition, with a foreword by Sidney Forman, appeared as *The Earliest Printed Catalogue of Books in the United States Military Academy Library* (West Point, 1962?). DLC, ViW.   **2561**

United States Military Academy. A Catalogue of Books in the Library of the Military Academy at West Point. June, 1824. New York: Joseph Desnoues, 1824. 47 p. Shoemaker 19109. MB, MH, N, WHi.**2562**

United States Military Academy. Catalogue of the Library of the U.S. Military Academy at West Point. May 1830. New-York: J. Desnoues, 1830. 132 p. Cooper 5253, Rink 574. DLC, MHi, MWA, NWM, PPAmP.   **2563**

United States Military Academy. Catalogue of the Library of the U.S. Military Academy,

West Point, N.Y., exhibiting its Condition at the close of the Year 1852. New-York: John F. Trow, 1853. viii, 403 p. Prepared by André Freis, Assistant Librarian. DLC, IU, InNd, LU, MH, MWA, MiU, NhD, NIC, NN, PHA, PP, VtNN, ViU.   **2564**

United States Military Academy. Supplement to the Catalogue . . . containing the Additions from the First of January, 1853, to the First of October, 1859 . . . New York: G. W. Wood, 1860. 155 p. DLC, LU, MH, NhD, NN, PPAmP, ViU.   **2565**

United States Military Academy. Catalogue of the Library, U. S. Military Academy, West Point, N.Y. 1873. Newburgh: C. Jannicky, 1873. viii, 723 p. DLC.   **2566**

United States Military Academy. Dialectic Society. Catalogue of Library of the Dialectic Society of the U.S. Military Academy, at West Point, New York. [New York: J. F. Trow, 1855]. 23 p. NWM. **2567**

Willets Point

United States. Battalion of Engineers. Catalogue of Books in the Library of the Battalion of Engineers. Willets Point: Battalion Printing Press, [1869?]. 31 p. DLC.   **2568**

Yonkers

Yonkers Library. Catalogue No. 2. Additions to April, 1857. [n.p., 1857]. 19 p. MWA (defective).   **2569**

NORTH CAROLINA

Chapel Hill

University of North Carolina. Dialectic Literary Society. A Catalogue of Books belonging to the Dialectic Society, at Chapel Hill. 1817. [n.p. , 1817]. broadside. S & S 41671. NcU.   **2570**

University of North Carolina. Dialectic Literary Society. Catalogue . . . 1821. 21 p. Not in Shoemaker. Cf. Cutter 83, Jewett, p. 149, Rhees, p. 308.   **2571**

University of North Carolina. Dialectic Literary Society. Catalogue of Books belonging to the Library of the Dialectic

Society at Chapel-Hill. 1827. Raleigh: J.
Gales & Son, [1827]. 32 p. Shoemaker
30089. NcU.   **2572**

University of North Carolina. Dialectic
Literary Society. A Catalogue of Books
belonging to the Dialectic Society, at
Chapel-Hill. May, 1835. Raleigh: J. Gales &
Son, 1835. 26 p. Rinderknecht 33411.
MWA, Nc, NcU, PP.   **2573**

University of North Carolina. Philanthropic
Society. Catalogue . . . 1822. 18 p. Not in
Shoemaker. Cf. Cutter 90, Jewett, p. 149.
                                     2574

University of North Carolina. Philanthropic
Society. Catalogue of Books belonging to
the Library of the Philanthropic Society at
the University of North Carolina. Taken 23d
February, 1829. Raleigh: J. Gales & Son,
1829. 25 p. Shoemaker 39879. NcU. **2575**

Forestville

Wake Forest College. Euzelian Society.
Catalogue . . . 1853. Cf. Rhees, pp. 308-9.
                                     2576

Raleigh

North Carolina Law Library. Catalogue . . .
1873. 38 p. Cf. Cutter 866.   **2577**

North Carolina State Library. Catalogue of
Books belonging to the North Carolina
State Library. Prepared by O. H. Perry,
Librarian. Raleigh: W. W. Holden, 1854. 43
p. At head of title: Ex. Doc. No. Ses. 1854-
'55. MH, NNGr (uncat.).   **2578**

North Carolina State Library. Catalogue of
Books belonging to the North Carolina
State Library. Prepared by O. H. Perry,
Librarian. Raleigh: Nichols, Gorman &
Neathery, 1866, [2] p. NcGU, NcU,
NcWeW.   **2579**

North Carolina State Library. Catalogue.
[Raleigh, 1874?]. 120 p. Nc.   **2580**

Raleigh Academy. Laws of the Raleigh
Academy with the Plan of Education
annexed, as revised in the Year 1811.
Raleigh: Gales and Seaton, 1811. 23 p. "A
Catalogue of Books in the Polemic Library
in the Raleigh Academy" on pp. 17-23. Not
in S & S. NcU.   **2581**

OHIO

Akron

Akron Library Association. Catalogue. 1872.
Akron: Akron City Times Office, 1872. 40 p.
DLC.   **2582**

Public Library. Catalogue of the Public
Library of Akron, Ohio. Akron: Argus
Printing Co., 1874. 110 p. DLC.   **2583**

Ashtabula

Ashtabula Social Library. Catalogue . . . 1860.
23 p. Cf. Cutter 457.   **2584**

Athens

Ohio University. Catalogue . . . 1828. 12 p.
Not in Shoemaker. Cf. Jewett 168, Rhees p.
310, giving 1829 as year of publication.
                                     2585

Canton

Kaufmann's (Peter) Circulating Library. First
Catalogue of Peter Kaufmann & Co.'s
Circulating Library. [Canton, ca. 1838].
broadside. Not in Rinderknecht. OHi
(Peter Kaufmann Papers).   **2586**

Chillicothe

Chillicothe Circulating Library. Terms of the
Chillicothe Circulating Library. [Chillicothe,
1811]. 6 p. Catalogue of books on pp. [3]-6.
Not in S & S. PPRF.   **2587**

Public School Library. Catalogue of the
Chillicothe Public School Library.
Chillicothe: Board of Education, 1861. 30 p.
OHi.   **2588**

Cincinnati

Apprentices' Library. A Catalog of Books, in
the Apprentices' Library of Cincinnati.
Cincinnati: Printed at the Daily Times
Office, 1846. 37, 26 p. DLC, MA, OC,
OCHP.   **2589**

Catholic Institute. Katalog der Bibliothek des
Katholischen Instituts von Cincinnati,
Ohio. Catalogue of the Library of the
Catholic Institute of Cincinnati, Ohio.
[Cincinnati, 1865?]. viii, 45 p. DLC. **2590**

Cincinnati Historical Society, see Historical and Philosophical Society of Ohio.

Cincinnati Horticultural Society. A Brief History of the Cincinnati Horticultural Society, its Charter, Constitution and By-laws, Officers from 1841-1859, Life, Annual and Honorary Members, and Catalogue of Books in the Library. Together with its Transactions for the Past Year, and Premium Lists for the Year 1859. Cincinnati: Office of the "Cincinnatus," by Ongley & Shain, 1859. 127, [13] p. DLC, OCLWHi, PPL.   **2591**

Cincinnati Law Library Association. Catalogue of Law Books, belonging to the Cincinnati Law Library Association. October, 1852. Cincinnati: C. Clark, 1852. 21, [1] p. DLC (interleaved).   **2592**

Circulating Library Society of Cincinnati. A Systematic Catalogue of Books belonging to the Circulating Library Society of Cincinnati. To which are prefixed an Historical Preface, the Act of Incorporation, and By-laws of the Society. Cincinnati: Looker, Palmer and Reynolds, 1816. 36 p. S & S 37244. DLC, OC, OCHP, PPAmP.   **2593**

Common Schools of Cincinnati. Catalogue of the Educational Library of the Trustees and Teachers of the Common Schools of Cincinnati. [Cincinnati, 185-]. 7 p. OC (4 interleaved copies, each with ms. additions of varying length; entered under: Cincinnati Public Schools. Educational Library of the Trustees and Teachers).   **2594**

Deutscher Lese- und Bildungsverein. Katalog . . . Cincinnati, 1846. Cf. Robert E. Cazden, *A Social History of the German Book Trade in America to the Civil War* (Columbia, SC, 1984) pp. 136 and 153, note 52, based on a notice in *Volksblatt* (Cincinnati), March 11, 1846.   **2595**

Medical College of Ohio. Catalogue of the Library of the Medical College of Ohio, and the Rules adapted by the Trustees in Relation thereto. Also, Extracts from the College Regulations for the Government of the Medical Class. Cincinnati: Corey and Fairbank, 1832. 26 p. Bruntjen 11804. InU (photocopy), OCHP.   **2596**

Mount St. Mary's Seminary of the West. Catalogue of the Library of the Seminary of Mt. St. Mary's of the West, Cincinnati, Ohio. August, 1873. New York: Catholic Publication Society, 1873. 426 p. CtY, DLC, KyU, MBAt, MH, MWA, MiU, OC, OCHP, OClW, ONowdM, PLatS.   **2597**

Mount St. Mary's Seminary of the West. Catalogue of the Books added to the Library of Mount St. Mary's Seminary, during 1874 and 1875. Cincinnati: Robert Clarke, 1875. 24 p. DLC, MH, OC, OCHP.   **2598**

New England Society of Cincinnati. Catalogue of Books in the Library of the New-England Society of Cincinnati. November, 1847. Cincinnati: G. W. Tagart, 1847. 32 p. DLC, OC, OCHP, PHi.   **2599**

Ohio Mechanics' Institute. A Catalogue of the Library and Reading Room of the Ohio Mechanics' Institute. Cincinnati: J. B. & R. P. Donogh, 1841. 48 p. Rinderknecht 41-3919. OC, OCHP, OClWHi.   **2600**

Ohio Mechanics' Institute. Catalogue of the Books and Papers in the Library and Reading Room of the Ohio Mechanics' Institute, of Cincinnati. Cincinnati: Marshall & Langtry, 1851. 68 p. DLC, MA, OOxM.   **2601**

Ohio Mechanics' Institute. Catalogue . . . 1857. 100 p. A periodicals list appears in the Institute's *Annual Report* for 1867. Cf. Rhees, p. 316.   **2602**

Ohio School Library. Catalogue of the Books and Papers in the Library and Reading Room of the Ohio School Library, of Cincinnati. Cincinnati: C. F. Bradley, 1856. viii, 113, [1] p. Cover and preface dated 1857. DLC, OC (copy 4 interleaved with ms. additions), OCHP, PPL.   **2603**

Ohio School Library. Catalogue of the Ohio School Library at Cincinnati. Cincinnati: Robert Clarke, 1860. viii, 204 p. DLC, OC (also holds a 14 page ms. suppl., 1864?), OCHP, TxU.   **2604**

Public Library of Cincinnati. Catalogue of the Public Library of Cincinnati. Cincinnati: Wilstach, Baldwin, 1871. ix, 644 p. Lists of illustrated books appear in the Library's *Annual Report* for 1872-73. In many libraries.   **2605**

Turn-Gemeinde. Katalog der Bibliothek der Turn-Gemeinde in Cincinnati, O. Cincinnati: A. Frey, 1866. 75 p. DLC. **2606**

Wesleyan Female College. Young Ladies' Lyceum. Library of the Young Ladies' Lyceum of the Wesleyan Female College, Cincinnati, Ohio. Cincinnati: Methodist Book Concern, 1859. 16 p. MWA, NNC, OHi. **2607**

Woodward College. Epanthean Literary Society. A Catalogue of Books belonging to the Epanthean Literary Society of Woodward College. Cincinnati: Methodist Book Concern, 1847. 32 p. OC, OU. **2608**

Young Men's Mercantile Library Association. A Catalogue of Books belonging to the Young Men's Mercantile Library Association of Cincinnati, to which is prefixed the Constitution, By-laws, and Regulations of the same. Cincinnati: Daily Express Office, [1838?]. 40 p. Rinderknecht 49731. InU (photocopy), MoSHi, OClWHi. **2609**

Young Men's Mercantile Library Association. A Catalogue of Books, belonging to the Young Men's Mercantile Library Association of Cincinnati, to which are prefixed the Constitution, By-laws, and Regulations of the same. Cincinnati: Shepard and Stearns, 1841. 62, [2] p. Rinderknecht 41-1132. InU (photocopy), OC, OCHP. **2610**

Young Men's Mercantile Library Association. Catalogue of the Young Men's Mercantile Library, in Cincinnati. Cincinnati, 1846. 145 p. Suppl. (1848) containing pp. 146-260 at DLC, ICN, OC, OOxM. Lists of donations, valuable books added, or lists of periodicals usually appear in the Library's *Annual Report.* DLC (film), GU, ICN, KyU, O, OC, OCHP, OCU, OClWHi, OOxM, PPF, ViW. **2611**

Young Men's Mercantile Library Association. Catalogue of the Young Men's Mercantile Library Association, of Cincinnati. Cincinnati: Truman & Spofford, 1855. xxxi, 307, [1] p. Lists of donations, valuable books added, or lists of periodicals usually appear in the Library's *Annual Report.* In many libraries. **2612**

Young Men's Mercantile Library Association. Catalogue of the Books of the Young Men's Mercantile Library Association of Cincin-

nati. Cincinnati: [Caleb Clark], 1869. xxiii, 468 p. Lists of donations, valuable books added, or lists of periodicals usually appear in the Library's *Annual Report.* DLC, KyU, MB, MnU, NB, N, NN, OC, OCHP, OClWHi, OCY, OFH, PU. **2613**

Cleveland

Cleveland Library Association. Catalogue of the Library of the Cleveland Library Association. January, 1849. Cleveland: Steam Press of M. C. Younglove, 1849. 60 p. OClW. **2614**

Cleveland Library Association. Catalogue of the Cleveland Library Association. Organized in 1848. Cleveland: Fairbanks, Benedict, 1865. 207 p. MWA, OAU, OCl, OClW, OO. **2615**

Public School Library. Catalogue of the Public School Library of Cleveland, Ohio. April, 1857. Cleveland: Harris, Fairbanks, 1857. 42 p. CtY, NNC, OCl, OU. **2616**

Columbus

Columbus Public Library. Catalogue … 1873. 34 p. Cf. Cutter 867. **2617**

Columbus Public Library. Catalogue … 1874. 58 p. Cf. Cutter 946. **2618**

Ohio School Library. Catalogue of the Ohio School Library. [Columbus]: Printed by Order of the State School Commissioner, by T. Wrightson, Cincinnati, 1856. 69 p. A list of books selected for the District School Libraries. Preface by H. H. Barney, Office of State Commissioner of Common Schools. DLC, MB, OC. **2619**

Ohio State Library. Catalogue of Books in the Library of Ohio. Columbus: P. H. Olmsted, 1817. 11 p. S & S 41685. OCHP. **2620**

Ohio State Library. Catalogue of Books in the State Library of Ohio. December 25, 1823. Columbus: Printed at the Office of the Columbus Gazette, by P. H. Olmsted, 1823. 10 p. Shoemaker 13620. O, OCHP, OClWHi. **2621**

Ohio State Library. A Catalogue of Books, in the Ohio State Library. December 1, 1826. Columbus: Zechariah Mills, 1826. 19 p. Copies held by CSmH, OCHP, and OClWHi contain suppl., Dec. 1, 1827 (5 p.). Shoemaker 25623 (together with suppl. for 1827). CSmH, OCHP, OClWHi. **2622**

Ohio State Library. Catalogue of Books, in the Ohio State Library. December 1, 1828. Columbus: Zechariah Mills, 1828. 23 p. Shoemaker 34599. O, OMC. **2623**

Ohio State Library. Catalogue of the State Library of Ohio. December, 1832 . . . Columbus: Office of the State Journal, 1832. 30 p. Not in Bruntjen. OCHP, OClWHi. **2624**

Ohio State Library. Catalogue of the State Library of Ohio. December, 1834. Columbus: Office of the State Journal, 1834. 32 p. Not in Rinderknecht. OCHP. **2625**

Ohio State Library. Catalogue of the State Library of Ohio. December, 1837. Columbus: Samuel Medary, 1837. 42 p. Suppl. for Dec. 1837 (5 p.), Dec. 1838 (6 p.), and Dec. 1839 (5 p.), held by O. Rinderknecht 46067. O, OClWHi. **2626**

Ohio State Library. Catalogue of the Ohio State Library. December, 1840. Zechariah Mills, Librarian. Columbus: Samuel Medary, 1840. 60 p. Rinderknecht 40-5141. DLC, O, OClWHi. **2627**

Ohio State Library. Catalogue of the Ohio State Library. December, 1842 . . . Thomas Kennedy, Librarian. Columbus: Samuel Medary, 1842. iv, 75 p. OClWHi copy has suppl., 1843, forming pp. [77]-84. Rinderknecht 42-3843. DLC, O, OCHP, OClWHi, OFH, OMC. **2628**

Ohio State Library. Catalogue of the Ohio State Library. December, 1845. John Greiner, State Librarian. Columbus: C. Scott, 1845. iv, 87, [1] p. OCHP holds suppl., 1846 (6 p.). OC, OCHP. **2629**

Ohio State Library. Catalogue of the Ohio State Library. December 1848. John Greiner, State Librarian. Columbus: Thrall & Reed, 1848. iv, 91 p. DLC, InU (film). **2630**

Ohio State Library. Catalogue . . . 1849 . . . 96 p. Substantial annual catalogues of books purchased appear in *Report of the Commissioners of the Ohio State Library* beginning in 1867; earlier reports contain lists of exchanges and donations. Cf. Bowker, p. 209, Rhees, p. 324. **2631**

Ohio State Library. Catalog of Manuscript Papers deposited in the State Library from the Governor's Office. Columbus, [1871?]. 23 p. NN, O, OU (micro-opaque card). **2632**

Ohio State Library. Catalogue of the Ohio State Library. 1875. Compiled by William Holden. General Library. Columbus: Nevins & Meyers, 1875. 727 p. In many libraries. **2633**

Dayton

Dayton Public Library. Alphabetical Catalogue of the Dayton Public Library of Dayton, Ohio. Cincinnati: C. Clark, 1870. 93 p. DLC, ODa. **2634**

Dayton Public Library. Alphabetical Catalogue of the Dayton Public Library of Dayton, Ohio. First Supplement. Dayton: Dayton Herald and Empire Office, 1875. 69 p. DLC, ODa. **2635**

National Asylum for Disabled Volunteer Soldiers. Catalogue of the Putnam Library, National Asylum for Disabled Volunteer Soldiers (Central Branch). Dayton: National Asylum Printing Office, 1872. 64 p. DLC, MB, ODa. **2636**

Delaware

Ohio Wesleyan University. Catalogue of the Library of the Ohio Wesleyan University. Delaware: Gazette Job Office, 1870. 26 p. DLC, ODW. **2637**

Gambier

Kenyon College. Catalogue of Books belonging to the Library of the Theological Seminary of the Diocese of Ohio, Kenyon College, and the Preparatory Schools. MDCCCXXXVII. Gambier: George W. Myers, 1837. 76 p. Rinderknecht 45054. DLC, InU, MH, MWA, N, NRCR, OCHP, OOxM, PPAmP. **2638**

Kenyon College. Philomathesian Society. Catalogue . . . 1834. Not in Rinderknecht. Cf. Rhees, pp. 327-28. **2639**

Kenyon College. Philomathesian Society. Catalogue of the Library, and Names of Members, of the Philomathesian Society of

Kenyon College, from its Formation in 1827 to 1840. Gambier: Thomas R. Raymond, 1840. 44 p. Rinderknecht 40-3725. Rhees, p. 328, mentions a 1850 catalogue but this may really be the 1840 catalogue? CSmH, DLC, MB, MWA, O, OClWHi, OFH, OHi.
2640

Kenyon College. Philomathesian Society. History, Statistics, Library, and Honorary Members of the Philomathesian Society of Kenyon College. Gambier, 1853. 82 p. "Catalogue of the Library" on pp. [59]-80. DLC, MWA, OClWHi.
2641

Hillsborough

Oakland Library. Catalogue of Books contained in the Oakland Library, in Hillsborough. [Hillsborough]: W. W. Doggett, 1848. 8 p. DLC, InU, MWA. **2642**

Hudson

Western Reserve College. Catalogue of Books belonging to the Library of Western Reserve College. [n.p., 1830?]. 18 p. Cooper 5424. OClW, OClWHi.
2643

Western Reserve College. Catalogue of the Library in Western Reserve College. Hudson: W. Skinner, 1850. 62, [2] p. CtY, OClW.
2644

Western Reserve College. Catalogue of Books belonging to the Library of Western Reserve College. [Cleveland, 1851?]. 18 p. OClW, InU (photocopy).
2645

Marietta

First Religious Universalian Society. Catalogue of Books belonging to the Library of the 1st Religious Universalian Society, of Marietta, Ohio. [Marietta]: Dunlevy & Joline, 1827. 8 p. Not in Shoemaker. OHi (pagination is irregular).
2646

First Universalian Religious Library Society. Catalogue of Books, belonging to the First Universalian Religious Library Society of Marietta, Ohio. [Marietta?]: P. Lepham, 1835. 12 p. Rinderknecht 32819. OClWHi.
2647

Marietta College. Laws of Marietta College, and a Catalogue of the Library. Marietta: G.

W. Tyler, 1840. 56 p. Rinderknecht 40-4363. DLC, InU, MB, MWA, OMC. **2648**

Marietta College. Catalogue of Marietta College Library. Cincinnati: Moore, Wilstach, Keys, 1857. 166 p. DLC, MB, MH, O, OMC, PPAmP.
2649

Marietta College. Phi Gamma Society. Catalogue of the Phi Gamma Society, of Marietta College. Marietta, 1861. 24 p. DLC, NjP, OMC.
2650

Marietta College. Society of Inquiry. Constitution, By-laws, and Catalogue of the Society of Inquiry of Marietta College, with Catalogues of Library and Cabinet. Marietta: Printed at the Intelligencer Officer, 1850. 32 p. DLC, NjP, PPPrHi.
2651

Marietta Library. Catalogue of Marietta Library. [n.p., 1855?]. 37, [1] p. DLC, OMC.
2652

Oxford

Miami University. Catalogue of the Books contained in the Library of Miami University, arranged according to Subjects. Oxford: W. W. Bishop, 1833. 24 p. Bruntjen 20120. ICU, IU, KyU, MH, MiU-C, Mo, MoU, N, OCl, OClWHi, OCU, OHi, OKentU, OOxM, RPB.
2653

Miami University. Erodelphian Society. Catalogue of the Members and Books of the Erodelphian Society, in Miami University. March 21st, 1829. [Oxford]: Printed at the Society's Press, 1829. 14 p. Shoemaker 39579. PPPrHi.
2654

Miami University. Erodelphian Society. Catalogue of the Honorary and Ordinary Members of the Erodelphian Society, with a List of the Books belonging to the Society's Library. Cincinnati: Corey & Webster, 1835. 17 p. Rinderknecht 33004. ICHi, MeB, OClWHi, PPPrHi.
2655

South Amherst

South Amherst Library. Catalogue of the South Amherst Library. Organized, 1865. South Amherst, 1875. 8 p. DLC. **2656**

Springfield

Springfield Library. Catalogue . . . 1873. 52 p. Cf. Cutter 670.
2657

Wittenberg College. Excelsior Society. Catalogue of the Members and Library of the Excelsior Society of Wittenberg College, Springfield, Ohio, from its Formation, November 20, 1845, to January 1, 1851. Springfield: "Republic" Office Print, 1850. Library catalogue on pp. 13-22. Cf. Catharine Penniman Storie, "What Contribution Did the American College Society Library Make to the History of the American College Library? A Supplementary Chapter in the History of the American College Library," Master's Thesis (M.S.L.S.), Columbia University, 1938, pp. 42, 99. OSW (location per Storie, p. 42). **2658**

Steubenville

Steubenville City Library Association. A Catalogue of the Steubenville City Library. Accompanied by the Rules and Regulations adopted by the Association. Steubenville: Daily and Dollar Messenger Book and Job Office Print., 1850. 23 p., [1] p. of "Rules." DLC. **2659**

Toledo

Toledo Library Association. Catalogue of the Library of the Toledo Library Association, organized, October 1864. Toledo: Spear, Johnson, 1867. xv, 151 p. OT. **2660**

Zanesville

Zanesville Atheneum. Catalogue . . . 1831. 20 p. Not in Bruntjen. Cf. Cutter 144, Rhees, pp. 341-42. **2661**

Zanesville Atheneum. A Catalogue of Books in the Zanesville Atheneum, to which are added its Charter, Articles of Association and Rules, and a List of its Officers and Stockholders. Zanesville: Edwin C. Church, 1843. 72 p. DLC holds undated suppl. (8 p.). Rinderknecht 43-5443. CtY, DLC, InU (photocopy), OClWHi. **2662**

Zanesville Atheneum. A Catalogue of Books in the Zanesville Atheneum, to which are added its Charter, Articles of Association and Rules, and a List of its Officers and Stockholders. Zanesville: Watson C. Church, 1855. 107 p. DLC, NN. **2663**

OKLAHOMA
(Formerly Indian Territory)

Fort Sill

Post Library of Fort Sill, Indian Territory. [Catalogue]. [n.p., 1875?]. 15 p. DLC. **2664**

OREGON

Portland

Library Association. Catalogue . . . Portland, 1852. Cf. George N. Belknap, *Oregon Imprints, 1845-1870* (Eugene, 1968), "Lost Oregon Imprints," p. 284, #L68a. **2665**

Portland Library. A Classified Catalogue of the Portland Library, of Portland, Oregon, with an Index of Authors and Subjects, consisting of about Twenty-five Hundred Volumes. Made by the Librarian, January, 1868. Portland: A. G. Walling, 1868. viii, 49 p. Lyle W. Gilliland, Librarian. OrHi, OrL, OrP, OrPFM, OrU. **2666**

Salem

Oregon State Library. "Librarian's Report." In: *Journal of the Proceedings of the House, of the Legislative Assembly of Oregon, during the First Regular Session, commenced September 10, 1860* (Salem: Asahel Bush, 1860), pp. [1]-5. Catalogue submitted by B. F. Bonham, State Librarian. Or. **2667**

Oregon State Library. "Librarian's Report." In: *Journal of the Proceedings of the House, of the Legislative Assembly of Oregon, for the Session of 1862* (Salem: Asahel Bush, 1862), pp. [89]-94. Catalogue submitted by John C. Peebles, Librarian. Or. **2668**

Oregon State Library. "Librarian's Report." In: *Journal of the Proceedings of the House, of the Legislative Assembly of Oregon, for the Third Regular Session, 1864* (Portland: Henry L. Pittock, 1864), pp. [175]-83. Catalogue submitted by P. L. Willis, Librarian. Or. **2669**

Oregon State Library. *Report of the State Librarian to the Legislative Assembly of Oregon. Fourth Regular Session, September, 1866,* contained in *Journal of the Senate Proceedings of the Legislative Assembly of Oregon for the Fourth Regular Session, 1866* (Salem: W. A. McPherson, 1866). Catalogue on pp. 39-49 of the *Report.* Or.   **2670**

Oregon State Library. *Report of the State Librarian to the Legislative Assembly of Oregon. Fifth Regular Session, September, 1868,* contained in *Message of the Governor of Oregon, to the Legislative Assembly. Fifth Regular Session, September, 1868* (Salem, W. A. McPherson, 1868). Catalogue on pp. [7]-66 of the *Report.* Or.   **2671**

Oregon State Library. *Report of the State Librarian, to the Legislative Assembly of Oregon. Sixth Regular Session, September, 1870,* contained in *Biennial Report of the Secretary of State of the State of Oregon, to the Legislative Assembly . . . Sixth Regular Session, September, 1870* (Salem: W. A. McPherson, 1870). Catalogue on pp. [7-55] of the *Report.* Or.   **2672**

Oregon State Library. *Report of the State Librarian to the Legislative Assembly of Oregon. Seventh Regular Session, 1872,* contained in *Biennial Message of His Excellency L. F. Grover, to the Legislative Assembly of Oregon. Seventh Regular Session, 1870* (Salem: Eugene Semple, 1872). Catalogue on pp. 12-75 of the *Report.* Or (contained in a volume with the general title: *Messages and Documents*).   **2673**

Oregon State Library. *Report of the State Librarian, to the Legislative Assembly of Oregon. Eighth Regular Session,* contained in *Biennial Message of Gov. L. F. Grover to the Legislative Assembly. Eighth Regular Session, 1874* (Salem: Mart. V. Brown, 1874). Catalogue on pp. 5-64 of the *Report.* Or.   **2674**

Oregon Territorial Library. "Report of the Territorial Librarian, made Dec. 11th, 1854." In: *Journal of the House of Representatives of the Territory of Oregon during the Sixth Regular Session of the Legislative Assembly, begun and held at Salem, December 4, 1854* (Corvallis: Asahel Bush, 1855), pp. [57]-70. Catalogue submitted by Milton Shannon, Territorial Librarian. Or.   **2675**

Oregon Territorial Library. "Librarian's Report." In: *Journal of the House of Representatives of the Territory of Oregon, during the Eighth Regular Session, 1856-7* (Salem: Asahel Bush, 1857), pp. [116]-19. Catalogue submitted by F. S. Hoyt, Territorial Librarian. Or.   **2676**

PENNSYLVANIA

Allegheny

Allegheny Public School Library. The Rules and Regulations, and Catalogue of the Allegheny Public School Library and Reading Room. Allegheny: John Ogden, 1872. 108, [1] p. DLC.   **2677**

Allentown

Academy of Natural Science, Art and Literature, of Lehigh County. Catalogue of Library . . . Allentown: E. B. Harlacher, 1874. 59 p. DLC, PAtL.   **2678**

Fratres Literarium. Catalogue of the F. L. Library, Allentown, Pa. 1866-67. Incorporated April, 1866. Allentown: F. D. Leisenring, 1866. 22 p. PAtL.   **2679**

Presbyterian Church. Library Catalogue, Presbyterian Sunday School, Allentown, Pa. January 1, 1872. [Allentown?, 1872]. 8 p. PAtL.   **2680**

Altoona

Mechanics' Library and Reading Room Association. Constitution and Catalogue of Books of the Altoona Mechanics' Library and Reading Room Association. Philadelphia: W. Mann, 1870. 77 p. DLC, PAlt (also holds a suppl. of undetermined date).**2681**

Attleborough

(later Langhorne)

Attleborough Library Company. Constitution and By-laws of the Attleborough Library Company, instituted Eighth Month 30, 1800, and a Catalogue of Books belonging thereto. Doylestown: W. W. H. Davis, 1859. 50 p. CU-SB, CtY, PDoBHi, PSC.   **2682**

Bedford

Bedford County Law Library. Catalogue of the Bedford County Law Library. [Bedford?, 1875?]. 7 p. DLC.   **2683**

Byberry, see Philadelphia.

Canonsburg

Jefferson College. Franklin Literary Society. A Catalogue of Books belonging to the Franklin Literary Society of Jefferson College. Pittsburgh: D. & M. Maclean, 1832. 13 p. Bruntjen 13149. PWW.   **2684**

Jefferson College. Franklin Literary Society. Catalogue of the Members and Library of the Franklin Literary Society of Jefferson College, Canonsburgh, Pa,, from its Formation, November 14, 1797, to June 3, 1839. Pittsburgh: Alexander Jaynes, 1839. 32 p. Rinderknecht 56587. MnSM, NNGr, PPiPT, PPiU, PPL, PPPrHi, PWW.   **2685**

Jefferson College. Franklin Literary Society. Catalogue ... 1854. 83 p. Cf. Rhees, p. 345.   **2686**

Jefferson College. Philo Literary Society. Catalogue of Books in the Library of the Philo Literary Society of Jefferson College. January 1, 1831. [Pittsburgh]: D. & M. Maclean, 1831. 8 p. Includes list of members on pp. 7-8. Bruntjen 7738. PHi.   **2687**

Jefferson College. Philo Literary Society. Catalogue of Books, in the Library of the Philo Literary Society, of Jefferson College, together with Lists of the Regular and Honorary Members. Canonsburgh: Printed at the College Press, 1835. 12 p. Not in Rinderknecht. PSt.   **2688**

Jefferson College. Philo Literary Society. A Catalogue of Books in the Library of the Philo Literary Society, of Jefferson College, together with Lists of the Regular and Honorary Members. Washington, [Pa.]: John Grayson, 1838. 13, [1] p. Rinderknecht 51056. CSmH, PHi.   **2689**

Jefferson College. Philo Literary Society. Catalogue of the Members, and Library, of the Philo Literary Society of Jefferson College, Canonsburgh, Pa., from its Formation, August 23, 1797, to July, 4, 1840. Pittsburgh: A. Jaynes, 1840. 32 p. "Catalogue of Books" on pp. 17-32. Rinderknecht 40-3597. DLC, MnSM, NjP, NN, OCHP, PHi, PPiU, PPL, PWW.   **2690**

Jefferson College. Philo Literary Society. Catalogue of Books in the Library of the

Philo Literary Society of Jefferson College. July, 1854. Pittsburgh: J. T. Shryock, 1854. 87 p. DLC.   **2691**

Jefferson College. Philo Literary Society. A Catalogue of Books in the Library of the Philo Literary Society of Jefferson College, together with Lists of the Regular and Honorary Members. Washington, [Pa.]: John Grayson, 1856. 13 p. CSmH, PHi.   **2692**

Carlisle

Dickinson College. Belles Lettres Society. A Catalogue of Books, belonging to the Belles Lettres Society, of Dickinson College, Carlisle. To which is annexed a List of the Members of the Society, Honorary, Graduate and Active, from its Establishment in 1783, until the Year 1825. Hagers-town: W. D. Bell, 1825. 31, 5 p. Not in Shoemaker. PCarlD.   **2693**

Dickinson College. Belles Lettres Society. Catalogue of the Library of the Belles Lettres Society, Dickinson College. July, 1839. Carlisle: G. W. Crabb, 1839. 52 p. Not in Rinderknecht. PCarlD (lost).   **2694**

Dickinson College. Oratorical Society. Catalogue of Books belonging to the Library of the Oratorical Society of Dickinson Institute, Carlisle, Pa. Founded 27th February, 1836. Carlisle: George M. Phillips, 1838. 27 p. Rinderknecht 50088. MdBP, MWA, MnHi, PCarlD.   **2695**

Dickinson College. Union Philosophical Society. A Catalogue of Books, belonging to the Union Philosophical Society of Dickinson College, Carlisle, to which is annexed, a List of the Members of the Society, from its Establishment to the Year 1816, inclusive. Carlisle: George Phillips, 1816. 18, 6 p. Not in S & S. PCarlD.   **2696**

Dickinson College. Union Philosophical Society. A Catalogue of Books belonging to the Union Philosophical Society, of Dickinson College, Carlisle. To which is annexed a List of the Members of the Society, both Honorary and Regular, to the Year 1823. Carlisle: Printed at the Office of the Religious Miscellany, by Fleming & Geddes, 1823. 32 p. Not in Shoemaker. DLC, PCarlD.   **2697**

Chester

Chester Library Company. Charter, Constitution, By-laws, and Catalogue of Books of the Chester Library Company. July 1, 1845. Chester: Y. S. Walter, 1845. 27 p. DLC, PCDHi. **2698**

Chestnut Hill

Christian Hall Library. Catalogue of the Christian Hall Library, Chestnut Hill. January, 1871. [Philadelphia, 1871]. 62 p. NNGr (uncat.), PPL. **2699**

Christian Hall Library. Catalogue of the Christian Hall Library of Chestnut Hill . . . May, 1875. Philadelphia: Collins, 1875. iv, 116 p. DeU, DLC, PHi. **2700**

Concordville

Concord Library Company. A Catalogue of Books belonging to the Concord Library Company of Delaware County. Chester: Y. S. Walter, 1846. 24 p. CSmH. **2701**

Coudersport

Coudersport Library and Literary Association. Constitution, By-laws and Catalogue of the Coudersport Library and Literary Association, organized May 5, 1850. Coudersport: S. F. Hamilton, 1874. 20 p. DLC. **2702**

Darby

Darby Library. A Catalogue of Books, belonging to Darby Library in Pennsylvania. Philadelphia: R. & W. Carr, 1811. [36] leaves. Not in S & S. ICN (interleaved with ms. additions), PHi (interleaved). **2703**

Doylestown

Society Library Company. Act of Incorporation of the Society Library Company, established at Doyl-Town, County of Bucks, with their Instrument of Partnership, Catalogue of Books, &c. Doyl-Town: Asher Miner, 1804. 12, [4] p. S & S 6192. PDoBHi. **2704**

Society Library Company. The Catalogue of Books, and List of Members' Names. Doylestown: Simeon Siegfried, 1819. 12 p. Not in S & S. PPL. **2705**

Easton

Easton Library Company. Catalogue of the Books belonging to the Easton Library Company; containing, also, the Articles of Association, and the Rules and Regulations of the Library, Easton, Pa. Phillipsburg: Cooley & Wise, 1855. 98, [1] p. CU, DLC, NRU, PE. **2706**

Lafayette College. Franklin Literary Society. Catalogue of the Library of the Franklin Lit. Society, Lafayette College. Easton: Geo. W. West, 1875. 55 p. MWA. **2707**

Erie

Irving Literary Institute. Catalogue . . . 1848. 16 p. Cf. Cutter 303, Jewett, p. 109, Rhees, p. 349. **2708**

Young Men's Christian Association. Catalogue of the City Library, (Young Men's Christian Association), Erie, Penn. Library and Reading Rooms . . . Organized in 1867. Erie: Republican Book and Job Printing House, 1868. 134 p. DLC, PEr. **2709**

Young Men's Christian Association. Supplementary Catalogue of the City Library, Young Men's Christian Association, Erie, Penn'a. Erie: Daily Dispatch Steam Printing House, 1872. 16 p. DLC, PEr. **2710**

Fallsington

Fallsington Library. Constitution of the Fallsington Library Company. 1802. Trenton: Sherman & Mershon, 1803. 18 p. "Catalogue of Books" on p. 18. S & S 4178. MWA. **2711**

Fallsington Library. Catalogue of Books belonging to the Fallsington Library. Newton: S. J. Paxson, 1844. 31 p. Not in Rinderknecht. DLC. **2712**

Fallsington Library. A Catalogue of Books belonging to the Fallsington Library. Trenton: Printed at the True American Office, 1854. 28 p. DLC (two copies with ms. additions). **2713**

Fallsington Library. A Catalogue of Books belonging to the Fallsington Library, Fallsington, Pa. Trenton: Murphy & Bechtel, 1875. 34 p. DLC, PDoBHi. **2714**

Germantown

Christ Church. Catalogue of the Parish Library of Christ Church, Germantown. Philadelphia: King & Baird, 1863. 16 p. PHi (Wg* vol. 11; interleaved). **2714a**

Friends, Society of. Catalogue of Books belonging to the Library of the Friends of the Preparative Meeting at Germantown. Philadelphia: J. Rakestraw, 1853. 24 p. PHC, PHi. **2715**

Friends, Society of. Catalogue of Books belonging to the Library of the Germantown Preparative Meeting of the Society of Friends. Philadelphia: William H. Pile, 1871. 92 p. DLC, PSC-Hi. **2716**

Gettysburg

Pennsylvania College. Philomathaean Society. Catalogue of the Members and Library of the Philomathaean Society of Pennyslvania College, Gettysburg, Penna. Gettysburg: H. C. Neinstedt, 1846. xxvi p. DLC, NjP. **2717**

Pennsylvania College. Philomathaean Society. Catalogue of the Members and Library of the Philomathaean Society of Pennsylvania College, Gettysburg, Pa. Gettysburg: H. C. Neinstedt, 1849. xxviii p. "Catalogue of Books" on pp. xx-xxviii. PHi. **2718**

Pennsylvania College. Philomathaean Society. Catalogue of the Philomathaean Society, of Pennsylvania College, Gettysburg, Pa., from its Formation, February, 1831, to February, 1853. Harrisburg: J. J. Clyde, 1853. 40 p. "Catalogue of Books" on pp. [27]-40. PPL. **2718a**

Pennsylvania College. Philomathaean Society. Catalogue of the Philomathaean Society of Pennsylvania College. Gettysburg: H. C. Neinstedt, 1862. 72 p. "Catalogue of Books" on pp. 45-72. P, PHi. **2719**

Pennsylvania College. Phrenakosmian Society. Catalogue of the Members and Library of the Phrenakosmian Society of Pennsylvania College, Gettysburg, Penn., from its Formation, February 1831, to April 1846. Gettysburg: H. C. Neinstedt, 1846. xxv p. "Catalogue of Books" on pp. xix-xxv. PHi. **2720**

Pennsylvania College. Phrenakosmian Society. Catalogue of the Members and Library of the Phrenakosmian Society of Pennsylvania College, Gettysburg, Penn., from its Formation, February 1831, to August 1849. Gettysburg: H. C. Neinstedt, 1849. xxxiv p. "Catalogue of Books" on pp. xxi-xxxiv. PHi. **2721**

Pennsylvania College. Phrenakosmian Society. Catalogue of the Phrenakosmian Society of Pennyslvania College, Gettysburg, Penna., from its Formation, February 1831, to November, 1852. Hagerstown, Md.: Cooke, 1852. 49 p. DLC (lost; unable to confirm presence of a library catalogue). **2722**

Theological Seminary. Catalogue of Duplicate Books from the Library of the Theological Seminary, at Gettysburg, Pa., offered for Sale by Order of the Board. Gettysburg: Printed at the "Star and Sentinel" Office, 1869. 19 p. DLC, PGL. **2723**

Harrisburg

Locust Street Methodist Episcopal Church. Catalogue of the Sabbath School Library of the Locust Street Methodist E. Church at Harrisburg. Harrisburg: Theo. F. Schefer, 1864. 66, 12, 26 p. FU (Baldwin Library; lost). **2724**

Pennsylvania State Library. A Catalogue of the Miscellaneous Books in the Pennsylvania State Library. Harrisburg: John Wyeth, 1818. 34 p. S & S 45263. MWA, PPAmP. **2725**

Pennsylvania State Library. A Catalogue of the Miscellaneous Books in the Pennsylvania State Library. Harrisburg: E. F. Cryder, 1829. 32, 34 p. "A Catalogue of the Law Books in the Pennsylvania State Library" (34 p.) has separate title page. Not in Shoemaker. P, PHi. **2726**

Pennsylvania State Library. Catalogue of the Pennsylvania State Library. To which is annexed a Copious Index. Harrisburg: E. Guyer, 1839. xii, 168 p. Rinderknecht 57877. DLC, ICL-R, MWA, MnU, P, PP, PPAmP, PPiU, RPB. **2727**

Pennsylvania State Library. Catalogue of Miscellaneous Books in the Pennsylvania

State Library. Harrisburg: Royal & Schroyer, 1853. xvi, 124 p. Supplemented by *Report of the State Librarian, to the Legislature of Pennsylvania, with a Catalogue of Books for the Year . . .*, 1854-60. FBoU, MB, N (with ms. additions), OCl, P.   **2728**

Pennsylvania State Library. Catalogue of the Pennsylvania State Library. Compiled and classified by Wallace De Witt. Harrisburg: A. Boyd Hamilton, 1859. xiv, 264, 440 p. In many libraries.   **2729**

Pennsylvania State Library. Catalogue of the Pennsylvania State Library. In Two Parts, Part I: Law Books and Papers. Part II: Miscellaneous Books. Compiled and classified by O. H. Miller. Harrisburg: Benjamin Singerly, 1873. xvi, 332, 600 p. Part II, Catalogue of Miscellaneous Books of the Pennsylvania State Library, also issued separately. MdU copy of vol. 1 is interleaved with ms. additions. In many libraries. **2730**

Hatboro

Union Library Company. Catalogue . . . Doylestown: Asher Miner, 1813. Not in S & S. Cf. Ruth Robinson Ross, *Union Library Company of Hatborough: An Account of the First Two Hundred Years* . . . (Hatboro, 1955), p. 37.   **2731**

Union Library Company. The Charter, Laws and Catalogue of Books, of the Union Library Company of Hatborough. To which is prefixed a Short Account of its First Establishment. Fourth Edition. Norristown: Henry S. Bell, 1831. 46 p. DLC.   **2732**

Union Library Company. Charter and Laws, with a Catalogue of Books of the Union Library Company of Hatborough. To which is prefixed a Short Account of its First Establishment. Fifth Edition. Philadelphia: T. Ellwood Chapman, 1847. 64 p. DLC.
                                    2733

Union Library Company. The Charter and Laws, with a Catalogue of Books, of the Union Library Company, of Hatborough, to which is prefixed a Short Account of its First Establishment. Sixth Edition. Norristown: Printed at the "National Defender" Office, 1858. 116 p. CU, DLC, NNGr, PHatU, PHi, PP, PPL.   **2734**

Union Library Company. The Charter and By-laws, with a Catalogue of Books of the Union Library Company of Hatboro, Pa. To which is prefixed a Short Account of its First Establishment. 7th ed. Hatboro: Printed at the "Public Spirit" Office, 1874. xx, [31]-186, [1] p. DLC, MB, MBAt, MWA, PHi, PP.   **2735**

Haverford

Franklin Library Company. Constitution of the Franklin Library Company of Delaware County. Philadelphia: Book and Job Printing Office, 1843. 8 p. Not in Rinderknecht. MWA (lost; unable to confirm presence of a catalogue section).   **2736**

Haverford College. Catalogue of the Library of Haverford School. Printed by Order of the Managers. 10th Mo. 1836. Philadelphia: William Brown, 1836. 40 p. Rinderknecht 37945. MH, MWA, PHC, PPAmP, PSC-Hi, WHi.   **2737**

Haverford College. Loganian Society. Catalogue of the Haverford Loganian Library . . . Philadelphia: Kite & Walton, 1854. 23 p. PHC, PPL.   **2738**

Haverford College. Loganian Society. A Catalogue of the Library of the Haverford Loganian Society of Haverford College. Philadelphia: Collins, 1859. 45 p. PHC, PHi, PPL.   **2739**

Haverford College. Loganian Society. Supplementary Catalogue of the Library of the Haverford Loganian Society, at Haverford College. Philadelphia: William K. Bellows, 1862. 10 p. PHC (bound with copy 1 of the Loganian Society's Catalogue of 1854), PHi.
                                    2740

Horsham

Horsham Library Company. The Constitution, Bye-laws, and Catalogue of Books, of the Horsham Library Company, established in the Year 1808. Philadelphia: J. Rakestraw, 1810. 24 p. Not in S & S. NNC.   **2741**

Jenkintown

Abington Library Society. The Constitution, Bye-laws, and Catalogue of the Books of the

Abington Library, established in the Year MDCCCIII. Philadelphia: William M'Culloch, 1804. 16 p. S & S 5642. MWA, NHi (defective), PHi.   **2742**

Lancaster

Apprentices' Library. Catalogue of Books belonging to the Apprentices' Library of the City and County of Lancaster. Instituted 1829. Lancaster: Forney, 1839. 15 p. See also entry 2744. Not in Rinderknecht. MWA.   **2743**

Franklin and Marshall College, see under Mercersburg.

Mechanics' Library Association. Constitution, By-laws, and Rules and Regulations, for the Government of the Mechanics' Society of the City and County of Lancaster. Incorporated, June 10, 1831. Lancaster: T. Feran, 1831. 24 p. "Catalogue of Books, belonging to the Apprentices Library" on pp. 18-24. Not in Bruntjen. CtY.   **2744**

Mechanics' Library Association. Catalogue of the Mechanics' Library Association, of Lancaster, Pa. Instituted in 1828. Lancaster: Examiner & Herald Print., 1870. 79, [1] p. DLC.   **2745**

Young Men's Christian Association. Catalogue of the Library of the Young Men's Christian Association of Lancaster. Lancaster: Pearsol & Geist, 1874. 104 p. PL.   **2746**

Lewiston

Lewiston Library Association. Catalogue of Books of the Lewiston Library Association. Lancaster: Gazette Job Office, 1870. 39 p. DLC.   **2747**

Lititz

John Beck's School Lyceum. Catalogue of the Library . . . & Apparatus, belonging to John Beck's School Lyceum, at Lititz, Lancaster County, Penn'a. Columbia: J. L. Boswell, 1835. 22 p. Rinderknecht 32399. DLC.   **2748**

Mauch Chunk

Minerva Lyceum. Catalogue. 1870. Mauch Chunk: Lynn, [1870]. [32] p. DLC. **2749**

Meadville

Allegheny College. Catalogus Bibliothecae Collegii Alleghaniensis. Catalogue of Books . . . Meadville: Thomas Atkinson, 1823. 139 p. Compiled by Timothy Alden and contains separate catalogues of volumes presented by James Winthrop, William Bentley, and Isaiah Thomas. Copy 2 owned by MWA contains a sheet of addenda on p. [140]. Shoemaker 11574. In many libraries.   **2750**

Meadville City Library. Catalogue of the Meadville City Library. Established 1868 . . . Meadville, 1873. 63 p. Printed in Lancaster by the Inquirer Printing and Publishing Co. DLC, Meadville Public Library.   **2751**

Meadville Theological School. Catalogue of the Library of the Meadville Theological School. Meadville: Republican Printing House, 1870. 134 p. CtY-D, DHEW, IU, MB, MH, NN, PP.   **2752**

Mechanicsburg

Mechanicsburg Literary Association. Catalogue . . . 1873. 57 p. Cf. Cutter 872. **2753**

Mercersburg

Marshall College. Diagnothian Literary Society. Catalogue of the Members and Library of the Diagnothian Literary Society of Marshall College, Mercersburg, Pa., from its Formation, June, 1835, to May, 1841. Gettysburg: H. C. Neinstedt, 1841. 24 p. Rinderknecht 41-3363. De, DHEW, DLC, ICJ, MBAt, NRU, PHi, PLF, PLT, PWW.   **2754**

Marshall College. Diagnothian Literary Society. Catalogue of the Members and Library of the Diagnothian Literary Society of Marshall College, Mercersburg, Pa., from its Formation, June, 1835, to September, 1843. Baltimore: Woods & Crane, 1843. 24 p. Rinderknecht 43-1942. DLC, PHi, PLF, PPL, PSt.   **2755**

Marshall College. Goethean Literary Society. Catalogue of the Members and Library of the Goethean Literary Society of Marshall College, Mercersburg, Pa., from its Formation June, 1835, to March, 1844. Chambersburg: Printed at the Office of the

"Weekly Messenger," [1844?]. 32 p. Rinderknecht 44-2445. CSmH, DeU, MB, MH, MoWgT, PHi, PLF, PLT, PPL, PWW.
2756

Montgomery Square

Montgomery Library Company. The Laws and Catalogue of Books, belonging to the Montgomery Library Company. Doylestown: Lewis Deffeback, 1819. 28 p. Not in S & S. PSC-Hi (with ms. additions).   **2757**

Montgomery Library Company. Catalogue of Books to be Sold by the Montgomery Library Company, at Montgomery Square . . . [Philadelphia: J. Richards, 1843]. 16 p. Not in Rinderknecht. PPL.   **2758**

Moyamensing

Moyamensing Literary Institute. Catalogue of the Moyamensing Literary Institute. Philadelphia: Sickels & Reading, 1854. 47 p. DLC.   **2759**

Moyamensing Literary Institute. Catalogue of Books of the Moyamensing Literary Institute . . . Philadelphia: G. S. Harris, 1870. 56 p. DLC holds suppl., Feb. 1873 (8 p.). DLC.   **2760**

Newtown

Newtown Library Company. Catalogue of Books in the Newtown Library. 1808. Newtown: William Coale, 1808. 11 p. Not in S & S. PHi (photocopy), PNt.   **2761**

Newtown Library Company. Constitution and By-laws, of the Library Company of Newtown, Bucks County. Doylestown: James Kelly, 1829. 23 p. "Catalogue of Books" on pp. 12-23. Not in Shoemaker. PNt.   **2762**

Newtown Library Company. Catalogue . . . Newtown, 1845. Fifty copies were printed, per George A. Jenks, "The Newtown Library," in *A Collection of Papers Read before the Bucks County Historical Society*, vol. 3 (Riegelsville, 1909), pp. 327-28.   **2763**

Norristown

Norristown Library Company. Catalogue . . . 1853. Cf. Rhees, p. 364.   **2764**

Northern Liberties

Library and Reading Room. Catalogue of Books in the Library and Reading Room of the Northern Liberties. Philadelphia: Thompson, 1835. iv, 48 p. Rinderknecht 33414. PP.   **2765**

Philadelphia

(see also listings under Chestnut Hill, Germantown, Moyamensing, Northern Liberties, Southwark, Spring Garden)

Academy of Natural Sciences. "Catalogue of the Library of the Academy of Natural Sciences." *Journal of the Academy of Natural Sciences of Philadelphia* 1 (1817): 203-11; 2:1 (1821), xv p. at end; 3:2 (1824): 463-67; 4:2 (1825): [391]-96. In many libraries. **2766**

Academy of Natural Sciences. Catalogue of the Library of the Academy of Natural Sciences of Philadelphia. Philadelphia: J. Dobson, 1837. 16, x, 300 p. Includes Act of Incorporation and By-laws. Copy 2 owned by PPAN has ms. additions. Supplemented, in part, by "Donations to the Library" or "Additions to the Library" in the Academy's *Proceedings* for 1841/43-1875, etc. Rinderknecht 42662. In many libraries.
2767

American Baptist Historical Society. Catalogue of the Books and Manuscripts in the Library of the Baptist Historical Society. Philadelphia, June, 1872. [Philadelphia: W. Syckelmoore, 1872]. 108 p. DLC, IC, IHi, MWA, NRAB, NcWaW, OO, RPB, TNSB, TxWB.   **2768**

American Baptist Historical Society. Catalogue of the Books and Manuscripts in the Library of the American Baptist Historical Society. August, 1874. Philadelphia, 1874. 108, 40 p. The catalogue of 1872 with "Addenda" (40 p.). DLC, KyLoS, MWA, NNC, NcWsW, PCC, PHi.   **2769**

American Entomological Society. Catalogue of Works in the Library of the American Entomological Society. Philadelphia, 1868. 32 p. Also published in the Society's *Transactions*, vol. 1. PPAN.   **2770**

American Mechanics' Library. Catalogue of the American Mechanics' Library . . . Philadelphia: Holland & Edgar, 1869. 28 p. MB.   **2771**

American Philosophical Society. Catalogue of the Library of the American Philosophical Society, held at Philadelphia, for promoting useful Knowledge. Philadelphia: Joseph R. A. Skerrett, 1824. xv, 290 p. PPAmP has copies with ms. additions. Shoemaker 15088. In many libraries. **2772**

American Philosophical Society. Catalogue of the American Philosophical Society Library. Philadelphia, 1863-84. 4 vol. Compiled by J. P. Lesley. In many libraries. **2773**

Apprentices' Library Company. Catalogue of Books, belonging to the Apprentices' Library Company, of Philadelphia. [Philadelphia]: Jesper Harding, 1823. 84 p. DLC has undated suppl. (28 p.) Shoemaker 11630, Rink 518. DLC (Rare Book col., AC901.P3 vol. 18), PHi, PP. **2774**

Apprentices' Library Company. Catalogue of Books, belonging to the Apprentices' Library Company of Philadelphia. Instituted in 1820. Philadelphia, 1830. 88 p. Cooper 3031, Rink 563. PHi, PPL. **2775**

Apprentices' Library Company. Catalogue of Books, belonging to the Apprentices' Library Company of Philadelphia. Instituted in 1820. Philadelphia: [E. G. Dorsey], 1833. 118 p. Not in Rinderknecht. PHi. **2776**

Apprentices' Library Company. Catalogue of Books, belonging to the Apprentices' Library Company of Philadelphia. Instituted in 1820. Philadelphia: Joseph and William Kite, 1838. 126 p. Rinderknecht 52268. MBAt, PHi, PP. **2777**

Apprentices' Library Company. Catalogue of Books, belonging to the Apprentices' Library Company of Philadelphia . . . Philadelphia: Joseph & William Kite, 1842. 135 p. Rinderknecht 42-4002. PHi. **2778**

Apprentices' Library Company. Catalogue of Books in the Girls' Library belonging to the Apprentices' Library of Philadelphia . . . Philadelphia, 1845. 46 p. PHi. **2779**

Apprentices' Library Company. A Catalogue of Books, belonging to the Apprentices' Library Company of Philadelphia. March 4, 1847 . . . Philadelphia: Joseph Kite, 1847. 120 p. PHi. **2780**

Apprentices' Library Company. A Catalogue of Books belonging to the Boys' Department of the Apprentices' Library Company of Philadelphia. Philadelphia, 1847. 143 p. Cf. Jewett, p. 124, Cutter 292. **2781**

Apprentices' Library Company. Catalogue of Books belonging to the Girls' Department of the Apprentices' Library Company of Philadelphia. March 1st, 1849. Philadelphia, 1849. 52 p. PHi. **2782**

Apprentices' Library Company. A Catalogue of Books belonging to the Apprentices' Library Company of Philadelphia. June 1st, 1850 . . . Philadelphia: Kite & Walton, 1850. 159 p. DLC, PHi. **2783**

Apprentices' Library Company. Catalogue of Books belonging to the Boy's Department. Philadelphia, 1850. DLC and PHi hold suppl., April 1, 1852 (23 p.); PHi copy bound at end of the Catalogue of 1850 (entry 2783). DLC (lost with the suppl.?), PHi. **2784**

Apprentices' Library Company. Catalogue of Books belonging to the Girls' Department of the Apprentices' Library Company of Philadelphia. April 1st, 1850. Philadelphia, 1850. 57 p. DLC, PHi. **2785**

Apprentices' Library Company. Catalogue of Books belonging to the Girls' Department of the Apprentices' Library Company of Philadelphia. January 1st, 1853. Philadelphia, 1853. 74 p. PHi holds suppl., March 1, 1855 (23 p.) and "Donation," 1857 (24 p.). DLC, PHi. **2786**

Apprentices' Library Company. A Catalogue of Books belonging to the Boys' Department of the Apprentices' Library Company of Philadelphia. January 1, 1854. Philadelphia, 1854. 176 p. DLC. **2787**

Apprentices' Library Company. Catalogue of Books belonging to the Girls' Department of the Apprentices' Library Company of Philadelphia. March 1, 1858. Philadelphia, 1858. 90 p. PHi. **2788**

Apprentices' Library Company. A Catalogue of Books belonging to the Boys' Department of the Apprentices' Library Company of Philadelphia. January 1, 1859. Philadelphia, 1859. 188 p. PHi. **2789**

Apprentices' Library Company. A Catalogue of Books belonging to the Boys' Department of the Apprentices' Library Company of Philadelphia. October 1, 1863 . . . Philadelphia, 1863. 176 p. PHi holds suppl., Oct. 15, 1863 (32 p.). MB, PHi (interleaved with ms. additions). **2790**

Apprentices' Library Company. Catalogue of Books belonging to the Girls' Department of the Apprentices' Library Company of Philadelphia. March 2, 1863. Philadelphia, 1863. 91 p. PHi. **2791**

Apprentices' Library Company. A Catalogue of Books belonging to the Boys' Department of the Apprentices' Library Company of Philadelphia. January 1, 1866 . . . Philadelphia, 1866. 208 p. PHi. **2792**

Apprentices' Library Company. Catalogue of Books belonging to the Boys' Department of the Apprentices' Library of Philadelphia. June 1, 1871 . . . Philadelphia: Merrihew & Son, 1871. 266 p. PHi. **2793**

Apprentices' Library Company. Catalogue of Books belonging to the Girls' Department of the Apprentices' Library Company of Philadelphia. May 2, 1872. Philadelphia: W. H. Pile, 1872. 129 p. DLC, PHi. **2794**

Apprentices' Library Company. Catalogue of Books belonging to the Boy's [sic] Department of the Apprentices' Library of Philadelphia. July 1st, 1874 . . . Philadelphia: Merrihew & Son, 1874. 248 p. DLC, PHi (interleaved). **2795**

Athenaeum of Philadelphia. Charter and By-laws of the Athenaeum of Philadelphia, to which are added, a List of the Directors, Stockholders, and Annual Visiters [sic] and of Persons who have presented to, or deposited at the Athenaeum, Books, Maps, Medals, &c. Together with a Catalogue of the Books, Maps, Minerals, &c. belonging to the Institution. Philadelphia: W. Fry, 1817. 35 p. S & S 41783. DLC, MWA, MnU, NHi, PHi, PPA, PU. **2796**

Athenaeum of Philadelphia. Charter and By-laws of the Athenaeum of Philadelphia, to which are added, a List of the Directors, Stockholders, and Annual Visiters [sic] and of Persons who have presented to, or deposited at the Athenaeum, Books, Maps,

Medals, &c. Together with a Catalogue of the Books, Maps, Minerals, &c. belonging to the Institution. Philadelphia: S. Roberts, 1820. 80 p. Shoemaker 159 (duplicated by 2741). DLC, ICN, MH, MHi, MWA, MiU-C, N, P, PHi, PPA, PPL, RNR, RPA. **2797**

Baptist Historical Society, see American Baptist Historical Society.

Brotherhead's Circulating Library. Catalogue of W. Brotherhead's Circulating Library . . . Philadelphia: W. Brotherhead, 1862. 60 p. MWA. **2798**

Brotherhead's Circulating Library. Brotherhead's Circulating Library, embracing all kinds of Literature, numbering over 32,000 Volumes . . . Philadelphia, 1872. 143 p. Running title: Brotherhead Library Catalogue. DLC copy has "32,000" corrected in ms. to read "33500." DLC. **2799**

Brotherhead's Circulating Library, see also entry 2340.

Byberry Library Company. The Constitution, Rules and Regulations, List of Members, and Catalogue of Books of Byberry Library Company. Philadelphia: William Brown, 1821. 23 p. Shoemaker 4890. PPL. **2800**

Byberry Library Company. Constitution of the Byberry Library, Rules and Regulations to be observed, List of Members, and Catalogue of Books belonging to the Institution. Philadelphia: J. Richards, 1840. 36 p. Rinderknecht 40-1222. PSC-Hi.**2801**

Byberry Library Company. Constitution of the Byberry Library Company, Rules and Regulations to be observed, List of Members, and Catalogue of Books belonging to the Institution. Philadelphia: William W. Axe, 1870. 86 p. PHi copy has [2] p. suppl. at end. DLC, PHi. **2802**

Carpenters' Company. Reminiscences of Carpenters' Hall, in the City of Philadelphia, and Extracts from the Ancient Minutes of the Proceedings of the Carpenters' Company of the City and County of Philadelphia. Philadelphia: Crissy & Markley, 1858. 41 p. Usually issued with Rules for the Library of the Carpenters' Company of the City and County of Philadelphia (57 p.) [1857?], containing

"Catalogue of Books in the Library of the Carpenters' Company of the City and County of Philadelphia" on pp. [3]-57. However, the same library catalogue in the copy at PPL (with ms. notes) is issued with An Act to Incorporate the Carpenters' Company . . . Philadelphia: T. Ellwood Chapman, 1857 (21 p.). DLC, PHi, PPL, PSC. **2803**

Carpenters' Company. An Act to Incorporate the Carpenters' Company of the City and County of Philadelphia; By-laws, Rules and Regulations; Together with Reminiscences of the Hall, Extracts from the Ancient Minutes, and Catalogue of Books in the Library . . . Philadelphia: J. Richards, 1866. 153 p. DLC, InFw, NcD, P, PHi, PHuJ, PP, PPLas, PSt (defective; lacks all after p. 114). **2804**

Carpenters' Company. An Act to Incorporate the Carpenters' Company of the City and County of Philadelphia; By-laws, Rules and Regulations; Together with Reminiscences of the Hall, Extracts from the Ancient Minutes, and Catalogue of Books in the Library . . . Philadelphia: H. C. Coates, 1873. 192 p. DLC (film), NBuU, P, PHi, PP, PPiU. **2805**

Central High School. Catalogue of the Library of the Central High School. November, 1841. Philadelphia: T. B. Town, 1841. 39 p. Not in Rinderknecht. DLC, PHi. **2806**

Christ Church. A Catalogue of Books belonging to the Library of Christ Church and to that of the Society for the Advancement of Christianity in Pennsylvania, with the Rules of the same. Philadelphia: J. Crissy & G. Goodman, 1823. 28 p. See also entry 2910. Shoemaker 13747. PHi, RPB. **2807**

Church of the Atonement. Constitution and By-laws of the Sunday School Association, and Catalogue of the Sunday School Library of the Church of the Atonement. Philadelphia: Merrihew and Thompson, 1848. 22 p. P. **2808**

Church of the Holy Trinity. Preliminary Catalogue of the Parish Library of the Church of the Holy Trinity . . . September

1st, 1862. Philadelphia: Deacon & Peterson, 1862. 31 p. MWA, PHi (Wg* vol. 10), PPL. **2809**

Deutsche Freie Gemeinde. Verfassung und Neben-Gesetze . . . nebst Bücherverzeichniss der Gemeinde-Bibliothek. Philadelphia: B. G. Stephan, 1874. 16 p. Also known as the Independent German Congregation of Philadelphia. NN, PU. **2810**

Deutsche Gesellschaft von Pennsylvania, see German Society of Pennsylvania.

English and French Family Circulating Library. Catalogue of the English and French Family Circulating Library and Cabinet de Lecture. Philadelphia: Marian M. Monachesi, Agent, [186-?]. iv, 66 p. PHi. **2811**

First Methodist Protestant Church. Constitution and Catalogue of Books of the Sabbath School attached to the First Methodist Protestant Church of Philadelphia, with Rules for the Government of the Library and a List of Officers of the Association. [Philadelphia]: Crozet, 1849. 26 p. PPL. **2812**

First Society of Unitarian Christians. Catalogue of Books in the Library of the First Society of Unitarian Christians in . . . Philadelphia. [Philadelphia], 1822. 12 p. Shoemaker 9893. PPAmP. **2813**

Franklin Institute. Catalogue of the Books belonging to the Library of the Franklin Institute of the State of Pennsylvania, for the Promotion of the Mechanic Arts. Philadelphia: S. D. Steele, 1847. 117 p. MWA, N, PHi, PPAmP, PPL, PU. **2814**

Franklin Institute. Catalogue of the Books belonging to the Library of the Franklin Institute of the State of Pennsylvania, for the Promotion of the Mechanic Arts. With an Appendix, containing the Works added since the Year 1847. Philadelphia: R. W. Barnard & Sons, 1851. 117, 68 p. ICh, NjP, N (misc. pamphlet box, 017.1), NN, OClWHi, PHi, PP, PPA, PPL. **2815**

Friends' First-Day School. Catalogue of Books in the Library of Friends' First-day School at Race Street. Philadelphia: T. W. Stuckey, 1871. 16 p. PSC-Hi (with mounted corrections). **2816**

Friends' First-Day School. Catalogue of Books in the Library of Friends' First-Day School at Race Street. Philadelphia: T. W. Stuckey, 1872. 23 p. PSC-Hi (with mounted corrections). **2817**

Friends Library, see Library of the Three Monthly Meetings of Friends; Library of the Four Monthly Meetings of Friends.

Friends, Society of (Hicksite), see Library Association of Friends.

George Institute. Catalogue . . . West Philadelphia, 1872. 31 p. Cf. Cutter 789. **2818**

German Society of Pennsylvania. A Catalogue of the Books, belonging to the Incorporated German Society, contributing for the Relief of Distressed Germans in the State of Pennsylvania, to which are prefixed the Rules, enacted by the Society, in Relation to the Library. Philadelphia: Conrad Zentler, 1826. 28 p. Shoemaker 24683. PHi. **2819**

German Society of Pennsylvania. A Catalogue of the Books, belonging to the Incorporated German Society, contributing for the Relief of Distressed Germans in the State of Pennsylvania, to which are prefixed the Rules, enacted by the Society, in Relation to the Library. Philadelphia: Conrad Zentler, 1831. 86 p. Not in Bruntjen. PPL. **2820**

German Society of Pennsylvania. Catalogue of the Library of the German Society, contributing for the Relief of Distressed Germans in the State of Pennsylvania, to which are prefixed the Rules, enacted by the Society in Relation to the Library. Philadelphia: Conrad Zentler, 1839. 218 p. Rinderknecht 55346. NHi, NNNAM, PHi, PP, PPP, PU, R. **2821**

German Society of Pennsylvania. An Additional Catalogue of the Library of the German Society, contributing for the Relief of Distressed Germans in the State of Pennsylvania. Philadelphia: King and Baird, 1850. 60 p. PPL. **2822**

German Society of Pennsylvania. Second Additional Catalogue of the Library of the German Society in Philadelphia. Philadelphia, 1859. 50 p. PU (27.2748 P385a). **2823**

German Society of Pennsylvania. Catalogue of the Library of the German Society, contributing for the Relief of Distressed Germans in the State of Pennsylvania. Philadelphia: Hoffman & Morwitz, 1864. viii, 272 p. Supplements appear in *Jahresbericht der Deutschen Gesellschaft von Pennsylvanien für das Jahr 1866-67.* PHi, PHuJ, PP, PPL. **2824**

German Society of Pennsylvania. Catalogue of the Library of the German Society, contributing for the Relief of Distressed Germans in the State of Pennsylvania. (With Supplement.) Philadelphia: Hoffman & Morwitz, 1868. 248, 42 p. Supplements appear in *Jahresbericht der Deutschen Gesellschaft von Pennsylvanien für das Jahr 1868,* etc. PHi, PPDrop, PU (27.2748 P385b). **2825**

Girard College. Inventory of Philosophical Instruments, Experimental Apparatus, Models, Books, and all other Property placed under the Control of the Building Committee of the Girard College for Orphans, by a Resolution of the Select and Common Councils of Philadelphia, passed January 20, 1842. Philadelphia: L. R. Bailey, 1842. 92 p. "Catalogue of Books, Maps, &c." on pp. 13-49. Rinderknecht 42-2008. DLC, PHi, PPAmP, PPF, PPL. **2826**

Hahnemann Medical College. Catalogue of the Museum and Library of the Hahnemann Medical College, of Philadelphia . . . C. M. Thomas, A.B., Curator of Museum and Librarian. Philadelphia: William P. Kildare, 1869. 45 p. DLC, DNLM, MiU, Nh, NN, PPL. **2827**

Harwood's Circulating Library. A Catalogue of Harwood's Circulating Library, comprising a Choice Selection of the most approved Modern Books . . . Philadelphia: William Duane, 1803. 120 p. Operated by John E. Harwood. S & S 4348. MWA. **2828**

Hicksite Friends' Library, see Library Association of Friends.

Historical Society of Pennsylvania. Catalogue of the Library of the Historical Society of Pennsylvania. Part I. History, Biography and Manuscripts. Philadelphia: Merrihew & Thompson, 1849. 36 p. CtY, DLC, MH, P, PHi, PPAmP, PPL, WHi. **2829**

Independent German Congregation, see Deutsche Freie Gemeinde.

Institute for Colored Youth. Catalogue of the Library in the Reading Room of the Institute for Colored Youth. Philadelphia: J. Rakestraw, 1853. 36 p.   DLC, PHi (interleaved).   **2830**

Law Association of Philadelphia. Catalogue of the Books belonging to the Law Association of Philadelphia. To which are added, the Charter, Regulations, and a List of the Members. Philadelphia, 1828. 39 p. Shoemaker 33823. MWA, NN, PHi.   **2831**

Law Association of Philadelphia. Catalogue of the Books belonging to the Law Library Association of Philadelphia. Philadelphia: Joseph & William Kite, 1837. 32 p. Rinderknecht 46269. PHi.   **2832**

Law Association of Philadelphia. Catalogue of the Books belonging to the Library of the Law Association of Philadelphia, &c., &c. Burlington, [Pa.]: J. L. Powell, 1842. iv, 67 p. Rinderknecht 42-2873. CtY-L, DLC, MWA, PPL.   **2833**

Law Association of Philadelphia. Catalogue of Books belonging to the Law Library Association of Philadelphia. Philadelphia: L. R. Bailey, 1846. 53 p. PHi, PPL.   **2834**

Law Association of Philadelphia. Catalogue of the Library of the Law Association of Philadelphia. With Rules and Lists of Members, etc. Founded A.D. 1802. Philadelphia: C. Sherman, 1849. [viii], 64 p. DLC, P, PPL.   **2835**

Law Association of Philadelphia. Catalogue of the Library of the Law Association of Philadelphia. With Rules and List of Members, etc. Founded A.D. 1802. Philadelphia: Henry B. Ashmead, 1861. vii, 113 p. DLC, PHi, PP, PU-L, TxU-L.   **2836**

Law Library Association, see Law Association of Philadelphia.

Law Library Company. Catalogue of the Books belonging to the Law Library Company of the City of Philadelphia. To which are prefixed the Charter, Regulations, and a List of the Members. Philadelphia: James Humphreys, 1805. [22] p. S & S 8766. DLC, PHi, PPAmP.   **2837**

Law Library Company. Catalogue of the Books belonging to the Law Library Company of the City of Philadelphia. To which are prefixed, the Charter, Regulations, and a List of the Members . . . Philadelphia: J. Maxwell, 1811. 35, [1] p. Not in S & S. PPL.   **2838**

Law Library Company. Catalogue of the Books belonging to the Law Library Company of the City of Philadelphia, to which are prefixed, the Charter, Regulations, and a List of the Members. Philadelphia: J. Crissy & G. Goodman, 1823. 34 p. Shoemaker 13071. PHi, PPL.   **2839**

Library Association of Friends. A Catalogue of Books in the Hicksite Friends' Library, Cherry Street, below Fifth . . . [Philadelphia]: Bersch & Pounder, 1837. 32 p. Rinderknecht 44410. Bruntjen 20686 for Friends' Library, Catalogue of Books (Philadelphia, 1833), appears to be a ghost edition. PHi, PPL.   **2840**

Library Association of Friends. A Catalogue of Books in Friends' Library, Cherry Street, below Fifth . . . Philadelphia: J. Richards, 1839. 64 p. PSC-Hi holds an undated suppl. (16 p.). Rinderknecht 57916 and 57917 are both for this edition? MiD-B, PHi, PSC-Hi.
2841

Library Association of Friends. Catalogue of Books in Friends' Library, Cherry Street, below Fifth . . . Philadelphia: Joseph Rakestraw, 1853. 82 p. DLC has additions to Nov. 1, 1858; NN has 15 suppl. lists of new books to 1868; PHi has lists, #1-9, to 1860?; PSC-Hi has additions to Nov. 1, 1863. Additions also listed in *Annual Report of the Library Association of Friends, of Philadelphia,* 1851-71, etc. DCU, DLC, IC, NN, PHC, PHi, PPL, PSC-Hi.   **2842**

Library Company of Philadelphia. Sixth Supplement to the Catalogue of Books, belonging to the Library Company of Philadelphia. Philadelphia: Zachariah Poulson, jun., 1801. 23 p. S & S 826. MWA, PPAmP, PPL.   **2843**

Library Company of Philadelphia. Catalogue of the Books, which have been added . . . since the First of January, 1801. [Philadelphia, 1802?]. 13 columns (galley proof?). Not in S & S. PPL.   **2844**

Library Company of Philadelphia. A Catalogue of the Books belonging to the Library Company of Philadelphia, to which is prefixed, a Short Account of the Institution, with the Charter, Laws, and Regulations. Philadelphia: Bartram & Reynolds, 1807. xl, 616 p. S & S 12918. In many libraries.
2845

Library Company of Philadelphia. A Catalogue of Books, belonging to the Library Company of Philadelphia, Volume II--Part I. Philadelphia: Thomas T. Stiles, 1813. 128 p. Supplements the Catalogue of 1807 (entry 2845). S & S 28943. DeU, MB, MH, NBu, PHi, PPA, PPAmP, PPL, PU, Vi.   **2846**

Library Company of Philadelphia. Supplement to Volume II-Part I of the Catalogue of Books, belonging to the Library Company of Philadelphia. Philadelphia: M. Carey, 1815. 46 p. Not in S & S. MH, PPAmP, PPL (also holds a 1829 reprinting, incorrectly dated 1825), PU.   **2847**

Library Company of Philadelphia. Second Supplement to Volume II . . . Part I of the Catalogue of Books, belonging to the Library Company of Philadelphia. Philadelphia: Mathew Carey and Son, 1817. 40 p. Not in S & S. DLC, MH, NBu, PPA, PPAmP, PPL, PU, Vi.   **2848**

Library Company of Philadelphia. Third Supplement to Volume II . . . Part I of the Catalogue of Books, belonging to the Library Company of Philadelphia. Philadelphia: Mathew Carey and Son, 1818. 34 p. S & S 44581. DLC, MH, MWA, NBu, PPA, PPAmP, PPL.   **2849**

Library Company of Philadelphia. Fourth Supplement to Volume II . . . Part I of the Catalogue of Books, belonging to the Library Company of Philadelphia. Philadelphia: Printed by Clark & Raser, for Littell & Henry, 1820. 27, [1] p. Shoemaker 1958. DeU, MH, MWA, PPA, PPAmP, PPL, PU, Vi.
2850

Library Company of Philadelphia. Fifth Supplement to Volume II-Part I of the Catalogue of Books, belonging to the Library Company of Philadelphia. Philadelphia: E. Littell, 1822. 34 p. Not in Shoemaker. PPA, PPAmP, PPL, PU, Vi.
2851

Library Company of Philadelphia. Sixth Supplement to Volume II-Part I of the Catalogue of Books, belonging to the Library Company of Philadelphia. Philadelphia: Printed for E. Littell by Clark & Raser, 1825. 55 p. Not in Shoemaker. PPAmP, PPL, Vi.   **2852**

Library Company of Philadelphia. Seventh Supplement to Volume II-Part I of the Catalogue of Books, belonging to the Library Company of Philadelphia. Philadelphia: Printed for E. Littell by Clark & Raser, 1828. 47, [1] p. Not in Shoemaker. PPAmP, PPL, PU, Vi.   **2853**

Library Company of Philadelphia. Eighth Supplement to Volume II-Part I of the Catalogue of Books, belonging to the Library Company of Philadelphia. Philadelphia: Judah Dobson, 1829. 112 p. Shoemaker 40050. PPAmP, PPL.   **2854**

Library Company of Philadelphia. Ninth Supplement to Volume II-Part I of the Catalogue of Books, belonging to the Library Company of Philadelphia. Philadelphia: Garden and Thompson, 1831. 33, [1] p. Not in Bruntjen. PPAmP, PPL, PU.   **2855**

Library Company of Philadelphia. Tenth Supplement to Volume II-Part II [i.e. I] of the Catalogue of Books, belonging to the Library Company of Philadelphia. Philadelphia: Adam Waldie, 1832. 217 p. Not in Bruntjen. MWA, PPAmP, PPL.   **2856**

Library Company of Philadelphia. A Catalogue of the Books Belonging to the Library Company of Philadelphia, to which is prefixed, a Short Account of the Institution, with the Charter, Laws, and Regulations. Philadelphia: C. Sherman, 1835. 2 vol. For vol. 3, see entry 2862. Rinderknecht 33693. In many libraries.   **2857**

Library Company of Philadelphia. Importation of Books for the Library Co. of Philadelphia. [Philadelphia]. A bulletin of new acquisitions, including "Books procured in America, by purchase or donation." DLC (Oct. 1838-Oct. 1855, inc.), NN (Sept. 1852-Oct. 1855), PHi (March 1852).
2858

Library Company of Philadelphia. Supplement to the Catalogue of Books, belonging to the Library Company of Philadelphia . . . Philadelphia: A. Waldie, 1838. 45 p. Cover title: First Supplement to the Large Catalogue of Books. PPL holds 2d ed., 1840, also printed by A. Waldie. Rinderknecht 52279. DLC, NBu, PPAmP, PPL, ViU.**2859**

Library Company of Philadelphia. Catalogue of Books added to the Library of the Library Company of Philadelphia, since the Large Catalogue of 1835. To January 1844. Third Edition. Philadelphia: C. Sherman, 1844. 182 p. On cover: First Supplement. Rinderknecht 44-4917 (duplicated by 44-4920, 44-4921). DLC, MWA, NjP, OKentU, P, PPAmP, PPL, PU, RPB.　　　**2860**

Library Company of Philadelphia. Second Supplement to the Catalogue of Books of the Library Company of Philadelphia, comprising the Books added to the Library from January 1844 to January 1849. Philadelphia: C. Sherman, 1849. 130 p. DLC, MWA, PHi, PPAmP, PPL, PU, RPB.
　　　　　　　　　　　　　2861

Library Company of Philadelphia. Catalogue of the Books belonging to the Library Company of Philadelphia. Vol. III: Containing Titles added from 1835 to 1856, together with an Alphabetical Index to the Whole. Philadelphia: [T. K. and P. G. Collins], 1856. xx, [985]-2103, [1] p. For vol. 1-2, see entry 2857. In many libraries.　　　　　　**2862**

Library Company of Philadelphia. List of Books added by Purchase and Donation since the Publication of the Third Volume of the Catalogue. June 1856-Jan. 1878. Title varies slightly. Some lists are devoted in their entirety to periodicals and continuations. Superseded July, 1878, by its Bulletin. New Series. Lists for Jan. 1871-July 1876, etc., contain additions to the Loganian Library. DLC, ICJ (June 1856-July 1865), IU, MB (1858-78, lacking only Jan. 1864, July 1870), MH (Jan. 1867-Jan. 1868, Jan.-July 1869, July 1870, Jan. 1871, Jan. 1872, Jan. 1873, Jan.-July 1875, MiU (1871/72, 1876/78), MWA (1856-66, inc., 1868-76), N (June 1856-Jan. 1878), NN, PHi (June 1856-Jan. 1878), PU (June 1856-July 1865), PPL (June 1856-July 1876).　　　　**2863**

Library Company of Philadelphia. Monday and Tuesday Afternoons, September 10th and 11th, 1866, at 4 o'clock. Catalogue of Miscellaneous Books, being mostly Duplicates belonging to the Library Company of Philadelphia . . . to be sold at Auction . . . by Bangs, Merwin & Co. . . . New-York. [New York, 1866]. 19 p. PPL (entered under: Bangs, Merwin).　　　　　　**2864**

Library of the Four Monthly Meetings of Friends. Catalogue of the Books belonging to the Library of the Four Monthly Meetings of Friends of Philadelphia, with the Rules for the Government of the Library. Philadelphia: Joseph Rakestraw, 1831. x, 152 p. Bruntjen 8725. DLC, InRE, KU, MH, MWA, N, NN (defective), NNC, NcD, OKentU, P, PHC, PHi, PPL, PPT, PSC-Hi, UPB, WaU.　　　　　　　**2865**

Library of the Four Monthly Meetings of Friends. Catalogue of the Books belonging to the Library of the Four Monthly Meetings of Friends of Philadelphia. Philadelphia: Kite & Walton, 1853. x, 349, [1] p. In many libraries.　　　　　　　　**2866**

Library of the Four Monthly Meetings of Friends. Supplementary Catalogue of Books belonging to the Library of Friends of Philadelphia. From 1853 to 1873. Philadelphia: W. H. Pile, 1873. 73 p. DLC, InRE, NN, PHC, PHi, PSC-Hi.　　　**2867**

Library of the Three Monthly Meetings of Friends. Catalogue of the Books belonging to the Library of the Three Monthly Meetings of Friends of Philadelphia, to which is prefixed a Brief Account of the Institution with the Rules and Regulations. Philadelphia, 1813. vi, 117 p. S & S 28586. DLC, ICN, PHC, PPAmP, PPL, PSC-Hi.
　　　　　　　　　　　　　2868

Loganian Library. A Catalogue of the Books belonging to the Loganian Library, to which is prefixed, a Short Account of the Institution, with the Law for annexing the said Library to that belonging to "The Library Company of Philadelphia," and the Rules regulating the Manner of conducting the same. Philadelphia: Zachariah Poulson, 1795-1829. 2 vol. Vol. 1, pt. 2 and vol. 2 have imprint: Philadelphia: J. Dobson, 1828-29. Shoemaker 34762, 40051. MH-H, MWA, PPL, PU, RPA.　　　　　　**2869**

Loganian Library. A Catalogue of the Books belonging to the Loganian Library, to which is prefixed, a Short Account of the Institution, with the Law for annexing the said Library to that belonging to "The Library Company of Philadelphia," and the Rules regulating the Manner of conducting the same. Philadelphia: C. Sherman, 1837. xvi, 450 p. Rinderknecht 46259. In many libraries. **2870**

Loganian Library. First Supplement to the Catalogue of Books belonging to the Loganian Library, to which is prefixed the Deed of Trust constituting the Foundation of the Library, etc., etc. Philadelphia: Collins, 1867. xxix, 32 p. MH, MWA, MiD, MiU-C, P, PHi (defective), PP, PPAmP, PPL, WHi. **2871**

Loganian Library, see also entry 2863.

Mercantile Library of Philadelphia. Catalogue . . . Philadelphia, [1821 or 22]. Not in Shoemaker. Cf. Cutter 84, Rhees, p. 414. **2872**

Mercantile Library of Philadelphia. Catalogue of the Mercantile Library of Philadelphia. April, 1823. Philadelphia: I. Ashmead, [1823]. 28 p. Shoemaker 13301, Rink 521. PPL. **2873**

Mercantile Library of Philadelphia. Catalogue . . . 1824. Not in Shoemaker. Cf. Cutter 98, Rhees, p. 414. **2874**

Mercantile Library of Philadelphia. Catalogue of the Mercantile Library of Philadelphia. Philadelphia: I. Ashmead, 1828. 76 p. Shoemaker 34765, Rink 550. MH, NN, PHi, PP, PPL, PU. **2875**

Mercantile Library of Philadelphia. Supplement to Catalogue of the Mercantile Library of Philadelphia. [Philadelphia, 1832?]. iv, 60 p. Not in Bruntjen. MH, PP, PPL.**2876**

Mercantile Library of Philadelphia. Catalogue of the Books belonging to the Mercantile Library Company of Philadelphia. With a General Index of Authors, and containing the Constitution, Rules, and Regulations of the Association accompanied by a Sketch of its History. Philadelphia, 1840. xxii, 182 p. Rinderknecht 40-5383. IU, MdBP, MB, MH, MiU, NjP, OKentU, PHi, PP, PU, WaU. **2877**

Mercantile Library of Philadelphia. A Catalogue of Books of the Mercantile Library of Philadelphia. Published April, 1850. Philadelphia, 1850. xxiv, 308, 139 p. Annual lists of books purchased, donations, and periodicals often appear in *Annual Report of the Mercantile Library of Philadelphia* beginning in 1851. In many libraries. **2878**

Mercantile Library of Philadelphia. Catalogue of Books added to the Mercantile Library of Philadelphia since April, 1850. Philadelphia: T. K. and P. G. Collins, 1856. 132 p. DeU, DLC, MWA, PHi, PP, PPA, PPAmP, PPL, PU. **2879**

Mercantile Library of Philadelphia. Second Supplement. Catalogue of Books added to the Mercantile Library of Philadelphia, 1850-1860. With an Alphabetical List of Novels. Philadelphia, 1860. 139 p. DeU, DLC, MWA, PU. **2880**

Mercantile Library of Philadelphia. Alphabetical List of Novels belonging to the Mercantile Library of Philadelphia . . . Philadelphia: Merrihew & Thompson, 1864. 48 p. PPL, PU. **2881**

Mercantile Library of Philadelphia. Catalogue of the Mercantile Library of Philadelphia. Philadelphia: [King & Baird], 1870. 4, 707 p. In many libraries. **2882**

Methodist Episcopal Church. A Catalogue of Books, contained in the Library of the M.E.U. Church. Philadelphia: S. W. Neall, 1836. 19 p. Rinderknecht 39541. DeU. **2883**

Odd Fellows Hall Association. Catalogue of Books in the Library of the Odd Fellows Hall Association . . . Philadelphia: S. N. Foster, 1864. 97 p. MWA has suppl., June 1866 (35 p.). MWA. **2884**

Pennsylvania Horticultural Society. Catalogue of the Library of the Pennsylvania Horticultural Society. Philadelphia, 1840. 24 p. Rinderknecht 40-5336. DeU, DLC, MBH, MH-A, MWA, PPAmP, PPL, PU, Vi. **2885**

Pennsylvania Horticultural Society. By-laws of the Pennsylvania Horticultural Society. Philadelphia: Stavely and M'Calla, 1844. 48 p. Regulations and library catalogue on pp. [30]-48. PPL, WHi. **2886**

Pennsylvania Horticultural Society. Catalogue of the Library of the Pennsylvania Horticultural Society. Philadelphia: Stavely and McCalla, 1850. 48 p. DLC, MBH, MH-A, PPL. **2887**

Pennsylvania Hospital. A Catalogue of the Medical Library, belonging to the Pennsylvania Hospital . . . Also, a List of Articles contained in the Anatomical Museum, and the Rules of the Museum, and of the Library. Philadelphia: Archibald Bartram, 1806. 127 p. S & S 11131, Austin 1533. CtY-M, DLC, DNLM (with ms. additions to "Rules"), ICAH, MBAt, MH-M, MWA, MiU, MnU-B, NNNAM, PPAmP, PPC, PPL (interleaved), PU. **2888**

Pennsylvania Hospital. A Catalogue of the Medical Library, belonging to the Pennsylvania Hospital . . . Part II. Philadelphia: James P. Parke, 1818. 108 p. For first part, see entry 2888. S & S 45262, Austin 1534. CtY-M, DNLM (with one ms. addition), FU-HC, LNT-M, MH-M, MWA, NNNAM, PHi, PPAmP, PPC, PPL, PU. **2889**

Pennsylvania Hospital. Catalogue of the Medical Library of the Pennsylvania Hospital. Philadelphia: T. A. Conrad, 1829. xiv, 322 p. Shoemaker 40012. Shoemaker 21844 for a 1825 catalogue published by T. A. Conrad (426 p.) is a ghost edition, apparently a conflation of the 1829 ed. and the suppl. of 1837. In many libraries. **2890**

Pennsylvania Hospital. Supplement to the Catalogue of the Medical Library of the Pennsylvania Hospital, published in 1829. Philadelphia: Joseph and William Kite, 1837. [323]-426 p. Rinderknecht 46213. CtY-M, DLC, KyLoU-HS, MWA, PHi, PP, PPC, PPL, PU, PWcS. **2891**

Pennsylvania Hospital. Catalogue Raisonné of the Medical Library of the Pennsylvania Hospital. By Emil Fischer . . . Philadelphia: T. K. & P. C. Collins, 1857. xxvii, 750 p. DLC, PPC, and PU hold suppl. compiled by August F. Müller in 1867 (paged 713-810). CU, CtY-M, DNLM, ICAH, MnU-B, NN, NcD-MC, PPA, PPAmP, PPC, PU-Med, WU. **2892**

Pennsylvania Library of Foreign Literature and Science. Catalogue of the Pennsylvania Library of Foreign Literature and Science.

Instituted November 1831. Philadelphia: John Bioren, 1835. 23 p. Rinderknecht 33648. PHi, PPAmP, PPL. **2893**

Philadelphia Almshouse. A Catalogue of the Medical Library belonging to the Philadelphia Alms-House . . . Philadelphia, 1824. 52 p. Shoemaker 17603. DNLM, PPC, RPA. **2894**

Philadelphia Almshouse. A Catalogue of the Medical Library of the Philadelphia Alms-House. Prepared agreeably to a Resolution of the Board of Managers, by E. F. Rivinus . . . Philadelphia, 1831. vii, 174 p. Bruntjen 8993. DLC, DNLM, DSG, MWA, MnU-B, NNNAM, PPC, PPL, PU, WHi. **2895**

Philadelphia Circulating Library. Catalogue of the Philadelphia Circulating Library . . . Philadelphia: Thomas H. Palmer, 1824. 162 p. Conducted by Margaret Palmer Parry. PPL holds suppl., April, 1828 (12 p.). Shoemaker 17608. MWA, PPL. **2896**

Philadelphia College of Pharmacy. Catalogue of the Library of the Philadelphia College of Pharmacy. Philadelphia, 1859. 12 p. PHi, PP, PPL. **2897**

Philadelphia County Prison. Catalogue of the Books in the Library of the Philadelphia County Prison. Philadelphia, 1855. 22 p. NN. **2898**

Philadelphia School of Design for Women. Prospectus of the Philadelphia School of Design for Women, containing a Programme of the Courses of Study, the Rules and Regulations, Constitution and By-laws, and a Catalogue of the Collection of Materials for Art Study in the Possession of the Institution . . . Philadelphia, 1875. 24 p. "Catalogue of Books belonging to the Philadelphia School of Design for Women" on pp. 14-16. Cf. Cutter 875 for a 1873 catalogue (20 p.) MCR-S, PHi, PU. **2899**

Phillips, John. Phillip's New and Increasing Book Store and Circulating Library Catalogue . . . Germantown: W. F. M'Laughlin, 1802. 59 p. Not in S & S. P. **2900**

Phillips, John. Phillip's New and Increasing Book Store and Circulating Library Catalogue . . . Philadelphia, 1805. iv, 91 p. Not in S & S. P. **2901**

Presbyterian Historical Society. Catalogue of Books in the Library of the Presbyterian Historical Society. Philadelphia: J. B. Rodgers, 1865. 107 p. DLC, MiU-C, NjTS, NN, OClWHi, OFH, PPL, PPPrHi.   **2902**

Public Library for People of Color, see Institute for Colored Youth.

Religious Historical Society. The First Annual Address, read before the Religious Historical Society, May 20th, 1817, by Samuel B. Wylie, D.D. With an Appendix published agreeably to an Order of the Society. Philadelphia: John W. Scott, 1818. 22 p. "The Library" on pp. 20-22 is a catalogue. S & S 46887. DLC, MWA, MiU, ViAlTh.**2903**

St. Andrew's Church. A Catalogue of the Parish Library of St. Andrew's Church, Philadelphia. Philadelphia: Stavely & McCalla, 1851. 18 p. Private Collection.   **2904**

St. Andrew's Church. Catalogue of the Library of the Female Sunday School of St. Andrew's Church. Philadelphia, 1861. 21 p. PHi (Wg* vol. 10).   **2904a**

St. Andrew's Church. Catalogue of the Parish Library of St. Andrew's Church, Philadelphia. Philadelphia, 1865. 53 p. PHi (Wg* vol. 1).   **2905**

St. Paul's Church. Catalogue of Books belonging to the Library of the Male Sunday School of St. Paul's Church. [Philadelphia, 183-?]. 18 p. Not in Cooper, Bruntjen, or Rinderknecht. PPAmP.   **2906**

Shallus's Circulating Library. Regulations of Shallus's Circulating Library, comprising a Choice Selection of the most approved Authors . . . Philadelphia: Thomas Town, 1809. 140 p. Operated by Francis and Ann Shallus. Not in S & S. DLC (lacks title page?).   **2907**

Shallus's Circulating Library. [Catalogue . . .]. Philadel- phia, 1810. 263 p. Operated by Francis and Ann Shallus. Not in S & S. ICN (lacks title page).   **2908**

Sixth Presbyterian Church. Catalogue of the Sabbath School Library . . . Philadelphia: Ashmead, 1840. Rinderknecht 40-5392. PPPrHi (lost and withdrawn?).   **2909**

Society for the Advancement of Christianity in Pennsylvania. Catalogue of the Library . . . Philadelphia, 1823. 8 p. See also entry 2807. Shoemaker 13877. PHi, PPL, RPB.   **2910**

Soldiers Home. Catalogue of the Library of the Soldiers Home. Philadelphia: King & Baird, 1867. 137 p. PHi.   **2911**

Trinity Church. Catalogue of the Library of Trinity Chapel Sunday School. Philadelphia: King & Baird, 1863. 18 p. PHi (Wg* vol. 11).   **2911a**

Union Circulating Library. Catalogue of the Union Circulating Library. Philadelphia: W. Pelham, 1812. 94 p. Operated by William Pelham. Not in S & S. DLC, PHi.   **2912**

Union Circulating Library. Catalogue of the Union Circulating Library. Philadelphia: G. Palmer, 1814. 94 p. Operated by Christiana Neal. S & S 32983. DLC, PHi, PPL.   **2913**

Union Circulating Library. Catalogue of the Union Circulating Library . . . Philadelphia: Thomas H. Palmer, 1824. 102 p. Operated by Christiana Neal. Shoemaker 18263. DLC, PPL.   **2914**

Union Circulating Library. Catalogue of the Union Circulating Library . . . Philadelphia: Mifflin and Parry, 1832. 103 p. Operated by Christiana Neal. Not in Bruntjen. MWA, NN.   **2915**

University of Pennsylvania. Catalogue of Books, belonging to the Library of the University of Pennsylvania. Philadelphia: Judah Dobson, 1829. 103 p. Shoemaker 40018. DLC, NN, PP, PPA, PPAmP, PPC, PPL, PU, RPB.   **2916**

University of Pennsylvania. Philomathean Society. A Catalogue of the Books belonging to the Philomathean Society of the University of Pennsylvania. Philadelphia: William F. Geddes, 1840. 17 p. Rinderknecht 40-5236. PHi, PU.   **2917**

University of Pennsylvania. Philomathean Society. Catalogue of the Library of the Philomathean Society, University of Pennsylvania. Philadelphia: King & Baird, 1870. 90 p. MnU (interleaved), PHi, PU.   **2918**

University of Pennsylvania. Rogers Engineering Library. Catalogue of the Rogers Engineering Library of the University of Pennsylvania. July, 1875. Philadelphia: Finley, 1875. 57 p. N, PP, PPL, PU. **2919**

University of Pennsylvania. Zelosophic Society. Catalogue of the Library of the Zelosophic Society, University of Pennsylvania. Philadelphia: Walz & Ketterlinus, 1850. 16 p. DLC, PPAmP, PU (photostat of DLC copy). **2920**

West End Sunday School Library. Catalogue of the West End S. S. Library, at Gray's Lane. Philadelphia: Ringwalt & Brown, 1863. 8, [1] p. DeU. **2921**

West Philadelphia Institute. Catalogue of the Library of the West Philada. Institute. February, 1856. Philadelphia: M'Laughlin, 1856. 59 p. PP, PPL, PPWa. **2922**

Young Men's Christian Association. Catalogue of the Library, Young Men's Christian Association of Philadelphia. 1870. [Philadelphia]: Jas. B. Rodgers, [1870]. 247 p. DLC, MWA, PPL. **2923**

Pittsburgh

Associate Presbyterian Church Seminary. Catalogue of Books in the Library of the Seminary of the Associate Presbyterian Church. December, 1854 . . . Pittsburgh: J. T. Shryock, 1854. 29 p. DLC (with ms. additions to the catalogue and to the regulations). **2924**

Young Men's Mercantile Library and Mechanics' Institute. Charter, Constitution and By-laws of the Young Men's Mercantile Library and Mechanics' Institute, of Pittsburgh, Penn'a, With Catalogue of Books. [Pittsburgh]: Johnston & Stockton, 1850. 28 p. DLC. **2925**

Young Men's Mercantile Library and Mechanics' Institute. Classified Catalogue of Books in the Young Men's Mercantile Library and Mechanics' Institute, of Pittsburgh, together with Charter, Constitution, By-laws, and Brief History of the Association. Pittsburgh: W. S. Haven, 1858. 59 p., [1] p. DLC, PPL. **2926**

Young Men's Mercantile Library and Mechanics' Institute. Catalogue of the Young Men's Mercantile Library Association and Mechanics' Institute, of the City of Pittsburgh . . . Compiled by G. E. Appleton, Librarian. Pittsburgh: W. S. Haven, 1866. 130 p. DLC. **2927**

Pottsville

Pottsville Scientific Association. Bulletin of the Pottsville Scientific Association, Schuylkill County, Penna., for January & February, 1855, including the Constitution and By-laws, together with the Officers and Members, and a Catalogue of the Library & Museum. Pottsville: B. Bannan, 1855. 10, 14, ii p. CLSU-H, CU, DLC, DNLM, PHi, PPAN, WHi. **2928**

Reading

Readinger Deutschen Lese-Gesellschaft. Grundregeln der Readinger Deutschen Lese-Gesellschaft. Gegründet im May, 1804, nebst dem Catalogus der Bücher, so der Gesellschaft eigen. Reading: Johann Ritter, 1807. 31, 4, 8 p. S & S 13465 (S & S 8572, under 1805, is a ghost edition). PHi, PPG (with ms. additions), PR. **2929**

Library Company of Reading. Constitution and Rules for the Government of the Library Company of Reading. Instituted in April, 1808. Likewise, a Catalogue of Books in the Reading Library. Reading: Gottlob Jungman, [1808]. 35 p. S & S 16038. CSmH (with ms. additions), MWA, P. **2930**

Library Company of Reading. Constitution and Rules for the Government of the Library Company of Reading. Instituted April, 1808, and incorporated December 14, 1819. To which is added, a Catalogue of Books, belonging to the Company. Reading: George Getz, 1821. 24 p. Shoemaker 6593. DLC (film), P, PHi (with ms. additions). **2931**

Southwark

Southwark Library Company. Constitution, By-laws and Catalogue of the Southwark Library Company, with the By-laws of the Directors. Incorporated February 22, 1831. Philadelphia: Barrett & Jones, 1847. 82 p. Cover title: Catalogue of the Southwark Library Company for 1847, with the Constitution and By-laws . . . DLC, MWA. **2932**

Southwark Public School Library. Catalogue of Books in Southwark Public School Library. Philadelphia: J. Coates, jr., 1833. 24 p. Bruntjen 21312. MnU, PP. **2933**

Spring Garden

Free Reading Room Association. Catalogue of Books belonging to the Library of the Free Reading Room Association of Spring Garden . . . Philadelphia: John Richards, 1851. 24 p. PHi (blank leaves for additions at end). **2934**

Free Reading Room Association. Catalogue of Books belonging to the Library of the Free Reading Room Association of Spring Garden. Philadelphia: Joseph Rakestraw, 1856. 40 p. DLC, PHi. **2935**

Spring Garden Institute. Catalogue of Books in the Library of the Spring Garden Institute . . . Incorporated April 12th, 1851. Philadelphia: Thomas William Stuckey, [ca. 1867]. 58 p. DLC. **2936**

Spring Garden Library. Bell's New Auction Rooms . . . Sale of the Spring Garden Library . . . Catalogue of a Large Collection of Miscellaneous Books . . . Feb. 8 & 9, 1843. Philadelphia: T. U. Baker, 1843. 8 p. Not in Rinderknecht. PPL. **2937**

Springfield

Library of Friends. A Catalogue of Books belonging to the Library of Friends at Springfield, Delaware County, Pennsylvania. Philadelphia: Joseph Rakestraw, 1850. 20 p. PHC, PSC-Hi. **2938**

Swarthmore

Swarthmore College. Catalogue of the Swarthmore College Library. 1871. Philadelphia: Merrihew & Son, [1871]. 32 p. PHi. **2939**

Titusville

Hurd's Circulating Library. Catalogue of Circulating Library, situated in the Book and Stationary Store, West Spring Street, Titusville. [Titusville, 187-?]. Operated by B. N. Hurd. DLC (lost). **2940**

Upper Dublin

Union Library Company. Constitution and Catalogue of Books, belonging to "The Union Library Company," of Upper Dublin. Instituted March 1st, 1834. Norristown: Robert Iredell, 1835. 8 p., [9] leaves. Rinderknecht 34648. PHi (with ms. additions to the Catalogue and names of members). **2941**

Warren

Young Men's Christian Association. Y.M.C.A. Public Library. Catalogue of Books. Warren, Pa. Lancaster: Wylie & Criest, 1872. 19 p. DLC holds "Additions," April 15, 1874 (9 p.) and Jan. 8, 1875 (10 p.). DLC. **2942**

Washington

Citizens' Library Association. Catalogue of Books belonging to the Citizens' Library Association of Washington, Penn'a. Chartered May 27, 1870. Washington, Pa.: M. A. Cooper, 1873. 47 p. PPiHi. **2943**

Washington College. Union Literary Society. Catalogue of Books in the Library of the Union Literary Society of Washington College, Pa. July, 1858. Washington, 1858. CtY (lost). **2944**

Westchester

Chester County Athenaeum. Catalogue . . . [Westchester?, 185-]. A published catalogue, per *Norton's Literary Gazette and Publishers' Circular,* Sept. 1853; text also appears in Larry Barr, et al., *Libraries in American Periodicals Before 1876: A Bibliography with Abstracts and Index* (Jefferson, NC: 1983), entry 1081. **2945**

West Chester Library Association. First Semi-Annual Statement of the Executive Committee of the West Chester Library Association with Catalogue. October, 1873. West Chester: W. C. Hickman, 1873. 74, [2] p. DLC, MB, PWcS. **2946**

West-Chester Library Company. Articles of Association of the West-Chester Library Company. Westchester: Charles Miner, 1819. 24 p. Library catalogue on pp. 9-24. S & S 50092. MWA, PWcS, PWcT. **2947**

Westtown

Westtown Boarding School. Catalogue of the Library of Friends' Boarding-School, at West-Town. 1856. Philadelphia: E. C. & J. Biddle, 1856. v, 98 p. InRE, PSC-Hi. **2948**

Westtown Boarding School. Catalogue of Books belonging to the Library of Westtown Boarding School. 1873. West Chester: F. S. Hickman, 1873. 84 p. InRE. **2949**

Whitpain

Whitpain Library Company. The Act of Incorporation, Bye-laws, and Catalogue of Books, of the Whitpain Library Company. Norriston: D. Sower, jr., 1826. 16 p. Not in Shoemaker. MWA. **2950**

Wilkesbarre

Wyoming Athenaeum. Catalogue of the Wyoming Athenaeum's Library, in Wilkes-Barre, with Extracts from the Articles of Incorporation, By-laws, Rules and Regulations. Wilkes-Barre: Printed at the Record of the Times Office, 1875. 42 p. DLC, PHi. **2951**

York

York County Library Company. Charter of the York County Library Company, together with a Catalogue of Books now on its Shelves, and the Bye-laws which have been adopted for its Present Regulation. York: Eli Lewis, 1823. 16 p. Not in Shoemaker. MWA. **2952**

RHODE ISLAND

Ashton

Reading Room and Library Association. Catalogue of Books in the Reading Room and Library Association, Ashton, R.I. Central Falls, 1871. 19 p. RHi. **2953**

Barrington

School District No. 2. Catalogue of the Library in School District No. 2, Barrington, R.I. [Barrington, 185-?]. 20 p. CtHT, DLC. **2954**

Block Island

First Baptist Church. Catalogue of the Sunday School Library, First Baptist Church . . . [Providence, 187-?]. [11] p. RPB. **2955**

Bristol

St. Michael's Church. Catalogue of the St. Michael's Church Sunday School Library. Providence: Knowles, Anthony, 1866. 28 p. RHi. **2956**

State Street Methodist Episcopal Church. Catalogue of the State Street M. E. Sabbath School Library, Bristol, R.I. January 1, 1868. Providence: Hammond, Angell, 1868. 23 p. RHi, RPB. **2957**

Young Men's Christian Association. Catalogue of the Library of the Young Men's Christian Association, Bristol, R.I. Providence: Providence Press Co., 1867. 44 p. DLC, RHi. **2958**

Centerdale (Centredale)

Union Library. Catalogue of Books in Union Library, Centredale, R.I. Providence: A. Crawford Greene, [1870?]. 12 p. RPB. **2959**

Centreville

Centreville Methodist Episcopal Church. Catalogue of the Centreville M. E. Sunday School. Providence: Gladding, Brother and Co., 1872. 14 p. RHi. **2960**

Cranston

St. Bartholomew's Church. Catalogue of St. Bartholomew's Sunday School Library. Providence: Knowles, Anthony, 1867. 11 p. RHi. **2961**

Cumberland, see Ashton.

East Greenwich

Providence Conference Seminary. Catalogue of the Library of the Providence Conference Seminary, with an Alphabetical List of the Authors. 1859. Providence: A. Crawford Greene, 1859. 32 p. MWA, RPB (entered under: East Greenwich Academy. Library). **2962**

East Providence

(see also Providence)

Second Baptist Church. Catalogue of the Second Baptist Sunday School Library, East Providence, R.I. Providence: S. M. Millard, 1870. 24 p. RPB.   **2963**

Foster

Foster Manton Society. Catalogue of the Foster Manton Library, together with the Constitution and By-laws of the Society. Providence: Benj. T. Albro, 1849. 26 p. DLC, MWA, RHi.   **2964**

Gloucester

Manton Harmony Library. Catalogue of Books in the Manton Harmony Library. [Gloucester, 187-?]. 47 p. DLC.   **2965**

Kingston

(see also South Kingstown)

Library (Kingston, R.I.). Catalogue of the Library at Kingston, R.I. Established 1852. Wakefield: Thomas P. Wells, 1856. 20 p. DLC, MWA, RHi, RPB.   **2966**

Lincoln, see Lonsdale, Manville, Slatersville.

Little Compton

Methodist Episcopal Church. Catalogue of Books in the M. E. Sabbath School Library, Little Compton, R.I. [n.p., 187-?]. 15, [1] p. MNBedf.   **2967**

Lonsdale

Lonsdale Athenaeum. Catalogue of the Lonsdale Athenaeum. December, 1847. Providence: H. H. Brown, 1847. 18 p. DLC (marked copy), RPB.   **2968**

Lonsdale Athenaeum. Catalogue of the Lonsdale Athenaeum. December, 1854. Pawtucket: A. W. Pearce, 1854. 26 p. RPB.
2969

Lonsdale Library and Reading Room Association. Catalogue of Books in the Lonsdale Library & Reading Room Association, with the Rules and Regulations. Central Falls: E. L. Freeman, 1871. 45 p. DLC, RHi, RPB.
2970

Manville

Emmanuel Church. Catalogue of the Sunday School Library, of Emmanuel Church, Manville, R.I. Providence: Providence Press Co., 1870. 16 p. RHi, RPB.   **2971**

Emmanuel Church. Catalogue of the Sunday School Library, of Emmanuel Church, Manville, R.I. Providence: Providence Press Co., 1873. 22 p. RHi, RPB.   **2972**

Manville Library and Reading Room Association. Catalogue of Books in the Manville Library and Reading Room Association, with the Rules and Regulations. Woonsocket: W. H. Crapon, 1874. 21 p. RHi.   **2973**

Newport

Callahan's Circulating Library. Catalogue of W. Callahan's Circulating Library, Newport, R.I. July, 1834 . . . [Newport, 1834]. 18 p. Not in Bruntjen. Cf. Hammett, p. 34. **2974**

Emmanuel Sunday School. Catalogue of Emmanuel Sunday School Library, Newport, R.I. 1871. Newport: James Atkinson, 1871. 19 p. RHi, RPB.   **2975**

Free Public Library, see Newport Free Public Library.

Hammond's Circulating Library. Catalogue of James Hammond's Circulating Library . . . Newport, R.I. [Newport]: James Atkinson, 1830. 71 p. Additional catalogue for 1836 (8 p.) recorded by Hammett, p. 37. Cooper 2843. RHi.   **2976**

Hammond's Circulating Library. Catalogue of James Hammond's Circulating Library. [Newport: James Atkinson, 1844]. 84 p. Not in Rinderknecht. CtY, RPB.   **2977**

Hammond's Circulating Library. Catalogue of James Hammond's Circulating Library, No. 84, Thames-Street, Newport, R.I. . . . 4000 Vols. [Newport, 184-?]. 90 p. MH.   **2978**

Hammond's Circulating Library. Catalogue of James Hammond's Circulating Library, 142 Thames Street, Newport, R.I. 8,000 Volumes. Newport: Mason & Pratt, 1853. 108 p. MH, MWA (defective).   **2979**

Hammond's Circulating Library. Catalogue of James Hammond's Circulating Library, No. 142 Thames Street, Newport, R.I. 8000

Volumes. Newport: Coggeshall & Pratt, 1854. 108 p. [RPB copy renumbered in ms. to read 112 p.]. RPB.   **2980**

Hammond's Circulating Library. Catalogue of James Hammond's Circulating Library, No. 142 Thames Street, Newport, R.I. 8000 Volumes. Newport: Coggeshall & Pratt, 1855. 107, 7 p. CtY.   **2981**

Hammond's Circulating Library. Catalogue of James Hammond's Circulating Library, No. 142 Thames Street, Newport, R.I. 9000 Volumes. Newport: Coggeshall & Pratt, 1856. 107, 10 p. NN, RNR.   **2982**

Hammond's Circulating Library. Catalogue of James Hammond's Circulating Library, No. 142 Thames Street, Newport, R.I. . . . 10,000 Volumes. Newport: Coggeshall & Pratt, 1858. 127 p. MH.   **2983**

Hammond's Circulating Library. Catalogue of James Hammond's Circulating Library, No. 142 Thames Street, Newport, R.I. 10,000 Volumes. Newport: Fred'k A. Pratt, [ca. 1860]. 127 p. RPB copy includes "Additional Catalogue" (16 p.). MWA (125 p. only), RPB (all pages after p. 120 missing).   **2984**

Hammond's Circulating Library, see also entry 2434.

New Circulating Library. Catalogue of the New Circulating Library, No. 93, Thames Street, Newport, Rhode Island. Bristol: Golden Dearth, 1808. 74 p. Presumably operated by Nathaniel Dearborn based on advertisements for his bookstore on pp. 72-74. S & S 15708. RNHi.   **2985**

Newport Association of Mechanics and Manufacturers. Catalogue of the Library, of the Newport Association of Mechanics and Manufacturers. (Incorporated, 1792.) Library Founded, 1828. Newport: Cranston & Norman's Power Press, 1850. 43 p. DLC, MWA, RHi, RPB.   **2986**

Newport Free Library, see Newport Free Public Library.

Newport Free Public Library. Catalogue of the Free Public Library, Newport, R.I. Newport: Daily News Steam Printing Press, 1867. 38 p. Also known as the Newport Free Library; the collection was absorbed by the People's Library, per Hammett, p. 153.   **2987**

Newport Mechanics' and Apprentices' Library. Catalogue of the Newport Mechanics' and Apprentices' Library, established by the Newport Association of Mechanics and Manufacturers . . . Newport: James Atkinson, 1835. 16 p. Rinderknecht 33385. RNHi.   **2988**

Newport Mechanics' and Apprentices' Library. Catalogue of the Newport Mechanics' and Apprentices' Library, established by the Newport Association of Mechanics and Manufacturers . . . Newport: James Atkinson, 1841. 16 p. Not in Rinderknecht. DLC.   **2989**

Newport Reading Room. Catalogue of Books, Newport Reading Room. October, 1858. [Newport]: F. A. Pratt, [1858]. 24 p. PPL.   **2990**

"Parish" School. Library Catalogue of the "Parish" School, Newport, R.I. Newport: Charles E. Hammett, Jr., 1863. 35 p. Cf. Hammett, p. 34.   **2991**

People's Library. Catalogue of the Books in the People's Library, Newport, R.I. Providence: Hammond, Angell, 1870. iv, 338 p. Cutter 675 and Hammett, p. 126, report a 52 p. suppl., Dec. 1870 (Courtlandt, NY, 1871). DLC, MB, MWelC, MWA, N, NNC, NcD, RHi, RN, RPB, RU.   **2992**

Redwood Library and Athenaeum. Charter of the Redwood Library Company, granted A.D. 1747. Newport: Rousmaniere & Barber, 1816. 36, [3] p. Catalogue of books on pp. [15]-36. S & S 38763. InU, MB (with ms. additions), MHi, MWA, NHi (with ms. additions), NNC, PHi, PPL (has four additional blank leaves), RHi, RNHi, RNR, RPB.   **2993**

Redwood Library and Athenaeum. Appendix to the Catalogue of Books, belonging to the Redwood Library Company, Newport, R.I. Sept. A.D. 1829. Newport: W. & J. H. Barber, 1829. 14 p. Not in Shoemaker. PPL (interleaved), RNR, RPB (bound with the Charter . . . 1816).   **2994**

Redwood Library and Athenaeum. A Catalogue of the Books belonging to the Company of the Redwood Library and Athenaeum, in Newport, R.I. To which is prefixed a Short Account of the Institution; With the Charter, Laws and Regulations. Providence: Knowles and Vose, 1843. xix, 95 p. Rinderknecht 43-3810. CtNbC, CtY,

DeWint, MH, MBAt, MWA, NjR, NN, NNUT, PBL, PHi, PPA, PPL, RHi, RNR, RPB.   **2995**

Redwood Library and Athenaeum. A Catalogue of the Redwood Library and Athenaeum, in Newport, R.I., together with a Supplement, Addenda, and Index of Subjects and Titles: showing all the Books belonging to the Company on the First of June, 1860. To which is prefixed a Short Account of the Institution; With its Charter, Laws and Regulations. Boston: John Wilson and Son, 1860. liii, 383 p. Cutter 429 reports suppl., 1863 (18 p.). In many libraries. **2996**

Redwood Library Company, see Redwood Library and Athenaeum.

Spring Street Church. Catalogue for the Library belonging to Spring Street Church Sabbath School, Newport, R.I. [Newport, 1868?]. 23 p. MB.   **2997**

North Providence, see Centerdale.

North Scituate

Aborn Library. Catalogue of the Aborn Library, of North Scituate, R.I. With an Appendix, containing a List of the Officers and the Constitution and By-laws of the Association. Providence: Albro & Hall, 1849. 12 p. RPB.   **2998**

Aborn Library. Catalogue. [n.p., 185-?] 20 p. MWA (defective; title from caption). **2999**

North Smithville, see Slatersville.

Olneyville

Broadway Baptist Church. Catalogue of Books in the Sabbath School Library, of the Broadway Baptist Sabbath School, Olneyville, R.I. 1870-71. Providence: Providence Press Co., 1870. 16 p. RPB.   **3000**

Broadway Baptist Church. Catalogue of Books in the Sabbath School Library of the Broadway Baptist Sabbath School, Olneyville, R.I. 1872-3. Providence: A. Crawford Greene, 1873. 18 p. RPB.   **3001**

Pascoag

Methodist Episcopal Church. Library Catalogue, Pascoag Methodist Episcopal Sunday

School Library. [Providence?, 187-?]. 8 p. RHi, RPB.   **3002**

Pawtucket

Methodist Church. Catalogue of Methodist Sabbath School Library, Pawtucket, R.I. Providence: Hammond, Angell, 1867. 15 p. RHi.   **3003**

Pawtucket Library. Catalogue of the Pawtucket Library, to which are prefixed the Charter, By-laws, and an Historical Sketch of the Institution. Pawtucket: Robert Sherman, 1860. xxiii, 152 p. Compiled by Sidney S. Rider. Cutter 876 reports suppl., 1873 (12 p.). DeU, DLC, MWA, MiD, RHi, RPaw, RPB.   **3004**

Trinity Church. Catalogue of the Sunday School of the Trinity Church, Pawtucket, R.I. June 1871. Central Falls, 1871. 22 p. RHi (lost).   **3005**

Pawtuxet

Baptist Church. Catalogue of the Baptist Sunday School Library, Pawtuxet, R.I. Providence: Providence Press Co., 1874. 16 p. RPB.   **3006**

Providence

(see also East Providence)

All Saints' Memorial Church Choir Guild. Library of All Saints' Memorial Church Choir. [Providence, 187-?]. [8] p. RPB. **3007**

Beneficent Congregational Church. Catalogue of the Beneficent Congregational Sabbath School Library. 1873. Providence: Rhode Island Printing Co., [1873?]. 28 p. RPB.   **3008**

Berean Baptist Church. Catalogue . . . [Providence, 187-?]. 8 p. RPB.   **3009**

Boston Circulating Library. Catalogue of Books in the Boston Circulating Library . . . Providence, R.I. . . . S. C. Glover & Co. Pawtucket: Nickerson & Sibley, 1871. 16 p. RPB.   **3010**

Boston Circulating Library. Catalogue of Books in the Boston Circulating Library . . . Providence, R.I. . . . S. C. Glover & Co. Pawtucket: Nickerson & Sibley, 1872. 24 p. RPB.   **3011**

Boston Circulating Library. Catalogue of Books in the Boston Circulating Library . . . Providence, R.I. . . . S. C. Glover & Co. Pawtucket: Nickerson & Sibley, 1873. 48 p. RPB.   **3012**

Brown University. Catalogue of Books in the Library of Brown University. Providence: Walter R. Danforth, 1826. 60 p. Shoemaker 23948. CtY, ICN, MH, MHi, MWA, MnU, PBL, PPAmP, RHi, RPB, RPJCB.   **3013**

Brown University. A Catalogue of the Library of Brown University, in Providence, Rhode Island. With an Index of Subjects. Providence, 1843. xxvi, 550 p. Printed in Andover by Allen, Morrill and Wardwell. Compiled by Charles Coffin Jewett. Rinderknecht 43-817. In many libraries.   **3014**

Brown University. Franklin Society. Catalogue of the Books in the Library of the Franklin Society, with the Names of its Members, Brown University. September, 1826. Providence: Literary Cadet Office-- Smith & Parmenter, 1826. 20, [5] p. Shoemaker 23950. MB (defective), MNBedf, MWA, RHi.   **3015**

Brown University. Philermenian Society. Catalogue of the Books in the Library of the Philermenian Society, together with the Names of its Members. Brown University. Providence: Jones & Wheeler, 1810. 16 p. S & S 19655. RPB.   **3016**

Brown University. Philermenian Society. Catalogue of the Books in the Library of the Philermenian Society, together with the Names of its Members. Brown University. Providence: Miller, Goddard & Mann, 1814. 19 p. S & S 31015. MWA, RPB.   **3017**

Brown University. Philermenian Society. Catalogue of the Books in the Library of the Philermenian Society, together with the Names of its Members, Brown University. September 1817. Providence: Miller and Hutchens, 1817. 22 p. S & S 40340. MWA, RPB.   **3018**

Brown University. Philermenian Society. Catalogue of the Books in the Library of the Philermenian Society, together with Names of its Members, Brown University. April 1821. Providence: Miller and Hutchens, 1821. 32 p. Shoemaker 4855. MH, RPB.   **3019**

Brown University. Philermenian Society. Catalogue of the Books in the Library of the Philermenian Society, with the Names of its Members. Brown University. April, 1824. Providence: Barnum Field, 1824. 36 p. Shoemaker 15580. MWA, RPB.   **3020**

Brown University. Philermenian Society. Catalogue of the Books in the Library of the Philermenian Society, with the Names of its Members, Brown University. September, 1828. Providence: Office of the Christian Telescope, 1828. 47 p. Shoemaker 32498. DLC, MHi, RPB.   **3021**

Brown University. Philermenian Society. Catalogue of the Books in the Library of the Philermenian Society, with the Names of its Members. Brown University. January, 1833. Providence: H. H. Brown, 1833. 45 p. Bruntjen 17989. MWA, MiD-B, RPB. **3022**

Brown University. Philermenian Society. Catalogue of the Library of the Philermenian Society, with the Names of its Members. Founded A.D. 1794. Providence: E. A. Marshall, 1835. 40 p. Rinderknecht 30694. MWA, RPB.   **3023**

Brown University. Philermenian Society. Catalogue of the Library and Members of the Philermenian Society. Founded A.D., 1794. Boston: William S. Damrell, 1838. 46 p. Rinderknecht 49474. MB, MBAt, MWA, RPB.   **3024**

Brown University. Philermenian Society. Catalogue of the Library and Members of the Philermenian Society. Founded A.D., 1794. Boston: John Putnam, 1841. 55 p. Cover title: Triennial Catalogue of the Philermenian Society, Brown University. Not in Rinderknecht. MB, MWA, RPB.   **3025**

Brown University. Philermenian Society. Catalogue of the Library and Members of the Philermenian Society, Brown University. Founded A.D., 1794. Boston: Samuel N. Dickinson, 1844. 60 p. Not in Rinderknecht. MB, MWA, NNC, RPB.   **3026**

Brown University. Philermenian Society. Triennial Catalogue of the Library and the Members of the Philermenian Society in Brown University. Founded A.D. 1794. Providence, 1849. 92 p. Printed in Boston by Damrell & Moore. DLC, MB, MHi, MWA, NN, OClWHi, OO, PHi, RPB (copy 2 interleaved with ms. notes).   **3027**

Brown University. United Brothers' Society. Catalogue of the Books in the Library of the United Brothers' Society, together with the Names of its Members, Brown University. Providence: H. Mann, 1814. 16 p. Not in S & S. CSmH (with ms. additions to names of members), MWA, RPB.   **3028**

Brown University. United Brothers' Society. Catalogue of the Books in the Library of the United Brothers' Society, together with the Names of its Members, Brown University. Providence: Miller & Hutchens, 1818. 24 p. Not in S & S. CSmH (contains mounted errata slip).   **3029**

Brown University. United Brothers' Society. Catalogue of the Books in the Library of the United Brothers' Society, together with the Names of its Members, Brown University. April, 1821. Providence: Printed at the American Office, [1821]. 24 p. Shoemaker 4856. MB, MWA, RHi, RPB.   **3030**

Brown University. United Brothers' Society. Catalogue of the Books in the Library of the United Brothers' Society, with the Names of its Members. Brown University. July, 1824. Providence: Barnum Field, 1824. 35, [1] p. Shoemaker 15581. MB, MWA, RPB.   **3031**

Brown University. United Brothers' Society. Catalogue of the Books in the Library of the United Brothers' Society, with the Names of its Members. Brown University. September, 1829. Providence: H. H. Brown, 1829. 39 p. Shoemaker 37970. MB, RPB.   **3032**

Brown University. United Brothers' Society. Catalogue of the Library, with the Names of its Members. Founded A.D. 1806. Providence: Weeden and Cory, 1835. 36 p. Rinderknecht 30695. MHi, MWA, RPB.
                3033

Brown University. United Brothers' Society. A Catalogue of the Library of the United Brothers' Society of Brown University, with the Names of Members. Founded A.D. 1806. Providence: Knowles, Vose, 1837. 40 p. Rinderknecht 43441. DLC, MdBP, MBAt, MBC, NN, RPB.   **3034**

Brown University. United Brothers' Society. A Catalogue of the Library and Members of the United Brothers' Society of Brown University. Founded A.D. 1806. Providence: Knowles & Vose, 1839. 51 p. Rinderknecht 54692. MeB, MNBedf, MWA, PCA, RPB.
                3035

Brown University. United Brothers' Society. Catalogue of the Library and Members of the United Brothers' Society of Brown University. Founded A.D. 1806. Providence: Knowles & Vose, 1841. 59 p. Not in Rinderknecht. CtY, IU (film), MWA, NNC, RPB.   **3036**

Brown University. United Brothers' Society. Triennial Catalogue of the United Brother's Society of Brown University. Instituted A.D. 1806. Providence, 1848. 64 p. Library catalogue on pp. 23-64. MHi, NNC, RPB (copy 2 has ms. additions).   **3037**

Brown University. United Brothers' Society. Catalogue of the Library and the Members of the United Brothers' Society, Brown University. Instituted A.D. 1806. Providence: A. Crawford Greene, 1853. 84 p. NN, PHi, RPB.   **3038**

Central Congregational Church. [Catalogue of the Central Congregational Sabbath School Library]. [Providence, 1863]. 24 p. First page begins with list of officers. "Regulations" dated November 1, 1863. MB (defective without title page).   **3039**

Central Congregational Church. Catalogue of the Central Congregational Sunday School Library. Providence: S. S. Rider, 1875. 21 p. RPB.   **3040**

Chestnut St. Methodist Episcopal Church. Catalogue of the Library of the Chestnut St. M. E. Sunday School. Providence: Providence Press Co., 1871. 46 p. RHi, RPB.   **3041**

Church of the Redeemer. Catalogue of the Church of the Redeemer Sunday School and Parish Library, Providence, R.I. Providence: Knowles, Anthony, 1863. 19 p. MWA, RPB.   **3042**

Church of the Redeemer. Catalogue of the Church of the Redeemer Sunday School and Parish Library, Providence, R.I. Providence: Knowles, Anthony, 1866. 20 p. RPB. **3043**

Cranston Street Baptist Church. Catalogue of Books in the Sunday School Library of the Cranston Street Baptist Church. January 1, 1874. Providence: Providence Press Co., 1874. 24 p. RPB. **3044**

Dana's Circulating Library. Catalogue of Dana's Circulating Library, No. 29, Market-Street, Providence, October, 1824 . . . Providence: John Miller, 1824. 36 p. Operated by George Dana. Not in Shoemaker. NHi (with ms. notes and additions). **3045**

Dana's Circulating Library. Catalogue of Dana's Circulating Library . . . 1828. Providence: Smith and Parmenter, 1828. 40 p. Operated by George Dana. RPB holds Catalogue of Additions, 1832 (8 p.). Shoemaker 32886. MB, RPB. **3046**

Eighth Baptist Church. Catalogue of the Eighth Baptist Sabbath School Library, taken October, 1867 . . . Providence: A. Crawford Greene, 1867. 23 p. Cover title: Catalogue of the Jefferson Street Sabbath School Library . . . RPB (entered under: Providence. United Baptist Church). **3047**

Elmwood Congregational Church. Catalogue of the Sabbath School Library, of the Elmwood Congregational Church. Providence: Providence Press Company, 1870. 26 p. MWA, RHi, RPB (entered under: Providence. Elmwood Christian Church). **3048**

First Baptist Church. Catalogue of the First Baptist Sabbath School Library, taken January, 1852. Providence: H. H. Brown, 1852. 16 p. RPB. **3049**

First Congregational Church. Catalogue of the Juvenile Library of the First Congregational Society in Providence. Providence: Knowles & Vose, 1839. 14 p. Rinderknecht 58124. RP, RPB (with ms. additions). **3050**

First Congregational Church. Catalogue of Sunday School Library of the First Congregational Society. [Providence, 186-?]. 20 p. MBAt. **3051**

First Congregational Church. Catalogue of the Society Library. First Congregational Church. 1870. Providence: Hammond, Angell, 1870. 8 p. RPB. **3052**

First Universalist Church. Catalogue of Books in the Library of the First Universalist Sabbath School, Providence, R.I. January, 1858. School Established in 1825. Providence: Hall & Pierce, 1858. 47 p. RPB. **3053**

First Universalist Church. Catalogue of the Library of the First Universalist Sunday School, Providence, R.I. [Providence]: Gladding Bros. & Tibbitts, 1874. 31 p. MWA. **3054**

Foster's Circulating Library. A Catalogue of Foster's Circulating Library . . . selected from 4000 vols. Providence: Edward and J. W. Cory, 1833. 55 p. Conducted by Adams Foster. Bruntjen 20866. MWA, RPB. **3055**

Franklin Lyceum. Catalogue of the Library of the Franklin Lyceum, Providence . . . Providence: A. Crawford Greene & Brother, 1857. 45 p. CSt, DLC, MWA, NN, RHi, RPB. **3056**

Franklin Lyceum. Charter, Constitution, By-laws, and Catalogue, of the Franklin Lyceum, Providence. Providence: A. Crawford Greene, 1859. vi, 129 p. Catalogue of books on pp. [29]-129. MWA, NN (film), RHi, RPB. **3057**

Franklin Lyceum. Charter, Constitution, By-laws, and Catalogue, of the Franklin Lyceum, Providence. Providence: A. Crawford Greene, 1871. 186 p. DLC, MWA, N, RHi. **3058**

Free Evangelical Congregational Church. Catalogue of the Sabbath School Library, of the Free Evangelical Congregational Church, Roger Williams Hall. Providence: Hammond, Angell, 1869. 23 p. RHi, RPB. **3059**

Friends' First-day School Association. Catalogue of the Library of Friends' First-day School Association, of Providence. 1872. Providence: Ferrin & Hammond, 1872. 21 p. RHi, RPB. **3060**

Grace Church. Catalogue of Grace Church Sunday School Library, Providence, R.I. Providence: B. Cranston, 1838. 19 p. Rinderknecht 52544. RHi. **3061**

Grace Church. Catalogue of Grace Church Sunday School Library. Providence: Benjamin F. Moore, 1841. 24 p. Rinderknecht 41-4367. RPB.   **3062**

Grace Church. Catalogue of Books in the Library of Grace Church Sunday School, Providence. 1844. [Providence, 1844]. 12 p. Rinderknecht 44-5179. RPB.   **3063**

Grace Church. Catalogue of the Library of Grace Church Sunday School, Providence. Providence: John F. Moore, 1851. 25 p. RHi, RPB.   **3064**

Grace Church. Catalogue of Grace Church Sunday School Library, Providence, R.I. Providence: Henry L. Tillinghast, 1856. 24 p. RPB.   **3065**

Grace Church. Catalogue of Grace Church Sunday School Library, Providence, R.I. Providence: A. Crawford Greene & Brother, 1859. 30 p. RPB.   **3066**

Grace Church. Catalogue of the Sunday School Library of Grace Church, Providence. Providence: A. Crawford Greene, 1864. 48 p. RHi, RPB.   **3067**

Grace Church. Catalogue of Grace Church Sunday School Library, Providence. Providence: Sidney S. Rider, 1874. 42 p. RPB.   **3068**

Greenwich Street Free Baptist Church. Catalogue of Books contained in the Greenwich St. Free Baptist Sunday School Library. [Providence, 186-?]. 12 p. RPB (entered under: Providence. Elmwood Avenue Free Baptist Church).   **3069**

High Street Congregational Church. Catalogue of the High Street Congregational Sabbath School Library. January 1, 1868. Providence: Hammond, Angell, 1868. 16 p. RPB.   **3070**

Mechanics' and Apprentices' Library. Catalogue of the Mechanics' and Apprentices' Library. Established by the Association of Mechanics and Manufacturers in Providence, R.I., 1821. [Providence]: Miller and Hutchens, [ca. 1821-23]. 14 p. Not in Shoemaker. MWA.   **3071**

Mechanics' and Apprentices' Library. Catalogue of the Mechanics' and Apprentices' Library, established by the Providence Association of Mechanics and Manufacturers, in the Year 1821. Providence: Cranston & Knowles, 1830. 22 p. Not in Cooper; Rink 572. MWA (defective), RPB.   **3072**

Mechanics' and Apprentices' Library. Catalogue of the Mechanics' and Apprentices' Library, established by the Providence Association of Mechanics and Manufacturers, in the Year 1821. Providence: B. Cranston, 1840. 36 p. Rinderknecht 40-5619. RPA, RPB.   **3073**

Mechanics' and Apprentices' Library. Catalogue of the Mechanics' and Apprentices' Library, established by the Providence Association of Mechanics and Manufacturers, in the Year 1821. Providence: M. B. Young, 1847. 50 p. RPB.   **3074**

Mechanics' and Apprentices' Library. Catalogue of the Mechanics' and Apprentices' Library, established by the Providence Association of Mechanics and Manufacturers, in the Year 1821. Providence: M. B. Young, 1857. 77 p. RPB holds suppl. (12 p.). RPB.   **3075**

Mechanics' and Apprentices' Library. Catalogue of the Mechanics and Apprentices' Library, established by the Providence Association of Mechanics and Manufacturers, in the Year 1821. Providence: Knowles, Anthony, 1866. 176 p. DLC, MWA, NNE, RHi, RPB.   **3076**

Perrin's Circulating Library. Catalogue of Perrin's (late Dana's) Circulating Library . . . Established in 1820 . . . Daniel Perrin, Bookseller & Stationer . . . [Providence]: M. B. Young, 1850. 47 p. Operated by Daniel Perrin. MWA, RHi, RPB.   **3077**

Perrin's Circulating Library. A Catalogue of Books in Perrin's (formerly Dana's) Circulating Library . . . Daniel Perrin, Bookseller & Stationer . . . [Providence]: Young, 1854. 40 p., 4 p. of adv. At head of title: Established in 1820. Operated by Daniel Perrin. RHi (40 p.), RPB.   **3078**

Perrin's Circulating Library. A Catalogue of Books in Perrin's Circulating Library . . . Providence: A. Crawford Greene, 1858. 52 p. Operated by Daniel Perrin. MWA, RHi.   **3079**

Perrin's Circulating Library. Catalogue of Books in Perrin's Circulating Library . . . Daniel Perrin, Bookseller and Stationer . . . [Providence]: Knowles, Anthony, 1866. 48 p. At head of title: Established in 1820. Operated by Daniel Perrin. RHi, RPB.
3080

Perrin's Circulating Library. Catalogue of Books in Perrin's Circulating Library . . . Daniel Perrin, Bookseller and Stationer . . . Providence: A. Crawford Greene, 1874. 60 p. At head of title: Established 1820. Operated by Daniel Perrin. DLC, MWA, RPB.
3081

Pilgrim Congregational Church. Catalogue of the Pilgrim Congregational Sabbath School Library. January, 1875. Providence: Providence Press Co., 1875. 16, [2] p. RPB.
3082

Power Street Methodist Episcopal Church. Catalogue of the Sunday School Library, of the Power Street Methodist Episcopal Church. Providence: B. F. Moore, 1844. 16 p. Rinderknecht 44-5181. RHi.
3083

Providence Athenaeum. Catalogue of the Providence Athenaeum Library. Providence: William Marshall, 1833. 67 p. Bruntjen 20875. MBAt, N, RPB.
3084

Providence Athenaeum. Catalogue of the Athenaeum Library with an Appendix, containing the Library Regulations and a List of the Officers and Proprietors. Providence: Knowles, Vose, 1837. 116, iv p. Rindeknecht 46471. CU-S, DLC, IU, KPT, MBAt, MH, MWA, N, NN, PPL, RNR, RPA, RPB, WHi.
3085

Providence Athenaeum. First Supplementary Catalogue of the Athenaeum Library with an Appendix, containing the Library Regulations and a List of the Officers and Proprietors. Providence: Knowles, Vose, 1839. 107, v p. Rinderknecht 58123. MBAt, MBC, MH, MH-AH, N, NN, NNS, PPL, RP.
3086

Providence Athenaeum. Catalogue of the Library of the Providence Athenaeum. To which are Prefixed the Charter, Constitution and By-laws of the Institution and a List of Proprietors. Providence: Knowles, Anthony, 1852. xii, 452 p. OKentU.   **3087**

Providence Athenaeum. Catalogue of the Library of the Providence Athenaeum. To which are prefixed the Charter, Constitution and By-laws, and an Historical Sketch of the Institution. Providence: Knowles, Anthony, 1853. xxxiv, 557 p., "Appendix," [449]-453 pp. This ed. has an "Alphabetical Index of Subjects." In many libraries.**3088**

Providence Athenaeum. First Supplementary Catalogue of the Library of the Providence Athenaeum. Providence: Knowles, Anthony, 1861. xiv, 374 p. Supplemented by "List of Books added . . ." in *Annual Report of the Directors of the Providence Athenaeum* beginning with no. 27; 1862. CtHT, DeU, DLC, IU, MBAt, MWA, N, NB, RHi, RPB, RU.
3089

Providence Female Benevolent Society. Catalogue of the Library. Providence: W. Simons, 1833. [7] p. Bruntjen 20876. RPB.
3090

Providence Library Company. Charter and By-laws of the Providence Library Company, and a Catalogue of the Books of the Library. Providence: Miller and Hutchens, 1818. 46 p. S & S 45450. MWA, NN, RPB. **3091**

Providence Reform School. A Catalogue of Books belonging to the Library of the Providence Reform School. 1861. Providence: Knowles, Anthony, 1861. 33 p. DLC.
3092

Rhode Island State Prison. Catalogue of Library. Providence: Knowles, Anthony, 1857. xii p. Copy held by M is appended to *Report of the Board of Inspectors of the State Prison of Rhode Island, with the Accompanying Documents, at the January Session of the General Assembly. 1857* (Providence: Knowles, Anthony, 1857). M, RHi, RPB.   **3093**

Rhode Island State Prison. Catalogue of the Library of Rhode Island State Prison. Providence: Providence Press Co., 1867. 25 p. MWA.   **3094**

Rhode Island State Prison. Catalogue of Books in the Library of Rhode Island State Prison. January 1st, 1871. Providence: Hammond, Angell, 1871. 29 p. RHi, RPB.
3095

Rhode Island State Prison. Catalogue of Books in the Library of Rhode Island State

Prison. January 1st, 1874. Providence: Hammond, Angell, 1874. 29 p. RPB. **3096**

Richmond Street Congregational Church. Catalogue of the Richmond-St Congregational Sabbath School Library. January, 1849. Providence: B. T. Albro, 1849. 33 p. RPB.   **3097**

Richmond Street Congregational Church. Catalogue of the Richmond Street Congregational Sabbath School Library. January, 1860. Providence: M. B. Young, 1860. 24 p. RPB.   **3098**

Rider's Select Library. Catalogue of Rider's Select Library . . . [Providence, 187-?]. 41 p. Operated by Sidney Smith Rider. RHi, RPB.
3099

Robinson's Circulating Library. Catalogue of M. Robinson's Circulating Library, consisting of about 3000 Volumes . . . Providence: John Miller, 1823. 52 p. Shoemaker 13886. RPB.   **3100**

Robinson's Circulating Library. Catalogue of Additions to M. Robinson's Library from 1823 to January, 1825. [Providence, 1825]. 11 p. Shoemaker 22004. RPB.   **3101**

Robinson's Circulating Library. Catalogue of Additions to M. Robinson's Library, from Jan. 1825 to Jan. 1827. [Providence, 1827]. 6 p. Shoemaker 29558. RPB.   **3102**

Robinson's Circulating Library. Additions to M. Robinson's Library, for 1827. [Providence, 1827]. 7 p. Not in Shoemaker. RPB.
3103

Robinson's Circulating Library. Additions to M. Robinson's Library, for 1829. Providence: Eastman & Hall, 1829. 9 p. Shoemaker 40197. RPB.   **3104**

Robinson's Circulating Library. Catalogue of Additions to M. Robinson's Library, for 1830 & 1831. Providence: Cranston & Hammond, 1831. 16 p. Bruntjen 8899. RPB.   **3105**

Robinson's Circulating Library. Catalogue of Additions, for 1832. [Providence?, 1832?]. 8 p. Bruntjen 14419. RPB.   **3106**

Roger Williams Free Baptist Church. Catalogue of Books in the Library of Roger

Williams F. W. B. Sunday-School, Providence, R.I. Providence: A. Crawford Greene, 1853. 16 p. RPB.   **3107**

Roger Williams Free Baptist Church. A Catalogue of the Books, belonging to the Roger Williams Freewill Baptist Sabbath School Library . . . Providence: A. C. Greene, 1860. 20 p. RPB (defective).**3108**

Roger Williams Free Baptist Church. A Catalogue of the Books, belonging to the Roger Williams Free Baptist Sabbath School Library. Providence, 1870. 27 p. MHi.**3109**

St. Andrew's Church. Catalogue of Saint Andrews Sabbath School Library. [Providence?, ca. 1860]. 8 p. RPB.   **3110**

St. Andrew's Church. Catalogue of Sunday School Library of Saint Andrew's Church. Providence: H. H. Thomas, 1865. 19 p. RPB.   **3111**

St. Gabriel's Mission. Catalogue of Sunday School Library Books, of St. Gabriel's Mission, Providence, R.I. Providence: Tillinghast & Mason, 1871. 8 p. RHi, RPB.
3112

St. James' Church. Catalogue of the Sunday School Library of St. James' Church, Providence, R.I. Providence: Hammond, Angell, 1869. 12 p. RPB.   **3113**

St. John's Church. Catalogue of St. John's Church Sabbath School Library. Providence: H. H. Brown, 1843. 17 p. Not in Rinderknecht. RPB.   **3114**

St. John's Church. Catalogue of Saint John's Church Sunday School Library, Providence, R.I. Providence: Knowles, Anthony, 1866. 22 p. RPB.   **3115**

St. John's Church. Catalogue of the Sunday School Library of Saint John's Church, Providence, R.I. Providence: J. A. & R. A. Reid, 1875. 20 p. RPB.   **3116**

St. Joseph's Church. Catalogue of Books in St. Joseph's Church Library. December, 1875. Providence: Providence Press Co., 1875. 16 p. RHi, RPB.   **3117**

St. Stephen's Church. Catalogue of St. Stephen's Sabbath School Library. 1857. [Providence, 1857]. 24 p. RPB.   **3118**

St. Stephen's Church. Catalogue of Saint Stephen's Church Sunday School Library, Providence, R.I. Providence: Cooke & Danielson, 1862. 19 p. RPB.   **3119**

St. Stephen's Church. Catalogue of Saint Stephen's Church Sunday School Library, Providence, R.I. Providence: A. Crawford Greene, 1866. 26 p. RPB.   **3120**

South Providence Methodist Episcopal Church. Catalogue of the Library of the South Providence M. E. Sunday School. 1870. [Providence, 1870]. 11 p. RPB (entered under: Providence. St. Paul's M. E. Church).   **3121**

Stewart Street Baptist Church. Catalogue of the Stewart St. Baptist Sunday School Library. Providence: John F. Greene, 1869. 19 p. RPB.   **3122**

Third Baptist Church. Catalogue of the Third Baptist Sunday School Library, Providence, R.I. Providence: Gladding, Brother and Co., 1871. 21 p. RPB.   **3123**

Trinity Methodist Episcopal Church. Catalogue of the Library of the Trinity M. E. Church Sunday School, Providence, R.I. Providence: Millard & Harker, 1869. 31 p. RPB.   **3124**

Trinity Methodist Episcopal Church. Catalogue of the Library of the Trinity M. E. Church Sunday School, Providence, R.I. Providence: Providence Press Co., 1872. 43 p. RPB.   **3125**

Westminster Circulating Library. List of Books added to the Westminster Circulating Library . . . since the former Catalogues were Printed. Laban W. Winsor, Proprietor. Providence: Laban W. Winsor, 1849. 32 p. At head of title: September, 1849. No. 2. MWA, RHi, RPB.   **3126**

Westminster Circulating Library. A Catalogue of Books in the Westminster Circulating Library . . . Providence: Elisha S. Winsor, 1852. 52 p. At head of title: Established May, 1848. No. 3. Operated by Elisha S. Winsor. See also entry 3130. DLC, RHi, RPB. **3127**

Westminster Congregational Church. Catalogue of the Libraries connected with the Westminster Congregational Sunday School and Church, Providence, R.I. Prepared

September, 1859. Providence: George H. Whitney, 1859. 44 p. RPB.   **3128**

Westminster Congregational Church. Catalogue of the Libraries connected with the Westminster Congregational Sunday School and Church, Providence, R.I. Prepared August, 1868. Providence: Providence Press Co., 1868. 37 p. RPB.   **3129**

Wheelock's Circulating Library. Catalogue of Books in Wheelock's (late Winsor's) Circulating Library . . . Providence: Knowles, Anthony, 1855. 55 p. At head of title: Established May, 1848. No. 4. Operated by Elijah Wheelock. See also entry 3127. RHi, RPB.   **3130**

Woonasquatucket Reading Room. Catalogue of the Circulating Library belonging to the Woonasquatucket Reading Room. Providence: Sidney S. Rider, 1875. 62 p. RPB.   **3131**

Woonasquatucket Reading Room. Catalogue of the Circulating Library belonging to the Woonasquatucket Reading Room. Providence, 1875. 36 p. RPB.   **3132**

Young Men's Christian Association. Catalogue of the Young Men's Christian Association of Providence . . . Providence: M. B. Young, 1856. 48 p. Cover title: Catalogue of the Young Men's Christian Association Library of Providence. DLC, RPB.   **3133**

Young Men's Christian Association. Catalogue of the Library of the Providence Young Men's Christian Association. Providence: Knowles, Anthony, 1860. 95 p. DLC, RPB.   **3134**

Young Men's Christian Association. Catalogue of the Young Men's Christian Association, Providence, R.I. Organized September, 1853. Central Falls: E. L. Freeman, 1873. 129 p. DLC, RPB.   **3135**

Young Men's Christian Union. Catalogue of the Free Library of the Providence Young Men's Christian Union. Providence: Pierce and Berry, 1859. 21 p. DLC, RPB.   **3136**

Slatersville

Slatersville Library. Catalogue and Regulations of the Slatersville Library, established in 1848. Slatersville: Lincoln & Hickcox, 1848. 19 p. MWA.   **3137**

Slatersville Sabbath School. Catalogue of Books contained in the Slatersville Sabbath School Library. September, 1869. Providence: A. Crawford Greene, 1869. 24 p. RHi.   **3138**

Smithfield, see Slatersville.

South Kingstown

(see also Kingston)

Narragansett Library Association. Catalogue of Books belonging to the Narragansett Library Association, South Kingstown, R.I. Wakefield: Duncan Gillies, 1861. 24 p. RHi, RPB.   **3139**

Warren

Methodist Episcopal Church. Catalogue of the Sunday School Library. Warren M. E. Church. [Providence?, 186-?]. 10 p. RHi, RPB.   **3140**

Methodist Episcopal Church. Catalogue of the Sabbath School Library, Warren, R.I. (Revised 1872). Providence: Providence Press Co., 1872. 24 p. RPB.   **3141**

St. Mark's Church. Catalogue of Books in the Library of St. Mark's Church Sunday School, Warren, R.I. Providence: M. B. Young, 1852. 12 p. RHi.   **3142**

Warren Baptist Church. Catalogue of Books in the Warren Baptist Sabbath School. Providence, 1870. 20 p. RHi (lost).   **3143**

Warren Public Reading Room Association. Catalogue of the Warren Public Reading Room Association Library. Established 1871. Providence: Providence Press Co., 1872. 43 p. RPB holds incomplete file of supplements to 1887.   MWA, RHi, RPB (entered under: George Hail Free Library).   **3144**

Warwick

Old Warwick Library Association. Catalogue of Books, belonging to the Old Warwick Library Association. Instituted, A.D. 1847. Providence: John F. Moore, 1848. 12 p. RHi.   **3145**

Old Warwick Library Association. Catalogue of Books in the Old Warwick Library

Association. Jan. 1, 1870. Providence: A. Grawford [sic] Greene, [1870]. 20 p. DLC, RHi, RPB.   **3146**

Union Library Association. Catalogue of Books in the Library of the Union Library Association, Phenix Village, Warwick, R.I., with a Sketch of the Rise and Progress of the Association, and a Copy of its Constitution and By-laws. Providence: A. Crawford Greene, 1852. 36 p. RHi, RPB.   **3147**

West Warwick, see Centreville, Warwick.

Westerly

First Baptist Sabbath School. Catalogue of the First Baptist Sabbath School Library, Westerly, R.I. 1870. Providence: A. Crawford Greene, 1870. 13 p. RPB.   **3148**

Pawcatuck Library Association. Catalogue of Books in the Library of the Pawcatuck Library Association, Westerly, R.I., with a Sketch of the Organization of the Association, a Copy of its Constitution and By-laws, and Hints respecting Reading. Providence, 1849. xviii, 92 p. Sabin 59258 records an unlocated 1848 ed. of 120 p. CtHT, CtY, DLC, RHi, RPB.   **3149**

Woonsocket

Carrington Library Association. Catalogue of Books in the Library of the Carrington Library Association, Woonsocket, R.I., with a Sketch of its History and Organization; A Copy of its Charter, Constitution, By-laws, and Rules and Regulations; and Hints respecting Reading. Woonsocket: Samuel S. Foss, 1854. xxxii, 56 p. Printed in Boston by John Wilson and Son. MB, RHi.   **3150**

Harris Institute Free Library. Catalogue of Books in the Harris Institute Free Library, Woonsocket, R.I., with Rules and Regulations. Woonsocket: S. S. Foss, 1869. 92 p. DLC holds suppl., Nov. 1869-March 1, 1875; RHi holds 1869-1871 (lost). DLC, MB.
3151

Universalist Church. Catalogue of Books belonging to the Universalist Sabbath School Library, Woonsocket, R.I. [Woonsocket?, 186-?]. 15 p. MWA.   **3152**

Universalist Church. Catalogue of Books in the Library of the Universalist Sabbath

School, Woonsocket, R.I. Boston: Bazin & Chandler, 1862. 20 p. RHi, RPB.   **3153**

Universalist Church. Supplementary Catalogue of Books belonging to the Library of the Universalist Sabbath School, Woonsocket. October 1st, 1870. Woonsocket: Patriot Steam Press, 1870. 32 p. RHi. **3154**

Woonsocket Baptist Sabbath School. Catalogue of the Woonsocket Baptist Sabbath School Library. April, 1866. Worcester: Evening Gazette Office, [1866]. 11 p. MWA.   **3155**

SOUTH CAROLINA

Beaufort

Beaufort Library. A Catalogue of the Books and Maps in the Beaufort Library. Charleston: Steam Power-Press of Walker and James, 1852. 24 p.; suppl., 12 p. On cover: Charleston: Steam Power Press of Walker, Evans, & Co., 1859. DLC, MH-AH, NcD.   **3156**

Beaufort Library. Government Sale. Catalogue of an immense Collection of Library Books in all Departments of Literature, Arts and Sciences . . . to be sold at Auction, by and under the Direction of Hiram Barney, esq., Collector of the Port of N.Y., on Monday Evening, Nov. 17th, 1862 and the succeeding Evenings of the Week, by Bangs, Merwin & Co. [New York]: C. C. Shelley, [1862]. 95 p. Seized by the Union army during the Civil War; see Sabin 28159 for additional information. DLC, MiU-C, NN. **3157**

Charleston

Apprentices' and Minors' Library Society. Catalogue of Books in the Apprentices' and Minors' Library Society, of Charleston, S.C. Charleston: Walker, Evans & Cogswell, 1873. 19 p. DLC, NcU.   **3158**

Apprentices' Library Society. Catalogue of the Books belonging to the Apprentices' Library Society of Charleston, S.C. Charleston: B. B. Hussey, 1840. 336 p. Cover title: Catalogue of the Books belonging to the Charleston Apprentices' Library Society . . . January 1st, 1841 . . . Charleston: B. B.

Hussey, 1841 (ScCC copy). Rinderknecht 40-1364. DLC, ScCC, ScU.   **3159**

Charleston College. Catalogue of Books in the Library of the Charleston College. Charleston: Miller & Browne, 1849. 36 p. DLC.**3160**

Charleston Library Society. Catalogue . . . 1802. 62 p. Not in S & S. Cf. Cutter 44.
3161

Charleston Library Society. A Catalogue of Books belonging to the Charleston Library Society. May, 1806. Charleston: W. P. Young, 1806. 79 p. S & S 10118. MBAt, NcU, PPL.   **3162**

Charleston Library Society. Supplement. 1st October 1806. [Charleston, 1806]. 4 p. PPL holds 2d suppl., 1st July, 1807 (7 p.). S & S 50658. NcU, PPL.   **3163**

Charleston Library Society. A Catalogue of Books, belonging to the Charleston Library Society. January, 1811. Charleston: W. P. Young, 1811. 146 p. S & S 22515. CFlS, GU, MWA (interleaved), NN (interleaved), NNGr (interleaved), NNS, NdU, PPAmP, PPL (interleaved), ScC, ScG, ScU, TxU, ViU,   **3164**

Charleston Library Society. Supplement. Antiquities, Arts and Sciences, Books of Charts, Maps, and Prints. [Charleston, ca. 1816-18]. [approx. 23 p.]. Not in S & S. ScC.   **3165**

Charleston Library Society. Supplementary Catalogue of Books, belonging to the Charleston Library Society. which have been purchased, or presented since January, 1811. Charleston: J. Hoff, 1816. 21 p. Caption title: Supplement to the Catalogue of Books, belonging to the Charleston Library Society. S & S 37214. MH-H, MWA, ScC.   **3166**

Charleston Library Society. Supplementary Catalogue of Books which have been purchased or presented since January, 1816. Charleston, 1818. Not in S & S. WU (School of Library and Information Studies; lost).   **3167**

Charleston Library Society. A Catalogue of the Books belonging to the Charleston Library Society . . . Charleston: A. E. Miller, 1826. xvi, 375, [1] p. Shoemaker 24063.

CtY, DLC, LNT, MBAt, MH, MWA, MiU-C, NHi, NIC, NN, PPAmP, PPL, ScC, ScHi, ScU, TxU. **3168**

Charleston Library Society. A Supplemental Catalogue, alphabetically arranged, of all the Books, Maps & Pamphlets which have been procured by the Charleston Library Society, since the Publication of the First Volume of their Catalogue in 1826. Charleston: J. S. Burges, 1831. 46, [1] p. Bruntjen 6470. DLC, MWA, NN, PPAmP, PPL, ScHi, ScU. **3169**

Charleston Library Society. A Second Supplemental Catalogue, alphabetically arranged of all the Books, Maps and Pamphlets, procured by the Charleston Library Society, since the Publication of the First Supplement in 1831. To which is annexed a List of the Names of the Present Officers and Members of the Society . . . Charleston: A. E. Miller, 1835. 76 p. Rinderknecht 30877. MWA, NN, PPAmP, PPL. **3170**

Charleston Library Society. A Catalogue of the Books of the Charleston Library Society, purchased since 1826, with a List of Present Officers & Members. Volume II . . . Charleston: Miller & Browne, 1845. xi, 144 p. DLC, KyLoS, LU, MiU-C, ScC, ScCF, ScU, TxU. **3171**

Charleston Library Society. A List of Books obtained by the Charleston Library Society, since the Publication of the Second Vol. of the Catalogue of Books, being the First Supplement to the same . . . Charleston: Miller & Browne, 1847. 21 p. DLC, MWA, ScC. **3172**

Charleston Library Society. A List of Books, Maps and Pamphlets, obtained by the Charleston Library Society, since the Publication of their last Supplement in 1847, to the First of January, 1854. Prepared by William Logan, Librarian . . . Charleston: A. E. Miller, 1854. 62 p. DLC, ScC. **3173**

Charleston Library Society. List of Books received by the Charleston Library Society, from October 20, 1874 to June 1, 1875. [Charleston?, 1875?]. 4 p. Sc. **3174**

Döscher, B. Catalog der Deutschen Leih-Bibliothek von B. Döscher . . . [Charleston]: Gedruckt in der Office der "Deutschen Zeitung," 1872. 16 p. DLC, LNT. **3175**

Kappelmann, Moritz Heinrich. Verzeichniss von Büchern, welche in der Leihbibliothek von M. H. Kappelmann & Co. Nr. 119 Meetingstrasse zum Lesen zu haben sind. Charleston: H. M. Hinck, 1850. 8 p. MWA. **3176**

Medical Society of South Carolina. Laws and Resolutions, of the Medical Society of South-Carolina, instituted at Charleston, December 24, 1789. Incorporated 10th May, 1794. With a List of the Members, and a Catalogue of the Books annexed. Charleston: Printed at the Courier Office, 1806. 31 p. S & S 10843, Austin 1266. NNNAM, PPL. **3177**

Medical Society of South Carolina. Laws and Resolutions, of the Medical Society of South-Carolina, instituted at Charleston, December 24, 1789. Incorporated 10th May, 1794. With a List of the Members, and a Catalogue of the Books annexed. Charleston: Printed at the Courier Office, 1820. 44 p. Shoemaker 2202, Austin 1267. DNLM, ScCM. **3178**

Medical Society of South Carolina. By-laws of the Medical Society of South-Carolina, instituted at Charleston, December 24, 1789. Incorporated 10th May, 1794. To-gether with a List of its Officers and Members. Also, Rules and Resolutions of the Medical College of South-Carolina. A Catalogue of the Society's Books, and the Charleston Fee Bill. Charleston: C. C. Sebring, 1826. 69 p. Shoemaker 25295. DLC, ScCM. **3179**

Medical Society of South Carolina. By-laws of the Medical Society of South-Carolina, instituted at Charleston, December 24, 1789. Incorporated 10th May, 1794. To-gether with a List of its Officers and Members. Also, Rules and Resolutions of the Medical College of South-Carolina. A Catalogue of the Society's Books, and the Charleston Fee Bill. Charleston: J. S. Burges, 1834. 87 p. Rinderknecht 25654. CtY-M (photostat of catalogue only), MHi, NN, ScCC, ScCM. **3180**

Medical Society of South Carolina. Constitution & By-laws of the Medical Society of South-Carolina, instituted at Charleston, Dec. 24, 1789. Incorporated May 10, 1794. Together with a List of its Officers and

Members. Also, a Catalogue of the Society's Books, and the Charleston Fee Bill. Charleston: Hayden & Burke, 1842. 100 p. Rinderknecht 42-3334. CtY-M (photostat of catalogue section only), MBCo, MH-M, ScCM.   **3181**

Medical Society of South Carolina. Constitution and By-laws of the Medical Society of South-Carolina, instituted at Charleston, December 24, 1789. Incorporated May 10, 1794. Together with a List of its Officers and Members. Also, a Catalogue of the Society's Books, and the Charleston Fee Bill. Charleston: Walker and James, 1850. xii, 82 p. DLC, DNLM, ScCM.   **3182**

Protestant Episcopal Society for the Advancement of Christianity in South-Carolina. The Ninth Annual Report of the Board of Trustees of the Protestant Episcopal Society for the Advancement of Christianity in South-Carolina, made at the Anniversary of the Society, January 6th, 1819. To which are annexed, the Constitution of the Society, incorporated Dec. 19, 1810; Instructions for the Regulation of the Missionaries employed by the Society . . . Rules respecting the Theological Library, and a Catalogue of the Books purchased the Past Year; A Plan to Establish a Permanent Fund for Building Episcopal Churches in the Diocese of South-Carolina; and a List of Members & Benefactors for the last Year. Charleston: A. E. Miller, 1819. 24 p. S & S 49215. MWA, PPAmP, ScCC.   **3183**

St. John's Lutheran Church. Catalogue of the St. John's Lutheran Sunday-School Library, Clifford Street, Charleston, S.C. Charleston: S.C. Walker, Evans & Cogswell, 1874. 24 p. ScHi.   **3184**

Unitarian Church. Rules of the Library of the Unitarian Church, Charleston, S.C., together with a Catalogue of the Books. Charleston: E. J. Van Brunt, 1835. 26 p. Rinderknecht 30874. MH-H.   **3185**

Columbia

Legislative Library, see South Carolina. General Assembly.

South Carolina. General Assembly. Catalogue of Books, belonging to the Legislative Library, at Columbia. June 10, 1826.

Columbia: D. & J. M. Faust, 1826. 12 p. Not in Shoemaker. MWA.   **3186**

South Carolina. General Assembly. Catalogue of Books and Pamphlets, belonging to the Legislative Library. Columbia: I. C. Morgan's Book and Job Office, 1841. 24 p. Rinderknecht 41-4878. DLC.   **3187**

South Carolina. General Assembly. Catalogue of Books and Pamphlets in the Library of the Legislature of South Carolina. January 1, 1850. Columbia: A. S. Johnston, 1850. 68 p. Sc, ScU.   **3188**

South Carolina College. Catalogue of Books belonging to the South-Carolina College Library. Columbia: Daniel and J. J. Faust, 1807. 36 p. S & S 13621. DLC (with ms. additions), IU (film of DLC copy with ms. additions?), MWA (defective), ScU (defective).   **3189**

South Carolina College. Catalogue of Books, in the South-Carolina College Library. August 23, 1814. Columbia: Daniel and J. J. Faust, 1814. 47 p. Not in S & S. MH, N, NN.
                                      3190

South Carolina College. Catalogue of Books in the South-Carolina College Library. September 1, [18]19. Columbia: Daniel Faust, 1819. 54 p. S & S 49465. ScU. **3191**

South Carolina College. Catalogue of the Library of the South Carolina College . . . Columbia: Telescope Print., 1836. xii, 112, xxxv p. Rinderknecht 40261. DLC (lacks group of xxxv p. at end), GDecCT, ICU, IU (film), N, ScCMes, ScU.   **3192**

South Carolina College. Catalogue of the Library of the South Carolina College. Columbia: A. S. Johnston, 1849. 151 p. DLC, DSI, IU (film), KyU, LU, MWA, N, NN, NcD, NcG, NcWsW, PPL, RPB, ScFlM, ScG, ScU.   **3193**

Greenwood

Hodges Institute. Catalogue . . . 1855. Cf. Rhees, pp. 461-62.   **3194**

Society Hill

Society Hill Library Society. Catalogue of Books, belonging to the Society-Hill Library Society. July 11th, 1840. Charleston: A. E.

Miller, 1840. 23 p. Rinderknecht 40-6223. NcU, ScHi. **3195**

Society Hill Library Society. Catalogue of Books belonging to the Society Hill Library Society, Society Hill, South Carolina. July 1850. Philadelphia: C. Sherman, 1850. Cf. Barrett Wilkens, *A Bibliography of South Carolina Library History* (Tallahassee, 1973), #298. **3196**

TENNESSEE

Nashville

Mechanics Library Association. Constitution and By-laws of the Mechanics Library Association, Nashville. Nashville: Hogan & Heiss, 1842. 32 p. Library catalogue on pp. [15]-32. Not in Rinderknecht. TU. **3197**

Nashville Library Company. Catalogue of Books in the Nashville Library. March 1825. Nashville: Joseph Norvell, 1825. 18, [2] p. Not in Shoemaker. TN (photocopy of original held by the late Stanley Horn, Tennessee State Historian). **3197a**

Tennessee State Library. Catalogue of the Tennessee State Library. October, 1855. Nashville: [A. A. Stitt], 1855. xiv, 119 p. Ct, DLC, M, MBAt, MH, MWA, Nh, N, NN, OKentU, T, TU, ViU. **3198**

Tennessee State Library. Catalogue of the General and Law Library of the State of Tennessee. Prepared by Order of the Judges of the Supreme Court, Mrs. Paralee Haskell, State Librarian. Nashville: Jones, Purvis, 1871. viii, 432 p. Compiled by George S. Blackie. In many libraries. **3199**

TEXAS

Galveston

Galveston Mercantile Library. Bulletin of Books. No. 1-2; Jan.-July 1871. Galveston, 1871. Bulletin for Jan. 1871 has cover title: Bulletin of Books in the Galveston Mercantile Library. With a List of Newspapers and Periodicals on File in the Reading Rooms. Established, 1870. Galveston: Printed for the Library Department of the Chamber of Commerce by Robert Clark, 1871. DLC

(undetermined holdings), MB (#1-2), MHi (#2), TxU (#2). **3200**

UTAH

Salt Lake City

University of Deseret. Catalogue of Books in the Library of the University of Deseret. Salt Lake City: Deseret News Steam Printing Establishment, 1875. 86 p. DLC, MB, UU. **3201**

Utah Territorial Library. Catalogue of the Utah Territorial Library. October, 1852. Great Salt Lake City: Brigham H. Young, 1852. 62 p. MnU, UPB. **3202**

VERMONT

Barre

Congregational Church. Catalogue of Books in Congregational S. S. Library, Barre, Vt. Montpelier: Argus and Patriot Job Printing House, 1874. [4] p. VtHi. **3203**

Bennington

Bennington Free Library. Catalogue of the Free Library, donated to the Citizens of Bennington, by Seth B. Hunt, Esq., and Trenor W. Park, Esq., June 23d, A.D. 1865. Troy: Troy Daily Times Establishment, 1866. 52 p. Bennington Free Library, VtHi (24 p. only), VtU. **3204**

Bennington Free Library. Catalogue of the Free Library, donated to the Citizens of Bennington, by Seth B. Hunt, Esq., and Trenor W. Park, Esq., June 23d, A.D. 1865. Bennington: C. A. Pierce, 1872. 120 p. Bennington Free Library, DLC, MWA, VtHi, VtU. **3205**

Brandon

Congregational Church. Catalogue of the Brandon Congregational S. S. Library. March, 1873. [n.p., 1873]. 11 p. VtHi. **3206**

Brattleboro

Brattleboro Library Association. Catalogue of Books, belonging to the Brattleboro'

Library Association, founded, October, 1842. [Brattleboro: Wm. E. Rythed, 1845?]. 12 p. Not in Rinderknecht. MWA. **3207**

Brattleboro Village Library. Catalogue of the Brattleboro Village Library. Brattleboro: F. D. Cobleigh, 1871. 62 p. On cover: Catalogue of the Brattleboro Library Association. Brattleboro: F. D. Cobleigh, 1872. MWA. **3208**

Brattleboro Village Library. Catalogue of the Brattleboro Village Library. E. J. Carpenter, Librarian. Brattleboro: J. H. Capen, 1860. 43 p. MWA. **3209**

Brattleboro Village Library. Catalogue of the Brattleboro Village Library. Brattleboro: F. D. Cobleigh, 1871. 62 p. DLC, MWA. **3210**

Brookfield

Brookfield Library. A Catalogue of Books in the Brookfield Library. [Windsor?, 1812]. 16 p. S & S 24940. MWA. **3211**

Burlington

Burlington Mechanics' Institute. A Catalogue of the Library of the Burlington Mechanics' Institute, with the Constitution of the Association. Organized December, 1842. Burlington: Stilman Fletcher, 1845 [i.e. 1847]. 16 p. Cover title: Constitution and Catalogue of Books, of the Burlington Mechanics' Institute, with the By-laws of the Library, and a List of Members, January 4, 1847. "Additions to the Library from March, 1845, to January 4, 1847" on pp. [13]-16. VtU. **3212**

First Congregational Church. Catalogue of the Parish Library of the First Congregational Society, Burlington, Vermont. Burlington: George J. Stacy, 1852. 42 p. VtU. **3213**

First Congregational Church. Catalogue of the Sunday School Library, of the First Congregational Society, Burlington, Vt. Burlington: Stacy & Jameson, 1854. 26 p. Cf. Gilman, p. 45. **3213a**

First Congregational Church. Catalogue of the Sunday School Library of the First Congregational Society in Burlington, Vt. Burlington: Times Press, 1868. 30 p. VtU. **3214**

First Congregational Church. Catalogue of Books in the Teacher's Library, First Calv. Congregational Church, Burlington, Vt. April, 1873. Burlington: Free Press Steam Job Printing House, 1873. 15 p. VtU copy contains "Additions to July, 1879" ([2] p.). VtU. **3215**

First Congregational Church. Catalogue of the S. S. Library of the First Congregational Church, Wincoski Avenue, Burlington, Vt. Burlington: Free Press Steam Printing House, 1875. 16 p. VtU. **3216**

Methodist Episcopal Church. Catalogue of Sunday School Books of the M. E. Church, Burlington, Vt. June 1, 1871. Burlington: R. S. Styles, 1871. 23 p. VtU. **3217**

St. Paul's Church. Catalogue of Books belonging to St. Paul's Parish Library, Burlington, Vt. Burlington: Chauncey Goodrich, 1847. [12] p. VtU (lost?). **3218**

St. Paul's Church. Catalogue of the Sunday School Library of St. Paul's Church, Burlington, Vt. [Burlington, 186-?]. 28 p. VtU has suppl., 1868 (9 p.). VtU (lost?). **3219**

St. Paul's Church. Catalogue of the Sunday School Library of St. Paul's Church, Burlington, Vt. October 10th, 1874. [Burlington, 1874?]. 12 p. VtU (lost?). **3220**

University of Vermont. Catalogue of the Books belonging to the Library of the University of Vermont. Burlington: Vernon Harrington, 1836. 93, [1] p. Rinderknecht 42266 (based incorrectly on the 1843 ed.). In many libraries. **3221**

University of Vermont. Catalogue of the Books belonging to the Library of the University of Vermont. Burlington: Vernon Harrington, 1836 [i.e. 1843]. 93, [1], 24, [1] p. Second group (24 p.) is an "Alphabetical Supplement. 1842" issued with the reprinted catalogue of 1836 (Burlington, 1843). Rinderknecht 42266 (under 1836). DLC, MH, MWA, NNC, RPB, VtU. **3222**

University of Vermont. Alphabetical and Analytical Catalogue of the Library of the University of Vermont, Burlington. Burlington: Free Press Office, 1854. iv, 163, [1] p. In many libraries. **3223**

University of Vermont. Phi Sigma Nu Society. A Catalogue of Books, in the Library of the Phi Sigma Nu Society, of the University of Vermont. Burlington: University Press, 1846. 40 p. MA, MH, MHi, MWA, NNUT, VtU. **3224**

University of Vermont. University Institute Society. A Catalogue of Books belonging to the Library of the University Institute Society of the University of Vermont. Burlington: Chauncey Goodrich, 1851. 26, [1] p. MA, MB, MBC, MH, NB, VtU. **3225**

Young Men's Association. Catalogue of the Library of the Young Men's Association of Burlington, Vermont. Burlington: R. S. Styles' Steam Job Printing House, 1872. 48 p. DLC, MWA, VtU. **3226**

Young Men's Association. Supplement to Catalogue of the Young Men's Association of Burlington, Vermont. May 1st, 1873. [Burlington, 1873]. 8 p. DLC. **3227**

Castleton

Castleton Congregational Church. Catalogue of Books in the Castleton Congregational Sabbath School Library, Castleton, Vermont. Rutland: McLean & Robbins, 1867. 7 p. N (misc. pamphlet box, 027.8). **3228**

Cavendish

Fletcher Town Library. Catalogue of the Fletcher Town Library of Cavendish, with the Regulations. Ludlow: Gazette Job Dept., 1871. 46 p. Vt, VtU. **3229**

Chester

Stone Chapel. Catalogue of Oberlin Sabbath School Library, Stone Chapel, Chester, Vt. [Boston?, 1868?]. 8 p. MB. **3230**

Cornwall

Lane Library Association. Constitution and By-laws of the Lane Library Association, with a Catalogue of its Library. Middlebury: Printed at the Register Book and Job Office, 1860. 30 p. N, Vt, VtMiS, VtU. **3231**

Ludlow

Baptist Sabbath School. Catalogue of the Baptist Sabbath School Library, Ludlow, Vt.

March 1st, 1875. Ludlow: R. S. Warner, 1875. [20] p. VtHi. **3232**

Middlebury

Goodrich, Chauncey. Catalogue of Books belonging to the Circulating Library of C. Goodrich. Middlebury, (Vt.) April, 1828. [Middlebury?, 1828]. 8 p. Not in Shoemaker. Vt. **3233**

Ladies' Circulating Library. Catalogue of the Ladies' Circulating Library, Middlebury, Vt. Organized March, 1866. Middlebury: Printed at the Register Job Office, 1870. 20 p. VtU. **3234**

Middlebury College. The Laws of Middlebury College. Middlebury: T. C. Strong, 1811. 16, xi p. "Catalogue of Books in the Library of Middlebury College" (xi p.) at end. S & S 23384 does not call for the extra xi p. CtY, MH, NjP, VtHi, VtMiM (defective). **3235**

Middlebury College. Catalogue of Books in the Library of Middlebury College. April 1st, 1823. [Middlebury], 1823. 18 p. Not in Shoemaker. VtMiM, VtU. **3236**

Middlebury College. Laws and Catalogue of the Library of Middlebury College. 1823. [Middlebury, 1823]. 24 p. Shoemaker 13331. WHi. **3237**

Middlebury College. Catalogue of Books in the Library of Middlebury College. 1833. [Middlebury, 1833]. 16 p. Bruntjen 20136. MBC, NN, VtMiM, VtMiS, WHi. **3238**

Middlebury College. Catalogue of Books in the Library of Middlebury College. 1833. [Middlebury, 1833]. 29 p. Printed in a single column on left hand side of page. Unrecorded variant of Bruntjen 20136. MH (lost?), MWA. **3239**

Middlebury College. Catalogue of the Library of Middlebury College. Middlebury: Printed at the Register Book and Job Office, 1859. 37 p. DLC, MBC, MH, VtMiM, VtMiS, VtU, WHi. **3240**

Middlebury College. Philological Society. Catalogue of Books belonging to the Library of the Philological Society of Middlebury College, together with those deposited for the use of itsMembers. Middlebury: J. W. Copeland, 1823. 15, [1] p. Shoemaker 13333. NhD, NN, VtMiM.   **3241**

Middlebury College. Philological Society. Catalogue of Books belonging to the Library of the Philological Society of Middlebury College, together with those deposited for the use of its Members. Middlebury: J. W. Copeland, 1824. 60 p. Shoemaker 17154. ICRL, M, MA, MBC, MWiW, NN, NNG, OCHP, RPB, Vt, VtHi, VtMiM, VtU, ViU, WHi.   **3242**

Middlebury College. Philomathesian Society. Catalogue of Books, in the Library of the Philomathesian Society, in Middlebury College. Middlebury: Francis Burnap, 1819. 13 p. S & S 48690. MWA.   **3243**

Middlebury College. Philomathesian Society. Catalogue of Books belonging to the Philomathesian Society, of Middlebury College. May 17, 1827. [Castleton: Press of the Vermont Statesman, 1827]. 12 p. Not in S & S. Vt.   **3244**

Middlebury College. Philomathesian Society. Catalogue of Books belonging to the Library of the Philomathesian Society, Middlebury College. 1832. Middlebury: H. H. Houghton, 1832. 12 p. Bruntjen 13742. MWA, VtMiM, VtMidSm, VtMiS.   **3245**

Middlebury College. Philomathesian Society. Catalogue of the Library of Philomathesian Society of Middlebury College. Middlebury: Office of the People's Press, 1837. 24 p. Rinderknecht 45609. NN, VtMiM, WHi.   **3246**

Middlebury College. Philomathesian Society. Alphabetical Catalogue of the Library of the Philomathesian Society, Middlebury College. 1844. Middlebury: Ephraim Maxham, 1844. 27 p. Rinderknecht 44-4236. NNC, Vt, VtHi, VtMiM, VtU.   **3247**

Montpelier

Bethany Church. Catalogue of the Bethany Church Sunday School Library, Montpelier, Vermont. January 1, 1871. Montpelier: Journal Print., 1871. 12 p. Cf. Gilman, p. 176.   **3247a**

First Congregational Society. Catalogue of the Sabbath School Library of the First Congregational Society, (Brick Church,), Montpelier, Vt. Montpelier: Walton's Steam Printing Establishment, 1861. 18 p. VtHi.   **3248**

Montpelier Agricultural Library. Catalogue of Books of the Montpelier Agricultural Library. [n.p., 185-?]. broadside. Cf. Gilman, p. 175 (no dating provided).   **3248a**

Vermont State Library. Catalogue of the Vermont State Library, 1850. Arranged and prepared by the State Librarian, under the Direction of the Governor, agreeably to an Act of the General Assembly. Montpelier: E. P. Walton & Son, 1850. 86 p. Ct, DeWint, DLC, M, MH, MWA, MnU, NNGr, T, VtNN, VtU.   **3249**

Vermont State Library. Catalogue of the Vermont State Library, with a List of Duplicates for Exchanges. 1858. Montpelier: E. P. Walton & Son, 1858. 63 p. M, MWA, NN (film).   **3250**

Vermont State Library. Catalogue of the Vermont State Library. September 1, 1872. Montpelier: J. & J. M. Poland, 1872. xiv, 200 p. In many libraries.   **3251**

Washington County Grammar School. Catalogue of the Washington County Grammar School Library. May 1, 1860. Montpelier: E. P. Walton, 1860. 15, [1] p. Vt, VtHi, VtU.   **3252**

Pittsford

Maclure Library. Catalogue of Books in the Maclure Library, Pittsford, Vermont. Boston: Tuttle, Dennett & Chisholm, 1840. 46 p. Not in Rinderknecht. MWA.   **3253**

Maclure Library. Catalogue of Books in the Maclure Library, Pittsford, Vermont. Rutland: Tuttle's Book and Job Office, 1852. 47 p. DLC, Vt.   **3254**

Rutland

Rutland High School. Catalogue of Rutland High School Library. 1857. Rutland: George A. Tuttle, 1857. 15 p. MB, VtU.   **3255**

St. Albans

St. Albans Free Library. Catlaogue of the St. Albans Free Library, with Appendix. St.

Albans: Messenger Print, 1871. 26, [2] p. DLC. **3256**

St. Johnsbury

St. Johnsbury Athenaeum. Catalogue of the Library of the St. Johnsbury Athenaeum. Cambridge: Riverside Press, 1875. xviii, 397 p. DeWint, DLC, ICN, MBAt, MWA, NhD, NCH, NN, Vt, VtStjA, VtU. **3257**

Springfield

Springfield Town Library. Catalogue of Springfield Town Library. [Springfield, 1874?]. 40 p. DLC, Springfield Town Library. **3258**

Williamstown

Williamstown Library. Catalogue of the Williamstown Library, Williamstown, Vt. . . . Montpelier: E. P. Walton, 1858. 32 p. VtHi. **3259**

Windsor

Franklin Circulating Library. Catalogue of the Franklin Circulating Library, at the Windsor Book-store . . . [Windsor, 1829?]. broadside. Not in Shoemaker. MWA. **3260**

Windsor Athenaeum. Windsor Athenaeum Library. Windsor: Printed at the Journal Office, 1854. 10 p. VtHi. **3261**

Windsor Circulating Library. Catalogue of the Windsor Circulating Library . . . Windsor, March 27, 1827. [n.p., 1827]. broadside. Operated by Preston Merrifield. Not in Shoemaker. VtU. **3262**

VIRGINIA

Alexandria

Alexandria Library Company. A Catalogue of the Books, belonging to the Alexandria Library Company, to which are added, the Act of Incorporation, the Laws of the Company, and the Names of the Members. Alexandria: Cottom and Stewart, 1801. 54 p. S & S 33. DLC, ViAl (microfilm), ViU. **3263**

Alexandria Library Company. A Catalogue of the Books, belonging to the Alexandria

Library Company, to which are prefixed, the Act of Incorporation, the Laws of the Company, and the Names of the Members. Alexandria: John A. Stewart, 1815. 46 p. S & S 33820. DLC (also holds an undated 16 p. suppl.), ViAl (microfilm, with the 16 p. suppl.). **3264**

Alexandria Library Company. A Catalogue of the Books, belonging to the Alexandria Library Company, to which is prefixed, the Act of Incorporation, the By-laws of the Company, and the Names of the Members. Alexandria: Alexandria Gazette Office, 1840. 46 p. Not in Rinderknecht. N. **3265**

Alexandria Library. Catalogue of the Alexandria Library (Founded 1794). Washington: Geo. S. Gideon, 1856. 61 p. DLC, ViAl, ViW. **3266**

Charlestown, see under WEST VIRGINIA.

Charlottesville

Albemarle Library Society. Catalogue of Books, presented to the Committee appointed for that purpose, and received by the General Meeting of the Albemarle Library Society. Approved, April 5, 1823. [Charlottesville, 1823]. broadside. Shoemaker 11567. ViU. **3267**

University of Virginia. Catalogue of the Library of the University of Virginia. Arranged alphabetically under different Heads, with the Number and Size of the Volumes of each Work and its Edition specified. Also, a Notice of such Donations of Books as have been made to the University. Charlottesville: Gilmer, Davis, 1828. 114 p. Shoemaker 37040. Facsimile edition, with an introduction by William H. Peden, published in 1945 by the Alderman Library of the University of Virginia. AAP, CSmH, DLC, MH-H, MiU-C, NjMD, NN, NNGr, RPB, Vi, ViHi, ViU, ViW. **3268**

Christiansburg

Christiansburg Circulating Library. Catalogue of the Christiansburg Circulating Library . . . [n.p., 185-?]. broadside. Cf. Ray O. Hummel, ed., *Southeastern Broadsides Before 1877: A Bibliography* (Richmond, 1971), #4165. Vi. **3269**

Emory

Emory and Henry College. Catalogue . . .
1846. 28 p. Cf. Cutter 278, Rhees, p. 481.
3270

Emory and Henry College. Catalogue of the
Library of Emory and Henry College,
Washington County, Virginia . . . Wytheville:
D. A. St. Clair, 1869. 39 p. DLC, N.   **3271**

Emory and Henry College. Calliopean
Society. Catalogue of the Library of the
Calliopean Society of Emory and Henry
College. Wytheville: D. A. St. Clair, 1872.
46 p. DLC, Vi.   **3272**

Emory and Henry College. Hermesian
Society. Catalogue of the Hermesian
Library of Emory and Henry College. 1872.
Bristol: Bristol News Book and Job Office,
1872. 24 p. DLC.   **3273**

Harper's Ferry, see under WEST VIRGINIA.

Lexington

Virginia Military Institute. Catalogue of
Library, Virginia Military Institute. Lexing-
ton: Smith & Fuller, 1855. 81 p. DLC (film),
IU (film).   **3274**

Norfolk

Norfolk Athenaeum. Catalogue of the Books
belonging to the Norfolk Athenaeum, with
a Brief Compend of the Laws of the
Institution. Norfolk: Shields & Ashburn,
Beacon Office, 1828. 28 p. PHi holds
undated "Addenda," 1829 or 30? (8 p.).
Shoemaker 34564. PHi.   **3275**

Norfolk Law Library. Catalogue . . . Norfolk,
1863. 44 p. Cf. Cutter 497.   **3276**

Norfolk Library Association. Catalogue of the
Library of the Norfolk Library Association,
with an Historical Sketch, containing the
Charter, Constitution, By-laws, and Regula-
tions of the Institution. Norfolk: Landmark
Printing House, 1875. 88 p. DLC, KyU, N,
Vi, ViN, ViU, WU (School of Library and
Information Studies).   **3277**

Ohio County, see under WEST VIRGINIA.

Petersburg

Library of Petersburg. Catalogue of the
Library of Petersburg, Virginia. April 13th,
1854. New York: D. Appleton, 1854. 82 p.
CtHT, DLC, MA, N, T, VtHi, Vi, ViU, ViW.
3278

Prince Edward

Union Theological Seminary. Catalogue of
the Library belonging to the Union
Theological Seminary in Prince Edward, Va.
Richmond: J. MacFarlane, 1833. 107 p.
Bruntjen 20968. In many libraries.   **3279**

Richmond

Mercantile Library Association. Catalogue of
Books. November 15, 1839. Richmond:
Shepherd & Colin, 1839. 20 p. Rinderknecht
58229. CSmH, ViHi, ViU.   **3280**

Mercantile Reading Rooms. List of the
Newspapers, Periodicals and Reviews, kept
on file at de Valcourt & Wiltz's Mercantile
Reading Rooms . . . [Richmond, 1872].
[4] p. ViRVal.   **3281**

Richmond Library. A Catalogue of Books
belonging to the Richmond Library.
Richmond: Thomas Nicolson, 1801. 24 p. S
& S 1254. CSmH.   **3282**

Richmond Library. A Catalogue of Books in
the Richmond Library, Athenaeum Building. Richmond: Macfarlane & Fergusson,
1855. 107 p. CSmH, DLC, IU, MiU, NcU
(two copies, each with extensive ms. notes),
Vi, ViR, ViU.   **3283**

Richmond Library Company. Catalogue of
Books of the Richmond Library Company.
July 1, 1845. Richmond: P. D. Bernard,
1845. 24 p. ViU.   **3284**

Richmond Library Society. A Catalogue of the
Books, belonging to the Richmond Library
Society, with the Rules and Regulations,
and the Act of Incorporation. Richmond:
John O'Lynch, 1811. 34 p. Not in S & S.
NNGr.   **3285**

Richmond Library Society. A Catalogue of the
Books, belonging to the Richmond Library
Society, with the Rules and Regulations and
Act of Incorporation. Richmond: John

Warrock, 1827. 56 p. Shoemaker 29497 (duplicated by 30456). CSmH. **3286**

Virginia State Library. A Catalogue of the Library of the Stat Virginia . . . To which is prefixed, the Rules and Regulations provided for its Government . . . Richmond: Sam'l Shepherd, 1828. 31 p. Shoemaker 37029. Vi, ViU, ViW. **3287**

Virginia State Library. A Catalogue of the Library of the State of Virginia . . . To which are prefixed, the Rules and Regulations provided for its Government. Richmond: Samuel Shepherd, 1829. 51 p., [1] p. of "Donations." Shoemaker 41382. DLC, MnU, OClWHi, ViHi, ViU. **3288**

Virginia State Library. A Catalogue of the Library of the State of Virginia . . . To which are prefixed, the Rules and Regulations provided for its Government. Richmond: Samuel Shepherd, 1831. 70 p. Not in Bruntjen. DeU, MWA, Vi, ViHi, ViW. **3289**

Virginia State Library. A Catalogue of the Library of the State of Virginia. Supplement, containing Addition of 1831. Richmond: Samuel Shepherd, 1832. 7 p. Not in Rinderknecht. MWA, Vi, ViHi, ViW. **3290**

Virginia State Library. A Catalogue of the Library of the State of Virginia . . . To which are prefixed, the Rules and Regulations provided for its Government. Richmond: S. Shepherd, 1835. 77 p. Rinderknecht 35211. DLC. **3291**

Virginia State Library. A Catalogue of the Library of the State of Virginia . . . To which are prefixed, the Rules and Regulations provided for its Government. Richmond: Shepherd & Colin, 1839. 94 p. Not in Rinderknecht. CSmH, Vi. **3292**

Virginia State Library. A Catalogue of the Library of the State of Virginia, arranged alphabetically under Different Heads, with the Number and Size of the Volumes of each Work specified. To which are prefixed, the Rules and Regulations provided for the Government of the Library. Richmond: Colin, Baptist and Nowlan, 1849. 157 p. DLC, NcU, PPL, Vi, ViW. **3293**

Virginia State Library. A Catalogue of the Library of the State of Virginia, arranged alphabetically under Different Heads, with the Number and Size of the Volumes of each Work specified. To which is prefixed the Rules and Regulations provided for the Government of the Library. Richmond: John Nowlan, 1856. 370 p. CSmH, DLC, MnU, Vi, ViW, WvU. **3294**

Young Men's Christian Association. Third Annual Report of the Young Men's Christian Association of Richmond, Virginia, with the Report of the Treasurer, presented May 11th, 1858, and the Constitution, By-laws, Names of Officers and Members of the Association, together with the Catalogue of the Library. Richmond: William H. Clemmitt, 1858. 50 p. "Catalogue of Library" on pp. [33]-50. ViW. **3295**

Young Men's Christian Association. Catalogue of Library . . . [Richmond: Clemmitt, 1858 or 59?]. 24 p. DLC (defective without title page?). **3296**

Young Men's Christian Association. Catalogue of Library, together with the Constitution & By-laws of the Young Men's Christian Association . . . Richmond: Gary & Clemmitt, 1868. 25 p. MWA, ViHi. **3297**

Romney, see under WEST VIRGINIA.

Salem

Roanoke College. Catalogue of Books in the Roanoke College Library, Salem, Virginia. Lynchburg: Schaffter & Bryant, 1869. 68 p. PPLT. **3298**

Wheeling, see under WEST VIRGINIA.

WASHINGTON

Olympia

Territorial Library, see Washington State Library.

Washington State Library. "Report of the Territorial Librarian." In:*Journal of the House of Representatives of the Territory of Washington, being the Second Session of the Legislative Assembly, begun and held at Olympia, December 4th, 1854* (Olympia: Geo. B. Goudy, 1855), pp. [151]-72. Transmits a catalogue of holdings. In many libraries. **3299**

Washington State Library. "Report of the Territorial Librarian." In: *Journal of the Council, of the Territory of Washington, being the Third Session of the Legislative Assembly, begun and held at Olympia, December 3d, 1855* (Olympia: Geo. B. Goudy, 1856), pp. [185]-94. Transmits a catalogue of holdings. In many libraries.   **3300**

Washington State Library. "Report of Territorial Librarian." In: *Journal of the Council of Washington Territory, Fourth Session of the Legislative Assembly, begun and held at Olympia, the Seat of Government, upon the First Monday of December, to-wit, the First Day of December, anno domini, 1856* (Olympia: Edward Furste, 1857), pp. [xxv]-xxvii. Transmits a catalogue of books added during the year. In many libraries.   **3301**

Washington State Library. Catalogue of Books, Maps, &c., belonging to the Territorial Library. February 1st, 1859. Olympia: E. Furste, 1859. 110 p. CU-B, DLC.
                                                        3302

Washington State Library. Catalogue of Books, Maps, Charts, etc., belonging to the Territorial Library. December 1, 1867. Olympia: C. Prosch, 1868. 85 p. Annual additions appear in *Report of the Territorial Librarian,* issued annually as an appendix to the *Journal of the Council* . . . CU-B, DLC.
                                                        3303

WEST VIRGINIA

Charlestown, see entry 3306.

Harper's Ferry, see entry 3306.

Ohio County

Ohio County Law Library. Catalogue of Law Books contained in the Ohio County Law Library and the Libraries of the Ohio County Bar, together with the Rules of Practice in West Virginia Courts. Wheeling: Frew, Hagans & Hall, 1871. 84 p. WvU.
                                                        3304

Romney

Romney Literary Society. A Catalogue of the Members and Library . . . 1849. 16 p. Cf. Jewett, p. 148, Rhees, pp. 489-90, Cutter 327, under "Romney Library Society." **3305**

Shepherdstown

Benevolent Society of the Parish of St. Andrew's. First Annual Report of the Managers of the Benevolent Society of the Parish of St. Andrew's. Shepherd's-Town, (Va.) : John N. Snider, 1817. 16 p. Catalogues of books in three church libraries (Trinity Church Library in Shepherd's-Town, Zion Church Library in Charles-Town, and St. John's Church Library in Harper's-Ferry) on pp. 12-14. S & S 42030. MWA.   **3306**

Wheeling

First Presbyterian Church. Catalogue of Books in the Library of the First Presbyterian Church Sabbath School Wheeling, W. Va. Wheeling: J. W. Ewing, 1865. 16 p. ViHi.
                                                        3307

Second Presbyterian Church. Catalogue of the Second Presbyterian Church Sunday School Library, Wheeling, Va. [Wheeling: Wheeling Intelligencer Book and Job Office, 1854?]. 7 p. DLC.   **3308**

Wheeling Library Association. Catalogue of the Books of the Wheeling Library Association. Established 1859. Wheeling: Frew, Hagans & Hall, 1873. 61 p. DLC.   **3309**

WISCONSIN

Appleton

Lawrence University. Catalogue of the Library of Lawrence University, Appleton, Wis. Appleton: Ryan & Co., 1855. 30 p. DLC, WAL.   **3310**

Lawrence University. Catalogue of the Library of Lawrence University, Appleton, Wis. Appleton: Appleton & Co., 1855. 43 p. DLC, WAL.   **3311**

Lawrence University. Catalogue of the Library of Lawrence University, Appleton, Wis. Menasha: B. S. Heath, 1859. 48 p. DLC, WAL, and WHi hold suppl., 1861 (10 p.). CU (film), DLC, MB, MH, MHi, WAL, WHi.
                                                        3312

Lawrence University. Catalogue of the Library of Lawrence University. Chicago:

Methodist Book Depository, 1869. 60 p. MB, WAL, WHi. **3313**

Lawrence University. Supplementary Catalogue of the Library of Lawrence University. 1874. [n.p., 1874]. 26 p. MB, WAL. **3314**

Clinton

Baptist Sunday School. Catalogue of the Library of the Baptist Sunday School, Clinton, Wisconsin. Janesville: Veeder & St. John, 1868. 24 p. MnU. **3315**

Delafield

Nashotah Theological Seminary, see entry 3340.

Janesville

Young Men's Association. Catalogue . . . 1870. 39 p. Cf. Cutter 676. **3316**

Young Men's Association. Catalogue of Books in the Library of the Young Men's Association, City of Janesville, Wisconsin. Janesville: Veeder & Leonard, 1875. 48 p. DLC, WJa. **3317**

La Crosse

Young Men's Library Association. Catalogue of the Young Men's Library Association, La Crosse, Wis. Organized October, 1868. La Crosse: Democrat Book and Job Printing, 1869. 22 p. WHi. **3318**

Young Men's Library Association. Catalogue of Books of the Young Men's Library Association, La Crosse, Wis. Organized, November, 1868. La Crosse: Democrat Book and Job Printing Office, 1872. 62 p. DLC, WLac. **3319**

Madison

Madison Institute. Catalogue of the Library of the Madison Institute, Madison, Wisconsin. [Madison]: Atwood & Rublee, 1867. 26 p. WHi. **3320**

State Historical Society. Catalogue of the Library of the State Historical Society of Wisconsin. Prepared by Daniel S. Durrie, Librarian, and Isabel Durrie, Assistant. Madison, 1873-87. 7 vol. (vol. 3-7 are suppl., 1873-87). In many libraries. **3321**

University of Wisconsin. "Catalogue of Books in the Library of the University of Wisconsin. January 1st, 1851." In: *Journal of the Assembly, of Wisconsin. Annual Session, A.D. 1851. With an Appendix* (Kenosha: C. Latham Sholes, 1851), pp. 974-84. Prefaced by "Report of Curator and Librarian" submitted by H. A. Tenney and forming part of the "Third Annual Report of the Board of Regents of the University of Wisconsin." In many libraries. **3322**

Wisconsin Library, see Wisconsin State Library.

Wisconsin State Library. Catalogue of Books in the Wisconsin Library . . . William T. Sterling, Librarian. Madison, December 22, 1840. [Madison, 1841?]. 7 p. Not in Rinderknecht. WHi. **3323**

Wisconsin State Library. Catalogue of the Wisconsin State Library, in Three Parts. Madison, May 1852. William Dudley, State Librarian. Madison: Charles T. Wakeley, 1852. 55 p. CU, DLC, MWA, MnU, NNGr (uncat.), W, WHi, WM. **3324**

Wisconsin State Library. Catalogue of the State Library of Wisconsin. 1858. Horace Rublee, Librarian. Madison: Atwood and Rublee, 1859. 122 p. ICJ, IaHi, MB, MH, MWA, MiD-B, MiU, N, NN, PHi, PP, PPAmP, WHi. **3325**

Wisconsin State Library. Catalogue of the State Library of Wisconsin. 1872. Madison: D. Atwood and Culver, 1872. 319 p. CSmH, DLC, ICJ, MB, MH, MWA, MiU, NcD, PPAmP, PPF, WM. **3326**

Manitowoc

Jones' Library Association. A Catalogue of Books. Jones' Library Association, Manitowoc, Wisconsin. January, 1871. Milwaukee: Milwaukee Publishing Co., 1871. 31 p. WHi. **3327**

Milwaukee

National Home for Disabled Volunteer Soldiers. Catalogue of the Library, belonging to the National Home for Disabled Volunteer Soldiers, (Northwestern Branch) near Milwaukee, Wisconsin. Near Milwaukee: National Soldiers' Home Printing

Office, 1875, 103, [2] p. Catalogue of the Hospital Library, July, 1875, onpp. [99]-103. DLC, M, MH, MiU, NNC, OO, WM. **3328**

Public School Library. Catalogue of Books in the Public School Library, of the City of Milwaukee. Also, Rules and Regulations of the Library. Milwaukee: Sentinel and Gazette Power Press Print, 1851. 18 p. DLC, MB, WHi. **3329**

Young Men's Association. Constitution, List of Officers, By-laws of the Library and Reading Room and Catalogue of the Library. Milwaukee: Daily Wisconsin Book and Job Printing Office, 1848. viii, 18 p. On cover: 1849. DLC, MB, WHi. **3330**

Young Men's Association. Supplementary Catalogue. Library of the Young Men's Association. Nov. 1, 1849. [Milwaukee, 1849?]. 7 p. WHi. **3331**

Young Men's Association. Charter, Rules and Regulations of the Association, and Board of Directors, with a Catalogue of the Library. Milwaukee: Starr's Book & Job Office, 1852. 39 p. DLC, ICHi, WHi. **3332**

Young Men's Association. Charter, Rules and Regulations of the Association, and Board of Directors, with a Catalogue of the Library and List of Members. Milwaukee: R. King, 1855. 92 p. DLC, IaHi, MA, MHi, MWA, MnHi, MnU, WHi, WM. **3333**

Young Men's Association. Supplementary Catalogue of the Library of the Young Men's Association, of the City of Milwaukee, with the Annual Report for the Year ending May, 1857. Milwaukee: Daily News, 1857. 28 p. DLC, IaHi, WHi. **3334**

Young Men's Association. Second Supplementary Catalogue of the Library of the Young Men's Association, of the City of Milwaukee, with a Corrected List of Periodicals & Newspapers, the revised Rules and Regulations, and the Annual Report for the Year ending May, 1859, List of Officers, &c. Milwaukee: Burdick, Townsend, 1859. 62 p. DLC, IaHi, MB, MWA, NNC, WHi, WMHi. **3335**

Young Men's Association. Catalogue of the Library of the Young Men's Association of the City of Milwaukee. Organized, Dec., 1847, Incorporated, March, 1852. Milwau-

kee: Daily News Book and Job Printing Establishment, 1861. 179, [1] p. In many libraries. **3336**

Young Men's Association. First Supplement to the Catalogue of the Library of the Young Men's Association of the City of Milwaukee . . . Milwaukee: Daily News Book and Job Steam Printing Establishment, 1863. 80 p. MB, MWA, NBu, PP, PPL, WHi. **3337**

Young Men's Association. Second Supplement to the Catalogue of the Library of the Young Men's Association of the City of Milwaukee . . . Milwaukee: Daily News Book and Job Steam Printing Establishment, 1865. 91 p. DLC, MB, MH, MWA, WHi. **3338**

Young Men's Association. Catalogue of the Library of the Young Men's Association of the City of Milwaukee, together with the Annual Reports, Rules, etc. Organized Dec., 1847, Incorporated March, 1852. Milwaukee: Daily Wisconsin Print, 1868. 391, [1] p. DLC, ICJ, M, MB, MH, MWA, NB, OClWHi, WHi, WM. **3339**

Nashotah

Nashotah Theological Seminary. Catalogue of Books and Pamphlets in the Nashotah Library . . . Compiled by L. P. Tschiffly, Librarian. Delafield: S. C. Hawks, 1861. 60 p. MnHi, NNGr (uncat.). **3340**

Platteville

Young Men's Library Association. Catalogue . . . 1870. 11-18 p. Cf. Cutter 677. **3341**

Racine

Racine Public School. Catalogue of Books in the Racine Public School Library . . . Racine: Z. C. & H. M. Wentworth, 1872. 53 p. DLC (marked copy). **3342**

NAVAL LIBRARIES

(see also entries 309-10, 598, 2234-35)

Narrangansett's Circulating Library. U. S. Steam Ship Narrangansett's Circulating Library. Norfolk, Va.: Argus Print, [1860]. 15 p. Printed while in drydock. MWA.
3343

RAILROAD LIBRARIES

Boston and Albany Railroad Library. A Catalogue of the Circulating and Consulting Departments of the Boston & Albany R. R. Library. December, 1868. Boston: David Clapp & Son, 1868. 45 p. M, MB, MWA, NN, NRU.
3344

Boston and Albany Railroad Library. An Appendix to the Catalogue of the Boston & Albany Railroad, showing the Works added since December, 1868. Boston: David Clapp & Son, 1869. 8 p. MB holds Appendix No. 1 (Revised Edition) for the Circulating Department (6 p.). M, MWA, NRU.
3345

Boston and Albany Railroad Library. Appendix. No. 2, showing the Works added since May, 1869. [Boston 1870]. 4 p. MB holds an 11 p. ed. for the Circulating Department. M, NN, MWA.
3346

Boston and Albany Railroad Library. Appendix. No. 3, showing the Works added since Jan. 1, 1870. Boston: David Clapp and Son, 1872. 11 p. M, NN.
3347

Boston and Albany Railroad Library. Fourth Appendix to the Catalogue of the Boston & Albany Railroad Library, showing the Books added from February 26, 1872, to March 1, 1873. Boston: David Clapp and Son, 1873. 6 p. MB.
3348

Boston and Albany Railroad Library. A New Revised Catalogue of all the Books in the Circulating Department of the Boston & Albany R. R. Library. March 1, 1873. Boston: David Clapp & Son, 1873. 16 p. MB. **3349**

REGIMENTAL AND MILITARY LIBRARIES

(see also entries 34, 100, 238-39, 431, 2561-67, 2664, 3274)

Illinois Infantry Regiment, 36th. Catalogue of Books in Regimental Library of the 36th Illinois. Chicago: Church, Goodman & Cushing, [186-?]. 16 p. DLC, OCHP. **3350**

STATE NOT IDENTIFIED

Hielbury Town Library. Catalogue. 1873. [n.p., 1873]. 12 p. DLC (defective; title page lacking). **3351**

Hielbury Town Library. Catalogue. 1875. [n.p., 1875]. 12 p. DLC (defective; title page lacking). **3352**

HAWAII, KINGDOM OF

Honolulu

American Board of Commissioners for Foreign Missions. A Catalogue of Books in the Library of the American Board of Commissioners for Foreign Missions at the Sandwich Islands. 1836. [Honolulu, 1836]. 7 p. DLC, NN. **3353**

American Board of Commissioners for Foreign Missions. Catalogue of Books in the Libraries of the A.B.C.F.M. and the Maternal Association, at the Sandwich Islands. Honolulu, 1837. 12 p. HU, NN.
3354

Oahu

Sandwich Island's Mission. Catalogue of Books belonging to the Circulating Library, of the Children of the Missionaries of the Sandwich Island's Mission. Oahu: Mission Press, 1835. 10 p. DLC. **3355**

Chronological Index

DELAWARE

DISTRICT OF COLUMBIA

GEORGIA

1872: 444, 459
1873: 462, 466
1875: 445

LOUISIANA

1838: 474
1840: 473
1848: 475
1858: 471-72
1869: 469
1871: 467, 470
1874: 468

MAINE

1806: 562
181-: 521
1811: 563
1815: 564
182-: 554
1820: 519
1821: 495, 565
1822: 497
1823: 503, 507
1824: 498
1825: 504
1826: 566
1828: 555, 571
1829: 508, 570
1830: 499, 505, 535
1831: 493a, 532
1832: 556
1834: 500, 506, 509, 533, 575
1835: 572, 581, 584
1836: 486, 514
1837: 526, 531
1838: 501
1839: 478, 557, 576
1840: 513
1841: 527
1842: 586
1843: 479, 510, 520
1845: 528, 582
1846: 480, 558
1847: 512, 515
1848: 491
1849: 559
1850: 481, 573
1852: 583
1853: 488, 536, 578
1854: 482, 530, 547

1855: 492, 522, 543
1856: 483, 516
1859: 477, 511, 544, 548
1860: 489
1861: 502, 523
1862: 484
1863: 494, 496
1865: 549
1866: 560
1867: 545, 550, 553
1868: 485, 517, 537, 574
1869: 524, 561, 568, 577
1870: 490, 539, 551
1871: 525, 529
1872: 569, 579
1873: 487, 493, 518, 552, 567, 587
1874: 476, 534, 540-42, 580, 585
1875: 538, 546

MARYLAND

1801: 649
1802: 601, 614
1804: 615
1807: 602
1809: 603, 608, 611-12, 616
1810: 609, 613
1812: 604
1813: 605
1814: 606
1816: 617, 642-43
1818: 644
1819: 645
1822: 599, 623-24, 641
1823: 618, 646
1827: 588, 600
1828: 646a
1830: 646b
1831: 619
1832: 589
1833: 590
1835: 628-29
1837: 591
1839: 647
1841: 620, 650
1842: 631
1843: 651
1844: 632
1847: 597
1848: 633
1851: 592, 621, 634
1852: 630, 637

1853: 610
1854: 625, 652
1857: 626
1858: 635
1860: 598, 622
1861: 639
1862: 593
1863: 594, 640
1865: 595, 627, 648
1869: 607
1872: 638
1874: 596, 636

MASSACHUSETTS

180-: 995, 1186
1801: 898, 1038, 1111, 1451
1802: 707, 729, 1365, 1474, 1605
1803: 1101
1804: 893, 899
1805: 701, 725, 730, 1064
1806: 700, 932
1807: 715, 731, 746, 1112, 1473, 1503, 1640
1808: 747, 913, 929
1809: 710, 1481, 1506
181-: 1306, 1530
1810: 716, 748, 868, 933, 1271, 1359, 1366, 1491
1811: 856, 914, 1367, 1482
1812: 934, 1153, 1331, 1606, 1704
1813: 1452
1814: 919, 989
1815: 732, 814, 915, 935, 990, 1018
1816: 749, 997, 1002, 1217, 1272, 1361, 1364, 1594
1817: 708, 733, 938, 1281
1818: 1102, 1368, 1402, 1453, 1460, 1483, 1489
1819: 665, 734-35, 916, 1019, 1442
182-: 1357
1820: 826, 872, 917, 936, 1461
1821: 882, 928, 1188, 1332, 1455, 1492, 1607
1822: 666, 869, 1024, 1462, 1559
1823: 663, 750, 923, 991, 1096, 1428, 1493
1824: 736, 920, 953, 996, 1465
1825: 667, 940, 1396, 1415
1826: 941, 984, 1017, 1136, 1362, 1463, 1484, 1511, 1557

1827: 656, 672, 717, 904, 969, 1003, 1277, 1333
1828: 793, 1072, 1092, 1273, 1358, 1608
1829: 718, 737, 840, 918, 948, 1001, 1443, 1469, 1574, 1600
183-: 1095, 1534
1830: 668, 673, 738, 794, 903, 942, 992, 1490, 1494
1831: 848, 924, 1004, 1228, 1456, 1563, 1615
1832: 1000, 1123, 1334, 1444, 1495, 1697
1833: 789, 792, 795, 939, 1097, 1378, 1505
1834: 719, 798, 930, 985, 993, 1005, 1085, 1090, 1238, 1485, 1525
1835: 739, 986, 1016, 1025, 1103, 1113, 1170, 1302, 1580, 1653, 1656, 1668, 1698
1836: 659, 873, 954, 1067, 1201, 1335, 1411, 1445, 1466, 1542, 1609, 1655
1837: 664, 783, 786, 796, 835, 846, 883, 1089, 1278, 1441, 1457, 1496, 1568, 1675, 1699
1838: 669, 740, 874, 998, 1131, 1470, 1676, 1693
1839: 674, 849, 852, 884, 1006, 1336, 1388, 1700
184-: 1389
1840: 670, 720, 818, 824, 1037, 1140, 1241, 1339, 1497
1841: 784, 790, 875, 987, 999, 1029, 1078, 1303, 1360, 1516, 1543
1842: 714, 860, 956, 1079, 1171, 1475, 1486
1843: 851, 1080, 1141, 1320, 1337, 1467, 1581, 1617, 1701
1844: 713, 741, 885, 1044, 1100, 1172, 1572, 1623, 1702
1845: 675, 791, 876, 981, 1232, 1247, 1261, 1610
1846: 797, 850, 886, 895, 988, 1007, 1049, 1051, 1081, 1086, 1242, 1393, 1601
1847: 799, 861-62, 866, 877, 1249, 1338, 1527, 1618, 1624
1848: 800, 819, 827, 887, 1050, 1211, 1233, 1239, 1286, 1356, 1375, 1564, 1589, 1632
1849: 671, 742-43, 752, 823, 853, 921, 925, 988, 1013, 1026, 1057, 1266, 1431, 1440, 1458, 1487, 1687
185-: 684, 689, 709, 937, 1071, 1073, 1179, 1292, 1645, 1661

1850: 801, 828, 888, 901, 943, 1008, 1045, 1062, 1082, 1178, 1526, 1619, 1625, 1680
1851: 753, 833, 841, 878, 889, 1243, 1317, 1498, 1633
1852: 1063, 1068, 1267, 1304, 1551, 1595, 1611, 1616, 1644, 1652, 1662, 1674
1853: 855, 977, 1030, 1034, 1052, 1059, 1087, 1116, 1118, 1183, 1234, 1244, 1248, 1533, 1566, 1570, 1604, 1620, 1626, 1677, 1694, 1705
1854: 677, 754, 802, 863, 867, 890, 909, 982, 1009, 1014, 1060, 1107, 1120, 1139, 1152, 1192, 1208, 1222, 1237, 1369, 1374, 1499, 1657, 1688
1855: 657, 660, 744, 788, 842, 1069, 1084, 1132, 1174, 1185, 1212, 1214, 1221, 1235, 1250, 1403, 1419, 1596, 1602, 1671, 1685
1856: 695, 702, 857, 879, 947, 949, 1031, 1039, 1124, 1184, 1240, 1245, 1255, 1279, 1318, 1448, 1476, 1582, 1621, 1627, 1634, 1641, 1649
1857: 755, 787, 834, 902, 951, 964, 970, 973, 1010, 1035, 1108, 1115, 1119, 1142, 1205, 1307, 1309, 1363, 1371, 1394, 1404-5, 1410, 1412, 1549, 1647, 1672, 1678, 1689
1858: 678, 756, 820, 847, 854, 891, 910, 971, 974, 983, 1121, 1173, 1204, 1236, 1294, 1310, 1327, 1340, 1372, 1420, 1422, 1450, 1459, 1488, 1508, 1591
1859: 813, 815, 858, 900, 906, 944, 952, 955, 965, 975, 1036, 1043, 1053, 1117, 1137, 1143, 1156, 1288-89, 1298, 1321, 1344, 1349-50, 1406, 1518, 1547, 1550, 1597, 1635, 1703
186-: 843, 1099, 1206, 1295, 1384
1860: 679, 703, 825, 844, 870-71, 905, 1027, 1074, 1093, 1157, 1187, 1200, 1246, 1262, 1269-70, 1319, 1377, 1512, 1565, 1583, 1636, 1663, 1669, 1684, 1695
1861: 690, 757, 803, 896, 907, 931, 976, 1028, 1061, 1133, 1193, 1218, 1229-30, 1345, 1460, 1509, 1579, 1612, 1628, 1664
1862: 696, 721, 911, 926, 1020, 1054, 1144, 1167, 1175, 1274, 1314, 1390, 1413, 1423, 1425, 1479, 1622, 1650, 1706

1863: 704, 711, 722, 816, 821, 830, 845, 908, 1021, 1083, 1098, 1114, 1125, 1158, 1191, 1253, 1353, 1471, 1477, 1586
1864: 726, 751, 758, 812, 822, 897, 927, 950, 1094, 1223, 1315, 1323, 1341, 1373, 1478, 1577, 1637, 1681, 1686
1865: 685, 691, 759, 804, 922, 966, 978, 1011, 1070, 1109, 1209, 1324, 1407, 1418, 1427, 1500, 1523, 1560, 1571, 1573, 1651, 1690, 1696
1866: 653, 655, 693, 760-63, 810, 817, 838, 957, 1022, 1055, 1122, 1181, 1257, 1308, 1312, 1342, 1346, 1397, 1435, 1532, 1544, 1578
1867: 682-83, 686, 705, 764-66, 809, 832, 836, 864, 880, 962, 1012, 1146, 1259, 1275, 1316, 1383, 1421, 1446, 1449, 1514, 1538, 1613, 1629-30, 1648
1868: 767-70, 785, 912, 945, 972, 1047, 1148, 1163, 1176, 1182, 1189, 1198, 1210, 1215, 1251, 1254, 1322, 1354, 1391, 1432, 1575, 1603, 1642-43, 1654, 3244
1869: 728, 771, 808, 892, 1040, 1042, 1104, 1130, 1159, 1168, 1180, 1202, 1219, 1225, 1260, 1285, 1296, 1328, 1343, 1347, 1398, 1408, 1519, 1531, 1558, 1631, 1638, 1670, 3345
187-: 1015, 1207, 1264, 1311, 1351-52, 1436, 1553
1870: 680, 697, 772-74, 806-7, 811, 859, 979, 1032-33, 1110, 1150, 1263, 1355, 1380-81, 1385, 1433, 1510, 1540, 1561, 1567, 1658, 1660, 1665, 3346
1871: 658, 706, 712, 775-78, 961, 967, 993a, 1041, 1126, 1129, 1138, 1154, 1164, 1224, 1226, 1258, 1265, 1276, 1280, 1282, 1297, 1325, 1348, 1370, 1376, 1400, 1414, 1472, 1501, 1507, 1513, 1520, 1522, 1524, 1584, 1593, 1598, 1673, 1682, 1691
1872: 688, 692, 698, 779, 831, 958-59, 963, 1023, 1127, 1149, 1151, 1162, 1195, 1287, 1293, 1299-1300, 1379, 1386, 1409, 1416, 1429, 1438, 1464, 1556, 1659, 1683, 3347
1873: 662, 681, 687, 727, 780-81, 805, 829, 865, 881, 968, 1046, 1048, 1065, 1075, 1088, 1145, 1160, 1166, 1197,

1213, 1220, 1231, 1256, 1268, 1290,
1395, 1417, 1439, 1447, 1515, 1521,
1528, 1537, 1545, 1548, 1585, 1588,
1592, 3348-49
1874: 654, 676, 723-24, 946, 960, 1058,
1077, 1134, 1147, 1165, 1169,
1190, 1196, 1199, 1216, 1284,
1326, 1329-30, 1392, 1399, 1401,
1424, 1434, 1437, 1480, 1517,
1529, 1539, 1546, 1554-55, 1576,
1587, 1590, 1639, 1646, 1666-67
1875: 661, 694, 699, 745, 782, 837, 839,
894, 980, 994, 1056, 1066, 1076,
1091, 1105-06, 1128, 1135, 1155,
1161, 1177, 1194, 1203, 1227,
1252, 1283, 1291, 1301, 1305,
1313, 1382, 1387, 1426, 1430,
1454, 1502, 1504, 1535-36, 1541,
1552, 1562, 1569, 1599, 1614,
1679, 1692

MICHIGAN

1828: 1747
1839: 1718
1842: 1719
1846: 1711, 1725, 1748
1850: 1749
1851: 1720, 1726
1853: 1740
1854: 1750
1856: 1741
1857: 1721, 1751
1858: 1752
1859: 1722, 1753
1860: 1727
1861: 1754
1862: 1730, 1732, 1755
1864: 1756, 1763
1865: 1715, 1723
1866: 1757
1867: 1744
1868: 1716, 1736-37, 1758
1869: 1708, 1731, 1765, 1768
1870: 1713, 1728, 1759, 1764
1871: 1709, 1712, 1717, 1735, 1738, 1767
1872: 1729, 1733, 1745
1873: 1710, 1739, 1742-43, 1760, 1762,
1766
1874: 1707, 1724, 1746, 1770
1875: 1714, 1734, 1761, 1767

MINNESOTA

1850: 1781
1858: 1774
1861: 1783
1863: 1777
1864: 1778
1867: 1772
1868: 1779
1870: 1771, 1784
1872: 1782, 1786
1873: 1776, 1780
1874: 1773, 1785

MISSISSIPPI

1839: 1787
1840: 1801
1841: 1788
1845: 1789
1847: 1790
1849: 1791
1851: 1792
1854: 1793
1857: 1794
1858: 1795, 1799
1868: 1800
1869: 1796
1872: 1797
1873: 1798

MISSOURI

1824: 1816
1834: 1817
1839: 1818
1842: 1808
1845: 1813
1850: 1819
1851: 1820
1853: 1814
1857: 1803
1858: 1821
1860: 1810
1866: 1811, 1823
1870: 1815, 1824
1871: 1805, 1812
1872: 1807, 1820
1874: 1804, 1809, 1822
1875: 1802, 1806

NEBRASKA

1871: 1826
1872: 18279

NEVADA

1865: 1828
1872: 1829
1874: 1830

NEW HAMPSHIRE

1802: 1977
1804: 1881
1806: 1835, 1998
1807: 1854
1808: 1831, 1841, 1956
1809: 1887, 2015
1810: 1893
1811: 1834, 2025
1812: 1903, 1999
1813: 1894
1815: 1855, 1904
1817: 1832, 1895
1818: 1837
1819: 1904a
1820: 1896, 1905, 1991
1821: 2012
1822: 1869
1823: 1992, 2001
1824: 1897-98, 1906, 2000
1825: 1888
1826: 1838, 1993
1827: 1994, 2002
1828: 1995
1829: 1996
1830: 1839, 1859, 1916, 1997
1831: 1899, 1917
1833: 1866, 2003, 2018
1834: 1918
1835: 1907, 1910, 1957
1837: 1979, 2022
1839: 1882, 2004
1840: 2013
1841: 1900
1843: 2008
1845: 1939
1847: 1856, 1885
1848: 2005
1849: 2006
1851: 2009
1852: 1850, 1901, 1908, 1970, 1988, 2019
1853: 1851, 1863, 1875, 1912, 1940
1854: 1934, 1958, 2020
1855: 1870, 1923, 1941, 1971

1856: 1871, 1886, 1902, 1942, 1959, 1976, 1989, 2016
1857: 1842, 1857, 1873, 1884, 1931, 1975, 1981
1858: 1843, 1846, 1943, 1966
1859: 1867, 1909, 1919, 1944 1953
186-: 1833, 1836, 1883
1860: 1935, 1972, 1980, 1982
1861: 1932, 1945, 1978
1862: 1862, 1868, 1891, 1960, 2007, 2010, 2027, 2071
1863: 1844, 1946, 1984
1864: 1848, 1852
1865: 1865, 1987, 2014
1866: 1877, 1926, 1950, 2011
1867: 1849, 1858, 1860, 1922, 1927, 1936, 1955, 1983
1868: 1847, 1889, 1947, 1961, 1964, 1968
1869: 1874, 1878, 1880, 1928
1870: 1876, 1911, 1924, 1929, 1951, 1954, 1962, 1967, 1985, 1990, 2023
1871: 1861, 1872, 1921, 1973
1872: 1892, 1913, 1915, 1937, 1952, 2024
1873: 1840, 1890, 1930, 1965, 1974
1874: 1845, 1853, 1864, 1914, 1925, 1948, 1969, 2021
1875: 1879, 1920, 1933, 1938, 1949, 1963, 1986, 2017

NEW JERSEY

1802: 2040
1804: 2049, 2108
1805: 2044
1807: 2033
1809: 2056
1811: 2095
1812: 2052
1813: 2029
1815: 2111
1816: 2034
1818: 2096
1819: 2109
1821: 2039, 2061, 2076
1824: 2031, 2035
1825: 2094
1828: 2093
1830: 2077, 2101
1832: 2063
1835: 2112

1836: 2058
1838: 2103
184-: 2082
1840: 2087
1842: 2102
1845: 2059
1846: 2100
1847: 2062, 2069, 2104
1849: 2070
185-: 2097
1850: 2032, 2057, 2071
1852: 2072
1853: 2042, 2083, 2105, 2107
1855: 2088
1857: 2073
1858: 2067
1859: 2089
1860: 2081
1861: 2074, 2080
1862: 2036, 2045, 2084
1863: 2051
1864: 2068, 2090
1865: 2085
1866: 2026, 2106
1868: 2026, 2047, 2075
1869: 2038, 2098
1870: 2065, 2086, 2091
1871: 2028, 2043, 2054, 2066
1872: 2027, 2030, 2037, 2110
1873: 2048, 2055, 2079, 2092, 2113
1874: 2050
1875: 2041, 2046, 2053, 2060, 2064, 2078, 2099

NEW YORK

1802: 2119, 2341
1803: 2336, 2343, 2409
1804: 2342, 2417
1805: 2542
1806: 2120, 2491
1807: 2528
1809: 2335, 2444
1810: 2455
1811: 2418
1812: 2514
1813: 2354, 2370, 2412, 2427
1815: 2371, 2502
1817: 2307, 2346, 2361
1818: 2149, 2178, 2337, 2372, 2419
1819: 2150
1820: 2151, 2319, 2515

1821: 2121, 2205, 2385, 2492, 2543
1822: 2114, 2407, 2561
1823: 2378, 2408, 2435, 2516, 2539, 2551
1824: 2200, 2300, 2368, 2562
1825: 2355, 2386, 2428, 2448
1826: 2201, 2256, 2369, 2373, 2377, 2437
1827: 2257, 2429, 2465, 2505
1828: 2122, 2202, 2362, 2387, 2517
1829: 2293, 2420, 2436, 2449, 2495, 2555
1830: 2366, 2379, 2388, 2563
1831: 2374, 2421, 2506
1832: 2115, 2277, 2507, 2540
1833: 2320, 2443, 2518
1834: 2389, 2469
1835: 2116, 2265, 2282, 2382, 2556
1836: 2199, 2258, 2508
1837: 2134, 2173, 2187, 2239, 2244, 2288, 2304, 2308, 2347, 2390, 2476
1838: 2117, 2152, 2266, 2352, 2383, 2430
1839: 2255, 2259, 2321, 2422, 2452, 2487, 2526
1840: 2125, 2188, 2206, 2243, 2338, 2391, 2413, 2498, 2501, 2519, 2544, 2557
1841: 2315, 2431, 2520, 2559
1842: 2148, 2203, 2260, 2267, 2376, 2503
1843: 2135, 2189, 2425, 2463, 2509, 2552
1844: 2144, 2208, 2261, 2268, 2384, 2392, 2474
1845: 2423, 2475, 2499, 2545
1846: 2153, 2322, 2339, 2504
1847: 2269, 2438, 2482-83, 2510
1848: 2190, 2231, 2245, 2262, 2313, 2466, 2521
1849: 2154-55, 2162, 2209, 2294, 2323, 2329, 2522
1850: 2136, 2156, 2171, 2393, 2432, 2440, 2484, 2500, 2546-47
1851: 2123, 2145, 2182, 2210, 2263, 2270, 2330, 2348, 2477, 2533, 2553
1852: 2137, 2142, 2168, 2316, 2394, 2441, 2445, 2451, 2511, 2523
1853: 2191, 2204, 2564
1854: 2174, 2273, 2331, 2446, 2485, 2489
1855: 2118, 2169, 2232, 2264, 2295, 2309, 2324, 2332, 2380, 2442, 2460, 2534, 2567

1856: 2157, 2163, 2172, 2234, 2395-97,
      2512, 2524
1857: 2138, 2158, 2166, 2211, 2230,
      2274, 2311, 2314, 2317, 2333,
      2360, 2471, 2535, 2569
1858: 2124, 2126-27, 2159, 2215, 2233,
      2271, 2286, 2398, 2458, 2462,
      2467, 2472, 2478
1859: 2139-40, 2143, 2146, 2183, 2216,
      2240, 2287, 2349, 2414, 2548
186-: 2359
1860: 2128, 2175, 2224, 2302, 2305,
      2325, 2351, 2399, 2405, 2410,
      2530, 2565
1861: 2160, 2207, 2222, 2252, 2283,
      2301, 2358, 2363, 2400, 2406,
      2424, 2433, 2439, 2459
1862: 2165, 2236, 2296, 2345, 2481
1863: 2129, 2275, 2310, 2401, 2525
1864: 2170, 2179, 2183a, 2223, 2276
1865: 2164, 2176, 2186, 2246, 2326
1866: 2147, 2180, 2185, 2214, 2291,
      2334, 2381, 2402, 2450, 2457,
      2470, 2486, 2490, 2549
1867: 2212, 2227, 2454, 2494
1868: 2181, 2253, 2415, 2434, 2464,
      2513
1869: 2131, 2217-18, 2242, 2279, 2356,
      2365, 2403, 2447, 2473, 2480,
      2531, 2537, 2568
187-: 2318
1870: 2133, 2167, 2196, 2226, 2247,
      2280, 2340, 2411, 2479, 2488,
      2496, 2538, 2541
1871: 2132, 2225, 2248-49, 2284-85,
      2289, 2298, 2350, 2416, 2456,
      2550, 2560
1872: 2161, 2184, 2235, 2237-38, 2250,
      2278, 2292, 2297, 2303, 2327,
      2404, 2453, 2461, 2527, 2529, 2532
1873: 2130, 2177, 2193-94, 2213, 2219,
      2228, 2254, 2281, 2290, 2299,
      2367, 2497, 2558, 2566
1874: 2141, 2192, 2195, 2197-98, 2220,
      2241, 2306, 2328, 2353, 2375,
      2426, 2468, 2493
1875: 2221, 2229, 2251, 2272, 2312,
      2344, 2357, 2364, 2536, 2554

NORTH CAROLINA

1811: 2581

1817: 2570
1821: 2571
1822: 2574
1827: 2572
1829: 2575
1835: 2573
1853: 2576
1854: 2578
1866: 2579
1873: 2577
1874: 2580

OHIO

1811: 2587
1816: 2593
1817: 2620
1823: 2621
1826: 2622
1827: 2646
1828: 2585, 2623
1829: 2654
1830: 2643
1831: 2661
1832: 2596, 2624
1833: 2653
1834: 2625, 2639
1835: 2647, 2655
1837: 2626, 2638
1838: 2586, 2609
1840: 2627, 2640, 2648
1841: 2600, 2610
1842: 2628
1843: 2662
1845: 2629
1846: 2589, 2595, 2611
1847: 2599, 2608
1848: 2630, 2642
1849: 2614, 2631
185-: 2594
1850: 2644, 2651, 2658-59
1851: 2601, 2645
1852: 2592
1853: 2641
1855: 2612, 2652, 2663
1856: 2603, 2619
1857: 2602, 2616, 2649
1859: 2591, 2607
1860: 2584, 2604
1861: 2588, 2650
1865: 2590, 2615
1866: 2606

1867: 2660
1869: 2613
1870: 2634, 2637
1871: 2605, 2632
1872: 2582, 2636
1873: 2597, 2617, 2657
1874: 2583, 2618
1875: 2598, 2633, 2635, 2656

OKLAHOMA

1875: 2664

OREGON

1852: 2665
1855: 2675
1857: 2676
1860: 2667
1862: 2668
1864: 2669
1866: 2670
1868: 2666, 2671
1870: 2672
1872: 2673
1874: 2674

PENNSYLVANIA

1801: 2843
1802: 2844, 2900
1803: 2711, 2828
1804: 2704, 2742
1805: 2837, 2901
1806: 2888
1807: 2845, 2929
1808: 2761, 2930
1809: 2907
1810: 2741, 2908
1811: 2703, 2838
1812: 2912
1813: 2731, 2846, 2868
1814: 2913
1815: 2847
1816: 2696
1817: 2766, 2796, 2848
1818: 2725, 2849, 2889, 2903
1819: 2705, 2757, 2947
1820: 2797, 2850
1821: 2800, 2872, 2931
1822: 2813, 2851, 2872

1823: 2697, 2750, 2774, 2807, 2839, 2873, 2910, 2952
1824: 2772, 2874, 2894, 2896, 2914
1825: 2693, 2852
1826: 2819, 2950
1828: 2831, 2853, 2869, 2875
1829: 2726, 2762, 2847, 2854, 2869, 2890, 2916
183-: 2906
1830: 2775
1831: 2687, 2732, 2744, 2820, 2855, 2865, 2895
1832: 2684, 2856, 2876, 2915
1833: 2776, 2933
1835: 2688, 2748, 2765, 2857, 2893, 2941
1836: 2737, 2883
1837: 2767, 2832, 2840, 2870, 2891
1838: 2689, 2695, 2777, 2858-59
1839: 2685, 2694, 2727, 2743, 2821, 2841
1840: 2690, 2801, 2859, 2877, 2885, 2909, 2917
1841: 2754, 2806
1842: 2778, 2826, 2833
1843: 2736, 2755, 2758, 2937
1844: 2712, 2756, 2860, 2886
1845: 2698, 2763, 2779
1846: 2701, 2717, 2720, 2834
1847: 2733, 2780-81, 2814, 2932
1848: 2708, 2808
1849: 2718, 2721, 2782, 2812, 2829, 2835, 2861
185-: 2945
1850: 2783-85, 2822, 2878, 2887, 2920, 2925, 2938
1851: 2815, 2904, 2934
1852: 2722
1853: 2715, 2728, 2764, 2786, 2830, 2842, 2866
1854: 2686, 2691, 2713, 2718a, 2738, 2759, 2787, 2924
1855: 2706, 2898, 2928
1856: 2692, 2862-63, 2879, 2922, 2935, 2948
1857: 2803, 2892
1858: 2734, 2788, 2803, 2926, 2944
1859: 2682, 2729, 2739, 2789, 2823, 2897
186-: 2811
1860: 2880
1861: 2836, 2904a

1862: 2719, 2740, 2798, 2809
1863: 2714a, 2773, 2790-91, 2911a, 2921
1864: 2724, 2824, 2881, 2884
1865: 2902, 2905
1866: 2679, 2792, 2804, 2864, 2927
1867: 2871, 2911, 2936
1868: 2709, 2770, 2825
1869: 2723, 2771, 2827
187-: 2940
1870: 2681, 2745, 2747, 2749, 2752, 2760, 2802, 2882, 2918, 2923
1871: 2699, 2716, 2793, 2816, 2939
1872: 2677, 2680, 2710, 2768, 2794, 2799, 2817-18, 2942
1873: 2730, 2751, 2753, 2805, 2867, 2943, 2946, 2949
1874: 2678, 2702, 2735, 2746, 2769, 2795, 2810
1875: 2683, 2700, 2707, 2714, 2899, 2919, 2951

RHODE ISLAND

1808: 2985
1810: 3016
1814: 3017, 3028
1816: 2993
1817: 3018
1818: 3029, 3091
1821: 3019, 3030, 3071
1823: 3100
1824: 3020, 3031, 3045
1825: 3101
1826: 3013, 3015
1827: 3102-3
1828: 3021, 3046
1829: 2994, 3032, 3104
1830: 2976, 3072
1831: 3105
1832: 3106
1833: 3022, 3055, 3084, 3090
1834: 2974
1835: 2988, 3023, 3033
1837: 3034, 3085
1838: 3024, 3061
1839: 3035, 3050, 3086
184-: 2978
1840: 3073
1841: 2989, 3025, 3036, 3062
1843: 2995, 3014, 3114
1844: 2977, 3026, 3063, 3083
1847: 2968, 3074

1848: 3037, 3137, 3145
1849: 2964, 2998, 3027, 3097, 3126, 3149
185-: 2954, 2999
1850: 2986, 3077
1851: 3064
1852: 3049, 3087, 3127, 3142, 3147
1853: 2979, 3038, 3088, 3107
1854: 2969, 2980, 3078, 3150
1855: 2981, 3130
1856: 2966, 2982, 3065, 3133
1857: 3056, 3075, 3093, 3118
1858: 2983, 2990, 3053, 3079
1859: 2962, 3057, 3066, 3128, 3136
186-: 3051, 3069, 3140, 3152
1860: 2984, 2996, 3004, 3098, 3108, 3110, 3134
1861: 3089, 3092, 3139
1862: 3119, 3153
1863: 2991, 3039, 3042
1864: 3067
1865: 3111
1866: 2956, 3043, 3076, 3080, 3115, 3120, 3155
1867: 2958, 2961, 2987, 3003, 3047, 3094
1868: 2957, 2997, 3070, 3129
1869: 3059, 3113, 3122, 3124, 3138, 3151
187-: 2955, 2965, 2967, 3002, 3007, 3009, 3099
1870: 2959, 2963, 2971, 2992, 3000, 3048, 3052, 3109, 3121, 3143, 3146, 3148, 3154
1871: 2953, 2970, 2975, 3005, 3010, 3041, 3058, 3095, 3112, 3123
1872: 2960, 3011, 3060, 3125, 3141, 3144
1873: 2972, 3001, 3008, 3012, 3135
1874: 2973, 3006, 3044, 3054, 3068, 3081, 3096
1875: 3040, 3082, 3116-17, 3131-32

SOUTH CAROLINA

1802: 3161
1806: 3162-63, 3177
1807: 3189
1811: 3164
1814: 3190
1816: 3165-66
1818: 3167

1858: 3295-96
1860: 3343
1863: 3276
1868: 3297
1869: 3271, 3298
1872: 3272-73, 3281
1875: 3277

WASHINGTON

1855: 3299
1856: 3300
1857: 3301
1859: 3302
1868: 3303

WEST VIRGINIA

1817: 3306
1849: 3305
1854: 3308
1865: 3307
1871: 3304
1873: 3309

WISCONSIN

1841: 3323
1848: 3330
1849: 3331
1851: 3322, 3329
1852: 3324, 3332
1855: 3310-11, 3333
1857: 3334
1859: 3312, 3325, 3335
1861: 3336, 3340
1863: 3337
1865: 3338
1867: 3320
1868: 3315, 3339
1869: 3313, 3318
1870: 3316, 3341
1871: 3327
1872: 3319, 3326, 3342
1873: 3321
1874: 3314
1875: 3317, 3328

STATE NOT IDENTIFIED

1873: 3351
1875: 3352

❖

Types of Libraries, Collections, and Formats

ACADEMY LIBRARIES

(includes student society and club libraries) (see also INSTITUTE LIBRARIES; SCHOOL LIBRARIES. For scientific and learned academies, see SCIENTIFIC AND NATURAL HISTORY LIBRARIES; for military academies, see MILITARY, POST, AND REGIMENTAL LIBRARIES)
Connecticut: 65
Delaware: 200
Massachusetts: 677-80, 1178, 1217, 1292, 1298, 1321, 1603
New Hampshire: 1873-74, 1957-60, 1973-74
New York: 2251, 2282, 2410
North Carolina: 2581

AFRICAN-AMERICAN LIBRARIES

Pennsylvania: 2830

AGRICULTURAL AND HORTICULTURAL LIBRARIES

Massachusetts: 661, 847, 860-65, 1071, 1156-58, 1173, 1295, 1390-91, 1458-59, 1685
New Hampshire: 1862
New York: 2148
Ohio: 2591
Pennsylvania: 2885-87
Vermont: 3248a

ALMSHOUSE LIBRARIES

Pennsylvania: 2894-95

APPRENTICES' LIBRARIES

see MECHANICS' AND APPRENTICES' LIBRARIES

ARMY POST LIBRARIES

see MILITARY, POST, AND REGIMENTAL LIBRARIES

ART LIBRARIES

New Hampshire: 1938
New York: 2307
Pennsylvania: 2899

ASYLUM LIBRARIES

see HOSPITAL AND MENTAL ASYLUM LIBRARIES

ATHENAEUM LIBRARIES

Maine: 515, 554-59, 573-74
Maryland: 600
Massachusetts: 715-24, 973, 1108-10, 1131-32, 1139, 1183-84, 1302-3, 1359-60, 1416-17, 1439-40, 1482-88, 1582-84, 1592
New Hampshire: 1916, 1939-40, 1946, 1970-72, 2001-7
New York: 2204, 2286, 2483-86
Ohio: 2661-63
Pennsylvania: 2796-97, 2945, 2951
Rhode Island: 2968-69, 2995-96, 3084-89
Vermont: 3257, 3261
Virginia: 3275

AUCTION AND SALE CATALOGUES

Kentucky: 465
Massachusetts: 721, 797, 918, 938, 990-91, 1073-74, 1097, 1367, 1451-53, 1460
New Hampshire: 1998, 2015
New York: 2312, 2341, 2352, 2409, 2437, 2447
Pennsylvania: 2723, 2758, 2864, 2937
South Carolina: 3157

BAR ASSOCIATION LIBRARIES

see LAW, BAR ASSOCIATION, AND COURT LIBRARIES

BIBLICAL COLLECTIONS

see RELIGIOUS AND BIBLICAL COLLECTIONS; THEOLOGICAL AND SEMINARY LIBRARIES

BOOK CLUBS

see CLUBS

BROADSIDE CATALOGUES

Connecticut: 51, 54, 86, 159
District of Columbia: 222, 310
Illinois: 367
Maine: 521
Massachusetts: 708, 724, 948, 1071, 1156, 1173, 1217, 1367, 1402, 1534
New Hampshire: 1833, 2005
New Jersey: 2047, 2076
New York: 2465
North Carolina: 2570
Ohio: 2586
Vermont: 3248a, 3260, 3262
Virginia: 3267, 3269

CARTOGRAPHIC COLLECTIONS

see MAP COLLECTIONS

CHAMBER OF COMMERCE LIBRARIES

New York: 2345

CHILDREN'S LIBRARIES

see JUVENILE COLLECTIONS AND LIBRARIES FOR YOUTH; SUNDAY SCHOOL/SABBATH SCHOOL LIBRARIES

CHURCH AND PARISH LIBRARIES

(see also MISSION LIBRARIES; SUNDAY SCHOOL/SABBATH SCHOOL LIBRARIES)

California: 42
Connecticut: 115, 187
Iowa: 419
Massachusetts: 675, 711-14, 798, 819-20, 895, 901, 904, 909, 940-44, 982, 988, 1013-14, 1092-94, 1113, 1137, 1171-72, 1179, 1237, 1247, 1266-68, 1281, 1294, 1356, 1372, 1469-70, 1511, 1550, 1640-42, 1675-76
Missouri: 1811
New Hampshire: 1849, 1954, 1963, 1993-97, 2013-14
New York: 2135, 2144, 2222, 2288, 2306, 2318, 2348, 2351, 2462, 2469, 2474
Ohio: 2646-47
Pennsylvania: 2714a, 2807, 2809-10, 2883, 2904-5
Rhode Island: 3007, 3042-43, 3117, 3128-29
South Carolina: 3185
Vermont: 3213, 3218
West Virginia: 3306

CIRCULATING OR RENTAL LIBRARIES

Connecticut: 50-51, 70, 112, 116, 173
District of Columbia: 208, 210-12, 215-17, 227-29
Illinois: 351, 358
Kentucky: 455, 465
Louisiana: 467-68, 473
Maine: 486, 493a, 519, 531-33, 570-71, 575
Maryland: 601-6, 608, 610, 623-24, 641-47, 649
Massachusetts: 709, 725, 793-97, 806-7, 823-24, 826, 831, 840, 843-44, 870-71, 893, 898-900, 915-18, 925, 928, 932-39, 973-75, 1017-19, 1029, 1073-74, 1085, 1096-97, 1107, 1181, 1185, 1191-93, 1238-40, 1287, 1357-58, 1361, 1368, 1441, 1451-53, 1460-63, 1568, 1647-48, 1658-60, 1668, 1680, 1684
Minnesota: 1776
Missouri: 1806, 1808
New Hampshire: 1850, 1869, 1917-18, 1988, 1991-92, 1998-99, 2008-12, 2015
New Jersey: 2041, 2058-59, 2106
New York: 2205, 2240, 2243, 2300, 2335-43, 2346-47, 2361-62, 2370-73, 2376-77, 2407-9, 2424, 2437, 2444, 2447-48, 2452, 2455, 2458, 2476, 2494-95, 2501, 2539-40, 2551, 2558

CITY LIBRARIES

see   FREE/PUBLIC/CITY/TOWN/ COUNTY LIBRARIES

CLUBS (BOOK, LIBRARY, READING, AND SOCIAL CLUBS)

COLLEGE AND UNIVERSITY STUDENT SOCIETY AND CLUB LIBRARIES

COLLEGES AND UNIVERSITIES

COMMERCIAL LIBRARIES

see MERCANTILE AND COMMERCIAL LIBRARIES

COMPANY LIBRARIES

see LIBRARY COMPANIES

COUNTY LIBRARIES

see   FREE/PUBLIC/CITY/TOWN/ COUNTY LIBRARIES

COURT LIBRARIES

see LAW, BAR ASSOCIATION, AND COURT LIBRARIES

DISABLED VETERANS' HOMES

see SOLDIERS' AND DISABLED VET-
ERANS' HOMES

DUPLICATES, CATALOGUES
OF LIBRARY

Massachusetts: 721, 758, 797, 865, 990-91
New York: 2352
Pennsylvania: 2723, 2864
Vermont: 3250

ENGINEERING LIBRARIES

see SPECIAL, TECHNICAL, AND
RESEARCH LIBRARIES

FACTORY LIBRARIES

see MILL, FACTORY, AND MANUFAC-
TURERS' LIBRARIES

FEDERAL GOVERNMENT
LIBRARIES

(see also MILITARY, POST, AND
REGIMENTAL LIBRARIES)
District of Columbia: 238-330
Maryland: 598
New York: 2234, 2561-68

FIRE COMPANY LIBRARIES

New York: 2366

FOREIGN LANGUAGE
COLLECTIONS AND LIBRARIES

California: 36
Illinois: 344-45, 373, 381
Indiana: 397
Maryland: 607, 649
Massachusetts: 709, 733, 735, 765, 823-
24, 937
Missouri: 1806, 1809-12
New York: 2242, 2308-10, 2341, 2351,
2377, 2400-2401, 2429
Ohio: 2590, 2595, 2606
Pennsylvania: 2810-11, 2819-25, 2893,
2929
South Carolina: 3175-76

FREE/PUBLIC/CITY/TOWN/
COUNTY LIBRARIES

California: 16
Colorado: 47
Connecticut: 49, 62, 94, 111, 169, 175-
77, 180-81, 189-90
Illinois: 343, 349-50, 364, 368, 370, 374,
378-80, 386-88
Indiana: 408
Maine: 494, 518, 561
Massachusetts: 653, 662, 676, 681-82, 687-
99, 703-6, 752-82, 957-60, 962-68, 971-
72, 978-80, 1015, 1020-23, 1040-41,
1048, 1051-56, 1058, 1065-66, 1068-70,
1075-77, 1091, 1105-6, 1127-29, 1133-
35, 1143-45, 1150-51, 1159-65, 1174-
77, 1182, 1189-90, 1194, 1197-99,
1201-3, 1209-10, 1213, 1216, 1218-20,
1222-27, 1229, 1251-54, 1258, 1265,
1274-76, 1279, 1282-84, 1289-90, 1293,
1296-97, 1299-1301, 1305, 1307-8,
1327-30, 1363, 1370, 1379, 1382-85,
1390-92, 1395, 1398-1401, 1403-9,
1413-14, 1418, 1420-21, 1424, 1428-30,
1433-34, 1438-39, 1447, 1512, 1515,
1517-24, 1529, 1532, 1535-41, 1544-46,
1548, 1552, 1554-56, 1558, 1560-62,
1569-71, 1576, 1582-84, 1586-87, 1590,
1592-93, 1597-98, 1630-31, 1635-39,
1649-51, 1663-66
Michigan: 1715-17, 1763
Minnesota: 1772-73
Nebraska: 1827
New Hampshire: 1839-40, 1842-45,
1870-72, 1879, 1915, 1919-22, 1941-
46, 1955, 1961-62, 1968-69, 1978-83,
1987, 2021, 2024
New Jersey: 2026-27
New York: 2272, 2281, 2330-34, 2375,
2456, 2464, 2471-72, 2530-32, 2569
Ohio: 2583, 2605, 2617-18, 2634-35,
2656-57
Oregon: 2666
Pennsylvania: 2751, 2934-35
Rhode Island: 2987, 2992, 3144, 3151
Vermont: 3204-5, 3208-10, 3229, 3256-58
Virginia: 3277

FREEMASONS

see MASONIC LIBRARIES

LAW, BAR ASSOCIATION, AND COURT LIBRARIES

LEARNED SOCIETY LIBRARIES

see SCIENTIFIC AND NATURAL HISTORY LIBRARIES; SPECIAL, TECHNICAL, AND RESEARCH LIBRARIES

LIBRARY ASSOCIATION LIBRARIES

LIBRARY CLUBS

see CLUBS

LIBRARY COMPANIES

Pennsylvania: 2682, 2698, 2701, 2704-6,
    2711, 2731-35, 2736, 2741, 2757-58,
    2761-64, 2800-2802, 2837-39, 2843-
    64, 2930-32, 2941, 2947, 2950, 2952
Rhode Island: 2993-94, 3091
Tennessee: 3197a
Virginia: 3263-65, 3284

LIBRARY SOCIETIES

see SOCIAL LI-BRARIES AND LIBRARY
    SOCIETIES

LITERARY ASSOCIATIONS, INSTITUTES, AND SOCIETIES

Illinois: 382
Iowa: 424
Maine: 583
Massachusetts: 661, 1034-35, 1045,
    1118-19, 1596
Michigan: 1745-46, 1764
Missouri: 1803
New Hampshire: 1973, 1975
North Carolina: 2570-73
Ohio: 2608
Pennsylvania: 2679, 2684-94, 2702,
    2707-8, 2753-56, 2759-60
West Virginia: 3305

LYCEUM LIBRARIES

Indiana: 396
Louisiana: 471-72, 475
Massachusetts: 1411, 1591, 1616, 1698-1703
New Jersey: 2048
New York: 2234-35, 2255, 2305, 2365,
    2378-79, 2475, 2537-38
Ohio: 2607
Pennsylvania: 2748-49
Rhode Island: 3056-58

MANUFACTURERS' LIBRARIES

see MILL, FACTORY, AND MANUFAC-
    TURERS' LIBRARIES

MANUSCRIPT COLLECTIONS

Connecticut: 103

District of Columbia: 313, 319-20
Maryland: 625
Massachusetts: 772, 852, 856, 993a,
    1428, 1455-57
New York: 2147, 2154-55, 2158, 2298,
    2412-13, 2467-68, 2502, 2504
Ohio: 2632
Pennsylvania: 2730, 2768-69, 2829

MAP COLLECTIONS

District of Columbia: 246-50, 328, 332
Kentucky: 446
Maryland: 625
Massachusetts: 853, 856, 992
New Hampshire: 1856-57
New York: 2145-46, 2152, 2158, 2412-13,
    2438-39, 2502, 2504, 2544
Pennsylvania: 2796-97, 2826
South Carolina: 3156, 3165, 3169-70, 3173
Washington: 3302-3

MASONIC LIBRARIES

Iowa: 429

MECHANICS' AND APPRENTICES' LIBRARIES

California: 27
Connecticut: 75, 117-19, 161-66
Illinois: 354-56
Kentucky: 453-54
Maine: 488-90, 515-17, 523-24, 528, 543-
    46
Maryland: 599, 626-27
Massachusetts: 855, 872-81, 1062-63,
    1078-82, 1241-46, 1492-1502, 1525,
    1589, 1687-92
Michigan: 1725-28
New Hampshire: 2000
New Jersey: 2031, 2057
New York: 2114-17, 2200-2203, 2208-13,
    2239, 2319-28, 2382-84, 2440-42,
    2463, 2483-86
Ohio: 2589, 2600-2602
Pennsylvania: 2681, 2743-45, 2771,
    2774-95, 2803-5, 2814-15, 2925-27
Rhode Island: 2986, 2988-89, 3071-76
South Carolina: 3158-59
Tennessee: 3197
Vermont: 3212

REFORM SCHOOL LIBRARIES

see PRISON, REFORMATORY, AND REFORM SCHOOL LIBRARIES

REFORMATORY LIBRARIES

see PRISON, REFORMATORY, AND REFORM SCHOOL LIBRARIES

REGIMENTAL LIBRARIES

see MILITARY, POST, AND REGIMENTAL LIBRARIES

REFORM SCHOOL LIBRARIES

see PRISON, REFORMATORY, AND REFORM SCHOOL LIBRARIES

RELIGIOUS AND BIBLICAL COLLECTIONS

(see also CHURCH AND PARISH LIBRARIES; FRIENDS, SOCIETY OF; MISSION LIBRARIES; SUNDAY SCHOOL/SABBATH SCHOOL LIBRARIES; THEOLOGICAL AND SEMINARY LIBRARIES; YOUNG MEN'S CHRISTIAN ASSOCIATIONS)

RENTAL LIBRARIES

see CIRCULATING OR RENTAL LIBRARIES

RESEARCH LIBRARIES

see SPECIAL, TECHNICAL, AND RESEARCH LIBRARIES

SABBATH SCHOOL LIBRARIES

see SUNDAY SCHOOL/SABBATH SCHOOL LIBRARIES

SALE AND AUCTION CATALOGUES

see AUCTION AND SALE CATALOGUES

SCHOOL DISTRICT LIBRARIES

(see also SCHOOL LIBRARIES)

SCHOOL LIBRARIES

(see also ACADEMY LIBRARIES; INSTITUTE LIBRARIES; SCHOOL DISTRICT LIBRARIES)

SCIENTIFIC AND NATURAL HISTORY LIBRARIES

SEMINARY LIBRARIES

see THEOLOGICAL AND SEMINARY LIBRARIES

SHIP LIBRARIES

see NAVAL AND MERCHANT MARINE LIBRARIES

SOCIAL CLUBS

see CLUBS

SOCIAL LIBRARIES AND LIBRARY SOCIETIES

(included here are also libraries of unknown types) (see also ATHENAEUM LIBRARIES; INSTITUTE LIBRARIES; LADIES' ASSOCIATIONS AND SOCIETIES; LIBRARY ASSOCIATION LIBRARIES; LIBRARY COMPANIES)

49, 1166, 1180, 1195, 1200, 1205-6, 1248-49, 1257, 1259-60, 1262-64, 1269-70, 1285, 1291, 1309-20, 1323-26, 1339-55, 1362, 1369, 1371, 1373-76, 1380, 1410, 1425-27, 1431, 1435-36, 1446, 1448-50, 1454, 1467-68, 1471-72, 1475-80, 1505, 1507-10, 1513-14, 1531, 1547, 1550, 1553, 1566, 1572-73, 1577-78, 1585, 1599, 1601, 1643, 1654, 1656-57, 1661-62, 1667, 1670-74, 1677-79, 1681-83, 1706
Michigan: 1724
Minnesota: 1774-75
New Hampshire: 1833, 1846-48, 1859-61, 1865, 1868, 1883-84, 1911, 1924-37, 1947-54, 1964-67, 1984-86, 2014, 2017
New Jersey: 2036-38, 2043, 2047, 2051, 2053, 2060, 2067-68, 2080, 2099, 2113
New York: 2123-34, 2136-43, 2165, 2171-77, 2179-86, 2196, 2222-24, 2227-30, 2254, 2279-80, 2289-91, 2349-50, 2363-64, 2380-81, 2405-6, 2445-46, 2449-50, 2457, 2480, 2493, 2527, 2536, 2560
Pennsylvania: 2680, 2724, 2808, 2812, 2904a, 2906, 2909, 2911a, 2921
Rhode Island: 2955-57, 2960-61, 2963, 2967, 2971-72, 2975, 2997, 3000-3003, 3005-6, 3008-9, 3039-44, 3047-54, 3059, 3061-70, 3082-83, 3097-98, 3107-16, 3118-25, 3128-29, 3138, 3140-43, 3148, 3152-55
South Carolina: 3184
Vermont: 3203, 3206, 3213a-14, 3216-17, 3219-20, 3228, 3230, 3232, 3247a-48
West Virginia: 3307-8
Wisconsin: 3315

TEACHERS, COLLECTIONS FOR

(see also SCHOOL DISTRICT LIBRAR-IES; SCHOOL LIBRARIES)
Connecticut: 69, 110
Massachusetts: 1448, 1504, 1591
New York: 2453
Ohio: 2594
Vermont: 3215

TECHNICAL LIBRARIES

see SPECIAL, TECHNICAL, AND RESEARCH LIBRARIES

TERRITORIAL LIBRARIES

see STATE AND TERRITORIAL LI-BRARIES

THEOLOGICAL AND SEMINARY LIBRARIES

(includes student society and club libraries)
Connecticut: 103
Illinois: 389
Iowa: 423
Maine: 572
Massachusetts: 665-71, 777, 830, 929, 1378, 1604, 1612
Missouri: 1809
New Hampshire: 1851, 1882, 1973-74
New York: 2255, 2293, 2301, 2368-69, 2466, 2529, 2541
Ohio: 2597-98, 2638
Pennsylvania: 2723, 2752, 2924
Rhode Island: 2962
South Carolina: 3183
Virginia: 3279
Wisconsin: 3340

TOWN LIBRARIES

see FREE/PUBLIC/CITY/TOWN/ COUNTY LIBRARIES

UNION LIBRARIES SERVING TWO OR MORE TOWNS

Massachusetts: 653-54, 948, 1107
New Hampshire: 1970, 2020

UNIVERSITY LIBRARIES

see COLLEGES AND UNIVERSITIES

UNIVERSITY SOCIETY AND STUDENT CLUB LIBRARIES

see COLLEGE AND UNIVERSITY STUDENT SOCIETY AND CLUB LIBRARIES

VATTEMARE'S INTERNATIONAL BOOK EXCHANGE

Massachusetts: 752, 853

❖

Proprietors of Circulating and Rental Libraries

Allis, George C., 50
Appleton, John S., 1460-61
Attree, William H., 2376
Bagley, A. C., 1239
Baker, George M., 870-71
Baker, T. M., 1017-19
Baldwin, J. B., 51
Barlass, William, 2335
Barnes, Samuel, 608-9
Bartholomew, Lucius B., 112
Bartlett, Richard, 2338-39
Bedortha, N., 2494
Benton, Henry, 70
Berrian, Samuel, 2336
Bixby, Nathaniel P., 623-24
Black, Robert, 2240
Blagrove, William, 898-99, 932-33
Blake, William P., 725, 2337
Brotherhead, William, 2340, 2798-99
Callahan, W., 2974
Callender, Charles, 915-18
Campbell, James, 806-7
Caritat, Hocquet, 2341-43
Chamberlin, Lottie, 1658-59
Charter, George, 2346
Chisholm, Alexander F., 531
Clark, [?] (Holliston, MA), 1191
Cobb, Lucius M., 351
Colman, George, 531
Colman, Samuel, 532-33
Cox, Edward, 465
Cruikshank, Charles, 208
Cushing, Thomas C., 1460-61
Dabney, John, 1451-53
Dana, George, 3045-46, 3077-78
Da Ponte, Lorenzo, 2377, 2429
Davenport, Benjamin, 826
Davis, William A., 215-17, 229
Davison, Gideon Miner, 2495
Dearborn, Nathaniel, 2985
Deforest, De Lauzin, 116
Dietrick, James D., 649

Dorman, Mrs. James A., 1660
Döscher, B., 3175
Duren, E. J., 486
Eastburn, James, 2361
Ellis, George, 467-68
Emerson, George W., 358
Emmell, S. B., 2058-59
Flanders, O. W., 1185
Force, Peter, 215-17, 229
Foster, Adams, 3055
Francis, David, 793-97
Francis, George C., 974-75
Fülling, Carl, 1806
Gideon, George E., 227-28
Gill, Caleb, 925
Gill, William, 1441
Gilman, John, 1357-58
Gilman, Whittingham, 1357-58
Glazier, Franklin, 519
Glover, S. C., 3010-12
Goodale, Ezekiel, 519
Goodrich, A. T., 2370-73
Goodrich, Chauncey, 3233
Goss, Sylvester T., 826
Grant, Francis, 1869
Grosvenor, J. M., 1648
Haldeman, Walter N., 456
Halliday, William H., 831
Hammond, James, 2434, 2976-84
Harrington, J. B., 1568
Harris, Clarendon, 1668
Harris, John, 1029
Harvey, John S., 1988
Harwood, John E., 2828
Hastings, Charles, 2551
Hawes, Noyes P., 493a
Herring, James, 2362
Hosford, Jasper, 2540
Howe, Hezekiah, 116
Hunt, Howard A., 1776
Hunter, James A., 611-13
Hurd, B. N., 2940